The Haitian Revolution and the Early United States

EARLY AMERICAN STUDIES

Series editors:
Daniel K. Richter, Kathleen M. Brown,
Max Cavitch, and David Waldstreicher

Exploring neglected aspects of our colonial, revolutionary, and early national history and culture, Early American Studies reinterprets familiar themes and events in fresh ways. Interdisciplinary in character, and with a special emphasis on the period from about 1600 to 1850, the series is published in partnership with the McNeil Center for Early American Studies.

THE HAITIAN REVOLUTION AND THE EARLY UNITED STATES

Histories, Textualities, Geographies

Edited by

Elizabeth Maddock Dillon

and

Michael J. Drexler

PENN

UNIVERSITY OF PENNSYLVANIA PRESS

PHILADELPHIA

Copyright © 2016 University of Pennsylvania Press

All rights reserved. Except for brief quotations used for purposes of review or scholarly citation, none of this book may be reproduced in any form by any means without written permission from the publisher.

Published by
University of Pennsylvania Press
Philadelphia, Pennsylvania 19104-4112
www.upenn.edu/pennpress

Printed in the United States of America on acid-free paper
10 9 8 7 6 5 4 3 2 1

A Cataloging-in-Publication record is available from the
Library of Congress
ISBN 978-0-8122-4819-7

CONTENTS

Introduction. Haiti and the Early United States, Entwined   1
Elizabeth Maddock Dillon and Michael J. Drexler

PART I. HISTORIES   17

Chapter 1. Revolutionary St. Domingue and the Emerging
Atlantic: Paradigms of Sovereignty   23
Carolyn Fick

Chapter 2. (Mis)reading the Revolution: Philadelphia and
"St. Domingo," 1789–1792   42
James Alexander Dun

Chapter 3. "The Mischief That Awaits Us": Revolution, Rumor,
and Serial Unrest in the Early Republic   58
Duncan Faherty

Chapter 4. "Entirely Different from Any Likeness I Ever Saw":
Aesthetics as Counter-Memory Historiography and the
Iconography of Toussaint Louverture   80
Ivy G. Wilson

Chapter 5. Frederick Douglass, Anténor Firmin, and the
Making of U.S.-Haitian Relations   95
Laurent Dubois

PART II. GEOGRAPHIES   111

Chapter 6. The Louisiana Purchase and the Haitian Revolution   117
David Geggus

Chapter 7. Republic of Medicine: Immunology and National
Identity in the Age of Revolution   130
Cristobal Silva

Chapter 8. The Occult Atlantic: Franklin, Mesmer, and the
Haitian Roots of Modernity   145
Kieran M. Murphy

Chapter 9. In the Shadow of Haiti: The Negro Seamen Act,
Counter-Revolutionary St. Domingue, and Black Emigration   162
Edlie Wong

Chapter 10. *The Haytian Papers* and Black Labor Ideology
in the Antebellum United States   189
Colleen C. O'Brien

PART III. TEXTUALITIES   209

Chapter 11. The Constitution of Toussaint: Another Origin
of African American Literature   213
Michael J. Drexler and Ed White

Chapter 12. Haiti and the New-World Novel   232
Gretchen J. Woertendyke

Chapter 13. Dispossession and Cosmopolitan Community
in Leonora Sansay's *Secret History*   250
Siân Silyn Roberts

Chapter 14. Theatrical Rebels and Refugees: *The Triumphs
of Love*, the Haitian Revolution, and Early American
Performance Cultures   266
Peter P. Reed

Chapter 15. The "Alpha and Omega" of Haitian Literature:
Baron de Vastey and the U.S. Audience of Haitian Political
Writing, 1807–1825   287
Marlene L. Daut

Epilogue. Two Archives and the Idea of Haiti   314
Anthony Bogues

Notes	327
Works Cited	385
Contributors	411
Index	415
Acknowledgments	421

Introduction

Haiti and the Early United States, Entwined

ELIZABETH MADDOCK DILLON AND MICHAEL J. DREXLER

It should no longer be possible to write a history of the early republic of the United States without mentioning Haiti, or St. Domingue, the French colonial name of the colony known as the "pearl of the Antilles" and the site of a world historical anticolonial, antislavery revolution that occurred between 1789 and 1804. In repeating this, we join a distinguished cohort of writers who have made similar claims in the past, though historically, such claims have tended to rise to the fore only to recede beneath subsequent waves of amnesia. Today, Haiti is known, in the words of Haitian poet and historian Jean-Claude Martineau, as the only country in the world with a last name—"Haiti, poorest country in the western hemisphere."[1] Haitian exceptionalism, as Michel-Rolph Trouillot recounts, has effectively singled out Haiti as a place apart from the rest of the world and defined Haiti in strikingly negative terms—as "bizarre, unnatural, odd, queer, freakish, or grotesque . . . erratic, and therefore unexplainable."[2] This tendency to place Haiti out of relation to and in isolation from other cultures and histories masks a deep history of connection between Haiti and a host of other countries. Unquestionably, Haiti bears strong historical ties to France, but the country's relation with the United States has been historically decisive as well. Moreover, the United States has, in turn, been shaped in cultural and political terms by its Caribbean neighbor. It is this early and far-reaching history of mutually entwined relations between Haiti and the United States that we explore in this volume.

Haitian exceptionalism has its double in American exceptionalism, a doctrine that holds that the United States embodies the world-exceptional origin and purest form of political liberty and democracy. While this doctrine still holds sway in contemporary popular political debate, it has been widely criticized in the field of American studies in recent decades. Nonetheless, it is fair to say that these twin exceptionalisms—one superlatively negative and the other superlatively positive—wield considerable force in the popular imagination of Haiti and the United States today. This polarization of the United States and Haiti has substantive effects: it places Haiti conceptually far, far away from the United States, thereby erasing both the geographical proximity of the two states and their historical and political contiguity and interrelation.

In contrast to this image of two distinct and unrelated societies with disparate histories, let us conjure two prosperous eighteenth-century colonial societies—French St. Domingue, and British North America—marked by compelling similarities to one another. In fact, the political histories of the two colonial societies are remarkably parallel for a period of time. At the close of the eighteenth century, colonists in both locations began to find exclusion from metropolitan seats of political power increasingly burdensome. "No taxation without representation" is a phrase that might be understood to have launched the Haitian Revolution as surely as it did the American Revolution that preceded it. In the case of the North American colonies, British colonials were rebuffed by the English Parliament in their attempt to achieve representation there, precipitating outrage and, eventually, armed insurrection against British colonial rule. In the case of St. Domingue, French colonials demanded representation in the French Estates General in Paris in 1788—amidst the political ferment of the French Revolution—and were, in contrast to North American British colonials, granted this right. But together with the right to representation in the French metropole came a second question: Which inhabitants of St. Domingue—white, black, mixed race, free, enslaved, and/or property-owning—would count as the citizenry of the colony? It was over this question that violence first erupted in St. Domingue, marking the beginning of a revolution that lasted from 1789 to 1804—a revolution that eventually succeeded, like the American Revolution, in throwing off colonial rule.[3]

At the very moment when French colonials secured the right to representation in the Estates General, Honoré Mirabeau, a prominent French statesman, underscored the contradictions inherent in a political system that operated on a principle of democratic representation while countenancing slavery. According to C. L. R. James, Mirabeau attacked the logic of the slaveholding proprietors of St. Domingue who sought representation for themselves and denied it to free and enslaved blacks: "You claim representation proportionate to the number of the inhabitants. The free blacks are proprietors and tax payers, and yet they have not been allowed to vote. And as for the slaves, either they are men or they are not; if the colonists consider them to be men, let them free them and make them electors and eligible for seats; if the contrary is the case, have we, in apportioning deputies according to the population of France, taken into consideration the number of our horses and our mules?"[4] Two aspects of Mirabeau's speech are worth noting: first, he succinctly points out that slavery operates by what we might call a "differential distribution" of the human—that is, some humans count as human, and others do not, or they count in different ways, as, for instance, animal bodies rather than voting citizens. In so doing, he reveals a core aspect of European colonialism: the uneven and racialized distribution of humanity across white, black, and indigenous peoples. Second, we might note that Mirabeau's critique of the contradiction between democracy and slavery is one that the United States faced at the same historical moment: in 1787, during the drafting of the U.S. Constitution, statesmen grappled with precisely the question of how to enumerate whites and blacks in apportioning representational power to the states. The problem of how to count citizens and dis/count slaves was infamously resolved in the case of the U.S. Constitution by enumerating disenfranchised slaves as three-fifths of a person. At the moment of revolution, then, white colonials and free and enslaved blacks in St. Domingue and British North America confronted precisely the same situation: how to reconcile the development of modern doctrines of universal political liberty and equality with the economic engine of modernity—namely, a colonial system of labor and production premised upon dehumanizing practices of race slavery.

Despite their related origins, and the geopolitical similarities of St. Domingue and the British colonies of North America within the imperial Atlantic world of the late eighteenth century, the American and Haitian Revolutions ultimately charted very different courses, most particularly with regard to slavery. The specific history of how Haitian blacks achieved freedom from slavery while enslaved U.S. blacks remained in bondage is worth attending to. A measure of freedom arrived for some enslaved blacks in the North American colonies during the American Revolution when the British freed slaves in order to allow them to fight against white colonials on behalf of the Loyalists.[5] However, as is well known, many of the white colonials who fought the British in the name of independence and later engineered the creation of the U.S. state were slaveholding men. Indeed, as Edmund Morgan argued long ago, slavery itself may have (ironically) facilitated republicanism in the United States insofar as race- and not class-based division characterized the deepest form of social hierarchy in the colonies: rather than overcoming this hierarchy in order to enable popular sovereignty for all persons, U.S. racial politics permitted a restricted white, male republicanism to masquerade as universal. In short, by writing off a sizeable portion of the population by means of racialization, a smaller, less diverse group of men were able to agree that they were "all created equal."[6] The unequal distribution of humanity, upon which colonial economic systems were erected, was written into the founding political documents of the United States.

In St. Domingue, freedom for the enslaved initially arrived in the form of a decree from the French Revolutionary government: much as the British in North America emancipated some slaves in hopes of turning the tide of war in their direction, in 1793, the French Republican commissioners in St. Domingue, Léger-Félicité Sonthonax and Étienne Polverel, issued decrees freeing slaves in St. Domingue in order for them to assist French Republican troops in fighting off challenges from counter-revolutionary French planters and from British and Spanish troops who were then invading St. Domingue. In 1794, the National Convention in Paris voted to end slavery in all French territories. Notably, then, the division between French Revolutionary Republicans and French monarchists as well as the division between French and British imperial forces, were both judged to be of greater significance (by Sonthonax and Polverel) than the divide between free whites and enslaved blacks. And it is worth underscoring that, at various points within the long and complex unfolding of the Haitian Revolution, a variety of factions faced off in a dizzying array of oppositions and alliances: forces were, at different moments during the war, fractured along European imperial lines (French, English, Spanish), French political lines (Republican, monarchist), geographical lines (metropolitan, creole—both white and black), class lines (petit blancs, grand blancs, property owners, and nonproperty owners), status lines (*gens de couleur* or free mulattos, enslaved blacks), and racial lines (white, black, mixed race). The decision to emancipate the slaves on the part of the French Republican government was largely pragmatic: Sonthonax and Polverel sought to consolidate the fractured military and political landscape by aligning (newly freed) enslaved blacks with their own faction of French Republicans.[7] And in this regard they succeeded. The skilled black military leader, Toussaint Louverture, had previously joined forces with the Spanish who were supporting black revolutionary fighters in attacking the French on St. Domingue. When Toussaint learned that the French had emancipated the slaves in 1794, however, he deserted the Spanish and joined forces with Sonthonax and Polverel to fight the Spanish and the British. Toussaint quickly became the most powerful military and political figure in St. Domingue, consolidating his authority as a leader of the freed slaves and as the top-ranking French officer in colonial St. Domingue.

With this brief account, we do not mean to summarize the whole of the Haitian Revolution (excellent accounts of which exist elsewhere). Nonetheless, we do mean to underscore a few key points. First, the Haitian Revolution was a long and complex series of events that pitted not just blacks against whites, but many Atlantic world factions against one another. It is important, then, to understand the colonial Atlantic context of the revolution as one that was decidedly far-reaching: French, British, Spanish, and African soldiers died by the tens of thousands in St. Domingue, not because St. Domingue was an isolated, exceptional place apart from the world, but because it was an island that stood at the very center of the network of the developing capitalist world economy.[8] Second, the tension between the revolutionary politics of republicanism and an economy fueled by slave labor was a constitutive one in the broader Atlantic world: both revolutionary Haiti and the revolutionary early U.S. republic were sites where this contradiction rose to the fore. How each fledgling state addressed this contradiction would serve to chart its relations with the Atlantic world for centuries to come.

The end of slavery in St. Domingue did not mark the end of the Haitian Revolution. Rather, the revolution took a new turn—a turn not just in an antislavery, but in an anticolonial direction as well—as Toussaint consolidated his authority in St. Domingue. While officially serving as the leader of St. Domingue under the aegis of the French government, Toussaint exercised authority with increasing independence and distance from France in the years from 1797 to 1802.[9] Indeed, U.S. officials in the Adams administration established diplomatic relations with Toussaint despite the fact that the United States was at political loggerheads with the French, in the midst of the so-called Quasi-War with France. As Ronald Angelo Johnson argues, "By 1798 . . . [officials in Adams's cabinet] concluded among themselves that the Louverture regime was moving to declare eventual independence from France. They consented to the United States' helping establish the first nation-state with a majority-black government and citizenry."[10] In effect, then, the Adams administration sought to make common cause with what they anticipated would be another newly independent, postcolonial American nation. Trade between the United States and St. Domingue reached new heights as U.S. merchants supplied Toussaint with both foodstuffs and armaments.[11] And in 1799, John Adams signed into law a bill, ratified by the U.S. Congress, which included language known as "Toussaint's Clause," authorizing the United States to trade and conduct independent diplomatic relations with Toussaint, despite an embargo against doing so with the French.[12]

This tenuous alignment of two independent, postcolonial American nations was short-lived. Two regime changes—one in France and one in the United States—were to have radical effects on St. Domingue in the years from 1799 to 1804. In France, Napoleon came to power in 1799, ceased war with England in 1801, and sought to reinstate slavery in the colonies.[13] The armed resistance of black citizens in St. Domingue to Napoleon's efforts to reinstall French colonial rule and eradicate black leadership in the military there ultimately resulted in the final defeat of the French and the establishment of the Republic of Haiti in 1804 under the leadership of Jean-Jacques Dessalines. In the United States, Thomas Jefferson took office in 1801. A southern, slave-owning president, Jefferson would ultimately assist in efforts to eradicate both trade and diplomatic relations with the free black government of Haiti. It would be another sixty-two years before the United States formally recognized Haiti as an independent sovereign nation.

For a brief moment, then, it appeared that Haiti and the United States were (or would be) two newly minted American nations moving from colonialism to independence and sharing resources in charting parallel paths. However, this story was rapidly and decisively overwritten in the United States by a quite different narrative—one in which Haitian and U.S. histories were not parallel but antithetical. And this is the story that continues to appear on the front pages of newspapers around the world today. What caused this sharp turn toward a revisionary narrative? And why has the story of the deep relation between Haiti and the United States been so insistently and repeatedly "forgotten" and eclipsed from public view? As we indicate above, the most proximate cause of the shifting narrative of the relation between the United States and Haiti involved the presidency of Thomas Jefferson together with the military and political decisions of Napoleon regarding French involvement in the Caribbean. When Napoleon came to power in France, he laid plans to reconstruct a French Caribbean empire, linking Louisiana, France, and the Antilles. According to Napoleon's "Western Design," Louisiana would serve as the breadbasket for the French colonies in the Caribbean, including St. Domingue. Because St. Domingue's plantations were geared toward the production of sugar and coffee, the island could not feed itself and had long relied upon the North American colonies for provisions of all kinds. Rather than support U.S. commercial gain in this trade, however, Napoleon envisaged a closed French circuit of production and profit: provisions from Louisiana would feed the Caribbean colonies; the Caribbean colonies would produce sugar and coffee for sale in Europe, the profits of which would enrich the French metropole. Napoleon's plan relied upon the reassertion of French control of St. Domingue and Louisiana, an effort that he undertook with a massive military intervention, sending forty thousand troops to St. Domingue in 1801 under the leadership of his brother-in-law, General Charles Victor Emmanuel Leclerc. Although it is not entirely clear whether or not Napoleon intended to reinstate slavery in St. Domingue, he certainly aimed to depose Toussaint and black military leaders in the colony: "Rid us of these gilded negroes," Bonaparte wrote to Leclerc in July 1802, "and we will have nothing more to wish for. . . . Once the blacks have been disarmed and the principal generals sent to France, you will have done more for the commerce and civilization of Europe than we have done in our most brilliant campaigns."[14]

Napoleon's massive military expedition to St. Domingue inaugurated the final phase of the Haitian Revolution. Despite successfully capturing Toussaint and imprisoning him in France (where he later died), the Leclerc expedition ultimately ended in spectacular failure. Leclerc died of yellow fever within eight months of arriving in St. Domingue, as did thousands of French soldiers, and, energized by rumors of the reinstatement of slavery, as well as the cruelties of Leclerc's successor, Donatien-Marie-Joseph de Rochambeau, black troops ultimately defeated the French and drove them from St. Domingue. General Jean-Jacques Dessalines, leader of the black rebel army, pronounced the independence of the state of Haiti in 1804, and in 1805 the first constitution of the sovereign and free state of Haiti was declared the law of the land. Following the defeat of French troops in Haiti, Napoleon abandoned his plans for a French empire in the Americas. In 1803, Napoleon famously expostulated, "Damn sugar, damn coffee, damn colonies."[15] That same year he abruptly sold the whole of Louisiana to Jefferson for roughly fifteen million dollars, thereby washing his hands of the American empire he had imagined.

With the purchase of the Louisiana Territory from Napoleon, Jefferson doubled the size of the United States and opened the way for a geographical and economic reconfiguration of the nation. Lauded today as "the greatest real estate deal in history," the Louisiana Purchase is portrayed in popular accounts of U.S. history as an event that "confirms our national self-image as a republic expanding benignly, bringing the gospel of freedom to people long deprived of its incalculable benefits. We *purchase*d Louisiana; we did not *conquer* it. . . . The Louisiana Purchase . . . supports a story of a free people accepting land freely sold to them."[16] The irony of such an account is that it ignores the bloody backdrop of the Haitian Revolution out of which the Louisiana Purchase emerged. Moreover, the new reach of U.S. territory westward sustained the maintenance and extension of slavery in those territories, even as such an expansion was enabled by the antislavery revolution in Haiti. Nearly one hundred years after the event, Henry Adams still felt that the connection between the Louisiana Purchase and Haiti remained untold: "Toussaint exercised on [the history of the United States] an influence as decisive as that of any European ruler," wrote Adams. Without the black rebellion, "Ten thousand French soldiers . . . might have occupied New Orleans and St. Louis before Jefferson could have collected a brigade of militia at Nashville."[17] Arguably, then, black freedom fighters in Haiti are in part responsible for the continental shape of the U. S. today.[18]

The irony with respect to Jefferson's presidency is also profound. Whereas the Adams administration pragmatically sought the benefits of trade with St. Domingue regardless of matters of race, Jefferson and southern Republicans were ultimately willing to forego the profits of a thriving trade between the United States and St. Domingue out of fear that an antislavery revolt might spread from Haiti to the southern United States. Jefferson's policy toward Toussaint has been the subject of some debate, in part because his motivations and actions shifted over time. Initially willing to assist the French with "starving" Toussaint out of power, Jefferson later supported Toussaint against the Leclerc expedition after gleaning a sense of Napoleon's ambitions for Louisiana.[19] Following Haitian independence, however, Jefferson became more willing to accommodate French demands that the United States cease trade with Haiti. In agreement with both French and southern slave-owners' entreaties to keep munitions out of the hands of Haitians, the Jefferson administration sought to regulate and curtail trade between U.S. merchants and Haiti. Although Federalists ardently supported the continuation of trade with Haiti, southern Republicans cited the violence of Jean-Jacques Dessalines against white colonials at the close of the Haitian Revolution as evidence of the peril represented by antislavery revolution. In 1806, Senator George Logan introduced a bill to prohibit all trade with Haiti, which played upon the fear of slave rebellion in the United States. At the center of the pro-embargo policy was a fundamental embrace of the racism that allowed many white Americans to support slavery: "Is it sound policy to cherish the black population of St. Domingo whilst we have a similar population in our Southern States?" asked Logan.[20] Despite the objection of Federalists, the 1806 embargo bill passed, and trade between the United States and Haiti plummeted; diplomatic relations between the United States and Haiti ended altogether.[21] As then Secretary of Treasury Albert Gallatin later noted, "One of the principal motives for passing [the embargo of 1806] was the apprehension of the danger which at that time (immediately after the last massacre of the whites there) might on account of our numerous slaves, arise from the unrestricted intercourse with the black population of that island."[22]

The imposition of a political and economic break between Haiti and the United States marked a turning point of significant dimensions—one that changed the shape of slavery in the United States as well as the geography of the U.S. nation and its place in the world. Indeed, a fundamental shift in the nature of slavery occurred in the United States following the Haitian Revolution. We might characterize this shift as occurring in three separate (albeit related) registers: in the *geography* of slavery, in the *economics and labor practices* of slavery, and in the *ideological justification* of slavery. First, the geography of slavery shifted decisively given the expansion of the slave economy westward with the Louisiana Purchase and the simultaneous shutting down of the slave trade between the Caribbean and the United States. Anxiety concerning the spread of antislavery revolution to the United States caused a flurry of legislation in southern states barring the importation of slaves (or the migration of free black persons) from the Caribbean to the United States.[23] And in 1808, when the U.S. federal government closed the slave trade with Africa, what had formerly been a largely Atlantic trade in slaves became one of decidedly continental dimensions: slaves from the Chesapeake were, in growing numbers, sold "down the river" to territories southward and westward. Second, the end of the Haitian Revolution marked the advent of what historians have recently begun to describe as the "second slavery"—a slavery in which labor regimes were intensified as they were integrated with industrial technologies and international capital markets. In the United States, in particular, this took the form of the rapid growth of cotton production, pushing westward along the so-called "cotton frontier."[24] And third, slave owners shifted from apologetic defenses of slavery to aggressive ones that described slavery as a positive good. Coupled with this ideology was a strong set of claims that antislavery revolution was not a result of the action of slaves or a response to the oppressive conditions of slavery, but rather the result of white abolitionist agitation.

These three changes, which followed on the heels of the Louisiana Purchase and the 1806 embargo, were interrelated and had far-reaching consequences in the United States. The fear that the specter of antislavery revolution in Haiti had generated in the southern plantocracy mobilized a new discourse concerning slavery—one that took aim at abolitionists and defended slavery as part of a core American identity in the United States. Republican Senator John Taylor from Virginia vigorously asserted this new set of claims regarding slavery in a series of essays published in 1803. Taylor argued that blacks were incapable of liberty and that the Haitian Revolution had been caused by white abolitionists; consequently, he concluded, slavery could not peacefully be abolished in the United States. As Tim Matthewson suggests, Taylor's writings "set the stage for the positive-good proslavery argument; they suggested a fundamental shift in southern thought about the place of slavery in America, and they encouraged a consensus of the view that antislavery sentiment was directly responsible for the bloodbath in Saint Domingue."[25] Perhaps more importantly, in conceding to French and southern demands to cut diplomatic ties with Haiti and thus to shape international policy around the defense of slavery, the Jefferson administration embraced slavery as a core aspect of the national economy.

The economic and diplomatic turn away from the Caribbean and toward the Mississippi and westward regions effected a significant reconfiguration of the geography of the United States: the Haitian Revolution, the Louisiana Purchase, and the 1806 embargo fundamentally redefined the *geographical imaginary* of the United States. Once consisting of thirteen states lining the North Atlantic littoral (an orientation that turned the United States toward an Atlantic economy in which the Caribbean was central), the United States was redrawn on a continental, rather than Atlantic, scale in the early nineteenth century: the Caribbean disappeared from this map of the United States and areas west of the Mississippi, in turn, assumed increasingly distinct and prominent contours. Following the Haitian Revolution and the Louisiana Purchase, then, the geography of the United States assumed a westward face, and it was this westward face that would, in turn, cement itself in the mythology of the American frontier and the doctrine of manifest destiny central to the history of the nineteenth-century United States.

The new geographical imaginary coincided—not incidentally—with a new geography of slavery and the emerging economic and labor regimes associated therewith. Historians including Dale Tomich and Anthony Kaye have defined the "second slavery" in terms of a post-eighteenth-century shift in the economics and labor practices of slavery—a shift that involved the industrialization of production, together with the development of increasingly intensive labor regimes and the integration of slave labor/production into international capital markets.[26] Cotton was the motor of the U.S. economy between the 1790s and the Civil War, and in the words of Sven Beckert, its value "catapulted the United States onto the center stage of the world economy."[27] The forced migration of enslaved African Americans to the cotton frontier provided the labor to cultivate and harvest the cotton that changed the place of the United States in the world economy: between the American Revolution and the Civil War, slavery "grew from 800,000 captives to four million, and from a narrow coastal strip of mostly declining plantations to a subcontinent-sized expanse of factories in the field; slave labor camps whose productivity per worker expanded every year."[28] Not only did the territorial geography of the United States shift away from an Atlantic orientation, so too did the U.S. slave trade and the economy as a whole.

Indeed, once the federal government closed the international slave trade in 1808, the internal slave trade became the primary means of supplying the expanding cotton industry with slave labor: between 1790 and 1860 roughly one million slaves were torn from their homes and families within the United States and forced to move southward and westward. The internal slave trade was on a scale, and at a level of social violence for slaves forced to move, that has led Ira Berlin to describe it as a "second middle passage."[29] Furthermore, as slavery expanded westward, new and more brutal labor regimes for slaves—what Edward Baptist evocatively calls the "whipping machine," also known as the "pushing system"—replaced previous task-based labor systems as cotton production ramped up. The destruction of families and social worlds of slaves who were uprooted by the funneling of labor to the cotton frontier also enabled the destruction of existing work patterns and their replacement by harsh regimes aimed at increased productivity.[30] As Baptist points out, the narrative that enshrines the cotton gin as the source of the booming cotton industry in the nineteenth century is one that fails to recognize the source of the cotton that is fed into the gins—a source found in the increased labor of slaves whose bodies were forcibly bent to the work of the industrializing second slavery. For our purposes in understanding the effects of the Haitian Revolution on the United States, it is particularly significant that the new "whipping machine" is coincident with (and indeed, relies upon) the geographical reconfiguration of the United States away from an Atlantic economic and spatial regime to a continental one.

The production of cotton was central to the new geography and economy that we describe here. Baptist argues that cotton created the United States as we know it in the nineteenth century: "The expansion of U.S. slavery made the U.S., in no small part because it also made more of the industrial revolution's key product—cotton, which was its petroleum, its most widely-traded, most important, most price-setting commodity."[31] The value of cotton shot up just after the Haitian Revolution and was fundamental to the growth of the U.S. economy. Cotton was the "driving piston that pushed the U.S. economy" for decades prior to the Civil War, and the wealth generated by cotton enabled the United States to import goods from England, establish credit in foreign markets, and ultimately attract foreign capital investment in U.S. industry.[32] In short, cotton and the second slavery enabled the United States to assume a core role in the developing capitalist world economy.

As the U.S. economy was propelled forward by global investment in the cotton industry, the economy of Haiti suffered from being cut off from trade with former partners such as the United States and France. Isolated from an Atlantic economy in which it once served as a key node of production and consumption, the Haitian economy struggled. And a debilitating blow to it was delivered in 1825, when the government of France (with the assistance of threatening French gunboats floating off Haitian shores) secured from Haitian President Jean Pierre Boyer the promise of an "indemnity" payment of 150 million francs to recompense the French for their loss of property—including the "property" of slaves—during the Haitian Revolution; in return, France granted Haiti official recognition of its independence. Boyer agreed to these terms so that Haiti could rejoin the world economy; however, the indemnity repayments, by all accounts, proved crippling. Boyer was forced to obtain a loan from France to make the first payment in 1825; the French charged interest and fees on top of the loan, which increased the debt further. A decade later, fully 30 percent of Haiti's annual budget was spent servicing the national debt while less than 1 percent was spent on education.[33] And indeed, Haiti did not finish paying off the debt until the following century: the last payment to France was made in 1922, when Haiti took out a loan from the United States for $16 million: that loan, in turn, was paid off in 1947.

According to Randall Robinson, in 1915, as much as 80 percent of the Haitian government's resources were devoted to debt repayments to French and American banks.[34] The effects of the indemnity payments were significant. Unable to invest in infrastructure, the Haitian government was forced, instead, to devote funds to debt repayment: "Year after year, Haiti's population watched as money that could have been used to build roads, ports, schools, and hospitals simply vanished."[35]

Although ostensibly aimed at repaying French colonials who had lost property during the revolution, the indemnity was in fact aimed at bringing Haiti back into the economic orbit of France, by creating, in the words of one scholar, "an independence debt." Frédérique Beauvois argues that the 1825 indemnity ordinance was a concerted effort on the part of France to take Haiti "economic hostage" and thus to "retain an official hegemony over a rebellious colony become sovereign state."[36] In short, with the indemnity ordinance, economic authority came to stand in for what was once the direct political control of France with respect to Haiti: we know this structure today by the name of "neocolonialism." Twenty-five years after the Haitian Revolution, then, the United States was catapulted into a starring role as a leader of the global economy, propelled there by the "petroleum" of the antebellum economy—cotton—and by the labor of slaves in the fields of the cotton frontier. Haiti, whose slaves had freed themselves, was, in contrast, exiled from the global economy until the moment when the nation agreed to assume the yoke of debt. "With the indemnity," concludes Laurent Dubois, "Haiti suddenly became a debtor nation, an unlucky pioneer of the woes of postcolonial economic dependence."[37] In 1825 Haiti was readmitted into the world economy on the condition that it assume a neocolonial position therein, and it is this configuration that has held sway, under the rule of debt (and occasionally gunboats and military occupation as well), since then.

From a narrative in which the United States and Haiti could be seen as parallel colonial states seeking independence and freedom from metropolitan authority, we have moved, then, to one in which the United States is a core state in the world economic system and Haiti is moved to the periphery and recolonized, in no small part due to racism and the utility of racism to the development of capitalism on an Atlantic and (later) world scale.[38] The story that has been poorly narrated, or not narrated at all, is thus the story of this transition—from Haiti as world historical site of antislavery and anticolonial revolution to Haiti as neocolonial debtor nation. This is a story that begins with revolutionary Haiti as the double of the revolutionary United States but shifts suddenly to a nineteenth-century Haiti literally written off the map of the continental United States, and ultimately to a contemporary Haiti seen as a poor and obscure space antithetical to "America" as we know it—a nation whose flickering encroachments on U.S. consciousness appear in the form of refugees, disease, and disaster. In accounts of the impoverished contemporary Haiti, no mention of the history of the French indemnity or the U.S. embargo of 1806 appears.[39] We contend that the un-narrated story of Haiti and the United States is one of a continued relation sustained under the guise of antithesis: it is not that the relation between Haiti and the United States suddenly ends with the embargo of 1806; rather, this relation is reconstructed in terms that construe the United States and Haiti as opposites. This is not a non-relation but a relation of obscured interdependence, and it is one that deserves our attention. As Troulliot has eloquently argued, "Haitian exceptionalism has been a shield that masks the negative contribution of the Western powers to the Haitian situation. Haitian exceptionalism functions as a shield to Haiti's integration into a world dominated by Christianity, capitalism, and whiteness. The more Haiti appears weird, the easier it is to forget that it represents *the longest neocolonial experiment in the history of the West*."[40]

We have argued that a continental geographical imaginary of the United States—one that underwrites the story of U.S. nationhood as one of westward progress—effectively erased an earlier, Atlantic configuration of colonial North America and the early United States. However, placing the Haitian Revolution and the American Revolution next to one another enables us to bring this earlier geography back into focus. Moreover, such a move also opens up the possibility of viewing alternative geographies taking shape from the period of revolution onward. For instance, with the Atlantic context in view, we can trace what Edward Rugemer has described as a "geography of freedom" inaugurated by the Haitian Revolution—one created and sustained in the writings and performances of diasporic Africans in the United States and the larger Atlantic world in the years after 1804.[41] The recent volume of writings edited by Maurice Jackson and Jacqueline Bacon on African American literature and the Haitian Revolution documents the depth and significance of a geography connecting Haiti and the United States following the Haitian Revolution.[42] In related terms, work by scholars including Colin Dayan, Susan Buck-Morss, Sibylle Fischer, David Scott, and Nick Nesbitt, among others, has argued for the centrality of the Haitian Revolution to modernity and the development of Enlightenment thought.[43] This is important scholarship that draws Haitian history and culture into narratives of world history—scholarship that places Haiti in a central position with respect to the geography of modernity and its countercultures and erasures. Trouillot's description of the Haitian Revolution as "unthinkable" within (racist and colonial) Enlightenment thought is perhaps the most often repeated phrase in current scholarship in this area.[44] Trouillot argues that the Haitian Revolution was silenced at the time that it occurred and in subsequent history. But the silencing to which Trouillot refers is not an erasure and it would be a mistake to understand it as such. As the scholars cited above demonstrate, what is required to redress the silencing (and here we would include geographical isolation as part of that silencing) of the Haitian Revolution, is the evocation of new ontologies, new narratives, and new geographies. In fact, the archive is replete with evidence of alternative narratives that allow us to see more than the familiar account of erasure, isolation, and negative exceptionalism. In this volume, then, we collect essays that explore alternative narratives to the one that places the United States and Haiti conceptually, historically, and geographically distant from one another. By drawing Haiti and the early United States into sustained relation, however, we do not so much offer a corrected narrative or geography as open a series of debates that allow us to speculatively redraw the map on which Haiti and the United States do not appear to share any spatial or historical relation.

We organize the essays that follow into three categories: Histories, Geographies, and Textualities. In each of these instances, we imagine the essays collected under these headings to approach the relation of Early America and the Haitian Revolution, as, in the words of cultural geographer Doreen Massey, a "realm of multiple trajectories."[45] Each section begins with an introduction that sketches the conversation in which the essays that follow are engaged. In Histories, the essays tackle how the Haitian Revolution was encountered in the early United States as it unfolded in time. These essays explore issues including perspectival bias and the influence of genre on the representation of history. In the Geographies section, essays consider how the Haitian Revolution led to new ideas about center and periphery or to reconceived pivotal or focal spaces of influence. And finally, in Textualities, the conversation turns to creative acts of appropriation, inspiration, and transposition, which extend the influence of the Haitian Revolution beyond the common historical archive and allow us to examine the way in which the national literary imaginary of the United States is traversed by a shared U.S./Haitian history.

PART I

Histories

WHEN JEAN-JACQUES DESSALINES declared the independence of Haiti in 1804, 165 newspapers in the United States were vying for readers. This number represented a vast increase over what had been available just half a century earlier. At the beginning of the Seven Years War, 21 newspapers circulated in the North American colonies. Over the next two decades, that number more than doubled; by the end of the American War of Independence in 1783, there were 44 outlets. Less than a decade later, the number of newspapers nearly doubled again. Editors from Maine to Georgia were publishing 73 papers as the first news of the slave rebellion on St. Domingue broke. Of the seventeen states admitted to the Union by 1804, only Delaware had but one paper in print; Boston had 4, Philadelphia 7, New York 15, Richmond 3, Augusta, Georgia 2, and Charleston, South Carolina 4.

News traveled with increasing speed over this period, too. The treaty ending hostilities between the Kingdom of Great Britain and the United States was reported in London on September 27, 1783, but news reached the United States only on January 6, 1784. By contrast, it took only twelve days for the first U.S. newspaper, *The Albany Gazette*, to report Jean-Jacques Dessalines's January 1, 1804, Declaration of Independence. The news traveled west, with the *Tennessee Gazette and Metro-District Advertiser* reporting it on February 22. Though news still lagged behind the events of the day (with distance still accounting for that differential), U.S. readers had become exponentially more aware of their changing world.

The essays in this section address entwined and competing encounters with the Haitian Revolution in the developing public sphere of the early United States. They take us from theories of state sovereignty to the street, from the economic interests of U.S. merchants to the diplomatic chambers of the elite, from the ad hoc flow of rumor and the migration of refugees and consequent syncretizing of cultural practices to the informal, if not illicit, communication networks among the enslaved.

Carolyn Fick opens the section by looking at Toussaint Louverture's relations with the United States, as well as with Great Britain and France from roughly 1797 to 1801. This was the period when Louverture was steering the colony toward the brink of independence. Her essay raises questions about the economic foundations of national sovereignty as well as the political foundations of popular sovereignty, individual rights, and freedom; she also explicates the complex set of relations that bound the United States and colonial St. Domingue at the close of the eighteenth century.

James Alexander Dun examines the reception and understanding of the Haitian Revolution by U.S. citizens and readers in Philadelphia. Dun explains the sources of Americans' fascination with violence in St. Domingue and explores their impact as frames through which subsequent events would be understood. Dun argues that in the effort to correlate these events with the French Revolution, Americans came to emphasize the issue of civic equality for *gens de couleur*, making it central to their debates over developments in France, while at the same time limiting white Americans' capacity to see the truly revolutionary nature of the challenge raised by the slaves.

In "'The Mischief that Awaits Us': Revolution, Rumor, and Serial Unrest in the Early Republic," Duncan Faherty surveys U.S. newspaper reportage on the Haitian Revolution during 1802 and tracks efforts to literally and figuratively quarantine the West Indies from North America. Examining how rumors about frigates from Haiti generated waves of social unrest, Faherty explores how a preoccupation with their presence reflected and encoded national anxieties about revolution in the West Indies. In the case of both Dun's and Faherty's essays, which focus on Philadelphia, it is clear that relations between Haiti and the United States during the Haitian Revolution were triangulated through the French Revolution. The Haitian Revolution precipitated a new understanding of and relation to the French Revolution for many in the United States—one that was routed through the Caribbean and foregrounded the politics of race and colonialism.

In his essay on historiography, counter-memory, and aesthetics, Ivy G. Wilson looks at the larger history of the Haitian Revolution and its place (or lack thereof) in histories of the United States, arguing that insofar as Haitian history strains against an exceptionalist account of the United States, it may be more accessible by way of art and aesthetics than by way of official knowledge. Turning, then, to the history of the iconography of Toussaint Louverture in U.S. culture, Wilson demonstrates that such an iconography can serve as a revisionary counter-memory that both rewrites the past and underwrites alternative futures concerning Pan-Africanism, black independence, and sovereignty in the United States and elsewhere.

Laurent Dubois closes this section with an essay placing postcolonial Haiti in relation to the United States and recounting the diplomatic interactions between the Haitian intellectual Anténor Firmin and the U.S. consul to Haiti, Frederick Douglass, in the period following the U.S. Civil War. Looking forward to the end of the nineteenth century, Dubois tracks the continuously linked histories of Haiti and the United States in terms of race, economics, and geopolitics.

CHAPTER I

Revolutionary St. Domingue and the Emerging Atlantic

Paradigms of Sovereignty

CAROLYN FICK

In attempting to examine the aspirations embodied in the Haitian Revolution and the contingencies of the late eighteenth-century Atlantic world within which its foremost leader, Toussaint Louverture, struggled to achieve their full realization, this essay focuses on a crucial period in the early histories of the first two emerging nations of the Americas: the one, the United States, already independent since 1783 and engaged in charting the course of its future development; the other, St. Domingue, still formally a colony of France and struggling to become independent, while, in the process, creating the foundations of the Haitian "state-to-be." In particular, it looks at Toussaint Louverture's relations with the United States, as well as with Great Britain and France, from roughly 1797 to 1801, when Toussaint, standing at the helm of St. Domingue's government, brought the colony increasingly toward the brink of independence. Ultimately, he sought to make St. Domingue into an emancipated black self-governing territory of the French empire. His economic relations with the United States and with Great Britain were crucial in the elaboration of his foreign policy for which the short-lived contingencies of the "Quasi-War" between the United States and France from 1797–1798 to 1800, as well as the prolonged war in Europe, provided the immediate opportunity. In addition to examining the economic foundations for national sovereignty during this period, this essay focuses equally on the political foundations for popular sovereignty, individual rights, and freedom. In the process, it also considers the extent to which St. Domingue under Toussaint Louverture came close to achieving any of these goals, on the one hand, and the extent to which they were undermined by the force of historical circumstances or his own will, on the other.

First, however, a brief review of Toussaint's position in St. Domingue at this point in time may help to explain why the Federalist administration of John Adams would be engaged in nearly official diplomatic relations with a former slave and revolutionary black emancipator and, conversely, why the latter should be engaged in diplomacy with a major slaveholding power. Toussaint began his revolutionary career while fighting alongside rebel slave leaders Jean-François and Biassou under the banner of Spain and monarchy during the first years of the 1791 slave rebellion. By the end of August 1793, the black rebel armies were still allied with Spain (now at war with France in Europe) and in control of significant portions of the colony's northern province. Counterrevolutionary and secessionist factionalism among planters and other groups of colonial whites, combined with the mounting threat of a British invasion, had pushed the French civil commissioner, Léger-Félicité Sonthonax, to declare slavery abolished in the northern part of the colony, a step that his colleague, Étienne Polverel, followed in October by declaring general emancipation in the remaining parts of the colony under French control. By so doing, the commissioners had hoped to combine the strengths of free plantation laborers, who would now be earning a small wage, with those of the black insurgents, each counterpart acting as soldiers in defense of the Republic and the colony. It was not until May 1794, however, that Toussaint deserted his allies of convenience, joined the French Republican army, and embraced the cause of revolutionary France, whose government had decreed slavery abolished on February 4, 1794, thereby extending universal French citizenship to former slaves in all French territories.

Thus, with Toussaint's defection from Spain, most of the rebel-occupied northern territories were liberated and soon back under French control, but the real military threat for republican St. Domingue came from the British, whose invasion at the end of 1793 was facilitated by an alliance with white secessionist colonists, as well as pro-British factions among the formerly free colored property owners, who opposed general emancipation. By now the British were in possession of the extreme western peninsular portion of the south, Môle St.-Nicolas at the western extremity of the north, and critical portions of the middle coastal areas and port towns of the western province. In 1796, following a coup led by a mulatto faction in the north to depose French Governor General Étienne Laveaux and take control of the capital, Toussaint was named lieutenant governor of St. Domingue and then, on May 1, 1797, commander in chief of the French colonial army in St. Domingue. In May 1798, with the final defeat of the ill-fated British occupation, Toussaint personally negotiated the terms of the British evacuation, thus overriding the authority of the newly arrived agent of France, General Marie-Théodore-Joseph Hédouville. He had thus risen to a position of overpowering authority, and from this point on, he single-mindedly exercised his power to begin laying the groundwork for what he ultimately envisaged would be a prosperous self-governing territory of France, *but* under sovereign black rule.

One reason for this critical distinction was that Toussaint no longer had much trust in the conservative post-Jacobin government of the Directory, which was responsible for the reorganization of the colonies into overseas departments of the French Republic, "one and indivisible," as well as for the implementation of universal citizenship and equality among the former slaves, most of them African-born. In addition, the Directory had sent a military, rather than a civil, agent to represent French Republican authority in St. Domingue and had come very close to suspending application of the French Constitution of Year 3 (1795), which sanctioned the abolition of slavery.[1] Toussaint rightly feared the resurgence of royalist and other proslavery factions, both inside and outside the government, which were pushing for a restoration of the slave trade and the pre-1789 colonial regime. Fully aware of the dangers that lay ahead so long as St. Domingue remained subject to the aleatory laws of the metropolis regarding the colonies, he took it upon himself to create the foundations for St. Domingue's political autonomy and, ideally, the economic basis for bringing the colony into the modern Atlantic world as an emancipated black state. But *how*? And how could a former slave colony in the midst of revolution and international warfare give itself an independent state structure? With what powers, and with what consequences? What kind of a society would it be? In the absence of any metropolitan guarantees, how would such an entity on its own be able to defend general emancipation, which was, after all, the basis of its new existence? And would there not be fundamental contradictions in the very concept and exercise of colonial sovereignty?

Toussaint's state-in-the-making, as it were, revolved around three overriding and interlocking objectives. The first, of course, was, the defense of general emancipation, which in the uncertain world of colonial slavery and

Atlantic imperialism—not to mention the uncertainties of the French Revolution—would require both supreme black rule and a well-fortified indigenous army. For this, Toussaint needed to restore the economy, revive exports, and accumulate sufficient foreign reserves with which to sustain the emerging state and military, but the path he chose toward economic recovery and, optimally, economic growth was neither innovative nor was it particularly liberating for the newly freed laborers. It was built on the ruins of the pre-1789 regime of large-scale plantation agriculture and commodity exports, as well as on the post-1793 emancipationist regime first instituted by the French civil commissioners, Léger-Félicité Sonthonax and Étienne Polverel, which relied exclusively upon collectivized plantation labor and the suppression of individual liberties.[2]

Thus, to restore the colony's war-torn economy, which by 1795 had left St. Domingue's exports virtually nonexistent, Toussaint sought to reinforce, rather than reform, the existing agrarian structure; in addition, in order to repress the implacable popular drive toward independent peasant smallholding among the masses, which, if left unchecked, would eventually undermine his regime, he placed the laborers under military, rather than civil administration. Moreover, he created a new category of landholders by leasing to his leading generals and high-ranking officers the abandoned or sequestered estates of the white émigré and exiled planters, thus further reducing the laborers to a condition of quasi-feudal serfdom, despite the provision that they receive a small portion of crop revenues as wages.[3]

And so, if increased exports and the capacity to generate foreign reserves were essential to building the state and to sustaining an indigenous black army to defend antislavery goals in the colonial Atlantic, then in Toussaint's domestic policy, it was the army that would coerce the freed workers to produce the exports, the army that would repress internal dissent or resistance, and the army that would deter individual initiatives toward an alternative model of agricultural production based on independent smallholdings and domestic markets. For, the unavoidable fact was that, with or without slave emancipation, the colony's prosperity depended on its agricultural exports. By their very nature, plantation labor and agriculture in the colonial Atlantic were tied to international commerce, and without commerce, Toussaint's own hands were tied.

Thus exports were vital for St. Domingue to reenter the commercial Atlantic as an international player, but for these to flourish, Toussaint needed wider markets and all of the advantages of free-market trade relations, notably with neutral countries like the United States. Clearly, so long as France was engaged in continental warfare, it could barely furnish the basic needs of the colony, let alone the military ones. Moreover, trade with French merchants, when it did transpire, was costly, as the terms of trade meant that Toussaint would have to buy dearly, sell cheaply, remain dependent upon mercantile price-fixing, and cope with inadequate supplies of basic goods. Such a disadvantage was even further compounded by the fact that French colonial currency was worth only two-thirds that of French metropolitan currency, the net result being a serious drainage of colonial currency at a time when Toussaint was committed to a program of renewed prosperity, the revival of plantation exports, and an accumulation of foreign reserves.[4] All of this inevitably brought him into the entangled world of international diplomacy and the vortex of a new Atlantic colonialism. He would have to contend with three major powers, Great Britain, the United States, and France, each motivated by particular national interests, in order to consolidate his own government and preserve the freedom of his people.

Thus, at the time of the British evacuation in August 1798, Toussaint sought to maximize his options and, to the extent that he could, turn the terms of Britain's military troop withdrawal to his advantage. To this end, as commander in chief of the French colonial army, he entered into direct negotiations—putatively, as equal to equal—with General Maitland, deliberately bypassing the authority of France's legally constituted agent, General Hédouville. Then, in exchange for the evacuation of Britain's troops and in order to allow Great Britain an honorable withdrawal, Toussaint negotiated and signed a mutually expedient convention with General Maitland that would guarantee Great Britain *protected and exclusive* trading relations with St. Domingue. Additionally, however, several secret clauses were attached in which Great Britain promised not to attack St. Domingue for the remainder of the war with France in Europe and, more to the point for Toussaint, not to intervene in any way in the internal governance of the colony. Toussaint, for his part, promised the same with regard to Jamaica, which meant that he would not try to export general emancipation beyond the shores of St. Domingue. Finally, Maitland promised to induce the British government to allow provisions to be brought to St. Domingue ports, to enter without risk of privateer attack, and to be paid for in colonial exports that would also leave the ports unhampered.[5] The convention was, in effect, a kind of hermetic free-trade agreement with an enemy of France. By acting in his own name, without consulting—and without the consent of—any higher French authority, Toussaint had virtually assumed the powers of a head of state and was exercising one of the functions that normally define a sovereign state—namely, that of negotiating international treaties.

Effectively, he had neutralized Hédouville as an agent of French authority and, after the latter committed a series of blunders that further envenomed relations not only between the two of them but, more seriously, between the French agent and the black officers of his army, Toussaint placed Hédouville under arrest and forced his departure for France, thus leaving himself with undisputed administrative power.[6] Then, without hesitation, Toussaint took another step to secure the expansion of St. Domingue's commerce, this time with the Americans. Again moving boldly in the direction of sovereignty, he personally addressed a letter to U.S. President John Adams on November 6, 1798, and sent it by his treasurer general, Joseph Bunel, who was accompanied by American consul Jacob Mayer. In the letter, he lamented the recent cessation of commerce between the United States and St. Domingue, the motives for which he claimed to be unaware of, and argued persuasively in favor of a reopening of trade between the two states for the mutual benefit of each party. He evidently was aware of the diplomatic hostilities between the United States and France in their Quasi-War against each other's shipping, since he went to considerable lengths personally to promise protection for American ships "in the ports of the French republic" in St. Domingue. "You can be assured," he wrote to Adams, "that the Americans will find [here] protection and security; that the flag of the United States will be respected here as would that of any other friend or ally of France; that orders will be given to this effect by our cruising corsairs; that I will facilitate, by all the means in my power, the prompt return [of American ships] to their country, and they will be paid in full for the cargo they will have brought."[7]

Basically Toussaint sought to circumvent the interruption of commerce with U.S. merchants that resulted from the Quasi-War and to officialize and expand such trade as was now being conducted clandestinely. For the Americans, as a neutral power, ongoing unhampered trade with St. Domingue was above all a matter of business and profits. The West Indian trade had always been crucial to the development of American commerce, and by now U.S. trade with St. Domingue ranked second in importance only with that of Great Britain in the commercial relations of the young republic.[8] The foreign policy adopted under the Adams administration with respect to St. Domingue reflected these commercial concerns, just as the cautious formulation of diplomatic relations with a virtually sovereign black state also exposed embedded contradictions in early American attitudes toward slavery, slave emancipation, and race. For his part, Toussaint sought favorable trade relations with the United States, above all, as a means to an overriding goal: the preservation of general emancipation and the survival of St. Domingue as a free and autonomous black state with the capacity to secure for itself a position as a player, if only a subordinate one, in the uncertain Atlantic environment of colonialism and slavery, dominated by the commercial powers of Great Britain, France, and the United States.

American trade with St. Domingue, though, was not one of Toussaint's innovations. Since the early 1790s, with the initial outbreak of slave rebellions across the colony and white colonial factions fighting each other, and then, in 1793, with the looming threat of the British invasion, the French authorities were utterly dependent on U.S. supplies, without which, they feared, the colony would be lost, most likely to Great Britain at that point.[9] In May 1793, the two French civil commissioners had written in distress to Edmond Genêt, the French minister in Philadelphia, that "if the English in the New World [Americans] do not come promptly to our aid, the ruin of St. Domingue is consummated." Later that year, Genêt resigned himself to the fact that "all of the commerce is already in their [the Americans'] hands as a result of the war and of the necessity for us to open the ports so that they would not perish from famine."[10] Thus, he had little alternative but to foster and facilitate commerce between the United States and St. Domingue, while offering protection for American vessels. But the war against France in Europe and the British invasion of St. Domingue in 1793–1794 tended to undermine French control over the colony, as did the Jay Treaty between the United States and Great Britain in November 1794, which American merchants interpreted as allowing trade with British colonial possessions, including the British-occupied territories of St. Domingue. What this meant for American merchants was expanded opportunities for trade. In fact, the Americans had been more than eager to supply both sides, in spite of French condemnations of U.S. merchants for trading with British-occupied zones of the colony and in spite of British condemnations of American merchants for trading with French-held St. Domingue. All of this, of course, led to the escalation of tensions between the United States and France and the outbreak of open hostilities on each other's shipping. Relations were further exacerbated by the exposure of the so-called XYZ Affair, which led Congress on July 7, 1798, to break off U.S. treaty arrangements with France and thereby officially to suspend all trade to St. Domingue.[11] These were the perfect conditions for Toussaint to negotiate in his own interests with the United States and Great Britain, and it is why he had taken it upon himself on November 6, 1798, to write to President Adams in favor of resuming normal and healthy trade relations between the two countries.

Renewed commerce depended, of course, upon the colony's capacity to produce plantation crops with which to pay for sorely needed basic goods and provide the means by which to feed and clothe Toussaint's army. In one of the first of a series of proclamations relating to the colony's land and labor resources, issued on November 15, 1798, Toussaint began to reorganize and reinforce the plantation structure by placing it increasingly under the supervision, if not directly into the hands of, the military and, in the process, began transforming the civil basis of the society into a military one. In this proclamation, Toussaint charged his lieutenants, the military police, and local parish commanders of the army with enforcing work discipline and overall submission of the plantation laborers, along with forcing those workers who had abandoned their estates for other opportunities to return.[12] Further, he began farming out, or leasing, properties that had been sequestered by the state to the superior officers and leading generals of his army, who, as leaseholders, now constituted a new category of proprietorship and, as far as the plantation laborers were concerned, a new category of mastership over them.[13]

In conjunction with these measures aimed at restoring colonial exports, Toussaint passed other ordinances, beginning with one on November 17, 1798, by which he sought to redress the colony's balance of trade, offset the drainage of colonial currency, and increase government revenues. In it he lamented: "The small volume of trade [at present] with the Americans and the Danish tends only to drain the colony of its specie. These foreign traders bring mostly luxury goods and very few staples, of which the colony is constantly deprived to meet its basic needs."[14]

This "mercantilist maneuver," as Toussaint aptly called it, had the threefold detrimental effect of maintaining the high cost of basic staples by reducing the supply, thereby creating scarcity and increasing the demand; of draining the colony of its specie by the high cost of the luxury goods; and of driving down prices for colonial export commodities by virtue of restricted outlets for plantation production. In consequence, Toussaint restricted the disembarkment of luxury goods to one-third of a ship's cargo, prohibited the exportation of colonial specie in any form, and, to counter fraud and corruption, tightened administrative controls over customs and treasury officials, who were, however, authorized to purchase foreign cargoes by paying in colonial commodities and to sell for specie any luxury goods they had purchased.[15]

As important as these regulatory measures were to strengthening his government and his army, without official normalization and therefore expansion of trade with neutral powers like the United States, such measures remained insufficient.

Finally, on February 9, 1799, the U.S. Congress passed and President Adams signed a law that exempted St. Domingue from the U.S. embargo on trade with France (known as "Toussaint's Clause") and therefore reopened normal trade with the colony. Adams then appointed Edward Stevens as consul general to St. Domingue, giving him a title that might imply, although it did not actually confirm, official recognition of independent status for St. Domingue. It was at any rate a de facto recognition. So now, Toussaint had two major economic allies, the one a declared enemy, the other a quasi-enemy of France. As for Stevens, the reopening of trade with Toussaint was not only good policy but an absolute necessity for the U.S. merchant houses that had been doing business clandestinely anyway since the initial American embargo on French ports, and he urged that a common agreement be reached with Great Britain "in the interests of America." For Maitland, on the British side, trade with St. Domingue, if properly regulated and contained within a United States-Great Britain-St. Domingue triangle, would not only be economically beneficial to Britain, as it would strike a blow at French commerce, but would also isolate St. Domingue and prevent the spread of slave emancipation elsewhere in the Caribbean, not to mention the southern United States. Thus, a three-way alliance, known as "Heads of Regulation," was signed on June 13, 1799. Essentially, it expanded the earlier Louverture-Maitland agreement and now opened direct trade with St. Domingue to both British and American shipping. Specifically, the agreement formally required Toussaint to protect British and American vessels against French privateering; prohibited all French and other foreign traders from doing business with the island without passports delivered by Toussaint, Great Britain, and the United States; designated two ports, le Cap and Port-au-Prince, both under Toussaint's control, through which British and American goods would pass; and finally, reiterated the containment of slave emancipation to St. Domingue.[16]

However, the arrangement was not without significant drawbacks for Toussaint. Certain clauses of the agreement (among other prohibitions) formally prohibited St. Domingue from having its own merchant marine or navy by restricting the size of its ships to fifty tons and their navigation to five leagues from the northern coastline.[17] So, although Toussaint had broadened his trading partners and widened his markets, Anglo-American commerce with St. Domingue, including the carrying trade of Toussaint's colonial exports, would nonetheless be handled exclusively aboard British and American bottoms. At the same time, though, the agreement did permit Toussaint to pursue another aim on his agenda. This aim stemmed from a particular set of domestic concerns, both political and military, and it involved consolidating his supremacy over the colony's former free colored elite, led by the staunchly pro-French mulatto military commander of the south, General André Rigaud. For one thing, slave emancipation had made St. Domingue a multiracial egalitarian society, and with Toussaint Louverture as commander in chief of the military and supreme administrative authority in the colony, there were in effect two elites vying for the power to govern and direct the destiny of the colony: the former free coloreds and the emergent black military elite. Toussaint had put it to Edward Stevens that Rigaud, even though subordinate in rank, would not guarantee protection of American vessels from privateering attacks in the ports under his command and, anticipating the impending civil war between them, insisted that these ports be excluded from the new trade agreement so as to prevent Rigaud from supplying his army and to ensure his defeat.

Other considerations also came into play in Toussaint's efforts to neutralize his rival. The Directory in France had recently issued orders for an invasion of Jamaica to be spearheaded by an expeditionary army from St. Domingue, purportedly in the name of republicanism and slave emancipation. If Rigaud were in command, he most certainly would carry out the invasion, given both his unwavering pro-French position and the backing he had received from Hédouville prior to his expulsion by Toussaint. Such a situation would wreck Toussaint's treaty arrangements with Maitland, which hinged upon a mutual agreement not to meddle in each other's territory and for Toussaint, explicitly, not to touch Jamaica. Writing to Secretary of State Timothy Pickering, Stevens reasoned that the projected Jamaica expedition was probably a ploy of the Directory, in conjunction with Rigaud, to get rid of Toussaint Louverture and his chief military officers, who were now running the colony.[18] One way or another, it was a "no-win" proposition for Toussaint, for if he and his army succeeded, this would separate Jamaica from Great Britain and diminish the latter's colonial and commercial resources. It would also mean that he had broken his treaty engagements with Maitland and lost his credibility. Alternatively, if Toussaint and his army failed, they would likewise be diminished and discredited and would cease to be a force with which to be reckoned. The old order, Stevens surmised, might even be restored as a consequence and slavery reestablished.[19] In any event, Toussaint wisely refused to carry out the orders of the Directory so that he could steer his course independently with the United States and Great Britain, preserve his integrity, and maintain the trade agreements he had just concluded. As Stevens put it to General Maitland: "Toussaint is determined to prevent this expedition, in conformity to his treaty with you. He has forbidden Rigaud to continue his preparations, and is resolved to march against him and reduce him to obedience."[20] This issue was only one among other far more serious ones that would precipitate the outbreak of civil war between the two rival leaders, and Toussaint's trade agreements with the United States and Great Britain, along with his secret clauses to exclude the southern ports under Rigaud's command, were crucial to his winning it.[21]

The Americans, for their part, had good reason to want to ensure Toussaint's victory over his rival. Clearly they saw in him the stronger of the two protagonists: he had the support of most of the blacks in the colony and, importantly, of all of the whites, many of whom had been allowed by Toussaint to return to the colony and repossess their properties. "Were [Toussaint's] power uncontrolled," Stevens wrote, "he would exercise it in protecting commerce, encouraging agriculture, and establishing useful regulations for the internal government of the colony." But, "if Toussaint should prove unsuccessful, all the arrangements we have made respecting commerce must fall to the ground. The most solemn treaty would have little weight with a man of Rigaud's capricious and tyrannical temperament."[22] Thus it was absolutely necessary to support Toussaint "by every legal measure" possible, not only to make sure that he win the civil war, but that he bring it to a quick and decisive end so that agricultural production and commerce could again take off. For one thing, a considerable number of plantation laborers had been drafted into Toussaint's army, plantation animals and equipment had been requisitioned for military use, crops in the fields remained unharvested, while existing harvests like coffee remained in entrepôts, and grinding on the sugar estates had come to a halt. Referring to the huge unexported quantities of coffee at the southern port towns of Jérémie, Grand and Petit Goâve, Miragoâne, and Léogane, Stevens remarked that "all this will be lost to the commercial world" so long as the civil war lasted.[23]

Furthermore, from the vantage point of the Americans, and the British as well, Toussaint was seeking to separate himself from the orbit of French authority, and "as soon as Rigaud falls," Stevens opined, "Roume [the last remaining French agent] will be sent off, and from that moment, *the power of the Directory will cease in this colony.*"²⁴ Then, Stevens believed, or at least anticipated, Toussaint would declare independence. Thus, insofar as Toussaint continued to defy French authority, American support for him was at least as much anti-French as it was pro-American. Writing to the secretary of state, Stevens announced what *he* understood to be Toussaint's intentions: "He is taking his measures slowly but securely. All connection with France will soon be broken off. If he is not disturbed he will preserve appearances a little longer. But as soon as France interferes with this colony he will throw off the mask and declare it independent."²⁵ From the American point of view, so long as it was *Toussaint* who declared independence, the colony would then no longer be under French dominion, and the United States could carry on business with St. Domingue without having to extend official diplomatic recognition. For a high Federalist like Alexander Hamilton, the best situation would be one in which Toussaint would declare independence first. Writing to Pickering on February 9, 1799, the day the act of Congress reopening trade with St. Domingue was passed and roughly four months before the civil war actually broke out, Hamilton expressed the view that the United States should give Toussaint verbal but nonetheless explicit assurances that, upon his declaration of independence, the commercial intercourse of the United States with the island would continue so long as Toussaint maintained this independence and protected U.S. vessels and property. But the United States should *not* take the initiative to extend formal recognition.²⁶ Thus, if Toussaint should declare independence, the United States could not be held responsible; St. Domingue would no longer be French, and therefore trade with the island would be licit and unimpeded. Secretary of State Pickering held a similar view, though he stopped just short of using official diplomatic measures to urge such a declaration of independence. He explained himself quite candidly to Rufus King, American consul to Great Britain at that time, "We meddle not with the politics of the island. T——T will pursue what he deems is in his best interests and that of his people; he will probably declare the island independent. It is probable that he wishes to assure himself of our commerce as the necessary means of obtaining it. Neither moral nor political considerations could induce us to discourage him; both would warrant us in urging him to the *Declaration. Yet we shall not do it.* We shall go no further than the Act of Congress allows."²⁷ He was especially concerned with the possible repercussions that direct involvement in a St. Domingue declaration might have on the United States, for then, he argued, America would never receive indemnities from France for the damages incurred on U.S. shipping: "The commerce of Saint Domingue presents us the only means of compensation, and this we shall obtain." So, free trade with Toussaint was commercially beneficial, and having Toussaint declare independence himself would be diplomatically pragmatic with regard to United States-French relations, and, as far as any potential threat to slavery was concerned, a safe bet. Pickering went on to point out that, for the time being, St. Domingue's needs were military ones: "The Government must be a military one during the present war, and perhaps for a much longer period. The commerce of the United States and of other nations . . . will amply supply all their wants, and take off all their produce." In this light, the population of St. Domingue would be tied to agriculture and nothing more. In fact, the terms of the Heads of Regulation concluded by Toussaint, Stevens, and Maitland in June 1799 ensured that St. Domingue would never have a navy or merchant marine capable of posing a threat to U.S. commerce since Toussaint's own ships would not be allowed to engage in the carrying trade between their respective countries. Thus, confined to themselves, "The Blacks of St. Domingo will be incomparably less dangerous than if they remain subjects of France." The reason for this, in Pickering's view, was that France could always mobilize and use such a powerful black army in some future war to conquer "all the British Isles and put in jeopardy our Southern States." On this account, Pickering was probably feeling a bit paranoid, for, in the only instance where there was any evidence at all for a French colonial expedition against a British isle, it was more likely a maneuver of the Directory to get Toussaint out of the way than to conquer Jamaica to spread slave emancipation. President Adams, for his part, was also very much against formal recognition of St. Domingue independence in that it would strain U.S. relations with other slaveholding European nations, not to mention France, with whom Adams genuinely sought a peaceable outcome to the Quasi-War.[28]

On the latter point Thomas Jefferson, then vice president under John Adams, was equally circumspect, but for slightly different reasons. On the whole, he was against reopening trade with "Toussaint and his black subjects," as he put it, if by so doing, the United States should aid and endorse their independence movement and thereby strike a blow at France.[29] Moreover, given that the United States already had armed vessels stationed around the French islands to protect her commerce in the ongoing Quasi-War, the reopening of trade with Toussaint, who was in rebellion against French authority, would surely be more than the Directory would bear. Potentially, it could provoke a full declaration of war by France against the United States at a time when it seemed that France was on the verge of reconciling its differences with the Americans.[30] But once trade was officially reopened with St. Domingue in February 1799, Jefferson's fears centered more pointedly on the repercussions of free trade with a nominally sovereign black state upon its black brethren still in slavery in the southern United States.[31] Thus, as opposed to his Federalist counterparts, who feared that France might deploy Toussaint's powerful black army against the United States if St. Domingue remained under French control, and who therefore fostered the separation of St. Domingue from France, Jefferson feared the influence on the South of an independent St. Domingue doing business with free white Americans, for "We may expect therefore black crews, supercargoes and missionaries thence into the Southern states; and when that leven [sic] begins to work . . . we have to fear it."[32] Already Toussaint had sent Joseph Bunel, his secretary treasurer—a merchant and former white plantation manager in St. Domingue—as special envoy to negotiate with President Adams on the reopening of trade with the United States. Bunel was, incidentally, married to a former free black woman, Marie Franchette Estève, herself a merchant in le Cap and in Philadelphia. But the real problem for the Americans, whether Federalist or Republican, was the uncertain political status of St. Domingue at this particular juncture.

Meanwhile, Toussaint was pursuing his own ends. He took advantage of U.S. commercial interests in the context of political and maritime hostilities between the United States and France and of war between France and Great Britain to foster trade with both. Thus, with a restoration of plantation exports, he would be able to obtain the foreign exchange revenues necessary to supply and equip his army, not only to win the war against Rigaud but to strengthen St. Domingue's overall military defenses and preserve general emancipation in an imperialist slaveholding world. He pursued these ends by dealing with two major slaveholding nations, while defying France and still refusing to declare St. Domingue independent.

Only two months into the civil war, in a letter of August 14, 1799, Toussaint used his good relations with the Americans, and with Consul General Edward Stevens in particular, to request from President Adams several warships as naval aid with which to crush Rigaud and, at the same time, protect commerce outside the two treaty-designated port cities of le Cap and Port au Prince, while his army continued to wage war on land.[33] Although Toussaint did not receive the warships at that time, U.S. naval aid was instrumental, perhaps even decisive, in Toussaint's winning the campaign against Jacmel

(Rigaud's stronghold) early the following year and in turning the tide of the war definitively in his favor. By early January 1800, the town was under full siege by some ten thousand of Toussaint's troops. Edwards clearly anticipated that Toussaint would secure not only the surrender of Jacmel, but the final defeat of Rigaud as well, and thus reign supreme. Writing to Secretary of State Timothy Pickering, the consul general asked for instructions should there be any alteration in U.S. relations with St. Domingue, for, he asserted, "I foresee that a new order of things will shortly take place here, and should wish to be prepared for the event."[34] By the "new order of things," Stevens was referring to an eventual declaration of independence by Toussaint. While this may have been wishful thinking on Stevens's part, it did not deter the United States from lending Toussaint decisive support in the fall of Jacmel. In March 1800, the Adams government gave instructions to allow American naval commanders to go beyond the mere blockading of southern ports and to engage their ships in battle in order to guarantee Toussaint's victory over Rigaud.[35] According to an officer aboard the American battleship the *General Greene*, commanded by Captain Christopher Perry, "We were ordered . . . to make a cruize around Hispaniola . . . for the purpose of aiding General Toussaint in the capture of Jacmel. We cruised off that port a considerable time to intercept supplies [destined] for Rigaud. This had the desired effect. Jacmel, closely besieged on the land side by Toussaint's army, and blockaded by the *General Greene*, was reduced to a state of starvation." Despite a last desperate effort to force Toussaint's lines, more than five thousand of Rigaud's men fell into Toussaint's hands. The *General Greene* opened fire and bombarded three of Rigaud's forts for a good half hour, forcing Rigaud's men to evacuate the town and two of the forts and to concentrate themselves in the strongest of the three: "This fort, however, soon hauled down its colors." The officer then declared that "the capture of Jacmel [was of] infinite consequence to Toussaint, and of high importance to the commerce of the United States to this island," no doubt because it prefigured the overthrow of Rigaud.[36] The extent of U.S. complicity with Toussaint was further exemplified by Toussaint's expression of gratitude in a letter to Edward Stevens for the aid he received from Captain Perry and the *General Greene*: "Nothing could equal his [Captain Perry's] kindness, his activity, his watchfulness and his zeal in protecting me, in unhappy circumstances, for this part of the colony. He has contributed not a little to the success by his cruise, every effort being made by him to aid me in the taking of Jacmel."[37] Then, when Toussaint wished to send two of his agents to the United States, Perry went against the orders of his superior commanding officer, delayed departure of the *General Greene* until Toussaint's agents were ready, and, just before leaving, received Toussaint on board with a "federal salute," a gesture tantamount to the official twenty-one-gun salute of the American government.[38]

Finally, to hasten Rigaud's final defeat and the opening of all St. Domingue's ports to full unfettered commerce, a good number of American warships that were in the Caribbean hunting down French vessels were redeployed to St. Domingue to choke out the remaining ports of the south that were still under Rigaud's command.[39] Thus, beginning with Jacmel, as other ports fell into the hands of Toussaint, they were thrown open to American commerce; on August 1, 1800, Rigaud surrendered at les Cayes and left in exile for France, leaving Toussaint with supreme political and military authority over the colony.

At this point, Toussaint could have declared independence *had he wanted to*. We may never know whether he was actually on the verge of preparing an eventual declaration of independence or not, but he was dealing with France's enemies for trade. He was defying French authority in the colony, while maintaining deferential relations with the metropolis, and he kept both British and American diplomats speculating about the consequences and ramifications of St. Domingue independence for their own interests. Even President Adams had this to say about the black statesman during the course of the civil war in July 1799: "Toussaint has evidently puzzled himself, the French government, the English Cabinet, and the Administration of the United States. All the rest of the world knows as little what to do with him as he knows what to do with himself."[40] Toussaint had indeed entered the world of nation-states and plunged himself into the vortex of imperialist politics, but to claim he did not really know what he was doing at this point is perhaps disingenuous. He certainly was not a dupe to the ultimate aims of British-American commercial interests, and even less so to those of British imperialism. Had he broken his ties definitively with France in 1799 or 1800, St. Domingue would have been little more than a convenient protectorate of the United States and Great Britain, a pawn serving the interests of American commerce and British imperialism, not the least of which interests (with regard to the latter) may have been an eventual restoration of the prerevolutionary regime of white racial supremacy and perhaps even slavery. An independent St. Domingue in the hands of British-American interests would have been left without the political counterweight of an equally powerful European mother country that, up to this point, had not officially revoked slave emancipation. Neither the United States nor Great Britain had ever encouraged St. Domingue independence for the sake of black emancipation and self-determination, but rather, in order to wrench the colony away from France and further their own commerce. They accepted slave emancipation on the single island of St. Domingue because at that point there was nothing that could be done about it, and, if contained to St. Domingue alone, they hoped to preempt the potential dangers for their own slaveholding territories of an independent black state born of slave revolt. And once the war in Europe would be over, a St. Domingue under British dominion would hardly be impervious to the colonialism and racialism of imperial rule. Thus, so long as France maintained slave emancipation, Toussaint remained deferential and stopped just short of breaking formal ties with the metropolis, but in 1801 he wrote and promulgated a constitution that gave him supreme legislative and executive powers, made him governor general for life, brought the Spanish part of the island under his jurisdiction, and nominally turned the colony into a black self-governing territory of the French Empire in which slavery was forever banished.

Of course, by now, too many other events had already occurred to undermine Toussaint's project of black self-determination. On September 30, 1800, only two months after his victory over Rigaud in the civil war, the Treaty of Mortefontaine was signed in Paris ending the Quasi-War between the United States and France, as well as Toussaint's exclusive trade alliance with the Americans. The very next day, on October 1, the Treaty of Idelfonso was signed to confirm the transfer of Louisiana from Spain to France; then came the presidential election victory of Thomas Jefferson over John Adams in early 1801 and, the final thunderbolt for Toussaint, the signing in October 1801 of the Amiens peace preliminaries between France and Great Britain. With Napoleon Bonaparte in power, and with Louisiana in the hands of France, St. Domingue was to become the cornerstone for a wider French empire in the Mississippi Valley. But that, of course, depended upon a French victory over the emancipated blacks of St. Domingue and a restoration of slavery. Here, the implications for Jefferson of Haiti's engaging in a real war of independence from France were problematic. While he let it be known initially that he would support a French expedition against St. Domingue to remove Toussaint and restore the colonial regime, he withdrew such support when he realized that a French victory in St. Domingue would then mean an expedition to occupy Louisiana and therefore cut off the security and well-being of the young republic, if not threaten its existence. The fact was, Jefferson needed the victory of the Haitian masses over Bonaparte's army in their life-and-death struggle for freedom in order to make Louisiana worthless to France. As Henry Adams put it retrospectively, "Without that island, the system [of France] had hands, feet, and even a head, but no body. Of what use was Louisiana when France had clearly lost the main colony which Louisiana was meant to feed and fortify?"[41] Referring to Henry Adams's monumental history of the United States, the Haitian historian and diplomat Dantès Bellegarde wrote that it was Adams who "clearly revealed the undeniable fact that the Haitians, by exterminating the army in St. Domingue of Captain-General Leclerc, had at the same time destroyed the dream of Napoleon to create a great French empire in the Mississippi Valley. The result was the sale of Louisiana to the United States for the miserable sum of $18,000,000; thus Haiti contributed to the maintenance and development of the American nation."[42] For Adams, "It was the prejudice of race alone [that] blinded the American people to the debt they owed to the desperate courage of five hundred thousand Haytian negroes who would not be enslaved."[43] The perverse irony was that the Haitian victory over Bonaparte also contributed to the maintenance and expansion of American slavery, while nonrecognition of Haiti's independence by the United States lasted yet another fifty-eight years.

What Toussaint had achieved for a brief period was a quasi-sovereignty that would in fact persist long after formal Haitian independence. His commercial relations with Great Britain and the United States, for one thing, were dependent on an international environment created by the French Revolution and the Napoleonic Wars. He exploited the advantages afforded by such an environment, but he could control neither the pace nor the direction of events once Bonaparte came to power, and with trade supremacy in the hands of the British and his trade relations with the United States limited to those of a captive junior partner, it was more the pretense of sovereignty than the real thing. Moreover, the state Toussaint built by which to buttress any such sovereignty and to defend black emancipation ultimately relied upon the suppression of popular sovereignty, upon the denial of individual liberties, and above all upon the denial of proprietorship and independent smallholding, which were the foundations of personal freedom for the greater mass of Haiti's agrarian laborers. Ironically, that which guaranteed the rights of citizenship in France and the early American republic and potentially could have provided a basis for citizenship in the newly independent black state was subverted under Toussaint's regime. In the process of building a sovereign, yet still colonial, black state to defend antislavery—in itself a supremely revolutionary act in the advancement of human freedom—civil society was curtailed.

By the mid-nineteenth century, Haiti did become a nation of small peasant producers with access to land for large segments of the peasantry, but by this time, the gap between "state" and "nation," as Michel-Rolph Trouillot put it, had become virtually an unbridgeable one.[44] By this time, too, having suffered for two decades without international recognition and without access to foreign capital or to external commercial markets on equitable terms of exchange, then having been crippled first by Thomas Jefferson's trade embargo of 1807 and after that by an outrageous indemnity to France in exchange for recognition in 1825, the country was left without the means by which to assert its political independence, let alone maintain economic stability and growth.

By the very terms of its existence, Haiti stood proudly as a nation that had overthrown its colonial status in the names of both human freedom *and* racial equality; and as a beacon of black liberation, it stood in stark contrast to the early American republic in which slavery remained foundational in the process of constructing the nation. Revolutionary Haiti exposed the interdependent and interlocking relations between slave emancipation and the construction of a sovereign state in the slaveholding Atlantic. The problems of defining citizenship and the rights of citizenship, the difficulties in laying the foundations for a political economy of the state and the nation, and the necessity of taking one's place and defending it as a recognized player in the daunting dimensions of the slaveholding Atlantic were all undertaken by Toussaint in his relations with the United States. In so doing, he exposed both the potentialities and the limitations of the time; in all of this, the Haitian revolutionary paradigm exposed the many hidden faces of modernity.

CHAPTER 2

(Mis)reading the Revolution

Philadelphia and "St. Domingo," 1789–1792

JAMES ALEXANDER DUN

Pulses quickened in Philadelphia after William Davis, captain of the brig *Hetty*, arrived in July 1791 from the French colony of St. Domingue. While this physiological impact was due in part to the sugar and coffee unloaded from the vessel's hold, other stirrings came from a portion of Davis's cargo not listed on the *Hetty*'s manifest: information. Having left the brig with a pilot who would bring it up the Delaware, Davis sped ahead to Philadelphia in order to tell of "a great disturbance" in the colony. Just before he sailed, Davis related, the governor had made public the fact that the National Assembly in Paris had passed a decree that "gave to the free negroes and mulattoes in [the] colonies equal rights with the other inhabitants." In response, the local government had made moves that seemed to place the colony on a path towards civil war. Not only did the Provincial Assembly resolve to reject the decree; it also voted to prepare to fight the 45,000 French soldiers rumored to be en route to enforce it and to send representatives "to the different European Courts, inviting their assistance to render their opposition effectual."[1] Subsequent arrivals seconded and amplified Davis's news. Another captain reported that French regulars at Martinique were about to embark to force St. Domingue to accept the decree, which ensured "*that the mulatoes* [sic] *and negroes were to enjoy every right of free men.*" Colonists in Cap-Français, enraged, had taken possession of a French naval ship, "plucked the national cockades from their hats, mounted black British ribbons," and made overtures to England and Jamaica.[2]

While these portraits of disloyalty and disorder were contested over the following weeks, the breathless quality of this news was maintained as readers in Philadelphia sought to understand the meaning of the National Assembly's Decree of May 15, 1791, in St. Domingue.[3] Their scrutiny was intense. When, two months later, news arrived of a massive slave insurrection on the Plaine du Nord around Cap-Français, Philadelphians were already aware of the island as a place of "disturbances." If the protagonists had changed, the general tenor of the news remained the same.

That the Decree of May 15 received as much attention in Philadelphia as the beginning of the slave insurrections is jarring to modern understandings of the Haitian Revolution. The risings on August 22 are typically posed as an important start to the series of events by which the colony of St. Domingue became the nation of Haiti. The Decree of May 15, at best, is depicted as background to this opening. This makes sense. Over the early 1790s, the National and Constituent Assemblies treated colonial issues fleetingly and as peripheral to the greater business of the domestic revolution. The extent of their notice of West Indian affairs lay in their efforts to determine the new government's relationship to its colonies. Only haltingly did they address the implications of the ideals of the French Revolution for slavery or racial discrimination, and, in general, their efforts were reactions to colonial initiatives. The Decree of May 15 was an important moment in the French Revolution, but more as a signal of its limits than for its actual results. For one thing, contemporary Philadelphians had it wrong: not only did it expressly protect slavery; it granted political rights only to *gens de couleur*[4] born of free parents and owning property. At most, several hundred were enfranchised by the measure, and probably fewer exercised their rights as citizens in the conflict-ridden colony.[5] The decree itself was the product of an alliance between those in the assembly who were tied to the slave regime (merchants and absentee planters) and administrators interested in securing colonial allegiance. As such, it was predicated on the preservation of racial hierarchies as the best source of stability. Even this timid effort, however, was modified and limited in the tumult after Louis XVI's flight to Varennes. Newly empowered, Colonial Committee chair Antoine Barnave successfully moved French policy in even more conservative directions almost immediately, and the decree was repealed entirely in the last days of the Constituent Assembly.[6]

This, then, was hardly a grant of *"every right of free men"* to the *gens de couleur* in St. Domingue. In the weeks after William Davis arrived with his news, however, the Decree of May 15 was discussed nearly every day in Philadelphia's newspapers. The tenor of the initial reports continued: the decree was received as an epic shift in the course of events on St. Domingue and in France itself. Why did Davis get the news so wrong? And why did the Decree of May 15 garner so much attention in Philadelphia?

Answering these questions makes us fend off familiar narratives. Where historians have identified backstories, contemporaries witnessed current events. Readers in Philadelphia received news from St. Domingue in the city's numerous newspapers. A review of this record shows that Americans discerned a revolution in St. Domingue well before they saw Haiti. Paradoxically, parsing apart the character of that revolution re-weaves elements of contemporary understanding treated separately in later analysis. Readers in Philadelphia interrelated events in France with those in French St. Domingue, a fact that reveals both an early check to American enthusiasm for the French Revolution and a degree of acceptance among some white Americans toward elements of the unfolding Revolution in the French colony. This essay focuses on the issue of *gens de couleur* civic equality as a way to bring this dynamic to the fore and examines the public discourse that developed in Philadelphia's newspapers in order to understand contemporary ideas about the revolutionary goings on in "St. Domingo," as the colony was commonly known. This articulation would shape responses to subsequent developments. Its most significant consequence, however, operated in a negative sense. The "revolution" in St. Domingue that was described in Philadelphia's newspapers was a limited one; the understanding Americans had of developments there obscured the truly revolutionary developments taking place. In reading about the French Revolution in St. Domingue, Philadelphians misread the Haitian Revolution.

"Extravagant Pretentions": The French Revolution in St. Domingue, 1789–1791

Two figures encapsulate the news from St. Domingue in Philadelphia in the early 1790s. Both met a grisly end. On March 4, 1791, the Chevalier Antoine de Mauduit du Plessis, colonel of the Port-au-Prince regiment, was killed by his own troops. Cut down by a saber, he was set upon by a throng and dispatched by the thrust of a bayonet. He was then decapitated, and his body was dragged through the streets to his house, where the mob tore his body apart, posted his head, and proceeded to raze the building.[7] Five days later,

Vincent Ogé, a free man of color, died on the parade ground at Cap-Français. Bound to a wheel, his arms and legs were broken, and he was left exposed to the elements. When the end came, he too had his head removed and his property dispatched.[8]

These moments of intense violence evoke not only the disorder that Americans encountered when they looked to St. Domingue, but also the issues they understood as producing it. Mauduit's story was central to the news of the white factional struggles that developed in the colony as the Old Regime dissolved in France. The colonel was prominent among the *pompons blancs*, government officials and military men who sought to maintain control against the *pompons rouges*, self-proclaimed "patriots" who hoped to take advantage of the changes in Paris to secure greater economic autonomy. Beginning in the fall of 1789, observers in Philadelphia read of their respective maneuvers, straining colonial events through categories concurrently evolving on the continent. The letters, proclamations, and accounts in their newspapers paid close attention to which actors wore the national cockade, which proclaimed themselves "in favor of the People," which were "friends of the National Assembly," which engaged in tyrannical practices, and which seemed to "take the lead in the cause of liberty."[9] Americans looking to the French Caribbean inevitably saw it as French first and, given their general enthusiasm for the French Revolution at this stage, looked to see where virtue lay. The colonists of St. Domingue, one correspondent wrote, "feel, with unabating energy, the glorious cause in which their patriotic countrymen of old France are embarked."[10] They were actively seeking out "retainers to despotic and aristocratic tyranny," another told, in order to "convince [them] that the spirit of French liberty . . . must . . . have its full effects there as well as in the mother country." Events on the island were "little else than the revolution in Old France in miniature."[11]

Before his vivid demise, Mauduit's position in this spectrum was unclear. While some Americans may have held hopes that *rouge* control might have led to favorable changes in commercial regulations, most were unsure whether the loosening of metropolitan controls was revolutionary or counter-revolutionary. When the *rouge* General Assembly at St. Marc crafted a constitution that would have made St. Domingue independent in all but name, Philadelphians read that Mauduit's troops forced them to flee to France.[12] Later they would read disputes over who was in the wrong, as well as the National Assembly's rejection of the *rouge* constitution, despite the St. Marc delegates' assertions that they were "zealous citizens," who, as "saviors of the colony," had sought to "secure their infant liberty" against the "agents of executive power."[13] To American observers anxious to support this local expression of the French Revolution, the white factional struggles on St. Domingue offered slippery heroes and rapidly shifting grounds. The resulting impression was one of disorder. "This unhappy colony," one correspondent wrote near the end of 1790, "is distracted with parties."[14]

Vincent Ogé's position was less ambiguous to American observers, though the issues he raised would ultimately prove to be more divisive. Like white colonists, the *gens de couleur* of St. Domingue hoped to benefit from the changes in France. Having come under increasing legal and social discrimination over the prior decades, free men of color leagued together with the antislavery group Les Amis des Noirs to secure the rights of citizens. The planter-dominated Colonial Committee, however, stymied these efforts. The National Assembly's decrees over colonial affairs in 1790 consistently ignored their claims, subverting them to efforts to secure metropolitan control. On St. Domingue, while both *blancs* and *rouges* bid for their support, neither gave the *gens de couleur* representation in their competing assemblies, and all met their calls for equal treatment with increasing violence. Frustrated by these developments, Ogé traveled from France in the fall of 1790, first to Britain for an interview with abolitionist Thomas Clarkson, and then to the United States, where he purchased arms. In October he landed near Cap-Français and petitioned the *blanc* Provincial Assembly for equal rights. White divisions were erased in response, and Ogé's forces were quickly scattered. After a brief flight into Spanish St. Domingo, he was captured and returned to Cap-Français, where he was executed five days before Mauduit was killed.[15]

The "parties" that Philadelphians read about as having "distracted" St. Domingue therefore included the *gens de couleur*. If the commentary in the city's newspapers similarly interpreted their bid for civic equality as extending from the ideals of the French Revolution, most judged this attempt to be inappropriate and dangerous to the colony. "Auget," one depiction read, had grounded his claims in the French "bill of rights . . . by which all men are declared to be born free and equal." These high-minded "pretensions," however, were belied by the robbery, murder, and "plundering" done by the *gens de couleur*. Not only were these "very wrong methods"; they were fatal to the colony. "If this levelling [sic] principle should be adopted," the writer concluded, "the colony is lost for ever."[16] A pair of later writings identified Ogé as a "fanatic" with "extravagant pretentions [sic] to the rights and privileges of enfranchised citizenship" and his followers as "freebooters, in the most extended sense of the word."¹⁷ Significantly, the latter of these pieces seamlessly incorporated a Philadelphia piece, quoted above and dated five months previously, in which events in St. Domingue were characterized as "France in miniature." Originally an interpretation of white struggles, this synopsis had charted the course of the "spirit of French liberty" in the colony. Now its phrases were employed to demonstrate the limits of that spirit. If the Revolution in France was accepted as the motor of events on St. Domingue, this writing denied that the *gens de couleur* could act under the same rubric. While previous reports had "erroneously" placed the *gens de couleur* among white factions, "their whole deportment has proved this a fallacy." Theirs was a contest for personal gain, a "revolt" or "insurrection," not a "revolution" to determine the colony's future.¹⁸

Alternatives to this line of interpretation were modest at best. Benjamin Franklin Bache, a supporter of France and a close watcher of events in its most important colony, offered the public a "Concise Sketch of the POLITICS of St. Domingo" in the spring of 1791. While Bache's picture did imply that French liberty and *gens de couleur* equality were not incompatible or inconsistent, he simultaneously suggested that violence was an improper means to attain that goal. The troubles on St. Domingue, he wrote, derived from the clash between the new "system of equality" and the "spirit of subordination" that had long ruled the island. "The flame of Liberty, which broke out in France," had been "so suddenly communicated to the inhabitants of their West-India possessions as to threaten the ruin of those Colonies." This conception presented Ogé as neither a "fanatic" nor a "freebooter," but it also sidelined *gens de couleur* efforts. The chief focus of Bache's "Sketch" was the struggle between white factions—the "democratical" and "moderate republican" groups vying against the "aristocratical" and "monarchical" elements. Whereas these "disturbances" were explained as the product of legitimate clashes of interests, those caused by Ogé were the result of passions fanned by "the flame of Liberty." Like previous observers, Bache worried that the colony would be "ruined" by these efforts.¹⁹ If he accepted the logic of *gens de couleur* pursuits, he made their designs apolitical and derivative of emotions, not principles. Bache's preferred solution—the return to "old laws," in which racial subordination was to be reestablished—would create peace, leaving justice to fend for itself.

Observers in Philadelphia explicitly connected the "revolution" they saw in France with the struggles at play in the Caribbean. "A revolution having been effected in France," they read, "it ought to extend to all parts of the empire."[20] All agreed that the empire's future, however, lay in the hands of its white citizens. Though these actors might be judged overly zealous or tyrannical, they were the ones upon whom events were seen to hinge. Even when the coherence of the claims of the *gens de couleur* was recognized, their valid participation was not. Even if they appropriated the ideals of the French Revolution, they were not French.

"The Regeneration of the Empire Can No Longer Be Partial": *Gens de Couleur* Civic Equality and the Vanguard of Revolutionary Promise, 1791–1792

The charged atmosphere and dynamic environment in which these observers operated created room in which this perception could change. The early 1790s was a period of flux in the nascent United States. With the nation's own revolution receding into the recent past, Americans questioned the meaning of that event for their society and culture. Divisions over the Constitution evolved into and around new and newly defined rifts on the political landscape. Burgeoning splits within the federal government met and matched up with local groups' concerns. Beyond the specific issues that defined and energized these divisions, Americans were arguing over the character of their nation and the revolution that had brought it into being.[21] The city of Philadelphia sat at the epicenter of these discussions. As the national capital, a long-standing regional center, and an emerging commercial juggernaut, the city was an important site. It also served as an actor of sorts. Because of its prominence, Philadelphia was home to numerous and influential newspapers and magazines, making the city a distribution point for domestic and international news as well as a cultural center.[22] Of course, Philadelphian realities did not map directly onto the rest of the nation. The city's particularities, however, raised the possibility that it would be a bellwether in the young republic. During the 1790s, the *Encyclopedia Britannica* expressly identified Philadelphia as a leader in global efforts to better the human condition.[23] While observers could make reference to Philadelphian penal reforms, educational innovations, and ventures to improve public health, the campaign against slavery had a special resonance.[24] In the "Quaker" city, the American Revolution had further animated its founding sect, but had also produced a vaunted state abolition law and an active Abolition Society that spanned a greater segment of the populace. These developments led Philadelphia to become a haven for free and freed African Americans over the decade. As Philadelphians puzzled their way through events on St. Domingue and fervidly embraced those in France, their own recent revolutionary past was on their minds, raising questions about the place they were in and the directions they were heading. In the intense collective attention on St. Domingue in the city's newspapers, we can see some of the answers they produced.

Bache's "Concise Sketch," therefore, in enveloping both white and *gens de couleur* struggles within the rubric of the French Revolution, represents a space in Philadelphia in which ideas about that revolution could be articulated. The kinds of troubles that Bache worried would "ruin" the colony were increasingly depicted in Philadelphia's newspapers as products of nefarious counter-revolutionary efforts. Mauduit's changing reputation epitomizes this trajectory. Reading of his gruesome end, Americans learned that, in casting out the St. Marc Assembly the previous July, he had ordered his troops—who were identified as "aristocratically inclined"—to fire into a body of "the people." When troops arrived from France in the spring, they had broken with their officers, united with the "citizens" of Port-au-Prince in the cause of "greater freedom," and forced Mauduit into the confrontation in which he lost his life.[25] As this story was fleshed out in Philadelphia, Mauduit was marked as allied with those who were "attached to the ancient political order of things."[26] As such, his death would "serve as an example to all those who wish to stop the rapid progress of the revolution." Later he was revealed to have been in league with the Spanish crown.[27] As we will see, by November 1792 this portrait had been expanded in some circles into a detailed account of perfidious intrigues. Mauduit's efforts to secure metropolitan control of the colony were woven into a plot that incorporated the king's attempted escape, the massing of royalist troops along the Austrian border, and the continuing slave insurrections in the French West Indies—particularly those on St. Domingue.[28]

Sensationalism may have played a role in the attention paid to Mauduit's death, but the scrutiny given to the colonel's reputation, affiliations, and stance on (and in) the revolution demonstrates the importance American observers placed on the stage that was St. Domingue. Therein lies part of the answer to our question over the reaction to the Decree of May 15 in Philadelphia. The French troops involved in Mauduit's massacre had purportedly told the *gens de couleur* that "you are our equals, the National Assembly has declared it" upon their arrival.[29] While quickly discredited, this report raised important questions about the implications of the revolution in France for the colony's racial hierarchy. The level of tumult on the island, in fact, led the National Assembly to rethink its decision to let the colony have a greater hand in its own governance. During debates in April over the colonial question, Robespierre vowed to let the colonies "perish" before allowing them to dictate policy. The result—the Decree of May 15—was limited, but it did signal a shift towards applying revolutionary ideals, albeit tentatively, to the issue of *gens de couleur* civic equality.[30]

When this news arrived in Philadelphia, it entered an environment in which Americans were seeking to understand the relationship between the disruptions in the French West Indies and the ideals of the metropolitan revolution. Imperfectly understood, the Decree of May 15 made St. Domingue seem to be the leading edge of developments in France. What is more, the decree (incorrectly) elevated the importance of civic equality as a revolutionary moment. As both a historic moment and a marker of ideals, the granting of rights to the *gens de couleur* was accepted, both by critics and supporters of France, as an epic and profound development. Critics painted a picture of the anarchy unleashed by the application of the Rights of Man to a slave society. An opponent of the decree saw it as the product of a *"mistaken and fatal philanthropy, which is less calculated to benefit the human species, than to overthrow empires and governments."* Granting civic equality would ensure that the colony "would be lost for ever."[31] Edmund Burke articulated the danger with greater flourish. He saw in St. Domingue an opened *"Pandora's Box"* in which "confusion and disorder reigned" and in which "the fatal venom of democracy infected every breast, the free men and the slaves, the black, the white, the part[l]y colored inhabitants . . . alike."[32]

Supporters of the French Revolution, on the other hand, confronted questions that stimulated a new schema by which to understand St. Domingue's travails. Were Ogé's "levelling principles" the same as those Burke derided? Would French "philanthropy" cause the colony to be "lost"? Since his "Concise Sketch" in late April, Benjamin Franklin Bache had laboriously translated numerous documents in his *General Advertiser* in an attempt to balance the generally critical British sources featured in other newspapers.[33] The description of the decree that he found most reliable was a letter that echoed Captain Davis's original understanding: the National Decree had given "to negroes and people of color, the same rights, and the same weight in government, as belongs to the white colonists."[34] Davis's news evinced the violent response of colonial whites to this policy, but left open the question of whether or not it would lead to the colony's destruction. An address by merchants in Bordeaux, the city (after Paris) most closely identified with the decree, in fact, suggested a very different threat. In urging angry St. Dominguans to accept the decree, the merchants described a revolution whose logic was universal and irrefutable. The rights restored to whites had to be matched by those belonging to other "*free beings*," they explained. The *gens de couleur* were also "children of their country," and discrimination against them was no longer possible now that the revolution had occurred. "Once perhaps that condition was supportable to them. All classes of citizens being equally debased; what was then called liberty was only its shadow, and offered only to our eyes the varied shades of real slavery—but now all Frenchmen restored to the rights and justice of equality, will be governed, and at the same time protected by them." With the eyes of the world and the future upon them, the National Assembly had risen above local concerns, the merchants proclaimed, to create law that brought reason to racial rules. "What have you to oppose the claims of the heretofore intermediate class," the letter asked. "Is it their *colour*?" To sanction this would be to sully the universal claims that rooted the new order. "The regeneration of the empire," they declared, "can no longer be partial."[35]

If Davis's news suggested the potential loss of the colony because of this development, that loss was less related to Burke's portrait of chaos than it was to the resistance of white colonists to the new order. This vein of interpretation, in effect, made the counter-revolution, not the revolution, the chief threat in St. Domingue. The advent of large-scale violence on the part of the colony's slaves in the late summer of 1791, first in the northern and then in the western and southern provinces, intensified the disorder and complicated the pictures observers provided, but the issue of civic equality for the *gens de couleur* remained at the forefront of attempts to explain the tumult on St. Domingue and to characterize the dangers that beset the colony. Burkean depictions of anarchic slave violence often placed *gens de couleur* at the head of the insurgent hordes or blamed the doctrines of "liberty and philanthropy" as producing only "blood and cruelty" in the colony.[36] Even when judged negatively, however, the *gens de couleur* were described as rational actors and viable participants in both the colony's struggles and the revolution that framed them. When Port-au-Prince burned in November 1791, many observers castigated the city's white inhabitants for going back on their agreements to recognize "the rights and privileges of the people of colour."[37] The "flame of civil discord," not Bache's "Flame of liberty," was to blame for the carnage.[38] The *gens de couleur* were righteous, if enraged, combatants, or at least cognizant and competent political beings.

"The Contest Between Liberty and Despotism": Defining the Revolution in Philadelphia, 1792

The sense of the centrality of civic equality within the evolving French Revolution and to St. Domingue's fortunes was bolstered by news from France. Philadelphians read that the repeal of the Decree of May 15, which took place on September 24, 1791, was a measure designed to combat the threat of "counter-revolution" on the island by white colonists, who were using the issue to argue for secession.[39] Subsequent news that the repeal had led *gens de couleur* to question their allegiance reinforced the notion that granting civic equality was a vital part of ending the violence.[40] When, in early June 1792, Philadelphians learned of a French decree, affirmed by the king on April 4, that granted full political rights to all *gens de couleur* in the colonies, most observers were sanguine about the probable peace and stability that would result.[41]

Shifts in the domestic context impacted the tenor with which this news was discussed in Philadelphia. As 1792 progressed, emergent rifts among political leaders led to the rise of rival presses. While domestic issues were also discussed, events in France proved to be especially divisive. Benjamin Franklin Bache's Francophile *General Advertiser* was joined, and, in terms of florid prose, surpassed, by Philip Freneau, editor of the *National Gazette*. Prompted by Secretary of State Thomas Jefferson and Virginian Congressman James Madison, Bache and Freneau sought to counter a perceived British bias in publications such as John Fenno's *Gazette of the United States*, an inclination they attributed to the influence of Treasury Secretary Alexander Hamilton.[42]

In Francophilic hands the cautious welcome of civic equality on St. Domingue evolved quickly into open approbation. "The strict enforcement of the decree of the National Assembly, confirming the Mulattoes of the islands in their privileges," Freneau decided, "seems the only practicable method of restoring peace & good order."[43] Shortly thereafter, Bache printed a letter from "a warm aristocrat" in Paris to a correspondent in the colony in which the Parisian predicted that France would soon collapse before the armies surrounding it, allowing the nation's new leaders to invade St. Domingue to "put every one in his place again." Such opinions, Bache editorialized, "shew that all ENRAGES are not Jacobins." The writer's wild hopes illuminated his odious politics, as well as his harebrained imagination. To oppose the "levelling [*sic*] system" that had "overset all the pretentions [*sic*] of birth and fortune" in France and the colonies, he asserted, was to be on the wrong side in "the contest between liberty and despotism."[44] To stand against civic equality for the *gens de couleur* was to stand against the revolution. Looking to St. Domingue, Bache and Freneau let their affection for France trump their former tepid reactions to civic equality. In defining their loyalties in St. Domingue negatively—that is, by identifying and opposing enemies to France—they came to incorporate the goals of the *gens de couleur* as emblematic of a wider world-changing movement.

This response was facilitated, and intensified, by the presence of Girondin commissioners in the colony after September 1792. Led by the fiery Léger Félicité Sonthonax, the commission increasingly turned to the *gens de couleur* as allies in their tussles with white factions.[45] The advent of open war between Britain and France in early February 1793 added urgency to the situation, as it seemed likely that the commission would need to defend itself against external, as well as internal, enemies.

Over this period, St. Domingue, always interesting, was described in Philadelphia newspapers as important beyond its shores. Beginning in the fall of 1792, "ST. DOMINGO" was a constant heading in their columns, alongside Paris and London, and was considered a significant site of a global struggle between liberty and tyranny. Bache described one set of disorders at Cap-Français as "dictated by the same spirit, that shone so conspicuous on the 10th of August last in Paris."[46] Freneau marked the contending sides as the "patriotic party" and the "counter-revolution party," noting that the latter acted "in concert with the anti-revolutionists in the mother country."[47] For Bache and his audience, St. Domingue, which "must be interesting to those who feel for the fate of an important part of the French republic," was also vital to the "theoretical politician," who could look there to judge whether the "spirit of liberty and republicanism" was consistent with colony holding.[48] By these accounts, the issue of civic equality determined the sides of this war. At the heart of the commissioners' efforts—a "struggle of republicanism against perverted authority and an oppressive aristocratical interest"—was the inclusion of the *gens de couleur* in the new "democratical" government on the island.[49] Resistance to this new order was a guise for wider counter-revolutionary efforts. In this context, Mauduit, dismembered twenty months previously, was resuscitated and remembered as the essential royalist.[50] "In fine," a typical account ran, "doubting the courage of Frenchmen, these enemies of their country hoped . . . to annihilate the constitution."[51] With the sides and stakes of the battle delineated, American supporters of France seized upon civic equality as a litmus test for republican orthodoxy.[52] Opponents of *gens de couleur* rights were opponents of France; their "epidermocratical tyranny" made their loyalties transparent.[53]

The Limits of Equality

If some in Philadelphia came to accept *gens de couleur* equality as a reasonable, if remarkable, product of French Revolutionary ideals, the ramifications of that understanding in the United States would ultimately prove to be ambiguous. There is no evidence that white observers made any correlation between the *gens de couleur* they read about on St. Domingue and those "free Negroes" or "mulattoes" who inhabited Philadelphia.[54] Though a considerable number of squibs decrying slavery and supporting antislavery efforts in America and Europe came in and around the writings describing events on St. Domingue, any perceived relationship between French equality and the gradual, compensated liberty provided in some portions of the United States after its revolution remained unarticulated in Philadelphia's newspapers.[55] Emotional enthusiasm for the topics these writings described may have stood in for more explicit connections. In those few places where lines were hazily drawn, the resulting picture indicates the ways in which the embrace of civic equality as a vital measure of French revolutionary ideals would prove hollow. Furthermore, they suggest the fundamentally limited nature of white American antislavery efforts in this period.

One such writing, entitled "MULATTOES OF ST. DOMINGO," was printed in several Philadelphia newspapers and a literary magazine in March 1792.[56] "MULATTOES," its author argued, were the "motley" descendants of low-bred European adventurers, who, in addition to the pursuit of lucre, sought "the enslaved African female" to satisfy their carnal needs. The resulting "yellow race" was "neither European nor African," and therefore "felt no attachment to either." Elevated above the most degrading labor and educated by their indulgent fathers (which "always engenders discontent, where there is no equality of condition"), this group came to resent their oppressive condition. The violence on the island derived from their campaign to gain "equal privileges."

Opportunistically allied with the slaves, they had "carried fire and sword through the territories of the white inhabitants."

Newspaper editors eager to see the best in French activities had dealt with such charges before. Bache and Freneau paid assiduous attention to all notices that emphasized that the French decrees granting equality to the *gens de couleur* expressly maintained the institution of slavery.[57] While some evidence that the *gens de couleur* interacted with the insurgents was inescapable, the emphasis on the peace that was to come from equality once they and those whites who were truly patriotic were united made these moments exceptions. The next stage of the "MULATTOES" author's piece, however, moved from history to prognostication and suggested an American solution to St. Domingue's problems along the way. Perhaps reacting to the repeal of the Decree of May 15, the author guessed that white factions would coalesce around an effort to quash the *gens de couleur*. Crushed by collective white might, "the future condition of the mulattoes in the islands will be changed for the worse." Their privileged status would end, and they would be reduced to the "condition of the . . . negroes." This eventuality, however, would ultimately serve them well. Without free people of color as competition, St. Domingue would become more attractive to white colonists. Thus, he continued, "When once the colonial whites begin to consider the West-Indies as their only proper home, a legitimate offspring of *their own grade* will ensue, who may in time, as has happened on this continent, render some of the insular governments independent of European supremacy; and grant those natural rights of man to the negroes and mulattoes, which they will in vain look for from the justice, the humanity, or the philosophy of Europe."[58] White self-interest, properly cultivated, would give whites independence, after which they would grant liberty to the nonwhites around them. By harnessing the wheels of history and nature, freedom would come from slavery, equality from injustice.

This view was abutted in Benjamin Franklin Bache's *General Advertiser* by an address from Amis des Noirs leader Abbé Baptiste Henri Grégoire (or "M. Gregory") to the *gens de couleur* of the colonies. As a celebration of the Decree of May 15, Grégoire's oration was old news; it rehashed ideas already printed and, after all, was concerned with a measure that was known to have been repealed. Bache's publication of it at this point, therefore, suggests a new relevance. Railing against his opponents in Paris, Grégoire posed the Decree of May 15 as part of a renewal taking place across France. Prejudice, like all unnatural distinctions, was melting away, improving morals and energizing the citizenry as it went. This would be opposed, he continued, by those who wished "to perpetuate in America, the reign of despotism, crushed in France." They would, no doubt, "attempt a stroke, which, tearing the colonies from the mother country . . . will throw St. Domingo into confusion."⁵⁹

Consciously or not, Bache had placed together contradictory senses of the logic of revolution as it applied to the *gens de couleur*. What Grégoire described as counter-revolutionary "strokes" and "confusion" was, for the "MULATTOES" author, a natural reaction that would ultimately lead to revolutionary ends. Both conceptions, however, made the *gens de couleur* passive vessels. They had been *given* their rights, Grégoire explained. Freedom would be bestowed upon them, the "MULATTOES" author said, after they had been re-enslaved. If in both cases the *gens de couleur* were generally understood as viable political actors, the implications of this shift were fundamentally sapped. As an ideal, revolutionary egalitarianism was a radical extension of democratic ideology. As a marker of revolutionary politics, it lost some of its revolutionary capacity. Reduced to a signal of political position, it could not become a challenge to the future. Consequently, the debate in Philadelphia's newspapers over equality for the *gens de couleur* was over power in St. Domingue, not over justice in the world.

The Decree of May 15 was "bigger" news that the insurrections after August 22 because of the underlying assumptions behind what made an event important. Scholars, seeking to tell the history of events they term the "Haitian Revolution," look to the Plaine du Nord (or to the woods of Bois-Caïman) and see significance. White American observers (and the voices that they read), however, told the story of a revolution that was French, and hence they looked to Paris. Keeping that gaze steady was a difficult task. Between the opening of disruptions on the island and the end of 1792, news from St. Domingue pushed and pulled the frame through which observers would view the French Revolution. Modern histories of the Haitian Revolution "begin" with the slave insurrections and "end" with the creation of an independent state in which blackness defined citizenship. Contemporary tales from the period found that end "unthinkable."⁶⁰ This blindness was understandable, given that the result was more than a decade away. Their tales did end, as suggested by the "MULATTOES" author, with a new degree of freedom, albeit one that was mediated and granted by whites, and extended only to the *gens de couleur*. The frame of understanding had been moved, as much by the actions of the *gens de couleur* on their own behalf as by changes in France, so as to include civic equality within a revolutionary rubric.

The French Revolution affected the revolution in Haiti in many ways, but its impact on contemporaries' ascriptive capacities was critical. The qualities of the "revolution," when "French," played a role in determining what would be seen as "revolutionary" in St. Domingue. This explanatory device, however, was a restraining one. In the fall of 1790, Vincent Ogé was a "rebel Chief" whose "pretentions" threatened to "lose" the colony because of their potential to undo a delicately balanced system of racial subordination. By mid-1792, some observers viewed the colony as potentially "lost" unless that same system was undone, though they continued to see the *gens de couleur* as recipients rather than winners of their equality. Ironically, slave insurrection, even when massive, was probably more easily understood: it was an idea readers had encountered before. It existed as a mental framework upon which they could hang the information from St. Domingue, though not as a "revolutionary" act. Perhaps Captain Davis, and his audience, paid more attention to the Decree of May 15 because it required greater mental gymnastics. For observers of the Haitian Revolution in Philadelphia, steeper hurdles lay ahead.

CHAPTER 3

"The Mischief That Awaits Us"

Revolution, Rumor, and Serial Unrest in the Early Republic

DUNCAN FAHERTY

On October 20, 1802, under the banner headline, "We stop the press to publish the following," the *Washington Federalist* printed an alarming dispatch from South Carolina: "The infernal French are disgorging the whole of their wretched blacks upon our shores. An express arrived this afternoon to the Brigadier General, with information that a French frigate was landing negroes about 32 miles from this place. Every inhabitant of the town were ordered to equip themselves and march to oppose them; which they did this afternoon with the greatest cheerfulness, and I believe would have gone with more pleasure had they to combat with the French." Bearing a ten-day-old dateline and couched as "an extract of a letter" from an eyewitness, the report presumably incited a considerable panic. Depicting South Carolina as besieged by French Negroes—a racist label synonymous in 1802 with unbridled revolutionary violence—the letter registers an implicit threat to U.S. sovereignty. Even as it marks the ebullient morale of the citizen-soldiers, the declaration of universal mobilization accentuates the seriousness accorded to the purported encroachment. While its hyperbolic tone inculcates the anti-Jacobinism of the decidedly partisan *Washington Federalist*, the report is more than an instantiation of the parochialism of early nineteenth-century periodicals. Despite the shocking news, the *Federalist*'s editors fail to provide a contextualizing frame for their readers. They convey no surprise about French ships lurking off the coast, offer no explication of the phrase "whole of their wretched blacks," and register no astonishment over the conscription of private citizens. Indeed, the presentation of the story suggests the information was not wholly unexpected.[1]

Numerous reports concerning a flotilla of French warships laden with imprisoned black revolutionaries had circulated in dozens of U.S. cities and municipalities since the middle of August 1802. As these accounts appeared along coastal trade routes (and their interior arteries), newspapers openly speculated about the muddled intentions of the French. Increasingly concerned by rumors accusing the French of covertly trafficking their imprisoned revolutionaries, private citizens, socially connected merchants, and prominent local and national politicians (in both private and semi-public correspondence) anxiously discussed the consequences of Caribbean slave unrest infiltrating the Republic. For early nineteenth-century Americans, the unease surrounding French revolutionary excess was unendingly magnified when inflected through the Caribbean; this fact made the arrival of French military vessels crowded with black revolutionaries doubly troubling. By examining how rumors about these frigates generated waves of discontent, I hope to register how a preoccupation with their presence reflects and encodes national anxieties about revolution in the West Indies.

This essay exhibits that preoccupation by surveying a broad range of materials concerned with the appearance of these foreign frigates. My primary archive is the wealth of newspaper articles emanating from across the United States, which demonstrate a national fixation on the multivalent meanings of the imprisoned French Caribbean revolutionaries. These articles and notices range from partisan news stories to alarmed reports in commercial shipping columns; collectively, they suggest deep-seated concerns about disruptions to the body politic and to both internal and circum-Atlantic economic networks.

As the French frigates remained in stasis just offshore of a major American city, newspapers from across geographical and political spectrums debated the manifold dangers the re-enslaved revolutionaries posed to domestic tranquility. The effects of these accounts are, in part, registered in how civic leaders (on both a local and a federal level) responded to them. The public and private correspondence of a variety of prominent southerners and federal politicians, which I trace in the final turn of the essay, displays an overt preoccupation with these prisoners as a coded way of expressing larger anxieties about the Haitian Revolution. The event served as a flashpoint, and by recovering this forgotten episode, we can better understand how a fragile sense of national cohesion was formed by a widespread practice of negation—a process of forging translocal networks of association to coordinate the quarantine of foreign uncertainties. By consistently prognosticating about the prisoners' potential capacity for destabilization, reactions to this event were often predicated on projecting a false sense of stability onto the social nexus in existence prior to their arrival. The universal insistence on preventing any of the prisoners from disembarking onto U.S. soil reveals a domestic enthnoscape intent on securing futurity by keeping unwelcome foreigners and their revolutionary intrigues in abeyance. While Federalists and Democratic-Republicans differed on their attachments to France (and on official U.S. policy in regard to Haiti), there was no partisan division over the prospect of revolutionary "French Negroes" mingling with the domestic slave population. In uncovering this lost historical episode, I move to demonstrate how it encapsulates the ways in which many Americans imagined (and simultaneously feared) a causal relationship between national security and Caribbean turmoil. What initially seems like an intriguing historical aberration—ill-founded reports of a rumored invasion—demonstrates just how keenly observers in the United States monitored the Caribbean for signs of impending domestic destabilization.

For over sixty-three days in the late summer of 1802, three French frigates crowded with West Indian revolutionaries had—without solicitation—anchored in New York harbor. These vessels had departed Manhattan, for parts unknown, scant days prior to the *Federalist*'s report. Even before they sailed, southern harbormasters were warned about the threat these ships posed. Given the widespread circulation of reports about the French frigates and their revolutionary cargo, the readers of the *Federalist* likely recognized this arrival as the first iteration of a long prognosticated trauma. Collectively these scores of newspaper articles, written across a four-month period in the late summer of 1802, catalog how intensely Americans envisaged race, citizenship, security, and economic stability through the hazy filter of the Caribbean. The sheer volume of these stories arguably created a narrative temporality that prepared the nation for this prophesied invasion, engendering a structure of thought and feeling wherein many Americans—particularly those with (direct or indirect) ties to a domestic slave economy—found themselves anxiously awaiting an incursion. The French ships localized these barely submerged fears, attaching all the circumspection surrounding foreign contagions to a discernible object floating just offshore. Quickly, the frigates became an emblem of foreign revolutionary energy and its racially inflected notions of liberty and equality. For Americans, large-scale slave revolts were unquestionably a thinkable history by 1802, as they quite easily (and explicitly) imagined the consequences of that turmoil spreading to the United States.² By anchoring the seeds of racial revolution just off the coast, the French frigates injected a new, although not entirely unexpected, pressure that threatened to ignite barely repressed domestic tensions.

Flood Tide

The first substantiated report concerning the warships appeared in New York on August 10, when a harbor pilot recounted that he had "passed a French frigate off the hook last night, standing in, mounting 28 guns on her maindeck."³ In the busy New York waterways—crowded with European and U.S. ships crisscrossing along a variety of circum-Atlantic trade routes—the first sighting of the French frigate *La Consolante* seemed innocuous. Still, most of the other ships in New York harbor were smaller commercial vessels, and few, if any, possessed the armaments displayed onboard the French vessel. Moreover, given the uncertain state of Franco-American relations in light of the XYZ Affair and the Quasi-War, the flag flying from the mast of *La Consolante* must have prompted concern.⁴ While the Convention of 1800 had supposedly reestablished "a firm, inviolable, and universal peace, and a true and sincere Friendship between the French Republic, and the United States of America," it failed to overwrite the outrage and abounding skepticism resulting from years of fractured relations.⁵ In short, France was no longer popularly embraced, as one historian writes, as "a benevolent 'sister republic'"; instead, many Americans had, by 1802, become deeply cynical about France's unabashed revolutionary fervor.⁶ As the October 20 letter in the *Washington Federalist* recounts, South Carolina's citizen-soldiers were prepared to fight either "the infernal French" or "their wretched blacks." For the anonymous letter writer, at least, the two terms were interchangeable signifiers, equal threats to domestic tranquility because of the infectious insurgency they represented.

The inchoate tidings of *La Consolante* were benignly lodged amid the shipping news, fixing the frigate as a routine instance of the city's multivalent participation in the ebb and flow of circum-Atlantic economies. The notice abuts ancillary reports of cargoes recently arrived from Charleston, Richmond, St. Thomas, the River La Plate, Nantes, Liverpool, and Honduras, collectively framing a global catalog of new merchandise. The disembarking vessels are described as bearing flour, tobacco, rice, cotton, rum, sugar, specie, mahogany, dye, and coffee. When possible, the listings identify the speculators destined to receive the various consignments, and detail the current foreign market prices for the respective commodities. Other subsidiary announcements list ships outbound for Barbados, Curacao, Kingston, London, Philadelphia, and Charleston.[7]

While a few ship captains from as far south as Virginia had broadcast vague sightings of French vessels intermittently since late July 1802, no special notice was afforded the disclosure since only cursory contact had been made. Nonchalance abruptly turned into consternation, as details about the histories of the imprisoned men began to emerge in early August. As the *La Consolante* anchored off Governors Island, it transformed from a ghostly apparition into a fixed presence moored in a major U.S. city. Rampant rumors of French attempts to illicitly offload their prisoners created deep-seated fears about the consequences of any of these "French Negroes" intermingling with enslaved Africans in the United States. Persistent rumors of clandestine connections between domestic slave unrest and French insurgents and West Indian slaves surfaced throughout the early nineteenth century.[8] Wary of the instability associated with Jacobins and French Negroes, many Americans monitored events in the West Indies for signs of infiltration. These anxieties only increased as France's brutal attempts to re-enslave their former colonies—after over a decade of complex social upheaval—and reinstall a regime of racial hierarchy met staunch resistance. Accounts of these zealous counteractions circulated in U.S. newspapers across 1802, creating charged expectations for the term "French Negro." Although French "noirs" had composed the majority of the Republican army that repelled the 1794 British invasion of Guadeloupe, by the summer of 1802 (as Napoleon furtively ordered slavery reinstalled in the Caribbean), "French soldiers" (a term reclassified to again include only white troops) clashed with their former comrades. The prisoners onboard *La Consolante* were likely battle-hardened veterans of these struggles—former citizen-soldiers and self-emancipated "revolutionaries"—a lineage that undoubtedly heightened fears about their arrival in a U.S. port.

On August, 11, the *Daily Advertiser*, the *Commercial Advertiser*, the *New-York Gazette*, and the *New-York Evening Post* sketched *La Consolante*'s history. Three of the articles are almost identical in size and cursory tone, and all four outline how the frigate had accidently split from three other French ships and "put here for provisions." Citing the frigate's captain as their source, they all recount how a gale separated *La Consolante* from its group and that the others were apparently also destined for the harbor. While the *Daily Advertiser*, the *Gazette*, and the *Post* identify the ship by its homeport, Brest, the *Commercial*

Advertiser unveiled that she was "last from the Guadeloupe station." This brief mention of the frigate's most recent port of call marks the first printed instance of *La Consolante*'s connection to revolutionary unrest in the West Indies, an association that would shortly burn white hot up and down the eastern seaboard. On August 12, the *Philadelphia Gazette* informed its readers that *La Consolante* anchored in New York harbor by ostensibly reprinting the previous day's notice from the *New-York Gazette*. Readers in both cities were no doubt comforted by the news that the ships were in good health, as yellow fever scares (often associated with Caribbean ships) were recursive concerns for coastal U.S. cities in the late eighteenth and early nineteenth centuries.[9]

Three days after the arrival of the first frigate, two other French ships of war—the frigate *La Volontaire* and the sloop *Salamandre*—arrived at New York's quarantine ground. As one vessel morphed into three, and a few hundred loosely immured enemy combatants multiplied into over a thousand, tensions in the city escalated. Even as local officials, reporters, and concerned citizens alike struggled to comprehend why the French sailed to New York, rumors of invasions, uncorroborated stories of prisoner insurrections, and nervous grumbles about illegal slave trafficking became daily fixtures in the region's papers. Almost as rapidly, the connections between the French ships and West Indian revolutionary upheaval became the most frequently reprinted story about New York in newspapers from Maine to South Carolina to Kentucky. The event promptly became a flashpoint for U.S. paranoia about revolutionary unrest in both France and the West Indies. The abiding serialization of information concerning these frigates engendered narrative temporalities that overwrote other operant, perhaps more factual, accounts of episodic events connected to the Haitian Revolution. For a range of U.S. observers, the prisoners were mutagens, radical agents capable of breeding malignancies in the American polity. Reports of crimes and escapes traveled faster out of New York—if reprintings in nearby cities are accurate measures—than corrections and retractions intended to clarify erroneous reports. Such an asynchronous flow of information exhibits the prevalent fears about these prisoners and the hunger for information that proved the verisimilitude of those concerns.

Riptides

Shortly after *La Consolante*'s arrival, the ship accidently "drifted from her anchorage" and wafted "amongst the vessels" docked "within the quarantine limits." If the sporadic intelligence about prisoners had not yet alarmed New Yorkers, this accident galvanized their attention. As *La Consolante* wavered without purpose it ran afoul the American brig *Twins*, and only the high tide prevented them both from capsizing. The image of the aimless *La Consolante*, eluding the control of her crew, unnerved those already wary about her presumptuous arrival. Even more dismaying than the near wreck were reports that during the entanglement "a number of the Blacks got on board" the *Twins* "and secreted themselves in [its] hold." The majority of the escaped prisoners were recaptured, but at least one remained undetected, for "during the night, he took the Twin's boat, got on shore, and made his escape on Staten-Island." Further intelligence maintained that during "the squabble" one of the French sailors fell overboard and drowned and that "one of the Blacks who stood in the way, was thrown overboard by some of the crew, and perished." In short, when *La Consolante* heeled out of control, the accident was replete with thefts, escapes, an accidental death, and murderous revenge. Though the event was not a total disaster—the frigate could have scuttled or more prisoners escaped—the frightening episode amplified the attentiveness of local officials.[10]

The mishap occurred late on Thursday evening, too late for most Friday editions, and when newspapers resumed publication after the weekend they readdressed rampant speculations about the collision at the request of the mayor's office. While measuring the spread of information over the weekend is difficult, by Monday morning, news of the collision was widespread. On August 16, the majority of New York's papers included stories aimed at cooling some simmering level of public restlessness, even as they refrained from explicating what had happened (a register, perhaps, of the familiarity of the context). The brief article in the *Mercantile Advertiser*, echoing the majority of the stories, openly acknowledges that the paper had been "requested to inform the citizens of New York" about recent events. The story announces that the French commandant has, "of his own accord," ordered *La Consolante* "to moor closer to Staten Island, in order to remove the uneasiness which her proximity to this city appears to have given to the inhabitants." These reassurances move to assuage the spirits of a suspicious populace and stress the attentiveness of the city government. Assuming pronounced concern on the part of its readers, the coverage in the *Commercial Advertiser* more aggressively seeks to pacify them: "In consequence of a disposition shewn by the black prisoners on board the French frigate *La Consolante*, on Saturday last, to rise and effect their escape, we understand that the Mayor ordered the military in readiness to oppose their landing on our shores, if they should attempt it." The *Commercial Advertiser* depicts the incident as evidence of systematic organizing on the part of the prisoners, and its representation of the situation as a conspiracy suggests an audience expecting malevolent behavior. Similarly, the news that the mayor mobilized the city militia evinces a measurable fear on the part of regional administrators in the wake of the accident.[11]

The *New-York Gazette* endeavors to address the spiraling rumors more broadly, by outlining their content and contextualizing their origins. According to the *Gazette*, after Mayor Livingston learned of "some disposition on the part of the Blacks, to rise and force a landing," he issued an order on Saturday, August 14, "in case of such an attempt, to have the military in readiness to oppose the landing on shores of sets of men so much to be dreaded—men inured to plunder and familiar with the most bloody massacres—and ripe for every species of cruelty." Even as the *Gazette* conveys affective fears about the prisoners, it moves to alleviate concerns about the French crews and their commander. The article denies a series of fallacious narratives: that the French threatened to fire on the city if denied provisions, that they conspired with their prisoners to burn Manhattan to "ashes," and that they sought to "land the blacks, and let them shift for themselves." Decrying these reports of antagonism as "laughable," the article opines that "it would be advisable" for the government "to become *indorsers* [sic] for Bonaparte," both to "please" him and to "prevent his future power and vengeance from being directed against us." Perhaps no less wary of the French than the editors of the *Washington Federalist*, the correspondents at the *Gazette* hoped appeasement would forestall an otherwise inevitable conflict. By encouraging someone to accept the semi-worthless promissory notes "offered in payment," the article mollifies public concerns by plotting a means of accelerating the removal of the French. Without proper provisions, the flotilla would be hard pressed to depart, and the *Gazette* tenders its plan to abate the potential damage caused by its continued presence.[12]

The *New-York Gazette* story also thickens its description of the history of *La Consolante*, particularly in regard to the health of its passengers. Proclaiming that "very little sickness and no malignancy" existed aboard the vessels, the article outlines how the ships had originally departed Guadeloupe for Cartagena. Rebuffed by the Spanish, the French captain ordered the flotilla to alter course "to bring them out to America" and "remain in this port" until he received new "orders relative to the disposition of the Black prisoners." The article stresses the health of the prisoners and explains that only officers and their oarsmen were allowed to disembark. Whether these reports assuaged the fears of New Yorkers is difficult to gage, but the report from the *New-York Gazette* quickly circulated in adjacent cities. On August 17, the *Philadelphia Gazette* reprinted verbatim the *New-York Gazette*'s August 16 story. Two days later, both the *Alexandria Advertiser* and the *Connecticut Journal* repeated the same details. The following day, Friday, August 20, the *Albany Centinel* followed suit, bringing the news to readers in the state capital. As readers in Philadelphia, New Haven, and Alexandria were possibly pacified by the assurances of the *New-York Gazette*'s story, readers in other cities were learning about the French frigates anchored just offshore of Manhattan. Beginning on Monday, August 16, readers in Boston, Baltimore, and Norfolk, Virginia, encountered at least brief reports of the arrival of the French frigates; by the end of the week, newspapers in such secondary ports and interior towns as Salem, Hartford, Providence, Portland, Middlebury, Keen, Hudson, Norwich, Elizabethtown, Portsmouth, Greenfield, Trenton, New Bedford, Washington, D.C., and Walpole had apprised their readers of the situation. By the early part of September, readers as far west as Lexington, Kentucky, were informed about *La Consolante* and her cargo.[13]

The ships were an offshoot of what Laurent Dubois describes as the "mass executions and deportations" undertaken by the French to reestablish "the old world of slavery" in their former Caribbean colonies. As part of this effort, the French planned to forcibly remove black revolutionaries and reimport a new more docile African slave population, imagining this as the best method for resuming the lucrative production of sugar. While the program was short-lived and ultimately unsuccessful, tidings of it unsettled both the Spanish and the Americans. The idea that the French intended to recreate the West Indies as a tabula rasa only heightened the palpable distress over the mysterious French flotilla, because it meant that these ships were merely heralds and forerunners. Such a resonance may account for the exaggerated rhetoric surrounding the frigates, which increased exponentially as the French lingered in New York harbor.[14]

Quite simply, the French lacked the resources to resupply the provisions necessary for departure. Moreover, it remained unclear if they knew where to sail when restocked. As the ships tarried in New York harbor, many of the prisoners began to suffer acutely from dysentery. As sickened prisoners were begrudgingly admitted into the harbor's quarantine hospital on Staten Island, accounts of escapees emanated from waterfront byways across the metropolitan area. At least two murders in New Jersey, both fictitious, were attributed to a band of French Negro runaways.¹⁵ Given that prisoners were cramped in the hold of the frigates for months, undoubtedly malnourished and wary about re-enslavement, it is hardly surprising that they fled whenever an opportunity presented itself. A September 13 report in the *New-York Evening Post*, subsequently reprinted—in just a few days—in over a dozen cities as far north as Augusta Maine and as far south as Norfolk, Virginia, suggested that "14 French negroes" were discovered just outside Hoboken "utterly destitute of any means of subsistence." As the story continues, it relates sightings of other bands of escapees and balefully proposes that "they cannot be expected to yield quietly to starvation." Intimately understanding the racialized fears of its audience, the story need only imply the distressing consequences of the prisoners' projected resistance to convey its haunting message. In conclusion, the report underscores prevalent concerns that the French would offload their prisoners, leaving "2000 of these poor wretches" upon "our coast," and thereby fuels a variety of nightmares about destitute revolutionaries wandering the margins of metropolitan New York.¹⁶

Stories of marauding "half-starved French Negroes" lurking in a variety of sparsely populated precincts in New Jersey and Staten Island concurrently filtered their way into and out of newspapers across the region. One such report, printed under the headline "Black Ducks" in the *United States Chronicle*, a Providence, Rhode Island, paper, typifies the tenor of these articles. Citing "a person employed at the Quarantine ground" as its source, the article relates a scene ripped from the pages of a gothic novel. During a thunderstorm, the man observed "at every flash of lightning, the heads of Negroes who were swimming ashore from the French Frigates" like "flocks of black ducks making for the land." Reporting invisible bodies and heads only illuminated by lightening accentuates the sensationalism of the scene. For a largely maritime audience, to equate the fugitives with subaquatic dangers effectively likens them to hidden snags, concealed perils that all too familiarly posed grave threats to commerce, transportation, and overall mobility. Reports like this floated up from the waterfront every day, and these stories increasingly imagined New York as under siege and the frigates as hemorrhaging prisoners' intent on collective action and subterfuge.¹⁷

In the frenzied rhetoric that characterizes these inflamed reports, on September 10, the *New-York Evening Post* decried that "if murders and robberies, and every species of crime are not committed upon us, it ought to excite unaffected surprise. A horde of the most dreadful, desperate and bloody-minded wretches are daily and nightly disgorged upon our shores from the

French frigates, and no man can pretend to foretell the extent or the progress of the mischief that awaits us." The story recasts the pre-arrival city as semi-Edenic, predicting that now because of the frigates, "a constant additional watch will be found necessary the ensuing winter, to preserve our houses from conflagration, our dwellings from burglary, and every species of property from being plundered." Representing the problem as unflagging, the *Post* speculates about the literal and figurative costs of the continued presence of the frigates. Constructing a new temporality, based upon the changes wrought by the French frigates, the article renders the future as almost entirely determined by a foreign contagion. Strenuously objecting to the "dangerous and shameful species of traffic" ongoing "daily between the Long-Island people and the frigates," the article portrays an extreme situation with no visible resolution. This distress festered as the French offered no signal of departure. Instead, they appeared willing to remain indefinitely anchored in New York harbor. The *Post*'s story culminates with an unequivocal crescendo, italicizing the "one question" that "must occur to every citizen—*for what purpose were these cargoes of negroes brought here?*"[18]

Spring Tide

The question posed by the *New-York Evening Post* haunted a variety of New York officials and elite citizens, and a flood of correspondence poured out of Manhattan detailing those concerns. Some of those letters, like many of the ones written by Mayor Edward Livingston, were fashioned as public gestures aimed at both acquiring information and reassuring a troubled citizenry; others, particularly those written by southerners (such as those of Fontaine Maury of Virginia and Colonel Wade Hampton of South Carolina) who were temporarily in New York, fueled the nation-wide panic by promulgating the idea that the French intended to unload their prisoners somewhere along the southern coastline. These circuits of exchange, which developed simultaneously with the spread of newspaper reports across the country, helped establish the structure of thought and feeling that culminated in the mustering of South Carolina's militia. Within a week of the arrival of the French frigates, letters about the situation in New York reached a variety of cabinet officials and the office of every governor south of Pennsylvania. President Thomas Jefferson referenced a number of these letters in his correspondence, citing them as evidence of the exigency of convincing the French to depart.[19]

On August 16, the *New-York Evening Post* reprinted an exchange of letters between Mayor Edward Livingston and local French officials concerning the current state of affairs. The incident with the American brig *Twins* may have sparked the correspondence, and it certainly expedited its dispersion. In careful, yet pointed, language Livingston sought confirmation from First Citizen Archambal, the commercial agent for the French Republic, that New York was not in any imminent peril:

Sir,

I have been informed that the Frigates belonging to your nation, now in this harbour, have a great number of negroes (slaves or prisoners) confined on board.—You are acquainted Sir, with the scrupulous jealousy which our laws watch their introduction into our country, and will therefore perceive it be a duty, which as its first magistrate I owe this city, to request through you an assurance from the Commander of the squadron, that none of these people shall under any pretense be permitted to land.—I hope too it will not be deemed an indiscretion on a point so interesting to our police, to ask whether the force on board is fully adequate to prevent any risque of insurrection or escape!

I have the honor to be

With great respect,
Your most obedient serv't,
Edward Livingston

Livingston appeals for guarantees even as he implies the readiness of local police to assist with shipboard security. Still, Livingston's equivocation about how to identify the French Negroes raises the question of whether they were slaves, revolutionaries, or prisoners. As provocative as that enigma may now seem, for Livingston this troubling indeterminacy needed to remain cached below the decks of *La Consolante*. Livingston stressed that none of "these people" were to disembark because of the unnerving polysemy they would carry ashore. The reprinted letter (quickly published in out-of-town papers) also illustrates the attentiveness of New York officials to the threat posed by the frigates. In this regard, the public dissemination of the letter moves to establish an official municipal response.[20]

Upon receipt of the letter, Archambal immediately forwarded Livingston's queries to the French commander Captain La Caille of *La Consolante*. The Captain replied "that the most severe orders had been previously given to prevent any man of colour from having any communication with the land." He maintained that the prisoners have "behaved very peace-able since their importation—and that this country does not seem calculated to inspire them with any ideas of revolt."[21] Still, even as he assured Livingston that the French sailors were sufficient to curtail any unrest, the captain withdrew to the quarantine ground near Staten Island. Retreating from the heavily populated Manhattan waterfront may have been a calculated response to Livingston's letter, an evidentiary appeasement to ameliorate "the fears manifested by the inhabitants of this city."[22]

The rapid dissemination of the query, and the French responses, attests to the mayor's vigilant interest in the frigates. Livingston's audience was as much the panicked citizens of New York as the French foreign minister. The size of this secondary audience multiplied across the next few days, as Livingston's detente reappeared in virtually every local paper and subsequently in papers from New Haven to Charleston. The Philadelphia-based *Gazette of the United States* carried the letters on August 18. The *Federal Gazette* (Baltimore) and the *Columbia Advertiser* (Alexandria, Virginia) published the letters across the next two days, just as readers in Albany and Massachusetts learned about the inadvertent collision and subsequent escape. On August 21, Boston's *Columbian Centinel* carried news that the French were finding it "difficult to negotiate for subsistence" for the starving prisoners, and that since so much "anxiety" had been produced by "their introduction" the "Mayor has opened a correspondence." The account reproduces La Caille's guarantees concerning ship security, and his avowal that none of the prisoners would alight from the ships. Yet the article concludes by noting that "between 30 and 40 negroes from the French frigates have been removed to the Hospital at Staten Island." This coda demonstrates just how promptly Livingston's rapprochement unraveled; despite his best protests and hopes, the opacity Livingston so greatly feared—the fluidity of signifiers that the slaves/prisoners/revolutionaries/enemy-combatants threateningly embodied—had gained a footing in New York.[23]

Even as Livingston authorized the publication of his negotiations with the French, he concurrently addressed a more pointed letter to Secretary of War Henry Dearborn—a letter that rapidly circulated among numerous officials in Washington. In this missive, Livingston formally appeals for federal troops to execute the quarantine laws and prevent any of the sick prisoners, who had, of necessity, been relocated to Staten Island, from escaping and "taking refuge in our Country." The undercurrent of alarm demonstrates the strain on the city's resources created by the continued presence of over a thousand putative revolutionaries in the harbor. The state hospital was overwhelmed with sick foreign prisoners, and Livingston argued that this burden detracted from its intended mission to sequester infirm traders and emigrants. Livingston reminded Dearborn of his capacity to "employ the garrison troops" and confessed that he lacked the resources to manage the situation by disclosing that "numbers of these blacks are daily escaping."[24]

Undertows

Unlike many other New Yorkers engrossed by the immediate local dangers, Fontaine Maury envisioned the problem as one with serious national ramifications. As a member of a well-established Virginian family, a former slaveholder, and three-term mayor of Fredericksburg, Maury was deeply troubled by the prospect of any of these black revolutionaries—re-enchained and forcibly deported from Guadeloupe—intermingling with enslaved Africans in the United States. Maury had recently arrived in New York to work as a commodities trader—primarily invested in moving freight between Virginia, Port Royal, Jamaica, and New York—and while he may have initially feared that the French vessels were a harbinger of market disruptions, he quickly became fixated on the imprisoned revolutionaries. Less than a week after *La Consolante* anchored, Maury busily dispatched letters to a variety of federal officials and prominent southerners exhorting them "to guard against a measure which if carried into effect may considerably endanger the peace and tranquility of the Southern States." The concept of large-scale domestic slave revolt was far from "unthinkable" for Maury; indeed, he fetishized the prisoners as portents of calamity. Given how quickly Maury leapt from observing the frigates to portending a national catastrophe, obviously the economic crisis that had gripped France since the outbreak of Caribbean violence in 1791 deeply resonated with U.S. merchants. Indeed, if Maury's panic is any accurate measure, Americans could all too easily envisage a similar sort of economic devastation should the contagion of rebellion spread.[25]

On August 21, 1802, Maury directed letters to such notable figures as Virginia Governor James Monroe, Maryland Governor John Francis Mercer, and the former governor of South Carolina General William Moultrie. Maury also co-authored, with the wealthy South Carolina planter and former low-country congressman and sheriff Wade Hampton (coincidently also in Manhattan), a slightly more temperate letter to Secretary of State James Madison. Colonel Hampton directed a number of letters southward himself, most crucially one to Governor John Drayton of South Carolina (which seems to have brought the news about the frigates to Drayton's attention). Like Maury, Hampton was deeply troubled by the situation and warned southerners to take precautions. In his letter to Monroe, which exemplifies the tenor of Hampton and Maury's correspondence, Maury suggests that he took "dire pains to procure" the "best information," and he reports that the French are expecting "three other Ships of War," also carrying rebellious prisoners to soon rendezvous in the harbor. In total, Maury estimated that 1,500 of these "unfortunate half starved Wretches" were either currently in New York's waterways or shortly expected. Arguing that the presence of the frigates had fostered an "extreme adgitation of the Public mind," Maury reported hearing of "many instances" of the French offering their imprisoned revolutionaries "for sale in this city, in open violation of the Laws." Fearing the threat to domestic tranquility if the French did actually "dispose of a number of renegando negroes," Maury advised that he had "little doubt but they will attempt to disperse them along the Southern Coast in a Clandestine Manner." In his estimation, even a solitary escapee was capable of disrupting the social fabric of the Republic.[26]

As the third youngest son of the Reverend James Maury, who ran a famous boarding school in Albemarle County, Virginia, which counted Thomas Jefferson, James Madison, Dabney Carr, and James Monroe among its students, Fontaine Maury was intimately connected with a number of notable federal politicians and wealthy southerners. Maury also had a wide range of business connections, both among the Virginian planter elite and in Manhattan where his older brother James managed a successful mercantile business. Maury was well positioned to have his circumspections about "extreme agitation" and "clandestine" activities regarded as crucial intelligence from a politically active and well-connected southern merchant writing to familiar associates. James Monroe's actions upon receipt of Maury's letter manifest his implicit trust in the author. In acknowledging the "interesting communication," Monroe requested Maury apprise him of any further developments concerning "the insurgent slaves of St. Domingo." After the receipt of Maury's letter, the next two letters cataloged in Monroe's correspondence are dispatches to Colonel William Davies (the former commander of the First Virginia Regiment of the Continental Army and the collector of customs at Norfolk) and Colonel Thomas Newton of Norfolk, instructing them to repulse any unauthorized landings. Monroe reminds Newton of his authority over harbor traffic and directs him to "remonstrate against" any French attempts to anchor "at Norfolk, or elsewhere near you," in "the most explicit and strongest terms." Whether Monroe was aware of the situation prior to Maury's letter remains unclear, but, certainly, the letter spurred his command to intercept "the conspirators of St. Domingo" before they touched Virginian soil.[27]

Monroe apprehensively consumed news from the French Caribbean throughout his tenure as governor of Virginia. He had ordered the state militia to suppress Gabriel's Rebellion, perhaps the most extensive slave conspiracy in the American south. Many Americans believed that Virginia had narrowly avoided a massive uprising, and Gabriel's Rebellion culminated in the execution of twenty-seven conspirators and the increased juridical scrutiny of both free and enslaved blacks in the region. Like many other Virginians, Monroe doubtless envisioned a connection between Gabriel's uprising and Toussaint's reign in St. Domingue. The historian Gordon S. Brown speculates that President Thomas Jefferson gave "the French a green light to proceed" with their recolonization efforts in the Caribbean because of the "domestic security scare occasioned by the recent Gabriel Revolt."[28] The fixation on St. Domingue as the wellspring of all slave unrest inflected American reactions to domestic problems. Indeed, as Douglas R. Egerton notes, "It's not surprising that one scholar has identified Gabriel as a Dominguan slave brought to the mainland. The fact is wrong, but the logic is impeccable."[29] This associative reasoning was commonplace for early nineteenth-century Virginians and deeply inflected their perceptions of any event even remotely connected to St. Domingue. By associating the antecedents of domestic slave unrest with (black) Jacobinism, fantasies about a docile U.S. slave population remained intact, even as an easy scapegoat for turmoil was displaced onto a foreign threat.

Just six months prior to his receipt of Maury's letter, circumstances prompted Monroe to issue warnings about domestic instability and French Negroes.[30] Responding to a March 1802 communication from the mayor of Norfolk, concerning unease "occasioned by the presence of many people of colour there from the West India Islands," Monroe presupposed that "the scenes which are acting in Saint-Domingue must produce an effect on all the people of colour in this and the States south of us, more especially our slaves." Effectively, Monroe demarcates Virginia as the northern boundary of an inverted circum-Caribbean system: one turned topsy-turvy by the news of slave uprisings as well as by the exodus of refugee planters and their servants. Reminding the mayor that "it is our duty to be on our guard to prevent any mischief," Monroe affirms his unquestioned support for anticipatory action. This commitment to preemptiveness demonstrates just how predisposed Monroe was for the receipt of Maury's letter later that same summer. Like the editors of the *Washington Federalist* (who felt no need to contextualize the invasion narrative), Monroe awaited the receipt of such a letter about French Negroes because he entertained its arrival every day.[31]

Slack Water

A week after the *Washington Federalist* stopped the presses, readers in Manhattan once again encountered reports about "the Frigates that were some time ago at New York, and finding that they could not effect their design there, steered round to take advantage of a more defenceless place."[32] According to various accounts, the area near Georgetown, South Carolina, was under assault. The French were detected "landing brigand Negroes at Mr. Alston's sea shore plantation," with observers counting "not less than one thousand" landed prisoners.[33] Extracted letters from a variety of "respectable gentleman" on the scene registered everything from the immediate mobilization of the white citizenry of South Carolina to their sanguine fears about domestic slave rebellions.[34] Consistently, these accounts predicted catastrophic results if any of these foreign prisoners interacted with the domestic slave population. Georgetown County was overwhelmingly inhabited by enslaved Africans (approximately 88 percent of the population); thus, it is hardly surprising that the vastly outnumbered whites dreaded the dangerous influx of revolutionary intrigue.[35] Moreover, the county was the lone Federalist stronghold in the state, and so decidedly partisan that, in the words of historian Howard A. Ohline, the elite of Georgetown believed that "Republicanism would surely cause a racial holocaust." Residents in a situation mirroring that of prerevolutionary St. Domingue, the planters of Georgetown County unsurprisingly responded quickly—and "with the entire extent of [the county's] military capacity"—to rumors of invasion. Well aware of the fates of the burned-out colonizers of Cape François, the plantation owners in Georgetown assumed their self-preservation depended on decisive action.[36]

Tensions had risen weeks earlier, after Governor John Drayton received news of the French frigates from Colonel Wade Hampton, a wealthy low-country planter who was visiting Manhattan when *La Consolante* arrived. In response to the disturbing news, Drayton organized coastal patrols and ordered the state militia to be on ready alert. In a letter Drayton addressed to President Jefferson about the situation, he confesses his firm belief that "the French are intent" on offloading the prisoners "clandestinely on the coast of the southern States of our Union." Stressing that his public duty required him "to oppose their landing by force of arms," Drayton urged Jefferson to protect the Republic at all costs. Drayton's misgivings about the French frigates stimulated racialized fears across the state. In short order, a variety of paranoid testimonials filtered their way out of Georgetown County and sparked statewide unease in South Carolina.[37]

An "extract of a letter from Georgetown" typifies these reprinted narratives by informing newspaper readers in Augusta, Maine, that South Carolinians had been "summoned to turn out with the different companies" and instructed "not to take a single negro, but shoot them all." The anonymous South Carolina militiaman who reputedly drafted this letter describes both his abject fears and his cautious hopes when he concludes that "we are informed they have landed about 1000; by tomorrow morning there will be soldiers enough at the place to prevent any more landing—if they get scattered among our negroes it will be a dreadful thing." As they frantically mobilized to repel the rumored invasion, the residents of Georgetown assumed that the incendiary spark they long dreaded was finally working its way north from St. Domingue (and south from New York) in the form of the French frigates and their revolutionary cargo. While South Carolina's papers had refrained from providing much coverage of the situation in New York—a common suppression tactic, as Herbert Aptheker has aptly demonstrated, to control access to information by the domestic slave population—the citizens of Georgetown recognized that the French had lingered in Manhattan, and they had been warned about their intentions to offload the prisoners somewhere along the southern coast. Given their fear of even moderate republican sentiments about liberty and equality—and occupying an isolated county with an enormous racial imbalance—it is hardly surprising that the citizens of Georgetown believed that they were being invaded; like James Monroe, Edward Livingston, and Fontaine Maury, they had dwelt in anticipation of such a possibility for some time.[38]

South Carolina was never overrun by black revolutionaries from the West Indies. It did, however, prepare for an invasion. To give a sense of how absolutely entrenched South Carolinians were in a fantasy of anticipation—of ceaselessly projecting a dreaded infiltration of Caribbean-tinged notions of liberty and equality—it is important to note that the rumors of invasion were sparked, as historian Jed Handelsman Shugerman observes, by "the sighting of one black foreigner" in Georgetown county.[39] That one black stranger—one solitary (possibly) French-speaking Negro—arrested near an isolated lowcountry plantation on or about October 11, 1802, caused citizens to anxiously stand guard on the coast, induced Governor Drayton to marshal the state militia, and incited panic in newspaper readers as far north as Maine for weeks after his incarceration. Indeed, citizens across the country (like readers of the *Washington Federalist*, the *New-York Gazette*, and *Edes' Kennebec Gazette*) were presumably panicked well *after* the unfounded—but still inflamed—passions had cooled in South Carolina. Clarification about what had actually happened migrated north in the ensuing weeks, as a November 10, 1802, story in the Norwich, Connecticut–based the *Courier* demonstrates. No armada appeared, no French frigates materialized, and no invasion force of one thousand former enslaved citizen-soldier-revolutionaries landed in South Carolina; the rampant paranoia arose from the discovery of just one "French negro" who was now "supposed to be a run-away." Published as the lead story under a section heading entitled "Domestic Intelligence," the article concludes by praising the citizens of Georgetown for taking the threat seriously, even as it warns against the cost of such false alarms.[40]

Ebb Tide

As part of an engaging critique of Benedict Anderson's concept of seriality and the rise of "nationalist consciousness," Trish Loughran argues that "Anderson's formulations about imagined communities rely on a similar fantasy about the ability of print to erase local differences and to install, in their place, a formal homogeneity, whether in fact or fiction." As the reportage of the French frigates demonstrates, readers in disparate U.S. cities did not experience the event simultaneously (indeed, readers in Maine may have been first panicked about South Carolina's invasion the same week that readers in Connecticut learned the reports were false) or even homogeneously. So while it is true that this event does not represent an instance of "simultaneity-across-space," which would allow readers to conceive of themselves as connected to a "larger, translocal community," it does exhibit the ways in which texts circulated to underwrite national communities through a variety of spatial and temporal deferments. Describing an emblematic instance of late eighteenth-century postal communication, Loughran argues that the situation was marked by "attendant losses, delays, deferrals, and confusions"; she interprets these broken lines of communication as more accurately describing the realities of textual circulation in the early Republic than Anderson's famous notions of print transcending distance and discord. Newspaper coverage, personal and public letters, and civic reactions to the events (and supposed events) associated with the French frigates are rife with instances of losses of information, delays in communication, deferrals in interpretations, and confusions of all stripes. Yet, despite the fractured messages, inaccurate explanations, and general disarray, the event demonstrates how the perceived threat of Caribbean revolutionary unrest formed translocal and nonpartisan networks of association; these large-scale interpretative communities, although disjoined by time, were united by their paranoia. In essence, the circulation of information about the frigates helped forge—in both senses of the word—the idea of national identity based on a domestic order that needed to be immunized against foreign contagions. The threat of French Negroes was substantial enough to overcome sectarian, regional, and economic divisions and form a sense of translocal purpose.[41]

In the ebb and flow of information about actual and imagined events, half-truths and confused prognostications rushed in to fill the gaps created by the contending tides of facts and sophistry. Out of these countercurrents of information, ceaselessly beating back and forth, emerged a temporally disjointed community united by paranoia, suggesting a sense of national cohesion imagined out of the intermixing of negation, disavowal, and a cathecting of racialized fear. Contending with a recursive flux of fears about racial unrest and foreign incursion, in which one was utterly comingled with the other, readers in the early Republic forged a multivalent simultaneity across nonsimultaneous space. The fear that arose out of this blurred temporality activated a prevalent sense that the West Indian revolt was always floating just offshore, restlessly drifting toward the United States, always on the verge of making landfall, despite ever vigilant attempts at maintaining a quarantine. This lingering uncertainty over the French frigates in U.S. waterways embodies this process of deferred meaning, and as such underscores the ways in which information in the early Republic traveled along temporally disjunctive webs of exchange. Yet, the coverage of the event also asks us to think about how these disarticulated narrative temporalities were informed by a larger translocal fixation on the Caribbean. Citizens in both Manhattan and Georgetown came to believe that their lives were endangered and that their futures were destined to be overwritten by the influx of French Negroes—and they did so without much provocation or hesitation. The paranoia was not just a southern, not just a rural, not just a slave-holders' fear, but was much more widely shared than we commonly imagine. From Augusta, Maine, to the low-country of South Carolina, newspaper readers and letter recipients anticipated that they lived under the threat of invasion because of a pronounced fixation with Caribbean history—a preoccupation that has for far too long remained obscured in our representations of the early Republic. As long as the indeterminacy raised by Caribbean revolutionary violence remained quarantined offshore, the United States remained able to at least tangentially imagine itself as free from the vexing issues of racially inflected conceptions of equality and liberty. Yet as the entire nation seemed to understand, once that indeterminacy landed on the Republic's shores, the nation's future would be reordered by the eruption of change it would inaugurate. Indeed, if newspaper readers in Rhode Island accepted that New York was under siege, and several weeks later readers in northern Virginia believed that the low-country of South Carolina was similarly targeted, they shared a simultaneity across time and space if for no other reason than that they jointly embraced the idea of a causal relationship between Caribbean history and domestic stability. As the daily assemblage of shipping news made manifest to newspaper readers in the early Republic, distinctions between the domestic and foreign were at best fluid and porous. The concepts of domestic tranquility and foreign revolution were mutually constitutive elements of the same ecosystem, reflecting the literal ways in which the waterways on which they played out routinely washed into one another. In this regard, the fantasy of being able to forestall indeterminacy always flowed alongside an endless anticipation of its arrival.

* * *

The fate of the imprisoned revolutionaries onboard the French frigates remains a mystery. Newspapers in the United States continued to obsessively cover the Caribbean and the Haitian struggle for independence in the months that followed, but they never mention *La Consolante* again. Ships' logs and naval records demonstrate that French vessels carrying imprisoned combatants briefly appeared in Pedro Shoals, Kingston, Cape François, Corsica, and Puerto Rico across the latter half of 1802.[42] Undoubtedly prisoners continued to escape when presented with an opportunity, others were likely clandestinely sold whenever a profit could be turned, and many more assuredly perished because of illness and malnourishment. Other documents indicate that some ships were turned "into extermination camps," as officers were ordered to drown "prisoners surreptitiously" or to suffocate them "with sulfur inside [their] holds."[43] The specific histories of the nameless fifteen hundred (or more) prisoners who docked off New York harbor may never be written, even as the ships that held them continued to sail across the Atlantic in years to come. While sailors and newspaper reporters alike faithfully maintained records about ports of call and the fluctuating prices of commodities, they seldom registered detailed notes about imprisoned former slaves. Our sense of their haunting journey thus remains fragmented, even as their presence in U.S. waterways exposes the intimate ligatures binding the United States to the Caribbean. With their names and fates unrecorded, they still ghost our archives in ways that we are only beginning to recognize and disentangle.

CHAPTER 4

"Entirely Different from Any Likeness I Ever Saw"

Aesthetics as Counter-Memory Historiography and the Iconography of Toussaint Louverture

IVY G. WILSON

On November 10, 1864, in the midst of the American Civil War, the *New Orleans Tribune* featured a column about a portrait with "intrinsic value" of Toussaint Louverture.[1] In it, the author noted that Jacob Snider, Jr., a Republican of the "blackest and noblest" kind, had presented the Louverture portrait to a fund established to support the family of Washington Wilks, a prominent English abolitionist who died suddenly while giving an oration at the Freemason's Hall in London earlier in the year. Snider himself was not infrequently involved with the art world and had acquired the portrait from John Bigelow, who had been serving as U.S. consul in Paris under President Abraham Lincoln's administration.[2] One of the most noteworthy details of the column is the information that Snider had traded his portrait of George Washington in exchange for Bigelow's one of Toussaint Louverture. The author concluded the *New Orleans Tribune* piece with a wish that Snider's gift to the fund might prompt a sale to help support the Wilks family. As extraordinary as it is to imagine a portrait of Louverture in the possession of a U.S. consulate, and one stationed in Paris no less, the story also evinces how Louverture was being positioned as a black founding father, with the same iconic value as George Washington.

But perhaps the most salient aspect of the column is what it intimates about the intersection of counter-memory historiography and mid-nineteenth-century notions of politics when they are animated by questions of the aesthetic. The author's passing comment about the portrait's "intrinsic value" could have been meant to intimate a number of ideas, including the painting's monetary value (determined by the market), its own artistic value (determined by "aesthetic judgment"), or its semiotic value (determined in a field of symbolic order). On the one hand, the author's hope that some "American historical society of New England Abolitionist[s]" would make a bid to help support the Wilks fund is a reminder of the authority that entities like historical societies exercise not simply as archeologists of knowledge and curators of archives but as agents in contemporary political affairs. On the other hand, the author's admission that, beyond the fact that Bigelow had acquired the painting from an old Parisian curiosity shop, the provenance and history of the painting was "unknown," might be thought of as a reminder that the Haitian Revolution has too often been occluded from standard histories of the Age of Revolution.[3] More importantly, the notice about the painting itself accentuates that sources other than those traditionally used by historians are needed to more fully delineate Haiti's presence in accounts of the United States and the hemisphere of the Americas writ large, no less than of France and European colonialism. And no small part of these other counterarchives about Haiti have come from and been created by African American intellectuals and cultural producers from activist Anna Julia Cooper to musician Charles Mingus, from painter Jacob Lawrence to writer Ntozake Shange, among many others.

African Americans have challenged the popular, if not official, discourse on Louverture and the Haitian Revolution by fashioning alternative archives in an intellectual and political project that might be called "counter-memory historiography." "Counter-memory" is most often identified with Michel Foucault and his critical analyses of history, Friedrich Nietzsche, and the figure of the author. As Natalie Zemon Davis and Randolph Starn have noted, Foucault's definition of "counter-memory designated the residual or resistant strains that withstand official versions of historical continuity."[4] Foucault's notion of counter-memory, especially where he is concerned with the epistemological relationship between "history" and "genealogy," also has bearings on his later discussions of the policing mechanisms of the disciplines that produce "subjugated knowledges," and ultimately heuristically, the insurrection of these subjugated knowledges.[5] Engaging Nietzsche's consideration of history, Foucault defines genealogy as "the constitution of the subject across history which has led up to the modern concept of the self" and as a mode of critical inquiry to investigate those elements that "we tend to feel [are] without history."[6] We might turn this on its head somewhat to intimate that the constitution of history across subjects, themes, and chronologies have led to the modern concept of the self. In this sense, there is no universal history, only multiple genealogies from which a history emerges and masquerades itself as universal.[7]

How might the Haitian Revolution be thought of as a counter-memory, as a "discontinuity" or residual strain against the official histories of the United States? How might such counter-memories resist teleological narratives of American self-actualization and exceptionalism? What are the ways that the Haitian Revolution and other uprisings like the Irish Rebellion of 1803 belie common perceptions about the Age of Revolution as the apotheosis of European enlightenment discourse? And, inasmuch as Louverture and the Haitian Revolution are subjugated knowledges within the histories of the United States and France, how might we accommodate art and aesthetics as iterations of subjugated knowledges within the disciplinary regimes of history that privilege primary sources as history's most fundamental object of analyses?

Nineteenth-century African American intellectuals enacted a mode of political critique by engaging counter-memory historiography, and no exercise symbolized this more than the iconography of Louverture. Many of these illustrations or sketches invert the literal definition of iconography as "picture writing" into, instead, an aesthetic practice of "writing picture" with their biographical vignettes of Louverture and social histories of the Haitian Revolution.[8] Manipulating the aesthetic practice of iconography, writers crafted these images as discursive allegories to enter into debates about the diaspora and Pan-Africanism, black independence and sovereignty, and chattel slavery in the United States and elsewhere.

In what follows, I turn to portraits of Louverture as they are represented in speeches and orations as well as a wide range of literary genres including the novel, poetry, and nonfiction prose. The vast majority of these sketches were represented narratively, rendered through a robust textual constellation of mid-century periodical culture rife with newspapers, pamphlets, and magazines. With respect to the political project of counter-memory historiography, it is precisely the fact that these sketches cannot be said to constitute primary documents about Louverture or the Haitian Revolution, since most of them were produced decades later, that they warrant analyses for the ways they were positioned to be both axiomatic artifacts of the past and emblematic claims on the present.

Apparitions of Haiti and Toussaint Louverture

The specter of Haiti has had a latent presence in the imagination of the African American public sphere beginning immediately after the revolution's conclusion.[9] On July 4, 1804, after their white counterparts had celebrated American independence, black Philadelphians took to the streets to celebrate Haitian independence.[10] News from Haiti was also covered in the early African American press, at least from 1827, when *Freedom's Journal* began publishing pieces about it. In its short existence of only two years, the editors of *Freedom's Journal* included several features involving Haiti: a six-part series of articles about the country's history and present condition, a three-part biographical account of Louverture, and the short story "Theresa—A Haytien Tale," among others.[11] David Walker, who in his 1829 pamphlet *Appeal to the Coloured Citizens of the World* calling for U.S. black resistance to oppression, suggested that if blacks must "see fit to go away," they should do so with the English and, if not with them, then the Haitians, "who, according to their word, [are] bound to protect and comfort us."[12] And James McCune Smith, among others who would deliver orations about Louverture (including William Wells Brown, Frederick Douglass, and Wendell Phillips), offered the lecture "Toussaint L'Ouverture and the Haytian Revolutions" as his topic before the Stuyvestant Institute in 1841. Throughout the first half of the nineteenth century, then, Haiti circulated through a number of mediums including public performances and parades, periodicals, pamphlets, and oratory.

What becomes visible in these invocations of Haiti is how they constitute a concomitant cultural gesture that was at least as much an honorific, consecrating of Louverture and the Haitian Revolution, as it was an epistemic mechanism deployed to ensure that Haiti would not drop out of the public imagination, or, worse still, history altogether. As these invocations of Haiti indicate, African American intellectuals were acutely aware of the ways in which black subjects were being continually elided in national and global histories, and they imagined aesthetics as both a corrective and supplement, not only to standard historical accounts but also to normative practices of historiography.[13]

In an 1848 article in Frederick Douglass's newspaper, the *North Star*, the anonymous author of an essay on Toussaint Louverture worries that the same military forces that subdued Louverture were also suppressing the historical account by compromising the archives and records on the Haitian leader. "The same tyranny which meanly murdered him in a European dungeon, blotted out all the best sources of information as to the means by which he accomplished them. But the facts which are derived through this very enemy, unsmothered by avalanches of abuse, are quite sufficient for our purpose."[14] It is not clear if the author means to suggest that "the best sources of information" had been "blotted out" ex post facto or not created at the moment of a given historical event itself, but it is evident that the author is concerned about an uneven archive that ostensibly privileges only the French version of events. The writer here, then, would seem to prefigure some claims that the Haitian Revolution has been occluded, claims most often associated with Michel-Rolph Trouillot's seminal work.[15] Whereas the "silencing" that Trouillot addresses is decidedly more a problem of political ontology (inasmuch as the Haitian Revolution was "unthinkable" or unimaginable), the problem that the author of this *North Star* article evinces is an epistemic one concerning historiography. In using the word "blotted," the author means to convey the ways that, on the one hand, the sketch of Louverture's character or reputation is being sullied and, on the other hand, accounts of the country are being materially obscured from various official histories.

Yet, as important as these early representations of Haiti, Louverture, and the revolution remain, they increased in frequency and assumed particular currency in the decade before the American Civil War. Haiti circulated in the U.S. imagination during this period for a number of reasons including the heightened discourse about the annexation of Cuba and continued fears by the Southern plantocracy of looming black insurrections, in addition to African Americans themselves increasingly invoking Haiti in debates about political sovereignty. These debates about sovereignty principally centered on issues of self-governance and citizenship, underwritten by the political philosophical question of the Right of Revolution. If, as F. O. Matthiessen outlined decades ago, the central preoccupation that united writers of the classic period now identified as the "American Renaissance" was the question of democracy, African American writers of the same moment, including Frederick Douglass, William Wells Brown, and Frank J. Webb, frequently addressed this very question through both national and international registers.[16] During the "impending crisis" and the Civil War, the geographical proximity and political history of Haiti put this question into high relief with particular urgency.[17]

As the novel that famously, in the words of Abraham Lincoln, started the Civil War, Harriet Beecher Stowe's *Uncle Tom's Cabin* (1852) features apparitions of Haiti in two important moments to stage dialogues about black emigration and self-governance, respectively. In one instance, the escaped slaves George and Eliza Harris, after being reunited and now ensconced in Canada, have a tête-à-tête about their possible next steps, with George championing emigration. George's preference of Liberia over Haiti—the two sites most vigorously considered in the emigration debates during the African American convention movements—depends upon a depiction of Haiti as both an effeminate and a failed country. Desperately wanting to adopt "an African *nationality*," George tells Eliza that such a subjectivity cannot be found in Haiti but rather on the shores of Africa where there is "a republic formed of picked men, who, by energy and self-educating force, have, in many cases, individually, raised themselves above a condition of slavery. Having gone through a preparatory stage of feebleness, this republic has, at last, become an acknowledged nation on the face of the earth,—acknowledged by both France and England."[18] It almost seems as if George were indeed speaking of Haiti for, by the time of the publication of *Uncle Tom's Cabin*, it had in fact gained diplomatic recognition from France in 1825 and England some eight years later in 1833.

If George's doubts about Haiti stem from his desire to embody an "African nationality," Stowe's use of the trope of "sans culottes" in a conversation between the St. Clair brothers correlates the Haitian Revolution to the French. On the heels of watching young Henrique beat his slave Dodo, Augustine coolly warns his brother Alfred that the current social system may be up-ended and mentions Haiti as a foreboding example. When Alfred retorts that the "Haytiens were not Anglo Saxons; if they had been, there would have been another story," Augustine replies, "If ever the San Domingo hour comes, Anglo Saxon blood will lead the day."[19] The "San Domingo hour" has often been used as shorthand by critics to note white fear of black insurrection, while often leaving unacknowledged the second half of the conditional sentence, with Augustine's full espousal of racial romanticist discourse, part and parcel of a wider articulation of racial romanticism so central to the novel's ideological subtexts. Variants of the word "St. Domingo" were used by Stowe's contemporaries to signal white fear of black insurrection. This was certainly the case with Melville's *Benito Cereno* (1855), in which he sets the story of a slave revolt gone awry and off course aboard a ship named the *San Dominick* to adumbrate the already gothic foreboding language of his prose.

However, more salient to the relationship of aesthetics and countermemories to revealing subjugated knowledges is the visual work that the "sans culottes" image performs to underscore class stratification as a central issue of the Haitian Revolution. It is important to recall that the words immediately preceding the line about the "San Domingo hour" concern class; the brothers mention the upper- and underclass, machinery, and the masses. Thus, when Augustine summons Haiti as an example of the precipitating decline of the French noblesse, the most immediate context is class more so than race. The interpolation of Haiti into a discussion about class or of class into a discussion of race (taking the initial context of Henrique's reign of terror over Dodo as the starting point) should be taken not so much as a non sequitur as a glimmer of the kind of "insurrection of knowledges" that will come to the fore some ninety years later when C. L. R. James offers a Marxist reading of the Haitian Revolution as one of class struggle in *The Black Jacobins* (1938).[20] Thus, we can see James's *The Black Jacobins* as an act to correct the overdetermination of race in previous depictions of slavery by considering its class implications as well. The scene with the St. Clair brothers (one where race is interpolated into a discussion primarily about class in a novel that is ostensibly about race) functions in the same ways that Marx's marginalia on chattel slavery do in his analyses of class formation—as a subjugated knowledge of an imminent genealogy of a historiography on race and class to come.

Body and Soul; or, The Iconography of Toussaint Louverture

If Stowe was among those who invoked "St. Domingo" as an apparition of sorts, another group of writers was equally preoccupied with offering fuller biographical sketches of Louverture. *Freedom's Journal*'s first installment on him, for example, opened with lines advertising that it was "copying into our paper the following sketch of the character of TOUSSAINT L'OUVERTURE."[21] While essentially every account of Haiti also includes one of Louverture, these figurative sketches range from vignettes to more detailed portraits. In the first half of the nineteenth century these included William Wordsworth's sonnet "To Toussaint l'Overture" (1803), John Greenleaf Whittier's 1833 ballad stanzas, Harriet Martineau's novel *The Hour and the Man* (1840), and Alphonse de Lamartine's verse drama *Toussaint Louverture* (1850). Wordsworth's sonnet, which finds Louverture imprisoned in Joux, is essentially concerned with the corporeal dematerialization of his body and the ostensible freedom engendered by his transubstantiation into nature.[22] If Wordsworth's sonnet can be thought of as a vignette, whereby the principal image fades into its background, the vast majority of biographical sketches of Louverture employ a different tactic of representation; rather than the aesthetics of ethereality and dissolution, these other sketches embody an aesthetics of corporeality and adumbration. In contrast to Wordsworth's concentration on the ethereal, later portraits perceptibly attended to the physical, the body and soul of Louverture as it were. The three most recurrent features of Louverture that these portraits illustrate are his sagacity and wisdom, racial identity, and leadership in both military command and political office.

Considerations of Louverture's wisdom—whether learned or untutored—were pressing concerns during this period when claims about black intelligence were often indexed to claims about their humanity. In one of the Louverture portraits in the *North Star*, the author notes that a French writer had reproached Bayou de Libertas for "not being aware that his slave had learned to read."[23] The French writer was apparently mortified that Louverture had gained enough faculties that he was able grow familiar with Abbé Raynal. A little more than two years later, another piece in the *North Star* suggested that Bayou himself had instructed Louverture "in some of the first branches of education."[24] And earlier than these two pieces for the *North Star*, James McCune Smith's 1841 Stuyvesant Institute lecture made similar note of Louverture's literacy. Although detractors of the Haitian Revolution were dismayed by the idea of a slave learning to read and write, antebellum African American intellectuals took measures to accentuate Louverture's literacy as both a personal sign of his individual virtue and a symbolic sign of the social, if not radically subversive, value of literacy for all African Americans. When these portraits highlight Louverture's literacy, they evince the strategies that Robert B. Stepto calls "liberation through literacy."[25] In a metacritical sense, such abilities enable subaltern subjects to enter into, and engage with, the conventions of normative historiographic practices.

While observations about Louverture's intelligence attempted to illuminate his cerebral qualities, many of the sketches were also preoccupied with portraying his physical attributes, delineating them as "Negro" or "African." In the same 1848 issue of the *North Star* that noted the complaint of the French writer who lamented Louverture's ability to read, the author prefigured the entire piece by underscoring Louverture's blackness—"Not a drop of any other than African blood flowed in his veins."[26] This detail was reiterated in public lectures by both William Wells Brown and Wendell Phillips. "This man was the grandson of the king of Arradas," Brown proclaimed, "one of the most wealthy, powerful, and influential monarchs on the west coast of Africa."[27] And Phillips drew a similar picture, echoing that Louverture had "no drop of white blood."[28] In making at least a partial response to the science of phrenology and the discourse of racial romanticism, Phillips was at pains to reify Louverture's blackness as undiluted, "with no drop of white blood," in order to make a case that "the Negro race ... is entitled ... to a place close by the side of the Saxon." Brown's and Phillips's characterization seem almost to be a rejoinder to the scene of the St. Clair brothers in *Uncle Tom's Cabin*, where Augustine surmises that, should the San Domingo hour come, "Anglo Saxon blood will lead the day."[29]

But the most recurrent trace in these sketches was Louverture's position as a leader in political office and especially the battlefield, and, by employing techniques of effulgence, these sketches moved from the domain of mere biography to the realm of iconography. In *The Garies and Their Friends*, Frank J. Webb's novel about the tragic lives of middle-class African American families (the Garies who pass for white and the Ellises who do not), there is a crucial episode that is animated by a discussion of an image of Louverture. After arranging accommodations to stay at one of the homes of a wealthy black Philadelphian, Mr. Walters, Garie finds himself intrigued by a painting hanging on the parlor wall.

> "So you, too are attracted by that picture," said Mr. Walters, with a smile. "All white men look at it with interest. A black man in uniform of a general officer is something so unusual that they cannot pass it with a glance.... That is Toussaint l'Ouverture and I have every reason to believe it to be the correct likeness.... That looks like a man of intelligence. It is entirely different from any likeness I ever saw of him. The portraits generally represent him as a monkey-faced person, with a handkerchief about his head."[30]

Walters's comments to Garie about representation read dress and attire as social signifiers. Recalling the article in the *New Orleans Tribune* about Jacob Snider's acquisition of a portrait of Louverture that opens this essay, it is worth noting that the author of that article also took notice that "Toussaint [was] dressed in the uniform of a Haytien general."[31] Here, accoutrements designate social position—the uniform works as a political emblem against black caricature. Considering Maurice Wallace's acute analyses of the ways that the military uniform transformed the political noncomformist Martin Delany into a "disciplinary individual and model (black) citizen" of the U.S, one whose "corporal asceticism" no longer constituted "a menace to the representational integrity of the body politic," we might conceptualize Louverture's uniform as a sartorial symbol that proleptically indexes the yearned-for body politic of Haiti as a nation.[32] Walters's statement also discloses the efforts to not only dehumanize Louverture as "monkey-faced" but to render him effeminate through the symbol of the "handkerchief [tied] about his head," as some of Webb's American readers would have interpreted the rag. Another way to read the handkerchief, however, is in terms of class consciousness, as a sign that Louverture was unpretentious, modest, even humble in his appearance to promote a sense of egalitarianism through his visual representation as a man of the people, as Wendell Phillips noted—"He hated the restraint of his rank; he loved to put on the gray coat of the Little Corporal, and wander in camp. Toussaint also never could bear a uniform. He wore a plain coat, and often the yellow Madras handkerchief of the slaves."[33]

The Louverture image in *The Garies and Their Friends* amounts to an example of Webb's practice of literary portraiture, and the placement of the image itself is significant in a novel marked by what Sam Otter calls its "still-life aesthetics." In lucid readings of *The Garies*, Otter argues that the novel's meanings and unfolding are hinged by the two counterparts of the Georgia tea table and the Philadelphia supper episodes. "Across the novel," Otter writes, "Webb presents scenes that are characterized by what we might call a still-life aesthetics: meticulously arranged domestic interiors—visions of freedom, consumption, and constraint—whose surfaces, imbued with narrative and historical meanings, invite viewers to partake of their complex pleasures."[34] What pleasures might be taken in this key scene of literary portraiture? Walters's pleasures with the image seem to stem from at least two sources, one formal (that the picture was "the correct likeness") and the other a thematic anomaly (that "a black man in uniform of a general officer is something so unusual"). Webb accentuates literary portraiture as a political strategy that seeks to picture U.S. abolitionism as something akin to the Haitian Revolution, but to do so he must figuratively activate the still life, set it in motion as it were, as its calm serenity will soon be breached by the hurried, frantic activity of the race riot afoot.

In a more general sense, Webb's description of the Louverture portrait, no less than the placment of it, is meant to signal his singularity, almost as if there was no historical precedence for someone like the Haitian leader. This singularity is reinforced by its placement within the spatial domain of the home as the primary piece of art. By comparison, we might recall an important scene in *Uncle Tom's Cabin*, whose author also wrote the introduction for Webb's novel. In Stowe's novel, there are both biblical scriptures as well as a drawing of George Washington (fancifully colored, perhaps black) hanging on the wall of Aunt Chloe and Uncle Tom's cabin, offered as the necessary text and image discourse that underlines the sanctioned social logic of their positions as Americans. Both episodes illuminate Mitchell's notion of "iconology" as the relationship between "pictures" and "verbal or literary imagery" inasmuch as the word choice of Stowe's and Webb's respective prose both fashions and indexes the curatorial efforts of African Americans to approach interior decorating as an exercise of political articulation.[35]

While Webb stressed Louverture's singularity, he was frequently compared to other political actors, on scales of both national and global histories. In terms of narratives within national symbolic orders, Louverture was compared to French and American figures. The oratorical and literary portraits of Louverture drawn by Brown, Smith, and Phillips were markedly different from those created by Wordsworth and Webb, both in terms of aesthetics and political strategy. Inasmuch as Brown, Smith, and Phillips were preoccupied with situating Louverture in various honorific pantheons and as the apotheosis of a particular teleology, these acts of consecration illustrate the notion of what might be called "correlative historiography"; that is, methodological practices that put into high relief or resurrect subjugated knowledges by the representations of overdetermined or overwrought acts of analogy. In such overwrought moments, the very partiality of portraying history is revealed at each moment of comparison, as those histories can only approximate something like universal history through the logic of analogy or, with respect to art more specifically, semblance and verisimilitude.

In his speeches on the lecture circuit, Brown linked Louverture to Napoleon before publishing them under the title *St. Domingo: Its Revolutions and Patriots* in 1855. Brown's likening of Louverture to Napoleon depends upon the use of the rhetorical device of parallelism, less for establishing a comparison between the two than a contrast.[36] And, although Napoleon's name is not mentioned in Wordsworth's Louverture sonnet, the connection between the two is more fully borne out when it is later included in *Poems Dedicated to National Independence and Liberty* (1815). Within the pantheon of U.S. figures, Louverture was most often likened to George Washington. "He was truly the

Washington of Hayti," reads the 1848 feature of him in Douglass's *North Star*.[37] Perhaps more than any other mid-nineteenth-century figure, it was Brown who associated Louverture with Washington again and again, and there he deployed a similar tactic of contrast through parallelism.[38] Even when Louverture was not explicitly compared to a specific figure, his name was put into a circulatory orbit with other prominent figures. Such was the case with Douglass's lecture on "Self-Made Men" (1859), in which the famed orator spoke about Benjamin Bannaker and William Dietz and essentially made Louverture a black American by figuratively pulling Haiti closer to the orbit of the United States.

While Douglass's strategy in his lecture was to use the honorific space of the pantheon trope to bring Haiti closer to the United States, both Smith and Phillips employed the trope to illustrate Louverture as a world-historical figure whose iconography cuts across time and space. In his 1841 lecture before the Stuyvesant Institute, Smith lamented the rise of the caste system in the United States as something that is an antidemocratic or "unrepublican" practice. It is only in the last line of Smith's speech that it becomes less of an anecdote and more prophetic when he notes that Louverture had learned to read while a slave—a suggestion that there may yet be a Louverture amongst the ranks at the Colored Orphan Asylum if only they too were afforded the opportunity to be educated. While the message of Smith's lecture may not have been unanticipated, his tactic of illustrating Louverture and the Haitian Revolution as part of a world-historical constellation that included "Leonidas at Thermopylæ" and "Bruce at Bannockburn" was perhaps less foreseen. Smith announced that these events and figures were necessary study for "every American citizen," and he implored his audience to take notice that "among the many lessons that may be drawn from this *portion of history* is one not unconnected with the present occasion."[39]

Delivered some twenty years later in 1861, Phillips's speech hoped to convince his audience of the equality of the "Negro race" by revealing "the great men they produce." In the process, Phillips is almost too conspicuous in his efforts to make an icon of Louverture, contending that few men have been more deserving. Phillips notes that, with George Washington, there was "no marble white enough on which to carve the name of the Father of his Country," while Louverture languishes in relative obscurity with "hardly one written line."

> You think me a fanatic tonight, for you read history, not with your eyes, but with your prejudices. But fifty years hence, when Truth gets a hearing, the Muse of History will put Phocion of the Greek,

and Brutus for the Roman, Hampden for England, Fayette for France, choose Washington as the bright, consummate flower of our earlier civilization, and John Brown the ripe fruit of our noonday, then, dipping her pen in the sunlight, will write in the clear blue, above them all, the name of the soldier, the statesman, the martyr, Toussaint l'Ouverture.[40]

Phillips's speech is perhaps the most resonant nineteenth-century illustration of the practice of "correlative historiography." While the speech itself is marked by an oratorical style indebted to classical rhetoric, it depends upon an alternation between synecdoche and metonymy. In order to underscore Louverture's exceptionalism, Phillips must delineate his extraordinary features as a part that can stand for the whole, indeed as the species for the genus. But Louverture's exceptionalism must also operate metonymically, as something that could be closely related to the quotidian ranks of the "Negro race" to function as an argument for a larger claim about black humanity. Phillips's speech should be contextualized within the debates on the meanings of the Civil War and efforts to correlate it with the earlier American Revolution. Phillips offered his New York and Boston audiences a sketch that was "at once a biography and an argument"; the speech was intended as a biography of "a Negro soldier and statesman" as well as "an argument in behalf of the race from which he sprung." Not content with placing him in a pantheon of some of the most notable figures in world history, Phillips saw him as a combination of them all. Phillips's oratorical portrait of Louverture and the revolution are presented not simply in epic terms but as a world-historical phenomenon—a picture that might have struck his audience as somewhat hyperbolic, something that Phillips himself acknowledges in his closing words. Phillips's acknowledgement should be taken less as an apology for the formal properties of rhetoric per se, than for what it metacritically evinces about normative historiography as a practice that needs other things besides the official archives to approach an understanding of a moment or event.

Toward an Im/partial History

In 1863, Brown published the omnibus *The Black Man: His Antecedents, His Genius, and His Achievements*, returning to some of the biographical sketches he had outlined earlier in myriad publications, including his previous St.

Domingo lectures. Like Phillips, Brown was concerned that the monumental history of Louverture and the Haitian Revolution was being effaced by public memory, and he intended *The Black Man* to act as a corrective: "When impartial history shall do justice to the St. Domingo revolution, the name of Toussaint Louverture will be placed high upon the roll of fame." Of the fifty-three character sketches in *The Black Man*, seven of them are related to Haiti or the revolution. Published at a moment more fully entrenched in the Civil War, the catalogue of Brown's text reveals a preoccupation with black rebellion as a form of revolution with entries on Nat Turner, Joseph Cinque, and Denmark Vesey. Indeed, Brown essentially draws upon his early descriptions of Louverture for *The Black Man* compendium.

One of the sketches, however, that did not make it into the newer publication was the brief one of a woman named "Vida." Brown recounts her story in the earlier lecture, when he covers the period of the revolution in which Dessalines begins his campaign against Rochambeau, noting that she, like Lamour de Rance, was a native of Africa. Vida and Lamour were "mawons," alternatively known as *cimarróns* or maroons in different parts of the Caribbean. "Her face was all marked with incisions, large pieces had been cut out of her ears. Vida kept a horse, which she had caught with her own hands, and had broken to the bit. When on horseback, she rode like a man. . . . This woman, with her followers, met and defeated a battalion of the French, who had been sent into the mountains. Lamour and Vida united, and they were complete masters of the wilds of St. Domingo."[41] Why did Vida disappear from Brown's account? What ideological and curatorial undercurrents guided his editorial choices to republish aspects of Lamour in the newer book but not include ones about Vida? In crafting the *Black Man* compendium, a volume that might be called an attempt at Nietzschean "critical history," with dozens of sketches of male figures but less than a handful about women, Brown created a genealogy of the Haitian Revolution that was decidedly masculinist. But in creating such a gendered genealogy, he also diminished aspects of the archives that were deemed otherwise not normative: the savage (versus the civilized), the performative (versus the scripted), and "guerrilla" warfare (versus traditional military tactics). If Brown's sketches of Louverture and the revolution are emblematic of a process of hagiography, they are also reminders that all histories are counter-memories that move from moments of latency and incipience to degrees of seeming permanence and concretization. In this instance, the story of Vida and other women of the revolution would remain dormant in the archives until activated, as it were, by a practice of counter-memory historiography that sought to unfold a feminist genealogy.

More than simply illustrating the cultures of textual reproduction in African American letters, Vida's omission from *The Black Man* draws attention to the epistemic problematic that comes into being when the production of counter-memories operationalizes the Foucauldian distinction between genealogy and history. Inasmuch as Vida does indeed constitute part of the history of the Haitian Revolution, she, and others like her, became increasingly less representative of the particular genealogy Brown was constructing. And in this sense, the anecdote of Vida between Brown's *St. Domingo* and *Black Man* intimates that counter-memory historiographies—whether in guises ranging from revisionist history to subaltern history—can only persist as interventions inasmuch as they reveal their very partiality, as both an acknowledgment of the impossibility of a total history and as a declarative statement of a political position, and continually perform against the grain.

CHAPTER 5

Frederick Douglass, Anténor Firmin, and the Making of U.S.-Haitian Relations

LAURENT DUBOIS

In December 1859, an elaborate official funeral was held in the cathedral of Port-au-Prince, presided over by Haitian President Fabre Geffrard, along with his wife and daughters. As the U.S. *Anti-Slavery Reporter* explained, the Catholic priest of Port-au-Prince, a Senegalese-born, French-educated man named Abbé Moussa, officiated a High Mass. In the nave of the church was the coffin, draped in black, lit up by candles, decorated with a pen, a sword, and a Bible, and an inscription naming the deceased as a "martyr for the cause of the blacks." After a rousing eulogy, the coffin was carried to a cross at the edge of town by a large procession that gathered many of the town's prominent citizens, who wore black armbands. But it was never placed in the ground, for it was empty.[1]

The funeral was for abolitionist John Brown, who had been hung days earlier in Virginia. It was probably fitting that Brown's largest funeral service was held in Haiti, and that the president welcomed him posthumously as a kind of an honorary citizen. John Brown had never visited Haiti, but the country's history had long visited him. He knew the tale of its antislavery revolution "by heart," and enjoyed recounting it. According to an English journalist, it was the example of the 1791 uprising that convinced him that with the right trigger, slaves "would immediately rise all over the Southern States." According to a recent book by Matthew Clavin, when Brown chose the valley town of Harper's Ferry, he sought to imitate his Haitian forebears' military tactics, for he knew they had won against the French by attacking towns and then retreating into inaccessible mountains. And as he awaited his execution after his plan failed, Brown took solace in reading a biography of Toussaint Louverture. After his father's execution, Brown's son wrote that if they listened, the slaves of the United States would hear Louverture's voice speaking to them, "among the pines of the Carolinas in the Dismal Swamp and upon the mountain-tops, proclaiming that the despots of America shall yet know the strength of the toiler's arm, and that he who would be free must himself strike the first blow." A Haitian newspaper similarly announced to the slaves of the United States: "Liberty is immortal. Brown and his companions have sown this Slave-land with their glorious blood, and doubt not that there from avengers will arise."[2]

Brown was not the only abolitionist who admired Haiti. In May of 1861, Frederick Douglass wrote of his desire to visit Haiti. He wanted to see the true country, not the one refracted through the lenses of white racism, to find in "the *free, orderly and Independent Republic of Haiti*, a refutation of the slanders and disparagements of our race." Haiti, he wrote, was literally a part of his being, and that of African Americans everywhere. Haiti was "the theatre of so many stirring events and heroic achievements, the work of a people, bone of our bone, and flesh of our flesh."[3]

The outbreak of the Civil War derailed Douglass's plans to travel to Haiti, and it would take him years to finally visit the country he admired. But the Civil War also created an opening for Haiti's allies in the United States, who pushed through a bill finally recognizing the country's independence. Since 1804, even as U.S. merchants flowed in and out of Haiti, its governments had consistently been spurned, or simply ignored, when they requested political recognition. The initial 1806 embargo against trade and diplomatic relations with Haiti was put in place during Thomas Jefferson's presidency and subsequently maintained by presidents and congressmen who saw any form of reconciliation with Haiti as an invitation to the enslaved to revolt. For generations of leaders in Haiti, this was both a chafing insult and a barrier to the country's full accession to the rights and privileges of an independent nation. But all attempts to change the policy had foundered in Congress. Secession, however, changed the equation. In 1862, President Lincoln and Massachusetts Senator Charles Sumner pushed through a bill that finally recognized Haiti's independence. The United States was the last country in the world to do so— France had acknowledged Haitian independence, in return for the payment of a hefty indemnity, in 1825. And yet, in the coming decades, the United States would become the country with by the far the most direct and profound impact on Haiti.

"Be convinced, gentlemen," President Geffrard commanded Haiti's Congress in 1863, "it is no longer permitted today for any people to isolate itself from other peoples." Each nation on earth, from "the feeblest" to the "most powerful," had a "Providential Mission to fulfill among the mutual destinies of humanity." As president, he succeeded in creating the preconditions for that openness, gaining recognition not only from the United States but from the only other institution that still had not accepted Haitian independence: the Vatican. Now it was up to Haitians themselves to embrace the "tremendous progress" being achieved "throughout the globe," to open themselves up to trade and exchange with a changing world.[4]

For generations, Haitian elites were convinced—and insisted to their country's population—that they needed to prove to the world that they truly belonged in order to gain political recognition. Geffrard was finally able to win that recognition. And yet that victory did not put an end to the need for self-justification. Indeed, in a way it almost deepened it, as foreign visitors and governments both criticized and intervened in the country with increasing forcefulness. Recognition opened the way for an increasingly widespread, and influential, presence on the part of foreigners and foreign institutions within Haiti. In the end, it curiously diminished, rather than protected, Haiti's independence. The denial of sovereignty, it turned out, could take many forms.

* * *

In the sixty years since Haitian independence in 1804, the country's political, social, and economic life had been shaped by a deep conflict over the meaning of freedom. The Haitian Revolution represented a tremendous victory, overthrowing slavery and empire and establishing an independent nation founded on the self-evident principle that no one should be a slave. But the new nation's political culture was deeply shaped by the idea that freedom was fragile, and that both old and new enemies might well attempt to reestablish slavery. The refusal of recognition by France and the United States and the widespread racist representations of the country and its revolution were constant reminders of this threat. The question was how to best protect the country and solidify its autonomy. There developed, over time, two different approaches to that problem. Both were products of the Haitian Revolution itself, creations of the remarkable process of social and political transformation and reinvention that began in 1791 and culminated in Haitian independence. But, though born out of the same struggle, the two approaches were in many ways incommensurable. The conflict between them created an enduring stalemate within Haiti.[5]

The first approach, pioneered by Toussaint Louverture and maintained by figures such as Jean-Jacques Dessalines, Henry Christophe, and Jean-Pierre Boyer, was to attempt to establish a secure foundation for self-defense by seeking to maintain the plantation economy. Only through the production and sale of plantation commodities, these leaders insisted, could they maintain an army, build forts, and foster alliances with foreign powers that would keep Haiti safe. The most famous symbol of this approach is the Citadel la Ferrière built by Henry Christophe: a vast fortress, visible from miles away, it was meant to withstand a new invasion by the French, and just as much to stand as a forceful symbol of the determination of Haitians to remain free. Some of the stones used to build this fortress were literally carried from old plantations and sugar works from the plain below by former slaves rounded up to do the work under conditions many contemporaries described as brutal, and even a new kind of slavery.

The second approach was the creation and maintenance of what Haitian sociologist Jean Casimir has dubbed the "counter-plantation" system. It was built by the ex-slaves, mostly African born, who were at the center of the military struggles of the revolution, but who more broadly made use of the interstices opened up by the conflict to craft a new way of life on the plantations where they had once been slaves. The system—one that of course has parallels in all other post-emancipation societies in the Americas—was based not simply on dismantling the plantation, but on setting up structures organized to avoid its return—in any form. From the perspective of this majority, a plantation was still a plantation—whether its profits were meant to fend off the French or not. Practitioners of this system turned their backs on the plantation-based projects of their early political leaders, taking control of the land and putting it to their own uses. The counter-plantation system was, perhaps, the most radical production of the Haitian Revolution, since it was based on the insistence that only through a complete transformation of the social and economic order itself could real freedom actually be attained. Those who supported it refused the idea—one explicitly advanced by state leaders—that they had to accept serious limits on their liberty in order to preserve it. They built their own kind of citadel through a set of social institutions rooted in individual land ownership and anchored in a set of broader family and community institutions.

On that land, they did all the things that had been denied to them under slavery: they built families, freely practiced their religion, and worked for themselves. They grew food for themselves and for local and regional markets, but they also found that coffee, once a plantation crop, could be successfully grown on small family farms and bring in money that could be used to buy other goods from the towns. That combination guaranteed rural Haitians a better life, materially and socially, than that available to most other people of African descent in the Americas throughout the early nineteenth century. Over time, despite opposition from certain leaders and the institution of laws meant to save the plantation, rural Haiti was largely transformed into a space divided into small land-holdings, a space of striking social and political autonomy. And, despite many attempts—including those made during the twenty-year U.S. occupation of Haiti (1915–1934)—efforts to rebuild plantations in Haiti largely met with failure. The relative success of this system can perhaps be summarized by one crucial fact: during the nineteenth and early twentieth century, few people left Haiti. The country was, instead, a significant magnet for immigration: people came from as close as other parts the Caribbean, including Guadeloupe and Martinique, and from as far as Europe and the Middle East. Thousands of African Americans made the journey to Haiti as well, in the 1820s and early 1860s. Many of these migrants became part of Haiti's rural communities.

The success of the counter-plantation system in the countryside, however, created a stark problem for the country's elites. They were unable to secure power and profit as large-scale land-holders overseeing plantation production. The state, meanwhile, despite attempts to control the rural population through draconian laws such as Boyer's Code Rural, in fact exercised very tenuous power in much of the country. What governing elites were able to control, however, were the port towns: the outlets through which coffee and other products—notably dyewood—harvested by the rural population had to pass on their way to foreign markets. Over the course of the early nineteenth century, the main route to social and economic advancement was the import-export trade. Success in this area depended on ties with foreign merchants, often German, who came to settle in Haiti eager to take advantage of commercial opportunities. The state, meanwhile, largely abandoned attempts to tax individual revenues, and instead focused on heavily taxing coffee and other goods, thus profiting from rural production without needing to directly control it.

What developed, then, was an enduring stalemate between the counterplantation system, rooted in the countryside, and a network of economic institutions within the port towns, including regional elite and government structures. The state was quite weak, with its army divided into regional poles of power. Haitian writer and geographer Georges Anglade describes nineteenth-century Haiti as a confederation of eleven regions, each with its own port town. The political situation alternated between periods of stability under authoritarian leaders and bursts of instability during which generals from different regions, vying for power, raised armies to take over the central government in Port-au-Prince. But the chronology of shifting government regimes somewhat obscures a deeper stability: the conflicts within the elite seem to have had a relatively limited impact on the rural majority in much of the country, which was organized around and governed through a set of largely independent institutions and economic networks. The weakness of the state seems to have suited many in the countryside: between a strong state committed to some form of plantation model and a state that was weak and largely absent from their lives, the latter was preferable.

By the 1860s and 1870s, a new generation of political activists and leaders attempted to change this configuration. The more radical among them looked back to earlier attempts at political reform, especially the revolutions of the 1840s, and insisted that Haiti needed a more democratic system. For the most part, however, they also remained convinced that Haiti's rural culture was unsustainable, and an obstacle to their country's progress. Many were anxious that in a changing world and in the face of rising U.S. power, Haiti would simply be overwhelmed if it did not reform and modernize itself. Haitian leaders, however, also facilitated increasing foreign control and intervention in their country: both governments and rebels wanting to take power reached out to the United States, England, and Germany, seeking weapons and direct military support. At one point in the 1865, for instance, the government in Port-au-Prince secured support from the British navy in a bid to suppress a rebel army based in Le Cap, in the north of the country. A ship called the *Bulldog* bombarded Le Cap, reducing a fort and several buildings to rubble.

Watching from the shore that day was a teenager named Anténor Firmin, who in time would become one of Haiti's greatest intellectuals and statesmen. He was of modest background, the son of tailors, and a brilliant student. He distinguished himself a few years later by helping to lead an impromptu militia in defending the city from an incursion by a rebel group. By the 1870s, he was working as a lawyer and was admired for his eloquence in court. He also edited a major newspaper, *Le Messager du Nord* and became a key intellectual figure in the powerful Liberal Party, jousting with the opposing National Party. Throughout the final decades of the nineteenth century, these two parties battled for political power in Haiti. The National Party's activists demanded a more democratic system, clamoring to place more control of the country's institutions in the hands of the majority of its people. The countervailing slogan of the Liberals was "Government by the Most Competent," and was, in the evaluation of one historian, "frankly elitist and anti-populist in its implications." One of the Liberal Party's leaders and theorists argued in 1861 that Haiti was not ready for democracy: "The supremacy of numbers assures the supremacy of ignorance." What it needed to escape its dependency on foreign nations was a generation of "engineers, builders, industrialists, science teachers"—and fewer poets. Many of its members argued that it was the light-skinned members of Haiti's society that had the education and capacity necessary to confront Haiti's challenges and develop its economy. But the party attracted a few prominent black members, including Anténor Firmin. One of the most controversial topics of debate at the time concerned Haiti's long-standing constitutional ban on property ownership by foreign whites. While many saw this as a vital mechanism for defending Haiti's sovereignty, others—including Firmin—came to see it as a barrier to economic development.[6]

In the 1880s, Firmin left Haiti to study in Paris. There, he participated in a salon organized by the Puerto Rican nationalist Ramón Emeterio Betances, where various thinkers from throughout Latin America and the Caribbean gathered, talked, and plotted. Firmin was also invited to join the Anthropological Society of Paris. But though he had some welcoming allies, along with one other Haitian colleague in the society, Firmin found himself largely in hostile territory. The ideas of the Comte de Gobineau, who penned his famous *Essay on the Inequality of the Human Races* in the 1850s, were still popular. While Firmin did not openly confront the dominant racial ideas of anthropology at the society, the experience of being part of its discussions left him in a quiet fury. He was, he later admitted, in a "depressive mood" while in Paris. He responded in print, writing an impassioned refutation of the dominant racial theories of the day.[7]

Called *The Equality of the Human Races*, Firmin's work skewered the European intellectuals, some famous and others less so, who had lined up behind spurious theories of racial difference. In one short chapter called "Prejudices and Vanities," he simply listed racist comments by "men who are generally considered authoritative voices in science and philosophy," from Immanuel Kant to Ernest Renan. "The notion of the inequality of the human races is so deeply rooted in the minds of the most enlightened men of Europe that they seem incapable of ever discarding it." That, he argued, was not because it was reasonable or logical, but because of the history of slavery and colonialism had produced, shaped, and ultimately naturalized these ideas.[8]

Firmin insisted that there was only one human race and that in order to be a truly "positivist science," anthropology must free itself from the thrall of untenable racist theories based on scattered anecdotal evidence, and devote itself to what should be its true calling: the study of human societies, in all their complexity, through careful scientific method. Firmin's book took its readers on a journey from Egypt to India to Africa in order to unwind the theories that buttressed ideas of racial inequality. It argued that, among all the contemporary civilizations of the world, the United States was destined to become the richest and most powerful. But for Firmin, Haiti presented perhaps the most powerful refutation of racist ideas. Its writers had produced brilliant poetry and essays, he emphasized. He even listed some particularly good-looking Haitian men in order to refute the idea that whites were inherently more beautiful. He remembered seeing in 1883, among the aides-de-camp of a Haitian general, "a young Black man so mesmerizingly handsome that one could not take one's eyes of his face. I have never seen him again and I still do not know his name." He described how another "handsome specimen of the Black race" was a man who directed the customs office at Le Cap. "I still remember how visiting foreigners who came through the town's port often neglected the business at hand to gaze admiringly at this man whose handsome features were enhanced by his black skin." The "physical beauty" of such men, Firmin suggested, gave "the lie to the fanciful descriptions of ethnographers." Through such perhaps playful passages, Firmin was making a serious point. For each supposed "scientific observation" deployed to justify racist theories, Firmin could provide an opposite observation. While his were based on his personal experience as a Haitian, those of the supposed "scientists" on the other side were just as personal, based on the racial trap they were caught in as European observers.[9]

Though largely ignored by the dominant strands of European anthropology, Firmin's powerful attack on European racism gained him many admirers and established him as one of the country's most revered intellectuals. When he returned home in the late 1880s, that profile helped him emerge as an increasingly influential political figure in the country. And once back in Haiti, he paid particular attention to the question that increasingly preoccupied the Haitian elite: What was to be done about the rising power of the United States?

* * *

With the rise of the steamship in the decades after the Civil War, the United States turned its attention to the Caribbean in a search for adequate coaling stations. Because they were independent, the Dominican Republic and neighboring Haiti provided the greatest opportunity for U.S. designs. Before the Civil War, some Southerners had explored the idea of annexing certain Caribbean territories as a way to expand slavery. In the 1870s, however, the push for annexation came from rather different quarters. President Ulysses S. Grant avidly pursued a project to annex the Dominican Republic. And, perhaps surprisingly, he found an ally in Frederick Douglass. Though Douglass had vociferously attacked plans for Caribbean annexation before the Civil War, he now saw things differently. Like Grant, he of course understood the strategic motivations for the interest in the region. "Almost every great maritime nation," he noted, "has some footing and foothold in the Caribbean sea but our own." But Douglass also saw annexation as a way of spreading the progressive values of post–Civil War U.S. society and of helping to bring prosperity to the Caribbean. "It may, indeed, be important to know what Santo Domingo can do for us," Douglass declared in 1871, "but it is vastly more important to know what we can do for Santo Domingo." Douglass was part of a commission that traveled to the Dominican Republic to explore possibilities for annexation, and he lectured on behalf of the idea in the United States.[10]

Grant's attempts at annexation foundered on opposition in the United States. But Haitians of Anténor Firmin's generation watched all these developments closely, and with increasing anxiety. Many Haitians were both unimpressed by and suspicious of their neighbors to the north. One journalist described the United States as hungrily watching his country "with eyes lit up with desire." Intellectuals saw the United States as a hopelessly materialistic, uncouth, even backward country, not to mention a deeply racist one—a place driven, as one wrote, by "materialism without humanism." In 1873 the prominent politician Demesvar Delorme urged his compatriots to turn their backs on the United States and to focus instead on the common culture and language they shared with France. Traveling by train in France in 1892, a Haitian man had the misfortune of sitting next to an obnoxiously talkative tourist from the United States. The experience pained him so much that he wrote a passionate lament about the rising power of Haiti's neighbor. "You are good at making machines," he complained, "but have a hard time coming up with ideas."[11]

There were, however, those who took a very different few. They saw the United States as a potential source for economic development, arguing that the nation would be a much more useful partner than France had ever been for the country. One Haitian politician declared in 1883 that ultimately the Haitian elite, though it remained tightly connected to France, would realize that a "marriage of love" with France was simply impossible. Spurned, they would have no choice but to join in "a marriage of convenience" with the United States.[12]

Firmin was among those who believed the United States could, under the right circumstances, help Haiti to develop and modernize. In 1888, he joined an uprising led by Florville Hyppolite against the central government in Port-au-Prince. Firmin took on the task of negotiating with the United States for political and military support. In order to secure that backing, Firmin raised the possibility that if Hyppolite took power, he would give concessions to the United States—including access to a coaling station, perhaps at a long-coveted port at the Môle Saint-Nicolas, in the northwest of Haiti. The insurrection ultimately triumphed—in part thanks to a series of arms shipments from a prominent U.S. merchant named William Clyde, who supplied Gatling guns—and Firmin became the minister of foreign relations of Haiti.

* * *

In his inaugural address in 1890, U.S. President Benjamin Harrison declared that "the necessities of our navy require convenient coaling stations and dock and harbor privileges." The navy ordered one of its admirals, Bancroft Gherardi, to gather "full and detailed description of all coaling stations in the West Indies." One of the most sought-after locations was the Port of the Môle Saint-Nicolas in Haiti. Gherardi concluded that the Môle would be "invaluable," and that if the United States approached the Haitians with the right mixture of firmness and strategy, it could be acquired for the navy with little difficulty.

When Harrison chose a new minister to Haiti, he carefully considered who might be most able to successfully negotiate with the Black Republic. He found the perfect person in Frederick Douglass, who had endorsed him during the campaign. Stephen Preston, Haiti's ambassador in Washington, rejoiced when he heard the news, calling it a "miracle." He effused that, "for the moment" at least, the danger "of attempts to annex a part of our territory" had passed. Secretary of State Blaine wrote to Douglass himself that his diplomatic mission to Haiti "would be the most potent we could send hither for the peace, welfare, and prosperity of that warring and dissatisfied people."[13]

It had taken nearly thirty years, but Douglass would finally be able to spend time in the land he admired. He did so, however, in a very different context from either 1861 or the 1870s. By the late 1880s, many of the gains of Reconstruction had been reversed, and Douglass was much more subdued about the extent to which the United States could serve as a progressive and democratic force. As he arrived in Haiti, Douglass found himself in a curious and ultimately uncomfortable position, both somewhat distrusted by some in the U.S. government and somewhat distrusting himself of the true intentions of the government he served.[14]

Having promulgated the new constitution, Hyppolite and Firmin quickly turned to the pressing question of how to deal with the United States. In his first meeting with the Haitian president, Douglass made a pitch for happy globalization: "The growing commercial intercommunication of various nationalities, so important to the dissemination of knowledge, to the enlargement of human sympathies and to the extinction of hurtful prejudices," he declared, were not a "menace to the autonomy of nations." President Hyppolite was a little skeptical: in his reply, he agreed that there was nothing wrong with international exchange, but added that "each nation has the right to be proud of its autonomy."[15]

Sympathetic to and knowledgeable about Haitian history, Douglass was well aware that Haitians were rightly sensitive about the threat of external pressures and forces. He warned Secretary of State Blaine that it did not go over well when a U.S. Navy ship was sent to do a survey of the harbor of Môle Saint-Nicolas without permission from the Haitian government. It was too easy for opponents of the new regime in Haiti to seize on such actions as proof that the government was ready to "sell the country to the Americans."[16]

Douglass left Haiti for much of 1890, and returned at the end of the year with official instructions to begin negotiations for the Môle. On New Year's Day of 1891, he called on Firmin. It was a remarkable meeting of the minds: the two men, though of different generations, were major intellectual figures who had struggled to defeat racism throughout their lives. Firmin, however, only had time to express his worries about the intentions of the United States.

Douglass tried to reassure his Haitian colleague that, while his government was indeed interested in acquiring a coaling station, they would do so only through "proper means" that were "consistent with the peace and welfare of Haiti."[17]

Already, however, Douglass was getting a reputation back home for being a bit too sensitive to the perspective of the Haitians. One of his strongest critics was the U.S. entrepreneur William Clyde, the owner of the West India steamship line, who had supplied weapons to Hyppolite in 1889. Clyde had sought a monopoly over steamship transportation in Haiti, and when he realized the deal had fallen through, he demanded that the Haitian government pay him for "time and money" he had spent in the country. Douglass, with a dose of incisive humor, responded disbelievingly to Clyde: "Then, sir, as they will not allow you to put a hot poker down their backs, you mean to make them pay you for heating it!" Clyde was not amused. "In his eyes I was," Douglass wrote, "more a Haïtien than an American."[18]

In March 1891 an article in the *New York Herald* attacked Douglass for, among other things, being black. If it was to gain the respect of Haitians, the writer argued, the United States needed a white diplomatic representative, "for the people here look upon a colored man as one of themselves, whereas they unwittingly recognize the superiority of the white race, although they will never admit it." They needed, the author suggested, a strong white hand to guide them. "To let Haiti alone is to allow her to follow her own path back to barbarism." "Prejudice sets all logic at defiance," Douglass later wrote about such claims. "Haïti is no stranger to Americans or to American prejudice," and the country would see right through a white diplomat who tried to "play the hypocrite and pretend to love negroes in Haïti when he is known to hate negroes in the United States." "The American people are too great to be small," he declared hopefully, and should treat Haiti with respect and justice. If, instead, the United States planned on preying on the weaknesses and fears of Haiti, or of acquiring things through the "dread of our power," then Douglass admitted he was not the right person to represent the United States. "I am charged with sympathy for Haïti," Douglass declared. "I am not ashamed of that charge."[19]

But the attacks against Douglass worked. Though Secretary of State Blaine realized he could not get rid of Douglass without inciting an outcry in both Haiti and the United States, he also concluded he could not trust him to get the Môle. So he sent Admiral Gherardhi to Haiti, who took over the negotiations with the Haitian government. Looking back bitterly on the experience,

Douglass claimed that the overweening attitude of Gherardi had the opposite of the intended effect, undermining his government's chances of getting what it wanted. In the face of Firmin's hesitation about ceding the Môle to the United States, Gherardi responded with veiled threats, declaring ominously that if his request were refused, the United States would have to force Haiti into assuming its "moral obligation." He told Firmin that "it was the destiny of the Môle to belong to the United States." Douglass attempted to be more conciliatory, arguing that the concession would be "consistent with the autonomy of Haïti" and a "source of strength rather than weakness." "National isolation," Douglass insisted was a "policy of the past," and Haitian rulers should act "to touch the world at all points that make for civilization and commerce."[20]

Firmin agreed with Douglass about these broader points. But he also understood Haitian politics, and the particular bind his government was in, enough to realize that it was essentially impossible to accede to the U.S. request. He told Gherardi and Douglass as much in their first discussion. He admitted that "if some one must have" the Môle, it should be the United States, but explained that such a concession would be the end of Hyppolite's government. So he stalled for time, asking for further documentation from the U.S. government. In April 1891, Gherardi and Douglass once again went to see Firmin to press him on the issue. This time, they had back-up: the U.S. Navy sent four warships into the harbor of Port-au-Prince, adding to the three warships already stationed there. The population of the town was, of course, worried by the display of force, and Firmin, under pressure, promised a final response to the request. But to the surprise of the U.S. envoys, it was a polite but firm "No."[21]

Firmin agreed that, in principle, the cession of Môle Saint-Nicolas could easily have been arranged to the benefit of both countries. The problem, however, was the way the United States had approached the matter. President Harrison and Secretary Blaine had asked that, in addition to giving access to the Môle, the Haitian government promise not to rent or grant any "special privilege or usage rights" to any part of its territory to any other government. For Firmin, this was too much. To accept this condition would, he wrote, constitute an "outrage against the national sovereignty of Haiti and a flagrant violation of Article 1 of our Constitution for, in renouncing our right to dispose of our territory, we will have tacitly accepted its alienation." The other problem was that the United States was being a bully. The fact that it had sent warships to Port-au-Prince in a clear effort to threaten Haiti made it impossible for the government to accept the U.S. request, he explained. If Haiti did so, it would "seem to cede to foreign pressure and therefore, *ipso facto*, to compromise our existence as an independent people." Firmin ended his refusal by insisting that the refusal was not an act of "ill will" on Haiti's part, and that his country remained attached to "the most glorious and the most generous Republic of the New World and perhaps of the modern World."[22]

Firmin was clearly proud of his refusal: he reprinted it in his 1905 book as a reminder of what he had accomplished. And he was celebrated in Haiti for having stood up to the United States. "Firmin's pen," notes one historian, had "managed to displace the seven beautiful, brand-new warships, planted in the harbor of Port-au-Prince during the negotiations." The action gave him enormous political legitimacy—he became "a hero, a legend," even "a messiah" in the eyes of many Haitians, who had watched the U.S. warships nervously for several days. When the last of them left, there was a "great sigh of relief" in the town. Firmin emerged bearing the mantle of a new national hero.[23]

In fact, though, if Firmin succeeded, it was largely because he had an astute observer of U.S. policy in Washington itself. The Haitian minister to the United States, Hannibal Price—the son of an English man and a Haitian woman—was a skilled politician who had cultivated many connections in the capital. He concluded that U.S. public opinion would not support aggression against Haiti, and that the Republican Party would likely lose seats in the next election, and so Harrison and Blaine would be in a weak position to press the matter. Based on this analysis, he felt sure that the show of force the navy planned for Port-au-Prince was, in fact, just theater. When Firmin wrote his response to Douglass and Gerardhi, he had in hand a telegraph from Price that read simply: "The fleet for the purpose of intimidating. Do not yield. Nothing will happen."[24]

* * *

"Will Haiti work?" an anxious Anténor Firmin wondered in 1905. In exile in St. Thomas, he was far from his home in Le Cap and, perhaps most painfully, without his library. He had spent fifteen years of public life in Haiti, which culminated in a failed bid for the presidency, his successful mobilization of supportive citizens in the towns having proved no match for the entrenched machinery of the Haitian military. In the wake of this political defeat, unable to return home, he tried to analyze Haiti's past and find a way forward. What he ultimately produced was a remarkable work of comparative history analyzing the parallel development of the United States and Haiti. Published as a kind of long letter to President Theodore Roosevelt, it was also very much a warning issued to his countrymen in Haiti. The United States was now the most powerful political force in the region, he declared, and Haiti had to find a productive way to deal with it. He dismissed those who believed the United States was simply a threat to Haitian sovereignty. "The intelligent Haitian," he wrote, "rather than getting caught up in an irrational suspicion," should instead "study the question with history books in their hands." Among foreign powers, he argued, the United States was the one that had shown itself "most respectful of their rights as an independent people." The United States would remain true to its founding principles, which disposed them to respect the independence of other countries. "Americans," Firmin wrote, "respect forms where Europeans flaunt them with cavalier ease." Anyway, he added, the United States did not need Haiti. Of all the great "occidental powers," the United States had the lowest population density—less than ten people per kilometer—and therefore the least need for colonies.[25]

The key for Haiti was to figure out how to thrive under the "colossal shadow" cast by the United States. His country "must grow, develop, without ever letting itself be absorbed." While Haiti's "smiling concessions" to other "rich and civilized countries" had been a "pure loss," the United States could become Haiti's salvation by providing "everything we need" to become "an active and laborious civilization." "They have capital of all kinds: money, machines, experience of hard work and the moral energy necessary to confront difficult circumstances." They could "offer us that helping hand we have been looking for throughout the past century."[26]

The United States could also, for Firmin, be an institutional example for Haiti. The alternation of parties in power in the United States, he noted, guaranteed political stability. He effused that the United States was a place where people put the national good over individual ambitions, and combined liberty and equality to their greatest effect. He even downplayed the continuing racial discrimination in the country. He celebrated Lincoln, and while he admitted that the question of the rights of African Americans still had to be resolved, he noted passingly—and with a rather nonchalant long-term view— that within a century, the problem would be resolved with "justice." He went further, asserting that the United States actually provided a model of racial egalitarianism for Haiti, which he declared was weakened by its own form of color prejudice between mulattoes and blacks.[27]

As he watched the rising United States, Firmin did what some Haitian revolutionaries had done in their relationship to France a century earlier. He sought to conjure up the best of imperial powers, the one whose devotion to principles of democracy and equal rights would make it an ally in Haitian's own struggles. For all its optimism, though, Firmin's analysis also had an ominous undercurrent: under such a powerful shadow, Haitians urgently had to solve their own problems. Otherwise they would be inviting disaster, opening the way for the destruction of their precious sovereignty. The power of the United States, its "almost undisputed preponderance" in the hemisphere, was inescapable. "Whether we rejoice or mourn," he declared, Haiti had to "to accept it and act accordingly." "Instead of putting ourselves in the position of trying to block an impetuous and irresistible torrent," Haiti had to go with the flow, trying to put itself in a position to be "productively watered" by the torrent of U.S. power. Otherwise, Firmin warned, "We'll be carried away trying to block it, in a gesture as reckless as it is hopeless."[28]

Firmin ended his life watching events in his homeland, from afar, with a deep anxiety. Just before his death in 1911, he lamented that he was likely to "disappear" without even seeing a glimpse of a "new dawn" for Haiti. "After my death," he wrote with a note of warning to his countrymen, "one of two things will happen: either Haiti will fall under foreign control, or it will resolutely adopt the principles in the name of which it has always struggled and fought." "For in the twentieth century in the Western hemisphere," he concluded with a mix of hope and foreboding, "no people can live indefinitely under tyranny, injustice, ignorance and misery."[29]

Firmin's worst fears ultimately came to pass. Accelerating political conflict during the years after his death created an opening for the United States, which for both strategic and economic reasons occupied Haiti in 1915. The occupiers remained until 1934, transforming the country in profound ways and spurring on a new set of political and intellectual movements that would shape the country's twentieth century. But Firmin's insights into the challenges of Haiti, as well as its promise, remain as relevant today as ever.

PART II

Geographies

OVER THE LAST twenty years, scholars of U.S. culture have challenged the traditional view that the modern United States emerged primarily from the Puritan experience of colonial New England. In doing so, they confronted a narrative that has had tremendous and enduring appeal. This was a story of English North America based not on immersion in already existing colonial networks, but on an exceptional culture knit together against Old World tyranny. Even as Puritanism waned in the latter decades of the seventeenth century (so the story went), its theo-philosophical roots could still be seen in the "spirit of capitalism" that animated prerevolutionary homo economicus. And if the founding documents of American independence were inspired by the Scottish Enlightenment and a renaissance of classical republican ideals from the ancient world, they also could be shown to echo the sacred covenant that had driven the original Protestant separatists to the New World.

By the late 1980s, however, a new view gained traction. If New England was exceptional, it was, by definition, less characteristic of the larger imperio-English experiment and also less lastingly influential. The Mid-Atlantic colonies, it was argued, more successfully replicated and disseminated the English cultural and commercial ethos that continued to energize colonial expansion south and west. Moreover, once North American colonials were understood as European colonists engaged in imperial endeavors, and not early avatars of Emersonian American individuals, a new Atlantic geography emerged in literary and historical scholarship in the place of the previous one focused primarily on New England. Central to this geography is the Caribbean. And indeed, as scholars have shown, Caribbean networks from Barbados and St. Domingue to Charleston and Philadelphia, essential legs of the triangle trade, transformed Europe itself as well as the North American colonies. Witness alone the exponential growth in per capita sugar consumption during the eighteenth century to measure its impact. As North America moved to declare political and economic autonomy from Great Britain, the new United States remained enmeshed in hemispheric webs, alliances, and antinomies which it sought to negotiate in new ways. Not least among these was the management of the human trade and labor force of African slaves. If the Federal Constitution can be traced back to Athens and the Magna Carta, it can also be compared to the Barbados Slave Code and the French Code Noir.

As we suggest in the introduction to this volume, the Haitian Revolution was at the center of a reconfiguration of the *geographic imaginary* of the post-revolutionary United States: the closing of the slave trade with the Caribbean due to fear of slave insurrection in the United States, the Louisiana Purchase of 1804, and the U.S. embargo on trade and diplomatic relations with Haiti in 1806 all contributed to causing a shift away from an Atlantic imaginary of the North American colonies to an increasingly continentally imagined, westward-oriented United States. Each of the essays in this section explores the ways in which the Haitian Revolution shifted and rescripted understandings of a U.S.-Haiti geography; these essays explore how the space of Haiti and that of the United States, and the relation between the two, was imagined, described, inhabited, and policed in a variety of discursive registers.

David Geggus opens this section with a careful parsing of the history of the relation between the Haitian Revolution and the Louisiana Purchase. Geggus revisits what was at stake for Napoleon in ceding Louisiana to the United States, arguing that the growing threat of war with Britain in March 1802 caused the cancellation of Napoleon's expedition to the Mississippi Valley and precipitated his sale of Louisiana, because he did not want this territory in the hands of England. Accordingly, Geggus concludes, while the Haitian Revolution contributed to the reasons that Napoleon chose to sell the territory of Louisiana to the United States, it cannot be considered the main reason for Napoleon's action.

In a radically different and innovative approach to understanding the geopolitics of the Haitian Revolution, Cristobal Silva turns to the geography of disease rather than that of international territorial negotiation. Specifically, Silva explores the links between such revolutionary markers as "liberty, equality, and fraternity" and the racialized medical and epidemiological rhetoric of national identity and health: "herd immunity" to yellow fever at the time of the Haitian Revolution, he argues, itself generated a new geography defined by the transmission of and immunity to disease that did not map neatly onto territorial borders. Kieran M. Murphy, in turn, explores the link between mesmerism, Vaudoux, the Haitian Revolution, and the Enlightenment denigration of occult epistemologies. In so doing, he describes an unsettling link between eighteenth-century science and the enforcement of racialized terror on enslaved peoples. Murphy explores the role of the Société Royale des Sciences et des Arts du Cap François, run by the ruling elite of St. Domingue, in staging a key confrontation between the Enlightenment and its occult other that was performed in the names of Benjamin Franklin and Franz Anton Mesmer.

The final two essays in this section focus on the ways in which Haitian and African American writers and political leaders sought to define the boundaires between Haiti and the United States in the years following the Haitian Revolution. Edlie Wong offers an extensive account of the 1820s in this respect, analyzing fears among U.S. whites about the contagion of slave revolt in relation to efforts on the part of blacks in Haiti and the United States to redraw a new modernity in which blacks were modern citizen-subjects of a hemispheric America. Wong focuses on the 1822 Negro Seamen's Acts (laws drafted by southern U.S. states to prevent black sailors from stepping onto U.S. soil) and testimony regarding the Denmark Vesey Conspiracy, as well as writings concerning debates over African American emigration to Haiti by Haitian President Jean-Pierre Boyer and the African American writer William Wells Brown, among others. Finally, focusing on Prince Saunders' *Haytian Papers*, Colleen C. O'Brien argues that Saunders articulated a distinct black labor ideology related to land ownership, which developed in the first half of the nineteenth century. O'Brien contends that insufficient attention has been paid to Saunders, who has remained in the shadow of idealized representations of Toussaint. Reading Saunders' work closely, O'Brien demonstrates that a novel and important territorial and labor-based account of freedom emerged in Haitian and African American writings in the nineteenth century, one that differs sharply from republican ideals and articulations of liberty.

CHAPTER 6

The Louisiana Purchase and the Haitian Revolution

DAVID GEGGUS

A prominent theme in the last quarter-century of writing on the Haitian Revolution has been an effort to redress a perceived neglect, or undervaluing, of the event's significance. First, Yves Benot forcefully wrote the Caribbean into the narrative of the French Revolution, and Robin Blackburn claimed for Haiti a prime place in the ending of slavery. Rolph Trouillot then denounced a generalized "silencing" of the revolution in the ideological West.[1] Recent historians of the Atlantic revolutions, unlike their predecessors, now give ample space to Haiti's revolution in their analyses.[2] Some have argued that it played a key role in the history of democracy, or the Radical Enlightenment, or the making of modernity.[3] Even Napoleonic studies, once resistant, now has to take account of Bonaparte's Caribbean catastrophe.[4]

The currently popular idea that the Haitian Revolution was in large measure responsible for the Louisiana Purchase fits well with this trend.[5] Yet it has a much longer pedigree. Although not the dominant interpretation of the land sale that doubled the size of the United States, it has been frequently put forward since the 1880s, when Henry Adams claimed that the black leader Toussaint Louverture influenced U.S. history as much as any European ruler. Grandson and great-grandson of antislavery presidents, Adams argued that "the prejudice of race alone blinded the American people to the debt they owed to the desperate courage of five hundred thousand Haytian negroes who would not be enslaved."[6] It has been almost exclusively American writers, nonetheless, who have championed the black revolution's contribution to the Early

Republic.[7] Neither Haitian historians nor the few French writers who have studied the Louisiana Purchase have shown much interest in its connection with events in the Caribbean, although modern French historians of the Haitian Revolution certainly acknowledge the connection.[8]

Analyses of why Bonaparte decided to give up Louisiana, only six months after he had bullied the king of Spain into signing it over to him, tend to emphasize one of three explanations that center respectively on the United States, Great Britain, or St. Domingue (modern Haiti). As diplomatic historian Elijah Wilson Lyon put it some eighty years ago, the success of Bonaparte's plan to occupy the colony "depended on the friendship of the United States, peace with England, and the subjugation of St. Domingo."[9] Echoing the "silencing" trope of Trouillot and Adams, Laurent Dubois states that the sale of Louisiana "has traditionally been interpreted as primarily, if not exclusively, the result of European 'balance-of-power' politics,'" and Robert Paquette condemns as "parochial" "the idea that Louisiana's fate was determined solely by European considerations."[10] My sense of the voluminous purchase literature, however, is that American authors have almost always acknowledged a Haitian as well as an American and European component in the causation of the colony's transfer.[11] My purpose in this chapter is to examine the relative influence of these different factors and whether the Haitian Revolution was, as Dubois puts it, "the most important causal force in shaping France's sale of Louisiana."[12]

* * *

France first gave up its lands on the Mississippi in 1763, surrendering them to Spain without much remorse. The factors that then shaped government thinking still applied in 1803, when Napoleon Bonaparte was head of state. Louisiana seemed vulnerable to a British attack from the north and the south, and it cost its colonial rulers far more than it produced in revenue.[13] Spain, the new ruler, valued Louisiana chiefly as a buffer to protect Mexico—in other words, as empty space. In the 1790s, however, two developments changed Louisiana's prospects and French attitudes. The rapid growth of the U.S. population between the Alleghenies and the Mississippi created a burgeoning market that potentially could be controlled by whoever possessed New Orleans. The new settlements might even be detached from the United States, as some frontiersmen then wanted, and combined with Louisiana, which after 1763 stretched from the Mississippi to the Rockies. A French mainland colony could also be developed as a convenient source of supplies for St. Domingue. France's most important overseas possession, St. Domingue, dominated the Atlantic market for tropical produce but purchased much of its foodstuffs, lumber, and livestock from foreigners, chiefly Americans. This affront to mercantilist thinking could be removed and colonial trade more effectively monopolized if the French regained possession of Louisiana and developed its agricultural potential.[14]

During the French Revolution, a succession of regimes considered plans to get back the lost colony. Charles-Maurice de Talleyrand, foreign minister after 1797, viewed it as an opportunity to curb the expansion of the United States, which he felt would inevitably become a British ally. Spain proved intransigent, however; St. Domingue was convulsed in revolution, and war with Britain closed the Atlantic to French commerce. French attention shifted to Egypt, where imperialists hoped to create a replacement for Caribbean sugar and cotton, as well as gain a shortcut to India. The rising General Bonaparte was dispatched to the Middle East, where he spent most of 1798–1799.[15]

This question of east or west was strongly influenced by matters of war and peace. As the British navy controlled the Atlantic, whatever colonies France had or acquired in the Americas, it could not exploit them in wartime, since the sea-lanes were too unsafe. The French Revolution had given France an unstoppable army, but had seriously disorganized its navy. Because Britain's maritime reach was far weaker in the Mediterranean, it made more sense to switch to an eastern strategy, as long as France and England were at war. Unluckily for the French, the destruction of Bonaparte's fleet at the Battle of the Nile showed that, even in the Mediterranean, British naval power was an insuperable obstacle.

Defeated in Egypt, Bonaparte returned to France to seize power and, while forcing the British to make peace, to reinvigorate plans for a new empire in the west. He never gave up dreams of oriental conquest, however, and early in 1801, he and the Czar Paul discussed sending a Franco-Russian army overland into India. Historians disagree to what extent the eastern and western strategies were alternatives or simultaneously pursued. The conventional view depicts a concentration on Louisiana and the Caribbean from 1801 to 1803, that formed an interlude between periods when the Asian strategy dominated. Yves Benot argues that Bonaparte simply refused to choose; both projects were jointly pursued as part of a plan for world domination, and were symptoms of a chronic inability to confront reality.[16] There is no doubt that each strategy contributed to the failure of the other.

The first consul's plans for Louisiana built on those of the Directory. Like previous regimes, he hoped to acquire Florida from Spain at the same time as Louisiana. This was to facilitate the defense of the Mississippi and more effectively hem in the United States, while greatly strengthening the French position in the Caribbean. He intended to reassert metropolitan control in St. Domingue, the former powerhouse of the Atlantic economy, and deport to Europe most of its new ruling class of black military officers, who were products of the successful slave revolution of 1791–1793. In the case of Louisiana, the question of slavery did not arise—Bonaparte apparently was unaware if it existed there.[17] But in the Caribbean the issue loomed large.

Although the French Republic had abolished slavery in 1794, it had not been able to enforce emancipation in all its colonies, such as Martinique, then under British occupation. On coming to power, it gradually became clear that Bonaparte had no qualms about maintaining slavery wherever it still existed, and in May 1802 he reopened the French slave trade. But exactly when (and even whether) he decided to restore slavery in St. Domingue remains controversial. All his public pronouncements, even his secret instructions for the expeditionary force he sent there, declared that emancipation was inviolate. Many believe, however, that it was always his intention to reimpose slavery in St. Domingue and that he merely kept the project secret until the colony could be reoccupied.[18] Others claim that Bonaparte was a pragmatist who, through 1800 and 1801, kept an open mind on the subject until he was won over in spring 1802 by his advisers and the colonial lobby, and by the early surrender of the colony's black army.[19]

A recent treatment of the question by Philippe Girard depicts the clash between the first consul and the colony's black governor, Toussaint Louverture, as the result of successive missteps by each, not a foregone conclusion. Girard emphasizes that the consul never expressly ordered a restoration of slavery in St. Domingue and that he left the decision, contingent upon local circumstances, to Captain-General Leclerc. (Much the same, however, could be said of Guadeloupe and Guyane, where local commanders were also given discretion as to timing, and the word "slavery" was avoided, but the institution was nonetheless reimposed in 1802.)[20] Girard does help clarify the issue, but then blurs it with needlessly equivocal statements that Bonaparte "seemed" to prefer slavery, or "would probably have welcomed" its restoration.[21] By June 1802, his preferences were entirely clear, although their expression was delegated to his colonial minister and conveyed in partly encoded dispatches.[22]

Related to this question of re-enslavement is uncertainty as to whether Bonaparte ever genuinely considered the alternative of using St. Domingue's ex-slave army to project French power elsewhere in the Americas, "to make Britain and the United States tremble" in the words of historian Pierre Pluchon.[23] Late in life, Napoleon regretted he had not collaborated with Louverture and once claimed he could have sent him to conquer Jamaica.[24] Bonaparte's racism no doubt hindered his imagining the former slave as an ally, as Laurent Dubois argues, but with most plantations sequestered by Toussaint's administration and St. Domingue's trade in the hands of Americans, Bonaparte had reason to doubt how much benefit France would derive from its colony under Toussaint's continued rule.[25]

Although Napoleon needed U.S. commercial support to conquer St. Domingue, his secret aim was to restore mercantilist control and exclude U.S. trade from St. Domingue once France was in full control of it.[26] He showed no interest in Canada; Louisiana's role was to complement France's revived Caribbean empire, not to link up with a reconquered Quebec, as some American and English commentators feared.[27] Similarly, if Spain's decrepit empire beckoned, it could only have been in the long term. Bonaparte well knew that American expansionists called Louisiana the highroad to Mexico, but it does not seem that Spanish silver mines were among his immediate priorities.[28]

Within a year of his seizing control of the French government, Bonaparte had extracted from Spain a conditional promise to return (or "retrocede") Louisiana (Treaty of San Ildefonso, October 1, 1800), and in March 1801 the agreement was sealed by the Convention of Aránjuez. He had already (by the Treaty of Mortefontaine, September 30, 1800) ended France's Quasi-War with the United States, and, when Thomas Jefferson replaced John Adams as president, in March 1801, Franco-American relations looked set to become more friendly. In October 1801 peace preliminaries were signed with Britain, which finally enabled Bonaparte to send a large army across the Atlantic. It sailed in December. Yet no French official would reach New Orleans until March 1803, just a month before Napoleon suddenly sold the colony.

This brings us to our main question: Why, once the pieces of Napoleon's western design had thus fallen rapidly into place, did he abandon it in less than eighteen months? On April 11, he brusquely announced his decision to commit what he flippantly called "Louisianicide." Some, like Jefferson's backchannel to the French government, Dupont de Nemours, thought Napoleon always intended to sell New Orleans, but they were evidently wrong.[29] This is shown by the meticulous preparations in the closing months of 1802 for a Louisiana expedition that was to sail from the Netherlands. Some have stressed that the western design was never complete; the failure to force Spain to cede Florida together with Louisiana meant that the latter never could be adequately defended.[30] The point is important, but since the French continued with their plans for Louisiana long after it was clear Florida was unobtainable, it is not a good explanation of why those plans were finally abandoned. Instead, scholars generally have leaned toward one of three explanations that focus either on the United States, Great Britain, or St. Domingue. Because one factor influenced another, the issue is complex, and, since there is no direct evidence of Bonaparte's thinking on the matter preceding his decision, it remains open to dispute.

Scholars who stress the St. Domingue factor make two arguments. First, they attribute the French failure to effectively occupy Louisiana to the delay and loss of resources caused by France's disastrous attempt to reconquer St. Domingue. The military quagmire that became the Haitian War of Independence, it is argued, prevented Louisiana from being garrisoned and fortified, and its French population and Indian neighbors from being organized to resist external attack, as had been planned. The second argument is that the French defeat in the Caribbean at the hands of former slaves rendered the whole western strategy pointless, since St. Domingue was the reason for Louisiana's retrocession.

The first of these St. Domingue–related arguments is problematic, because several factors delayed the departure of troops for Louisiana, and much more has been attributed to the Haitian Revolution than seems warranted. Some have thought that the Leclerc expedition sent to St. Domingue was meant to detach forces for New Orleans, once it could spare them.[31] This is what Ambassador Robert Livingstone in London and Consul Tobias Lear in Cap-Français claimed to have learned from private conversations, what Alexander Hamilton surmised, and what Finance Minister Barbé-Marbois recalled in the 1820s.[32] However, there is no real evidence for it. Such an order was not part of General Leclerc's instructions; nor was it mentioned anywhere in his correspondence or in Napoleon's.[33] Perhaps it was conveyed orally (as may have been the case with the restoration of slavery in St. Domingue), so as not to alarm the United States or the British. Yet the later discussion (in January 1802) of detaching troops for Louisiana from the expedition being sent to Guadeloupe makes this questionable. The instructions, moreover, were top secret. In any event, in May 1802, at the (temporarily) successful end of his campaign,

Leclerc began sending shipping back to France because of the need there for troopships.[34] This suggests that the belief that the St. Domingue expedition was meant to provide forces for Louisiana is simply wrong.

If the fighting in St. Domingue hindered Louisiana's occupation, it could have done so only by delaying the sailing of the expedition specifically destined for Louisiana, that the French began assembling in the summer of 1802. This was after a new Spanish government that was hostile to the transfer eventually agreed to it in late May of that year.[35] Bonaparte had earlier considered sending a separate expedition to Louisiana in October 1801, even before Madrid made the retrocession legal, but the project was rapidly canceled. The reasons are uncertain but doubtless included the scarcity of shipping caused by the St. Domingue expedition and concern that such an early move might jeopardize the approaching peace with Britain, which was signed in March 1802. Not least was the fact that the Spanish had not finalized the transfer of power. For a year, down to July 1802, the first consul pressed them on this constantly but, in the event, he preferred to wait until the paperwork arrived from Madrid.[36] The recalcitrant Spanish government dragged this out, so that it did not reach Paris until October 25, 1802.[37] Legal niceties were not usually Napoleon's main concern, but on this occasion he had extra incentive to play by the rules. He was still hoping to cajole the Spanish into surrendering Florida; and to undercut U.S. and British opposition to the transfer, it was far better to arrive in New Orleans with legal title than without.

As this diplomatic obstacle was less visible than France's deepening problems in St. Domingue, contemporaries such as Alexander Hamilton and Thomas Jefferson more readily attributed to the latter the delay in occupying Louisiana. Like Henry Adams, Hamilton would later give much of the credit for the Louisiana Purchase to the resistance of St. Domingue's blacks and the colony's deadly climate. His judgment was skewed, however, by his belief that the Leclerc expedition was destined for New Orleans and, as most historians recognize, by his desire to minimize the role played by Jefferson.[38]

Only in the closing months of 1802, however, did the Haitian Revolution certainly impede the New Orleans expedition, and it was to a much smaller extent than usually supposed. Historians Robert Tucker and David Hendrickson, apparently misled by the ill-informed dispatches of the U.S. ambassador in Paris, write that "time and again ... the voracious demands" of the St. Domingue campaign caused the Louisiana expedition to be delayed and reduced in size.[39] Philippe Girard, the best historian of that campaign, similarly states that "thousands of troops earmarked for Louisiana were re-routed to

Cap[-Français]."⁴⁰ This, however, is unproven and would appear unlikely, as the initial force destined for New Orleans never seems to have exceeded three thousand. Five battalions of the Seventeenth and Fifty-Fourth Regiments were assigned to the expedition in August 1802, and they were still the intended expeditionary force in February 1803. Although it was decided on December 19 that one of the regiments should be diverted to St. Domingue before it reached Louisiana, this order was canceled on February 3, 1803, when the troops were still in Europe awaiting departure.⁴¹

The expedition did not sail when the transfer documents had arrived from Spain in October because of a succession of problems. The only one that can be attributed to the Haitian Revolution was a shortage of troopships. It probably would have prevented embarkation before late December. But even if enough vessels had been assembled earlier, another logistical problem would likely have delayed their departure. In late November, the port of embarkation was changed from Dunkirk to the River Scheldt, and it took more than a month to transfer the expedition's stores to the new location. In the meantime, winter storms damaged some of the ships. Undergoing repairs and awaiting supplies, the vessels then became icebound for close to two months.⁴² In view of this succession of diplomatic, logistical, and environmental difficulties, had there been no St. Domingue expedition, or if it had encountered only brief resistance, it is far from certain that Louisiana would have been garrisoned earlier.

As for the second argument concerning the Haitian Revolution, we do not know exactly when Napoleon gave up hope of success in the Caribbean. Conceivably, it was in the first half of January 1803, when he learned of General Leclerc's death (January 7) and shouted out at dinner (January 11) "Damn sugar! Damn coffee! Damn colonies!"⁴³ According to Yves Benot, "There could be no further doubt about the inevitable disaster"; for E. Wilson Lyon, it signaled a "radical change of outlook"; and Paul Hoffman makes this the cause of the decision to sell Louisiana.⁴⁴ Yet, according to historian Gustav Roloff, Napoleon then pushed his colonial policy with increased energy. The reports from St. Domingue were "far from entirely hopeless." In Thomas Fleming's view, Bonaparte became even more determined to have both St. Domingue and Louisiana. On January 14, the British ambassador in Paris reported that sending reinforcements to the Caribbean occupied the government "to the exclusion of almost every other object."⁴⁵

Robert Paquette argues that Bonaparte was merely salvaging what he could and that the western design had failed. Failed it had, but the key point is Napoleon's perception. Treasury Minister Barbé-Marbois recalled that Bonaparte slowed down the dispatch of reinforcements but did not change his plans.[46] On February 4, he wrote to Leclerc's replacement that St. Domingue was France's highest priority, that fifteen thousand reinforcements were en route or soon to sail, and that he would send another fifteen to eighteen thousand in the fall. He presumably meant it, as his papers contain calculations of how to raise this number and orders to begin preparations.[47] Above all, Bonaparte continued to push for the departure of the Louisiana expedition at least until February 24, and to rebuff American attempts to negotiate a sale.[48] The death toll in St. Domingue was certainly staggering, but one can hardly argue that it foreclosed expansion in Louisiana any more than it foreclosed expansion in Europe.[49]

Finally, failure in St. Domingue did not necessarily mean Louisiana lost its purpose. Some contemporaries saw it as a possible replacement for the pearl of the Antilles. These included General Thouvenot and the former prefect Wante in St. Domingue, the Cuban intellectual Arango y Parreño, and Bonaparte's war minister, Louis Alexandre Berthier.[50] On April 10, 1803, the night before Napoleon Bonaparte made up his mind to sell Louisiana, Berthier argued at length with him against such a move. He reminded the first consul how colonies had made France wealthy and how Louisiana could compensate for its past losses in India and those then threatening in the Caribbean. He called Louisiana potentially the most important of France's overseas possessions, both as an agricultural producer and as an outlet for the transAppalachian commerce of the United States. In the hands of others, it would be a commercial rival (even, Berthier fancifully asserted, for French grapes and olives). The minister, who had negotiated Louisiana's conditional transfer from Spain to France in October 1800, argued with more foresight that its value would increase, if ever a Panama canal were built. At the very least, he added, Louisiana could serve as a dumping ground for France's political dissidents.[51] Napoleon's foreign minister, Talleyrand, his colonial minister, Decrès, and his brothers Lucien and Joseph also opposed the sale.

E. Wilson Lyon's seminal study from 1934 is far from being monocausal, but, on balance, it emphasizes French fears of burgeoning U.S. hostility to the retrocession. The other main work in English, by Alexander DeConde, is more equivocal but also makes a strong case for the U.S. factor.[52] Since U.S. hostility to retrocession was well known to the French government, this argument implies that the French long believed they could outmaneuver the Americans but that they suddenly changed their minds. Both the Adams and

Jefferson governments had several times stated that a French acquisition of New Orleans would force the United States to ally with England and, sooner or later, seize the city by force. For this reason, the French aimed to keep the retrocession a secret until they could garrison and fortify the colony as a fait accompli. However, American anger, both in the capital and on the frontier, greatly increased in the winter of 1802–1803, when French intentions could no longer be doubted and when France was (wrongly) blamed for Spain's suddenly ending U.S. trading privileges in New Orleans. Mounting U.S. bellicosity was repeatedly emphasized in the reports sent to Paris by the French minister, Pichon, who opposed repossession of Louisiana.[53]

There is very little evidence of French government alarm on this score, but it is a persuasive coincidence that news of warlike motions in the U.S. Senate (the "Ross Resolutions" proposing the seizure of New Orleans) reached Napoleon just three days before his sudden decision to sell. Critical of the exaggeration of American nationalist historians, Robert Paquette discounts this factor. He notes that Pichon's dispatch regarding the Ross Resolutions arrived in Paris too late to affect the decision. Yet he seems unaware that the news of the Senate motion had already arrived by other channels.[54] The resolutions were defeated in the Senate but that was not known in France until later. The American factor has by far the best claim of the three explanations of the purchase to be considered its proximate cause.

President Jefferson's own bellicose gestures were more muted and ambivalent, and historians have long known that he was lucky and, in a sense, bluffing when pressuring the French. He was expecting only minor concessions from Bonaparte—no land at all west of the Mississippi—and he would not have attacked the French unless they were again embroiled in a war with Britain.[55] Although U.S. ambitions were limited, this does not mean that the American threat was negligible, as revisionists argue. For Bonaparte, it probably functioned as the last straw in his disenchantment with Louisiana. Beyond the approximately $10 million for France's depleted coffers, the sale also had benefits that included the conversion of U.S. antagonism to friendship, the consolidation of a pro-French ministry in the White House, and the strengthening of the only maritime power that might eventually rival Great Britain.[56] However, if American influence played a critical role in the chronology of Bonaparte's decision making, its importance was obviously less than that of the British factor, of which it was a dependent variable. It was the imminent outbreak of war with England that forced the French to take the American threat seriously.[57]

The official explanation generally given by Napoleon and Talleyrand for the sale of Louisiana was the imminence of war with England, which finally broke out in May. Lucien Bonaparte's memoirs leave a similar impression.[58] So do the recollections of the French minister who negotiated the Louisiana Purchase, François Barbé-Marbois.[59] Friction began building between Britain and France in late 1802 over their respective failures to carry out treaty obligations. The French retained troops in Italy and the Netherlands, contrary to the Treaty of Lunéville, and the British kept Malta, contrary to the Treaty of Amiens. Fearful of renascent French ambitions in Egypt and in Europe, the British began mobilizing in early March. This convinced a reluctant Napoleon, in the opinion of his apologists, that he could no longer avoid war.[60] Even historians who play down the British factor usually give early March as the date when the first consul probably "lost interest" in Louisiana.[61]

The resumption of a maritime war meant troops could no longer be sent either to St. Domingue or to Louisiana. Both colonies could be blockaded, and, if Haitian independence was not already inevitable, it became so once assured British naval support. Above all, Napoleon believed the British would quickly seize New Orleans and that this required a complete about-face in policy. In his *Histoire de la Louisiane*, Barbé-Marbois suggests that the city could have been more easily seized by the Americans than the British, but he explains the first consul's decision largely in terms of the British threat.[62] Although his American counterpart in the negotiations, James Monroe, denied that the British factor alone could have influenced the question, Barbé-Marbois claimed that, by March 8, Napoleon already thought war inevitable and that any Louisiana expedition would be captured at sea. A month later, Napoleon's priority had become preventing the British from taking New Orleans. Sale to the United States would achieve this end and help finance the forthcoming war. According to Barbé-Marbois, Napoleon also hoped the purchase would strengthen the ability of the United States to challenge Britain as a maritime power.[63]

Some of those, like Lyon, who minimize the importance of the British factor point out that an imminent seizure of New Orleans by Britain did not necessitate the sale of Louisiana, since captured French colonies were likely to be returned at the end of a successful war, as they had been in 1802. However, such an outcome was much less likely in the event of an American seizure of the city, facilitated by an Anglo-French war, and this is the prospect that France faced in early 1803. Others argue that, if the Haitian War of Independence had not prevented the garrisoning of the colony, it could have held out against

British or American foes, as was Napoleon's intention. Yet, as noted above, it is quite unlikely that the fighting in St. Domingue did prevent the dispatch of troops to Louisiana.

More important is such critics' argument that it was not the renewal of hostilities in Europe that determined colonial policy, but failure in the Americas that persuaded the first consul to abandon his western design and resume the struggle with Britain. Some add that European victories were needed to distract attention from defeat in the Caribbean.[64] In this view, Napoleon, not the British, was responsible for the breakdown of the peace of Amiens; and he decided to risk war, not because of irremediable conflicts in Europe but because, once he had written off St. Domingue, neither Louisiana nor peace with England was of use to him. Indeed, it is difficult to understand why Napoleon willfully antagonized the British by publishing in late January the Sébastiani report on Egypt, if he had not already decided to abandon the Caribbean and resume hostilities.[65] However, if he had truly written off St. Domingue at that time, one may wonder why he was sending fifteen thousand soldiers there, and also hurrying along the Louisiana expedition down to the moment when the British government began mobilizing for war.

* * *

Whether writing of "the heroic negro insurrectionists of San Domingo" or its "horrible servile war," most American historians have tended to acknowledge the influence of the Haitian Revolution on the Louisiana Purchase but have accorded it lesser importance as a causal factor than the imminent renewal of the Anglo-French war.[66] This judgment seems to me correct. For Napoleon Bonaparte, most of the news from St. Domingue was bad throughout the fall of 1802, and although it worsened in early January 1803, he still pursued his plans for Louisiana until at least late February. By that time, the Haitian Revolution may have rendered the colony's acquisition pointless, but there is no sign that Bonaparte thought so, and many of his advisers still did not think so six weeks later. In the intervening period, however, the likelihood of a European and maritime war rapidly escalated, and once this threat was compounded by the prospect of conflict with the United States, Bonaparte gave up his western project within days.

It is certainly difficult to separate cause and effect in this seamless web of influences surrounding the sale of Louisiana. The three main factors, American, British, and Caribbean, mutually reinforced one another. The success of the black insurgents in St. Domingue was partly due to Jefferson's decision to continue supplying them, which was entirely due to his opposition to French plans for Louisiana. The likelihood of Jefferson's seizing New Orleans was greatly increased, both by the French army's difficulties in St. Domingue and by the approach of war between France and England, just as the danger of losing Louisiana in a war with England was considerably magnified by the American threat.

Although the American threat was the proximate cause of the change in French policy, it was not a sufficient cause, since American action was contingent upon the outbreak of war between Britain and France. It was thus the least important of the three factors. The Haitian Revolution is more difficult to assess, because its role first in delaying the French occupation of Louisiana and then in persuading Napoleon Bonaparte it was not worthwhile remains open to question. The chronology of Bonaparte's actions suggests that the military quagmire in St. Domingue was not a sufficient cause, but in the long term it would probably have become one. If Britain and France had remained at peace, the French would still have lost St. Domingue and perhaps decided, therefore, that Louisiana was not worth keeping. But was it an essential cause of the purchase, without which the sale would not have occurred? This is less probable. Even if there had been no Haitian Revolution, the chances of France keeping Louisiana after the resumption of the maritime war with England were not strong. By 1811, the French had lost every one of their colonies.

The Louisiana Purchase grew out of a combination of developments in the United States, Europe, and the Caribbean. American, British, and Haitian nationalists can all claim a share of the credit. Jefferson handled the situation deftly, but he also owed an ironic debt of gratitude to the British government he detested, to his Federalist opponents, who had called loudly for the use of force, and to those he supposedly called (but actually did not) the "cannibals of the terrible republic."[67] There is little reason, however, to suppose that the Haitian factor was the most important of these influences, or that it has been particularly neglected by American historians. At the present time, in fact, historians who make a passing reference to the causes of the Louisiana Purchase seem more likely to mention Haiti than any other factor.[68] Though such statements may be perfectly legitimate, they produce their own variety of silencing.

CHAPTER 7

Republic of Medicine

Immunology and National Identity in the Age of Revolution

CRISTOBAL SILVA

If the late eighteenth century was the Age of Revolution—an age when national identities and allegiances proved to be remarkably unstable, constituting and reconstituting themselves along rapidly shifting political and economic axes—it was no less an Age of Epidemic—an age when diseases like smallpox, typhus, and yellow fever helped determine the outcome of revolutionary struggles throughout the Atlantic world, and had an equally significant impact on how categories like citizenship and community constituted themselves.[1] Where France, Britain, Spain, and the United States deployed military forces across the North Atlantic and Caribbean basins to protect their economic interests and enlarge their imperial ambitions during the last two and a half decades of the century, the rapid movement of armies and refugees entailed by these deployments led to broad demographic shifts that disrupted long-familiar epidemiological patterns and brought disparate populations into collision with new pathogens. It is not that late eighteenth-century epidemics were suddenly or significantly deadlier than they had been in prior eras. On the contrary, the period coincides with the continued professionalization of physicians, and with perhaps one of the most significant innovations in the history of Western medicine: Edward Jenner's 1796 development of the smallpox vaccine, which heralded an increasingly sophisticated approach to treating diseases that would transform public health policy in the nineteenth and twentieth centuries. But even as a familiar disease like smallpox became easier to manage, the complex commercial migration networks that emerged during the Age of Revolution reshaped global geographies and created the conditions for previously unfamiliar diseases like yellow fever and cholera to appear among European populations on both sides of the Atlantic. In the face of such shifting patterns, physicians, politicians, and military men alike found themselves compelled to reassess their understanding of how illness and health operated in familiar environments, and to extrapolate from their epidemiological observations about disease and reconsider what we might today call the biological—or immunological—foundations of citizenship and national identity.

This essay examines the decade-long yellow fever pandemic that struck the West Indies and the coastal United States between 1793 and 1804. Physicians throughout the Atlantic world formed independent and often contradictory theories about what the pandemic was, where it began, and how it spread, but my decision to focus on this particular decade frames these theories in the context of the Haitian Revolution.[2] Indeed, I would argue that neither the revolution nor the pandemic can be properly understood in isolation from one another, but that considering them together repositions the relationship between place and nation by introducing health and illness as a matrix for defining the terms of citizenship in the revolutionary era. For example, even as the revolution transformed St. Domingue into a contested space where competing imperial powers clashed for political and economic supremacy and where Africans fought to establish and protect their own liberty in the Americas, yellow fever complicated these battles on a number of axes. First, and most dramatically, it was a force that frustrated French and British colonial ambitions by decimating European troops sent to St. Domingue.[3] But just as significantly, yellow fever spread beyond the shores of St. Domingue, confounding national, territorial, economic, and racial boundaries as it surfaced throughout the West Indies and coastal United States.

I will examine the effects of the disease in Philadelphia, on French and British forces in the West Indies, and on the African revolutionaries who fought in St. Domingue itself. In doing so, I will purposely dislocate sites like Philadelphia and St. Domingue as stable geographic entities by unhinging the concept of national identity from territorial integrity. In this respect, I want to represent revolution-era Philadelphia and St. Domingue as the loci of pandemic: as the sites of movement and migration—of illness and health—rather than as fixed stages on which historical events unfolded. That is to say, even as I alternately situate Philadelphia and St. Domingue at the centers of the pandemic, these are centers without place because the very definition of a pandemic obviates the political and geographic boundaries of nationhood in favor of disease vectors, migrations, and transmission routes. And even as yellow fever disrupts seemingly natural geopolitical categories, the epidemiological writings of late eighteenth-century physicians that I examine here seek to relocate the bonds of communal and national identity in relation to shared immunities and susceptibilities.

I am being deliberate in my use of language when I make the distinction between "epidemic" and "pandemic" in this essay. Though related, these are two technical terms of medicine that I would frame geographically: epidemic signifies the unexpected surge of disease within a local space, and it is the term most familiar to scholars of the early Republic who write of the 1793 Philadelphia yellow fever epidemic. And yet, I would shift away from this term, which centers the outbreak in a fixed space (Philadelphia) and time (1793)—a space deliberately defined within the United States but severed from the remainder of the hemisphere—in favor of pandemic, which signifies a broader, more widespread outbreak that spills over geographic, territorial, and political borders. This is not to say that Philadelphia did not experience an epidemical outbreak of yellow fever—it did—but that this outbreak was only one incident in a much larger pandemic that raged through the western rim of the Atlantic world, and shook the foundations of empire in Europe. In other words, this essay makes an argument for reframing the way that we categorize and scale the outbreak: when we isolate the pandemic to Philadelphia—when we see it as a local epidemic—we skew our understanding of the event toward a familiar, but isolationist (or even exceptionalist) history of U.S. national identity, and away from the wider immunological and geopolitical dynamics that shaped it. Thus, epidemic comes to be *about* Philadelphia and *about* the United States, rather than about Philadelphia's relationship to the world around it.[4] On the other hand, analyzing pandemic requires us to consider Philadelphia from an alternate vantage point, which reveals that the geographies as well as the bodies of foreign soldiers, revolutionaries, and refugees were central to how Philadelphians negotiated their place in the world. What it means to read for pandemic rather than epidemic, then, is to reorient our analysis of illness away from received political and national boundaries toward a territorial geography of immunity that binds local spaces to one another through a complex set of military, commercial, and medical networks.

By way of reorienting these geographies, I concentrate on what Benjamin Rush called the "Republic of Medicine." For Rush, this term refers to the community of physicians dispersed throughout the Atlantic world who shared their knowledge with one another via correspondence and print publication.[5] The physicians whom I write about were primarily interested in the local outbreaks they each encountered, and so acted independently from each other, but circulated and responded to one another's texts to construct a transatlantic (or even transnational) body of knowledge about yellow fever. This diffuse Republic of Medicine was held together in print by common professional concerns, and yet the heterogeneity of approaches and conclusions that emerged from it dislocate this republic from any fixed geographic or national categories. In the aggregate, these epidemiological histories produced by the Republic of Medicine were neither the work of a British, French, American, or even a Black Atlantic. Instead, it might be more accurate to say that they represent a Yellow Fever Atlantic—a space in which the meaning of location itself comes to be contested while professional physicians work to reimagine what community and nation look like under the shadow of pandemic.

Such an analysis is available in large part because of the nature of yellow fever—an illness that is not native to the Americas, though its presence dates back to the sixteenth century, when it was imported aboard slave ships from West Africa.[6] Until the mid-eighteenth century, West Indian colonies were primarily dependent on migration from Europe to sustain their populations; regular migrations to the colonies produced periodic and virulent yellow fever epidemics.[7] By the last quarter century prior to the Haitian Revolution, however, the West Indian experience of yellow fever shifted in significant ways, as the disease became a chronic (that is, endemic) issue, rather than an acute (epidemic) threat.[8] But the arrival of French troops sent to quell the St. Domingue slave rebellion in 1792 changed this pattern yet again: the sudden influx of soldiers who were susceptible to the disease unleashed a new period of vigorous epidemic activity that soon spread throughout the West Indies and beyond. As refugees from Cap-Français left the colony in June and July of 1793, British forces prepared to land in September; by then, the pandemic was in full swing, and would shape the regional history of the Caribbean, France, Great Britain, and the United States.[9] I am less interested in the pandemic's direct effects on the revolution than I am in examining epidemiological writings about how yellow fever's observable symptoms and the mechanics of its transmission reflect an evolving understanding of the relation between nation and health in the Age of Revolution.

As a case in point, whereas British forces were sent to St. Domingue in 1793 with the expectation that they would easily undermine the French sphere of influence and redirect the colony's wealth toward Great Britain, the plan quickly proved to be more complicated than anticipated. By the late 1790s, yellow fever had decimated so many British troops that Hector McLean, an assistant inspector of hospitals for British forces in St. Domingue, acknowledged the toll that the disease had on the army's morale in his study of the pandemic, asserting that "already have groundless fears, terrified and subdued our countrymen; and rendered them more liable to fever, and more easily conquered. The name of St. Domingue is execrated, and dreaded by all descriptions. The officer and soldier bound for this service look upon themselves as doomed to certain destruction."[10]

McLean's description of the soldiers' fear does two things in the context of his narrative: first, it highlights the immunological bonds that tie his "countrymen" to one another. Susceptibility to yellow fever is what draws them together—indeed their shared susceptibility is what gives meaning to signs of national kinship like language, uniform, flag, or culture. The upshot of the immunological bond that McLean portrays is that it manifests itself publicly as fear—the very thing, he warns, that makes soldiers susceptible to the fever in the first place (not an uncommon belief at the time). By suggesting that this same fear would lead to British forces being conquered by their foes, McLean neatly packages the troops' immunological susceptibility with British identity by projecting the individual effects of illness as a matter of national character and security. In response, he takes pains to mitigate these fears by insisting that "it will be pleasing [for them] to know" that the yellow fever "IS NOT INFECTIOUS"—a claim that while technically true, was a distinction without a difference for the common soldier in St. Domingue.[11] Of the 20,200 British troops sent to the colony between 1793 and 1797, over 60 percent (12,700) perished on the island, and as many as 95 percent of those casualties succumbed to yellow fever; their fears were hardly unfounded.[12] McLean was technically correct in saying that yellow fever was not infectious because the disease does not spread directly from human to human. But the reason that mortality was so high among soldiers—in fact, the reason that the yellow fever pandemic spread so quickly with the arrival of European troops in St. Domingue—lies in its mechanics of infection.

Yellow fever is a hemorrhagic fever that presents initially as mild discomfort, headaches, vomiting, muscle aches, and jaundice. In the best-case scenario, these symptoms peter out, and patients regain full health, acquiring, in the process, a lifelong immunity to the disease. Significantly, the generally diffuse nature of these symptoms means that people living in the West Indies in the eighteenth century could recover from yellow fever without ever knowing they had been infected because they were essentially asymptomatic; they would go through life imagining themselves naturally immune to the disease as they remained unscathed while epidemics raged about them. On the other hand, acute cases of yellow fever present with the classic symptoms that define the disease: delirium, seizures, violent black vomits, bloody fluxes, and bleeding from the mouth, the nose, and the eyes before ending, in about 50 percent of cases, with death. Yellow fever requires three factors to thrive in a community: the yellow fever virus itself, a large pool of susceptible human subjects, and its vector of transmission, the *Aëdes aegypti* mosquito.[13] A final but significant detail in the history of this pandemic is that unlike the *Anophales* mosquito that lives in marshlands and spreads malaria, *Aëdes aegypti* prefers water from artificial, man-made containers, and thus congregates in urban environments such as low-lying port towns. These environments came to be encoded as epidemical sites because they were densely populated by humans and mosquitoes, and were therefore breeding grounds for yellow fever.[14]

Patients who survive yellow fever develop a lifelong immunity to it and become incapable of passing the virus on to others. This individual immunity is an important regulator of infection and epidemic, but tells only half the story because the presence of immune individuals in a community is critical to how yellow fever interacts with populations. The reason for this lies in a concept that modern epidemiologists call "herd immunity," a mechanism that describes the social—or collective—dynamics of immunity and susceptibility to disease. Herd immunity refers to a community's ability to withstand epidemic outbreak based on the rate of individual susceptibility among its inhabitants. The higher the ratio of immune to non-immune subjects in a given population, the more likely it will be protected from epidemic.[15] Applied to yellow fever in St. Domingue, this suggests that when herd immunity was high—when immunes significantly outnumbered non-immunes—it became statistically less likely that an infective *Aëdes aegypti* mosquito would encounter a susceptible subject and spread the disease to him or her. Conversely, when herd immunity was low—when a community was dominated by non-immune individuals—mosquitoes were much more likely to pass the virus on to one or more susceptible subjects, who in turn became carriers of the virus and potential links in a chain reaction of epidemical outbreak.

In practical terms, herd immunity offers a straightforward explanation for the epidemiological history of yellow fever among European populations in the West Indies. During the early period of colonial expansion, which was marked by the rapid migration of (non-immune) Europeans to the colonies, herd immunity was low, meaning that severe epidemics with high rates of mortality were common. However, in the latter half of the eighteenth century, as colonial populations stabilized and grew less reliant on migration to sustain themselves, yellow fever epidemics became fewer and farther between. The disease certainly remained a constant endemic presence in the West Indies, but adults raised there were generally immune to it, having been infected in childhood. Conversely, new immigrants from Europe often fell ill soon after their arrival to the West Indies because they were almost universally susceptible. If these new arrivals happened to survive infection, they too would join the population of immunes. Thus, when immigration rates were high, so too was the risk of epidemic; when rates were low, epidemics tended to remain in check. In practical terms, this dynamic can be observed by the fact that among its many names, yellow fever was also called the "seasoning fever," and that in St Domingue itself, physicians reported that "very rarely does a single person escape the tribute that [yellow fever] demands in return for creolizing oneself, as the native expression goes."[16]

The important point here is that herd immunity does not distinguish populations according to national origin: French troops were no more or less susceptible to yellow fever than British troops were, and no more or less susceptible than Philadelphians. Instead, the immunological fault lines were drawn geographically, separating West Indian Creoles from Europeans and Americans according to how much exposure a subject had to pathogens. French and British forces who began to arrive in St. Domingue in 1792 and 1793 thus came to an island where yellow fever was endemic, but where the general population was effectively immune. The influx of susceptible armies during this period could easily double the population of European inhabitants in St. Domingue port towns like Port-au-Prince, Saint Marc, and Môle-Saint-Nicholas, thus cutting herd immunity for those locations in half, and dramatically increasing the odds of outbreak.[17] And yet the reality was even more grim for the troops themselves, because herd immunity among their ranks was effectively zero. Worse yet, military camps became even more dangerous by virtue of the fact that they were both isolated from the civilian population and restricted to tight, unsanitary quarters. Likewise, the mosquito's preference for dusk helped make soldiers even more vulnerable. Responding to what he saw as disastrous behaviors that rendered his troops more vulnerable to the fever, French army physician Nicolas Pierre Gilbert, who was stationed in St. Domingue alongside General Leclerc in 1802, urged soldiers to avoid evening strolls by the sea, and reminded them that "nothing is more dangerous than going to bed and sleeping on humid ground."¹⁸ This mix of isolation with specific behaviors formed military micro-communities that soon became infested with *Aëdes aegypti* and provided an ideal environment for epidemics to erupt.

The pattern of infection and immunity was considerably different in Philadelphia than it was in the West Indies. There, refugees from St. Domingue arrived in June and July of 1793, and were soon followed by yellow fever in early August. The illness spread so quickly that by the end of the month, Benjamin Rush urged residents to flee the city—then the capital of the United States. Roughly 20,000 of Philadelphia's 45,000 inhabitants did so, including George Washington and Alexander Hamilton, though Hamilton not before he too was infected. By the time the contagion subsided after the first fall frost, more than 4,000 Philadelphians had died.¹⁹ Philadelphia's physicians erupted into debate almost as quickly as the yellow fever did, arguing over the origins of the disease and its contagiousness. According to Martin Pernick, these issues had important political implications, which he lays out as the division between Federalist "importationists," who believed the disease to have been brought to Philadelphia from abroad, and Republican physicians, who were convinced that its origins were local.²⁰ Importationists quite rightly linked the epidemic to the influx of refugees earlier that summer. This assumption divided the population of Philadelphia into two camps—infectious French foreigners and susceptible Americans. For importationists, the threat of epidemic foreshadowed a threat to national security and had to be met with a strong federal response; the importationists promoted policies such as the quarantine of (Creole) French ships as well as trading limits with French colonies.²¹ By the end of the decade, when the Alien and Sedition Acts were enacted as law, importation had become a trope of patriotic rhetoric, with one writer, according to Pernick, charging that "the doctrine of domestic fevers was 'treason.'"²²

On the other hand, the leading voice among Republican physicians was Rush, who bemoaned the parochialism of importationist dogma. His critique followed a two-pronged approach: first, he charged that importationists were following the whims of "self love" rather than the sober evidence of science by denying that Philadelphia could produce the disease. Not only did he believe that this was bad public health policy, but he complained about its pernicious effects, which had "unhappily corrupted the science of medicine."²³ Second, Rush sought to dismantle the primary concern of importationists—namely, that "if we admit the yellow fever to be of domestic origin, it will ruin the credit and commerce of our city." This was obviously a charged accusation during a time of economic uncertainty, but it was based on the belief that ships would avoid Philadelphia if it came to be known as an unhealthy city. Rush maintained that "the reverse of this opinion is true."[24] If the disease was imported, he explained, Philadelphians could do little to "remove its causes" beyond isolating themselves from the world and destroying commerce that way. On the other hand, a local disease was more easily managed from within the city, and therefore easier to overcome. Physician and St. Domingue refugee Jean Devèze may have had a personal stake in supporting Rush's opinion on the matter, even if the two did not agree on treatment methods. He was adamant that the fever "was neither brought in by men or vessels," and that "what proves the truth of this assertion is, that very few persons newly arrived were infected with the sickness."[25] Rush cited the same evidence to support his argument, noting that "no foreigners or sailors" had been infected in Philadelphia, and that "the refugees from the French West-Indies, universally escaped it. . . . [But] this was not the case with the natives of France, who had been settled in the city."[26]

By translating the debate between Rush and the importationists into the framework of herd immunity, we see that both parties were at least partially correct in their observations: the epidemic erupted in Philadelphia because infectious *Aëdes aegypti* mosquitoes followed refugees from the St. Domingue Revolution, and these refugees generally remained healthy in Philadelphia because of their previously acquired immunities. Such observations became increasingly pointed in the early nineteenth century, as French physicians published numerous treatises on yellow fever. André François, for example, drew the outline of the fever's epidemiological patterns most explicitly, writing that "in the West Indies . . . [it] spares the inhabitants of the land while furiously killing strangers—sometimes within a few days of their arrival. In the United States, it is the opposite: only the native seems susceptible to the fever, while the stranger remains free from it."[27] As François suggests, the infection patterns in Philadelphia were mirror images of St. Domingue's: where a susceptible population of soldiers migrated to an endemic environment in St. Domingue, the disease was brought to a susceptible community in Philadelphia. While the Philadelphia medical debates were invested in national politics, the dynamics of herd immunity frame this discussion as a story of hemispheric migration patterns. In this respect, I find the specific disagreement about epidemiological origins to be less interesting than the fact that both parties marshaled the evidence about patterns of migration, susceptibility, and immunity in order to reconsider the terms of communal and national identity.

The issue becomes increasingly complex if we consider David Nassy's writing on the epidemic. A French physician operating in Philadelphia, Nassy offers a hybrid position between the two parties. On the one hand, he suggests that diseases are endemic to specific geographic locations, but he is aware that such a theory clearly cannot account for the fact that St. Domingue refugees in Philadelphia were immune to infection. Indeed, Nassy's quasi-climatist view of epidemic leads him to conclude that epidemics emerge as a conjunction of body and location: "The disease is not contagious for foreigners, whose constitutions have little homogeneity with that dry air. We are convinced of it by the prodigious numbers abounding in this city, none of whom were attacked with that disease, whilst the most part of the natives, and those used to the climate, were taken ill with it."[28] Thus, for Nassy, colonial "experience has often shewed" that disease is bound to the relation between body and place—an attempt, perhaps to relocate or repatriate health and national identity within well-defined territorial borders.[29]

I stated at the outset of this essay that my reading of the yellow fever pandemic would dislocate the Haitian Revolution because I wanted to consider how communal and national identity were constituted as much along immunological as territorial axes in the late eighteenth century. The upshot of this approach has been that in focusing on the Republic of Medicine, I have swept St. Domingue itself to the margins of my reading of the revolutionary era. Perhaps even more problematically, Africans in St. Domingue and black Philadelphians have been equally marginalized and silenced. In what remains of the essay, I would like to offer a corrective for this marginalization because Africans were absolutely central actors in the history of the yellow fever pandemic and were deeply enmeshed in emerging nationalist discourses; the specters of St. Domingue and of slavery were never far from discussions of yellow fever in England or in the United States, and this produced significant racial anxieties about linking citizenship with health. Indeed by recuperating these African voices—and bodies—my intention is to demonstrate that demographic mechanisms such as herd immunity do not simply explain epidemiological events; they also recalibrate the rhetoric of national identity and produce an alternate way to conceive of the Republic of Medicine as an immunology of citizenship.

This vision of the Republic of Medicine builds on the work of Priscilla Wald, who has coined the term "imagined immunities" to describe what she calls the "central role of disease in the articulation of a national community."[30] Wald suggests that during moments of rapid demographic change—such as the era of late twentieth-century globalization in the case of her analysis, or the Age of Revolution in mine—communities rely on their shared susceptibilities and immunities to enact strategies for reimagining national bonds. These strategies often manifest themselves outwardly, in xenophobic narratives that pathologize strangers as potential threats to the state, or inwardly, as policing mechanisms designed to protect the integrity of territorial boundaries, even as epidemical outbreaks underscore the porousness of those borders. Wald's point is that disease and contagion are integral to the politics of nationhood, and while any number of medical metaphors, tropes, and allegories will attest to this fact, I would add that herd immunity, which acts as an epidemiological trigger during those moments of demographic instability, provides an important structural backstop for her observations. As Wald puts it, "The inextricability of disease and national belonging shapes the experiences of both; disease assumes a political significance, while national belonging becomes nothing less than a matter of health."[31] Nevertheless, the immunological reactions of Africans and black Philadelphians put pressure on eighteenth-century medical beliefs about the racial body and upended discussions about immunological communities.

* * *

Having dislocated St. Domingue in the Atlantic world to understand the relation between immunology and citizenship in the Age of Revolution, I would now turn back to yellow fever as a way of relocating the disease as a site for testing the limits of national identity in the Age of Epidemic. Unlike Europeans, whose immunity and susceptibility were split along an East-West hemispheric axis, immunity for Africans during the pandemic was assumed to be an essential racial trait. British physician Robert Jackson noted that "it has never been observed that a negro, immediately from the coast of Africa, has been attacked with this disease; neither have Creoles, who have lived constantly in their native country, ever been known to suffer from it."[32] Jackson's observations are not surprising, given that yellow fever was endemic to West Africa and that the vast majority of slaves arriving in the West Indies would have acquired immunities to the disease at some point in their lives. Due in part to observations such as these from his network of correspondents, Rush had been convinced that there is "something very singular . . . in the constitution of the

Negroes which renders them not liable to this fever," and he published this belief in the *American Daily Advertiser* as a "hint to the black people, that a noble opportunity is now put into their hands, of manifesting their gratitude to the inhabitants of that city which first planned their emancipation from slavery, and who have since afforded them so much protection and support, as to place them, in point of civil and religious privileges, upon a footing with themselves."[33] While he does not print a similar request of St. Domingue refugees, Rush's words are rife with the sentiments of Republican virtue, balancing immunological considerations alongside nobility, liberty, and civility. Indeed, the vision of community that he offers is one in which white citizens have already extended the hand of emancipation and equality to black people, who are now asked to return the favor with an act of public good—remaining in the city to care for their fellow Philadelphians—that justifies their citizenship in that community. But his patronizing tone reinforces the Africans' immunological difference in a way that alienates them from the community even as he invites them to demonstrate that they deserve to be part of it by repaying the good treatment they received at the hands of Philadelphians.

On the other hand, in his *Short Account of the Malignant Fever, Lately Prevalent in Philadelphia*, Matthew Carey built a great notoriety in the wake of the pandemic with his inflammatory remarks concerning black Philadelphians, a number of whom—"the vilest of the blacks," he called them—he accused of using their immunity to extort white Philadelphians.[34] Carey attacked the black nurses for failing to live up to Republican virtues of self-sacrifice, and in much the same way that Rush's request revealed a racial fault-line between immunity and citizenship, Carey pushed this fault line farther to specifically exclude black Philadelphians from the national community. It was this fact in particular that provoked Absalom Jones and Richard Allen to defend the actions of their community, and to reintegrate the narrative of African nurses back into a discourse of virtuous self-sacrifice.[35] Indeed, Jones's and Allen's response is keyed specifically to detailing the bonds of virtue that establish the shared citizenship of black and white Philadelphians, as well as to underscore their immunological bond, as evidenced by the number of black nurses who died from the fever in the performance of those duties.[36] It is this shared immunological susceptibility to yellow fever that forms the common communal bond between black and white Philadelphians for Jones and Allen.

Rush was, of course, disastrously wrong, and black Philadelphians were not inherently immune to yellow fever. Indeed, despite the racial difference, herd immunity would consider both white and black populations of Philadelphia to be part of the same immunological cohort. As Rush reports, many of the black nurses "took the disease, in common with the white people, and many of them died with it."[37] It is perhaps difficult to overstate just how counterintuitive this was to Atlantic-world physicians. Looking back on the last decade of the eighteenth century, William Pym would write that yellow fever was "a disease of rather a whimsical character" that raised a number of questions about "why it should attack whites in preference to blacks?—Why it should prefer a robust European to a languid Creole? And why it should respect the sable race of the West Indies, yet attack the negroes of North America?"[38] Why indeed? The fact is that black Philadelphians were no more similar to the Africans in St. Domingue than white Philadelphians were to West Indian Creoles. Immunities and susceptibilities to yellow fever mirrored one another on geographic, rather than racial lines, and the epidemiological kinships of Africans in St. Domingue were entirely different from Philadelphia's.

* * *

As I outlined earlier, French and British troops sent to St. Domingue during the 1790s unwittingly helped to spread the yellow fever pandemic throughout the western rim of the Atlantic world. When Napoleon sent troops to St. Domingue under the command of his brother-in-law General Leclerc in January of 1802, he had perhaps not anticipated that these troops were almost universally susceptible to yellow fever and that their arrival would revive an outbreak that literally stopped his armies dead in their tracks. This time, however, herd immunity, which had heretofore largely been described on a geographic axis (Creole-European) came to be figured explicitly in racial terms. As Jackson had observed, the black insurgents in St. Domingue were largely immune to yellow fever. As the revolution progressed to its conclusion in 1804, this immunity came to figure prominently in militarily encounters. Leclerc, whose mission from Napoleon was to recapture St. Domingue and to reintroduce slavery to the island, found that as with the British, yellow fever became epidemic soon after the arrival of French expeditionary forces. By the spring of 1802, he would complain to Bonaparte that he was losing between 30 and 50 soldiers to the disease every day—up to 1,500 a month.[39] By the time he died of the fever in November of 1802, an estimated 21,000 of 35,000 troops under his command had also perished from the disease—this in contrast to the 700 who died in combat.[40]

Out of this history emerged what we might call a third model for the Republic of Medicine—one perhaps not interested in the etiology and treatment of yellow fever, but one no less aware of its immunological dynamics, or of its military and nationalist implications. Soon after Toussaint Louverture was captured on May 2, 1802, French forces intercepted a letter of his that celebrated the return of the fever and its effects on the French army.[41] And in a story transcribed by C. L. R. James in his own rewriting of Caribbean identity, Jean-Jacques Dessalines, who would become the leader of a free Haitian Republic in January of 1804, harangued his troops as follows:

> Take courage, I tell you, take courage. The French will not be able to remain long in San Domingo. They will do well at first, but soon they will fall ill and die like flies. Listen! If Dessalines surrenders to them a hundred times he will deceive them a hundred times. I repeat, take courage, and you will see that when the French are few we shall harass them, and we shall beat them, we shall burn the harvests and return to the mountains. They will not be able to guard the country and they will have to leave. Then I shall make you independent. There will be no more whites among us.[42]

Scenes such as these have helped to create a narrative of the Haitian Revolution as a victory of black immunity over superior military power. While the mortality rates for French and British soldiers certainly underscore the fact that yellow fever played an important role in the outcome of the revolution, such narratives tend to minimize the agency of Africans and black Creoles in achieving their victory through insurgent warfare. While Dessalines's words echo the by-then widely known epidemiological patterns of yellow fever in the West Indies, it is equally significant that he highlights the military tactics and strategies that complement European yellow fever mortality. Dessalines's knowledge of yellow fever represents both him and his fighters as skilled, sophisticated agents in their revolutionary struggles, rather than as mere "brigands," or, as McLean would have it in his opening remarks on the fever, as an "enemy, inferior indeed in the art of war, but formidable from a frame of body which was adapted to the climate, and derived vigour and activity from that influence of the sun, by which foreign troops were enervated and exhausted."[43]

In counterpoint to such representations, Dessalines links immunity to yellow fever with his nation's independence, and in so doing, creates a model of black citizenship for the future Republic of Haiti. This is a republic that, if not built on the prevailing medical knowledge of the eighteenth century, is nevertheless grounded on an intimate understanding of the geographies of immunity in the colonial world. The boundaries of this Haitian Republic of Medicine become visible to modern scholars as we expand the scope and scale of our analysis, moving outward from individual epidemic events to account for the movements and migrations that shaped pandemics in the Atlantic world. Herd immunity is a powerful framework for explaining the epidemiological patterns of yellow fever in the late eighteenth and early nineteenth centuries, but I want to underscore that it is a twentieth-century analytical concept of which eighteenth-century physicians had no knowledge. On the other hand, understanding how herd immunity operates is critical for gaining insight into the way that yellow fever helped to redefine the political dimensions of community. I would therefore argue that although physicians did not understand the exact immunological dynamics at work during the pandemic, they were nevertheless keenly aware of the striking epidemiological patterns that herd immunity produced.

These patterns highlight the immunological fault lines that divided and reconstituted communal identity in St. Domingue and in Philadelphia, thus creating a strong paradigm for imagining the relation among immunity, ideology, and national identity. Ultimately, this bifurcating approach to herd immunity marks a site for interdisciplinary inquiry into the way that immunology regulates political spaces. In this model, national identity is not a function of linguistic or territorial kinship, but is constituted as a shared immunological response to the world. British and French troops arriving in St. Domingue between 1792 and 1804 and native Philadelphians in the late summer of 1793 were bound by their susceptibility to yellow fever despite their national differences. They were also bound by the narrative strategies that physicians and laymen alike employed to make sense of their susceptibility. Conversely, Creole, mixed-race, and African slaves who had lived in the West Indies for an extended period seemed immune to the disease, regardless of their national origins; whether they witnessed the pandemic in St. Domingue or Philadelphia, their immunity figured importantly in the histories of yellow fever that attempted to reestablish coherent narratives of national identity.

CHAPTER 8

The Occult Atlantic

Franklin, Mesmer, and the Haitian Roots of Modernity

KIERAN M. MURPHY

> Voodoo was the medium of the conspiracy
> —C. L. R. James, *The Black Jacobins*

In the 1820s, Balzac's go-to mesmerist, Doctor Chapelain,[1] published records from the Sociètè Magnétique du Cap-François that, I will argue, provide an overlooked yet critical perspective on one of the most important incidents leading to the Haitian Revolution. The records include a list of members of the society, descriptions of mesmeric treatments performed on the island, and a speech on Mesmer's doctrine of "animal magnetism" delivered in 1784 at various receptions. As we will see, this speech is an ardent statement of support of black self-emancipation and radical antislavery that should figure prominently in the history of human rights as a crucial event occurring between the 1781 publication of Condorcet's *Réflexions sur l'esclavage des nègres* and the 1788 creation of the Société des Amis des Noirs. Less than seven years before the Haitian Revolution (1791–1804), colonial authorities perceived Mesmer's doctrine and the spread of its "magnetic" practices among the slave population as a major source of civil unrest. In what follows I will show how those authorities proceeded to defeat the threat of mesmerism on scientific grounds, and how their rationale provides a critical case study for examining the complex interactions of colonialism, human rights, and modern science.

The French colony of St. Domingue stood as one of the leading scientific outposts of the New World when, in 1784, Mesmer's controversial hypnotic therapy known as "animal magnetism" made its official debut on the island.[2] Due to the alleged success of its cures, its practice quickly spread to all levels of colonial society. Colonial authorities considered animal magnetism a threat because it became a source of distraction and empowerment for slaves. The introduction of animal magnetism in St. Domingue also coincided with the arrival of a scientific report refuting Mesmer's theories and signed in Paris by a royal commission of luminaries headed by Benjamin Franklin. Franklin's report inspired the colony's leading scientists to form their own ad hoc scientific commission in order to purge mesmerism from the island. In its attempt to maintain control over the slave population, St. Domingue's scientists mimicked the Franklin commission and its occultation of hypnotic states rendered manifest by the mesmerized body.

As we will see, unwelcome similarities between animal magnetism and slave rituals also motivated the creation of the colonial antimesmerism commission. These similarities displayed an intimate link between master and slave cultures that undermined the sovereignty of colonial power and science. Significantly, these similarities—particularly those between magnetic somnambulism and Vodou possession—provide essential material for the Haitian revision of modernity undertaken by Colin (Joan) Dayan and Susan Buck-Morss because they open up a larger frame of reference that includes the genealogy of psychoanalysis and its contributions to trauma and mourning theory.

Saint-Méry's Conflation of Mesmerism and "Vaudoux"

The transgressive link between animal magnetism and slave rituals appears in the first detailed description of what we now refer to as "Haitian Vodou." A founding member of the colonial anti-mesmerism commission, Moreau de Saint-Méry, wrote this unprecedented account for his encyclopedic study of St. Domingue, which he published in exile during the Haitian Revolution. At the beginning of his wide-ranging study, Saint-Méry considers the subject of slave music and dance on the island, including what he calls the "Vaudoux dance."[3] Before this dance begins, the participants congregate around their

"King" and "Queen," and a box containing a snake (*une couleuvre*) that channels "Vaudoux"—"An all-powerful supernatural being on which depend all the events on earth" and "knowledge of the past, present and future." The devotees plead for the magical power of "Vaudoux" to help them solve their problems and fulfill their aspirations, as well as, Saint-Méry significantly notes, to give them the ability to control their master's mind. Then, the queen, possessed by the snake's spirit, enters into a trance and becomes the clairvoyant mouthpiece of "Vaudoux."[4] Once the queen responds to the solicitations and receives the tributes from her followers, the "Vaudoux dance" starts.

Saint-Méry refers to this scene as a "monstrous absurdity" and warns of the danger that such gatherings represent for the colony. In this passage, Saint-Méry inadvertently formulates a critique of his own position through the description of a slave ritual that clearly mirrors the structure of colonial power. For him, "Nothing is more dangerous in all its aspects than the cult of Vaudoux," especially due to the relationship established between the king, the queen, and their followers, which he describes as "on one hand a system of domination and, on the other, of blind submission." Saint-Méry's perception of Vaudoux as dangerous arises from his own complacent role in perpetuating the terror of slavery that made plantations in St. Domingue such a profitable undertaking for the Bourbon family. Saint-Méry's biased description of Vaudoux is, then, the site of a paranoid projection that expresses the power of fascination at work in domination and blind submission that keeps the vastly outnumbered king, queen, or master in control.

Saint-Méry's portrayal of the Vaudoux queen's possession inadvertently manifests another undesirable link between master and slave cultures, which becomes apparent as he comments on the contagious aspects of the Vaudoux dance: "What is very true of Vaudoux and at the same time very remarkable, is *the kind of magnetism*, which brings the members to dance right to the edge of consciousness. The prevention of spying is very rigorous. Whites caught ferreting out the secret of the sect and tapped by a member who has spotted them have sometimes themselves started dancing and have consented to pay the Vaudoux Queen to put an end to this punishment."[5] Saint-Méry conveys the irresistible contagious force exerted by the "Vaudoux dance" and the way it even dangerously attracts whites through its "magnetism." In addition to the reference to magnetism, the whole scene, with its descriptions of convulsive states and clairvoyant possession, recalls Mesmer's magnetic séances, which were wildly popular in Paris at the time. To better understand the importance of Saint-Méry's conflation of Vaudoux and animal magnetism,

I will now briefly examine Mesmer's polemical doctrine and its impact on colonial society in St. Domingue.

Magnetic Somnambulism and Transatlantic Mesmerism

Mesmer attributed illnesses to an obstruction in the circulation of the body's "magnetic fluid."[6] He believed that he could project his own "magnetic fluid" to help reestablish its harmonious flow, and in turn the patient's health. Such projection often provoked a "crisis" manifested by convulsions and swoons. The rapid success of animal magnetism brought it under the scrutiny of the medical establishment. For the most part, they saw animal magnetism as a threat to their own (often shaky) practices, and in turn forcefully tried to discredit animal magnetism with the publication of hostile reports. With the distance of history, Mesmer's "magnetic fluid" theory actually proved to be fruitful because it pointed to an imperceptible yet crucial influence at work in the healer-patient relationship. As the ancestor of hypnosis and suggestion, Mesmer's new therapeutic approach has also been recently acknowledged by historians as a major step toward modern psychotherapy and as an important precursor of psychoanalysis. Mesmer's loyal disciple, Armand-Marie-Jacques de Chastenet, Marquis de Puységur (1751–1825), is, in fact, now receiving credit for initiating what are now commonly called "talking cures."[7]

In May 1784, Puységur discovered that, with the help of "magnetic passes," some of his patients would fall into a state similar to sleep, but would retain their ability to interact with the magnetizer. In these first cases of artificially induced "magnetic" somnambulism, Puységur observed that his patients were developing remarkable gifts. Under the influence of the magnetizer, their oral communication skills improved; they started to diagnose their own cases, prescribe treatments, and predict their outcome. After coming back to their wits, they did not remember what happened during the somnambulic state. Puységur's claim that under magnetic sleep his patients turned into the mouthpiece of another self arguably became the first credible medical record of an entity that would later be labeled as the unconscious.[8]

The similarities between Puységur's account of magnetic somnambulism and Saint-Méry's description of the Vaudoux queen's possession are striking. In the same encyclopedic book that contains the description of the "Vaudoux dance," Saint-Méry also chronicled the official arrival of mesmerism in St. Domingue. In June 1784, a month after the discovery of magnetic somnambulism, Puységur's brother, Count Anne Chastenet de Puységur, at the head of a cartographical mission, brought with him the knowledge and the procedure of the hypnotic cure to the island.[9] His fourteen-month stay in St. Domingue helped spread the enthusiasm for animal magnetism to all levels of colonial society.

A 1785 letter from plantation owner Jean Trembley sums up Anne Chastenet's impact in the colony: "Marvelous cures that could hardly be attributed to any play of the imagination have been reported. A cripple brought from the plain to Cap-François on a litter walked freely afterward. A female slave paralyzed for fourteen years was entirely cured in a short time.... A plantation owner on this plain made a big profit in magnetizing a consignment of cast-off slaves he bought at a low price.... The rage for magnetism has taken hold of everyone here."[10] In addition to the profits masters gained, the slaves appear to have enjoyed the curative virtue of animal magnetism and incorporated some of its techniques in their rituals. A scandal eventually broke out in the parish of Marmelade, where, Saint-Méry reports, the European ideas of animal magnetism had particularly flourished.[11] Colonial authorities caught a "mulatto" and his black assistant promoting their own kind of magnetic treatment and, to dissuade others, severely punished them.

Karol Weaver has reason to argue that Mesmer was perhaps not too far off the mark when, later in his life, he boasted "that Haiti owed its independence to him." Colonial authorities quickly perceived the introduction of mesmerism as undermining their control over the slaves. For Weaver, mesmerism became a source of civil disobedience: "The practice of mesmerism by slaves was a political act of revolution. In order to participate in magnetist treatments, slaves violated numerous restrictions—they ran away, they assembled, they traveled without permission, they practiced an illegal form of medicine, and they carried weapons. All these undertakings paid off in the slave rebellion of 1791."[12] Slave mesmerism became a source of civil disobedience because, as with the "Vaudoux dance," it empowered and sidetracked its followers. To discredit animal magnetism, colonial authorities organized an ad hoc scientific commission that drew its inspiration from Benjamin Franklin's royal commission.

Robert Darnton has shown how the Franklin commission had also served political ends in France. During the years preceding the storming of the Bastille, the democratic tone of Mesmer's theory of a pervasive "magnetic fluid" accessible by all had become an important source of inspiration for French revolutionaries and pamphleteers who had been marginalized by the Enlightenment establishment and who saw in the backlash against mesmerism a despotic government working through its official institutions.[13] During the 1820s in France, records from the Société Magnétique du Cap-François established by Anne Chastenet upon his arrival in St. Domingue, surfaced in the leading journal dedicated to defending the cause of animal magnetism.[14] According to the editor, these documents came from Doctor Chapelain, one of the leading authorities of animal magnetism at the time. The documents include a list of members of the society, descriptions of magnetic treatments performed on the island, and an anonymous speech on Mesmer's doctrine delivered in 1784 at various "receptions." Although imbued with paternalist rhetoric, this forgotten speech should have a prominent place in the history of human rights due to its ardent support of black self-emancipation and radical anti-slavery—support that far surpasses the democratic aspirations of the Parisian pamphlets examined by Darnton. I quote at length this remarkable document:

> Humanity! How has the word echoed out in the new world? Ghosts of Americans out of the past, rise up from your native land! Miserable Africans, rise up from your chains! And you, white man, their oppressor, arrogant European . . . , listen to me: America displays the most terrifying contrast! In the north, the savage is free as the wind; in the south, the debased man is sold and treated like lowly cattle; Europe tears Africa's children away to have them water the soil of America with their sweat, that soil which is still stained with the blood of the first inhabitants.
>
> We detest these atrocities. . . . They are not the crime of the individuals governed by that policy. Although the disciples of Mesmer cannot emulate the children of Penn in freeing their brethren; *although that great act of justice* is forbidden to us, it is at least in our power, gentlemen, to allay the plight of our Negroes. America's power elite can still be benefactors to humanity. In overseeing our labor gangs let us retrace the patriarchal government of the first men; let the word *subject*, which, by the knots of mutual kindness, links the subordinate to the superior, replace the word *slave*. . . . The prosperity of the colonies and the multiplication of blacks that has been the necessary byproduct, each day changes the relationship between the power conferred on those applying the shackles and the weakness conferred on those receiving them.
>
> O my fellow citizens! Let us be fair, and let us prepare ourselves for the calamities that threaten us. Let us organize our estates on

the immutable basis of justice and humanity; they shall become legitimate, they shall become unshakeable; let us treat our Negroes with kindness, they shall cease to be our enemies, and they shall become both the foundation and the motor of our prosperity.
. . .

The levers of policy are not at all in our hands; it may well be however that certain members of the [Magnetic] Society do have influence with the heads of the public administration, the bureaus of the legislation. Let us avail ourselves of that influence, gentlemen, for the welfare of humanity; that welfare can never oppose that of the State. . . .

Let us formally commit ourselves, in the future and under all circumstances, to do all that we possibly can to bring the status of the Negro slaves to that of men governed by the normal laws of the State. Whenever we are unable to go all the way in this regard, let us promote, with all our strength, the emancipation of individual slaves, and let us procure, by all means authorized by the laws, the inalienable rights to be exercised by each man and by each citizen for our brothers who live in oppression and wretchedness.[15]

Less than seven years before the 1791 slave insurrection, this piece of mesmerist propaganda begins by invoking the first victims of white oppression, the ghosts of the decimated indigenous population of the Americas, and hinges on a revolutionary call for justice against slavery in the name of a shared humanity in order to prevent the looming catastrophe. This anonymous text shows clearly and to an unprecedented extent how some of Mesmer's missionaries operated against colonial power. Authorities quickly perceived the subversive influence of mesmerism in St. Domingue and planned to defeat it on scientific ground by mimicking the Franklin commission's refutation of Mesmer's theories.

Occulting Facts: The Scientific Refutation of the "Magnetic Fluid"

The Franklin commission, which included luminaries such as Antoine-Laurent Lavoisier and Jean-Sylvain Bailly, published a report that proved experimentally that Mesmer's "magnetic fluid" did not exist and that the magnetizer's influence on patients could be simply attributed to the latter's "imagination."[16] Whereas the report has been praised as a pioneering piece of modern scientific writing, it also shows its limits.[17] The Franklin commission can explain the strange states of convulsion, dissociation, and "sympathy" witnessed during the magnetic cure only in terms of the convalescent's "imagination" and its stimulation by dramatic staging (music, "le baquet"),[18] the magnetizer's touch ("magnetic pass"), and the imitation of other patients. An Enlightenment euphemism for the nonrational and the illusionary, the term "imagination" reduces liminal states to unreal causes and, in turn, dismisses what Joseph Breuer and Sigmund Freud would bring to the fore a century later in their studies of hypnotized hysterics, namely, the unconscious and the desiring body. In relegating mesmerism to mere occultism by rejecting the "magnetic fluid," the Franklin commission report also negated a foreign body, an occult other that it nevertheless rendered manifest through its multiple descriptions of the magnetized and desiring body, and through its perception of it as a danger to reason and public order.

The fact that Franklin, then the American ambassador to France, presided over the official refutation of Mesmer's "magnetic fluid" also helps to explain why mesmerism did not take hold in the United Sates until the 1830s. Franklin had actually met Mesmer a few years before the experiments he conducted in his home in Passy to refute animal magnetism. In 1779, Mesmer had made an early attempt to export animal magnetism to North America when he invited Franklin to discuss the glass harmonica. The influential American leader had contributed to perfecting the instrument that Mesmer played as background music during his magnetic treatment. But Franklin appears to have been more interested in listening to Mesmer's skillful performance than to his doctrine.[19] In 1784, the same year Anne Chastenet arrived in St. Domingue, another of Mesmer's most enthusiastic students, the Marquis de Lafayette, French hero of the American Revolution, crossed the Atlantic and presented the discovery of animal magnetism to Philadelphia's American Philosophical Society and personally to George Washington.[20] Thomas Jefferson, who was about to succeed Franklin as the American representative to France, had witnessed the Parisian craze for animal magnetism and sided with the staunch rationalism of Mesmer's opponents. It was he who most likely prevented the spread of mesmerism at home by sending the commission's report to influential friends in order to undermine Lafayette's proselytizing mission.[21]

As it did with Lafayette, the report of the Franklin commission also followed Anne Chastenet to St. Domingue, where it turned up during the fall of 1784.[22] For colonial authorities, the report became instrumental for protection against the emancipatory rhetoric declaimed by mesmerists and the disruptive appropriation of their hypnotic techniques by slaves. It was at this point, in 1785, that some of the leading scientific figures of St. Domingue formed the Cercle des Philadelphes to pay homage to Franklin, the president and founder of Philadelphia's American Philosophical Society and the internationally recognized bearer of the Enlightenment spirit. By 1787, the Cercle des Philadelphes, which counted Franklin as an honorary member, received official recognition and support from the crown, and was renamed the Société Royale des Sciences et des Arts du Cap François.

Saint-Méry was one of the founding members of the Cercle des Philadelphes. He deplored the introduction of animal magnetism in St. Domingue and, like the Franklin commission, rebuffed Mesmer's new cure as an "illusion" and "superstitious doctrine."[23] His aversion to slave rituals and mesmerism prompted him to conflate the two in his description of the "Vaudoux dance," where he can convey the phenomena of possession and of the white master's contagious attraction only in terms reminiscent of a séance of animal magnetism. In other words, the "monstrous absurdity" of slave rituals described in terms of the "superstitious doctrine" of mesmerism accounts for the presence of a foreign body that syncopates Saint-Méry's text and that, as in Franklin's report, he cannot acknowledge, even though he perceives it as a threat to colonial power and science.

Beyond their Caribbean and European specificities, Vodou and mesmerism established a transgressive transatlantic link between master and slave cultures. What slips out from Saint-Méry's paranoid description of slave rituals is an overlapping space between the "Vaudoux dance" and animal magnetism, and between Vodou possession and magnetic somnambulism.[24] Although they do not analyze Saint-Méry's passage on the "Vaudoux dance" and mention the 1784 speech quoted above, Gabriel Debien, who first chronicled mesmerism in St. Domingue in the 1960s, and François Regourd, who did so in 2008, argue that there is no clear evidence that Vodou incorporated any aspect of mesmerism. References in colonial records to "black mesmerism seem to have been nothing but a smokescreen set between the rationality of French judges, and the frightening manifestation of black Vodou nocturnal ceremonies," according to Regourd. "In that context, the use of words designating at that time a familiar and reassuring form of charlatanism was doubtless a way to publicly disqualify any kind of black occult knowledge and also gave words to judges to describe and condemn such hypnotic effects."[25] I would argue, however, that the debate concerning whether "mesmeric elements" were included in Vodou ceremonies appears to be a false one since the occult nature of the ceremonies' "hypnotic effects" made them highly compatible with mesmeric states while rendering the search for tangible proof very difficult.

Around the same time that Saint-Méry's antimesmerism commission struggled to protect the sovereignty of colonial power in St. Domingue, one of Mesmer's most enthusiastic students and future distinguished member of the Société des Amis des Noirs, the Marquis de Lafayette, promoted the achievements of mesmerism in North America. In a letter from Hartford dated October 12, 1784, Lafayette, evoking his visit to the sect of Shakers and to a Native American dance, candidly refers to a transatlantic cultural link made apparent by mesmerism: "I should talk to you of a new sect of Shakers who make contortions and miracles; all this is connected with the great principles of magnetism. I should tell you that I can make a book . . . having the title *Essay on the Savage Dances* and especially on the new dance brought here from the woods of the occident . . . applied to the principles of Doctor Mesmer."[26]

For Lafayette, consonant liminal states such as trance, possession, and magnetic somnambulism brought into contact transatlantic cultures that, for Saint-Méry, had to remain separate in order to protect the sovereignty of colonial and scientific authority. The Franklin scientific commission and its St. Domingue offshoot reinforced such a cultural split by occulting the mesmerized and possessed bodies.

Toward a Vodou Epistemology

Colin Dayan and Susan Buck-Morss have perceived the important political repercussions of such scientific shortcomings and have attempted to counteract their detrimental impact with the elaboration of a historical epistemology derived from Haiti's pioneering experience of modernity and its articulation in Vodou rituals.[27] In what follows, I examine some of the defining features of their groundbreaking mobilization of Haitian Vodou to rethink modernity and argue that their accounts might productively be amplified further by attending to ambiguous phenomena that Vodou possession makes apparent, specifically those associated with amnesia, melancholia, and healing. The similarities between Vodou possession and magnetic somnambulism that presented a threat to colonial and scientific authority in St. Domingue contribute essential material to the exploration of these ambiguous phenomena by opening a larger frame of reference that includes the genealogy of psychoanalysis and its contributions to trauma and mourning theory. Laurence Rickels has traced this genealogy back to a famous nineteenth-century mesmeric cure and emphasized how, much like Vodou possession, its healing power blurred the line between mourning and melancholia, the nonpathological and the pathological, truth and delusion.

In *Haiti, History, and the Gods*, Dayan reconstructs a rich and nuanced alternative history of modernity from the point of view of the slaves' brutal experience of "white enlightenment."[28] The traumatic experience of slavery has profoundly shaped Haiti's post-independence history. For instance, Haiti's color-coded society and its legacy of internal conflicts spring from the development of an elaborate and hierarchical taxonomy of colonial subjects based on skin, and were instigated by the Enlightenment's obsession with classification and the supposed natural order of things. From white to black, each descending gradation received a name—some like "Marabou" and "Griffe" closely tied with sorcery and the monstrous—that contributed to turning people into exploitable things.

Relations of proximity and promiscuity between master and slave in St. Domingue brought Africa, Europe, and the Americas into intimate contact and rendered boundaries between master and slave ambiguous, creating in turn, what Dayan calls a "reversible space," a kind of subversive space that eluded the scientific categories structuring Enlightenment classification. As seen above with the transgressive intermingling of mesmerism and Vodou in St. Domingue, the existence of reversible spaces in the Atlantic world has important political and epistemological implications. To tap into the critical energy of reversible spaces, Dayan's work displaces Enlightenment binary thinking and its logic of opposition and mastery with a more ambiguous historical epistemology issued from the slaves and their descendants, and embodied in Vodou syncretism and possession. Dayan writes the "vodou history" of colonialism in St. Domingue in order to demolish "such straightjacket pairs as victim and victimizer, colonized and colonizer, master and slave" and unearth the critical agency of those who had been silenced by history.[29]

Dayan's notion of "vodou history" hinges on syncretism and spirit possession. Vodou syncretism manifests the free association of "seemingly irreconcilable elements, taking in materials from the dominant culture even as it resists or coexists with it." The interpenetration and coexistence of African,

European, and Native American elements in Haitian divinities illustrate this principle of syncretism. Possession is the central event of the Vodou ceremony and occurs in a state of trance when the body of a practitioner is taken over by a spirit called a *lwa*. Each *lwa* of the Vodou pantheon has its own personality that becomes the practitioner's in the state of possession. Dayan considers the manifestation of Vodou divinities via possession a "ritual of knowing" and "collective physical remembrance" that reconnects slave descendants to their "unwritten history." As Dayan's study demonstrates, Vodou possession, along with Haitian folklore, provides legitimate and rich materials that give the silenced slaves of colonial Haiti a voice. Such unwritten materials also expose the limitation of Enlightenment science because the inherent ambiguity of memory and orality will always resist mastery.[30]

Beyond the retrieval of otherwise lost slave experiences, Dayan argues that "vodou history" dissolves the rigid opposition between master and slave. Her argument depends on a distinction between the phantasm of the "zombi" and the phenomenon of possession. In Haiti, zombies are bodies of victims who are collectively believed to have been brought back from the dead and turned into soulless slaves by sorcerers. As Dayan puts it, "The zombi tells the story of colonization." It reincarnates the structure of terror and control that Haitians' ancestors had successfully fought off during the revolution. From the proto-industrial plantations of Haiti to a global figure popularized by mass media during the American occupation of Haiti and the Great Depression, the zombie also tells the story of the monstrous side of modernity, particularly the commodification of the human workforce. Vodou possession, on the other hand, is "*not* another form of slavery."[31] She stresses that Vodou possession is in fact described by practitioners as a relation between rider and horse. Possession as spirit horse riding implies a more reciprocal relationship between the divine and the human.[32] The relation between the host who temporarily surrenders his or her body and the spirit who harnesses it expresses a form of reciprocity that is not based on ownership and domination but on "the enhancement of ambiguity" between dichotomies such as the sacred and the profane, memory and history, self and other, master and slave.[33]

Although she associates most of the critical potency of her revision of modernity and colonial history with her compelling account of Vodou possession, Dayan does not examine the function of the important event that takes place after the trance when the spirit departs: amnesia. The actions and words produced under the influence of a *lwa* will not be remembered by the host who welcomed it.³⁴ Amnesia is significant for two main reasons. First, it helps establish a communal space for freedom of speech by absolving the host from the transgressive actions that might have happened during the trance. Amnesia thus creates a state of exception where disenfranchised members of the community can have a voice.³⁵ Ordinary Haitians tend to mistrust the official legal system and rely on "alternative judicial orders" to solve local issues.³⁶ By undermining social norms and power relations, the unconscious host of a *lwa* provides at times such an alternative way to seek justice.

Amnesia is also significant in the way it blurs the line between the pathological and the nonpathological. This medical ambiguity is manifest in the reversal of the psychological and anthropological interpretation of Vodou possession from illness during most of the twentieth century to its recent rehabilitation as a healing practice.³⁷ To be under the sway of a foreign body while not being able to remember it is divine and serves a social purpose, but it can also express the symptomatic behavior of a melancholic fragmented self and community that have been profoundly marked by traumatic events. Vodou possession embodies both the symptom of a traumatic experience (amnesia, state of dissociation, haunting) and its treatment. The treatment occurs through the triangular exchange that takes place among the spirit, host, and congregation and through the cathartic experience of the trance.³⁸

The host's memory of what happened during the trance is not lost, but entrusted to the congregation, which provides a safety net for the profound crisis entailed by the displacement of the self by a foreign body. The congregation's bearing witness to the host's memory helps prevent amnesia from turning pathological. The amnesia that follows a traumatic experience blocks access to the event responsible for one's symptomatic behavior and, in turn, hinders an important step in the healing process. Such pathological amnesia appears to be at work in the cyclical alternation between oppression and emancipation that has marked Haitian history. The succession of brutal regimes and uprisings that followed Haitian independence manifests a melancholic compulsion to repeat, which, during the Duvalier era, Haitian authors such as Franketienne and René Depestre interpreted, through the trope of collective zombification, as the periodical return of a colonial past that still haunts Haitians.³⁹ As an influential religious network, Vodou often played an integral part in fomenting the cycles of both oppression and emancipation.⁴⁰ But, alongside the national melancholic history, a "vodou history" has thrived as a ritual of knowing and healing through spirit possession. Recognizing the therapeutic necessity of remembrance as well as temporary amnesia, "Vodou history" emphasizes the ethical imperative of bearing witness to the other's memory.

In *Hegel, Haiti, and Universal History*, Susan Buck-Morss builds upon Dayan's work when she invokes a Vodou inspired "syncretic epistemology" in her revision of the Enlightenment project of "universal history," particularly in its Eurocentric, teleological, and Hegelian form. To Dayan's account of composite gods linking transatlantic spiritualties in St. Domingue, Buck-Morss adds freemasonry as another significant example of syncretism. Unlike mesmerism, the influence of freemasonry on slave rituals is more apparent because it left visual evidence. Slaves adopted and adapted freemason practices and symbolism, particularly some of its emblems that were integrated in ceremonial Vodou cosmograms (*vèvè*).[41] Despite fundamental differences, such correspondences hint at "porous" boundaries between Vodou and freemasonry; these could be due to their shared role as secret transcultural societies, as well as to similarities in their respective syncretic philosophies.

Buck-Morss chooses to rethink modernity and "universal history" in terms of an epistemology she gleans from Vodou rituals because these rituals registered the catastrophes of modern slavery and the politically unprecedented events of the Haitian Revolution—specifically, the radical antislavery principle first articulated in Toussaint Louverture's 1801 constitution.[42] Vodou became the site where, beyond cultural and linguistic differences, a very diverse slave population could achieve a sense of recognition through its shared traumatic experiences of dispossession, loss, and meaninglessness. The melancholic compulsion to repeat the cycle of oppression and emancipation that characterizes Haiti's post-independence history, as explored through the trope of the zombie by Franketienne and Depestre, is a symptom of these past traumatic experiences. Buck-Morss notes that a melancholic compulsion to repeat also transpires in Vodou possession since remote divinities must constantly be brought back through the host's body, and the *vèvè* must continuously be redrawn at the beginning of each ceremony. Vodou emerged from catastrophes and diverse cultural ruins, giving rise to what Buck-Morss calls, building upon Walter Benjamin, an "allegorical mode of seeing"—that is, a mode of interpretation that registers the transience of life and meaning, repeatedly constructing it anew through syncretic connections or "porous" boundaries that resist mastery and totalization.[43]

Buck-Morss puts into practice her revised version of "universal history" as a Vodou "allegorical mode of seeing" when she turns her attention to the slave ceremony of Bois Caïman, which supposedly triggered the insurrection leading to Haitian Independence. This key event survives only in ruins, in disparate and fragmentary secondhand accounts that could never bring certainty to what happened during this fateful and perhaps imagined night of August 1791, and to the actual role it played in fomenting the revolution. The uncertainty informing what has been referred to as the founding moment or myth of the Haitian Revolution gave way to various jubilant and biased interpretations that fail to account for the extreme violence and the wars within the war that actually made up this historical event, and in turn are unable to think beyond the reductive opposition between "victim and aggressor." Through an exercise of inclusive "empathic imagination,"[44] whereby she makes a compelling yet speculative case for an important Muslim influence on the slave ceremony of Bois Caïman, Buck-Morss hopes to establish a politically subversive dialogue between the past and the present, which would undermine current Western views downplaying the role played by the Arab world in the emergence of modernity.

Unlike Dayan, who models her historical inquiry on and finds key materials in Vodou possession, Buck-Morss is more interested in Vodou as a syncretic philosophy based on an "allegorical mode of seeing," as well as being interrelated with the notion of modernity due to their common roots in the politically unprecedented events that marked the Haitian Revolution. However, by leaving out the centrality of the phenomenon of possession in Vodou ceremonies from her Haitian revision of "universal history," Buck-Morss ends her essay on a strange note: "The politics of scholarship that I am suggesting is neutrality, but not of the nonpartisan, 'truth lies in the middle' sort; rather, it is a *radical* neutrality that insists on the porosity of space between enemy sides."[45] The designation "*radical* neutrality" implies an "empathic imagination" attuned to all ambiguities but its own. In other words, it does not emphasize the haunting influences at work in the reversible space and time explored by Dayan, Franketienne, and Depestre, which, between possession and dispossession, can turn one into the medium of a spirit and of unwritten and silenced history, or into a zombie.

By providing a striking reversible space where the silenced dialogue between black and white spirits slips out, including Franklin's and Mesmer's, Saint-Méry's examination of a "Vaudoux dance" that took place not too long before the alleged ceremony of Bois Caïman contributes essential material to the Vodou revision of modernity by including the genealogy of psychoanalysis and its contributions to trauma and mourning theory to the discussion.

This inclusion is important because it adds a rich and nuanced conception of the modern self to the philosophical abstraction offered by "*radical* neutrality." Vodou possession, mesmerism, and psychoanalysis teach that the modern self can never wholly personify "*radical* neutrality" because it is haunted by remote divinities and unmourned losses. Possession manifests melancholic amnesia as well as, as Dayan's historical inquiry demonstrates, a legitimate medium to access unwritten history and heal. A Haitian revision of modernity must then retain the perplexing relation between unmourned losses and remembrance embodied in Vodou possession.

I would argue that this perplexing relation between loss and remembrance might be illuminated by using mesmerism as a relay between Vodou and the interfacing of Benjaminian allegory with Freudian "endopsychic perception," or what Laurence Rickels calls "endopsychic allegory." Rickels defines Freud's conception of endopsychic perception as "the inside-out view of the inner workings of the psyche projected outward as the delusional representation or mass mediatization of our funereal identifications."[46] As in Benjaminian allegory, Vodou myths and religious rituals mirror the psyche as a stricken world structured around the recent traumatic experience of catastrophe, loss, and meaninglessness. According to Dayan, they also mediate in part the "colonial myth" through delusional representations such as evil spirits that reflect the perverse logic and paranoid fantasies of the master.[47] Paranoid projections manifest psychotic symptoms as well as an engagement to negotiate with catastrophe that can lead to partial healing and that "offers another way to get around losses that's not the one-way consumer choice between mourning and melancholia."[48] To substantiate this latter claim, Rickels looks back at the genealogy of talking cures and the successful treatment of a psychotic patient reported by Justinus Kerner and enabled by the clairvoyant visions of his magnetic somnambulist.[49] Elaborating on Herbert Silberer's interpretation of this case, Rickels underscores that the healing process operated along the reversibility of the endopsychic structure of the somnambulist's prescriptive visions and the patient's delusions. Later, Freud would perceive the unsettling similarity between his own therapeutic science and the paranoid system developed by Daniel Paul Schreber, and thus address "Schreber's endopsychic perception at the undecidable intersection between the possible truth of Schreber's delusions and the possible delusional dimension of his own theories."[50]

Reciprocally, a Vodou revision of modernity might learn from Freud's moment of self-reflexive clarity and recognize "the undecidable intersection" between the truth of Vodou's delusions and the possible delusional dimension of its theories. The prerevolutionary intermingling of Vodou and mesmerism in St. Domingue provided the stage for a transatlantic confrontation between Franklin and Mesmer that, for its part, brought out the delusional dimension of Enlightenment science. Moreover, in addition to provoking civil disobedience, the reversibility of Vodou possession and magnetic somnambulism points to the compatibility of their endopsychic structures and, as in the magnetic treatment reported by Kerner, to the possible healing effect of their exchange. This reversibility also contributed to making master and slave cultures porous and, in turn, certainly contributed to breaking the spell of the "colonial myth" that was necessary to trigger the 1791 slave insurrection.

CHAPTER 9

In the Shadow of Haiti

The Negro Seamen Act, Counter-Revolutionary St. Domingue, and Black Emigration

EDLIE WONG

The Haitian Revolution emerged as a textual and historical flashpoint for a New World modernity that profoundly challenged the discursive frameworks surrounding race and slavery in the Americas.[1] For C. L. R. James, the antislavery radicalism of the Haitian Revolution was an unintended, yet powerful consequence of the brutal modernity of racial slavery in colonial St. Domingue.[2] Thirteen years of internecine warfare among enslaved blacks, *gens de couleur*, and French, English, and Spanish colonists and soldiers ended with the violent declaration of Haitian independence, which was marked by the massacre of the remaining white population on the island. Proslavery ideologues marshaled the violence of St. Domingue as a dire warning against slave emancipation and racial equality on U.S. soil. They exploited fears of "the lawless and simibarbarous [sic] population" of Haiti to justify growing states rights aggression over the preservation of slavery.[3] Even Anglo-American abolitionists who embraced the Haitian Revolution's egalitarian ideals were forced to contend with gruesome tales of the atrocities committed by the formerly enslaved. From the vantage of 1893, Frederick Douglass reflected that "Haiti and its inhabitants, under one aspect of another, have, for various reasons, been very much in the thoughts of the American people."[4] "While slavery existed amongst us, her example was a sharp thorn in our side and a source of alarm and terror," he continued. "She came into the sisterhood of nations through blood"

(*LH*, 206). The first among the New World nations to abolish racial slavery, Haiti was forced to wait another twenty-one years before France—the first among the Western nations—acknowledged its independence and sovereignty in exchange for a large indemnity that undermined Haiti's economic stability.

This essay examines the dynamic ways in which three different, yet at times overlapping discourses from various sites in the black Atlantic world contested the boundaries and routes of Haiti's revolutionary New World modernity. In the 1820s, the consolidation of a long-divided Haiti and the conquest of Spanish Santo Domingo (now the Dominican Republic) under the leadership of Haitian President Jean-Pierre Boyer reignited fears of slave revolt in the U.S. South. However, many black Americans welcomed these same events as a powerful portent of black political progress and possibility in the Atlantic. This essay begins by revisiting a controversial episode in American cultural history—the 1822 Denmark Vesey conspiracy and the black quarantine codes that emerged in its wake—to explore the changing significance of Haiti to the twofold expansion of a proslavery racial jurisprudence and the cultures of early black American resistance to it. Following upon Boyer's successful campaign in Spanish Santo Domingo, the public revelation of a secret slave conspiracy in Charleston, South Carolina, gave powerful form to the specter of a counter-revolutionary St. Domingue on U.S. soil. Southern slaveholders mobilized a racialized discourse of disease emergence and health security in their legal efforts to contain the "contagion" of slave revolution and black militancy associated with the idea of Haiti. These black codes constructed the South as vulnerable to the dangers of slave revolt (and hence different from the North) and jeopardized U.S. foreign trade relations with the other Atlantic nations.

The second half of the essay resituates these local events within a transnational geopolitical context, charting Boyer's efforts to recruit black American emigrants and reshape the counter-revolutionary St. Domingue of proslavery political discourse. Boyer repositioned Haiti within the histories of the modern West and emphasized the benefits of black American emigration to Haiti over competing schemes of African colonization to Liberia spearheaded by the American Colonization Society (ACS). In these emigrant recruitment campaigns, Boyer laid the discursive groundwork for countervailing representations of black militancy and revolution in early African American print culture. Black American editors and writers, including Samuel Cornish and John Brown Russwurm of the *Freedom's Journal*, Prince Saunders, and William Wells Brown celebrated this Haitian modernity as they readapted fears over U.S. slave revolts such as the Vesey conspiracy for the transatlantic antislavery campaign at mid-century. They transformed the counter-revolutionary St. Domingue that Anglo-American writers such as Leonora Sansay and Bryan Edwards depicted as gothic theaters of racial savagery into the free modern Haiti where the egalitarian promise of America might be fulfilled.

St. Domingue in Charleston

Early American writers and political commentators viewed the most wellknown of the averted slave conspiracies of Gabriel Prosser (1800) and Denmark Vesey (1822) and the failed slave revolt of Nat Turner (1831) as legacies of the racial violence that St. Domingue unleashed into the Atlantic world.[5] "Every community the other side of 'Dixon's Line' feels that it lives upon a volcano that is liable to burst out at any moment," wrote William Wells Brown of the events surrounding Vesey.[6] Comparisons to St. Domingue heightened the threat that these various plots posed to the slaveholding social order and legitimized the anti-black legal violence that followed swiftly in their wake. After discovery of Prosser's conspiracy, Virginia Governor James Monroe remarked that the "occurrences in St. Domingo for some years past . . . doubtless did excite some sensation among our Slaves."[7] Two decades later, the Vesey conspiracy was also linked to Haitian radicalism, and it remains the most controversial of the recorded slave plots.[8] For example, Michael P. Johnson's revisionist account challenges the narrative of black resistance generally associated with the Vesey conspiracy. By emphasizing the agency of the Charleston Court of Magistrates and Freeholders in the making of the plot, he argues that white officials colluded with convicted black men seeking commutation of death sentences to create testimonies affirming the plans for a nonexistent large-scale slave revolt.[9] For Johnson, Vesey and his conspirators were the victims of a court seeking to publicly vindicate its actions. This section does not attempt to resolve that historiographical controversy; rather, it revisits the pamphlet literature surrounding the Vesey conspiracy to examine how proslavery efforts to interdict the dangerous circulation of radicalizing black bodies and print culture contributed to the construction of a counter-revolutionary St. Domingue. A struggle over the interpretation of the American legacy of St. Domingue lay at the heart of the Vesey conspiracy and the racial jurisprudence that was passed in its wake.

In the hands of southern lawmakers, the anticolonial revolutionary black agency of St. Domingue became the discursive groundwork for the expansion of slave state power in the form of black quarantine codes referred to as the "Negro Seamen Acts." Following the suppression of the Vesey slave plot, South Carolina enacted the first of a series of laws "for the better regulation of Free Negroes and persons of color," targeting those engaged in the seafaring trade that soon extended to North Carolina, Georgia, Florida, Alabama, Louisiana, and Texas. These Seamen Acts barred the ingress of all free black sailors, regardless of their nationality, and interrupted long-standing commercial networks between the United States and European nations. South Carolina's Negro Seamen Act went so far as to direct that all black sailors be imprisoned until their vessels departed the state under penalty of being sold as "absolute" slaves if their confinement fees went unpaid. Protests condemned these Seamen Acts as infringements of the Constitution's Commerce Clause and international bilateral treaties. In response, southern lawmakers defended them as a legitimate exercise of police power, couching restrictions in the language of quarantine against the "Moral Contagion of Liberty," as Michael Schoeppner argues.[10]

These black codes served to proliferate (if not create) fears of Haitian antislavery radicalism as Carolinian planter politicians argued for health safety and the "law of self-preservation" against "foreign negroes" seeking "to disturb the peace and tranquility of the state."[11] The Negro Seamen Acts sought to prevent black foreigners from "infecting" domestic slave populations with ideas about freedom, and they popularized a racialized discourse of disease emergence and contagion associated with the specter of counter-revolutionary St. Domingue. Quarantine laws were not uncommon in the United States; however, the Negro Seamen Acts specifically racialized foreign bodies as carriers of revolutionary antislavery thought in the South. One legal advocate argued that "South Carolina has the right to interdict the entrance of such persons into her ports, whose organization of mind, habits and associations, render them peculiarly calculated to disturb the peace and tranquility of the state, in the same manner as she can prohibit those afflicted with infectious disease, to touch her shores."[12] These coastal slave states began prohibiting the circulation of free black sailors (as bearers of antislavery radicalism and "incendiary pamphlets") in their efforts to territorialize their racially based economies. They viewed black sailors as a menace to slaveholding localisms and used this racial threat to expand their sphere of power, fashioning a powerful discourse of self-preservation against the subversive hydra head of disorder long associated with Atlantic seafaring life. In this manner, changing representations of Haiti and the revolutionary antislavery upon which it was founded exerted a powerful shaping influence upon U.S. foreign policy and interstate relations in the 1820s.

Given the significance of black maritime labor to the capitalist world economy, the Negro Seamen Acts immediately affected U.S. trade relations with Britain and France as these nations began to reconsolidate their Atlantic empires in the wake of the Haitian Revolution and later West Indian emancipation. British merchant vessels plying the waters of these lucrative Atlantic economies were often crewed by those colonial subjects whom they once held as commodities. One writer noted that "thousands of coloured able bodied and expert seamen" regularly shipped along the North Atlantic currents that brought the coastal United States into contact with Europe and the Caribbean.[13] By 1865, black sailors, writes Jeffrey Bolster, had "established a visible presence in every North Atlantic seaport and plantation roadstead."[14] When harbormasters first began seizing black crewmen from their vessels in Charleston Harbor, representatives from Britain, France, and the U.S. North besieged the federal government with protests and petitions. Indeed, "Sundry masters of American vessels lying in the port of Charleston" delivered a joint petition to Congress, "in which they loudly complained of the existence and operation of a certain law of the state of South Carolina, affecting the persons of free colored mariners employed by them all—all such being liable to arrest and confinement in jail, *only because of their color*, though it might be that they were actual *citizens* of the United States."[15] Not only did this "obnoxious law" heighten sectional antagonisms, but it also placed further stress upon U.S. foreign relations with Great Britain as the British antislavery campaign for West Indian emancipation began to gather momentum.

Southern slave states insisted that the Negro Seamen Acts issued from their "right of self-preservation" and the doctrine of states' rights in studied disregard of both federal and international diplomatic appeals.[16] British Minister Stratford Canning angrily demanded that U.S. Secretary of State John Quincy Adams carry out the immediate suspension of these sanctions against British merchant vessels. Such appeals for federal intervention only encouraged the South Carolina governor to more energetically rally his slaveholding sister-states to resist any violation of their right of self-government. Coastal U.S. slave states acknowledged, in this negative fashion, the revolutionary possibilities of an Atlantic reshaped by the Haitian Revolution. The *Richmond*

Enquirer, for example, angrily justified South Carolina lawmakers: "Are they bound to receive *aliens*, who may carry the very seeds of insurrection into their bosom? Suppose our slaves returning from Hayti,—suppose suspected tools from that island should arrive in Charleston in a British vessel,—is there no right to guard against the danger?"[17] Proslavery lawmakers repeatedly invoked the racialized specter of counter-revolutionary St. Domingue to defend these regulations as necessary policing measures. In the beleaguered 1845 Congressional debate over the admission of Iowa and Florida, Mississippi Senator Robert Walker defended a similar prohibition in the Florida constitution as the only guarantee against the entry of "free colored seamen [who] were dangerous to a slaveholding community," including "runaway slaves from St. Domingo, who had been concerned in all the atrocities perpetrated there, and whose hands had been imbrued in the blood of their masters."[18] These proslavery ideologues portrayed averted slave plots such as the Vesey conspiracy as localized intensifications of St. Domingue and gave powerful form to the political discourses of southern jurisprudence at mid-century.

Planter politicians represented the Vesey conspiracy as a propitiously forestalled reenactment of the Haitian Revolution on U.S. soil. The *Official Report* of the Charleston Court of Freeholders and Magistrates related the events leading to the hanging of thirty-five men and exile of forty more "beyond the limits of the United States, not to return therein, under the penalty of death."[19] Because it is likely that the "testimonies" recorded in the *Official Report* were the results of either coercion or fabrication as Johnson argues, they illuminate the powerful ways in which the Haitian Revolution informed the southern imagination of this slave conspiracy.[20] For black witnesses and white court officials alike, the Vesey plot seemed unimaginable without reference to the example of St. Domingue, and the many sentences of exile reinforced the discourses of contagion and quarantine promulgated in the conspiracy's wake.[21] Historian James Sidbury argues that "it is almost as interesting to know that black Charlestonians imagining a conspiracy to overthrow slavery would include a letter to the president of Haiti as it is to know whether such a letter was sent."[22] In these various documents, Charleston officials sought to represent domestic unrest as the product of foreign, and specifically, Haitian, influence as they drew upon the "apocalyptical possibilities of slave emancipation" to garner local and state support for increasingly stringent black codes that included the controversial Negro Seamen Act.[23] In their efforts to consolidate southern slave state power, proslavery interests began expanding the historical and geographical scope of the Haitian Revolution.

The official pamphlet literature takes pains to construct Vesey as a product of New World slavery and a direct heir to the racial barbarism of counter-revolutionary St. Domingue. Vesey's biography takes the form of an extended footnote appended to the *Official Report*'s "Narrative of the Conspiracy and Intended Insurrection," which Magistrates Lionel Kennedy and Thomas Parker copied from *An Account of the Late Insurrection* published by the Corporation of Charleston. The fourteen-year-old Vesey was purchased from the Danish island of St. Thomas by Captain Joseph Vesey, who sold him, along with a cargo of 390 slaves, in St. Domingue's Le Cap-Français. A year later, Vesey was returned to the captain when the planter who purchased him found him subject to epileptic fits. The captain brought Vesey back to Charleston where he slaved for the next seventeen or eighteen years until Vesey purchased his freedom with prize money that he had drawn in a local lottery.[24] In linking Vesey's early life to St. Domingue, this biographical note emphasizes Vesey's foreign origins and imagines the Charleston plot as a means for the adult to reenact the "bloody events of San Domingo" that he had missed as an adolescent:

> As Denmark Vesey has occupied so large a place in the conspiracy, a brief notice of him will, perhaps, be not devoid of interest. The following anecdote will show how near he was to the chance of being distinguished in the bloody events of San Domingo. During the revolutionary war, Captain Vesey, now an old resident of this city, commanded a ship that traded between St. Thomas' [*sic*] and Cape François (San Domingo). He was engaged in supplying the French of that Island with Slaves. In the year 1781, he took on board at St. Thomas' 390 slaves and sailed for the Cape; on the passage, he and his officers were struck with the beauty, alertness and intelligence of a boy about 14 years of age, whom they made a pet of, by taking him into the cabin, changing his apparel, and calling him by way of distinction *Telemaque*, (which appellation has since, by gradual corruption, among the negroes, been changed to *Denmark*, or sometimes *Telmak*).[25]

In referencing colonial St. Domingue, the anecdote also locates Vesey squarely within another revolutionary moment: the *American* Revolution. Transported and sold during the War for American Independence in 1781, the young slave was given a name that unwittingly captured the difficult journeys of those caught up in the forced migrations of the Atlantic slave trade. "Denmark" was an Anglophone translation or "corruption" of the name of the eponymous hero of a popular didactic French tale *Telemaque* (1699). Writer François Fénelon based the story upon the *Odyssey*, and it charts the various trials of Telemachus in search of his father Ulysses. Other accounts further heightened the mythic St. Domingue dimensions of the conspiracy by emphasizing Vesey's longing to return to Haiti; one witness reported that the fifty-five-year-old Vesey yearned to "go back to his own country" once Charleston was plundered (*OR*, 121).

Kennedy and Parker's *Official Report* tells us much about the place of Haiti in narratives of slavery and freedom in the United States.[26] Nearly all accounts emphasize the powerful hold that St. Domingue exerted upon the imaginary of the black conspirators and white officials who recorded their testimony. According to the *Official Report*, "knowledge of an army from St. Domingo" prepared to "march towards this land" galvanized all those involved in the conspiracy, and they intended "to hoist sail for Saint Domingo" once they had overthrown Charleston (*OR*, 73, 68). Other witnesses testified that Vesey had opened a correspondence with Port-au-Prince, asking for military assistance. Vesey's co-conspirator, Peter Poyas, a slave, reportedly recruited insurgents with reassurances that "an army from St. Domingo" would join them (*OR*, 67, 73). Indeed, some men had joined the plot under the idea that Vesey had "a promise" from Boyer that Haiti "would receive and protect them" (*OR*, 83). According to these reports, Vesey had also secured the cooperation of a black sailor—a cook named William aboard an outbound vessel—to relay insurrectionary messages to Boyer (*OR*, 146). Yet another account recorded in the *Official Report* elevates this black sailor into the brother of a Haitian general (*OR*, 153). Such accounts lent additional force to the implementation of racialized maritime restrictions such as the South Carolina Negro Seamen Act.

The Haitian Revolution repeatedly appears throughout Kennedy and Parker's *Official Report* as a historic precursor to the Charleston conspiracy. For many of the alleged black conspirators, the Haitian revolutionaries had achieved what the American Revolution failed to do. Rolla Bennett, a slave, confessed that Vesey "said, we must unite together as the St. Domingo people did, never to betray one another," while the slave Jesse confessed that Vesey urged the men to "seek for our rights, and that we were fully able to conquer the whites, if we were only unanimous and courageous, as the St. Domingo people were" (*OR*, 67, 82). Other accounts recorded in the *Official Report* channeled the bloody horror of St. Domingue in their claim that no white men, women, or children were to be spared in Vesey's planned attacked upon the city for "*this was the plan they pursued in St. Domingo*" (*OR*, 82, emphasis in the original). While some witnesses seized upon Haiti as emblematic of the struggle for the liberty and equality called for in both the French Declaration of the Rights of Man and American Independence, other alleged conspirators channeled, with equally persuasive impact, the "indiscriminate massacre" and universal devastation brought about by the Haitian revolutionists.[27] Such conflicting yet complementary representations of St. Domingue express the deep ambivalence with which Americans, black and white, slave and free, negotiated the mixed legacy of the Haitian Revolution on U.S. soil.

These competing visions of Haiti shaped the structure and meaning of the Vesey conspiracy in early American print culture. References to the racial barbarism of counter-revolutionary St. Domingue suffuse the pages of the *Official Report*; however, the Charleston magistrates paid little attention to how the alleged black conspirators also drew powerful inspiration from Boyer's recent and successful reunification of postrevolutionary Haiti. Some accounts emphasized Boyer's thrilling capture of Spanish Santo Domingo over the more historically distant battles of the Haitian Revolution. Free black Saby Gaillard reportedly gave another informant "a piece of paper from his pocket; this paper was about the battle that Boyer had in St. Domingo . . . and said if he had as many men he would do the same too, as he could whip ten white men himself" (*OR*, 93).[28] Another witness reports that Vesey "was in the habit of reading to me all the passages in the newspapers that related to St. Domingo, and apparently every pamphlet he could lay his hands on, that had any connection with slavery. He one day brought me a speech which he told me had been delivered in Congress by a *Mr. King* [who] . . . declared . . . that slavery was a great disgrace to the country" (*OR*, 42, emphasis in the original). These testimonies cast racial slavery as incompatible with the tenets of a modern democratic nation. They, too, resonated with the image of a unified free Haiti that Boyer sought to present before the Western world. Black testimony from the earlier account published by the Corporation of Charleston further insisted that Vesey's plan included British reinforcements who would assist in their escape to Haiti: "The English were to come here and help them, . . . the Americans could do nothing against the English, and . . . the English would carry them off to St. Domingo."[29]

Proslavery U.S. lawmakers marshaled the specter of a counter-revolutionary St. Domingue—of irrational, dehumanizing black violence—to justify the various black codes passed in the wake of the Charleston plot. In this, they held onto the sensationalized "horrors of St. Domingo"—to borrow the subtitle of Sansay's novel, refusing to acknowledge the post-revolutionary black state of Haiti. In the public controversy over the Vesey trials, *Charleston Times* editor Edwin C. Holland utilized a discourse of white self-preservation against black barbarism in defense of the actions of the Charleston Court of Magistrates and Freeholders: "They were indubitably justified by every principle of the first and great law of nature—SELF-PRESERVATION."[30] Holland admonished that "every possible precaution should be adopted, that is calculated, in the remotest degree, to save us from a catastrophe which at all times threatens us, and of the horrors of which, the imagination can form no definite idea."[31] The "catastrophe" and "horror" to which Holland alludes is a second St. Domingue on U.S. soil. His *Refutation of the Calumnies Circulated Against the Southern Western States* described "our negroes as the '*Jacobins*' of the country, against whom we should always be upon our guard, and who . . . should be watched with an eye of steady and unremitted observation."[32]

The specter of the Haiti Revolution shaped such representations of a Manichean race struggle for life or death. Even an ardent critic of the Vesey court such as U.S. Supreme Court Associate Justice William Johnson, a Charleston native, was unable to elude these rhetorical snares when ruling in the case of Jamaica-born free black Henry Elkison—the first of many unsuccessful British lawsuits challenging the South Carolina Negro Seamen Act.[33] Johnson's ruling in *Ex parte Henry Elkison v. Francis G. Deliesseline* (1823) ultimately ceded authority to the slave state although he admitted, in what was tantamount to a declaration of the law's inherent law*less*ness, that Elkison's "right to his liberty" as a free black subject, yet without "remedy to obtain it" in a slave state, was an "obvious mockery" of law. Johnson sent a copy of his controversial opinion in *Elkison v. Deliesseline* to President Thomas Jefferson, expressing concerns over the mounting agitation in Charleston: "I fear nothing so much as the Effects of the persecuting Spirit that is abroad in this Place. Should it spread thro' the State & produce a systematic Policy founded on the ridiculous but prevalent Notion—that it is a struggle for Life or Death, [then] there are no Excesses that we may not look for—whatever be their Effect upon the Union. . . . They now pronounce the Negros the real Jacobins of this country."[34] The state's sovereign right to self-preservation became the cornerstone of the southern defense of its increasingly punitive racial jurisprudence, particularly of the Negro Seamen Acts. When the British Consul in Charleston again protested the seizure of black crewmen from British merchant vessels, the *Charleston Mercury* argued that this law "has its foundation in the right of every organized society to protect itself,—a right which no Government can be expected to surrender."[35] Periodic expansions to the Negro Seamen Act over the next thirty-four years (especially in 1835 and 1844) continued to respond to the changing geopolitics of the Atlantic world as black freedom in the Caribbean, following Haitian independence and West Indian emancipation threatened to drift westward to U.S. shores. Official accounts of the Vesey conspiracy illuminate how local fears over slave revolt were necessarily articulated with transnational anxieties over the dismantling of Europe's Atlantic slave economies.

For proslavery ideologues like South Carolina governor William Aiken, U.S. slaves could not envision freedom for themselves unless they were acted upon by a foreign—specifically, Haitian—influence. South Carolina's native slave population, Aiken insists, was vulnerable to the "seduction" of "foreign free persons of color."[36] The historic events of Vesey's plot had become, in his words, "the most irrefragable evidence" for the continued necessity of South Carolinian policy against these dangerous foreigners.[37] Aiken, of course, neglects to mention the presence of certain foreigners—"people of colour" and slaves of French colonial émigrés fleeing from St. Domingue—whom the city had welcomed into its midst during the turmoil of the Haitian Revolution.[38] Cities such as Charleston, Baltimore, Boston, New York, Norfolk, and Philadelphia received sizable shares of the roughly ten thousand refugee planters and their slaves fleeing St. Domingue.[39] Indeed, Creole French-speaking slaves supposedly numbered among the conspirators named in the Vesey conspiracy, and one witness threatened that a "French Band was armed throughout, and were ready" (*OR*, 112, 114). However, planter politicians, such as Aiken, sought explanations for domestic slave revolts or plots like the Vesey conspiracy that helped reinforce their worldviews.[40] Consequently, slave revolts on U.S. soil were phenomena unnatural to the South's paternalistic order as its politicians and lawmakers sought desperately to reinforce Michel Rolph Trouillot's oft-cited description of the Haitian Revolution as "unthinkable even as it happened."[41]

Aiken's "appeal to history," sought, among other things, to locate an insurrectionary desire for freedom in an external "foreign" population even though the depositions of suspects named in the conspiracy tended to "prove that this, like all other attempts of this kind, sprung from internal causes, for the existence of which the state alone was responsible."[42] Rather than acknowledge the local origins of slave unrest, southern legislators and officials represented "the rank and file of the conspiracy as the victims of *foreign seduction*" in the concerted effort to redirect the source of black antislavery radicalism on southern soil elsewhere beyond the boundaries of the U.S. nation-state.[43] Hence, the Vesey conspiracy serves as a focal point in a much longer history of Southern anxiety over the idea of Haiti and the Haitian Revolution, which imagined internal slave populations as vulnerable to the contagion of black radicalism. The following sections explore how a broad range of black and white American writers, activists, and commercial interests acted in concert with Haitian leaders such as Boyer to challenge these proslavery discourses of counter-revolutionary St. Domingue. They countered with representations of Haiti as a modern post-revolutionary nation fulfilling the ideals of Western enlightenment and coeval with the United States.

Atlantic Modernities

The specter of counter-revolutionary St. Domingue helped shape U.S. foreign relations in the 1820s as the federal government deferred to the individual states' sovereign authority to enforce their Negro Seamen Acts against the free black subjects of northern states as well as of foreign nations. According to Gordon S. Brown, the ensuing conflicts over U.S. foreign trade policies also aggravated disputes between northern mercantile interests and southern slaveholding interests over the diplomatic recognition of a sovereign Haiti under Boyer. These negotiations over the place of the modern black state in the Americas provided yet another discursive context for the Haitian dimensions of the Vesey conspiracy. In the immediate wake of the Haitian Revolution, Jean-Jacque Dessalines had initiated efforts to secure international treaties for the incorporation of the newly independent black nation into the Atlantic political economy. However, the various Atlantic nations at the time responded with the diplomatic isolation of Haiti in the effort to contain the political implications of a nation founded on slave revolution and governed by former slaves and free people of color.[44] By 1806, Spain, the Dutch and Danish Empires, and the United States had prohibited trade with Haiti. Shortly after assuming leadership of a reunified Haiti, Boyer undertook the difficult task of resolving the ambiguous diplomatic and economic status of Haiti in his post-revolutionary reconstruction efforts. In July 1822, Boyer's secretary general, Joseph Inginac, invited the United States to become the first Western nation to recognize Haiti's sovereignty and independence.[45] President James Monroe refused, and he later blocked Haiti's invitation to the Western Hemisphere Panama Conference of 1825.[46]

Northern petitions asking for U.S. recognition of Haiti often came before Congress, yet proslavery representatives consistently maligned them as "marks of incendiarism."[47] Between 1838 and 1839 alone, Congress received more than two hundred petitions asking for federal recognition of Haiti.[48] Those favoring Haitian recognition observed that "the people of Hayti are not yet fully understood" as they expressed their desire for "the United States . . . [to] acknowledge their Independence, with the full consent not only of the philanthropists, but of the sagacious Statesman."[49] In particular, northern merchants pressed for federal recognition of Haiti, arguing that it was in the country's "interest . . . to secure so very valuable a branch of our West India trade" with a commercial treaty.[50] These requests increased after the Haitian government began taxing commercial interactions with countries that refused to acknowledge its sovereignty.[51] When Boyer finally negotiated the contested French recognition of Haitian sovereignty in 1825—accorded in a Royal Ordinance delivered by no less than three French vessels of war—it came at the expense of a 150-million franc indemnity to the dispossessed French planters of St. Domingue. King Louis Philippe later reduced the indemnity to sixty million francs and extended Haiti full recognition in 1838.[52] U.S. newspapers reported these proceedings with great interest, and many were convinced that "if our government shall treat them [Haitians] judiciously, a very large portion of their commerce will fall into the hands of merchants of this country."[53] However, even after French diplomatic recognition of Haiti, the United States maintained its policy of disavowing Haitian sovereignty and its place among the Western nations.[54] In a letter widely reprinted in U.S. newspapers, Boyer stressed his desire for Haiti to be "elevated to the rank of civilized nations," with "the surest means of accomplishing that object" being the establishment of "mutual relations with other nations."[55] He asked that the "friends of liberty in the U. States" continue to pressure the federal government to disencumber itself from the "obstacles which, until now, have prevented it from pronouncing itself in favor of the independence of the Republic of Hayti."[56]

In his efforts to secure U.S. diplomatic recognition, Boyer challenged the idea of a counter-revolutionary St. Domingue that was proliferated by proslavery ideologues as a caution against slave emancipation in the Americas. One of Boyer's translated proclamations republished in U.S. newspapers denounced his country's "most embittered slanderers . . . the promoters of the horrid traffic in human flesh" who "imagine that they behold Hayti always ready to annihilate them."⁵⁷ In response to southern black codes like the Negro Seamen Acts, Boyer enforced restrictive economic trade policies against the slave states, claiming that he wished to avoid "every occasion for umbrage to other governments, in relation to the internal police of their colonies."⁵⁸ He specifically prohibited the transit of Haitian trade vessels "to North and South Carolina in the United States of America" after the enactment of the Negro Seamen Acts.⁵⁹ He also took these opportunities to publicly condemn the "unworthy and scornful treatment the Haytiens have received from foreign governments. . . . The outrage done to the Haytien character, is a deplorable effect of the absurd prejudices resulting from the difference of colours."⁶⁰ Boyer cited the Negro Seamen Acts among these new racial restrictions as a profound mark of U.S. national retrogression: "The proscription practiced, now, more than ever, in certain countries, against men of the colour of Haytiens . . . recently established in the middle portion of America . . . [are] strange proceedings, . . . [and] horrible as they are, would appear less surprising at a period less advanced than the present."⁶¹ Such public avowals of black racial pride stimulated fears that Haiti might instigate and support slave uprisings like the Vesey conspiracy, and such fears persisted in the U.S. South until the abolition of slavery.⁶² Thus, the localized events in Charleston over the summer months of 1822 may be understood as part of these broader geopolitical negotiations within the Atlantic world.

At the time of the Vesey conspiracy, Haiti had begun advertising for skilled black immigrants in U.S. newspapers in order to address its acute labor shortages.⁶³ In 1819, Boyer expressed an early interest in the recently established American Colonization Society (ACS) as he attempted to redirect the course of black colonization from Africa to Haiti. In encouraging black American emigration to Haiti, Boyer sought to strengthen the relations between the two countries, seeing in it "an infallible means of augmenting the commerce of the United States, by multiplying relations between two people." By 1821, Boyer's secretary of state had established a society at Port-au-Prince "to encourage the emigration of free Africans and their descendants from the United States."⁶⁴ Advertisements for emigrants continued throughout the 1820s as the Haitian government extended offers of free passage and generous land grants to skilled black Americans in hopes of revitalizing an economy compromised by years of internecine warfare. Many metropolitan black American writers and reformers began to embrace Boyer's recruitment efforts. They saw in Haiti the realization of the unfinished project of American egalitarian democracy.

From the time they began publication on March 16, 1822, until they ceased two year later, Samuel Cornish and Jamaica-born John Brown Russwurm, editors of the *Freedom's Journal*—the first black U.S. newspaper—listed among their many goals the dissemination of "correct information" on Haiti: "As the relations between Hayti and this country are becoming daily more interesting, it is highly important that we have correct information concerning the state of affairs there. Our readers may depend on our columns, as we shall never insert any news whatever, of a doubtful nature, concerning the island."[65] Accurate news was particularly needful given, in the editors' words, "the dissatisfied and envious in this country, who are continually forging 'News from Hayti,' . . . [and] unmanly attacks upon a brave and hospitable people."[66] Cornish and Russwurm often reprinted from abolitionist Benjamin Lundy's *Genius of Universal Emancipation* salutary reports promoting the advantages of Haitian emigration.[67] For many black Americans, emigration to Haiti was a far more promising alternative to Liberia and the American Colonization Society's undisguised efforts to draw "off the free people of colour from the United States."[68] "I have often asked myself," observed one emigration advocate, "why Hayti, whose climate is so mild, and whose government is analogous to that of the United States, was not preferred as their place of refuge."[69] Black writers encoded a powerful counternarrative to American national culture in their embrace of Haitian emigration. For example, David Walker, the *Freedom's Journal*'s fiery Boston agent, proclaimed that "Hayti, the glory of the blacks and the terror of tyrants," offered a far more invigorating example of revolutionary egalitarianism than the American Revolution.[70] In his radical *Appeal to the Coloured Citizens of the World* (1829), Walker also admonished those who had fallen for the American Colonization Society's "colonizing trick," although he endorsed emigration to Haiti for those "of us [who] see fit to go away . . . go to our brethren, the Haytians, who, according to their words, are bound to protect and comfort us."[71]

In the United States, the Haitian emigration movement commenced in earnest when Boyer began financing the emigration of some thirteen thousand black Americans to Haiti in 1824.[72] Earlier that year, Loring D. Dewey, a Presbyterian minister and ACS agent, had begun corresponding with Boyer in hopes of initiating a resettlement program in the black republic. Dewey helped oversee the establishment of the Society for Promoting the Emigration of Free Persons of Colour to Hayti in the United States (*CR*, 28, 30). The ACS did not support Haitian emigration and promptly "recommended the removal of Mr. Dewey from his agency" as a representative for the organization.⁷³ In her antislavery masterpiece *Uncle Tom's Cabin* (1852), Harriet Beecher Stowe likewise denigrated Haiti in order to sing the praises of African colonization. Her protagonist George Harris, a fugitive slave, embraces emigration to Liberia, rejecting Haiti, "For in Hayti they had nothing to start with . . . [and a] stream cannot rise above its fountain." "The race that formed the character of the Haytiens," he continues, "was a worn-out, effeminate one; and, of course, the subject race will be centuries in rising to anything."⁷⁴ The swift and intolerant actions of the ACS in the matter of Dewey and Haitian emigration gave the organization's more liberal supporters pause as they reconsidered the racial ideologies that underlay colonization to Africa: "But when we find the advocates for slavery in Missouri among its zealous friends—when we find it encouraged and patronized in South Carolina, a state that has passed a law to seize free negroes and sell them for slaves; and in Charleston, a city that has made it a penal offence to teach a slave to read or write;—and now, when the members of a Society think it necessary to dismiss an agent because he has corresponded with the free government of Hayti—we cannot prevent a lurking suspicion that all is not right."⁷⁵ Boyer subsequently sent his agent Jonathas Granville to New York with funds sufficient to defray the expenses of six hundred emigrants and the authority to arrange for the immigration of six thousand more within the year.⁷⁶ With this arrangement in place, Dewey continued promoting Haitian emigration, observing that "among the Coloured People themselves, a preference of Hayti over Africa was frequently expressed," given the "present peaceful state of the island, and the fair prospects before the Haytiens, of having their Independence acknowledged by other nations."⁷⁷

Boyer sought to use black American emigration to Haiti as a means to influence U.S. public sentiment and secure federal recognition of his country. He identified black Americans as fellow "children of Africa" and welcomed their immigration to Haiti as a refuge from racial oppression. America's failure to abolish slavery made it possible for Boyer to proclaim postrevolutionary Haiti as the "land of true liberty." Moreover, black freedmen, "who drag out in the United States a painful and degrading existence, will become, on arriving at Hayti, citizens of the Republic, and can there labour with security and advantage to themselves and children" (*CR*, 14). Boyer's letters fashion Haiti as a refuge for free blacks seeking the promised "happiness, security, tranquility" withheld from them in America: "the descendants of the Africans . . . are compelled to leave the country, because . . . far from enjoying the rights of freemen, they have only an existence, precarious and full of humiliation" (*CR*,

10, 6–7). Boyer went so far as to describe his emigration plan as a charitable act of humanitarianism toward a sister-nation. In rhetoric shaped by Enlightenment thought, Boyer crafted a utopian vision of black civility and social reproduction to be fulfilled upon Haitian soil:

> What joy it will give hearts like yours, to see these scions of Africa, so abased in the United States, where they vegetate with no more utility to themselves than to the soil which nourishes them, transplanted to Hayti, where they will become no less useful than estimable, because the enjoyment of civil and political rights, ennobling them in their own eyes, cannot fail to attach them to regular habits, and the acquisition of social virtues, and to render them worthy by their good conduct, to enjoy the benefits which their new country will bestow upon them! (*CR*, 16–17)

For Boyer, slavery was antithetical to Western modernity. Indeed, the emergence of a unified Haitian state facilitated the abolition of slavery throughout the island. In 1822, after taking the capital city of Spanish Santo Domingo, Boyer's first act was to proclaim the emancipation of all slaves.[78] Boyer's emigration rhetoric stressed the political and social progress of Haiti, and he also took pains to circulate his proposal widely through black as well as white agents. He later made "a verbal statement of the same offer" to Thomas Paul, the founder of Boston's African Baptist Church, who was to act "as an organ of communication to the free people of color in the United States."[79] A vocal advocate for Haitian emigration, Paul praised the independent black state as the ideal "asylum for the enjoyment of liberty and the common rights of man," urging his fellow "emancipated people of colour" to swiftly transplant themselves amongst those "who are determined to live free, or die gloriously in the defence of freedom."[80] Richard Allen, founder of the African Methodist Episcopal Church, later served as chair of the Haitian Emigration Society in Philadelphia.[81]

Boyer's discursive struggle to reposition Haiti within Western historiography was not without its shortcomings; it demanded that he cast out Africa from these discourses of New World modernity and revolution. Indeed, Joan (Colin) Dayan reminds us that Boyer's Haitian modernity must be viewed alongside the "codification of servitude" and repression of the black peasantry in his Code Rural, which placed labor and agriculture under state control.[82] Hence, these public discussions over black emigration to Haiti allowed Boyer to question modernity (and Haiti's place within this new world order) without necessarily challenging its Western racial biases. Boyer embraced his fellow black Americans who had suffered the forced migrations of the Atlantic trade even as he rejected the "barbarous" Africa from where they had been stolen. This discourse of African barbarism allowed Boyer to portray his island nation as coeval with other white Western nations. "Animated with the desire to serve the cause of humanity," reads Boyer's letter to Dewey, "I have thought that a finer occasion could not have presented itself to offer an agreeable hospitality, a sure asylum, to the unfortunate men, who have the alternative of going to the barbarous shores of Africa, where misery or certain death may await them" (*CR*, 11). In renouncing Africa as "barbarous," he emphasizes the similarity of the "principles of legislation and government" between Haiti and the United States, which "ought necessarily to render them friends, although a blind prejudice seems until now to have put obstacles in the way of more direct relations between the one and the other" (*CR*, 11). Indeed, black Americans and Haitians are the true products of New World modernity—men, who are, in Boyer's words, "accustomed to live in the midst of civilized people." Thus the emigration of black Americans to Africa—"the cradle of their fathers"—would be less a homecoming than a forced "exile" to a primitive land.

This ambivalence towards Africa is built into the very structure of Boyer's struggles to forge a political and social identification with the United States. Boyer felt compelled to differentiate his country from the undeveloped primitivism of the African continent and reposition Haiti within the progressive histories of the modern West. Haitian modernity is thus given shape and meaning against the specter of unenlightened Africa. It is not a coincidence that one of the more lurid accounts from the Vesey conspiracy had linked Haiti and Africa through its shared racialized barbarism: "St. Domingo and Africa would come over and cut up the white people if we only made the motion here first" (*OR*, 62). White officials granted freedom and immunity to the unnamed slave who offered this statement. This lead witness also maintained that the Vesey plot involved not only the savage murder of Charleston's white men, but also the rape of its white women (*OR*, 62–63). Against this ever-present specter of African barbarism, Boyer envisioned the futures of the United States and Haiti interlaced through hemispheric ties of commerce, government, and people. Indeed, his rhetoric struck a delicate balance between praise and critique of the United States as a sister-nation, and it persuaded many black Americans. Between 1824 and 1827, an estimated thirteen thousand immigrated to Haiti, although a "considerable number of these immigrants, and probably some of the best of them, and those who had means, returned to the United States" when the Haitian government suddenly halted its subsidies.[83]

Many black American writers saw Haiti as a successful example of self-government "hitherto unseen in these modern and degenerate days," while they stressed the failures of American democracy and rejected the prospects of African colonization.[84] Boyer's rhetoric of Haitian modernity found a ready home in the columns of *Freedom's Journal*. Editors Cornish and Russwurm reprinted various articles about Haiti, including a three-part biography of Toussaint Louverture.[85] One issue offered a "few lines on the past and present conditions of a people, who have bravely burst asunder the galling chains of slavery," especially given that "many of our New England friends believe, and practice the self-evident truths, 'that all men are created equal, that they are endowed by their Creator, with certain inalienable rights; that among these, are life, liberty, and the pursuit of happiness.'"[86] "The Haytiens," lauded another editorial, "can look back on the past with great satisfaction; they have fought the good fight of Liberty, and conquered: and all that is . . . required of them, is, to enjoy this invaluable blessing, as accountable beings, who look forward to what man, even the descendants of Africa, may be, when blessed with Liberty and Equality and their concomitants."[87] The newspaper also ran advertisements for agricultural workers to contract in Haiti, asking those interested to contact Russwurm.[88] In embracing Boyer's vision of black modernity, these black writers and editors saw in post-revolutionary Haiti the achievement of the American promise of egalitarian democracy and freedom.

French acknowledgement of Haitian independence further encouraged black American emigration to the island for it provided Western confirmation of Haiti's rightful place among the Atlantic nation-states. In public and private ceremonies, scores of black Americans commemorated this event as the realization of the emancipatory project that had begun with the Haitian Revolution in 1791.[89] For some, French recognition lent legitimacy to Haiti's founding revolutionary antislavery, and it energized literary efforts to remake the Haitian Revolution into the origins of what Paul Gilroy first described as a black "counterculture of modernity."[90] In four issues between January 18 and February 15, 1828, the *Freedom's Journal* serialized a short story entitled "Theresa—a Haytien Tale" under "Original Communication." Reserved for pieces written by black contributors, the "Original Communication" section included letters to editors, testimonials, wedding and death announcements, and poetry and short fiction.[91] Set during the Haitian Revolution, "Theresa—a Haytien Tale" crafts a domestic plot of black familial reunion that channels and amplifies the Haitian modernity of Boyer's emigration recruitment campaigns. It also predates the earliest known works of black American fiction, including Francophone writer Victor Séjour's "Le Mulatre," or "The Mulatto" (1837), Frederick Douglass's "A Heroic Slave" (1852), William Wells Brown's *Clotel; or The President's Daughter* (1853), and Frank J. Webb's *The Garies and Their Friends* (1857).

Frances Smith Foster speculates that American educator Prince Saunders may have been the author of "Theresa—A Haytien Tale," which was signed simply with the initial "S."[92] An early émigré to Haiti, Saunders (who married the daughter of Paul Cuffee, the earliest proponent of African colonization) became one of the most vocal advocates of emigration, preceding by several decades the work of well-known Haitian emigrationalist James Theodore Holly.[93] In 1816, Saunders became the official courier to the Court of St. James for Emperor Henri Christophe, who had control of northern Haiti (and was battling Alexandre Pétion for leadership of the south).[94] While in London negotiating British diplomatic recognition of Christophe's Haiti, Saunders associated with the likes of abolitionist luminaries William Wilberforce and Thomas Clarkson and oversaw the translation and publication of the *Haytian Papers* (1816), a compendium of selected official ordinances and legal codes, including extracts from the Code Henri. Saunders republished it in Boston in 1818. A public relations document, the *Haytian Papers* sought to refute the "gross misrepresentation[s]" circulated against Haiti by offering Anglophone readers "correct information with respect to the enlightened systems of policy, the pacific spirit, the altogether domestic views, and liberal principles of the Government" under Christophe.[95] In 1818, in Philadelphia, Saunders delivered an address advocating Haitian emigration before the American Convention for Promoting the Abolition of Slavery and Improving the Condition of the African Race. "Among the various projects or plans which have been devised or suggested, in relation to emigration," Saunders insisted, "there are none which appear to many persons to wear so much the appearance of feasibility, and ultimate successful and practical operation, as the luxuriant, beautiful and extensive island of Hayti, (or St. Domingo)."[96] Saunders went so far as to suggest U.S. intervention in Haiti to facilitate the consolidation of the "two rival governments of Hayti . . . into one well balanced pacific power."[97] A unified Haiti would become a refuge for the "many hundreds of the free people in the New England and middle states, who would be glad to repair there immediately to settle."[98] In 1823, Saunders returned to Haiti with clergyman Thomas Paul on a mission for the Baptist Missionary

Society. Boyer subsequently appointed Saunders the attorney general of Haiti, where Saunders remained until his death in 1839.[99]

"Theresa—a Haytien Tale" emphasizes the French atrocities committed against the Haitians in the "long and bloody contest . . . between the white man" and "the sons of Africa."[100] "French barbarity" destroys the domestic repose of an "unfortunate village" in Môle-Saint-Nicholas, the strategic northwestern harbor that the United States later sought to annex as a naval base in 1889, during Frederick Douglass's appointment as U.S. Minister to Haiti (*THT*, 639).[101] The merciless French even put Haitian mothers and their infants to the sword. Madame Pauline and her two daughters, Amanda and Theresa, are left without the protection of their father and uncle, revolutionaries who died in battle (*THT*, 639). In identifying with the Haitian people, "Theresa—a Haytien Tale" offers a meditation on revolutionary Haiti for the purposes of its black American audience. Moreover, it resignifies the Haitian Revolution through the American War of Independence by likening Toussaint Louverture's black freedom fighters to the American revolutionaries in their cries of "Freedom or Death!" as they charge into battle against the French (*THT*, 645).

The female protagonists and domestic plot of "Theresa—a Haytien Tale" emphasize the forms of black social reproduction engendered—not destroyed—by the Haiti Revolution, building upon the very promises that Boyer extended to all black American emigrants. In this, the story reads against the grain of Sansay's epistolary novel, *Secret History; or, The Horrors of St. Domingo* (1808), as well as Sejour's "Le Mulatre," which depicts the Haitian Revolution as an inter-racial domestic drama of parricide. Revolutionary impulses have often been channeled through the figurative act of parricide, according to Russ Castronovo, and patricide—specifically, the literary imagery of black sons killing white slaveholding fathers—emerged as one of the primary metaphors for the Haitian Revolution.[102] "Theresa—a Haytien Tale" also figures the Haitian Revolution as a familial drama; yet, it is one that ends by establishing Toussaint Louverture as the black patriarch of the reunited Haitian family as nation. It offers a powerful counternarrative to these plots of tragic familial drama characterizing the black and white literary imaginary of the Haitian Revolution. In this, "Theresa—a Haytien Tale" provides an earlier iteration of the plot of black familial reunion as hemispheric slave revolution found in Martin R. Delany's famously unfinished *Blake; or, The Huts of America*.[103]

The persuasive force of "Theresa—a Haytien Tale" lies in its female protagonists, for they are ordinary women caught up in the extraordinary events of the Haitian Revolution.[104] Believing the "salvation of her oppressed country" at stake, young Theresa temporarily forsakes mother and sister to travel the dangerous route to "the military quarters of the great Toussaint," where she conveys the secret intelligence leading to the eventual "destruction of the French, and their final expulsion from her native island" (*THT*, 644). Theresa's heroic actions reconcile the warring tensions between filial duty and revolutionary nationalism, for "the salvation of her oppressed country to her, was an object of no little concern; but she also owed a duty to that mother, whose tender solicitude for her happiness, could not be surpassed by any parent" (*THT*, 643). In this, the tale illuminates the interdependence of the social and political in the Haitian Revolution. In Louverture, Theresa finds a paternal substitute for the father whom she lost in war, and the tale ends with the reconstitution of Theresa's family writ large. The revolutionaries rout the invading French forces and rescue the captured mother and sister—a powerful portent of the independent black nation-state that was soon to emerge from the Haitian Revolution. This ending also aligns itself with the image of a reunified Haiti under Boyer. After the assassination of Dessalines in 1806, civil strife fractured the country into two warring regions. In 1818, Saunders stressed the urgency for Haitian pacification and unity, noting the detrimental effects of civil war upon families: "There is scarcely a family whose members are not separated from each other, and arrayed under the banners of the rival chiefs, in virtual hostility against each other," he observed. "In many instances the husband is with Henry, and the wife and children with Boyer."[105] Haitian civil unrest had discouraged earlier recruitments of black American emigrants. In celebrating Haitian (familial and national) reunification, "Theresa—A Haytien Tale" enhances the *Freedom's Journal*'s emigrationalist stance by figuring the promise and possibilities for black social reproduction in Boyer's unified Haiti.

In depicting the mutually constitutive forces of social reproduction and black revolution in Haiti, "Theresa—a Haytien Tale" worked in tandem with the political views of the *Freedom Journal*'s editors. The *Freedom's Journal* was an international print medium with a vast distribution network from Maine and New York to Washington, D.C., Maryland, North Carolina, Canada, England, and Haiti.[106] It provided crucial links between the United States and Haiti as well as between the U.S. North and South as sectional divisions over slavery and states's rights threatened to fracture the country like Haiti, dividing families and turning kin against each other. In the pages of the *Freedom's Journal*, editors Cornish and Russwurm "created for the black community a social and cultural space in which to articulate their opposition to white oppression while also providing an invaluable lesson in literary interaction and the power of print," according to Elizabeth McHenry.[107] In a publication dedicated to disseminating "correct information" on Haiti, "Theresa—a Haytien Tale" offers a fictional meditation upon the profound challenge that the Haitian Revolution and Boyer's post-revolutionary republic offered, in Trouillot's words, to "the universalist pretensions of both the French and the American revolutions."[108]

Revolution Revisited

At the height of the transatlantic antislavery campaign in the 1850s, black abolitionist William Wells Brown took up the power and potential of black militancy so long exploited by proslavery lawmakers to fashion a revisionist account of the Haitian Revolution that would stand as a precursor to C. L. R. James's *Black Jacobins*. "No revolution," writes Brown, "ever turned up greater heroes then that of St. Domingo. But no historian has yet done them justice."[109] Over the course of Brown's career as an abolitionist, he wrote extensively on the Haitian Revolution, especially during the prolific years of his self-described exiled from the United States. In advance of the implementation of the 1850 Fugitive Slave Act, Brown, a fugitive slave, fled to Europe where he remained until British philanthropists secured his manumission.[110] In his five years abroad, Brown traveled more than twenty-five thousand miles and delivered over one thousand lectures while authoring numerous essays, a travelogue, and *Clotel*.[111] He also served as the official delegate for the American Peace Society at its international conference in Paris. Like Frederick Douglass, Brown was fêted in Europe. He socialized with the likes of Victor Hugo, the president of the Peace Congress and acclaimed poet and author of the lesser known novel, *Bug-Jargal* (1826), based upon the tumultuous events of the Haitian Revolution. Once state governments began enforcing the new Fugitive Slave Law, interest in black American emigration abroad again revived, and the American Peace Society required a "talented man of colour" like Brown in Europe to challenge the American Colonization Society's promotion of imperialist resettlement schemes to Africa.[112]

On the eve of his long-awaited departure from England in May 1854, Brown delivered a lecture on Haiti entitled "Santo Domingo: Its Revolutions and Its Patriots" at the London Metropolitan Athenæum, which he repeated four months later at Philadelphia's St. Thomas Church. The speech sold rapidly in the United States.¹¹³ The second in a series of three highly successful lectures, "Santo Domingo" drew heavily upon John R. Beard's largely sympathetic biography, *The Life of Toussaint L'Ouverture, The Negro Patriot of Hayti* (1853), published in the same year as Brown's *Clotel*. Lara Langer Cohen has most recently traced the influence of Beard's text on *Clotel* to consider the fragmentation, juxtaposition, and reassembly at the heart of Brown's "patchwork aesthetic."¹¹⁴ *The Life of Toussaint L'Ouverture* remains the most frequently cited text in *Clotel*, and it also serves as a key intertext in Brown's "Santo Domingo" address. In *Clotel*, Brown draws directly from Beard's account of the 1802 Haitian yellow fever outbreak crippling Napoleon's forces in his description of the New Orleans epidemic that sends two of Thomas Jefferson's granddaughters to the auction block.¹¹⁵ Brown's transposition of Beard's account demands that we reread the novel's themes of racial amalgamation and the genealogical legacies of American slavery in relation to the Haitian Revolution.¹¹⁶ These intertextual references linking Haiti and New Orleans figure the U.S. South as dangerously open to the "infection" of slave revolt. In this, Brown offered powerful critical commentary upon the racialized discourses of contagion and quarantine established by the Negro Seamen Acts, which figured "foreign" black bodies as infectious carriers of revolutionary epistemologies.

In the face of increasing sectional strife over slavery, black American writers often turned to the Haitian Revolution in their efforts to rethink the meaning of the American Revolution in the decade leading to Civil War.¹¹⁷ For example, Webb's *The Garies* subtly infuses black revolutionary thought—in the figure of Toussaint Louverture—into its domestic plot of urban race riot. Decorating the handsomely appointed abode of wealthy black Philadelphian Mr. Walters, a majestic portrait of Louverture, purported to have been presented to "an American merchant by Toussaint himself," captivates Clarence Garie, a progressive-minded white Georgia planter.¹¹⁸ "'All white men look at it with interest,'" Walters remarks. "'A black man in the uniform of a general officer is something so unusual that they cannot pass it with[out] a glance.'"¹¹⁹ Like Webb's, Brown's writings crafted nuanced textual and geographical links between the United States and Haiti.¹²⁰ Brown could not imagine a revolutionary history of the West without the Haitian Revolution as its pivotal point. In perhaps the most unexpected citation of Beard in *Clotel*, Brown fuses two passages from *The Life of Toussaint* to anachronistically introduce Nat Turner's revolt during Clotel's heroic but failed rescue of her daughter.¹²¹ Like "Theresa—A Haytien Tale," Brown conjoins the domestic narrative of Clotel's self-sacrificing mother love to a historical plot of black militancy.

In "Santo Domingo," Brown drew upon both Beard's *Life of Toussaint* and *Clotel*'s fictional recontextualization of Turner's revolt to craft a radical vision of coeval revolutions. The lecture reinvents Haiti as the geographical and historical wellspring of revolutionary antislavery in the Americas. It offers a complex model of historiography that accounts for the contingent transnational interests vested in sustaining African slavery and the revolutionary antislavery that transformed the colony into a modern black republic. From a depiction of internal social strife *within* the island's "black" populations, Brown traces these local tensions in a transnational field of colonial relations with France, England, Spain, and the United States. He uses the adverbial form of "while" to conjoin multiple events, expanding the account's geographical and temporal scale. Variously comparing Toussaint Louverture to figures such as Nat Turner, Napoleon Bonaparte, and George Washington, Brown unites the nonsynchronous events of the American, French, and Haitian Revolutions within a single representational field that includes U.S. slave conspiracies and revolts.

Unlike Boyer's earlier efforts to locate Haiti within the developmental narratives of the West, Brown's historical account acknowledges the brutal violence that helped forge the country's revolutionary antislavery and propel it into New World modernity.[122] Neither does Brown shrink from detailed descriptions of the atrocities that Dessalines's black revolutionary forces committed against the white colonists of St. Domingue: "the banks of the Artibonite . . . strewn with dead bodies, and the waters dyed with the blood of the slain."[123] Exploiting the specter of black militancy used so effectively by proslavery politicians, Brown offers this image of white "slaughter" and "carnage" as a terrifying portent of what is yet to pass within the slaveholding United States: "Let the slave-holders in our Southern States tremble when they shall call to mind these events" (*SD*, 25). In this, Brown anticipates the militant antislavery of John Brown and justifies bloodletting in the cause of universal freedom. "Should we be obliged to shed rivers of blood; should we, to preserve our freedom, be compelled to set on fire seven-eighths of the globe," he proclaims, "we shall be pronounced innocent before the tribunal of Providence, who has not created men to see them groan under a yoke so oppressive and so ignominious" (*SD*, 31–32).

Unlike Delany, Henry Highland Garnet, and Alexander Crummell, Brown did not promote black American emigration to Africa or Haiti. Rather, his writings sought to reveal the historical connections between the United States and Haiti in ways that invigorated the revolutionary character of the

American antislavery struggle. In remapping the Haitian Revolution onto U.S. soil, Brown delineates the transnational contours of what Sibylle Fischer calls the "emancipatory project of revolutionary anti-slavery"—one that exists simultaneously in the Haitian past and the American present.[124] "The spirit that caused the blacks to take up arms, and to shed their blood in the American revolutionary war, is still amongst the slaves of the south; and, if we are not mistaken, the day is not far distant when the revolution of St. Domingo will be reenacted in South Carolina and Louisiana," warns Brown (*SD*, 32). The revolutionary antislavery unleashed in the Haitian Revolution—the sympathetic echo of which was sounded in the Denmark Vesey conspiracy and Nat Turner revolt—is a fundamental aspect of the "spirit" of radicalism that pervaded the Western world in the age of revolution. In this, Brown undermines the implicit claims of conventional historiography as a narrative of developmental progress. He conjures the specter of a *revolutionary* St. Domingue to haunt the topography of America's internal slave colony of the South: "Already the slave in his chains, in the rice swamps of Carolina and the cotton fields of Mississippi, burns for revenge" (*SD*, 37). Brown retrieves the Haitian past and projects it into the American future. By positing a future that doubles back upon itself as a repetition, or in his words, a "re-enactment" of a revolutionary Haitian past, Brown's "Santo Domingo" destabilizes a teleological narrative of U.S. national history that takes 1776 as its inaugural moment.[125]

Brown's "Santo Domingo" identifies Haiti as the radical epicenter for the complex spatial and temporal cartographies of the black Atlantic binding together the United States, Europe, and Africa. His revolutionary historiography of antislavery in the Americas is not invested in preserving a linear continuity of past, present, and future. Revolution and racial slavery destroy historical continuity and produce ruptures in the diachronic narrative of nation. The Haitian Revolution becomes a possible future for the United States— one that does not reenact the contradiction of America's founding and its uneasy reconciliation of democratic consciousness with racial slavery. "Toussaint's government made liberty its watchword, incorporated it in its constitution, abolished the slave-trade, and made freedom universal amongst the people," writes Brown, whereas "Washington's government incorporated slavery and the slave-trade, and enacted laws by which chains were fastened upon the limbs of millions of people" (*SD*, 37). The Haitian Revolution becomes a touchstone for the "unfinished revolution" of 1776: "The indignation of the slaves of the south would kindle a fire so hot that it would melt their chains, drop by drop, until not a single link would remain; and the revolution that was commenced in 1776 would then be finished" (*SD*, 38). In enforcing racial jurisprudence like the Negro Seamen Acts, U.S. slave states sought to purge from their boundaries the specter of black radicalism unleashed by the Haitian Revolution. However, these legal efforts to draw a racialized cordon sanitaire around the slaveholding South conjured a powerful imaginary of a counter-revolutionary St. Domingue that black American writers like Brown adapted into a rallying cry to end slavery and racial injustice.

Haiti's emergence as a post-revolutionary modern black state profoundly challenged the "ontological order of the West and the global order of colonialism," according to Trouillot.[126] The United States would deny Haiti diplomatic recognition until 1862, when the Civil War began to bring the era of legal slavery to an end.[127] However, official recognition served only to draw Haiti further into the bellicose sphere of U.S. overseas empire and neocolonialism. Forty years later, in 1893, Frederick Douglass echoed Brown in two speeches on Haiti and the Haitian Revolution for the Haitian Pavilion dedication ceremony at the Chicago World's Columbian Exposition.[128] Appointed as commissioner of the Haitian Pavilion by Haitian President Florvil Hyppolite, Douglass presented the "Lecture on Haiti" at the African Methodist Episcopal Church's Quinn Chapel in the evening before he gave a version of it as his keynote address. The lecture began by boldly asserting, "My subject is Haiti, the Black Republic; the only self-made Black Republic in the world," and condemned the United States for failing to accept Haiti as a "sister republic" at its founding (*LH*, 203). "Haiti is black," Douglass noted wryly, "and we have not yet forgiven Haiti for being black or forgiven the Almighty for making her black" (*LH*, 203). In a world reshaped by U.S. Jim Crow and the global diffusion of white supremacist ideologies, Douglass, in words hearkening back to Brown's "Santo Domingo," invoked the Haitian Revolution as a rallying call for Americans to complete the "unfinished revolution" of Reconstruction. Haiti "came into the sisterhood of nations through blood," and Douglass, like Brown, justified this bloodshed in the "cause of universal human liberty" (*LH*, 206, 208). In citing Haiti as example, Douglass portrays these early black revolutionaries as "linked and interlinked with their race, and striking for their freedom, they struck for the freedom of every black man in the world" (*LH*, 208). Of all the so-called Western nations, Haiti should be regarded as "the original pioneer emancipator of the nineteenth century" (*LH*, 209). In this, Douglass stressed the enduring power and significance of Haiti and its black revolutionary history to America after Reconstruction, for it remains "the greatest of all our modern teachers" (*LH*, 209).

CHAPTER 10

The Haytian Papers and Black Labor Ideology in the Antebellum United States

COLLEEN C. O'BRIEN

> The government of Hayti . . . I mean the Code Henri, [is] the most moral association of men in existence; nothing that white men have been able to arrange is equal to it. To give to the labouring poor of the country a vested interest in the crops they raise, instead of leaving their reward to be calculated by the caprice of the interested proprietor, is a law worthy to be written in letters of gold, as it secures comfort and a proper portion of happiness to those whose lot in the hands of white men endures by far the largest portion of misery.
>
> —Sir Joseph Banks to Prince Saunders, August 8, 1816

When Prince Saunders (Sanders) published *Haytian Papers: A Collection of the Various Proclamations, and Other Official Documents; Together with Some Account of the Rise, Progress, and Present State of the Kingdom of Hayti* in 1816, he made it a point to illustrate that the Haitian Constitution and government exemplified the "natural intelligence" of black men.[1] Yet his project was not exclusively about an exemplary cadre of representative men; it was about African American and Haitian laborers who would build the first free black nation in the Western Hemisphere. Saunders pointed out that "it especially appears to be [Henry Christophe's] object to ameliorate the condition and improve the character of the humblest class, namely, that of the plantation laborers" (*HP*, vi, iii).[2] The "Code Henri," according to Saunders's aristocratic British supporter, Sir Joseph Banks, was revolutionary in its mandate that, rather than being subject to the vicissitudes and exploitative practices of wage labor, Haitian cultivators were entitled to "a full fourth of the gross product" of their labor (*HP*, xiii). Although the work codes instated by the French colonial commissioner Étienne Polverel in 1794 and elements of the infamous Code Noir (1685) as well as its amendments had much in common with the Code Henri, Banks and Saunders insisted that the latter offered legitimate developments in the rights of the agricultural worker. In addition to profit sharing, cultivators were entitled to provision grounds and to legal recourse if their rights were violated by managers and planters. "It is the King's express order," reads Article 1, "that on every complaint of the cultivators against their landlords and farmers, the lieutenant commanding in the parish shall immediately attend to the circumstances of the case" (*HP*, xiii).

Banks's and Saunders's representations of this seemingly pro-labor code, however, neglect to mention that, as Kate Ramsey reminds us, "after independence, first Dessalines and then Christophe in the northern kingdom imposed their own versions of militarized agriculture that were likewise met with resistance and *marronage*."[3] Haitian independence did little to make the plantation system more egalitarian. Continuing a tradition of black leadership relying on forced labor that began with Toussaint, "Christophe feudalized the system and in the process created a new black landed nobility."[4] Pétion in the south enforced less restrictive labor practices and distributed more land, much because of ongoing peasant rebellions from 1807 to 1817.[5] Clearly, the realities of labor and rights in Haiti were not as peaceful and idyllic as Saunders claimed. Nonetheless, Saunders's rhetoric—or perhaps propaganda—reveals two important points. First, opportunities to work for themselves, and to eventually own the land where they labored, appealed more to African Americans than the prospects of wage labor. Second, rhetoric about the Haitian Revolution contributed to a black labor ideology in the New World that would appear over and over in the speeches and writings of black leaders in the United States. From the beginning of Saunders's emigration campaign to the late 1820s and beyond, the progress of the first black republic in the New World was incredibly important to African Americans as they considered the prospects for attaining equality outside the boundaries of an ever-whitening nation.

Saunders apparently compiled *Haytian Papers* for two reasons: to enlist the financial support of wealthy British philanthropists who could underwrite his American emigration project and to convince African Americans that their prospects were better in Haiti. Even though his is far from a complete picture, Saunders emphasizes the rights of laborers to appeal to free African Americans who, as skilled artisans, teachers, or agrarian laborers, could become citizens of Haiti.[6] Saunders reprinted *Haytian Papers* in the United States in 1818 and began lecturing there in that year, primarily to northern free black organizations formed for the purpose of starting free schools but whose members might be interested in emigrating to Haiti. The issue of free schools is a significant one that I will consider later; first, I will note that his attention to "agricultural interests" was probably meant to assure potential émigrés that they would prosper in Haiti. Compared to the conditions blacks faced as an unprotected labor force in the United States, the code's promise of recourse against unfair employers might very well have seemed superior to anything "that white men have been able to arrange" (*HP*, vi). Features including freedom from wage labor (because payment to cultivators came in the form of a portion of the produce), officially mandated hours of work and rest, and specific provisions to protect the aged, infirm, injured, or sick laborers were more than a "free laborer" in the United States could expect. Saunders's ally, Henri Christophe, welcomed black émigrés from the States and seemingly encouraged them to gain the ranks of farmers, whom the Code Henri (included in Saunder's collection) defined as "proprietors and farmers of land" who could "treat their prospective laborers with paternal solicitude" (*HP*, xiii).

While the concept of "paternal solicitude" rings of elitism, Saunders assured his American readers of Christophe's dedication to "the improvement of the hearts and lives, of all the various classes of society" and the American goal of "excit[ing] a more lively concern for the promotion of the best interests, the improvement, the definite independence, and happiness of the Haytian People." (*HP*, xi). This opportunity in Haiti offered African Americans an ideal of personal autonomy and a means of contributing to the common good, a position of virtue and respect that was increasingly difficult to attain in the United States (*HP*, vii).[7] In focusing on the promise of agrarian labor, Saunders's emigration plan prioritized land, labor, and freedom as the fundamental conditions for creating equality. As Kimberly K. Smith points out, while the Jeffersonian ideal of "workers [who] are not under a master's control but establish their own control over the natural world from a position of individual independence and political and social equality" applied to only about 10 percent of Americans and even less to African Americans, many black leaders throughout the nineteenth century participated in a "struggle [that] made the connection between nature and freedom—between possessing the land and possessing oneself—a central theme in black political thought."[8]

Therefore, *Haytian Papers* reflects a quintessential aspect of revolutionary Haitian political thought that would influence African American political thought—that property ownership, rather than wage labor, was the foundation of freedom and a guarantee of equality. As Anthony Bogues says of revolutionary Haiti, "Citizenship was linked to the capacity to own property, and a positive identification with blackness," whereas United States citizenship was clearly associated with whiteness.[9] Saunders's work contributed to the way that African Americans used the history of Haiti to fashion ideas about the relationship between property in land, property in the laboring body, and liberty; these ideas varied remarkably from the free labor ideology that developed concurrently among white abolitionists and laborers.[10] For one thing, while many forms of labor were associated with drudgery and indignity,[11] the agrarian ideal of labor that Saunders promoted locates dignity in cultivating the earth and asserts a sense of natural rights contracted through a relationship to the natural world and productive labor rather than government protection. This agrarian ideal constitutes a relationship to place, to labor, and to nature that supersedes national affiliations and locates freedom in self-sufficient labor. As Kimberly Ruffin says of early African American environmental thought, "Redemptive possibilities came from expressing natural affinities even in the absence of agency as U.S. citizens. Connections to nonhuman nature through work helped when coping with the lack of national belonging."[12]

This essay will read the *Haytian Papers* as part of a distinct black labor ideology that developed in the first half of the nineteenth century, one that drew from publications about Haiti to imagine property and liberty in alternative ways. The first section discusses how representations of Haiti in Saunders's compilation, while they may not have offered a very realistic portrait of the actual political conditions in Haiti, promised a space where African Americans could attain a distinct kind of freedom. The second section considers James McCune Smith's 1841 lecture on Haiti. I want to illuminate the ways that Smith draws from predecessors such as Saunders who contributed to the shaping of a radical black labor ideology grounded in ideas about labor, land, and a new "civilization" that they traced to Haiti. For Smith, who was not an emigrationist, the imagined connection between Haiti and the United States fortified a vision of land ownership as the foundation of citizenship and belonging that could stabilize a nation fraught by racial animosity and class conflict.[13]

The final section places Saunders's and Smith's work in context with their contemporaries, whose stories of Haiti had a very different focus—often the heroic and exemplary character of the "enlightened" Toussaint. Both Saunders and McCune Smith, however, focus on Haiti after independence, long after Toussaint was deposed and died in prison in France. Their depictions of the Haitian landscape and their emphasis on the work required to sustain free landscapes differentiate their writings from white abolitionists who were often proponents of a free labor ideology that perpetuated capitalism.

The Cultivators of Freedom

The idealized, and perhaps romanticized, belief that Haiti could embody a form of radical liberty and universal equality free from the constraints of racial prejudice or class animosity transformed the struggling nation into a symbol of hope for African Americans. As Elizabeth Rauh Bethel notes, "The Republic created by peoples of African descent, the slaves turned revolutionaries who had defeated Napoleon's army, and the succession of rulers who had guided the young nation into the international political arena, had been transformed in the Afro-American collective consciousness into figures and events of mythic stature."[14] Bethel rightly observes that Saunders's efforts to "advance Hayti . . . at every opportunity" were a means toward the "economic prosperity and political equality" that "proved continually elusive for Afro-Americans who remained in the United States."[15] Jacqueline Bacon further points out that reports from Haiti were of paramount importance to readers of *Freedom's Journal*, a New York publication widely accepted as the first African American newspaper.[16]

Yet this myth of Haiti failed to acknowledge the elusiveness of freedom and property for the revolutionaries themselves. Philippe Girard has depicted Toussaint as an ambitious emancipated slaveholder bent on his own self-preservation, willing to use force to put former slaves back to work, and as able to strike deals with the slaveholding British as he was to foil plans for insurrection on other islands.[17] As Laurent Dubois adds, "Committed to defending liberty at all costs, Louverture had turned himself into a dictator, and the colony he ruled over into a society based on social hierarchy, forced labor, and violent repression."[18]

Toussaint, Dessalines, and Henry Christophe profited financially from the practice of forced labor, yet the Haitian people who fought for freedom at any cost had different ideas about the value of their labor and their relationship to the plantation. What David Roediger, citing James Fenimore Cooper, calls the "subterfuge" that drove republican ideology—that property in the laboring body had value, or, as Paine claimed, that "man was free in large part because he held 'property in his own labor'"—may have assured white American workers of their liberty.[19] Yet formerly enslaved Haitians knew well that their labor could very easily be expropriated and exploited, just as African Americans who had fought in the Wars of Independence and of 1812 in the United States knew that they could not expect compensation for military labor. Thus, for African Americans, the ongoing example of Haitian struggles for freedom (documented through newspapers reports of Dessalines's proclamations and of repeated peasant revolts against plantation labor) suggested that Haiti had the potential to become the first truly free nation in the Western Hemisphere.

The notion of autonomy and self-sovereignty that characterized a revolutionary Haitian understanding of freedom has been linked to a system that many Haitians experienced in Africa, one that offered holdings of small parcels of land and the opportunity for self-sufficient subsistence agriculture. Laurent Dubois describes the *lakou* system as a social and cultural practice designed to control land and resist the plantation system, one that "guarantee[d] each person equal access to dignity and individual freedom."[20] In African American political rhetoric, Haitian freedom fighters appear as self-sacrificing republican citizens because they demonstrated the highest levels of military bravery to fight the Creoles, the French Republicans, the Spanish, or anyone who wanted to enslave them. But the goal of this sacrifice was no abstract Enlightenment ideal. Rather, as Carolyn Fick asserts, it was the "freedom to possess and to till their own soil, to labor for themselves and their families, with no constraints."[21] Nick Nesbitt adds that Haitian Bossales's "determined refusal to participate in wage-labor and to allow the reimposition of a state apparatus became so insurmountable that the elites were forced to abandon any hopes of reimposing large scale agriculture" after two decades of internal rebellion and resistance to the "Police Guards" cultivation system.[22] Saunders had to negotiate public relations somewhat skillfully to assure African Americans that Haiti could be a peaceful and safe home, and he did so in part by insisting that the vestiges of French greed were at the root of the problem. Anglo-African (African American) virtues were the panacea that could help Haiti fulfill its destiny and overcome its colonial past.

The ongoing resistance by Haitian workers to the concept and practice of a wage labor system evidences their rejection of a "free labor" system that relies on exchange between worker and employer. Saunders characterizes Dessalines and Henri Christophe as leaders who embody the will of the Haitian people, yet he does not readily acknowledge the tension between cultivators who resisted wage labor and their military leaders. He thus tries to depict Christophe in particular as a leader who will champion the rights of African Americans who come to Haiti to work the land.[23] While white abolitionists in the United States would promote erroneous assertions that free labor in the post-emancipation Caribbean was as lucrative as slave labor, Saunders defines the profits of Haitian emigration as beyond capitalist goals. He is likewise interested in productivity, yet *Haytian Papers* begins and concludes with an emphasis on the rights and role of the laborer; although it intimates that African Americans might become proprietors in Haiti, their mission is to create a truly free country. The Code Henri followed Toussaint's logic that "oblig[ing] my fellow countrymen to work . . . was to teach them the true value of liberty without license,"[24] yet Saunders acknowledges that the Haitian people had their own vision of liberty as something that one worked to create and that manifested in one's entitlement to property, to the land, to the very soil one tilled.

The concept of freedom that Saunders promised potential African American émigrés is also guaranteed, if not manifested, in the security of land ownership. The "Narrative of the Accession of Their Royal Majesties to the Throne of Hayti" (included in the American version of *Haytian Papers*) credits Dessalines for his part in redefining freedom and marks his assassination as a moment of rupture in the progress of the nation as it worked to assert those principles of freedom. The "Narrative" describes the period after the creation of a constitutional empire and before the assassination in terms that incorporate the idea of independence with an inalienable right to the land on which one labors. It says, "At length the Haytians, reunited, reconciled, perceived that there existed and could exist for them no other country on the globe than these happy and fortunate climes" (*HP*, 56). This passage asserts an agrarian ideal that joins political harmony among the "reunited" and "reconciled" Haitians with their implicit entitlement to "no other country on the globe" but Haiti, where they have worked and fought for freedom (*HP*, 56).

I want to reiterate that the authorship of the "Narrative of the Accession" is not quite clear; Saunders simply attributes all of the writings in *Haytian Papers* to Haitian men of color and about half of the documents included are signed by Henri Christophe. The point is that Saunders was confident in the power of these documents to persuade American readers that, in the words of the ambiguously authored "Reflections on the Abolition of the Slave Trade," "A new aera [sic] arises for Africa under the protecting shield of philanthropic men: its inhabitants may breath in the bosom of their country the pure air of liberty; they may enjoy the sweets and advantages of civilization in devoting themselves to the cultivation of the earth" (*HP*, 152–153). This agrarian ideal differs somewhat from Thomas Paine's proposition in *Agrarian Justice* (1797) that "the earth, in its natural, uncultivated state was . . . *the common property of the human race.*"[25] Just as the Haitian revolutionaries fought for their land and worked to improve it, African American émigrés would have to labor in Haiti to establish claims to land ownership. *Haytian Papers* depicts Haiti as a naturalistic, Edenic space, "which the sun delights to illumine, abundantly, pouring forth, with a complacent heat, all the benignity of his beneficent rays" and ripe with "fields in which are to be found, in unparalleled plenty, those fruits of delicious flavour, and those trees loaded with the precious aromatic juices of Arabia, which produce the real nectar so much esteemed, and so generally prized" (*HP*, 56). But God did not intend for Haiti to be a leisurely Eden, for "its cottons, cacaos, &c. and so many other productions with which bounteous Nature hath endowed Hayti, in the measure of its goodness, [are] the true attribute of Divine Providence" (*HP*, 56). The commodity crops that one must work to cultivate, the "productions" of labor, evidence the "true attribute"—that Haiti belongs to the laborers who have undertaken its cultivation. More than naturalistic, uncultivated space, a productive landscape is the sign of "Divine Providence" and the proof of entitlement to property (*HP*, 56).

The passage described above emphasizes the natural bounty of the island—a gift that exemplifies the favor of "Divine Providence" and the right to the land that one earns through productive labor, but a reference to Dessalines's murder, "when our happiness was all at once totally and utterly subverted," disrupts the idyllic scene (*HP*, 56). While the passage locates peace and freedom both among the "reunited, [and] reconciled" Haitians and within a nurturing landscape, that freedom is tenuous and mutable (*HP*, 56). Particularly when greed or sloth interrupt the production of freedom, the right to the land and the enjoyment of political harmony and equality also fall into danger. It is this vulnerability that Saunders exhorts African Americans to correct by transporting their pure principles of industry to Haiti, where they can establish a right relation to the land.

Saunders's American audience had reason to suspect, however, that civil strife between Christophe and Boyer would make it unlikely for them to encounter peace upon arrival in Haiti. In his *Memoir to the American Conven-*

tion for Promoting the Abolition of Slavery, Saunders criticizes Christophe and Boyer and seems to hint that their leadership is tainted by a French colonial legacy. "The present spirit of rivalry which exists between the two chiefs in the French part of the island, and the consequent belligerent aspect and character of the country," Saunders admits, "may at first sight appear somewhat discouraging to the beneficent views and labours of the friends of peace" (*HP*, 13). These rivalries are mere remnants of "the abominable principles, both of action and belief" that the French instilled on the "present inhabitants" (*HP*, 12). Notably, these are the same actions and beliefs that yielded the profits of 1789. To ameliorate what is essentially greed, one of the lingering "abominable principles" of the French, British philanthropists who have "the best interests of the descendants of Africa deeply at heart" will, according to Saunders, support the efforts of the black Philadelphians (and New Englanders) who might become through their "beneficent views and labors . . . friends of peace" (*HP*, 13). Due to a shared destiny with the people of Haiti, and a different set of principles and beliefs than the French, African Americans can "be made the instruments of the pacification and reunion of the Haytian people," thereby earning them their right to Haitian citizenship and land" (*HP*, 13).

This anticipated intervention of British and United States actors in the political and economic life of Haitians, unfortunately, displaces the role of the Haitian people in creating a republic that both controverts the racist logic of Atlantic slavery and defines freedom through land ownership. Although Saunders consistently refers to the British as "philanthropists" who will bankroll Haitian emigration and African Americans as the "actor[s]" or "labour[ers]" (*HP*, 7, 12, 13, 16) who will effectively rescue Haiti from the legacy of the French, the seductive language of prosperity and profit does slip into the papers. In the "Narrative" section of *Haytian Papers*, the author speaks effusively of Christophe's palace, perhaps to inspire awe and pride in his African American audience as he draws a portrait of the illustrious Sans Souci and a regal black kingdom. In his *Memoir*, however, Saunders far more critically attributes the "divisions which exist in Hayti" to "men [who] forsake the true worship and service of the only true God, and bow down to images of silver, and gold" (*HP*, 14). This criticism of the "actual moral, political, and above all . . . religious character of the Haytians" seems to refer critically to the "rival chiefs" whose personal wealth, particularly in the case of Christophe, devastated many Haitian lives. Saunders's confidence that free blacks from the United States can fix Haiti, however, still suggests that U.S. emigrants, not the Haitian freedom fighters, are destined to "fix" Haiti.

It is unfortunate that Saunders dissociates Haiti's revolutionary accomplishments from the people who struggled, lived, and died for them. At the same time, adopting a revolutionary definition of freedom that locates it not in an abstract principle or natural right, but in the opportunity to forge a connection to the land and to build a free nation through productive labor and a sense of shared destiny among people of African descent in the New World is a somewhat noble project. Nor is the avowed entitlement, on the part of "Free Persons of Colour" in the United States, to a nation that God has consecrated for the "African race" ignoble if one looks at it from the perspective of a sincere desire to safeguard the "stability and independence" of the first free black nation in the Western Hemisphere (*HP*, 3, 11). This nascent sense of identification with an "African race" that might define freedom differently is part of U.S. emigrants' political desire; it is a desire to work toward completing the project of the revolution, and not necessarily a desire to subordinate and capitalize on or to set aside the natural rights of the Haitian people.

Plagued by reports of the violence and strife that characterized Christophe's regime, Saunders could attribute Haiti's problems only to "the mysterious operation of [God's] providence" which (in addition to wreaking havoc on Africans for a couple hundred years), "has seen fit to permit the most astonishing changes to transpire upon that naturally beautiful, (and as to soil and productions,) astonishingly luxuriant island" (*HP*, 12). Saunders calls upon African Americans to take part in this sacred work, so that "they may revive, by their labours, the recollection of our illustrious ancestors" (*HP*, 12). It is a rallying call of "Haiti for the Africans," an Ethiopianist exhortation to prove that "*the Deity hath created, of one blood, the whole human race, to dwell over every part of the earth*" (*HP* 154, original emphasis).[26] Echoing Dessalines's proclamation in the constitution of 1805, that the "Supreme Being, before whom all mankind are equal and who has scattered so many species of creatures on the surface of the earth for the purpose of manifesting his glory," Saunders engages his audience in the work of restoring those "considered as outcast children" (*HP*, 19). While Wilson Moses attributes economic motives to Paul Cuffee's and James Forten's emigrationist plans, explaining that "their enterprising spirit was a product of the environment, ideological and material, that generated the nationalism of white Yankee businessmen,"[27] Prince Saunders's experience in and familiarity with alternative productions of nationalism—with Haitian ideals—suggests that early black nationalism and Ethiopianism in the United States had more hemispheric underpinnings.

Like Saunders, James McCune Smith looked to Haiti in his articulations of labor ideology and political theory. For Smith, the illegitimate claim that the French made to the island of Haiti—through conquest—and their cruel denial of natural rights to captives from Africa illustrate the failings of natural rights theory. Instead, Smith upholds a system wherein one draws from the power of a sacred landscape to locate, and enact, the laborious practice of liberty. In many ways, this story is also an allegory for the struggles of African Americans in McCune Smith's home, New York.

Haiti and Black Labor Ideology in the 1840s

A black labor ideology founded in the principles of the Haitian Revolution continued to develop in the 1840s. James McCune Smith's "Lecture on the Haytian Revolutions; with a Sketch of the Character of Toussaint L'Ouverture" (1841) figures land, labor, and freedom in a manner much like Saunders's.[28] As I will discuss below, both men emphasized the importance of education in their public speeches. Smith's speech concludes with a discussion of Toussaint's literacy and the importance of learning as well as outrage that African American children were excluded from New York City's school system. Saunders was helping Henri Christophe recruit schoolteachers to create an educational system in Haiti. So intellectual labor emerges as an important and indispensable subtext in these works, although their main focus is on work, belonging, and rightful land ownership.

Slavery is the obvious evil in Haitian and United States history, but racism and ignorance that are fed by and contribute to caste prejudice and result in exclusionary politics and economic practices are also endemic to both histories. In Smith's history of Haiti, there are three "Haytian Revolutions" rather than one. The first, and least important, was of the whites and *petit blancs* who wanted to establish "republican principles"; the second was emancipation of the slaves; the third, and most important, "achieved independence of the colony from the mother country."[29] In contrast to the self-serving and greedy behavior of white and free black revolutionaries who aspired toward "republican principles," the insurgent slaves aspired toward a very different form of freedom (*LHR*, 9). The impetus for freedom, in the third case, is not a derivative of the French Revolution; rather, it is a wish to belong. Belonging, in this sense, encompasses a sacred connection to the land where one labors and a sense of self-sovereignty, or self-determining human activity.

According to Smith's account, black revolutionaries were not in need of government protection or orders from above (republican principles) to assert this freedom, "For at the very moment, and for some time before the Commissioners declared them emancipated, there were in the plain of the Cape upwards of 100,000 people who held their freedom and the soil by *force of arms*, a title as good as, because identical with, that by which the planters had held it in their possession" (*LHR*, 8, emphasis in the original).[30] This de facto freedom comes from the process—and work—of becoming free rather than republican principles of assumed freedom, and it is notably not just a matter of holding onto abstract principles, but of people holding "freedom and the soil . . . in their possession." Smith detects some signal differences between the former slaves who considered themselves free and organized into work brigades on plantations (after chasing away the so-called owners) and Ogé's uprising or the French Revolution. The French conquerors, like their free black offspring, intended and proceeded to extract every bit of wealth from that soil; they did so by ruthlessly dominating and exploiting both the people and the soil. This system, according to Smith, was the first cause of the revolution.

Since conquest or "*force of arms*" rather than a natural right to property gave French colonists original title to the land, and inheritance had endowed the free people of color with property, the act of insurgents taking the land by insurrection was equally justifiable. Since the 100,000 people who "held their freedom and the soil by *force of arms*" did not engage in any gross violations of natural rights, however, their natural right to the land remained intact and even pure, unlike the contaminated French definition of their natural right (*LHR*, 18). This lesson distinguishes the relationship to the land of the people who "held their freedom and the soil" from the claims of the French (*LHR*, 18). Ironically, French "civilization" was based on the premise that government could protect natural rights when, in fact, the government authorized a system of slavery that negated natural rights. Rather than in government, McCune Smith finds "natural right" in the soil and landscape of Haiti and the entitlement to it that the Haitian people establish through their righteous rebellion and the force of their labor. The proper expression of these natural rights is facilitated by literacy and education, which is why Toussaint is important to the equation.

While, according to Smith, the horrors of slavery and the particularly unnatural state of cruelty and disregard for human life were a first cause for insurrection, the second cause was the "topographical structure of the island"—a different manifestation of "natural right" (*LHR*, 4). At first glance, this characteristic might seem like a matter of military strategy—the maroons, for example, took advantage of the "mountainous regions of the island" to prove that "there was such a thing as successful resistance against their masters, and such a thing as compelling their masters to yield to them their liberty" (*LHR*, 8). It is important to note that *marronage* itself asserts liberty; it is the application of an intellectual principle that blacks did not need to learn from the French. Yet Smith does not endow the maroons with the same kind of belonging to the mountains of Haiti as he does the slaves who rose up to fight. Even though the mountains provided the maroons a place of freedom, they compromised their own liberty because treaties with the French and Spanish had "grant[ed] them liberty and a portion of territory for their exclusive use" if they agreed to aid in returning runaway slaves to their masters (*LHR*, 8). The slaves who would rise up to fight, however, recognized the pure principles of liberty in the topography and beauty of the mountains and established a true sense of belonging to Haiti. The very presence of the mountains inspired the "eager, restless" desire for liberty that the slaves of the plains saw in "access to those lofty heights" (*LHR*, 8). They accurately and fully understood the significance of freedom, and of the land's relationship to it.

The reason that the mountains themselves are so important harkens to Dessalines's and Saunders's representation of Haiti as the manifestation of an abundant natural world created by Divine Providence for the express purpose, or destiny, of building a land of freedom. Smith says that "the island is nearly intersected by a lofty range of mountains thickly serried by primeval forests, amid which are many strongholds only approachable by narrow and easily defended passes," but the significance of this topographical structure exceeds practical strategic benefits (*LHR*, 8). "These lofty recesses, these altars which nature in all ages has consecrated to liberty" left the men and women on the plain "restless and panting for liberty and for access to those lofty heights on which experience had taught them she made her dwelling" (*LHR*, 8). A land that is sacred, marked by mountains that are "altars" and "consecrated to liberty" (*LHR*, 8) is the same holy place where Saunders promises that the descendants of Africa are destined to "breath in the bosom of their country the pure air of liberty" (*HP*, 19). It is the location where Dessalines's "Supreme Being . . . has scattered so many species of creatures on the surface of the earth for the purpose of manifesting his glory" (*HP*, 19). The liberty that this place embodies is inseparable from the land; it is a title to the island that guarantees a space in the world for the creation of independence. This idea of liberty comes directly from Haiti's mountains and soil and is cultivated by revolutionaries in more ways than one. It establishes a mutual sense of belonging between the island and the cultivators who claim it, and it corrects the errors of the French and the maroons.

While the role of the slaves in recognizing the true meaning of liberty is clear, Smith credits Toussaint with the development of independence as a concept presentable to the outside world. Smith, unlike Saunders, skims over Dessalines's infamous actions other than to classify them as a response to French precedents of savagery. Yet the lessons are similar: the French "hid beneath a republican exterior a longing after the spoils," while black Haitians persisted, as "industrious laborers," to "overthrow an ERROR which designing and interested men had craftily instilled into the civilized world, a belief in the natural inferiority of the negro race" (*LHR*, 21, 22, 24). There is an intellectual principle at work here—a point that only the Haitian revolutionaries seem to get when they look at the mountains.

Smith scrutinizes French republican principles and focuses on Haitian labor as a challenge to those principles. He depicts Haiti as a sacred place consecrated to liberty and equality rather than as a financial resource ripe for capitalist exploitation. The accomplishments of the revolutionaries demarcate Haiti as the site where a positive identification with blackness can manifest itself, but that positivity needs to be translated into a representation that the rest of the world can learn from. This is why Smith concludes the *Lecture on the Haytian Revolutions* with a brief celebration of literacy.[31] Lamenting the exclusion of "colored children" from the "privileges" of a free education, he concludes with the declaration that Toussaint brought peace to Haiti in part because he was a "FREEDMAN, WHO HAD BEEN TAUGHT TO READ WHILE IN SLAVERY!" (*LHR*, 28). Not just land, but also a concept of property in knowledge helped to bring Haitian freedom into being and also shaped black labor ideology in the United States.

Black abolitionists from Prince Hall at the turn of the century to Saunders and the contributors to *Freedom's Journal* in the late 1820s had a specific interest in Haiti's progress in the arena of education, and this emphasis on Haiti remained critical to black political thought well into the twentieth century.[32] Saunders and McCune Smith both connected the need for land and labor with the need for education to create a free country. Education, as the meeting point between intellectual and manual labor, was as important an issue in 1818 as it was forty years later, when the *Anglo-African Magazine*'s inaugural issue would herald the success of the system that Christophe and Sanders worked to establish. McCune Smith was a contributor to the *Anglo-*

African, which reported: "In the *Concours* of the colleges of France in 1858, the laurels once worn by Abelard, fell upon the brow of a black youth from Hayti, M. Faubert, who won the highest prize, two other young Haytiens winning other prizes."[33] The editors of the *Anglo-African* turn to Haiti to refute the charges of race "scientists" like phrenologist Josiah Nott. Pointing out that many white American students have had the opportunity to study in Paris and that "none of these has yet won the distinguished honor" conferred upon the "black youth of Hayti," they take the opportunity to "formularize for Dr. Nott" the inferior performance of white Americans in this particular educational realm.[34] It goes something like this: black Haitians 2: white Americans 0. Considering the much larger number of white American scholars who could have been candidates for the awards, the result is embarrassing for the white Americans.

Unlike Saunders's, however, James McCune Smith's objective is not to encourage emigration, but to highlight the rapid elevation of Haitian people from "the lowest condition of slavery" to "all the functions which belong to free citizens," a progress that he wants to see take place in the United States and that, once again, requires a particular form of knowledge, which can be spread through education.[35] As John Stauffer points out, "McCune Smith emphasized that 'we are not a migrating people. The soil of our birth is dear to our hearts, and we cling to it with a tenacity which no force can unhinge.'"[36] Even though he celebrates Toussaint, Smith's objective is consistent with the objectives of black Haitian revolutionaries—to assert a positive identification with blackness, one that hinges on a particular working relationship to the land of freedom as well as the intellectual work of understanding that relationship.[37] Toussaint's literacy helped him only to articulate these intellectual principles to the rest of the world.

McCune Smith's 1841 "Lecture," furthermore, asserts a distinct relationship between the political and economic forces that preceded the Haitian Revolution and similar forces that he identifies in the antebellum United States.[38] For McCune Smith, the problem of masters was not exclusive to slavery—black belonging in the United States was coming unhinged. The political economy of New York in the 1840s, as McCune Smith describes it, exemplifies the dire need for land reform and an alternative to free labor ideology as articulated by white Republicans. It depicts the 1840s—the decade that witnessed the Dorr Rebellion and labor riots—as another revolutionary moment in which labor must be reinvented and in which people must relearn what freedom is.

Going back to the point about Smith's list of three Haitian Revolutions—the republican uprising against France, emancipation, and independence—there is something valuable to be learned from the first revolution. Conflicts over caste *prior* to the Haitian Revolution, which Smith characterizes as racism, were endemic to the failures of the French Revolution. While McCune Smith's second and third revolutions provide the positive example of liberty, the first returns as a cautionary tale about the errors and lies of caste, which also include racism. As he reveals in his conclusion, referring to the "first revolution," or the conflict between *petit blancs* and *gens de coleur libre*, "this portion of history, is one not unconnected with the present occasion. From causes to which I need not give a name, there is gradually creeping into our otherwise prosperous state, the incongruous and undermining influences of *caste*" (*LHR*, 28, emphasis in the original).

McCune Smith finds free labor ideology complicit in the crisis of the 1840s. From the Age of Jackson onward, as David Roediger illustrates, white working-class hostility toward free blacks, race riots, and an exclusive platform of white manhood suffrage further compromised the rights of northern African Americans. Eric Foner, furthermore, points out that free blacks in the North who had been skilled craft workers prior to emancipation suffered a serious economic downturn after emancipation due to exclusionary practices by white artisans, crasftsmen, and employers. By mid-century, says Foner, "The vast majority of Northern blacks labored for wages in unskilled jobs and personal service."[39] Thus the story of three revolutions in Haiti becomes an allegory of sorts for the "present occasion" in United States politics because the animosity between *petit blancs* and *gens de coleur libre* anticipates the racism that the black citizens of New York face in 1841. Smith's agenda in the speech is rather clear: slavery is evil beyond question; yet the damage caused by slavery extends beyond fundamental deprivations of natural rights and violations of natural law. A racist mythology about Africans that was created to justify and perpetuate slavery occludes the tremendous contributions—intellectual and physical—that black laborers have made and will continue to make in Haiti and the United States, and it destroys the foundations of freedom. Those contributions, and the political economy of the United States, are in jeopardy due to the caste prejudices perpetuated by republican free labor ideology and by the intellectual segregation of black and white.

While Smith condemns "the curse of caste," he does not hide his disdain for the *petit blancs* of St. Domingue, who "suddenly embraced the republican revolutionary principles," forming "Liberty Clubs" that much resemble groups like the U.S. "Sons of Liberty" (*LHR*, 10).⁴⁰ He berates the *petit blancs* for their artificial self-importance, as when they formed an army "in which every officer became at least a general, and every soldier an officer" (*LHR*, 10). Generally referring to them as "scum" and echoing historian J. Brown's assessment of *petit blancs* as "subordinate," "idle," and "dissolute," Smith also notes the passage of laws that deprived free blacks in Haiti of many forms of public employment, privileging *petit blancs* and ushering them into the labor market at the expense of free black men (*LHR*, 13, 6). This system, too, has much in common with the "present occasion" (*LHR*, 28). Smith is rather condescending toward working-class whites (either in revolutionary Haiti or in New York City in 1841). But his point, as a black intellectual, is this: due to its irrational racial prejudice, which is expedient because it protects the economic interests of a riotous and uneducated class of poor whites and the wealthy capitalists who employ them, the United States sells itself short.

As a particularly grievous example of white privilege and prejudice, Smith specifies that, in New York City, "800 children, chiefly of foreign parents, are educated . . . at the expense of all the citizens," while "colored children are excluded from these privileges" (*LHR*, 28). It is important to emphasize that a system that privileges whiteness, even among "foreigners," manifests what Smith perceives as the "unrepublican sentiment" of free labor ideology. In contrast to Toussaint, who, Smith claims, "abolish[ed] caste" and "proved the artificial nature of such distinctions," white politicians in the United States create artificial distinctions, not just between free men and slaves, but contingently between free white men and free black men. Whiteness, Smith seems to intuit, has become a commodity of sorts—conveying unearned privileges even to immigrants. Meanwhile, this denial of educational opportunity is one example of the prejudice that hinders intellectual exchange, a process of black/white cultural commerce that would otherwise build up a legitimate American civilization.

The Myth of Haiti and the Romance of Toussaint

Beginning in 1791 and continuing well into the twentieth century, the fate of Haiti as the first free black nation in the New World was a source of wonder for politicians, abolitionists, proslavery historians, and eugenicists in the United States. This was because Haiti represented both the potential for an egalitarian post-slavery republic that fulfilled the promises of the Declaration of Independence and what Eric Sundquist calls "the fearful precursor of black rebellion throughout the New World."[41] Much writing about Haiti by white abolitionists, as Bogues points out, focuses on the figure of Toussaint Louverture and very often neglects to discuss the progress of the island nation after Toussaint's death in 1802. The horrors that befell Haiti when Napoleon Bonaparte dispatched ten thousand troops to depose Toussaint, reassert French control of the island, and reinstate slavery tend to fall out of the white abolitionist picture, as does the story of how Jean Jacques Dessalines and Henri Christophe fought for independence. Most troubling, however, is the forgetfulness about the men and women, many of whom were born in Africa, who came together to demand a radically egalitarian form of freedom based in land ownership. In his poem "Toussaint L'Ouverture," John Greenleaf Whittier (an excerpt from whose *Songs of Labor* graces the address that Gerrit Smith delivered in 1846) depicted the Haitian slave as fundamentally different from Toussaint. Alienated from the Edenic landscape and dehumanized by the whip, "While in his heart one evil thought / In solitary madness wrought," the slave fought for revenge rather than liberty. Toussaint, the exception, transcended the fierce desire for vengeance and chose "the lowlier and the purer way" toward freedom, pausing in the process to save his master.[42]

Similarly, much of the nineteenth-century literature on the revolution—including Harriet Martineau's influential novel *The Hour and the Man* (1841)—focuses on Toussaint as an enlightened and genteel leader, overlooking the complexities of a diplomatic policy that employed plantation labor in order to provide the tropical commodity crops that could be traded for munitions from the United States, autonomy from the French metropole, or protection from the British navy. Even in recent scholarship, the overwhelming emphasis on Toussaint over Dessalines or Christophe is in part responsible for lack of attention to, or comprehension of, the *Haytian Papers* and what I interpret as Saunders's vision that African Americans could provide better leadership than the "rival chiefs" (*HP*, 13). Instead, this emphasis privileges Toussaint's inclusion among an "enlightened" intelligentsia over the goals of Haitian revolutionaries. Few sources that mention Saunders consider his contribution to Christophe's educational endeavor or how that may have been a mechanism for leveling the hierarchies of labor and property ownership that the Americas inherited from Europe, although they do hone in on his introductory celebration of Haiti's "enlightened" politics.[43]

An overwhelming silence about Haiti's black laborers likewise pervaded European and Anglo-American accounts of the Haitian Revolution in the nineteenth century.⁴⁴ Haiti's implicit republican assertions of revolutionary social change, based in laborers' demands for the redistribution of land, were somewhat inscrutable to proponents of free labor in the United States. Haitians established their right to property through simple standards: a responsibility to work the land and to respect the equal right of all people to do the same.⁴⁵ This helps explain Michel-Rolph Trouillot's well-known claim that for whites in Europe and the Americas, "the Haitian Revolution . . . entered history with the peculiar characteristic of being unthinkable even as it happened."⁴⁶ The appearance of an exotic romantic hero who reaffirmed republican values appealed to white reformers, but a population of freedom fighters who claimed an inalienable right to property was another story entirely.

Matthew Clavin notes the role of *Haytian Papers*, both as a testament to the republican potential of Haiti, and within a "bifurcated" archive that includes either saintly stories of Toussaint or gothic stories of horror. In the latter case, the actions of Haitian freedom fighters were better understood by antislavery whites in the northern United States as a reaction to brutality (which was itself a recapitulation, on the part of slave owners, to the entitlements of an aristocratic past) than as an expression of an a priori understanding of freedom that connected the sovereign self to sovereign land.⁴⁷ Either position conveniently avoids questions of land and labor rights, much less black agency or intentionality.⁴⁸

While the establishment of schools and the dissemination of knowledge or "enlightenment" was a critical accomplishment for northern free blacks (like James McCune Smith) who published papers like *Freedom's Journal* in the 1820s and *Anglo-African Magazine* in the 1850s, the acquisition of property was equally important. *Haytian Papers*, then, is unusual for its focus on Henri Christophe and agricultural labor. It seems to be one of the first sources in which a third archive, in addition to Clavin's "bifurcated archive," appears in African American references to Haiti. Regardless of the actual conditions in Haiti, the island nation offered, at least in Saunders's and McCune Smith's imaginations, more optimal conditions than the United States. Political sovereignty was an essential component of Haiti's allure, as was its geography. While many of Saunders's contemporaries had supported Paul Cuffee's exodus to Sierra Leone, Haiti's proximity to the United States and the relative familiarity of its landscape to African Americans made it a more appealing destination. When the American Colonization Society, an organization comprised mainly of white proslavery men, began to promote Liberian colonization, "People who had supported Cuffe—James Forten, Peter Williams—and people who would support Haytian emigration—Richard Allen, Russell Parrott, Samuel Cornish—led a solid opposition to" it.[49] This opposition stemmed from an aversion to white control in Liberia, but a connection to the geography of the New World may have also influenced the reaction. As Bethel notes, black Philadelphians declared that "our ancestors (not of our choice) were the first successful cultivators of the wilds of America [and] we, their descendents feel . . . entitled to participate in the blessings of her luxuriant soil."[50] For James McCune Smith as well, such references to the soil and a sense of entitlement to the New World landscape are as integral to the myth of Haiti, particularly as it pertains to black labor ideology, as are examples of Toussaint's genius.

PART III

Textualities

THE ESSAYS IN this final section propose that reading and writing about slavery, rebellion, emancipation, and Haiti in particular had wide-reaching consequences for the reception and production of literary culture in both the United States and Haiti. The range of actants and subject matter, as well as the shape of the imagined audience shifted as writers and readers struggled with new dreams and nightmares. The constraints of genre were bent to accommodate new methods of storytelling.

Michael J. Drexler and Ed White note that Toussaint Louverture's 1801 Constitution for a quasi-independent St. Domingue may have been the most widely read text authored by a Caribbean or African American writer up to the publication of Frederick Douglass's 1845 *Narrative*. Together with the satires, commentaries, and elaborate literary fantasies that accompanied its publication, the Haitian constitutional text illustrates how politics and aesthetic form shape one another. Gretchen J. Woertendyke also explores changes in genre, arguing that the Haitian Revolution influenced the development of the form of historical romance. Charles Brockden Brown's novels, essays, and criticism are central to understanding the development of the early American novel during the romantic interregnum, as well as to later nineteenth-century Romantic writers like Edgar Allan Poe, Nathaniel Hawthorne, and Herman Melville. In Woertendyke's essay, Brown is drawn into dialogue with the sclerotic, but wildly popular newsman William Cobbett to show how news and rumors about Haiti shaped the early American novel at the intersection of the genres of romance and realism.

Leonora Sansay's *Secret History; or, the Horrors of St. Domingo* (1808) has gained much attention for being among the most explicit literary registers of the Haitian Revolution. Siân Silyn Roberts notes that the West Indies of Sansay's novel are littered with broken families. The islands are sites where war, privation, and geographic dispersal expose the household as a wholly fragile model for the community at large when called upon to extend across deep cultural and spatial divides. Silyn Roberts proposes that Sansay's *Secret History* offers an alternative model of social relations in which people, goods, and information circulate freely through a circum-Atlantic world, in something akin to "the rhizomorphic, fractal structure" of the transcultural formation that Paul Gilroy calls the "Black Atlantic" and that the essay defines as "cosmopolitan sociability." Peter Reed takes us to the Philadelphia theater scene in 1795, where the crisis in St. Domingue was already being represented on stage. John Murdock's otherwise conventional sentimental comedy, *The Triumphs of Love; or, Happy Reconciliation*, features unusual supporting characters embodying American understandings of slave revolts and suggests that the Haitian Revolution had already begun to infiltrate and alter American conventions even before its final historical impact had become fully evident.

Maureen L. Daut explores the complicated interactions between early Haitian political writers and the northern U.S. newspaper press in the first two decades of Haitian independence and argues that the idea of Haiti as a powerless "apparent state" with an unimportant literary tradition is a concept of more recent vintage that belies the history of Haitian literature. U.S. readers living in the northern states were well acquainted with Haitian authors generally and with the works of the Baron de Vastey (1781–1820) in particular. Vastey composed at least ten prose works, all of which circulated either in the original or in English translation in the Atlantic world: his ideas were thus crucial to the development of northern U.S. American attitudes towards Haitian independence in the early nineteenth century—one reviewer of his works called him "the 'Alpha and Omega' of Haitian intellect and literature." Rather than a nonrelation between Haiti and the United States, Daut traces the substantive interaction—in intellectual and literary terms—between the two nations in the early nineteenth century.

CHAPTER 11

The Constitution of Toussaint

Another Origin of African American Literature

MICHAEL J. DREXLER AND ED WHITE

In the summer of 1801, Toussaint Louverture, the rebel leader of the slave revolt on the French colony of St. Domingue, promulgated a constitution that signaled the quasi-independence of the island. By January of 1804, Haiti would become the second independent republic in the Western Hemisphere, the culmination of the first anticolonial insurgency carried out by former slaves. The 1801 Constitution has generally been overshadowed in the history books—in the rare cases that the Haitian Revolution garners any attention in histories of the early United States—by the story of Toussaint's ascendancy, his arrest and deportation to France, and the rise of his successor, Jean-Jacques Dessalines. But as a document of the age of revolutions, the 1801 Constitution, known as "Toussaint's Constitution," deserves to stand alongside the Declaration of Independence, the Declaration of the Rights of Man and the Citizen, and the U.S. Constitution as a signal text. Our interest here, however, is to make a perhaps more modest claim, but one that could have significant repercussions for the study of early African American literature. Our claim will be that, following its dissemination throughout the United States in the fall of 1801, Toussaint's Constitution became the most widely read piece of literature authored by an African American and may have remained so until the publication of *Narrative of the Life of Frederick Douglass* in 1845.[1]

Several caveats might be immediately raised regarding such a suggestion. Most obviously, the text was neither written in, nor published in, nor even ostensibly about the United States. Moreover, not only was Toussaint not from, in, or of the United States, he was not the author of "his" constitution in any traditional sense. How, then, does a work prepared in the West Indies by a committee of mostly white planters warrant consideration as an important African American text? We would note that similar analogous objections have been raised, together or in isolation, about any number of African American writings. Phillis Wheatley's first book of poetry had to be published in London because neither sufficient subscribers nor willing printers could be found for a North American edition. Despite the popularity and impressively wide dissemination of her elegy on the death of George Whitefield (1771), Wheatley's book would not be published in the United States until after her death.[2] Olaudah Equiano's *Interesting Narrative* is now considered a crucial text of an Atlantic, not to mention U.S., literary canon, not because he visited Pennsylvania or Georgia, nor even because he may have been born in the Carolinas. As Vincent Carretta argues, Equiano wrote of himself, and appealed to those of African descent, as "citizens of the world" at a moment when "trans- or supra-national identities" partly indicated that "national identities were denied them."[3] Likewise, simpler models of authorship have been problematized by African American studies, such that few would dismiss the narratives of Venture Smith and Sojourner Truth, for example, due to the major roles of their amanuenses, Elisha Niles and Olive Gilbert. As we will see, Toussaint's Constitution should also be viewed as a text dictated to amanuenses—in this case, the assembly committee strictly directed by the general. All of these examples demonstrate the necessary reconceptualization of textual and authorial classification demanded by African American writing. Texts written or published outside of the United States are often so precisely because of institutional or cultural hostility, and these difficult conditions in turn necessitate broader understandings of authorship and spatial identity or self-affiliation.[4]

Each of these critiques informs our view that Toussaint's Constitution joins, if not inaugurates, a tradition in African American letters of holding white social and political morality to account for its more abstract and universalizing strands. The appearance of the 1801 Constitution represents a strategic inversion of foundational documents and principles of the West. From Equiano, who leveraged the golden rule to castigate "nominal Christians," to Jones and Allen's appeal for civic recognition, and to the redirection of the U.S. Constitution and the Declaration of Independence in David Walker's *Appeal* and Douglass's Fourth of July oration, Toussaint's Constitution ought to take a place as a most powerful example. It offers students of African American literature both a strong articulation of black agency in letters as well as an unprecedented archive of responses from white audiences in the United States. One might reasonably consider the committee that drafted the constitution as Toussaint's collective amanuensis, albeit under very different conditions than one normally encounters with, say, a fugitive slave narrative. Certainly, too, the 1801 Constitution exemplifies one possible and important manifestation of paranational identity germane to the U.S. context, articulating as it did a revolutionary state determined to protect those of African descent from chattel slave status.

It is difficult to assess the impact of Toussaint's Constitution among the nine hundred thousand or so black residents of the United States in 1801. It is certainly plausible that both slaves and free people of color may have identified more with the emergent black republic of Haiti than with the U.S. republic, which held them in bondage. Gabriel Prosser's slave rebellion in Virginia in 1800 suggests a possible earlier awareness of events in St. Domingue, as do the nineteenth century's numerous plans for relocation to and colonization of Haiti. If African American poetry can trace its roots to Wheatley, the protest tradition in African American letters ought to extend back from James Forten, David Walker, Henry Highland Garnet, Martin Delany, and others to the actions and words of Toussaint. Certainly William Wells Brown suggested as much in the first edition of *The Black Man, His Antecedents, His Genius* (1863), which included extensive profiles of six Haitians (Toussaint, Dessalines, Henri Christophe, Andre Rigaud, Alexandre Pétion, and Jean Pierre Boyer).

What is notable about the 1801 Constitution, however, is that it profoundly intervened in the political self-awareness of the white citizenry and elite as well. Indeed, it arguably challenged the U.S. understanding of revolution and race more than any work prior to (or even including) Douglass's "What to a Slave Is the Fourth of July?" or William Wells Brown's *Clotel*. We get some sense of the text's remarkable impact from its migration through U.S. newspapers, Federalist and Republican alike. The first reports about the constitution appeared as early as August 3, 1801, in the *Baltimore American*. About a week later, it appeared in the national Democratic Republican standard-bearer, the *National Intelligencer*, as well as the chief Federalist organ, the *Gazette of the United States*. Within months, it had appeared in at least twenty-four newspapers from Virginia, Maryland, and the District of Columbia, northward to Philadelphia, New Jersey, New York, Connecticut, and Massachusetts, and even into New Hampshire, Vermont, and the territory of Maine. Such a proliferation dwarfs, for instance, the readership of Equiano's narrative, the first American edition of which ran to but 336 copies, with no second edition until 1829.

Before we return to the circulation and reception of the constitution, let us turn to a description of what we consider to be the text at issue. We do not isolate just the text of the 1801 Constitution itself as the critical text, as it typically appeared as one component within a textual cluster. In this larger grouping, four texts seem particularly important. The first of these reports on events of April 6, 1801—the 17th Germinal in the French Revolutionary calendar—when Toussaint ordered the preparation of a new form of government. In this text, of just under 800 words, Toussaint appoints a committee of eight deputies—two each from the four departments—and orders it to prepare "a constitution suited to [the] climate, soil, culture, trade, and to the manners" of the inhabitants of the "Island of St. Domingo." The second text, running just under 4,000 words, is a full English translation of the constitution itself. There appears to have been only one translation, appearing first in the *National Intelligencer* before its extensive circulation. No indication is given of its translator. The third text, of just over 3,500 words and sometimes appearing in two installments, describes the formal acceptance and promulgation of the constitution on July 7, 1801 (19th Messidor). This textual sequence begins with Toussaint's arrival at Cap-Français and his formal reception; a speech (just over 1,100 words) by the president of the central assembly, Citizen Borgella; an answer from Toussaint (just over 650 words) accepting the new constitution and calling on the citizens of the island to honor the new system; a concluding speech again by Borgella (just over 1,000 words); and a quick summary of the closing ceremonies. Finally, a fourth text (of slightly more than 800 words) sometimes appeared proximate to the above texts: this is the "Character of the Celebrated Black General, *Toussaint L'Ouverture*." The three auxiliary segments—the Germinal convocation, the Messidor promulgation, and the character sketch—were essential to the reception of the constitution itself, and they should be considered part of the larger textual apparatus, just as prefaces, notes, testaments, and accounts of speeches or meetings are essential parts of later fugitive slave narratives.

What, then, is this text? One should first note that it does contain some of the organizational features of the U.S. Constitution and would therefore have been readily identifiable as belonging to the same "family" of texts. Titles 7 through 9, for example, outline St. Domingue's legislative, executive, and judicial branches, albeit with important distinctions. Most notably, power is concentrated in the executive branch—here forcefully equated with the "Government" itself—and, at the moment of the constitution's enactment, the supreme executive, "the Governor," is Toussaint. Indeed, not only is Toussaint named in the text six times, but his "firmness, activity, indefatigable zeal, and . . . rare virtues" earn him the office until "the melancholy event of his decease," at which point his successor will have been named by Toussaint himself.[5] As for the governor's powers, he oversees the military (§ 34), "proposes laws," even those that change the constitution (§ 36), "promulgates" them (§ 34), and "exacts the observation" of all laws and obligations (§ 35). In these points, the constitution codifies its own creation: it exists because it has been called forth and then promulgated by Toussaint. Toussaint is furthermore granted the duties and powers of overseeing finances (§ 38), monitoring and censoring "all writings designed for the press" (§ 39), and suppressing any "conspiracy" against the state (§ 40). With this tremendous, individual concentration of power, the responsibilities of the legislature and the tribunals are definitively subordinated to the governor. The assembly, for instance, "votes the adoption or the rejection of laws which are proposed by the Governor" (§ 24). They are further granted the power of providing opinions on existing laws (§ 24) and of managing the details of the national budget (§ 26). Tribunals shall exist in three tiers: those of "first demand," then of "appeal," and finally of "cassation" or annulment (§§ 44–45). But "special tribunals" organized by the governor shall oversee all military infractions, as well as "all robberies and thefts," "house-breaking," and "assassinations, murders, incendiaries, rapes, conspiracies and rebellions" (§ 47). Furthermore, Titles 10 through 12 extend the power of the governor over local or "municipal" government, the armed forces, and the basic financial matters of the island. Toussaint is granted the authority to nominate all "members of the municipal administration" (§ 49), to control with total authority the armed forces (§ 52), and to appoint a commission of three to "regulate and examine accounts of the receipts and expences of the colony" (§ 62).

The hegemonic hermeneutic of the U.S. Constitution makes many readers today read Toussaint's Constitution cynically. The U.S. text implies a series of beliefs about politics and human nature, laboriously expounded in accounts of Florentine political thought, early modern British history, and principles of the Scottish Enlightenment. Whereas the U.S. Constitution, therefore, enacted theories of collective power and private property, the 1801 St. Domingue text concentrates power in the hands of an autocrat and, read through the same U.S. hermeneutic, seems a power grab. It would be more productive to see Toussaint's governmental apparatus enacting a different hermeneutic, one based not on political principles inflected by a theory of human nature and commerce, but on a particular local history and a state of society that might be called "ethnographic." Indeed, this latter foundation becomes clear when we consider the stunning departures of the 1801 text from that of 1789. For Toussaint's Constitution's opening segments detail St. Domingue's territorial extent (Title 1), its "Inhabitants" (Title 2), its religion and morals (Titles 3 and 4), "Men in Society" (Title 5), and its "Agriculture and Commerce" (Title 6). As even these headings indicate, it would have been difficult not to see the parallels between the 1801 Constitution and the older colonial genre of the ethnography, which structured its analyses of the indigenous other within a similar progression from region and demographics, to morality and religion, and then economy. The insertion of these elements—associated in the turn-of-the-century United States with nonwhite peoples—demonstrated a competing hermeneutic with an unusual defamiliarizing potential.

What is more, this ethnographic strand was peculiarly accentuated by its association with the slave code. The latter, from the memorable moment of the Barbados Code of 1661, demonstrated a transmutation of ethnographic genres, taking a descriptive analytic frequently tooled to penetration and mastery and rendering it a supervisory code for better management and domination. This may be the most remarkable aspect of the 1801 Constitution, which can be read as a revolutionary, emancipatory answer to the French Code Noir, accepting its strictures and structures in order to emphasize its repudiation. Article 2 of Louis XIV's well-known 1685 code enjoined, "All slaves that shall be in our islands shall be baptized and instructed in the Roman, Catholic, and Apostolic Faith," while subsequent articles outlined the rules for marriage, bastardy, and ownership. Article 6 of the 1801 text echoes its predecessor—"The Catholic, Apostolic and Roman religion, is the only one publicly professed"—while subsequent articles elevate marriage, ban divorce, and declare the need to address illegitimate children. This is the slave code rewritten for ex-slaves—an antislavery code in which abolition is emphatically announced at the outset. Section 3 declares, "Slaves are not permitted in this territory; servitude is forever abolished—All men born here, live and die freemen and Frenchmen." As abstract as this principle is, the overall context of the document shows that this revolutionary assertion must be understood as a moral and practical resistance to a specific history of slavery. So Toussaint's Constitution challenges its more abstract counterpart to the north, which is so uneasy with historical and sociological details as to veil these realities with euphemisms like "Persons as any of the States now existing shall think proper to admit" through "Importation" (Article 1, § 9) or the "Person held to Service or Labour in one State ... escaping into another" (Article 4, § 2). From this perspective, the details of Title 8, "General Dispositions," display not odd particularities inappropriate to political theory, but a particular historical consciousness that wants to reward innovations in agricultural technology (§ 70), punish the arbitrary seizure of persons (§ 65), and monitor local "associations inimical to public order" (§ 67). When Section 76 proclaims "that every citizen owes his services to the country that has given him birth, and to the soil that nourishes him, to the maintenance of liberty, and the equal divisions of property, whenever the law calls him to defend them," it is also insisting that allegiance and service to the state have a very particular meaning at a crucial point in the revolution. This is a constitution assuming crisis, not stasis.

One should already be able to anticipate the impact of the 1801 text on a U.S. readership, for whom the constitution may have seemed less a poor cynical imitation than a stunning historical and social revelation about the 1789 U.S. Constitution. Yet, before turning to the 1801 Constitution in its U.S. context, we must outline a final important generic strain to the textual complex—the characterological romance in the portrait of Toussaint himself. As we have indicated, the institutional-ethnographic text of the constitution itself was consistently presented in the U.S. press with auxiliary texts that developed a necessary narrative frame confirming the label of "Toussaint's Constitution." These texts operated on several levels.

The simplest narrative is that of the constitutional ceremonies, summarized above: Toussaint greets the eight members of the assembly (seven of whom were white, one "mulatto," and all former slave owners); he demands that they draft a constitution, "consult[ing] past events to avoid their repetition"; he warns them against "publish[ing] any of the legislative acts you may think proper to make" before receiving Toussaint's approval. After the constitution has been drafted, Citizen (Bernard) Borgella, the head of the assembly, greets Toussaint in a public ceremony of tremendous pomp and circumstance: "The croud was immense.... There existed the most profound silence." Borgella delivers two long speeches, and Toussaint one, somewhat shorter. In fact, the text of Borgella's longer speech concludes by noting that Toussaint offered yet another speech, "which being little more than a reiteration of the sentiments of the orator who preceded him, it would be superfluous to give a translation of."

On another level, these declamations offer a situational explanation of the new constitution. Toussaint and especially Borgella summarized details of colonial history, the Revolution in France (including Bonaparte's return to France from Egypt), the difficult relations between the two realms, and the struggle for order on the island. It is clear that the concern in these speeches is the legitimation of the constitutional enterprise itself, since, despite all assertions of fidelity to France, the "unfortunate colony" has suffered from the "perverse influence" of "the Metropolis." This more broadly colonial narrative confirms and reinforces the ethnographic elements of the constitution summarized above. For a major problem of governance heretofore was the old French constitution, in which a "multiplicity of wheelworks" had "run afoul of each other . . . giv[ing] rise to popular cabals, diversity of opinion, and public Calamities." In short, it was the mechanical differentiation of structures that had provoked first "the Spirit of Party," as devious politicians had known how to "interpret [laws] according to their interests"; conflict, anarchy, and disorder had followed. These catastrophes had been averted by the actions of Toussaint, who, at every moment of seemingly terminal chaos, had risen "like a phoenix from the ashes." He had "take[n] charge of the rein of an abandoned colony," suppressing unrest, unifying the regions, and even "conquer[ing] inveterate prejudices," replacing them with "the most tender fraternity." The new constitution would enact in writing the heroic achievements of Toussaint himself, specifically addressing the demands of the immediate colonial situation: "[Toussaint] announces to you that the time of convulsions is past; he demonstrates the necessity of giving you laws of convenience; and adopting this constant maxim, that laws are conventions established by men, to conform themselves to, for the regulation of the order of society. He makes you conceive that it is with them as it is with the production of the earth, that every country has its manners, its statutes, as well as its appropriate fruits." Inspired by and modeled upon Toussaint, this new text thus answered those "circumstances which present themselves but once during a long series of ages, to fix the destiny of mankind"—not embody timeless principles, as the U.S. Constitution might have it. Finally, the Messidor speeches made clear the pressing demands of the near future: the need for new planters, unification of the island, property regulation, and reestablishment of the plantation system.

Thus the texts of convocation and promulgation together told the story of the constitution as a kind of textual analogue or extension of Toussaint: he had requested, assessed, endorsed, and proclaimed it; his action was demanded and affirmed within it; and its internal logic and propositions reflected those of his behavior in resisting French interference. He was even cast as the local counterpart to "the re-edifying genius" of Bonaparte, who had restored order and unity to France. It is not surprising, then, that these texts were at times accompanied by the "Character of the Celebrated Black General *Toussaint L'Ouverture.*" This short sketch describes the "extraordinary man" in terms of his intelligence, achievements, gratitude, and humanity, but above all his practicality. It mentions his childhood education in France,[6] his rise to military leadership, and his attempts to restore economic order. The key anecdote, however, concerns the request by the British general Thomas Maitland, for the favor of the restoration of twelve planters to their estates. Upon their return, Toussaint "clapped them in prison," but within days had them brought to a church in which he preached a sermon of reconciliation: "We were for a while Spaniards, (the blacks fled to the Spanish protection, in the beginning of the troubles), but we were missed. We were born Frenchmen, and now we are Frenchmen again. These twelve men have also been missed. They were born Frenchmen. For a time they have been British; but now they have returned, and are Frenchmen again. Let us embrace." Here Toussaint embraced them, and reconciled his followers—he restored them to their estates, and gave them negroes as servants. The episode exemplifies a pragmatism consistent with the ethnographic formulations of the other texts, and in contrast to which patriotic affiliations are fickle and relatively meaningless. Even as the sketch affirms Toussaint's service to the French Republic, it likewise stresses that same republic's incompetence and antagonism toward Toussaint. Insisting that Toussaint is *not* concerned with amassing power for its own sake—he "did not treat as an independent prince as some of the papers have said"—the sketch presents him as the most practical of figures, ultimately concerned with restoring "commerce and prosperity." Thus, the character sketch simultaneously emphasizes Toussaint's self-effacing qualities and his heroic actions, such that he becomes the paradigmatic republican.

Such was the textual aggregate that arrived in the United States in August of 1801, with a remarkable circulation through newspapers. If the constitutional text appeared in at least twenty-four papers, the promulgation texts appeared in at least twenty-two, the character sketch in at least seventeen, and the convocation texts in at least five. Newspapers printing these texts ranged across much of the United States: at least seven papers in Connecticut, fourteen in Massachusetts, four in New Hampshire, two in Maine, one in Rhode Island, four in Vermont, two in New Jersey, nine in New York, and five in Pennsylvania. The text even appeared in some of the southern states: in at least three papers in the District of Columbia, two in Maryland, one in Virginia, and three in South Carolina.[7] Though the character sketch appears in papers as early as June 11 (the *American Intelligencer* of Massachusetts), most of the texts appeared in sequential issues of newspapers from August into December.

The impact of the text was surely related to the fractious political context it entered. The conflicts and turmoil of the Federalist era are well known, but three dimensions of that moment—all relevant to the reception of Toussaint's Constitution—may be briefly rehearsed here. Most obvious was the emergence of political parties from the mid-1790s onward. The split had numerous causes, consequences, and manifestations, including an increasingly partisan press and the growing association of the competing factions with Britain (the Federalists) and France (the Democratic-Republicans). Several other dimensions are particularly germane to Toussaint's Constitution, including the increasing formulation of partisan difference in terms of constitutional hermeneutics—for instance, in the 1792 debates over the "general welfare" clause, prompted by Alexander Hamilton's 1791 "Report on the Subject of Manufactures." Also important was President Washington's 1794 attack on the Democratic-Republican societies, widely associated with the so-called Whiskey Insurrection, the largest domestic insurrection in U.S. history prior to the Civil War. Washington's Message to the Third Congress, in November of 1794, explained his oversight, as "Commander-in-Chief of the Militia," of the expedition to suppress the insurrection, while condemning "certain self-created societies" that incited opposition to the state. Four years later, the Kentucky and Virginia Resolutions further highlighted Constitutional disagreements, raising the specter of the dissolution of the union in responding to the Adams administration's Alien and Sedition Acts. The 1800 election could justly seem like a referendum on (among other things) the interpretation of the U.S. Constitution. Within the first year of Jefferson's administration, an assault on the lame-duck Sixth Congress's Judiciary Act was anticipated; Republicans of various stripes would target judges and the very notion of the separate judiciary. In these and other conflicts, basic components of the Constitutional order and its interpretation were challenged: individual freedoms had uncertain foundations, as did the separation of powers; "self-created societies" seemed a threat to the Constitutional order, which apparently did not extend far enough, yet efforts to centralize power had provoked a major domestic insurrection and the first signs of a state secession movement.

During this period, too, political conflicts were increasingly codified in terms of the cult of personality. This characterological fixation had long been a feature of North American political culture, with Washington emerging as an iconic figure even before the Declaration of Independence. But a new wave of character-oriented politics emerged in the 1790s, which is the moment when we see the emergence of that constellation we today know as "the Founding Fathers." "Washington" and "Franklin" were slightly reconfigured from their earlier formulations, as each was appropriated or condemned by a party culture, and as each became the subject of biographical sketches or edited collections of writing. When the actual persons conveniently died (Franklin in 1790, Washington in 1799), they were increasingly lionized and vilified: Washington as the Federalist leader holding together the country or betraying the revolution, Franklin as the true voice of democracy or the hidden seed of revolutionary licentiousness. At the same time, the cults of "Hamilton" and "Jefferson" rapidly took shape, codifying the major figures of the succeeding generation. Both were subjects of much characterological writing from the mid-1790s through the Jefferson administration, in works like John Wood's *History of the Adams Administration* (1801/1802), not to mention a host of pamphlets and newspaper pieces. Other figures were significant in this emerging constellation as well—Thomas Paine, who arrived back in the United States in 1801; Aaron Burr, who emerged as an intriguing foil for both Jefferson (after the 1800 electoral tie) and Hamilton (whom he was to kill); and Adams and Madison, among others. Our point, however, is that these figures had become a symbolic system for thinking about political conflicts, just at the moment that Toussaint's Constitution arrived in the United States.

Finally, and relatedly, U.S. political definitions became increasingly regionalized, specifically around the question of race. This was particularly true with the 1800 election, in which New England was solidly Federalist against the Democratic-Republican South and mid-Atlantic, these divisions reflecting the candidates' regional associations. The Kentucky and Virginia Resolutions demonstrated a regional resistance to the Adams administration that would be answered, during the Jefferson administration, by hints of a New England secession movement. This regional differentiation was thus understood in terms of competing views of the Constitution: what the northern emphasis on a stronger government promoting commerce and naval protection and the southern stress on state authority and agricultural production revealed was the different economic lifestyles of the regions. The difference was in a basic sense a racial one, as was evident in the northern discourse about Jefferson's election as the "Negro President"—that is, elected because of the three-fifths representation clause—not to mention the eventual conflicts over the

1807 Act Prohibiting Importation of Slaves. Furthermore, the regional–racial divide was manifest in the construction of cultic political figures, above all with news of Jefferson's relationship with Sally Hemings, the insinuation that Hamilton was a "creole bastard," the celebration of Washington as benevolent slave owner, or the concomitant sense of Franklin as an abolitionist. In such a climate, the New England writer William Jenks could pen, in 1808, an alternative future history, *Memoir of the Northern Kingdom*, in which a Napoleonic, French-speaking, slave-owning South was imagined at odds with a Britain-affiliated, English-speaking North of commercial and yeoman prosperity.

Each of these dimensions of U.S. political life would contribute to the disruptive power of Toussaint's Constitution. The appearance of the U.S. Constitution and the election of George Washington as the first president had encouraged an elaborate ex post facto mythology of an orderly revolution and its aftermath. But subsequent events seriously undermined this sense. The Constitution was the subject of deep interpretative controversy. As the Massachusetts Regulation seemed to find a more forceful avatar in the Whiskey Rebellion, the 1789 text suddenly seemed sparse, unable to regulate states or even local political associations. The unified myth of Toussaint as the great revolutionary general was suddenly fragmented: either he was the strongman holding together a disintegrating nation, or he was the tool of the old authorities, fostering a newly repressive system of control. The United States, in this context, was increasingly understood in terms of an economic divide that informed most legislative and diplomatic battles. In such a context, events in France and St. Domingue were semiotically charged, seeming to offer a foil for events at home.

The revolution in St. Domingue was also understood through these emerging perspectives. Early accounts of the revolution, following the massive slave uprising of 1791, were informed by the arrival of French Creole refugees fleeing for their lives. Unsurprisingly, these accounts were filled with graphic descriptions of rapacious brutality committed against the white ruling class. As news of black-against-white violence increased, northern states moved to limit slavery, explore various schemes of gradual emancipation, and ban the slave trade. Southerners by contrast began a vigorous defense of their slave-based economies and moved to limit the importation of slaves from the West Indies, fearing that that population would bring a rebellious culture to domestic plantations. By the end of the decade, however, a more accommodating view of the revolution in St. Domingue was taking shape. In the wake of Francophobia and the condemnation of French Revolutionary "excess," Federalist merchants successfully appealed to Congress to consider ways to limit French control over the West Indian carrying trade. What had once seemed a portent of a broadening race war now signaled an irresistible opportunity: to sever French colonial holdings from imperial France, while thwarting long-term French plans to revive ambitions in the Mississippi valley. In 1799, the Federalist-dominated Congress passed what became known as the Toussaint Clause, which allowed trade to continue with French West Indian islands while restricting trade with France. The clause was the first move by the United States to recognize the de facto economic independence of St. Domingue and endorse the legislation's eponymous partner, a black general and former slave. Commercial self-interest for the moment trumped race. But Jefferson's inauguration in 1801 ultimately destroyed any friendly relationship between Haiti and the United States, which would refuse formally to recognize the Caribbean state until after the American Civil War. To be sure, trade policy changed little prior to 1806, when legislation to prohibit direct mercantile trade with the island was sought and implemented. And Jefferson's ambivalence toward Haiti was inflected by his own plans for westward expansion. The official administration position was that Bonaparte would ideally maintain control of the island, but it was quickly understood that St. Domingue would be the base for a renewed French presence in Louisiana, just as it was understood that only Toussaint could make possible the Louisiana Purchase.

In this divided context, in which U.S. political conflicts were refracted through events in the Caribbean, Toussaint's Constitution emerged as a profoundly catalytic text. As we have suggested, the reception of the text was deeply partisan and bivocal. To be sure, few newspapers from the early republican period included editorial commentary in their formats, but this is not to say that opinion-driven content was absent. Opinion pieces, propaganda, or rumor-mongering proliferated through reproduced letters from unnamed correspondents, commentary on articles in rival papers, and the strategic organization of articles within tight-margined pages. Most partisan papers also featured parodies and satires alongside reports of events both foreign and domestic. It is to such ancillary commentary that we now turn, to illustrate at least two competing inflections that emerged.

Federalist newspapers—the most likely to reprint the Toussaint cluster, at a rate of about five to one—were most inclined to place the texts in a positive light. After the passage of the Toussaint Clause in 1799, Federalist papers fairly consistently defended trade with St. Domingue against Republican opposition, regularly voiced for example in the Democratic-Republican

Aurora of Philadelphia. But with the new constitution, the broader political ramifications became evident through the placement of other key storylines.

Discovering "The Character of the Celebrated Black General," for example, printed alongside attacks on Jefferson and Thomas Paine was not uncommon. Writers juxtaposed Paine with hagiographic portraits of George Washington that, like other biographical sketches proliferating since his death, featured the former president's moral and religious virtues.[8] Jefferson made himself an easy target by association when he decided to allow Paine, that international revolutionary and Christian apostate, to return to the United States from France aboard a U.S. Navy vessel. Federalists viewed Jeffersonian support for Paine as an endorsement of the radical antireligious views espoused in *The Age of Reason*, as well as a quiet approval of Paine's criticisms of Washington.[9] To cite another example, the August 4, 1801, *Independent Gazetteer* (Worcester, Massachusetts) published a defense of Washington and Adams, singling out the Alien and Sedition Acts for special praise, while attacking the hypocrisy of Jacobins, democrats, whigs, and other mock republicans.[10] But we might most usefully illustrate the Federalist response with reference to a fascinating piece appearing in the August 13 *Gazette of the United States* in Philadelphia, alongside the promulgation text from St. Domingue. The editors leave no doubt about the relevant context for the excerpt:

> [The following outlines of a Constitution, framed after the model of modern systems of government, are extracted from a work lately published and entitled, "*My Uncle Thomas:*" *a Romance. From the French of Pegault Lebrun*. It will be observed that *My Uncle Thomas* is to *make* the Constitution, and then the people are to *obey* it. This is doubtless the natural and necessary result of persuading the people at large that they are able to govern themselves, and of flattering them with titles of sovereignty till they have wearied themselves out with their own commotions and are glad to gain tranquility by a quiet submission to the constitution of an *Uncle Thomas*, an Uncle *Buonaparte*, an Uncle *Gallatin*, or any body else who will be at the trouble of taking the burthen off their own shoulders. The basis of this excellent Constitution is: "*We are all free and equal**—*but you shall obey me; because*—*I will have it so*"]
> * That is, "all Republicans, all Federalists."
> EXTRACT.
> "You Uncle! You make a Constitution!

"S'death, why not as well as another?
"I fear it will not answer.
"Well, then, I will make a second.
"Which will be no better.
"Then I will try a third.
"Which will not last longer than the other.

"After meditating *two hours* he produced the following:

Rights of Man—"Every man has a right to live in plenty, and without doing any thing for his livelihood.

Of the Government—"General *Thomas* having been proclaimed Grand Regulator, shall regulate and misregulate just as he pleases.

Civil and Criminal Code—"As the only difference among men consists in one wanting what another possesses, no man shall have any exclusive possessions of his own.
 "As Magistrates are useless where there are no disputes, there shall be no Magistrates among us.
 "As there can be no occasion for prisoners, or goalers, or attornies, or hangmen, where there are no Magistrates, there shall be neither hangmen, attornies, goaler or prisoner.
 "We have thus got rid, in a moment, of what has embarrassed the whole world from the earliest period.

Of the Finances—"There shall be established, in extraordinary cases only, a *general* and *voluntary tax*.

Upon Breathing—"My tax is purely voluntary, for those who do not chuse to breath will have no occasion to pay any thing." &c. &c.
 The same humourous writer observes: "Vanity and self-love transform us into strange creatures. There is no man, however low his condition, but thinks himself superior to every one else. I have no doubt but my shoe-black would accept the office of first Consul. All I hope is that it will not be offered to him."

Can Americans *rationally* hope so of their shoe-blacks?

As the text itself admitted, the source here was a 1795 comic romance, Pigault-Lebrun's *Mon Oncle Thomas*.[11] Now the continuum of anti-Jacobin satire is extended to include the U.S. context, with Uncle Thomas referring to Jefferson, as is made clear by the reference to Gallatin and the well-known citation ("all Republicans, all Federalists") from the 1801 inaugural address. Uncle Thomas's constitution becomes a weapon of irrationality and political domination, deliberately denying the social or ethnographic realities of commercial society. Magistrates imply conflicts—so let us do away with magistrates.

What is perhaps most notable about this satire, though, is how close it veers to the St. Domingue text. Toussaint's Constitution might fit the imperious model presented here, from the above dictation to the final reference to the plebeian, perhaps even racialized, figure of the shoe-black—a seeming commentary on the ex-slave-turned-general. But the *Gazette*'s treatment of the Caribbean constitution is consistently positive, revealing several important contrasts. Most obviously, Jeffersonian rule implies a potentially radical constitutional hermeneutic whereby political principles ignore or dominate social realities, thereby reflecting the dangerously idealistic character of the ruler. But Toussaint's Constitution seems to be read very differently, as a properly Federalist text well adapted to existing conditions and emergencies, rather than to the promotion of abstract principles. Of course, such a reading necessitates the repression of Article 3: "Slaves are not permitted in this territory; servitude is forever abolished—All men born here, live and die freemen and Frenchmen." But perhaps as importantly, it necessitated the repression of Toussaint's race as a factor, and a transference of his blackness to Jefferson. Both gestures—deradicalization and reracialization—were necessary for the celebration of Toussaint as counter-revolutionary, as Larry Tise observes. In Tise's view, the Federalists turned to Toussaint as an antidote for both the new administration's republican enthusiasm and the Federalist losses in 1800.[12] Conceived as a counter-revolutionary, Toussaint had successfully reinstituted the rights of property, established a state religion, and re-elevated economic elites: he instated himself as ruler for life with the right to appoint his successor. This is the Toussaint of "The Character of the Celebrated Black General," in which the imperative "to restore the planters, and revive the trade" displaces Toussaint's race, mentioned only in the title and the first paragraph.

We may contrast this configuration with that implicit in the Democratic-Republican press. Few Toussaint texts appeared in those papers, but they were printed in the national partisan journals, like William Duane's *Aurora General Advertiser*. An early opponent of the Toussaint Clause, Duane remained contemptuous of Toussaint, so much so that the *Aurora* was one of the few papers to dedicate space for what might today be called an editorial.[13] His response to the promulgation of the constitution began with a principled objection to its anti-republican articles, but ended with a race-conscious warning to his compatriots in the southern states: "We are among those who deny the competency and question the legality of the authorities assumed by the extravagant organization which has lately been set up in St. Domingo," Duane wrote, launching an attack on Toussaint's character and executive authority. "In the new system of what is called a constitution, we see nothing to respect, nothing to admire, and much to excite abhorrence and disgust." Rather, the constitution was "a spurious mimicry" of its French antecedent, "a new made monster . . . a despotism of the worst kind, formed in the worst manner, conceived in treachery and masked by hypocrisy." The constitution is furthermore "a bitter and malignant satire on free government," foremost because it instates Toussaint governor for life.

Despite the ideological republicanism that drives the first half of Duane's response, the matters of race and slavery are not far away. The 1801 Constitution "ought to suggest to the union the necessity of providing every possible means of security," he continues, advocating liberal naturalization policies to encourage white emigration to the southern states. Toussaint's Constitution may "concentrate the force, ignorance, and superstition, in the great body of the unfortunate and injured descendants of Africa, and capacitate them for mischief—and it may spread some day the storm of retaliating destruction upon the heads of the whites, who may be . . . extirpated. . . . *Woe to the countries in its neighbourhood.*"[14] The argument here essentially inverts the Federalist configuration, which maintained that a constitution must pragmatically respect the social order. By contrast, Duane sees Toussaint's Constitution bracketing true republicanism to serve the aberration of a slave society achieving emancipation. Like the Federalist position, however, the onus of this relationship between constitution and ethnographic orders is placed upon the character of Toussaint, who is implicitly associated with Washington in an adjacent article entitled "TORYISM called FEDERALISM." This piece condemns Federalist editors for assaulting the republican values of the American Revolution, "while frequently the same editors in the same papers eulogize *Washington* as the greatest and best of men."

This split partisan response to the Toussaint texts reveals a fundamental parallax, by which we mean a different perspective orientation due to a change in the position of the observer. In the Federalist configuration, the character of Toussaint (and one might say republicanism) worked to subordinate constitutionality to ethnography, and emerged as an ideal: a heroic military leader fashioned in the model of Washington, but even more lastingly effective than the latter in having more correctly fashioned his constitution. Such a figure could be contrasted with Jefferson or Paine, Francophile Republicans signaling the worst excesses of French Jacobinism. Toussaint's republicanism was Washingtonian Federalism, rejuvenated overseas, but such a fantasy required the suppression of the racial realities of Toussaint's actual achievement. Here, Toussaint was a black *Washington*. For the Democratic-Republicans, however, Toussaint was a *black* Washington. Cynically devaluing republicanism, his agenda was the concentration of power: his obviously authoritarian constitution revealed the Federalist hermeneutic seeking to amass and concentrate power at the expense of the states and the decent associations of white people, who were destined to become de facto slaves. This Federalist elitism, serving mercantile interests and undermining those of the plantation economy, could only mean, eventually, rule by violent slaves, state religion, and an essentially monarchical executive. Republicans openly associated Toussaint with fears of racial warfare and widespread social instability; Federalists envisioned a figure superseding political anarchy, and reestablishing the unification of culture and government. In each instance, Toussaint elevated political conflicts to a far-reaching political fantasy: paranoid race war in the one instance, authoritarian narcissism in the other.

In the U.S. context, the reception of Toussaint's Constitution was, thus, fantastically revealing. Its circulation and that of the auxiliary texts we have identified elicited a partisan bivocal response, one that split upon nothing less than contrary fantasies about the future of the republican experiment in the United States, if not also in the Americas. Most significantly, these reactions to Toussaint's Constitution disclose a pattern that would continue up to and through the Civil War: despite Constitutional compromises designed to postpone reckoning with U.S. slavery, race would symptomatically emerge and define disputes about signal issues of the nation's future.

Considered from another perspective, however, Toussaint's Constitution joins, if not inaugurates, a tradition in African American letters of holding white social and political morality to account for its more abstract and universalizing strands. The appearance of the 1801 Constitution represents a strategic inversion of foundational documents and principles of the West. From Equiano, who leveraged the golden rule to castigate "nominal Christians," to Jones and Allen's appeal for civic recognition, and to the redirection of the U.S.

Constitution and the Declaration of Independence in David Walker's *Appeal* and Douglass's Fourth of July oration, Toussaint's Constitution ought to take a place as a most powerful example. It offers students of African American literature both a strong articulation of black agency in letters as well as an unprecedented archive of responses from white audiences in the United States.

CHAPTER 12

Haiti and the New-World Novel

GRETCHEN J. WOERTENDYKE

To place the Haitian Revolution, rather than the French or American Revolution, at the center of revolutionary studies is to remap American literature. This new map, at base, features "blackness" and calls for investigation of the extent of its influence on the emerging American romance, particularly in its most ambiguous form: the gothic. In this essay, I argue that the Haitian Revolution provides both a political subtext and a generic template for the emerging gothic romance. That is, not only does the black revolution resonate with the specific concerns of the Early Republic, but it can also account for the form's temporality, one quite apart from the British gothic.

At the conclusion of the slave revolution in St. Domingue in April 1804, as the last vestiges of colonial rule were eliminated, the head of state, Jean-Jacques Dessalines, vowed that no European would ever again rule the island's native inhabitants, and then pronounced: "I have avenged America."[1] Dessalines' remarkably explicit connection between the St. Dominguan revolutionary battle for independence from France and slaves in the Americas not only signified his desire to destroy colonial classifications of phenotype, but also served to make "blackness" the defining feature of—and model for—a new nation. Indeed, the 1805 Constitution defined Haitian citizenship as "black," an extraordinary detail that highlights the radical postcolonial possibilities and intentions suggested by the early post-independence document.[2] The reversal of power attained by the black and mixed-race peoples of the former French colony was a potent model for the end of slavery and colonialism beyond the new nation's boundaries and as a result, became a specter of possibility and horror across the Atlantic world.

While Dessalines's provocative claim made this connection explicit, writers and readers in the Early Republic had long grasped the connection implicitly. Tales of violence stemming from St. Dominguan refugees, travel writers, and slave traders crossing the Atlantic made references to "St. Domingo" ubiquitous across a range of 1790s early republican print. Even before the 1793 destruction of Le Cap by insurgents, white southerners were beginning to connect St. Domingue to the building unrest by the creolized black slaves in the States. In a letter to Virginia Governor Henry Lee, Thomas Newton warns of the insidious "example in the West Indies" contaminating local blacks.[3] Pamphlets such as Bryan Edwards's *An Historical Survey of the French Colony in the Island of St. Domingo* (1797) made the extreme violence against the planter class the premise for strengthening slavery in the early republic. A fervent anti-abolitionist, Edwards claimed that "upwards of 100,000 savage people, habituated to the barbarities of Africa . . . [attacked] the peaceful and unsuspicious planters, like so many famished tygers thirsting for human blood."[4] Echoing Jefferson's prediction in *Notes on the State of Virginia* (1785), Edwards concludes that if abolitionism continues to spread, particularly in the new nation where British and French antislavery influences had already sown seeds, slave revolution would become infectious and both whites and blacks would be "exterminated."[5]

Northern abolitionists too mobilized the image of "St. Domingo" in order to undermine the logic of slavery. In a 1791 piece called "The Vision," published in the *New York Magazine, or Literary Repository*, the author, "M," imagines that he "procure[s] a Negro infant boy, and give[s] him the best education."[6] In the rest of the "vision" the now grown black boy introduces and defends the narrator's petition before parliament, on behalf of emancipating the slaves of the "West Indies." But while "St. Domingo" is the source and object of the narrator's ventriloquism, and British Parliament the audience for his hearing, he indicts "America as the principal theatre of our disgrace and of our miseries." The tale ends, like many other tales in the late eighteenth century and early nineteenth century, with the narrator waking up: "For it was nothing but a dream!" The use of "St. Domingo" alongside various associations with "vision"—as divine, prophetic, and a means through which New World slavery is policed—links what seems impossible to know in the future to an unsettling present, one in which early republicans must wake up to the deeper implications of the colonial contest in the West Indies. The latent power of black slaves, as model citizens or violent revolutionaries, is suspended by the sleeping narrator, but "The Vision" still challenges the image of a docile, vacuous slave. The tale also illustrates the interdependency of Britain, the Early Republic, and the French colony in early conceptions of the slave in the United States.

Whether represented as the premise for emancipation or as a rationale for its reinforcement, by the early 1800s, the Haitian Revolution features prominently not just in the Annals of Congress and private correspondence of Thomas Jefferson, but in newspapers, magazine tales, pamphlets, and travel narratives.[7] These popular print engagements with spectacular violence became the material out of which nascent literary forms like the romance emerged, in particular, the gothic, the genre already ripe for representing the anxieties of the new nation.[8] Tales like Edwards's of St. Domingue exacerbate the intensity and expand the context of hysteria over race, slavery, and the burgeoning Democratic-Republican "societies" proliferating throughout the 1790s. While oppositional newspapers such as the Philadelphia *Aurora*, the *New York Journal*, and Boston's *Independent Chronicle*—all fervently pro-French Revolution, Irish sovereignty, and antislavery—printed story after story connecting race with radical politics, Federalist venues like the *Gazette of the United States*, *Peter Porcupine's Gazette*, and the *Farmer's Weekly Museum* identified the "horror" of Jacobinism, Irish uprising, and slave revolt as inescapable consequences of republicanism.[9] The burgeoning gothic thrives on this hysteria and political tension, proliferating ambiguous racial formations for an environment of print already preoccupied with representations of spectacular violence.

Arguing that the "wider Romantic print culture was not merely a pretext for Romantic literary texts, but a significant cultural force in which many key tropes were circulated and consolidated," Ian Haywood suggests that one effect of this circulation and consolidation is a form of literature that "incorporates ineffability as one of the rhetorical devices . . . used to dramatize the 'evil' nature of [its] material."[10] The U.S. gothic romance, in its burlesque violence and sublime terror, also feeds off and reimagines tropes of blackness and foreign invasion circulating in newspapers and periodicals. In the matrix of revolutionary struggle, radical émigrés, antislavery discourse, and the explosion of print in the new nation, the Haitian Revolution was made to uniquely embody the anxiety such forces produced. It became a flexible and versatile short hand for impending violence in the developing U.S. romance.

In the 1790s, writers William Cobbett and Charles Brockden Brown both drew upon revolution and conspiracy, and both also made the alien central to their stories. While Cobbett "circulates and consolidates" tropes of race (blackness and whiteness) in his numerous pamphlets and editorials in the pages of *Peter Porcupine's Gazette*, Brown's novels borrow from—and make abstract—widespread hysteria found in popular print. That is, when Cobbett invokes the "black slave," he mobilizes the fear of large-scale slave revolution so that readers might recognize the potential for Irish uprisings against the British state. Similarly, when Brown uses Irish intruders in two of his novels, *Wieland; or, The Transformation: An American Tale* (1798) and *Edgar Huntly; or Memoirs of a Sleep-Walker* (1799), he invokes the "hordes of wild Irishmen" in order to awaken readers to the threat of slavery for the future of the Republic.[11] What Brown's *Arthur Mervyn; or Memoirs of the Year 1793* (1799) and "Louisiana pamphlets" (1803) make patent is that the Irish serve to screen the real horror of the black slave.

Equally immersed in the cultures of British romanticism and early republicanism, Cobbett and Brown help to integrate the British gothic with local suspicions—of émigrés, secret radical societies, and the moral and political threat of slavery. Reading the work of these contemporary Philadelphia writers together illustrates how the pervasive tropes of "spectacular violence," as they arrive from accounts of the Haitian Revolution, surface in—indeed, give rise to—the gothic romance in its distinctly American form.

William Cobbett's "Cant of the Pickpockets"

As one of the more popular writers of the early national period, William Cobbett helped to plot the romance of America's new nationhood. Despite his alarmist warnings about secret conspiracies, collective violence, and alien infiltration, he remains best known for his anti-Tory politics in *Political Register* and *Rural Rides* from the later period of 1803–1830s in Britain. After the anonymous publication of *The Soldier's Friend* (1792), a scathing satire of the British military, Cobbett fled Britain, narrowly escaping indictment for seditious libel. Fueled by his admiration for Thomas Paine's *Rights of Man*, Cobbett toured France before arriving in Philadelphia later that year. Remarkably, Cobbett immediately critiques the French, Republicans, Africans, the Irish, and begins writing against the general "coarseness" of the American population. As a result, editorials that appeared throughout Philadelphia in 1795–1796 lambaste his increasingly prevalent anti-American publications: Cobbett is referred to as "ass-brained, a booby, a nincompoop, a Lilliputian desperado, a mere adventurer, a monster, a murderer, and a headstrong horse."[12] James

Madison wrote of his "satirical scurrility," and Samuel Taylor Coleridge called him "the rhinoceros of politics with the horn of brute strength on a nose of scorn and hate."[13] Attempts to discredit him during the revolutionary decade underscore the extent of Cobbett's influence in 1796, as the most widely read political writer in the United States.[14]

Cobbett's pamphlets provide a sustained treatment of the more occasional pieces found in his *Peter Porcupine's Gazette*. The pamphlets also chart his transformation from the Painenite politics that motivated his settlement in Philadelphia to the Burkean counter-revolutionary politics that came to define his tenure in the United States. In *The Bloody Buoy* (1796), for example, Cobbett excoriates the French "sans-culottes" in order to warn of the dangers of democracy for the early republic. Speaking of revolutionary France, Cobbett writes, "Hardly had the word *equality* been pronounced, when the whole kingdom became a scene of anarchy and confusion."[15] The pamphlet summons a violent scene from the Abbé Baurruel's "The History of the French Clergy," in which priests are forced to eat the Countess of Perignan and her three daughters, "stripped, rubbed over with oil, and then put to the fire," while revolutionaries "shout and dance" around them.[16] These stark images of cannibalism and savagery echo those found in mid-eighteenth-century captivity narratives, as well as a familiar national narrative with which French "terror" became legible. Much of *The Bloody Buoy* "trac[es] all the Horrors of the French Revolution to their real Causes" found in the "doctrine of equality" and "the *name* of liberty."[17] Cobbett's critical focus lies in the seductive power of words, their ability to be empty signs—liberty exists only in "name"—even while their creative force yields threatening material consequences: not only do people kill and die for liberty, but also "birth, beauty, old age, all bec[ome] the victims" of its "destructive equality." Cobbett writes:

> Let this, Americans, be a lesson to you; throw from you the doctrine of equality as you would the poisoned chalice. Wherever this detestable principle gains ground to any extent, ruin must inevitably ensue. . . . Would you teach servants to be disobedient to their masters, and children to their parents? . . . Would you break all the bands of society asunder, and turn a civilized people into a horde of savages? This is all done by the comprehensive word *equality*. But they tell us we are not to take it in the unqualified sense. In what sense are we to take it then? Either it means something more than liberty or it means nothing at all. The miscon-

struction of the word *liberty* had done mischief enough in the world; to add to it a word of still more dangerous extent, was to kindle a flame that never can be extinguished but by the total debasement, if not destruction, of the society who are silly or wicked enough to adopt its use. We are told, that every government receives with its existence the latent disease that is one day to accomplish its death; but the government that is attacked with this political apoplexy is annihilated in the twinkling of an eye.[18]

Disobedient servants and children, uncivilized savages, ignorance, and idleness—all familiar tropes of terror in the early national period—become the source of "annihilation" in the future. Cobbett consolidates and circulates these tropes—eliding servants, children, and uncivilized savages, and linking the family, home, and domesticity with blackness, immaturity, and violence.[19] As Leonora Nattrass identifies in *William Cobbett: The Politics of Style* (1995), it is Cobbett's keen awareness of audience that shapes his political principles, rather than the reverse.

Cobbett's attention to the singularity of his historical moment—when the nation's "latent disease" threatens to destroy liberty and equality in the "twinkling of an eye"—is surprisingly similar in thematic and temporal structure to Jefferson's private correspondence. In a 1787 letter, Jefferson asks, "What country can preserve it's [*sic*] liberties if their rulers are not warned from time to time that their people preserve the spirit of resistance? Let them take arms." But then after the Haitian Revolution, Jefferson's revolutionary doctrine seems to change.[20] In a 1797 letter, Jefferson warns that "if something is not done, & soon done, we shall be the murderers of our own children.... The revolutionary storm sweeping the globe, will be upon us, and happy if we make timely provision to give it an easy passage over our land."[21] Jefferson's call for an urgent response to slave revolution, to act "soon" and in a "timely" manner, connects the absence of any national critical reaction to an unstoppable force—a "revolutionary storm"—and its devastating consequences.

The letters also make slave revolution teleological. For Jefferson, the ideological, economic, and political reality of the late eighteenth century is poised to produce, in the not-too-distant future, unimaginable violence of global significance. Slave revolution, as figured by Haiti, promises to reconfigure the American landscape. Jefferson concludes: "The day which begins our combustion must be near at hand; and only a single spark is required to make that day tomorrow."[22] Without an imagined future in which the nation is responsible for murdering its children, the motivation to transform the terms of slavery (for Jefferson) and democracy (for Cobbett) remains invisible.

Cobbett's pragmatism and artifice are most suggestive when he compares black slaves with the radical underground political group known as the United Irishmen. Drawing from the increasing paranoia over slave conspiracy, or the "negro slave to the Southward," Cobbett yokes a warning against the contaminating rhetoric of the United Irishmen to a future slave revolution. In *Detection of a Conspiracy, Formed by the United Irishmen, with the Evident Intention of Aiding the Tyrants of France in Subverting the Government of the United States of America* (1798), his conviction that the "French have formed a regular plan for organizing an active and effective force within these States" rehearses his own dark fantasies of Irish violence perpetrated on British soil.[23] In reading the United Irish constitution, Cobbett makes a case against Irish as a very real and present threat to American sovereignty. He relies on Burke's often cited and emotional "Speech on the Occasion of the recommitment of the Quebec Bill, 6 May 1791" as evidence of the danger implicit in the very form of the constitution, specifically its reliance on eighteenth-century systematizing.[24] Burke writes:

> The French Constitution . . . is founded upon what is called the right of man; but, to my conviction, it is founded on the wrongs of man; and I now hold in my hand an example of its effects on the French colonies. Domingo, Guadeloupe, and the other French islands, were rich, happy, and growing in strength and consequence, in spite of the three last distressing wars, before they heard of the new doctrine of the right of man; but these rights were no sooner arrived at the islands than any spectator would have imagined that Pandora's box had been opened, and that hell had yawned out discord, murder, and every mischief; for anarchy, confusion and bloodshed, raged every where; it was a general summons for: "Black spirits and white, blue spirits and gray, mingle, mingle, mingle, you that mingle may."[25]

Citing revolutionary St. Domingue and its "anarchy, confusion, and bloodshed" as the logical extension of rhetoric and constitutional doctrine, Burke connects the foundational documents of the nation with all forms of wrongminded violence and subterfuge and provides both the theory and method for Cobbett's focus in the *Detection*.

The key to understanding Cobbett's bait and switch, however, from a fear of black slave violence in the United States to a fear of Irish rebels expressed in the *Detection*, is found in his simultaneous critique of and reliance on "cant." The word "cant" in its differing connotations of hypocrisy, false piety, and jargon symbolically registers the various threats posed by the United Irishmen for the nation. He claims that "the words Ireland, Irishmen, &c. are mere substitutes for other words, like the cant of the pickpockets, according to which a hog means a shilling, a pig means a sixpence, and so on."[26] From geography to subjectivity—Ireland to Irishmen—"cant" facilities Cobbett's later relocation to St. Domingue and southern slavery.

Cobbett's pamphlet relies on logic of substitution, which allows him to activate several conspiratorial fears at once. He writes, "What renders the situation of America more favourable to the views of France than any other country is the negro slave to the Southward. On this it is that the villains ground their hope." He concludes, "I do not take upon me to say that these preparatory steps have been taken, but this I know, that nothing could be thought more hellish or better calculated to insure success."[27] In an argument against Irish and French Jacobins, the black slave is figured as the last "hope," the bastion of future possibility and horror. Cobbett's conflation of race, region, and history introduces readers to French revolutionary rhetoric and slaves in the south at once. Cobbett's easy movement between the Irish, black slaves, and French Jacobins suggests a quite conscious troping of hysteria. Poised between British nationalism and early American print culture of the eighteenth-century, Cobbett's "politics of style" contributes perhaps not coincidentally to the emerging form of romance in the United States.

"Vehicle" of Terror and the Plot of America's Romance

The singular relationship between gothic romance and revolutionary violence, in Britain and in the Early Republic, requires some explanation, for it is not only the genre's malleability that provides fertile ground for performing historically specific cultural work, but also its fictionality. More specifically, the relationship between romance and violence helps account for the proleptic temporality of the American gothic and its departure from the British form. While the British gothic used the anxieties produced by the French Revolution—anxieties rooted in concerns over the origins of British national identity—the emergence of the American genre relied on an extraordinarily unclear and volatile future, one manifest through a revolution far more threatening to the nation's present, and future, stability.[28]

British gothic novels, such as William Godwin's *Caleb Williams* (1794) and Mathew Lewis's *The Monk* (1796) never mention the French Revolution, but both nevertheless were read as invitations to British citizens to engage in violent protest and revolutionary struggle—to become Jacobins themselves. As Robert Miles outlines the rise of the 1790s British form, "The gothic vogue fed off of the revolutionary anxieties of its readership."[29] The Jacobin Terror (1793–1794), with its spectacle of mob and state violence, pointedly undermined the model of revolution in the Glorious "Bloodless" Revolution—and threatened to radically transform the nation's narrative of origins. William Godwin's suppressed original 1794 preface to *Caleb Williams* describes his "vehicle" as a response to the "spirit and character of the government [which] intrudes itself into every rank of society."[30] A year later, he explains why "the alarms of booksellers" forced its omission: "Terror was the order of the day; and it was feared that even the humble novelist might be shown to be constructively a traitor."[31] Dated May 12, 1794, the same day British Prime Minister Pitt suspended habeas corpus and arrested the leading radical of the London Corresponding Society, Thomas Hardy, Godwin's critique would have been widely understood by his readers.[32] The power of *Caleb Williams* lies in its barely concealed threats, threats that would resonate for British readers in the wake of the French Revolution. What drives the British gothic, however, is not what the French Revolution suggests for the future of the nation, but what it reveals about its origins in 1688.[33]

In his study of the British fiction, Ian Duncan argues that modern romance after novels is dialectical, or the "fulcrum against which—positioned on its edge, between inside and out—reality can be turned around."[34] In *Modern Romance and the Transformation of the Novel*, he suggests that the "essential principle [of romance] *is* fiction: its difference from a record of 'reality', of 'everyday life'." The novel, against which romance comes to be defined, "narrate[s] its historical formation through time." Duncan continues:

> But even as the novel began to totalize its mimetic range it reasserted fiction, and not mimesis, as its critical principle, in an elaborate commitment to plot. Fiction in these novels is the effect above all of plot, conspicuous as a grammar of formal conventions, that is, a shared cultural order distinct from material and historical contingency. To read a plot—to take part in its work of

recognition—is to imagine a transformation of life and its condition, and *not* their mere reproduction. Such is the rhetorical definition of romance."[35]

For Duncan, then, the primary effect of romance is that of plot, one so conspicuous that it becomes its grammar. Its cultural work is to render the transformation of the material world and its conditions rather than its reproduction. That is, at the core of romance is "fiction." Whereas the realist novel "narrates its historical formation through time," romance works diachronically in its use of archetype, which is a feature of its grammar and a trope that speaks to and from particular positions—or spaces—in history.[36] In this way, romance is always "purposeful and allegorical," even as it is situated in some local space and time. Put another way individual works are active inflections, rather than passive members, of the genre.[37]

What, then, is the plot of America's romance? As previous critics have noted, the American gothic is fundamentally shaped by anxiety over race; however, this racial anxiety has been based on a concept of nation largely confined within its geographic borders.[38] Looking at genre necessarily requires critical perspectives that go beyond these markers. To get at this complexity, form needs to be mapped not just spatially but temporally. Wai Chee Dimock offers a notion of "deep time" to account for the structural transformations of American literature, one that "highlights a set of longitudinal frames, at once projective and recessional, with input going both ways, and binding continents and millennia into many loops of relations, a densely interactive fabric."[39] Dimock also cautions against mapping genre since doing so risks "thinning" out this complex network, reducing the "fine grain" of textual nuance to a set of strict codes. But reading for genre does require a pause, a reinforcement of borders even if only temporarily, in order to access the thickening of time such forms manifest. At the same time, if we are to truly map genre temporally, the collapse of various histories, literary traditions, and political conflicts can, conversely, suggest a "thinning" out of time, one that opens up and connects not only past with present but past, present, and future.

While traces of the early nation's history seep through the fissures of the emerging romance, a focus on the past fails to account fully for the form's terrifying effects. As Leslie Fiedler famously notes, "The [British] gothic had been invented to deal with the past and with history from a typically Protestant and enlightened point of view, but what could one do with the form in a country [America] which, however Protestant and enlightened, had (certainly at the end of the eighteenth century!) neither a proper past nor a history?"[40] If the American gothic mirrored the British form insofar as it "felt for the first time the *pastness* of the past," then the Native American would seem the most likely vehicle for producing terror.[41] But Native Americans are by the late eighteenth century already "removed" from republican territory and imaginatively displaced as romantic figures of national origin. While images of the "savage" do remain scattered throughout antebellum literature, as in Brown's *Edgar Huntly; or the Memoirs of a Sleep-Walker* (1799), they persist as reminders of the violence and regeneration of early American literature and history.[42] In short, the amazingly effective management and removal of Native Americans in early national expansion relegate the "savage" to a mythological past-ness in literature as the gothic romance develops into a recognizable genre. The American form, lacking a substantive history to allegorize, is concerned with futures, not origins. I want to suggest that the spectral blackness that haunts early U.S. literature conjoins the West Indies and southern plantations, making alien and monstrous the nation's own worst fantasies over the future of slavery throughout the hemisphere.

Brockden Brown's "Traces of Futurity"

Brown's gothics, populated by strong female characters and Native American "savages," link the future of the nation to the future of slavery. Throughout his editorials and romances, the Haitian Revolution comes to represent this connection. As such, the Haitian Revolution is integral to Brown's theory of the new American romance. Well-versed in the cultural, political, and literary movements of the period, Brown was poised to join two of the governing tropes of Romanticism, sensibility and the sublime, with the spectacular violence and political instability of early republican culture. In a series of installments titled "The Rhapsodist," published in the *Universal Asylum, and Columbian Magazine* in Philadelphia from August through November of 1789, Brown establishes a temporal map of the rising national form.[43]

Here, he grounds the peculiarity of American romance as that which warns against an apocalyptic future. He explains that "we are too much interested in the scene that passes before us, to believe it unreal."[44] For Brown, our investment in the present prevents us from understanding how the nation's misreading of the past is already shaping its future. He continues:

The conclusion of every act, and the final catastrophe of the drama, affect much more nearly than the fading colours of a vision, and the unsubstantial images of sleep. But perhaps it is necessary to abstract our attention from surrounding objects, to transport ourselves some million years forward from the present date of our existence, in order to form a rational conception of the present life, and of our own resemblance to the phantom of a dream. But distance, in this case, will only magnify the prospect. We shall quickly discover, that the present state is built upon a firm and immortal basis; that its traces are forever visible, and its vestiges preserved entire to the remotest period of futurity. Such, in general, is the true opinion we should form of our present state.[45]

Brown's romance "transports" the narrative into "the remotest period of futurity" through some "final catastrophe." In his meditation on romance, Brown introduces a new aesthetic that compliments the political present of late-eighteenth-century America.

Brown's move to "grasp at futurity" is, in part, the result of an inability to conjure the past. Historiography of the Early Republic typically begins at its origin in the American Revolution; but for Brown, the prehistory of the nation is veiled from the American writer. In the absence of a national history, the "moral painter" must turn to "new springs of action, and new motives to curiosity."[46] Brown's essay concludes: "The life of the rhapsodist is literally a dream. If he wishes to review the transactions of any former period, he searches in vain for the memory of it—it is nought but a shadow."[47] The British gothic, motivated by an obsession with origins, contradicts the more triumphant, less ambiguous, and very recent origin of the new nation. This version of the story gets rehearsed in other literary forms, in the tales of Washington Irving and the historical romances of James Fenimore Cooper. Not until the dark romances of Nathaniel Hawthorne is the disturbing and distorting prehistory of the nation given form; however, Hawthorne's theory of romance also registers anxiety in the future. In his preface to *The House of the Seven Gables* (1851) he writes, "The point of view in which this Tale comes under the romantic definition, lies in the attempt to connect a by-gone time with the very Present that is flitting away from us."[48] Brown, very influential on later gothic writers such as Hawthorne and Poe, locates the anxiety of gothic romance in the anticipation of loss, horror, and instability; he locates it in the uncertainty of the future.

Nothing so captured this uncertainty like the future of slavery. The specter of Haiti compelled readers to contemplate the horrors of slave insurrection at a moment when the nation, forced to consider abolitionism, was beginning to polarize along political and regional lines. These tensions shape romance as the nation works to define itself against an array of contradictory needs (say, economic dependence on trade with St. Domingue but also political independence against slave revolt) and amidst various invisible threats, like those Cobbett attempts to make visible. In Brown's third novel, *Arthur Mervyn: or, Memoirs of the Year 1793* (1799–1800), these competing forces and tensions are marked, for this novel is Brown's most explicit novelistic engagement with St. Domingue as the locus of terror.

Phantoms with the power to transport readers and characters are pivotal to this novel. In it, the title character moves between a peaceful farming town outside the urban reaches of Philadelphia and the city central, which is in the grips of a yellow fever epidemic in 1793. With Arthur struck by a ghostly "West Indian phantom" at the height of the panic, the novel traces his gradual consciousness of race and follows him from Philadelphia to the South, along a path that corresponds with his evolution.[49] The novel is set against a backdrop fraught with anxiety over political dissent and foreign immigration, evidenced in the passing of the Naturalization Law of 1790, the Fugitive Slave Act of 1793, and the Alien and Naturalization Acts of 1798. The laws themselves reveal the tension between immigration and slavery, citizens and aliens, as statesmen struggled to maintain the integrity of the "peculiar institution" through segregation of native and foreign blacks.[50] In 1798, Secretary of the Navy George Cabot Lodge wrote: "The cursed foul contagion of French principles has infected us . . . [and] they are more to be dreaded than a thousand yellow fevers."[51] The threat is political, and it threatens to overturn the foundation of early republican democracy. Even so, real reports linking yellow fever to newly arriving ships were not uncommon. In a piece published in the *Pennsylvania Gazette* on September 3, 1800, hints of this connection surface: "The Governor of Virginia has issued his proclamation, enjoining all vessels going from the port of Norfolk, up James River, to perform quarantine at Jordan's point—and also the same to be observed in all other ports within the commonwealth, in consequence of the existence of the yellow fever, or some other contagious disorder, at that place." Brown's novel exploits this perceived relationship between the disease that afflicts thousands in urban Philadelphia and the St. Dominguan refugees.[52]

In the central plot of Part I, Arthur pursues the missing Wallace, not heard from since the onset of yellow fever, in the streets of Philadelphia. Among the ruins, paranoia, and horror of the disease-ridden city, Arthur arrives at a "mansion" and comes upon a dying man. He concludes instantly that, though scarred beyond recognition, he could not be Wallace: "The life of Wallace was of more value to a feeble individual, but surely the being that was stretched before me and who was hastening to his last breath was precious to thousands."[53] The dying man's obvious wealth, "intelligence," and "beauty," in addition to "traces of pillages" Arthur finds throughout the mansion gesture beyond the heart of the republic into the imperial reaches of old Europe and the British gothic. Arthur's confrontation with the dying man as a phantom from the West Indies, however, recodes these gothic conventions to suggest a fraught imperial future for the nation, rather than its fraught colonial past.

A fear of transformation into something alien is underscored by the following scene, as Arthur examines the dying man and his surroundings. Arthur glimpses an "appearance in the mirror":

> It was a human figure, nothing could be briefer than the glance that I fixed upon this apparition, yet there was room enough for the vague conception to suggest itself, that the dying man had started from his bed and was approaching me. This belief was, at the same instant, confuted, by the survey of his form and garb. One eye, a scar upon his cheek, a tawny skin, a form grotesquely misproportioned, brawny as Hercules, and habited in livery, composed as it were, the parts of one view.[54]

The near conflation of the dying man with the grotesque form of the apparition in the mirror tars the symbol of empire-—the dying man-—and makes him corporeally vulnerable to dissolution or transformation into the raced, "misproportioned" form of the West Indian phantom. This vision is experienced as a moment in time, collapsed into fear, with the "swiftness of lightening." To recognize the gross figure in the mirror is to be struck senseless: "A blow upon my temple was succeeded by an utter oblivion of thought and of feeling."[55] Lying unconscious, to be taken for "death" by hypothetical observers he introduces into his tale, Arthur is "haunted by a fearful dream," which he recollects upon returning to consciousness: "I conceived myself lying on the brink of a pit whose bottom the eye could not reach. My hands and legs were fettered, so as to disable me from resisting two grim and gigantic figures, who stooped to lift me from the earth. Their purpose methought was to cast me into this abyss. My terrors were unspeakable, and I struggled with such force, that my bonds snapt and I found myself at liberty. At this moment my sense returned and I opened my eyes."[56] His hands and legs fettered, Arthur's dream-state performs the kind of reversal of power that results from a single moment of violence at the hands of an unknown, partially seen West Indian apparition. Like the protagonist in *Edgar Huntly*, Arthur needs only wake up to be free. He reflects on how "the memory of recent events, was, for a time, effaced by my visionary horrors. I was conscious of a transition from one state of being to another, but my imagination was still filled with images of danger."[57] In Sean X. Goudie's discussion of the novel, Arthur's crucial "transition" ultimately consolidates imperial power and resists West Indian violence through an acceptance of systemic racial classifications and embodiment of white supremacist ideology.[58] But Arthur remains haunted by "images of danger" figured as a West Indian phantom, which leaves him in a state of apprehension about his own future. Like the disease that ultimately contaminates Arthur's body, the West Indian phantom perpetually threatens the body of the nation. The collapse between the fever epidemic, its origin in St. Domingue, and the unidentifiable "phantom"—imposing on the body of Arthur—makes separation of the West Indies from the Early Republic structurally impossible.

In the second half of the novel, Arthur attempts to discipline a "marauding West Indian slave" and his own connection to him. But the most startling use of a St. Dominguan as a harbinger of catastrophic disease occurs when Arthur, on his way to Baltimore from Philadelphia, shares a stagecoach with a "sallow Frenchman from Saint Domingo . . . an ape, and two female blacks."[59] During this trip, the Frenchman sings to the ape, while the "blacks . . . chattered to each other in a sort of open-mouthed, half-articulate, monotonous, and sing-song jargon."[60] Arthur is unable to make sense of the West Indian women, but understands when the Frenchman yells at the animal: "Tenez! Dominique! Prenez garde! Diablo noir!'"[61] The man's loss of control over the "ape," an obvious racial assignation, can be read as a metaphor for France losing control over its slave population in St. Domingue. In a way that he presented in greater detail in his Louisiana pamphlets, Brown suggests in *Arthur Mervyn* that black insurrection would not have been possible were it not for the irresponsible and ineffective managerial skills of French colonial power. The illegibility of the West Indian women's "jargon" conceals their agency, intellect, and intentions. Moreover, like popular conceptions of the slave throughout the south, their docile demeanor may or may not be authentic.[62]

In *Arthur Mervyn*, the racial anxiety embodied by the West Indian phantom and the threatening "ape" is prescient, for both the novel and the nation. For despite Arthur's arrogant objectification of his company in the stagecoach, the "ape" signals that such objectification may not suffice. Arthur's travel to the southern states relocates the narrative geographically where the infection of slave resistance becomes unambiguous and most ominous. In the end, slave violence in the future is reinforced by the parallel plot of the yellow fever epidemic in the first part of the novel. By reading the novel's two parts against and alongside one another, we see how *Arthur Mervyn* tacitly links "St. Domingo" and its explicit threat to slaves in the southern states with violation of the core of early republican Philadelphia through an infection, contamination, and annihilation.

Conclusion

In *An Address to the Government of the United States on the Cessation of Louisiana to the French, and on the Late Breach of Treaty by the Spaniards, Including the Translation of a Memorial, on the War of St. Domingo, and the Cessation of Mississippi to France, Drawn up by a Counselor of State* (1803), Brown writes under the guise of an "ordinary citizen" who accidentally discovers a French plot to infiltrate and colonize Louisiana.[63] This discovery is made in a letter (included in the pamphlet) written to Napoleon. Veiled behind a fictional character, the pamphlet indicts France for mismanagement of its colonies and also highlights an ambivalent history with the new nation. But it is Brown's transparent use of Haitian slave violence to urge early Americans "to awaken . . . from this fatal sleep" that suggests the source of terror in his earlier fiction.

The letter warns against any attempt to regain control of its former West Indian colony, arguing instead for the less bloody prospect of retaining Louisiana, recently brokered by Jefferson amidst much criticism from Republicans as well as Federalists. The letter reads,

> The eye will immediately be turned to St. Domingo. Alas! What have been the miseries of that devoted colony? Beneath what an

ignoble yoke does it now groan! And how lost are its inestimable treasures to the parent nation! And shall not our first efforts be directed to regain these treasures? to break the iron sceptre of the negroes; that has already nearly crushed all the fair fruits of European culture, and which in a few years, by a series of cruel wars and revolutions, will convert those beautiful plantations into an African wilderness?[64]

The violence at the hands of the "negroes" and the prediction of ongoing revolutions will finally destroy any former traces of European civilization: all financial gains will devolve into "African wilderness." Brown raises the specter of "quandon [sic] slaves and naked Banditti" to reinforce his position that France should avoid any more dealings with the "brutes" of St. Domingo, and should instead act with the "caution and deliberation. . . . [that] are the virtues of men."[65] The letter continues, "When I think upon the graves, the ignominious graves, that are gaping, in the plains of St. Domingo, for the conquerors of Egypt and Italy; the inevitable fate from the swords of banditti and slaves, or from the hovering pestilence, which awaits those veterans who have vied, in the usefulness and grandeur of their past exploits, with all that history or poetry has embalmed, I tremble with compassion. . . . and with fear."[66] Gruesome imagery of "gaping" graves, a result of either "swords of banditti and slave" or "the hovering pestilence," links the infectious conditions in St. Domingue during the revolution to yellow fever in the United States. In a final analysis, Brown concludes:

> Forty years has the genius of the French nation slept. Under the influence of the old government, all our faculties were benumbed. St. Domingo, indeed, was permitted to advance. Our islands prospered under that wretched policy, which converted men into cattle, and grasped at present benefits at the hazards of all the evils, by which they have since been overwhelmed. . . . It is time to awaken. Should this fatal sleep continue under the auspices of Bonaparte, fortune will have smiled in vain on that hero.[67]

Brown's attention to the relationship between French imperial domination, particularly its focus on economic prosperity at the expense of humanity (turning "men into cattle") and subsequent "torrents of blood," sends a clear message to early nineteenth-century readers: should the early republic refuse to read St. Domingue as a cautionary tale, it too will suffer.[68]

* * *

I have focused on the writing of William Cobbett and Charles Brockden Brown not because they provide the only, or most obvious, example of spectacular violence found in the wider print culture out of which gothic romance emerged. As the revolutionary decades faded and the nineteenth-century moved toward the crescendo of the Civil War, events like Nat Turner's slave revolt in Southampton, Virginia, and David Walker's publication of the *Appeal* (1829) inspired numerous engagements and fertile ground for imaginative literature.[69] But Cobbett and Brown are helpful models for understanding one genre of romance, the gothic romance, and a tension between origins and futures. As I briefly sketched in this essay, both writers trope race for their own ends, a rhetorical move that would seem to make race more broadly (rather than the Haitian Revolution specifically) constitutive of the American gothic. To be sure, images of Native Americans, underground reading societies, and seduced women, even blackness in general, provide important contexts for understanding an increasingly prevalent and increasingly collective anxiety. But, as I have argued, the effectiveness of these racial tropes draws energy from the spectacular uprisings in St. Domingue.

The example of Haiti illustrated that blacks were poised to join, and to lead, the modern nation-state.[70] Enslaved on the premise of a natural inferiority within an institution that directly challenged the principles of the nation's Enlightenment origins, the potential of both free and enslaved blacks was untapped; and unlike the successful marginalization of Native Americans, blacks in the new nation labored in homes, fields, and churches—very near to and conversant with Anglo-European institutions so important to the budding democracy. The Haitian Revolution and the radical violence it represents, then, over-determines the ways in which late eighteenth-century print was understood. The specter of Haiti conjoins already existing tropes of race and suspicion that define the temporal distinction of the American gothic romance. As such, Haiti's relevance for U.S. literature extends wider and deeper than our literary histories acknowledge.

CHAPTER 13

Dispossession and Cosmopolitan Community in Leonora Sansay's *Secret History*

SIÂN SILYN ROBERTS

In recent decades, literary scholarship has all but accepted the premise that the sentimental tradition authorized and naturalized the bourgeois subject and the contractual state at the level of the family.[1] Two people of equal merit and matching emotional property—Myra and Worthy in *The Power of Sympathy* (1789), say, or the Richmans in *The Coquette* (1797)—achieve individual perfection through marriage as each augments the other with something he or she lacked prior to the exchange, creating between them a certain kind of subject defined by its interiority, autonomy, and ability to regulate its desires. This subject, according to conventional accounts, is the constitutive component of a democratic republic.[2] Indeed, that a wide range of eighteenth- and early nineteenth-century American intellectuals found Enlightenment theories of individual sovereignty, property, and the regulation of emotion essential to their writings now passes for orthodoxy in critical circles.[3] By measuring an auto-generative national culture in terms of the individual and civil society, however, we have given a degree of theoretical privilege to the logic of sovereignty that is simply not supported by a large number of novels from the period. This logic proceeds on the assumption that the selective criteria of self-government and self-ownership are the exclusive grounds on which civil society can be formed. That, to the contrary, early American literary culture often calculated human life in terms other than the elite relationship of individual to contractual state is the starting point of this essay.

What follows is an argument to the effect that Leonora Sansay's epistolary novel, *Secret History; Or, The Horrors of St. Domingo* (1808), is part of an established American literary tradition at the turn of the eighteenth century that assaults the cultural institution of the self-contained, autonomous household; that is to say, the novel turns on the miniature version of the contractual state first imagined by John Locke, who established civil society as an assembly of self-governing, property-owning individuals whose freedoms and rights were produced and guaranteed by the paternal family. The works I have in mind—from *Wieland* (1798) to *Clotel* (1853)—take the family to task for its absolutism and exclusion in a nation defined by the diversity of its people. It is no coincidence that the West Indies of Sansay's novel is littered with broken families. War, privation, and geographic dispersal expose the household as a wholly fragile model for the community at large when the household is called upon to extend across deep cultural and spatial divides.[4] *Secret History* proposes a different model of social relations in which people, goods, and information circulate freely through a circum-Atlantic world, something akin to "the rhizomorphic, fractal structure" of the transcultural formation Paul Gilroy calls the "Black Atlantic" and which I am heuristically calling "cosmopolitan sociability."[5]

It is not my intention to enter the current scholarly debate over cosmopolitanism's viability as a political ethic.[6] I am more concerned with the ways early American authors challenge the presumed dominance of the sovereign nation-state when they question the cultural logic of individualism and familialism underwriting that formation. As Michael Drexler has argued, the Haitian revolution of 1791–1804 transformed the way authors like Charles Brockden Brown and Leonora Sansay conceived political authority, while Sansay's first-hand experience of the displacements and circulations produced by colonial trade and slave insurrection uniquely qualified her for the rhetorical task of reconceiving citizenship in the Atlantic world.[7] To this end, I argue that the two female protagonists of *Secret History*, Clara and Mary, represent a mobile form of humanity defined less by nation, origin, or the household to which they belong and more by the cultural information to which they are granted access. I want to consider how the novel's almost dizzying confluence of generic registers—specifically, the captivity narrative, the Barbary narrative, and the epistolary novel—yields valuable insights into the social dimensions of form; namely, the kind of political collectivity that inheres in the language of captivity.[8] Sansay draws on the conventions of the captivity narrative, I argue, to imagine a workable model of circumatlantic social relations that engages and negotiates the nature of individual freedom and the form of government best qualified to protect and guarantee that freedom.[9]

This argument rests on the claim that the novel helps expose the severe limitations of Enlightenment theories of the autonomous individual and contractual relations as a means of organizing human life in a circum-Atlantic world where people and things circulate a vast, politically volatile geography. In his *Second Treatise of Government* (1689), Locke describes the situation very differently: "Every man has a property in his own person: this nobody has any right to but himself. The labor of his body, and the work of his hands, we may say, are properly his. Whatsoever then he removes out of the state that nature hath provided, and left in it, he hath mixed his labor with, and joined to it something that is his own, and thereby makes his property."[10] When he declares that "every man has a property in his own person," Locke converts both material property and self-ownership into the original condition of individual sovereignty. The subject's uncontested ownership of property serves analogously as the basis for personal autonomy or self-possession, and these qualities make him eligible for citizenship. This model, Locke claims, holds especially true in America, which he imagines as a vacant space outside history and awaiting the inscription of culture by European settlers.[11] The social contract converts this model of self-formation into the means by which a group of such individuals enter into an agreement to respect each other's person and property. Locke would have us believe that the paternal family operates in a manner analogous to the social contract insofar as it produces and preserves both material property and the intellectual conditions of self-sovereignty, or property-in-oneself. Having dismissed patriarchal, hereditary prerogative as a legitimate form of authority in the *First Treatise of Government* (1689), Locke proceeds in the *Second Treatise* (1689) to install a logic of paternalism as a new, modern form of political authority, independent of bloodline or genealogy. We might see the family as a reproduction of the state in miniature, or a "little common-wealth," with all "subordinate" forms of life—namely women, children, servants, and slaves—accorded social status in relation to their proximity to the male authority figure.[12]

Literary critics have all but obeyed Locke's injunction to regard the family as a scale model of contractual social relations when they read the sentimental household as a paradigm for the nation-state.[13] As American authors were quick to recognize, however, this model of government works only if those who head it are the self-sovereign individuals Locke originally had in mind. It is, in other words, an exclusive form of government that presumes a stable and static group of like-minded individuals collectively united on the grounds that each shares similar notions of property and self-ownership. In *The Power of Sympathy*, for example, Worthy recognizes his counterpart in Myra on the grounds that they share similar aesthetic tastes and standards of emotional control. In *The Coquette*, the republican Mrs. Richman imagines her ideal male counterpart as nothing less than "a second self."[14] The sentimental couple Roswell and Lucretia in *Julia and the Illuminated Baron* "loved their own virtues in each other."[15] In each case, the domestic model of social relations demands constituents who are, for all practical purposes, little more than copies of one another.

The Collapse of the Contract

It should therefore come as little surprise to find the household failing, like the state, to govern a human population in the West Indies composed of different and competing cultural groups. The St. Domingue French Creoles, slaves, and military invaders constitute a collective body of incompatible but coterminous differences and interests. Where such difference exists, there can be no common understanding of the rules of citizenship; indeed, the slave insurrection is arguably proof of the dangers of making such an assumption. Key to my argument is the fact that Sansay defines the rival factions competing for political dominance in Saint Domingue in terms of different notions of "property" and "ownership." That she stages the Haitian conflict in this way would have told her readers that she was critiquing proprietary theories of citizenship associated with contractualism. Consider how the novel imagines the ground taken by the former slaves: "They have fought and vanquished the French troops, and their strength has increased from a knowledge of the weakness of their opposers, and the climate itself combats for them. Inured to a savage life they lay in the woods without being injured by the sun, the dew or the rain. The negro eats a plantain, a sour orange, the herbs and roots of the field, and requires no cloathing [sic], whilst this mode of living is fatal to the European soldiers."[16] This cultural geography is conceptually hostile to the "nature" that awaited Locke's settler in America. In St. Domingue, there is no sharp division between culture and nature that allows the individual to convert raw, passive nature into personal property. Rather, the slaves exist in somatic continuity with their surroundings ("they lay in the woods without being injured by the sun," and so on). Hardly the sum of its property-owning individuals, this group is depicted as a single social organism ("the negro"), which surfaces wherever there are resources to be exploited and advantages to be gained.[17] Sansay dismantles self-sovereignty as the measure of political agency when she converts racism into a form of autochthony that works to the slaves' advantage. For the liberated slave, occupation of the land is less a function of settlement and cultivation than opportunism and strategic intensification.

The presence of this social formation puts conventional notions of "property" on the defensive.[18] As Clara puts it, in prerevolutionary St. Domingue "every inch of ground was in the highest state of cultivation, and every body was rich" (*SH*, 144). The slave rebellion underscores the galling irony of such a statement: the five hundred thousand slaves whose forcibly extracted labor produced that wealth are not its beneficiaries and "every body" refers only to the slaveholding Creoles. In Locke's original paternal household, there is no distinction between the slaveholder's labor and that of his slaves because both belong to him alone as forms of property that authorize him as the head of a miniature contractual state imagined in familial terms. *Secret History* takes this logic to task by exposing "cultivation" as a measure of property that serves the plantation elite rather than those who actually mix their labor with the land. As a consequence, the ownership of property loses its rhetorical authority to make individuals. To put it another way, the novel makes it impossible to produce anything resembling Locke's civil subject. It is for this reason, I argue, that the slaves do not become sovereign individuals even once they have reclaimed their labor and the lands they cultivated.[19] For the same reason, the Creoles are unsuccessful in their efforts to repatriate the rebel-controlled island because such a campaign has become an untenable fantasy of a return to origins. This milieu, moreover, is necessarily hostile to the form of white, European masculinity produced and upheld by the laws of sovereignty. Thus, the invading French forces cannot remain in St. Domingue without endangering their cultural purity. Accordingly, they never intend to restore the plantation economy, but instead set out "to make a fortune, and return to France with all possible speed" (*SH*, 66).[20] Indeed, through a regime of embezzlement and extortion, the French exploit the collapse of conventional laws of property by unscrupulously converting St. Domingue's wealth into moveable articles easily inserted into an international economy.

The slave rebellion therefore proves an ideal rhetorical device for questioning "ownership" as the basis of humanity. The rebels' collective repudiation of being owned makes it clear that they cannot be regarded as property. The ancien régime hedonism of the French only partially obscures the fact that the population of St. Domingue has been reduced to endemic homelessness in a ruin of dilapidated buildings and temporary shelters. By transforming the Creoles' property into a wasteland, Sansay illustrates the precariousness of the notions of property on which Enlightenment epistemology was built. In short, the contest over St. Domingue raises the question of who can be properly said to "possess" property where there are contending definitions of ownership in play. Under such conditions, "property" cannot be an absolute foundation for sovereignty and citizenship. With property exposed as a radically exceptional rather than a natural basis of selfhood, the traditional social contract likewise loses ground because it functions only when its constituent members share similar notions of citizenship. To make this clear, Sansay sets out to expose the limits of contractual social relations maintained by the sentimental conventions of the family.

To my mind, the absolute and repeated failure of the paternal household in *Secret History* conveys deep skepticism about contractual relations as a model of civil society. Consider, for example, one of the novel's many interpolated tales in which a sentimental love story ends with the destruction of an entire family. Clarissa, the daughter of a white Creole planter, dies of a fever only days after her marriage. Her father, having abandoned his wife and daughter in Cuba, refuses them all financial and medical assistance.[21] As Mary notes, this father "has lost all sense of justice, reason, or humanity; who, regardless of his duties, or the respect he owes society, leaves his wife to contend with all the pains of want, and sees his child sink to an untimely grave" (*SH*, 115). He has abandoned those masculine qualities—namely "justice, reason, or humanity"—that should accompany a male into the marriage state. We encounter the same failed paternalism time and again in Mary's travels throughout the West Indies. Men are generally murdered or take mistresses as a matter of course, leaving wives and children destitute and vulnerable.

Indeed, nowhere do contractual social relations fail more spectacularly than in the marriage of St. Louis and Clara. Clara, like Clarissa, enters the novel in terms taken directly from sentimental literary convention. Refined, beautiful, and universally admired, she is a love object that, in a sentimental register, should generate the kind of desire in a man that compliments and completes her own emotional property. Her marriage has all the external accoutrements of an exchange based on merit: Clara brings nothing to the exchange other than her exceptional sensibility—she is all but destitute prior to her marriage—while her husband possesses the wealth and social status of a high-ranking French officer and colonial landholder. But St. Louis is also "vain, illiterate, [and] talkative," not to mention vicious, irrational, and violent (*SH*, 63). Clara's emotional property is not matched by any corresponding quality in her husband, who repeatedly assails her autonomy every time he abuses her, which amounts to treating her property-in-herself as his own. Neither is perfected by this exchange because St. Louis lacks the emotional properties of "justice, reason, [and] humanity" necessary to compliment Clara's sensibility and behaves more like a "monster" than a man. His subhuman nature converts their home into a gothic domain when he imprisons, beats, rapes, and threatens to disfigure his wife. These gothic interludes, taken straight from the pages of Radcliffe or Lewis, register the catastrophic failure of the contract when it encounters forms of humanity that do not meet the restrictive criteria of rational individualism.[22] Under such conditions, the contract becomes an altogether destructive force.

By means of countless abusive marriages, extramarital erotic intrigues, and severed familial ties, *Secret History* invites us to consider the other forms of collectivity that the collapse of the household throws into relief. To see how Sansay recuperates this situation as a new form of aggregation, it makes sense to begin with the spectacular obliteration of the sentimental family with which the novel opens.

Upon landing in the West Indies, Mary recounts in her first letter the infamous razing of Cap-François, a populous colonial settlement in northern St. Domingue burned by black general Henri Christophe when French forces invaded early in 1802. Sansay recasts this atrocity as a family tragedy—with the town aflame and the men captured, the liberated slaves force the remaining white Creole inhabitants to evacuate amid the destruction:

> The ladies, bearing their children in their arms, or supporting the trembling steps of their aged mothers, ascended in crowds the mountain which rises behind the town. . . . Here they suffered all the pains of hunger and thirst; the most terrible apprehensions for their fathers, husbands, brothers, and sons. . . . These horrors were increased by the explosion of the powder magazine. Large masses of rock were detached by the shock, which, rolling down the sides of the mountain, many of these hapless fugitives were killed. Others, still more unfortunate, had their limbs broken or sadly bruised, while their wretched companions could offer them nothing but unavailing sympathy and impotent regret. (*SH*, 62)

This scene encourages us to believe that the institution of the family is the first casualty in the war over property. Once the slaves have reclaimed the stolen labor on which domestic plantation sovereignty rests, the sympathetic social body collapses when Sansay reduces it to its constituent parts (women, children, and the elderly) and renders those parts vulnerable for lack of paternal protection ("fathers, husbands, brothers, and sons"). Detached from a home, these constituents lose the enclosure of the domestic sphere and become "fugitives," or part of a population that must keep moving for lack of a home to which it can return. As the emotional adhesive that conventionally binds together the domestic community, "sympathy" is rendered "impotent" and "unavailing" in a milieu where sentimental social relations have been dealt a catastrophic blow. In short, the novel's opening scene places center stage a rootless group of people who are not protected by civil society but who nonetheless cannot be separated from it. What is at stake in such a move?

This scene, I am convinced, registers a tension between civil society and a measure of humanity that lies, literally as well as figuratively, beyond the pale of the state. The rhetoric of the contract implies that all forms of life are protected by the head of the household in whose orbit they are enclosed, but the logic of the contract restricts that privilege to dependents of those who meet the contract's selective criteria of personal sovereignty. Thus the state cannot claim to protect all people, yet neither is it independent of those whom it excludes. *Secret History*'s opening scene puts flesh on this discrepancy. Here, the masculine authority on which the contract depends has been literally overwhelmed by the much larger social body of rebelling slaves who do not qualify as "human," as civil society defines that term. With contractualism's collapse, the domestic subordinates formerly protected by its operations are transformed into something resembling a mass body—or "crowds" of "fugitives"—that mirrors the aggregate of slaves, in that both groups exist in relation to civil society only as social nonbeings. Sansay's point, to put it another way, is that people defined under contractual logic as "citizens" only ever constitute a small subset of a much larger mass of humanity, and the epistemological logic that produces that subset is all too easily dismantled.

In *Society Must Be Defended*, Michel Foucault classifies such a category of human life as a "population," or "a multiplicity of men."[23] By this he means not a count of individual bodies but a "global mass that is affected by the overall processes of birth, death, production, illness, and so on."[24] Understood as a population, the social body conceptually contradicts the twin concepts of individual and nation-state, as Foucault goes on to explain: "The theory of right basically knew only the individual and the social body constituted by the voluntary or implicit contract among individuals. . . . [By contrast,] what we are dealing with in this new technology of power is not exactly society (or at least not the social body as defined by the jurists), nor is it the individual-as-body. It is a new body, a multiple body, a body with so many heads that, while they might not be infinite in number, cannot necessarily be counted."[25] The series of qualifications Foucault makes in claiming that the population is neither society nor a collection of biological bodies carefully extracts any residue of the individual from this new, "multiple body." When it comes to "man-as-species," there is "absolutely no question relating to an individual body."[26] As I see it, each time *Secret History* offers us an account of displaced and impoverished Creole, French, Spanish, American, British, and African refugees, we encounter the Atlantic world in just such terms.[27] When the family's constituents are expelled from the home and forced into nomadic exile through the West Indies and America, the novel mobilizes a vast and heterogeneous mass of people and converts them into a single common body collectively united by a lack of family, home, and property. They are, in other words, conspicuously lacking the entitlements guaranteed by a contractual form of government. The Haitian slave rebellion and consequent mobilization of humanity therefore offer a paradigm for a quantitative measure of people whose rights and freedoms must be protected by a form of government capable of regulating a restless body of inhabitants. In what follows, I want to show how Sansay converts this mass body into a viable form of aggregation.

The Politics of Captivity

As Sansay seems well aware, any form of sociability that displaces individual autonomy in favor of unlimited encounter across multiple coordinates is necessarily hostile to models of community that presuppose sameness, equality, and sympathy among self-sovereign individuals. In the following example, Sansay acknowledges her skepticism concerning contractual social relations even as she establishes the terms for a cosmopolitan collective. This is Mary's account of everyday marriage practices in the West Indies:

> Here female virtue is blasted in the bud by the contagious influence of example. Every girl sighs to be married to escape from the restraint in which she is held whilst single, and to enjoy the unbounded

liberty she so often sees abused by her mother. A husband is necessary to give her a place in society; but is considered of so little importance to her happiness, that in the choice of one her inclination is very seldom consulted. . . . [Once married] she is assailed by those whose only desire is to add another trophy to their conquests, and is borne away by the torrent of fashion and dissipation till all traces of her native simplicity are destroyed. . . . She is now given to the world, and in those who surround her she will find the destroyers of her delicacy, her simplicity, and her peace. (*SH*, 96–97)

The alleged promiscuity of St. Domingue's white Creoles poses much the same problem we encountered between Clara and St. Louis. Rather than producing, guaranteeing, and protecting individual freedoms under a paternal head, marriage subjects a woman to male tyranny that destroys her traditional value as a woman. Here, the practice of trading women to secure the social bonds between men has given way to a system in which women trade themselves in order to secure "unbounded liberty." This phrase, here associated with sexual license, transfers the female through many points of extramarital exchange, a practice Sansay likens to "the contagious influence of example." Such "liberty" proves disastrous to the cultural institution of the home because it is at odds with contractualism, where freedom rests on self-government or the regulation of desire. Even as Sansay uses the language of seduction to register the overthrow of contractual principles, however, she yokes one's detachment from the conventional protections of the home to the idea of dispersal and circulation. The sexual transaction whereby the girl is "given to the world" shifts marriage from a sentimental register to a cosmopolitan one. Sansay may abandon the contract as a model of government, but she nonetheless recuperates and rehabilitates this notion of "unbounded liberty" as freedom to circulate in a larger world. To authorize the novel's large community of detached and disenfranchised women as the cultural bearers of a model of the social body as circulatory system, Sansay removes it from the household—where it can only ever be destructive—and relocates it in a circum-Atlantic setting. To do so, she turns to the conventions of the captivity narrative.[28]

As we have seen, women in this novel are all too vulnerable to tyrannical forms of masculine power within the household—the very domain where they are supposed to be protected by virtue of their proximity to a male authority figure. As a result, the home in *Secret History* paradoxically takes on the function of the wilderness in captivity narratives in which savage men likewise exert despotic forms of power over isolated and helpless females. To think of *Secret History* as something akin to a captivity narrative, we need look no farther than the novel's own language. St. Domingue is a "place of . . . captivity," occupied by "monsters, thirsting after blood, and unsated with carnage" (*SH*, 135, 123). The predatory and rapacious French General Rochambeau is one such "monster from whose power," Mary tells us, "there is no retreat" (*SH*, 104). St. Louis likewise takes on the appearance and behavior of a savage when he tortures his wife: he is, Mary informs us, "more demon than a man," and "nothing can be more brutal than St. Louis in his rage" (*SH*, 84, 87). Prey to such bad men, both Mary and Clara lament their circumstances in language taken directly from the conventions of captivity. Mary "feel[s] like a prisoner" in St. Domingue, and longs to leave "this land of oppression." When her husband's brutality prompts Clara to declare, "My wearied soul sunk beneath the torments I endured and death would have been preferable to such a state of existence," she sounds strikingly similar to a female captive in the tradition of Mary Rowlandson, who prefers death before dishonor in the face of "other" cultural practices (*SH*, 77, 105, 138). To what end does Sansay so consciously engage the conventions of this narrative form?

By placing both Mary and Clara in the position of the female captive, Sansay employs the rhetorical power of the captivity narrative to define the nature of good government. Let us assume that tyrannical power (which invalidates the social contract) exists in the captivity narrative to define good government inversely. The captive comes to recognize legitimate authority by being deprived of its protection: in *The Algerine Captive* (1797), Royall Tyler enjoins his readers to understand Underhill's captivity in just such terms when his protagonist proclaims, "Let those of our fellow citizens, who set at nought the rich blessing of our federal union, go like me to a land of slavery, and they will then learn how to appreciate the value of our free government."[29] So too in John Williams's and Mary Rowlandson's accounts of captivity, the captive secures a place in his or her cultural home by deferring to God as the authority who determines who belongs to the Christian community. Rowlandson turns physical privation into a test of faith that testifies to her eligibility for membership among those favored in the eyes of God. This group is made imaginable through the exclusion and stigmatization of her Indian captors. In returning to a reconstituted English household, Rowlandson makes this social formation the seat of good sovereignty and hence the basis for American identity.

Given that 75 percent of the captivity narratives published in the eighteenth century appeared in the last two decades of that century, we must conclude that this narrative form spoke to the particular interests of its postrevolutionary readers. Indeed, that Rowlandson's narrative experienced a surge in popularity during this period suggests to me that her relatively static, exclusionary model of the nation held considerable appeal for a readership preoccupied with questions of political and social formation.[30] Yet the coincidental vogue for other variations of the captivity narratives likewise tells us that Rowlandson's was simply one of several competing notions for the composition of the new United States. Mary Jemison's 1824 narrative, for example, rewrites American identity from the periphery by proposing a model of community based on incorporation and assimilation. The very Indian practices that Rowlandson had to expel from her version of the nation become the basis of inclusion in Jemison's. In adopting native customs and abiding by their laws, Jemison converts cultural differences into new protocols for American identity.[31] By reproducing an English household in the wilderness, she reconfigures the elite and exclusionary social formation of Rowlandson's narrative into one that can tolerate diversity. Even as she overturns the absolutism of Rowlandson's narrative, however, Jemison nonetheless comes to resemble Rowlandson by imagining American identity in terms of stasis. Her narrative may be structured according to a series of removes west, but she continues to seek a place of permanent settlement. This goal is realized in her parting words: "I live in my own house, and on my own land."[32] The composition of their respective households may differ, but both Jemison and Rowlandson ultimately install some form of stationary, geopolitically circumscribed domain as a metonym for the new United States.

When Sansay turns the home into a wilderness populated by savage and predatory men, she turns this cultural logic of captivity on its head. Unlike the Rowlandson or Jemison models, her novel is conspicuously resistant to national boundaries and preoccupied with the perpetual motions of human displacement—hence the impossibility of permanent settlement. The letters comprising *Secret History* circumnavigate Europe, America, St. Domingue, Jamaica, and Cuba, and movement between these points frames the action: the novel begins with Mary and Clara's transatlantic crossing and ends in anticipation of their return to Philadelphia. Mary may long for the paternal protections afforded by Aaron Burr, but that narrative possibility is deferred by the novel's conclusion, which leaves the sisters once more poised on the verge of flight. This suggests a system that keeps bodies in constant motion between international nodes rather than a pattern of removal and return, while the promise of paternal protection is a fantasy of becoming that remains unfulfilled within the novel's narrative frame—or at the very least, can be fulfilled only in a vaguely utopian, democratic American republic in a distant and unspecified future. According to the logic of captivity, then, bad government in the West Indies emerges as any force that impedes the flow of people by restricting them to a single place or function: St. Louis imprisons Clara in their home, for example, and General Rochambeau refuses to issue the passports that would allow the island's inhabitants to escape. Where Rowlandson obeys a strict cultural imperative to return to her point of origin unchanged, that same imperative proves downright hazardous in this domain. Madame G–, for example, is one of those Creole refugees who returns to St. Domingue "lured by the hope of reinstating her children in their paternal inheritance" (*SH*, 124). In a remarkable reversal of the Rowlandson model, Sansay transforms this homecoming into a captivity narrative: stranded on the island with no means of escape, Madam G– and her daughters are enslaved and executed by the revolutionaries. This vignette tells the same story as Clara's captivity narrative: to pursue the protection and privilege supposedly guaranteed by paternalism in a cosmopolitan setting is chimerical, even dangerous, and stasis is tantamount to slavery and death. Both women clearly have everything to lose by being trapped in one place.

It therefore makes sense that, in contrast with Rowlandson, "removal" in *Secret History* does not threaten cultural identity but rather proves a source of vitality. Trapped with St. Louis, Clara is mentally stultified and physically tortured. Once she escapes her home and husband, however, she emerges with each successive step as a figure of remarkable cultural adaptability, effortlessly suturing herself into every new community to which she flees. It is for this reason, I am convinced, that Clara is permitted a narrative voice of her own only once she escapes her home in St. Domingue and dives into the human current of refugees en route to Cuba. No longer merely the object of her sister's letters, she becomes a subject with a story to tell; she sends her own correspondence into circulation at the very moment she enters the flow of people circumnavigating the Atlantic, as if to signal that one's membership in a mass body need not be a threat to one's own culture but can be indeed a genuine and viable alternative to contractual forms of life. Once her dispossession is complete ("deprived of everything we possessed, in a strange country, of whose language we are ignorant . . . with [no] money" [*SH*, 105]), Clara transforms into the kind of subject ideally suited to a system that favors movement over stasis and transfusion over autonomy:

> Whatever subject may engage her attention, she seizes intuitively on what is true, and by a sort of mental magic, arrives instantaneously at the point where, even very good heads, only meet her after a tedious process of reasoning and reflection. Her memory, surer than records, perpetuates every occurrence. She accumulates knowledge while she laughs and plays: she steals from her friends the fruits of their application, and thus becoming possessed of their intellectual treasure, without the fatigue of study, she surprises them with ingenious combinations of their own materials, and with results of which they did not dream. Her heart keeps a faithful account, not only of every word but of every look, of every movement of her friends. (*SH*, 105, 152)

Insofar as it abandons the processes of "reasoning and reflection"—language taken directly from Lockean faculty psychology and empiricism—Clara's method of collating information clearly opposes the Enlightenment model of the rational and autonomous subject. Rather, her knowledge is a function of spontaneous, and organic impulse. She absorbs and fuses ideas ("ingenious combinations") before sending them back into circulation, suggesting a fundamental continuity rather than contiguity with other minds. Accordingly, she opposes the principles of the social contract (whereby subjects agree not to encroach on the property of other constituents) when she "steals" the "intellectual treasure" of her associates. She comes to resemble the figure of the colonial plunderer we earlier encountered in the French soldiers, who intend "to make a fortune, and return to France with all possible speed." It seems plausible that Sansay recuperates this figure here for its rhetorical possibilities: Clara offers us a measure of humanity defined by its ability to mine information rather than illegitimate colonial spoils. Indeed, Clara's mind is singularly adept at recording and transmitting vast amounts of information (she can monitor every "word," "look," and "movement" of her personal encounters), making her the perfect constituent of a single, integrated social organism promoting the unimpeded circulation of people and ideas around the Atlantic circumference.

In this respect, *Secret History* more closely resembles the form of the Barbary narrative, an equally popular version of the captivity narrative tradition at the turn of the eighteenth century, which, from the vantage point of a white captive, construes an Atlantic world in terms of international commerce while offering an occasion for ethnographic observation. The Barbary narrative brings to a halt the circulation of people, goods, and information through a transatlantic world in order to inversely imagine good government as that which ensures the free circulation of people and things through different cultural spheres. Equal parts domestic drama, ethnographic survey, and intelligence report, *Secret History* likewise transforms the Atlantic world into an unimpeded relay of social, cultural, and political information. Much like conventional Barbary narratives, the novel catalogues the inhabitants and manners of different cultures according to ethnic group: the French, Mary informs Burr, possess an "elasticity" of character and "an inexhaustible flow of spirits"; the white Creole women of St. Domingue "have an air of voluptuous languor"; the Cuban Creoles are "false treacherous and revengeful"; Spanish women are "sprightly, and devoted to intrigue" (*SH*, 61, 70, 120, 112). Rather than hasten to condemn Mary's descriptions as reductive or ethnocentric, let us pause to consider their implications at the level of social relations.

By distilling the West Indies into concentrated cultural information, Mary arguably participates in a system of exchange that privileges contact between populations and ethnic groups over individual experience. We encounter the various constitutive groups in this world in much the same terms that Mary described "the negro": as generalizations in a mass body differentiated at the level of cultural practice rather than as individuals. This is not a matter of assuming that everyone in this system is the same. Rather, it acknowledges cultural difference exists and then provides the possibility that commonality can be found through a shared participation in this informational exchange.[33] Indeed, I would argue that the novel's disjunctive form illustrates the impossibility in this environment of the kind of intimate, sustained knowledge required of individuals in the sentimental tradition adapted from Adam Smith. Its many interpolated tales often read as narrative dead-ends when they, like the novel's many locations, are never revisited or resolved. This form, however, relays the reader through the West Indies with a kind of stochastic motion that moves in multiple directions to produce community as a weave of information that surfaces and submerges without discernable beginning or end.

Conclusion

I believe *Secret History*'s exclusion from the most influential accounts of the early American novel is due not only to the hitherto obscure cultural and political threads tying the colonial Caribbean to North America, but also to its refusal to comply with the nationalist framework that has for so long given the American novel its generic coordinates. I would argue, to the contrary, that the kind of circulations and displacements produced by the revolutionary West Indies and related by Sansay are an indelible feature of American literary production. From *Edgar Huntly* (1799) to *Sheppard Lee* (1836) to *Israel Potter* (1855), the American novel has long been characterized by itinerancy and a cynicism about the protections and rights supposedly safeguarded by the British domestic haven. It is therefore fair to say that authors like Charles Brockden Brown and Leonora Sansay left as their legacy to the early American novel an enduring skepticism about the sentimental household as a tenable paradigm for the American nation. Brown took the family to task on the grounds that the new American republic will include those, like Mervyn, Carwin, Ormond, and so on, whose origins are hidden, remote, or otherwise unrecoverable and who cannot be classified as the land-owning, elite, autonomous, and self-governing, hierarchically organized individuals that Enlightenment thought originally proposed. Sansay puts that skepticism to work in a cosmopolitan, transatlantic context to take into account the vast and heterogeneous groups of people who, dispersed across a wide geographic area, ostensibly lack the requisite qualities of autonomy and self-ownership and whose national affiliations and personal status have long since been eroded or creolized by distance, cultural acclimatization, or the forced extraction of labor. Under such conditions, it is impossible for the people inhabiting this world to meet the exemplary, qualitative political standard of the European Enlightenment.

In this sense, Sansay is part of a long literary tradition that extends well up to the Civil War invested in devising new models of subjectivity peculiarly suited to the shifting political and social needs of North America and a larger Atlantic world. As I see it, novelists like Stowe, Hawthorne, Melville, Warner, Wells Brown, and others all continue to address the question of what Giorgio Agamben and others call "bare life"—namely, the logical relationship of those excluded from civil society to the contractual model of political relations underwriting the U.S. Constitution.[34]

CHAPTER 14

Theatrical Rebels and Refugees

The Triumphs of Love, the Haitian Revolution, and Early American Performance Cultures

PETER P. REED

On May 22, 1795, Philadelphia's Chestnut Street Theatre saw a theatrical representation of the Haitian Revolution in John Murdock's sentimental comedy *The Triumphs of Love; or, Happy Reconciliation*.[1] Although Murdock's comedy does not directly depict St. Domingue's slave revolts of the 1790s, its hapless refugees and rebellious black characters dramatize subtle but meaningful shifts in the Atlantic social worlds during the age of the Haitian Revolution. *The Triumphs of Love*'s plot, though relatively conventional, features unusual supporting characters. Pointing to American understandings of the slave revolts then in progress, Murdock's characters suggest that the Haitian Revolution had begun to alter American conventions and cultural forms in the 1790s. Murdock's rebellious black characters provided audiences with a safe way of encountering Haiti's unthinkable violence, and his refugees, implicated as well in St. Domingue's disorder, allowed audiences to imagine their own local connections to the revolution's offstage refugees, who had begun arriving in significant numbers in American cities soon after the Haitian Revolution began.

The Triumphs of Love shows how popular entertainments operated as sites where the North American public responded to the Haitian Revolution, ridiculing racial revolution but also registering its profound impact through the conventional forms of popular theater. The play and its changing environs also point to ways in which audiences could imagine the points of connection and disconnection among the American, French, and Haitian Revolutions. Murdock's play registers the proximity of a radically changing Atlantic world, even as its stock dramatic devices and clichéd characters—the dissolute Frenchman, the wayward Quaker reformed, the beautifully suffering female stranger, the unruly freed slave—allow audiences to strategically disavow the full import of those changes.

John Murdock's play reached the stage just as early American theater re-emerged from its post–Revolutionary War doldrums. Under the managerial guidance of Thomas Wignell, the New Theatre (later known as the Chestnut Street Theatre) saw increasing success in the 1790s. Wignell, coming to Philadelphia from New York City, had imported a stable of English actors who would become America's first stage celebrities. Those players put on regular seasons of conventional English dramas, recycling Shakespearean favorites and Restoration comedies. Occasionally, the early national stage presented the work of homegrown playwrights, trumpeting their "native genius," but creativity cost more than imitation, and literary originality seems to have been a low priority for troupes, publics, and critics alike.[2] *The Triumphs of Love* exemplifies this phenomenon. Despite Murdock's self-promotional efforts, it appeared only once on any stage, failing to merit a longer production run. Even so, Murdock's play offered relatively distinctive fare for Philadelphia theatergoers. Its local scenes and topical subject matter departed from the general run of English-authored scripts. As Heather Nathans has observed, the play depicts "the Philadelphia Murdock knew, a hodgepodge of recent German and Irish immigrants, slaves and free blacks, Quakers, artisans, and wealthy elite."[3] Advertisements announced Murdock's script as presenting "several interesting subjects, such as Negro Slavery, and our glorious Revolution."[4] Although the ads do not trumpet the fact, Murdock's play also displays the profound impact of refugees from French St. Domingue, who had begun to arrive in Philadelphia in increasing numbers during the 1790s.

The slave revolts and political unrest that would later become known as the Haitian Revolution propelled between fifteen and twenty thousand French Caribbean islanders to North America during the 1790s and early 1800s.[5] Their numbers increased dramatically after June 1793, when slaves burned Cap-Français and forced many of its white residents to evacuate, sometimes in complete destitution. Refugees from St. Domingue arrived in a brief but spectacular influx. Then, according to Gary Nash, by the "spring of 1794, the exodus of French islanders to North America tapered off and by the late fall of 1795 had nearly ended."[6] Philadelphia, one of the epicenters for refugee arrivals, received around five thousand Caribbean exiles—a substantial addition to its forty-five thousand residents.[7] Although many of these refugees eventually returned to France, and some even went back to the Caribbean, those who remained exercised conspicuous influences on Anglo-American culture and theater. Speaking in French, Caribbean, and African accents, the islanders appeared foreign while also interacting and connecting with North Americans in distinctive ways.[8] Under the umbrella terms of "French" and "Creole," the Haitian Revolution thus propelled to North America a radically heterogeneous assortment of free, enslaved, black, brown, and white people—outsiders marked as different and tied together by shared experiences and memories of Caribbean slave revolt.

Murdock scripted *The Triumphs of Love*'s refugees and rebels amid the frictions and interactions generated by Philadelphia's distinctive French Caribbean newcomers. The play's direct attention to St. Domingue's revolution and its characters is rare—very few contemporary Anglo-American dramas refer to slave revolt, let alone to the Haitian Revolution.[9] The characters brought to Philadelphia by the slave uprisings offer Murdock's play more than topical interest, however. Slave revolt reconfigures the raw materials for the sentimental comedy, furnishing usable character types and key plot turns on the way to its titular happy resolution. Articulating subtly shifting structures of feeling, the play registers the impact of the Haitian Revolution's vexed, contingent, and displaced histories as they occurred. St. Domingue and its revolts pose problems and offer solutions for Murdock's play. In its early acts, for example, French Caribbean influences corrupt American characters: Thus, the rakish French dandy Beauchamp leads George, a young Philadelphia Quaker, in playful irresponsibility. George's reform from his youthful dissipation begins only when Beauchamp receives "some bad news" from St. Domingue, which forces him to leave Philadelphia; "cruel necessity" (presumably slave unrest and revolutionary disorder) compels Beauchamp to "sail direct for the Cape."[10] During Beauchamp's absence, George gradually renounces his unruly ways, even freeing his slave Sambo (who has imbibed the troubling revolutionary spirit of St. Domingue's rebels) in what Heather S. Nathans has identified as American drama's first emancipation scene.[11]

French Caribbean influences also assist in the play's resolutions. At the beginning of the final act, Beauchamp's beautiful and destitute sister, Clementina, arrives in Philadelphia, putting an appealing face on the consequences of Caribbean slave revolts. Clementina charmingly declares herself "wretched and unfortunate," deprived of her wealth and sent down a path strewn with "distress and sorrow" (69–70). George, infatuated with his friend's sister, completes his reform by marrying the lovely refugee just as Beauchamp returns to Philadelphia. *The Triumphs of Love*, although at first marking their difference, finally incorporates St. Domingue's refugees into the American social landscape. Murdock's play ultimately embodies them as strangely attractive aliens, victims of distant but somehow intimately familiar violence, outsiders finally naturalized into the American family through the performance of shared trauma.

As Murdock's script and other performances suggest, the Haitian Revolution exercised profound influences on American popular culture and everyday life. Those influences operated in complex, multifaceted, and sometimes repressed or obscured ways.[12] As Sibylle Fischer has persuasively argued, responses to the Haitian Revolution were characterized by "fantasy, paranoia, identificatory desires, and disavowal"; ultimately, "imaginary scenarios became the real battleground."[13] Moreover, the slow-moving processes of repression and substitution that Michel-Rolph Trouillot describes as the "general silencing" of the Haitian Revolution appear to have been already at work in the 1790s.[14]

Murdock's play, of course, is hardly innocent of such tendencies, nor would we expect it to be. On the contrary, it participates fully in the shared practices that formed, reformed, and deformed other representations of St. Domingue and its slave revolution. Even if, as Trouillot powerfully argued, the revolution was politically or historically "unthinkable," its histories have hardly been characterized by a simple lack of representation. Instead, the Haitian Revolution was transformed into the raw material for amusements, and Murdock's play shows just this: the Haitian Revolution becomes "diversion," first diverted or repressed, and then returning as play or entertainment—as seeming distraction. Of course, the entertaining deflection of St. Domingue's slave revolts into play does not necessarily make for resolution. The process does, however, seem to reroute representation into non-narrative, antidiscursive, and extralinguistic modes. In its diversion, the Haitian Revolution inspired pantomime, gesticulation, song, and dance. Staging scene and scenario, the theater indirectly embodied the effects of the Haitian Revolution. If the stage never contemplated the epic horror of the actual revolution, the ghostly presence of revolution nevertheless shaped costume, complexion, mask, gesture, accent, mannerism, and style. Making meaning through allusion, association, innuendo, and exaggeration, performances such as *The Triumphs of Love* trafficked in complex emotions, desires, and fantasies. Theater's paradoxical formal blend of disguise and open display lent itself to the task of characterizing the Haitian Revolution's broader impact on North American culture.[15]

The Triumphs of Love codes representations of the Haitian Revolution using theater's ambivalent forms. Taking those ambivalent and coded meanings into account usefully foregrounds the challenges of understanding how contexts and influences shape cultural expressions. *The Triumphs of Love*'s scenes appear within a matrix of related meanings. Murdock's own personal responses to the Haitian Revolution were no doubt important; his perspective, of course, appeared before readers and spectators, each with their own individual interpretations. At the same time, theatrical acts meet their audiences through preexisting theatrical conventions; those practices make acts legible not simply as individual actions but as variations on types. Plays and other performances also occur at sites that lend specific meanings to the act; other factors such as actors, troupes, and occasional contexts contributed to the meaning as well. Those specific scenarios of performance, moreover, are nestled within broader matrices of related cultural meanings. In the case of *The Triumphs of Love*, the broadly understood traits of French Atlantic people and unruly slaves articulate a complex of assumptions (many unspoken) about national identity, gender roles, racialized characteristics, socioeconomic standing, and political attitudes. Those assumptions were shaped, of course, by collectively held experiences, practices, discourses, perceptions, and assumptions, which drew upon—among other influences—theatrical and social performances.

Murdock's play carries out conflicted cultural work, gathering audience members around unthinkable scenes displayed in conventional forms. St. Domingue's refugees, fleeing scenes of racialized violence, act out nothing more perilous than the risk of not making an idealized love match, but their amusements seem dangerously freighted with the horrors of slave rebellion. Familiar characters, predictable plots, and recognizable generic forms seem loaded with implications in the context of the Haitian Revolution. Slavery and freedom, violence and revolution, all inform the comedic performance, although their threats are ultimately defused by happy reconciliations and marital unions.

At the same time, as the play enfolds the problems of the Haitian Revolution within dramatic conventions, those threats could just as well be seen as driving the plot, with the horrors of slave revolt steering the course of sentimental comedy. Anxieties about slave revolt transform dramatic tensions, heightening the stakes of traditional forms. Even as the play masks the revolution's full import behind lighthearted amusements, the Haitian Revolution has inexorably shifted the implications of such conventions, and Murdock's characters display St. Domingue's corporeal consequences. At the end of the play, the refugees, for example, form a Creole pairing—a potential transnational New World family, innovating upon the usual comic conclusion. The misbehavior of unruly slaves displays veiled threats, embodying the contagious influence of slave revolution. As a response to slave revolt, the play thus radically reimagines sentimental comedy as a product of, and perhaps a performative antidote to, revolutionary black violence.

The play's cultural work, moreover, surpassed the boundaries of the early national playhouse. Its characters and scenes permeated the popular imagination and shaped offstage social interactions. St. Domingue's refugees brought new social performances to everyday life in North America, new ways of presenting identity, and new cultural affiliations. Rebellious slaves and fleeing refugees operated as distinctive social types and enacted competing versions of the Haitian Revolution in public. Such offstage acts, independent from the stage but sharing its forms, techniques, and theatrical principles, show the dispersed kinds of cultural work in which theater took part—the business of embodying slave revolt, of transforming its consequences into entertainment, and of gathering audiences around those scenes. *The Triumphs of Love* shows theatrical texts and social performances each borrowing from and influencing the other. That interplay appears particularly intense in a Philadelphia setting shaped by the Haitian Revolution's radically new characters, scenes, and historical plots.

Performing Refugees

Typical of sentimental comedy, as Lisa Freeman has argued, *The Triumphs of Love* addresses the problems of "good breeding" in changing social contexts.[16] Murdock's play stages a struggle over the character of America's rising youth, setting its conflicts in an early national Philadelphia profoundly altered by slave revolt and the presence of problematic Creole intercultures. The play's early scenes center on the youthful follies and eventual reform of its Quaker protagonist, George Friendly Jr., George's elders worry that "the rank weeds of vice will overgrow the seeds of virtue" (14). Those vices are cultivated by George's friend Beauchamp, a cosmopolitan French planter with ties to

St. Domingue. George celebrates his attachment to Beauchamp, remarking that he is, of "all the young foreigners I am acquainted with, that youth I most esteem"(38). George's affection, cemented by "an hour in young Beauchamp's company," models a profound and immediate attraction to St. Domingue's refugees, a transcending of cultural and national differences through the bonding power of privileged male fraternization (38).

George's attraction to French style and culture spurs a sort of moral panic in the play's imagined world. Beauchamp underwrites a freewheeling, alluring, and rakish youth culture that leads George away from traditional Quaker ideals and into extravagant, dissolute bachelorhood. At times, their youthful sport takes on tones of boisterous homoeroticism, as when George poses as a "damn'd great Frenchman," donning a mask with a suggestively long nose and pursuing a friend with threatening swordplay (48–49).[17] French Caribbean influences seem both playfully rakish and suggestively threatening. Murdock's script seems itself ambivalent about such transgressive and entertaining influences, working to contain the threats even as it conjures them up for the audience's pleasure.

However, as if unable to resolve these tensions, Murdock's script temporarily dismisses Beauchamp, turning away from such dangerous fun. The unrest in St. Domingue requires his return to Cap-Français, the "very jaws of hell" (71). First bringing Beauchamp to Philadelphia, the exigencies of slave revolt then separate the young protagonists and enable George's reform. After the Frenchman's departure, the play displaces George's desires onto Beauchamp's sister, Clementina, another "of the late sufferers of St. Domingo" (81). First appearing in the play's fourth act, Clementina tearfully claims the "privilege of the wretched and unfortunate," to relate her journey to Philadelphia:

> I was in the full enjoyment of all the luxuries of life—and in one day, obliged to fly my country and possessions, with some few hundred dollars: thought myself fortunate in getting a passage for this famed country of liberty and tranquility. But was arrested by the way, by cruel pirates, and stripped of the remnant of my fortune, save a few dollars the relentful [sic] savages left me: and here I am, a wretched refugee; reduced almost to the last extremity. (69–70)

Alone, impoverished, and traumatized by pirates and rebellious slaves, Clementina tells a gripping tale of exceptional suffering. "Oh, who is like unto me," she asks rhetorically, "in so short a time to experience such a reverse of fortune?" (70). Clementina's predicament feminizes the refugee dilemma, turning the drama's attention from the pleasures of cosmopolitan debauchery to the more sentimental pleasures offered by helpless, destitute women.

Those pleasures, of course, produce their own consequences, effects whose seriousness it is a real challenge to decipher. George's friend Trifle, for example, enthusiastically pursues a mixed-race French woman, presumably one of the many slaves and servants of color brought to Philadelphia by the island insurrection. Alongside fantasies of pitiable but attractive white refugees like Clementina, Murdock's play suggests, slave revolution also produces erotic visions of exotic Caribbean women, racially marked characters whose complexion is "superior to all our boasted fair whites and reds" (19–20). Trifle's racialized desire adds interracial attraction to the list of slave revolt's consequences, enacting an illicit version of George's attraction to Clementina.

Taken together, Murdock's French-Caribbean brother and sister embody a beautified, culturally acceptable form of the trauma of slave revolt, distracting the audience's gaze from the Haitian Revolution's offstage horrors. As Clementina's self-indulgent monologue suggests, the play positions them as the distinctive victims of extraordinary hardships. At the same time, Murdock's script uses the refugees to promote transnational Creole identifications and transcultural sympathies, paradoxically converting the horrors of St. Domingue into refined cosmopolitan American pleasures. In the end, the play's exiles allow Anglo-Americans—both on and off the stage—to imagine the United States as itself proudly exceptional, a haven from slave revolt, a "great asylum of the unfortunate and persecuted of all the earth!"(56).[18]

Murdock and his audience responded to offstage slave revolts and refugees in varied ways. Especially before 1793, white Americans could envision St. Domingue's slave revolts as a kindred revolution along with the French Revolution, admiring their colorblind extension of universal rights. White radicals such as the New Englander Abraham Bishop, for example, could advocate black rights and openly praise the uprisings.[19] Other observers, however, reacted with fear and paranoia, while still others sympathized with refugees while condemning them for allowing the slave revolt to happen. Moreover, the presence of a certain number of free *gens de couleur* and mixed-race slaves troubled North American racial categories, and white Americans oscillated between expressions of solidarity and assertions of difference. In addition, local, national, hemispheric, and intercultural politics created reactions "rife with inconsistency and hairsplitting logic," as Ashli White has observed.[20] Of course, St. Domingue's slave revolts could carry entirely different connotations for black onlookers, who could see positive examples or inspiration in St. Domingue's uprisings. The slaves and servants of refugees, moreover, helped spread news of the Haitian Revolution and the political cultures of black Americans.[21] *The Triumphs of Love*, oscillating between sympathy for and suspicion of St. Domingue's refugees, dramatizes Americans' initial collective ambivalence about the Haitian Revolution.

Despite some ambivalence, the dominant American public mood seemed sympathetic toward the exiles after the 1793 burning of Cap-Français. Those refugees, moreover, took active roles in Philadelphia's public life, and Murdock's play participated in an emergent culture of refugee display. For example, theaters began offering benefit nights in the 1790s, donating proceeds to the "unfortunate St. Domingo sufferers" who had arrived in the United States.[22] Outside playhouses, newspaper announcements kept the sufferings of French refugees on exhibit, and the exiles themselves printed an impressive number of scholarly monographs, newspapers, broadsides, gazettes, songs, poems, speeches, and advertisements. In print and public performance, the refugees thus found or put themselves on display, sometimes achieving a sort of celebrity status.[23]

French newcomers also offered language, music, art, and dance lessons, attempting to use social performance to capitalize both upon their cultured reputations and their supposed victimization by rebellious slaves. One newspaper notice, for example, announced the 1794 arrival of a "young married Man," his wife, and three brothers, whom "the disturbances of St. Domingo have driven to America for an asylum." Hoping to "procure for his family those comforts to which they have been accustomed," he advertised music, dancing, and drawing lessons, the "fruits of his education."[24] Attempting to recreate or perpetuate prestigious performances of Caribbean gentility, the lessons also offered access to those leisure practices. In the end, such lessons attempted to translate a lost aristocratic plantation lifestyle into material wealth.

Exhibitions of Creole refinement did not always result in profit, of course, and former islanders sometimes resorted to more extreme measures. The same advertisement also offers for sale two dozen silver-handled knives, a "remnant of his fortune." As St. Domingue's refugees sometimes did, the advertiser performed elegant destitution, simultaneously displaying gentility and material want. The knives became props for the act, at once "handsome" reminders of former wealth and luxurious sublimations of the violence that had driven the refined sufferers into exile. The display of cultured misfortune before a backdrop of imagined black violence, of course, explicitly aimed at recreating the familiar luxuries of St. Domingue. Such acts suggest a certain resilience in exile, the ability to transport cultural performances and adapt them in a strange land. They also reveal the lines of cultural and economic continuity between Caribbean plantations and North American cities; with the sympathy and economic support of many Americans, exiles used cultural performances to restore lost modes of social dominance. Others noticed such connections as well. Leonora Sansay, the onetime companion to Aaron Burr and planter's wife who fled St. Domingue before fictionalizing her experiences in the 1808 novel *Secret History, or, the Horrors of St. Domingo*, remarked upon the exiles' urge to reproduce the "expensive pleasures" of St. Domingue.[25] Refugees transformed the consequences of slave revolt into resources for transcultural exchange, as Sansay (perhaps with some self-consciousness) both observed and demonstrated.

Refugee Theater

While *The Triumphs of Love* participates in the public reception of St. Domingue's refugees, the North American stage also saw visible and distinctive performances by and about those refugees. In the early 1790s, a prominent group of francophone actors appeared in North American cities from Charleston to Boston. Itinerant French actors, some fleeing the French Revolution, had appeared on American stages at the beginning of the decade, but Caribbean revolution made them a permanent, if peripatetic, presence in American theaters. From 1792 onwards, audiences in Boston, New York City, Philadelphia, and Charleston attended entertainments headlined by Alexandre Placide, who had achieved European success as the "first rope dancer to the king of France" before pursuing his trade for three years in St. Domingue.[26] Driven northward by the slave revolts, Placide and his imported actors settled in Charleston from 1794 to 1797. After a few years as a separate troupe, they integrated into Anglo-American companies and circulated among the cities of the eastern seaboard.

Those actors became some of St. Domingue's most visible exiles. Appearing night after night before American audiences, their performances evoked their misfortunes as well as their sophisticated, cosmopolitan ability to traverse boundaries between languages and cultures. St. Domingue's actor-refugees exercised an appeal reminiscent of Murdock's fictional exiles. Their hospitable reception in South Carolina, for example, reveals cosmopolitan attraction and sympathy. Announcing the actors' arrival from St. Domingue, the Charleston *City Gazette* argued that the twin titles of "French" and "unfortunate men" ought to "recommend them to the public benevolence."[27] Audiences in other locales also greeted St. Domingue's refugees with a sense of transnational mutuality based on common economic and racial privileges, shared fears of slave revolt, and the transcultural appeal of Franco-Atlantic theatrical styles. The refugee success also reveals the readiness of North American entertainment institutions to accommodate certain kinds of outsiders.

Although none of the actors in Murdock's play appears to be a known refugee, St. Dominguan actors had appeared regularly on Philadelphia stages during the decade, and thus, Murdock's refugee characters appeared in close proximity to both offstage refugees and refugee actors. The year before *The Triumphs of Love* premiered, French performers had appeared at Philadelphia's Cedar Street Theatre, a seasonal competitor of the New Theatre. A well-known dancer and pantomime performer, Madame Gardie, appeared at the New Theatre itself in 1794.[28] Gardie, displaying on stage "all the fascinating vivacity of her nation," became famous as the "principal attraction" of "the first introduction of serious pantomime on our stage."[29] In June 1794, Gardie had shared her season-ending benefit with Miss Willems, the Anglo-American actor who played Clementina in *Triumphs of Love*.[30] A few weeks after the premier of Murdock's play in 1795, Gardie moved northward, appearing in New York City theater notices.

The acting exiles had a significant impact on Anglo-American theater, and we might image Murdock's characters as appearing in the context of a North American entertainment industry that had been subtly but profoundly altered by the presence of the French performers. Primarily, they introduced their conventional repertoire, bringing French dramas and associated performance styles to American audiences.[31] Philadelphia audiences, for example, witnessed one of the more evocative productions of St. Dominguan exiles when they performed *Mirza and Lindor*, a Parisian operatic export dramatizing competition for the affections of a Creole woman against a background of black Caribbean violence. The play, first produced in 1779, predates St. Domingue's slave uprisings, but its themes were perhaps newly evocative in the 1790s, and even more so in the hands of exile actors.[32] Placide introduced the play to Boston in 1793, and the growing troupe then developed the play into a pantomime extravaganza by 1794. Set on Martinique, the "Grand, Historical, and

Tragi-Heroic Pantomime" staged colonial conflicts among French soldiers, Spanish privateers, and Caribbean "savages," some "dressed in the real custom of those in South-America." Under the direction of Jean Baptiste Francisquy, a French dancer and choreographer who had performed in France, Martinique, St. Domingue, and Charleston, the actors performed a "Military Evolution with the savages, to remind the Governor of the manner the Europeans and the Savages formerly went to War."[33] The play featured numerous blackface roles and dances in character, relying for effect on racial mimicry and performances presented as authentically Caribbean. Advertisements listed a "minuet de la nation," three "savage" dances (one a "pas de cinq" including a child actor), a "Negro dance" and a "Creole dance."[34]

When Philip Lailson, a Swedish circus entrepreneur who had come to the United States from France in 1796, brought the play to Philadelphia with other francophone actors, it carried the subtitle "The First Adventurers in America." The play still featured blackface roles; former Philadelphia star Susanna Haswell Rowson, for example, played Zoé, a servant (presumably darker-skinned), while some of the French actors appeared as six "Negro musicians." A number of local amateurs also appeared as supporting cast alongside the French refugees.[35] As an exile performance in the 1790s, the pantomime presents a wishful mythology of French Caribbean colonial conflicts. Dancing servants and Spanish corsairs stand in for rebelling slaves; only the "Savages," now cowed by the ceremonial exercises of French soldiers, represent the distant memory of island unrest. The scenes seem evocative and wishful, for, as revolts drove slaveholders from their St. Domingue plantations, actors in exile celebrated the supremacy of colonial masters over rebellious islanders and threatening outsiders.

The refugees also altered Anglo-American plays to feature threatening blackface and Caribbean conflict. In 1796, for example, they acted in a New York City production of Richard Brinsley Sheridan's pantomime version of *Robinson Crusoe*, in which exiles (including the famous Madame Gardie) arranged and executed "Negro" and "Savage" dances. In scenes that must have resonated with the refugees' estrangement from both France and St. Domingue, the pantomime staged the "deplorable situation" on Crusoe's island and ended by celebrating the hero's "return to his native country." Victor Pelissier, a musician from Cap-Français, and Monsieur Francisquy, another refugee who had co-managed the Charleston troupe with Placide, composed new music and dances for the pantomime, transforming Crusoe's English colonial adventure into a transcultural, trans-imperial display of Caribbean unrest and triumphal homecomings.[36] In effect, French refugees reenacted nostalgic, even reactionary, revisions of their contemporary revolutionary Caribbean. Such theatricals share with Murdock's play a subjunctive desire to reconstruct or deflect the horrors of Caribbean insurrection and exile.

Blackness, Blackface, and Revolutionary Performances

Those refugee performances literally profited from collective desires to stage the dramas and counter the traumas of St. Domingue. The trouble with representing the Haitian Revolution's refugees, however, was that they inevitably reminded audiences of the slave revolts whose presence they seem to want to repress. As Simon P. Newman has argued, the "very presence" of French refugees continued to evoke "the specter of black insurrection."[37] In *The Triumphs of Love*, the specter of Haiti arguably appears in the character of Sambo. As a conventional figure of blackness, Sambo operates in the stage tradition of wildly kinetic black servants, including most famously the servant Mungo in Isaac Bickerstaff's 1768 comic opera, *The Padlock*.[38] As David Worrall has noted, William Bates, the white actor who played Sambo in blackface in the Philadelphia production, had also written the successful *Harlequin Mungo*, a musical pantomime that premiered in 1787 at the Royalty Theatre in London's East End.[39]

Although a conventional type, Bates's character seems to have taken on edgy and tense overtones in his new American contexts. After Sambo gains his freedom in the American stage's first manumission scene, he parrots French radical slogans and songs, comically reenacting St. Domingue's black revolution. Following these cues, the play's producers presented Sambo as an example of the incendiary influence of the Caribbean; a prologue spoken before the play declares the slave "caught" by the flames of revolt spreading to the United States.[40] Sambo's misbehavior, though framed as comedy, also appears part of a northward-creeping contagion of slave revolt. As one reviewer wrote, Sambo seemed "calculated to irritate the risible muscles."[41] His antics, as the review's language suggests, appear at once exasperating and laughable, both provoking and pleasing. His disorder energizes the play against the white characters' ideals of sedate and sentimental behavior. Performing the pleasures of black rebelliousness, Sambo adds a shrewd and even celebratory brand of low comedy to the play.

Sambo's rebellion operates by imitation and mimicry; his behavior becomes for a time the play's primary joke as well as its overwhelming problem.

Sambo takes cues indiscriminately from his master, radical French republicans, and other freed slaves, threatening to hijack the plot. In his first scene, for example, he plays the trickster servant, reading George's confidential note and scheming to take over his master's role, becoming a "rogue among fair sex too" (19). Later in the first act, Sambo imitates George's song, a rakish celebration of the pleasures of elite misbehavior. Sambo declares his desire (in characteristic stage dialect) to "trife [trifle] time away" as his master does (19). The slave transforms servile imitation into kinetic, celebratory, and unruly blackness. Sambo's stage dialect and comic malapropisms, of course, may dilute any real social critique in scorn for his servile aping. Nevertheless, Sambo's act repeats with a difference—he does not simply imagine a life of privilege; he performs freedom from slavery. Significantly, his mimicry occurs after George's exit; then, Sambo dominates the stage for a brief scene, supplanting his master while imagining elite leisure.

Murdock's script presents Sambo as a counterfeiter mimicking an imitation—George's rakishness is itself a pose, a mannered performance of faux-roguishness. Sambo's mimicry thus answers George's act in kind while compounding his master's act with threatening black male sexuality. Moreover, the tangled composite of imitations and substitutions appears in a layered, black-on-white figure of stylized racial mimicry. Sambo's blackface appears in a sequence of masked acts with no discernible original, a hall of mirrors invoking extended Atlantic genealogies of racial performance. Of course, Murdock's play does not deploy its racial counterfeit as self-consciously as would minstrelsy of the 1820s and 1830s, with its knowing jokes about burnt-cork makeup and genuine imitations.[42] Nevertheless, *The Triumphs of Love* revels in the problems of George and Sambo's mirror-image mutual mimicry; the play seems aware of the complications and implications of racial representation on the American stage, but also willing to transform such tensions into casual entertainment.

Even as it presents Sambo's mimicking misbehavior, Murdock's play works to control that unruly knot of imitations. In one of the play's more sentimental and serious scenes, George manumits the still imitative (but now grateful) Sambo. In the act of freeing Sambo, the play tries to redirect the slave's energies, refiguring his imitative capacity as the desire for improvement. Sambo earns the respect of his master with an "untutored, pathetic soliloquy" that George overhears in the third act (52). It also reveals a keen understanding of the ways African Americans could appropriate conventions of black theatricality. Sambo declares himself "handsome" and "berry complish'd" in singing, dancing, and fiddling; his performance provides proof that "we negro improbe berry much" (52). Observing that he can "tink so, so, pretty well," he goes on to wonder in the third person, "why he slave to white man? Why black foke sold like cow or horse?" (52). Slavery, he asserts, opposes the will of "de great somebody above"; certainly, his bondage runs counter to the emergent abolitionism of the late eighteenth century (52). Although favored with the "bess massa in e world," Sambo laments his continued dependence and vulnerability to the harsh contingencies of a slaveholding society. Overhearing those ruminations "sensibly" affects George, and he grants Sambo his freedom, offering him the option of remaining on wages or leaving (52). Sambo's habitual mimicry, despite its unruliness, thus enables his freedom. George's friend Careless, for example, opposes manumission, declaring that slaves, "after they are set free, become vicious."[43] Although the more enlightened George rejects this as a justification for slavery, he still declares Sambo in "want of education" and post-emancipation guidance (52).

Sambo's sentiments echo the Quaker-inflected rhetoric of Philadelphia's abolitionists, including the prominent doctor and public figure Benjamin Rush, who supported the publication of Murdock's play with a subscription for six copies.[44] The sentiments reassuringly echo the conventional wisdom of late eighteenth-century abolitionism, which sometimes argued, as Benjamin Rush had, that slavery produced "habits of vice" which freedom would only exacerbate.[45] For George (and perhaps for the audience as well), the black mimicry of white thought becomes a gratifying demonstration of Sambo's capacity for humanity, proof he deserves freedom. More pointedly, it offers a critique of white abolition's appetite for pleasurably progressive performances. Sambo's manumission requires him to repeat abolitionist platitudes in another entertaining act, a sentimentalized counterpart to his singing, dancing, or fiddling. For George, the act of manumission itself becomes one of the most "luxurious gratifications" imaginable (53).

Participating in the pleasures of manumission, Sambo shares or mimics George's pleasure, declaring himself full to bursting with emotion. In another of the play's proto-minstrelsy scenes, the former slave declares his desire to "dance and sing," now "more happy dan a king" (53). Sambo sings complex sentiments; elevating slave above king, his lyrics articulate a kind of carnivalesque inversion. At the same time, Sambo declares himself satisfied with emancipation—imagining himself as a king may be just another act of servile mimicry. Sambo's celebratory injunction to dance and sing (made famous in plays such as George Colman's 1787 *Inkle and Yarico*) perhaps seemed a cliched act of ethnically or racially marked characters by the 1790s. At the same time, the moment also provides a foretaste of the nineteenth-century minstrel show as Sambo's act takes center stage, briefly advancing the alluring, charismatic stage presence of blackness. Despite the limitations of his performance, Sambo's act displays an appealing black theatricality. The freed slave dances around the politically charged desires to supplant his master and become a king, putting the theatrical charisma of blackness on display. Starting off as mere mimicry, Sambo's act quickly turns into a celebration of the pleasures and even the allure of black performance that would characterize later blackface minstrelsy.[46]

In freedom, Sambo's threatening antics trouble the play further. Baffling the constraints of racial paternalism, he eludes George's benevolence and makes the imagined consequences of black freedom central to the play's meaning. In the third act, the newly freed Sambo celebrates his manumission with Caesar and Pompey, two other black characters. Entering "with two candles, reeling and singing," he sings a garbled but recognizable rendition of "La Carmagnole" and drunkenly repeats "liberty and quality for eber and eber" (67). Read one way, the scene mocks black imitators of the French Revolution, ridiculing revolution's decline into hiccupping drunkenness— "liberty and quality, heighup, forever" (69). History's grand dramas repeat, as Marx would later observe, in the form of farce.[47] Sambo's slogans stage the dismissive notion that St. Domingue's "Black Jacobins" were merely servile imitators of the French Revolution.[48]

Such scenes can be seen as restaging early national anxieties about French-inspired black radicalism. The stage blackening of French radicalism appeared in other settings, as in a 1797 Boston production of John O'Keefe's *The Poor Soldier*. When local political disputes generated controversy over "Bagatelle," a white character satirizing French revolutionary republicanism, the managers rewrote him as the black valet "Domingo."[49] The move seems slippery, signaling the ongoing Haitian Revolution while somehow appearing more comedic and less controversial when masked behind burnt-cork makeup. Like Murdock's characters in *The Triumphs of Love*, the 1797 rewrite of *The Poor Soldier* reveals the ease with which conventions of performance and spectatorship could reconfigure radical blackness as light comedy. Such scenes participate in the general silencing of the Haitian Revolution, not simply by repressing it, but by reformulating dangerous behavior while nevertheless keeping it near at hand—by making a joke of black insubordination.

Although a drunken slave certainly does not seem very politically dangerous, Sambo's actions implicitly acknowledge the radical potential of black fraternization. Exercising their newfound freedom, Sambo and his inebriated cohort become "mischievous rogues" (68).[50] They appear in Murdock's script dangerously uncontrolled, literally intoxicated with revolution. When George orders him quieted, Sambo resists, violently hiccupping his right to liberty and equality. French radicalism and black freedom, the scene suggests, produce dangerously proud former slaves, and St. Domingue had made such combinations increasingly dangerous. Slaves from the French Caribbean, numbering perhaps a third of all St. Domingue's refugees, were widely regarded as an alien and potentially revolutionary presence. In the mid-1790s, reports reached North America, for example, of Caribbean rebels displaying French cockades; closer to home, "impudent" black Americans, as Simon Newman has observed, appropriated French revolutionary symbols such as Phrygian caps and liberty poles to promote "FREEDOM TO AFRICANS" in the 1790s.[51] In the nineteenth century, Americans increasingly heard of regular, organized black celebrations of French radicalism and Haitian independence. Observers linked St. Domingue's slaves to various plots and uprisings, ranging from spates of arson in the 1790s to Gabriel's 1802 rebellion in Richmond.[52] In Philadelphia itself, refugee slaves increased the black population by 25 percent.[53] Onlookers suspected that these "French Negroes," as they were often called, plotted revolt, spread unrest, and modeled general bad behavior for other black Americans.[54] Legal records indicate that slaves brought by St. Domingue refugees frequently resisted or fled bondage. Gary Nash has found at least 43 advertisements in Philadelphia newspapers for runaway francophone slaves between 1791 and 1797; during the same years, 90 of the 244 runaways listed in the city's Vagrancy Dockets were francophone slaves and servants.[55] With the disruption of mastery through gradual emancipation as well as immediate escapes, Philadelphia's francophone black population seemed increasingly uncontrolled and potentially insubordinate.

Slaves from the French Caribbean may have appeared conspicuously in public spaces; they may have spoken French, Caribbean, or African languages; when they spoke English, it may have been in patois or pidgin forms, or with distinctive accents. And they did not always need to speak, their identity often discernible by distinctive clothing and sometimes branding.[56] At times, such people parlayed their alien appearance into cannily staged performances. A young slave named Tower, for example, escaped from Baltimore in 1793 and headed toward Philadelphia. Wearing a "striped jacket, with sleeves, in the fashion of a sailor's" and walking "with a considerable swing" in his "somewhat bow leged [*sic*]" gait, Tower either had some maritime experience or passed as a sailor. Of course, both ability and pretense could help an escaping slave, especially if Tower intended to travel the same nautical routes that shuttled black sailors and news of revolution to and from St. Domingue. The owner also presumed that Tower, having absconded with some cash, would likely change his appearance. The slave apparently spoke "a little French" and was "known to have put a striped ribbon round his hat," and his owner speculated that Tower would "attempt to pass as one who lately came in the fleet from Cape François.[57] The owner suspected that his slave would take on multiple roles in his escape. Tower could pose as a sailor, manipulating the expectations of mobile and sometimes free sailors, and he must have appeared light-skinned enough to pass as a refugee, blending in with the recent dramatic arrival of mixed-race foreigners. If nothing else, the runaway could signal support of French republicanism with his tricolor ribbon and his repertoire of French phrases, perhaps stirring fellow feeling among American supporters of the French Revolution. Tower's theatrical escape reveals a subtle and cunning manipulation of the forms of theatrical self-display shaped by the Haitian Revolution. His act also reveals the potentially destabilizing effects caused by public displays of St. Domingue's refugees. Tower performed black freedom in a public arena that mustered spectators' abilities to detect runaways—a stage, as Tower knew, on which the field of possible social performances had multiplied radically with the arrival of the St. Domingue refugees.

Official records of St. Domingue's darker-skinned refugees, although certainly failing to capture their full experiences, suggest that outsiders perceived them to move in cryptic and sporadically visible circles. When they achieve visibility in the official record, "French Negroes" often appear as fugitives, running and dodging the policing regime of slavery. One of the more spectacular and apparently alarming performances of St. Domingue appears in an 1804 newspaper account of black Philadelphians who transformed Fourth of July festivities into a local reenactment of St. Domingue's revolutionary violence. The report echoes and perpetuates the notion that unrestrained blacks might enact violent imitations of St. Domingue, confederating and causing trouble in North American cities. The account claims "a considerable number of strange black people" loitering about, blaming the disturbance on intrusive outsiders. As the black celebrants gathered in the streets, they allegedly threatened bystanders and even performed acts of violence. Reaching a fever pitch, the outraged accounts culminate with the black celebrants' threats to "shew them *St. Domingo!*"⁵⁸ The event, with its display of threatening mimicry, constitutes theatrical behavior; the account itself seems unabashedly theatrical as well, displaying in print a crowd of threatening aliens whose unruliness finally erupts into violence. Ultimately, the suspicious account turns on the uttered threat to repeat and perhaps surpass the spectacular violence of St. Domingue.

Such reports of runaway, unruly, and theatricalized "French Negroes" reveal the depth of the alarm caused by St. Domingue. Caribbean revolt seemed to inspire formless fears of contaminating influences, secret communications, illicit associations, and underground networks. Working through those channels, St. Domingue's slave uprisings seemed to produce a performing black population whose acts escaped the regulation of playhouse conventions and benevolent masters. Against the background of those threats, *The Triumphs of Love* stages its own imitations of radical black performances. As white performers black up and give comedic form to representations of violent blackness, the stage seems compelled, at least for a brief moment, to respond to the rebellious black figures appearing just offstage.

Sentimental Stage Solutions

Sambo perpetrates his comic misbehavior until the play no longer requires (or tolerates) his presence. At the end of the third act, he disappears without explanation, shepherded offstage by the invisible hand of Murdock's script. Sambo's disappearance seems symptomatic of the play's anxieties—like contemporary advocates of African colonization, Murdock's plot seems unable to imagine freed slaves remaining on stage alongside the drama's white protagonists. The play's shift in focus also enfolds Sambo's black unruliness within the drama of refugee union and reunion, clearing the way for a dramatic revision of the Haitian Revolution's consequences. As if to neutralize the performative influence of Sambo's unruliness, the final act of Murdock's play returns to the marital storyline, resolving George's youthful rebellion and the refugees' penury. In the end, Murdock's Philadelphia plays host to the reconciliation of the tensions produced by the Haitian Revolution. Freed slaves disappear conveniently, leaving former slaveholders to work out their differences. George's marriage to Clementina allies the newly abolitionist reformed Quaker with the no-longer slaveholding French Caribbean, thereby imagining a creolized hemispheric union as a magical solution for slave revolt.

Sentimental comedy, as Lisa Freeman has argued, revolves around "the relations that sustain the public and private spheres, that is, who will breed with whom, on what basis, and with what prospects ensured for future offspring." Having finished with Sambo, *The Triumphs of Love* turns to those concerns with an almost manic energy.[59] George has fallen in love with Clementina sight unseen, before she arrives in Philadelphia; upon meeting her, he declares himself "caught in love's trap, at last" (71). Despite Clementina's impoverishment, George presses ahead with his suit, and the two engage in an accelerated courtship. The marriage seems remarkably rushed, George's offers of brotherly kindness and monetary assistance transforming into ecstatic hand-kissing and longing looks with almost satirical speed. George's union with Beauchamp's sister becomes the ready-made solution to the corrupting influences of slavery and French rakishness. Clementina's embodiment of "suffering virtue" and "honor" eclipses the play's earlier concern with transgressive desires (74). As a "young lady of most extraordinary beauty" whose race never comes under scrutiny, her match with George carefully avoids any insinuations of miscegenation (74). Clementina thus becomes the play's single antidote to the double problem of refugeeism: racially unmarked, virtuous, and heterosexually available, she solves the twin problems of St. Domingue's troubling blackness and dissolute homosociality that had earlier troubled the play.

Rescuing Clementina from her refugee hardships through marriage, the ending transforms George's earlier French-inspired dissipation into a newly virtuous kind of Francophilia. It seems significant, then, that Beauchamp returns in the closing moments of the play. Clementina, who has spoken unaccented English to this point, bursts into accented English ("my broder, my broder") before declaring her happiness in French (82). Beauchamp echoes her vocal performance, declaring his own gratitude in French accents. Audibly, the play scripts the marriage not as a performance of assimilation, but as the formation of a transnational, multilingual Creole cohort. Beauchamp's alien accents reintroduce French speech for the first time in the play since Sambo's raucous departure at the end of the third act. The accented dialogue serves as a reminder—at once threatening and reassuring—of the strangers brought to American shores by St. Domingue's slave revolution.

Perhaps predictably, those slave revolts remain in the realm of implication and rumor throughout the play; they never appear as more than a displaced (if not precisely unthinkable) horror, coded in suffering refugees and rowdy black Francophiles. Murdock's play works energetically to enclose the threats of St. Domingue within conventional theatrical forms. Celebrating an alliance of reformed slaveholders, the play ultimately diverts attention from the troubling forms of black violence that lurk on its margins. Even so, the play has accomplished a nimble piece of cultural work, not simply unthinking slave revolt, but imagining how slave insurrection provides critical motive forces for social change. In *The Triumphs of Love*, slave revolt first generates conflict and then provides for its resolution, displaying alien refugees and rebellious slaves before transforming them into a transnational and hemispheric (and decidedly white) extended family. Slave revolution, however suppressed its details, provides the comedy's symbolic complications and crucial opportunities. Perhaps most importantly, the play embodies the material consequences of the Haitian Revolution on stage before live audiences. The unruly black bodies and sentimentally suffering white refugees of St. Domingue appear intertwined in acts of mutual imitation, and St. Domingue's slaves and refugees alike become vectors of dangerous and pleasurable theatricality. Finally, *The Triumphs of Love* reveals North American theater's participation in circum-Atlantic networks that shaped and communicated various understandings of slave revolt. Clichéd dramatic conventions and novel social performances intersect in Murdock's play, dramatizing the theatrical qualities of rebel slaves and refugees as well as the stage's distinctive ways of displaying the Haitian Revolution's impact.

CHAPTER 15

The "Alpha and Omega" of Haitian Literature

Baron de Vastey and the U.S. Audience of Haitian Political Writing, 1807–1825

MARLENE L. DAUT

The Importance of Haiti

On February 17, 2004, the U.S. cable news network CNN covered the burgeoning coup d'état in Haiti that would eventually force Haitian president Jean-Bertrand Aristide from power and send him into exile in the Central African Republic. The broadcast began with CNN anchor Wolf Blitzer announcing that "increasing violence" was "pushing the country closer toward complete chaos." Blitzer then turned to David Ensor, a national security correspondent for CNN, who declared that though "Haiti is not strategically important . . . it is close by," and he noted that the U.S. Coast Guard was on the watch for "desperate Haitians" who might try to "make the dangerous journey to U.S. shores." Shortly afterward, the former ambassador to Haiti, William Jones, rather tersely used the myth of "Haitian exceptionalism" as a "shield that masks the negative contribution of the Western powers to the Haitian situation,"[1] when he suggested that he did not believe that the "American taxpayer should be saddled once again for coming in and trying to solve the problem in Haiti."[2] What the CNN broadcast did not mention is the fact that many of the people to whom Ensor referred as "rebels" had U.S.-backed "paramilitary training"³ or that U.S. dollars were used to support both repressive Duvalier regimes long before the United States had decided to, in Ensor's words, "help . . . to ease out a military government and oversee elections in the Caribbean nation."⁴ The broadcast equally omitted the fact that the United States had funded the opposition to Jean-Bertrand Aristide's candidacy in 1990 and had continued to fund opposition to him after he was democratically elected.⁵ Finally, there was no consideration given to the fact that the United States had been involved in destabilizing the Haitian government nineteen times between 1857 and the turn of the century alone (Bellegarde-Smith, 269), not to mention that the U.S. military had occupied Haiti from 1915–1934.⁶ By evoking such a notion of Haiti's essential disconnectedness from the United States, the CNN broadcasters continued to mask the deep historical, political, and cultural relationship between the United States and Haiti, ultimately making it seem as if Haiti's problems concerned the United States only insofar as the dollars of the U.S. "taxpayer" were concerned.⁷

Given the increasingly fractured interactions between Haiti and the United States that eventually culminated in what one critic has called the "alleged kidnapping of Aristide,"⁸ it would be more than tempting to conclude that Haitians have always been the victims of an unequivocally "bad press," which they have been powerless to influence or respond to.⁹ However, if we examine the complicated dialogic interactions between early Haitian political writers and the northern U.S. newspaper press in the first two decades of Haitian independence, we find that the idea of Haiti as a powerless "apparent state"¹⁰ and of its early literary tradition as unimportant emerge as concepts of more recent date.

Literary reviews of Haitian works in nineteenth-century U.S. newspapers, advertisements for their books, and inclusion of their texts in U.S. libraries indicate that early U.S. American newspaper editors and readers living in the northern states were intimately acquainted with Haitian authors and in particular with the works of the Baron de Vastey (1781–1820).¹¹ Vastey composed at least eleven different prose works that all circulated either in the original or in English translation in the Atlantic world.¹² These works were variously concerned with promoting Haitian arts and letters, responding to calumnious French writing, decrying the evils of the colonial system, arguing with journalists from Alexandre Pétion's republic, defending Africans and the "black race," and most importantly, narrating the history of Haiti from a Haitian point of view.

Vastey's works were reviewed on both sides of the Atlantic, and in fact, they were so powerfully received that a reviewer of his *Réflexions sur une lettre de Mazères* referred to him as "the Alpha and Omega of Haytian intellect and literature"; a reviewer of his *Le Système colonial dévoilé* lauded his works as well, calling Vastey "the most able Haytian of the present era."[13] The *Fireside Magazine or Monthly Entertainer* (1819) also announced *Le Système* to its readers as a worthy piece of literature, while the *Baltimore Patriot* added to its mention of Vastey's works that of all the "important State papers issued lately" by Haiti, Vastey's *Le Système* "excites our particular interest."[14] A prior review of Vastey's *Le Cri de la conscience* in the *Boston Daily Advertiser* and again in the *Alexandria Gazette* stated that Vastey's writing was characterized by a "great zeal and ingenuity."[15] Furthermore, the reviewer was pleased to find that Vastey "quotes Grotius and other writers on public law with familiarity, and applies their maxims, with a good deal of judgment."

In the eyes of Caleb Cushing, who provided a lengthy and much reprinted and referenced review of Vastey's *Réflexions politiques* in the *North American Review*, a U.S. magazine known for its interest in Latin America and the Caribbean,[16] "The works of M. de Vastey are very favourable specimens of the native mental force of a Haytian."[17] Yet another U.S. journalist wrote, after reprinting large passages of Vastey's *Réflexions sur une lettre de Mazères*: "We think these extracts cannot but leave a favourable impression on the minds of our readers, relative to the state of Haytian literature. And upon the whole, if we consider the state of the people in Hayti."[18]

Northern U.S. newspaper editors who published these kinds of reviews assumed not only that their readers would be interested in Haitian literature, but that they would also be "cheer[ed]" by the "rapid progress of the intellectual culture" and "literary state of the negro or mulatto empire of Hayti."[19] In other words, these editors assumed that the U.S. reading public would be interested in knowing about Haitian literature and pleased to learn that it was worthy of their attention and praise.[20]

Owing to what Meredith McGill has called a "culture of reprinting" in the early United States, "unauthorized"[21] reprints of Vastey's works were also disseminated across a broad spectrum by newspaper editors in the north, who printed his words sometimes with or sometimes without attribution. The numerous northern U.S. newspapers that referenced or otherwise made use of Vastey's work thus helped to generate a vibrant anglophone audience for his texts. In fact, by the time of the U.S. Civil War, although Vastey himself was already deceased, his writings formed a distinct part of Haitian revolutionary historiography circulating in the anglophone world. Vastey was mentioned by name in the U.S. press before the Civil War more than any other Haitian writer throughout the rest of the nineteenth century. From a literary standpoint, his ideas were remarkably effective in helping shape and influence not just a United States based abolitionist movement,[22] but northern U.S. discourse on Haitian recognition until at least 1825.

Because the early U.S. press was neither static nor homogenous, early nineteenth-century U.S. attitudes toward the existence of Haiti and Haitian writing were anything but monolithic. Before 1816 (and widespread circulation and reviews of Vastey's works), Christophe's government was highly criticized in the both the northern and southern U.S. presses. U.S. newspapers in the north that printed or reviewed Vastey's works after 1816, however, tended to view Haiti favorably, intimately tying his ideas to northern U.S. notions of national identity. Vastey's works thus became attached to and identified with some of the most important debates of the era—namely how best a nation-state should be governed, the meaning and consequences of revolution and universal emancipation, the emergence of national literary traditions, the capacity of blacks for self-rule, and the issue of international trade. Moreover, as this essay will show, Vastey's ideas were crucial to the development of northern U.S. attitudes toward Haitian independence after 1816.

The U.S. newspaper press can provide an adequate measure of Vastey's popularity and contribution to popular political opinion of Haiti in the United States precisely because, as Jeffrey Pasley has written, in early America the press "was the political system's central institution." In fact, according to Pasley, almost every little town in the early national United States had its own newspaper, which Pasley, quoting Alexis de Tocqueville, says helped "political life to circulate in every corner of the land." Furthermore, these newspapers were "not simply a forum or atmosphere in which politics took place"; instead, they were the "'linchpin'" of nineteenth-century politics.[23] Through the reproductions of Vastey's works in these early U.S. newspapers, we can essentially chart not only the way that his ideas moved from state to state in the northern United States, but how they affected U.S. political opinions on northern Haiti in the early nineteenth century.

By reconsidering early Haitian-U.S. relations, in light of the heavy circulation of Vastey's works in the northern United States, I find that the pro-recognition arguments that often preceded reviews or reprints of Vastey's publications complicates the idea that Haiti suffered a unilateral "bad press" in the nineteenth century that has influenced and overdetermined its relationship to the United States up until the present time.²⁴ For, contrary to popular belief, Haiti was not isolated by nonrecognition in the first two decades of independence, if by isolation we mean a lack of contact. Instead, Vastey—like the Emperor Jean-Jacques Dessalines and King Henry Christophe, the latter of whom addressed a letter to American merchants in the *Republican Watch-Tower* on July 28, 1809—understood the power of the U.S. press to influence popular ideas about Haiti and often used it to his own advantage.²⁵

The fact that both postcolonial and American studies have largely ignored a figure who was so central to the development of early U.S.-Haitian relations requires that we interrogate the silences surrounding Vastey's works on a level beyond simply his usage of the French language or his seeming imitation of European forms of discourse. As Deborah Jenson and Daniel Desormeaux have each pointed out, Haitian authors have often been critiqued for practices that are considered standard in European and U.S. American literature.²⁶ The attempt of Haitian authors to distance the country from the former metropole while simultaneously making use of its language, some of its literary traditions, and even its audience, for example, was a strategy of all early postcolonial states, including the antebellum United States²⁷ (and according to Bakhtin characterizes all thought),²⁸ and does not make Haitian authors mimic men or the strange proponents of "collective bovarysme."²⁹ Furthermore, the seeming absence of native readers for nineteenth-century political writing was not a singular feature of Haitian society either but was rather a constitutive element of most literate countries in the mid-nineteenth century.³⁰

The absence of early Haitian voices within the discourse of the Age of Revolution has led to a distortion of the Haitian intellectual's role in what would come to be called "postcolonial discourse." The silencing by the West of the Haitian revolutionists who, as Clinton A. Hutton has pointed out, were the first to argue for the cosmological basis of freedom and natural rights for all human beings regardless of skin color or "race," reinforces the myth of the West as the generator of knowledge and knowing in both the philosophical and postcolonial traditions.³¹ Perhaps the most salient example of this comes when Hegel or Spinoza is considered to have originated the idea of the absolute logic of freedom, even though Toussaint Louverture espoused such a concept when he wrote, "It is not a circumstantial liberty conceded to us that we wish, but the unequivocal adoption of the principle that no man, whether he be born red, black or white, can become the property of his fellow men."³² The silencing of Vastey's own "radical anti-colonial" discourse as a part of what we now call postcolonial theory obscures the "provocative recontextualization of the Enlightenment as an ideology both illuminated and refashioned" not just by "slaves or former slaves,"[33] but by the very real, as opposed to *apparent*, states of early nineteenth-century Haiti. As J. Michael Dash has written, Vastey's *Le Système* provides the "prototype of the voice of protest that would predict the end of the materialist Western World during the American Occupation."[34] The 1971 Annual Report of the Library Company of Philadelphia anticipates Dash's assessment of the *avant la lettre* nature of Vastey's works in writing of his *Réflexions sur une lettre de Mazères* that it was not only "a pioneer work in positive black thinking, but probably the first scholarly, serious socio-ethnological study by a Negro" and thus that it "deserve[s] a fate better than limbo."[35] Without an acknowledgement and understanding of how former slaves and eventual statesmen like Louverture, Pétion, Christophe and Dessalines, along with their sometime allies Vastey, Louis-Félix Boisrond-Tonnerre, Noël Colombel, Julien Prévost, and Jules Solime Milscent, theorized the postcolonial and indeed challenged the concept of Enlightenment humanism, we end up silencing their voices and thus reproducing the very power structures that we are striving to critique.

The silencing of Vastey's work indicates a serious disciplinary problem for early American studies as well, for it seems to me that the majority of studies concerning U.S.-Haitian relations have been too "U.S.-centric," to use Carol Boyce Davies's term.[36] In other words, too much attention has been paid to U.S. reactions to and readings of the Haitian Revolution—or what Mimi Sheller has called the "Haytian Fear"[37]—at the expense of analyzing the Haitian reaction to U.S. nonrecognition, on the one hand, and Haitian reactions and contributions to U.S. readings of their revolution, on the other.[38] In fact, U.S.-centricity or "one-centeredness" has had a particularly stifling affect upon Americanists who seek to "critique the insular and exceptionalist analyses of U.S. culture" and who have, according to Michael Drexler, "opened up new avenues for research" into the connection between the United States and the Caribbean basin.[39] In many studies of early Haitian-U.S. relations the Haitian Revolution, like the coup in 2004, seems to matter only insofar as it affected U.S. lives, U.S. slavery, U.S. politics, U.S. history, and U.S. literature. This reflects "a constantly expanding" center "logic" that in taking the United States as its primary and "most important" object of study, finds it increasingly difficult to imagine "multiple and *equal* centers."[40] Such a center "logic" also has the effect of placing the United States, its authors, its politicians, and its historians on center stage in studies of the Haitian Revolution, forcing the Haitian actors of this revolution into a secondary position whereby they operate behind the curtains of an independence movement that they not only scripted and staged and later theorized and historicized themselves, but for which they suffered and died.

Vastey's (Para)National Imagination

If Haiti was a prominent, if not vexed, symbol in the nineteenth-century U.S. political and literary imaginary, the United States formed a distinct part of the "initial burgeoning of hemispheric thought within the national imagination" in Haiti upon independence as well.[41] Like many early American writers, early Haitian authors believed in the power of literature, and specifically the press, to express nationhood and that "artists could be responsible agents for achieving national liberation."[42] In the minds of nineteenth-century Haitian authors like the poet, journalist, and historian Emile Nau (1812–1860), creating a distinctly Haitian literary tradition did not require immediately disavowing European or U.S. literary traditions or even the French language. Nau once wrote, "What a great day it will be when in every genre Haiti has its own original artists," and he compared the emergence of Haitian literature to the emergence of U.S. literature. Nau wrote that eventually Haiti would have its own Edgar Allan Poe and James Fennimore Cooper. He believed not only in the genius of the Haitian literary imagination, but also that over time Haitians would create their own national language, "a little bit darkened," and that the French, and ultimately the world, would read this writing.[43]

Nau's comments demonstrate that the early Haitian literary tradition shared with the early U.S. American literary tradition both a desire for foreign readers and a conception of itself in transnational terms.[44] The American Renaissance was, in fact, typified by a kind of "*inter*-American system of political relations" that was characterized by the "overlap" and "simultaneity of different national claims upon territories as well as upon literary texts and traditions," or what Anna Brickhouse calls "hemispheric thought."[45] Similarly, the emergence of the Haitian literary tradition was connected to a transatlantic and at times hemispheric political and territorial imaginary. In the United States this "hemispheric" imaginary was buttressed by imperial, expansionist, and, often even, colonial claims, but in Haiti it took the shape of a comparative nationalism, whose fantasy was a form of inter-Atlantic humanism that predates Glissant's theory of creolization as the recognition of difference and "diversity" rather than its "sublimation."[46]

If, as Sean Goudie has written, the United States had a "paracolonial" relationship with the West Indies in the eighteenth and nineteenth centuries—meaning that the United States's relationship to the Caribbean operated with a kind of proto-colonialism "alongside," "near," and "resembling" European colonialism[47]—then we might describe the relationship that early Haiti had with the antebellum United States as paranational. Haiti's process of imagining the nation in discursive terms grew up alongside and near—and in effect, resembled—the United States's own vibrant print culture, where the printing press "provided the technical means for 're-presenting' the *kind* of imagined community" that Haiti, like the United States, wanted to become.[48] While later Haitian authors like Dantès Bellegarde would view the looming presence of the United States as a distinct threat to Haitian sovereignty—in 1907 Bellegarde warned that "God is too far and the United States is too close"—early nineteenth-century Haitian writers used the United States as the only other independent nation of the hemisphere as a point of political comparison and departure.[49]

Although Europe was the most obvious referent in "measuring the new development of a national literature" for early Haitian authors as it had been for early U.S. writers,[50] Haitian authors from both the north and the south like Milscent and Nau, along with the Baron de Vastey, compared Haiti's origins as a former French colony wishing to create its own distinct culture to the United States' relationship with England. However, Nau importantly distinguished between U.S. and Haitian societies by noting that the American had been merely "transplanted" while the Haitian had been "treated like a veritable pariah of civilization" and had to build an entirely new society "upon the ruins of colonial society."[51] Nau's comment bespeaks the ambivalent effect of comparing the accomplishments of the descendants of Africans to white men of European descent who were a part of the very colonial system that had produced the subjugation of Africans.

Baron de Vastey, too, expressed ambivalence about Haiti's paranational relationship to the United States when he wrote: "We do not really know, if we would be able to gain certain advantages in seeing ourselves compared to the United States of America."[52] After all, he had asked, "Is it reasonable to expect that men who had been burdened under the weight of ignorance and slavery, who were even refused intellect, would have all of a sudden Franklins and Washingtons?" (*RP*, 31). Vastey pointed out that because the new nation of Haiti had suffered the paralyzing effects of slavery, which had stifled the kind of "wisdom" and "clarity" found in the writing of Franklin and Washington, it needed time to recover (*RP*, 30).

Though Vastey says that he hesitates to compare Haiti's national emergence to that of the United States, this is exactly what he does when he essentially argues that there is an ethical imperative to do so. For unlike those proponents of Haitian exceptionalism who hold that Haiti and its revolution lie beyond all comparison,[53] throughout his prose works Vastey calls attention to what Susan Gillman has identified as a lack of awareness or recognition on the part of American studies concerning the "unevenness of situations" that characterize the "imperial" and "neo-colonial histories" of the Americas. According to Gillman, such oversight produces a "misleading symmetry" and "static synchronicity" in comparative American studies, which elides the uneven development of nation-states, as well as the distinct histories of "slavery" and "racial relations" found across the myriad geographical locales of the Americas.[54] Vastey, in fact, recognized the effect of such "misleading symmetry" with respect to Haiti's position in the Atlantic world and attributed it to the fact that the French colonists had generated an entire written archive precisely in order to further subjugate the slaves and free people of color. He wrote that "the majority of historians who have written about the colonies were *whites, colonists* even. . . . The friends of slavery, those eternal enemies of the human race have written thousands of volumes freely; they have made all the presses in Europe groan for entire centuries in order to reduce the black man below the brute." "Now that we have Haitian printing presses," he countered, "we can reveal the crimes of the colonists and respond to the most absurd calumnies, invented by the prejudice and greed of our oppressors."[55] Vastey believed that Haitian writers had a duty, not only to themselves but to all of Africa, to counter such "calumnies" by producing their own histories of colonialism, slavery, and the revolution.[56]

Vastey's call for Haitian writers to pen histories of Haiti demonstrates not only his explicit comprehension of the "unevenness" of access to the public sphere, but the "unevenness" of the very comparative terms upon which Haiti was discussed in the first place. On that account, in his *Réflexions sur une lettre de Mazères*, he spoke of what he called the "fatal truth" of Haitian independence and wrote that the Haitian Revolution and the subsequent independence of Haiti were hardly remarkable in and of themselves.[57] Elsewhere, he pointed out that "all the changes that have taken place in Europe" since the classical age had been "the result of revolutions, revolts, wars, force" (*RP*, 22, 23). The culmination of the Haitian Revolution in the independence of Haiti was in his mind simply a part of the natural historical progression that had produced countless other changes to the maps of the world, including the one that had resulted in the creation of the United States. For Vastey, the Haitian revolutionists' creation of a new state in the Americas was hardly exceptional or remarkable in this comparative historical context. He wrote that what was exceptional instead was that when Switzerland separated itself from Austria, the United States from England, and Portugal and the seven provinces of the Pays-Bas from Spain, these changes were "undertaken under the aegis and sanction of European public opinion" (*RP*, 22). The Haitian revolutionists' creation of a new nation-state, on the other hand, was equated with "a political fiction" (*RM*, 90). So begins Vastey's assiduous documentation of the ways in which Haitian exceptionalism as a discourse promulgated by European colonists to mask their "negative contributions" worked to make the commonplace in Haiti extraordinary and the extraordinary mundane.

To the suggestion that the Haitians should monetarily compensate the French colonists for the loss of their plantations as U.S. American proprietors did for the English as part of Jay's Treaty (1794), Vastey pointed out that the Americans did this in a state of relative peace, as propertied men who themselves sought compensation from the British for the loss of their slaves and for the confiscation of American ships (*RP*, 48). Haitians, on the other hand, had been "deprived of everything . . . possessed nothing . . . were nothing, and . . . counted for nothing" (*RP*, 50). Consequently, Haitians had a right to the properties of the former French colonists since "we have conquered all over these vampires: country! liberty! independence and property" (*RP*, 50). Though Vastey acknowledged that the laws of modern warfare, as opposed to ancient practices, protected both the persons and the property of the vanquished, he pointed out that "we do not find any comparable example to ours in the annals of nations" (*RP*, 52).

Though Vastey's statement above may seem like a contradiction of his earlier position that Haiti was not so different from the other former European colonies, it actually reflects his acute awareness that comparison must always move upon a shifting axis of sameness and difference. For although the U.S. and Haitian Revolutions had similar historical antecedents, according to Vastey, there was an immeasurable difference between U.S. and Haitian independence. For him, the revolutions that had occurred in the United States and Haiti were both products of a "torrent and . . . coincidence of events" that had eventually culminated in the termination of a "bad marriage [*mauvaise ménage*]" with the metropole (*RP*, 31). However, there was no comparison to be made between the material conditions of Haitians and U.S. Americans at the moment of independence. At the moment of independence, Vastey observed, Haitians had been "mort civilement" or "civilly dead" and "inhabited this earth as if they did not really inhabit it; . . . lived as if they were not really living" (*RP*, 49–50). Vastey then asks, "Is it not a wish to distort everything, to find examples in subjects that are completely dissimilar?" (*RP*, 49). Vastey further pointed out that those who would become immediate citizens of the United States "were themselves white Englishmen, free and propertied [who] enjoyed their natural civil and political rights, [and] no one disputed them these rights" (*RP*, 49). In other words, the U.S. American Revolution was solely a question of independence, but not emancipation. Because Haitians, on the other hand, were what Orlando Patterson would later describe as "socially dead" beings,[58] any comparison between the two acts of independence that sublimated the racial distinctions of Haiti as a country populated mostly by Africans who were, "black and enslaved, without country, without property, deprived of their natural rights" (*RP*, 49). only contributed to Haiti's threatened position in the New World, while the United States enjoyed economic and political prosperity as one of the privileges of whiteness.

One of Vastey's most ardent, crucial, and effective engagements with his U.S. audience appears in those passages in which he connects critiques of Henri Christophe to white privilege. Some U.S. newspapers, like their French counterparts, were quite fond of ridiculing the fact that Christophe had instituted a monarchy—saying that "the black King of Hayti is as jealous of his royal titles, as any White Legitimate in any part of this world."[59] One newspaper even described Christophe as a "black emperor" who was "imitating his white brother [Napoleon]" in committing "robberies" against the United States.[60] Each of these judgments connects monarchy to tyranny in some form, suggesting that there was a kind of hypocrisy in a former black slave crowning himself king when it was a king who had subjugated him in the first place. The judgments above also cast aspersion on Christophe's character, linking his blackness to imitation, robbery, treachery, and jealousy.

In at least one U.S. periodical this disdain turned to all-out mockery when Christophe's entire court was ridiculed in the Baltimore-based *Niles Weekly Register*. The article of November 9, 1816, referred to Vastey as the "baroness Big Bottom," to Christophe as "king Stophel himself" and to Limonade as "Lime Punch." The article further stated that the "vast pomposity" of Christophe's court was being described for the "benefit of all who desire to '*laugh and to be fat'*, at the fools and knaves who applaud it—black or white."[61] The author of the *Niles* article even associated Christophe with primates, which had been a common "leitmotif" in the sixteenth and seventeenth centuries:[62] "Bonaparte once asked a West Indian how Christophe *aped royalty*—the newspapers can now inform him, for they give a long account of a set of black fellows at Hayti, the quondam grooms and scullions of the "legitimate" days, disguised as gentlemen and ladies, riding in somber processions, acting royalty with about as much display of sense as is usual on such occasions; that is little or none at all."[63] This passage renders the current government in Haiti illegitimate by referencing the "'legitimate' days" when "black fellows" did not "disguise" themselves as "gentlemen and ladies." The article also associates monarchy in Haiti with a form of mimicry or "ap[ing]" that was nonsensical. Even though the article in the *Niles Weekly* purportedly ridiculed anyone "black and white" who applauded the monarchy of Christophe, the article took specific aim at Haiti in such a way that it dealt explicitly with race, even poking fun at Christophe's personal physician: he was "no ordinary physician, but a negro" who specialized in "itch ointment."

In response to this kind of writing, in general, Vastey highlighted the idea that what was disturbing about Christophe's monarchy to the Atlantic World was decidedly: "The crown on the head of a Black man! There you have what the French publicists, the journalists, the creators of Colonial Systems cannot digest; one would say to hear them, that a black king is a phenomenon that has never been seen in the world! Who will therefore reign over the blacks, if the blacks cannot be kings. Is royalty such a privilege that it belongs exclusively to the white color? (*RP*, 17). Vastey also decried the historical revisionism taking place in European and U.S. discourse by reminding his readers that black kings had existed for a long time.

In pointing out the hypocrisy of those who criticized the black king while they showed deference to their own king, Vastey clearly spoke to a European audience. However, at the same time, the defense of monarchy as a system of government was explicitly directed at the United States, for Vastey knew that if he wanted to appeal to his U.S. audience, he would have to defend the monarchy on political, as well as racial grounds.[64] Vastey devoted an entire chapter in his *Essai* to defending the monarchy as a system of government. In his earlier *Réflexions sur une lettre de Mazères* he had already taken up the topic, writing that the method of government hardly mattered as long as it was "wise, just, enlightened, and benevolent, and the governees have religion, virtues and good morals!" (*RM*, 73). Vastey further wrote that since no two peoples were exactly alike, no single form of government could suit all nations. To that end, he paraphrased Montesquieu to prove that it would be an error to think that a republican government was always better than a monarchy since "the best constitution is not the one that is most beautiful in theory, but the one that suits itself the best to the people for whom it has been made."[65] This statement seems specifically aimed at the United States since Vastey appeared to view the country as having a democracy that was an exceptionally good form of government with "sage laws" that were specifically suited to the U.S. mindset. His point, however, was that such a democracy might not be exportable.[66]

Vastey's work challenges developing notions of "American exceptionalism"[67] by making the radical assertion that putative democratic republics could be just as flawed and tyrannical as monarchies. Vastey explained, for example, that Pétion's republic, modeled after that of the United States in theory, was a colossal failure precisely because through a series of what Vastey called "demagogical farces" (*Essai*, 297), Pétion broke the laws of republicanism. First, when he refused to step down in March of 1815 after three successive terms, and later, Vastey admonished Pétion for revising his constitution to state that the term of the Haitian presidency was "à vie," or "for life," rather than for four years, as the original constitution had mandated (*Essai*, 297, 315–316). Vastey's recitation of this relatively minor episode in Haitian history was supposed to demonstrate that it was rulers with their personal flaws and political ambitions and not systems of government that had the power to make a nation prosperous or to destroy its foundations.

In critiquing Pétion's mangled adoption of republican principles, Vastey also avoids appearing to criticize the United States's republican mode of government. Simultaneously, he also claims that "one finds this institution [monarchy] in all of the most free people, the most civilized and the most enlightened on the earth" (*Essai*, 153). Vastey continued to imagine the nation in paranational terms when he flattered the United States in claiming that Americans "have acquired a reputation for sagacity and prudence that is justly merited" (*Essai*, 153), but he still considered that each nation should develop its own government according to its own needs and not according to the doctrines or ideologies of another.

After 1816, many U.S. journalists began internalizing Vastey's own understanding of the meaning of Haitian independence for the hemisphere. Cushing repeated Vastey's very own words about Haitians needing time to produce a Franklin and Washington, he echoed Vastey's words again when he wrote that the French were responsible for all civil strife in Haiti, and he also bought into Vastey's ideas about compensating the French colonists when he wrote: "No man of course but a colonist can seriously think the king of Hayti was under the least obligations to restore the lands of the planters, or even give them an equivalent."[68]

A more radical adoption of Vastey's language and rhetoric occurs when Cushing defends Christophe's monarchy:

> A nation, which has attained considerable refinement, which is tranquil within and threatened by nothing but ordinary dangers from abroad, can enjoy a free and republican government; but when a country has been plunged for two centuries in the lowest degradation, when its inhabitants have been sunk below the level of ordinary political oppression, and when, although exalted to the rank of a nation, it has continued to be harassed by restless and able enemies,—in such a country, the firm hand of kingly power is needed to stifle faction, repel aggressors, and give energy, dispatch, and secrecy to the public measures.[69]

Cushing continued by repeating Vastey's very own words: "Little does it matter, indeed," he wrote, "what is the form of a government, if it be sagely conducted, and its only aim be the public happiness and peace."[70] This point is also to be found in a toast given by Rufus King, who, according to Michael Zuckerman, was, like many Federalists, "unabashed" in his "defiance of Jeffersonian policy towards Haiti": "To the government of Haiti, founded on the only legitimate basis of authority—the people's choice."[71] A prior review of Vastey's work in May of 1815, also published in the *North American Review*, had a more semantic reason for defending Christophe's monarchy: "There is as pretty and numerous a collection of Princes, Dukes, Counts, Barons as any country in Europe could produce," the article states; "indeed England is quite outdone; she has produced only one Black Prince, but in St. Domingo there are many. These titles sound as well as any similar appellations; and may wear as well as older ones. If the colour of the heart be right, that of the skin is of inferior importance."[72] Finally, an additional U.S. journalist even went so far as to defend the "military attitude" of the north of Haiti by writing that it was "necessary, perhaps, as a preservative against the attempts of France."[73]

It might at first seem astonishing that a monarchy, with its attendant "collections of Dukes, Counts, Barons" and many "Black Prince[s]," was so openly defended in a country whose origin story rests upon the opposition between monarchy and democracy. John Adams's very own "Defence of the of the Constitutions of the Government of the United States" (1787) had provided a harsh critique of "kingly power" by suggesting that the "American people" were too "enlightened" to ever allow the "executive power" to rest with "one single person."[74] The force of Vastey's argument, however, lies in his recognition that *true* international democracy rested not in imposing one nation's government on another, but in accepting that different peoples might choose to be governed in different ways. It is this idea of democratic relativity that was implicitly accepted by those in the United States who read, published responses to, and even adopted Vastey's words to defend the Haitian government of the north.

Perhaps even more telling than Cushing's adoption of Vastey's very own rhetoric to defend the Haitian monarchy was his joy at discovering that King Christophe wished to change the language of Haiti from French to English. Cushing wrote that Christophe "could not hesitate in adopting that language, which now possesses a literature unrivalled by the proudest in ancient or modern times, which is making rapid strides to a diffusion almost universal, and which is spoken in the first instance by two nations of which one is the noblest in the old and the other the noblest in the new world."[75] Here, Cushing actually argues for United States recognition of Haiti on the grounds that Haiti wanted to be more like the United States, with its "unrivalled" anglophone literature. Cushing invited Haitians to join in the imagined solidarity of England and the United States by adopting the English language and by degrees the anglophone literary tradition. This invitation hardly reflects the kind of isolation and non-recognition—cultural, diplomatic, and commercial— that is described by many scholars of early Haitian-U.S. relations. Instead it indicates that northern U.S. newspaper editors and contributors, through their engagement with Haitian writing, imagined and even acknowledged the independence of Haiti—a fact that thereby dismantles the fable of non-recognition propagated by the U.S. government.

Haiti and the Fable of Non-Recognition

Traditional historiography and political theory of early Haitian-U.S. relations suggest that Haiti (both the north and the south) suffered almost total diplomatic isolation in the early nineteenth century as the result of European and U.S. non-recognition. The United States's official non-recognition of Haiti until 1862 has led many scholars to conclude that the Haitian government was consistently undermined by the U.S. government—resulting in a "century of isolation"[76]—and thus that U.S. citizens and the people of Haiti have had a generally hostile relationship since 1804.[77]

Though I would not argue with Tim Matthewson's claim that antebellum U.S. foreign policy was undoubtedly "pro-slavery," nor with Paul Farmer's statement that as early as 1804 Haitians feared "Yankee imperialism,"[78] examining the literary-politico archive of the two nations forces us to consider the separation between the state and its formal authority and the private participants of a capitalist economy, for whom the market was king. McGill has written that the U.S. American "market" is a "tricky concept" precisely because "from the perspective of government seeking to regulate corporate behavior, the market is aligned with the private sphere and is often depicted as dangerously independent of public oversight."[79] U.S. trade with early Haiti, coupled by a press that was "dangerously independent," provides an interesting case study for the consequences of such a lack of oversight.

Haiti was extremely important to U.S. commerce throughout its early existence, as is illustrated by the fact that Haitian and U.S. trade continued to be robust throughout the early nineteenth century. Haitian trade was especially valuable for northern U.S. merchants because it represented the singular opportunity for the U.S. to have virtually "unrestricted" trade in the area.[80]

In the early nineteenth century it was not only merchants and corporations who often found themselves at odds with formal U.S. policy when it came to Haiti, but journalists whose right to free speech was protected by the First Amendment. In fact, as Donald Hickey has pointed out, while Congress was attempting to craft and then pass a trade embargo against Haiti in 1804 and again in 1805, "Newspapers in the North [of the United States] were especially vigorous in upholding the independence of Haiti and America's right to trade with her."[81] In addition, Sara Fanning tells us that in the early 1820s northern U.S. journalists launched a "modern media campaign" to urge official recognition of Haiti.[82] We might conclude, therefore, that in the nineteenth-century United States, the fact that the government refused to formally recognize Haitian independence did little to disrupt the intricate everyday interactions between private individuals in the United States—namely, journalists and merchants—and the government in Haiti.

This contradiction between what the U.S. government mandated and what private U.S. merchants and journalists—who were also permitted to travel to and from Haiti—were allowed to do under U.S. law was not lost on either the Haitian or the U.S. governments. According to Vastey, Milscent (a journalist from the Pétion's republic), and Julien Prévost (the Duke de Limonade who often wrote in an official capacity for Christophe's government), Haitian trade with the citizens of a foreign nation equaled recognition, and recognition equaled a state of peace. Milscent wrote, for example, that if a nation's citizens traded with Haiti, "It must be inferred from this reasoning that, by that fact, we are in a state of peace with the nations which have tacitly recognized the independence of Haiti . . . because their ships have been frequenting the ports of this island."[83] Vastey added that U.S. citizens "who have traded with Haiti for many years, who enjoy the protection of the government" were friends of Haiti who, "like us, had been brought to liberty and independence" (*Essai*, 356). Limonade echoed Milscent almost verbatim when he wrote to Clarkson that "for sixteen years the subjects of all maritime and trading nations (France alone excepted) have carried on a commerce with Haiti. These activities and mutual interchanges are in fact equivalent to a tacit, if not formal, recognition of our independence."[84] In other words, it was not possible to trade with Haiti if Haiti did not exist, on the one hand, and if a nation's "subjects" traded with Haiti this fact made a nation a friend and ally, on the other.

Joseph Clay of Pennsylvania acknowledged the danger of this "tacit" recognition as early as 1804 when he told Congress, "We cannot trade with them without acknowledging their independence;" but trade with them was exactly what U.S. merchants continued to do despite the fact that the U.S. government refused to recognize the sovereignty of either Christophe or Pétion.[85] The government of the United States, therefore, as Senator Clay remarked, unwittingly and "tacitly" recognized the sovereignty of the two Haitian governments every time its citizens engaged in trade with the country.[86] The fable of nonrecognition is noteworthy precisely because it demonstrates what Lauren Berlant has called the "contradiction between the sovereignty of abstract citizens" and "formal" state power.[87] It also reflects the power of what one nineteenth-century American politician called the "tyranny" of the U.S. "newspaper government."[88]

U.S. merchants' "tacit" recognition of Haitian independence was explicitly tied to articles about Vastey that appeared in the northern U.S. press. The powerful northern press argued for formal recognition using a similar logic to that found in the review of Vastey's works published in the *Analectic Magazine*: "The Americans enjoy the advantage of going into the West India markets, at the lowest possible scale of expense.... These circumstances combine to render the trade with Hayti advantageous at least in this point of view." The author of this particular article then explicitly states that since Vastey's works "cannot but leave a favourable impression on the minds of our readers relative to . . . the state of the people in Hayti the most cogent arguments which his Majesty could urge, in favour of such a recognition, would be, to present the other powers with a copy of le Baron de Vastey's Reflections."[89] Another U.S. writer, also in the context of Vastey's writings, stated that Haiti's "commercial importance is too well known to require any notice in this place.... Perhaps . . . a reciprocity of benefits may be secured.... Our statesmen and financiers should look to this business, with a steady and unquenching eye."[90] The same writer for the *Boston Commercial Gazette* took the point even farther in saying, "We must confess that we have not learned any principle in philosophy, that shows a natural incompatibility of black skin, or any other feature of this people, for excellence in government, or science, or military tactics."[91] These kinds of reviews of Vastey's work formed a part of a campaign by the northern press to urge that Haiti could govern itself and to prove that the only obstacle was that the country was populated with blacks.[92] Vastey's remonstrations were, therefore, reverberating in the U.S. national imagination in ways that resulted in measurable material consequences for both the northern kingdom and the southern republic.

Not only did the U.S. press use Vastey's works to argue explicitly for formal recognition of Haitian independence, but U.S. journalists themselves discursively recognized the independence of Haiti when they wrote articles acknowledging that there was a king or a president of the country. Journalists routinely referred to "the kingdom of Hayti"[93] and to Christophe as "the King" of Haiti.[94] One journalist even recognized that the country had a "written bill of rights."[95] A review of Vastey's *Réflexions sur une lettre de Mazères* also acknowledged that Haitian independence was a fact whether or not France or the United States wanted to accept it: "It was stipulated in the late continental treaty, that France should not be interfered with, in any attempts to recover her lost possessions; and she may flatter herself with an idea, therefore, that St. Domingo can be gathered again unto her dominion; but she will learn, we apprehend,—if, indeed, she has not already been taught,—that the Haytians are resolved upon the alternative of liberty or death, and that it is going to cost as much as the island is worth, to regain possession of it."[96] There is a fleeting dance here with the name of Haiti. When referring to what France believes, the author uses "St. Domingo"; but when discussing reality the author recognizes "the Haytians." Furthermore, northern U.S. newspapers began referring to the former colony of St. Domingue as Haiti as early as 1804.[97] In these small ways, northern Americans had actually been discursively recognizing Haitian independence and affirming Haitian sovereignty for quite some time.

Although the recognition of Haitian sovereignty by U.S. journalists, merchants, abolitionists, and other private individuals cannot be equated with official, government recognition, these discursive acts of recognition were not without political, national, or economic meaning. They exposed at once the delicate position of Haiti within the American hemisphere in the nineteenth century and the burgeoning neo-imperial relationship that was developing between Haiti and the United States. These acts of discursive recognition also ask us to consider what it meant for the United States to politically disavow the independence of a country while reifying that independence with everyday speech acts and commercial involvement. This informal recognition placed the sovereignty of Berlant's "abstract citizens" above the political will of the U.S. government (and the southern states), exposing a deep chasm between U.S. capitalism, when aligned primarily with the people, and U.S. democracy, when viewed as a system of governance.

Nineteenth-century Haitian writing from both the north and the south also fundamentally asks us to consider what recognition actually meant to post-independence Haitians. Milscent described the relativity and symbolism of nonrecognition perfectly when he wrote that

> the Independence of Haiti would not be able to produce the same effects in the eyes of different powers, nor furnish to each one of them the same degree of annoyance.... [Our independence] does not carry with it any attack on the United States. The peoples of that country, enlightened by the past, must tacitly applaud our resolution. Our principles of moderation are not a mystery for them; they know that we do not purport to intervene in causes that have nothing at all to do with the soil of our country. As such, those sage philanthropists can only smile at our prosperity. They are not interested in breaching the bounds of neutrality that have always procured for them real advantages. It is therefore quite consoling for us to be able to, for many reasons, consider them as neighbors whose system is generably favorable to the amelioration of the fate of mankind.[98]

Milscent's uses the language of pacification in this passage—a language that highlights the relative obsolescence of U.S non-recognition because Haiti and the United States are involved in what he sees as a mutually beneficial relationship that has "real advantages." He makes it clear, for example, that the Haitian government poses no real threat to U.S. interests. Milscent even makes an appeal to sameness, arguing that the two nations have much in common—a reference to their origins in revolution. In so doing, Milscent imagines a hemispheric solidarity that would make Haiti and the U.S. potential allies precisely because their citizens were imagined to be so.

Vastey also conflated the acts of U.S. citizens with the government.[99] He repeatedly sought to make it clear to his U.S. audience that the northern kingdom wanted to have a peaceful relationship with the government of the United States by welcoming U.S. citizens in Haitian ports.[100] Vastey also wanted the United States to equate Haitian treatment of U.S. subjects as a friendly overture to the U.S. government. Though his position seems contradictory—nonrecognition from France equals war but from the United States it was merely an annoyance—it reflects the wholly symbolic and relative nature of the elusive, transitory notion of recognition.[101] What Vastey sought from France on behalf of the Haitian government was little more than their acknowledgment, indeed their acceptance, of Haiti's right to be free and independent from them without clause. Vastey hoped to make it explicitly clear that the non-recognition, which he disdained in the conduct of France, could not be compared to the chimera of non-recognition propagated by the United States and England. The latter did not carry with it any perceived threat to Haitian sovereignty; instead, it was a political fable that allowed the United States and England to formally disavow the revolution and subsequent independence of Haiti while benefiting from it materially, as the nineteenth-century Haitian historian Beaubrun Ardouin observed.[102] If, as Milscent wrote, Haiti's independence could not provide the "same degree of annoyance" to each country, neither could non-recognition by those same countries carry the same "degree of annoyance" that it did coming from France.[103]

Although the idea that the U.S. had recognized Haitian independence when its citizens engaged in trade with the country may have been merely a powerful rhetorical move on the part of Vastey, Limonade, and Milscent, their political writings exposed U.S. nonrecognition for what it was as well: a powerful political fable that was contested by the everyday interactions between Haitian and U.S. merchants and journalists. While the official policy of the U.S. was to not recognize the independence of either Haitian government, U.S. American journalists and other private individuals discursively recognized the country's sovereignty on their own, thus accomplishing what their government would not.

Conclusion: The Uses of Vastey

Like the abolitionist publications that cited Vastey's works in the antebellum United States, early national newspaper editors and journalists from the north used Vastey's words to argue that Haiti had reached a sufficient level of civilization to deserve formal U.S. recognition.[104] The way in which these arguments were framed revealed the United States's own anxieties concerning its national identity.

Vastey's *Réflexions sur une lettre de Mazères*, for example, was described in several U.S. newspapers as being "perhaps the first work by a negro, on which the energies of the mind had been powerfully excited, and have found a proper scope for action, where sentiments favorable to freedom could be avowed without the immediate threat of the scourge, the axe, or the jibbet, and where in fact, this long oppressed race have not been suffered to say a word in defence."[105] This reviewer claimed that the "mind[s]" of blacks had so changed that they were now able to take revenge with their pens, rather than with weapons. This was an allusion to the violence of the Haitian Revolution, which was portrayed as exceptionally horrific in the U.S. media in the first few years of the nineteenth century.[106] The reviewer makes the claim that blacks no longer need violence to force access to what Nick Nesbitt has called the "global discursive sphere"[107] but could simply use their civilized pens to "avow" "sentiments favorable to freedom."

Cushing also connected Vastey's writings to the post-Enlightenment discourse of regeneration and degeneration circulating in the Atlantic World when he noted that Vastey was "self-educated" and applauded the fact that he had arisen out of the "lowest moral and intellectual degradation, by the force of his own powers." He wrote that "the vehemence of the once oppressed, but now victorious soldier, the fire of an emancipated slave, the vigorous pride of a regenerate African are all wrought into the style" of his works.[108] Cushing concluded that Vastey's works proved "the regeneration of Hayti," saying that "we may hope that before long they will have wiped away all the disgraceful stains contracted in a life of bondage."[109]

The word "regeneration" had a particular meaning in the late eighteenth and early nineteenth centuries. By "the [French] Revolution, regeneration had become an extremely popular and more general word, referring to improvement, a freeing from corruption, or societal renewal."[110] By the nineteenth century, regeneration was equally connected to both the abolition of slavery and racial miscegenation.[111] According to Robert Fanuzzi, early nineteenth-century U.S. writers were distinctly affected by the French discourse of "the elevation of the African race" through "structural" and "institutional philanthropy."[112] In fact, the idea that slavery had caused a corruption of humankind that only abolition and philanthropy could cure would become a favorite claim of abolitionists like the Abbé Grégoire, who claimed that slavery corrupted equally the masters, slaves, and the free people of color.[113]

Vastey had also internalized this idea that slavery had resulted in a complete corruption of humanity, and he understood Haitian independence as a part of a larger post-Enlightenment project of rehabilitating humankind. Vastey wrote that after the Haitian Revolution, humanity had triumphed and "the regeneration of a large part of the human race [was] beginning."[114] Not only did Vastey believe that humankind was being "regenerated," but he also believed that whatever happened in Haiti would mean something for the world and not just for Africans.[115]

Like early Haitians, the early American colonists had also spoken of themselves in connection with the concepts of regeneration and degeneration in the years immediately leading up to the U.S. War of Independence.[116] This regeneration was wholly connected in their minds to the emergence of a national literature after the American Revolution. In a famous essay entitled "American Literature," the Massachusetts politician Fisher Ames wrote: "Few speculative subjects have exercised the passions more or the judgment less, than the inquiry, what rank our country is to maintain in the world for genius and literary attainments. Whether in point of intellect we are equal to Europeans, or only a race of degenerate creoles."[117] Ames had lamented that despite the fact that "nobody will pretend the Americans are a stupid race," the country had not produced "one great original work of genius." He asked, "Is there one luminary in our firmament that shines with unborrowed rays?"[118] Later in the century Ralph Waldo Emerson would take up this theme as well when he wrote that "Americans" needed a poet to sing their glory, having "listened too long to the courtly muses of Europe." Emerson argued that U.S. writers needed their own scholarly traditions in order to end "our day of dependence, our long apprenticeship to the learning of other lands" and to prove that the "American freeman" was not "timid, imitative, tame."[119] The idea that literature was essential to nation-building did not evaporate after the Civil War either, for in "Democratic Vistas" (1871) Walt Whitman famously wrote: "Our fundamental want to-day in the United States . . . is of a class, and the clear idea of a class, of native authors, literatures, far different, far higher in grade than any yet known."[120]

This a priori conflation of literacy with humanity and civilization may have been part and parcel of the Enlightenment and the burgeoning science of race,[121] but it also formed a crucial element in early U.S. American assessments of Haiti's potential as an independent nation. Indeed, the *City of Washington Gazette* equated literature with civilization as well when the writer wrote of Vastey: "We have been gratified and surprised to find the author, not only well acquainted with the works of Buffon, [Bernardin de] St. Pierre, and Montesquieu, but also in some degree with those of Homer, Tacitus, Milton, etc., and possessing a degree of learning and classical knowledge, which we could not by any means have expected in a country which Europeans are in the habit of considering as in a very uncivilized state."[122] Knowledge of European writing here stands as evidence capable of refuting the belief that Haiti exists "in a very uncivilized state" precisely because it was supposed to have provided the same evidence for U.S. Americans.

Vastey wrote about the connection between literacy and civilization in much the same way when he suggested that Haitians were regenerated men precisely because "we write and we print. Even in our infancy our nation has already had writers and poets who have defended its causes and celebrated its glory" (*RM*, 84). It is perhaps not surprising that U.S. writers who were engaged in their own project of creating a "poetry and philosophy of insight" that was distinctly *American* and therefore not beholden to "*their*," meaning European traditions, were so willing to make the case that Vastey's writing was proof of "black" capacity for "civilization."[123] U.S. writers were infinitely willing to accept Haitian writing, in general, and Vastey's argument in particular, as proof of such capacities and as evidence of Haiti's right to nationhood precisely because they were involved in their own project of national consolidation through the development of a specifically American U.S. literary tradition.

In the United States this project of literacy as humanity was intimately connected to a "cultural milieu" that "sought alternately to solidify and to signify across the unstable boundaries of nation and race within a New World arena characterized by its transnationality."[124] Yet the consolidation of U.S.

American identity was also formed in conjunction with a fantasy of imperialism that was paradoxically bound in certain ways to the recognition of Haitian independence. An article in the *Boston Commercial Gazette* argued that it would be in the best interests of U.S Americans to recognize Haitian independence so that the Haitian government might allow "our ships of war" to be stationed in the port of Môle-Saint-Nicolas.[125] The expression of this desire to station U.S. troops in Caribbean waters seems now like a dangerous precursor of what Paul Farmer has called "the uses of Haiti." Almost immediately after Christophe's death in 1820 and again after the United States formally recognized Haitian independence in 1862, the United States "began showing great interest" in Môle-Saint-Nicolas.[126]

This stationing of U.S. troops, nevertheless, was curiously coupled with the stability and validity of U.S. democracy when the author of the article in the *Boston Commerical Gazette* continued:

> Under the influence of reason and sound sense, a more enlightened policy than has yet existed towards the Haytiens will arise, and the declaration of our bill of rights, that 'ALL MEN ARE BORN FREE AND EQUAL', [will] be considered as having some weight in the scales of justice and humanity. When this period arrives, it will become our duty, as a moral people, to seek their alliance, that we may the more readily aid them in the advancement of learning and Christian philanthropy.[127]

The article oscillates uncertainly between patrimony and militarization of Haitian-U.S. relations, coming dangerously close to proposing a civilization mission of "Christian philanthropy." This civilizing mission would perhaps provide closure to the project of the American Revolution that the continuation of slavery in the United States had stifled.

The United States's revolution was supposed to have brought liberty to the hemisphere, but as the Abbé Grégoire observed, the United States would have to do something about its enslavement of more than "one million six hundred thousand Africans" "to conciliate, as republicans, this contradiction of their principles, and to justify, as Christians, this profanation of evangelical maxims."[128] If it was true that, as Brissot de Warville observed during his visit to the United States, "Americans, more than any other people, are convinced that all men are born free and equal,"[129] then the philosophical underpinnings of the "American" identity were threatened by a policy toward Haiti that was viewed as devoid of "reason and sound sense."

As Nesbitt has written, the very existence of Haitian revolutionists and masses of revolting slaves who had written their own Declaration of Independence "presented freedom to the world as an absolutely true logic," and one that had to be made "universal": the Haitian Revolution had meant that "no humans can be enslaved."[130] If no humans could be enslaved and Haiti was both the argument and the proof, then the United States's revolution was not just incomplete, but as Sibylle Fischer has noted, was of spurious virtue.[131]

Vastey acknowledged that U.S. slavery confounded the meanings of liberty and revolution for the world, too, when he wrote: "The independence of the United States of America has been a source of goodness for Europe and the entire world; ours will contribute to the Happiness of the human race, because of its moral and political consequences" (*RP*, 15). Vastey refers to the fact that the American Revolution may have introduced the world to a useful political philosophy and form of governance, but that the Haitian Revolution had put into practice the moral ideals that underpinned such a democratic philosophy and system of governance. Vastey's comparative take on the Age of Revolution continued when he argued that the Haitian Revolution was good for humanity because it "thrust us into civilization and enlightenment," whereas the French Revolution was harmful for humanity because it caused the French to "descend into barbarity and the dark ages" (*RP*, 25). It was, therefore, the Haitian Revolution and not the U.S. or the French Revolution that signaled the "triumph of humanity."[132]

Vastey's most important reversal concerning the meaning of the Age of Revolution comes when he suggests that it was not Haiti that needed philanthropy, but that Haitians could instead provide "a base of support where the philanthropists will be able to plant the powerful lever which will lift up the moral world against the enemies of the human race" (*RM*, 41). People who are pro-slavery are here not just enemies of the African race, but enemies of humanity, and it is their world, not Haiti, that needs to be uplifted by philanthropists.

At heart, Vastey's argument illustrates what Ralph Bauer has called two different and competing conceptions of the nation-state in the Americas as it developed into the twentieth century: one as "the agent of hemispheric or global hegemony" and the other as "a protection against United States cultural, economic, and military expansion."[133] If the nation for early U.S.

Americans was defined and indeed "imagined" in terms of a limitless expansion, the nation-state in early Haiti was conceived of in terms of clearly defined unity within the borders of Hispaniola. In other words, in nineteenth-century Haiti, "cultural nationalism" might be considered what Simon During has called in another context "a mode of freedom" that was "developed *against* imperialism."[134] For, there was surely a desire in Haiti to unify the north and the south and even the eastern parts of the island, as Vastey noted in his 1819 letter to Clarkson,[135] but there was not a wish to expand the borders of the country beyond the limits of the island; nor was there any considerable effort made to transfer the Haitian ideals of universal emancipation and liberty for all human beings to other countries in any way that accorded with the U.S. American belief that it has to the right to "violently export" its democracy to other countries.[136] Vastey vehemently argued against the slave trade and the horrors of colonialism in *Réflexions sur une lettre de Mazères*, *Le Système*, and *Notes*, but simultaneously affirmed that Haitians were not going to meddle in the affairs of the other countries in the hemisphere. Furthermore, Vastey pointed out that the Codes of Christophe, as Dessalines' 1805 Constitution had already done, expressly prohibited Haitians from interfering with "affairs outside of our island."[137] Vastey also explicitly noted that Haitians did not desire to create a Caribbean empire when he wrote: "The revolution did not transfer from the whites to the blacks the question of control of the West Indies. . . . Haiti is one of the islands of this archipelago and is not itself the West Indies."[138] Vastey's point was that Haitian nationalism was not going to be defined by or based upon its ability to expand its territories, but rather upon Haitians' own particular claim to sovereignty over a small part of the region.

In the end, literature, like trade in Haiti, was about imagining the nation in dialogic, paranational terms, not about projecting an imperial fantasy that resembled the ever-creeping expansionism of the United States. Instead, in Haiti both literature and trade became metaphors for hemispheric, transatlantic, and ultimately humanistic interactions that would carry over to the later Haitian literary tradition, most readily seen in the works of Pierre Faubert, Joseph St. Rémy, Antènor Firmin, Demesvar Delorme, and Louis Joseph Janvier. In many respects, these authors were before their times in their beliefs that the nation-state was only "second-best to world unity"[139] and that trade and contact, or what Édouard Glissant has referred to as creolization,[140] would be the instrument to produce Aimé Césaire's "humanism made to measure the world."[141] The Haitian historian Joseph St. Rémy had this to say about trade as a metaphor for human relationships: "There is a law made by nature, that the races only ameliorate themselves in mixing, that well-being only increases by free commerce, that understanding is only enriched by the exchange of ideas, that populations only become more civilized by coming into contact with others."[142] His was a utopian vision of human contact articulated in an age of seemingly unending war, to be sure, but one that underscores the prescient cosmopolitanism of early nineteenth-century Haitian authors who at the very least imagined that they could have a relationship with the United States and indeed the Western world that was not based upon colonial domination.

The takeaway from this attempt to reconstitute and then make sense of the circulation of Vastey's works in the early United States, then, is that by not reading the very Haitian authors who addressed and described in the nineteenth century their understanding of Haiti's relationship with the United States, we tend to unwittingly propagate not only the fable of nonrecognition, but the fiction of Haiti's essential lack of importance. Perhaps renewed attention to the dialogic interactions between Haiti and the United States in the first two decades of the nineteenth century can serve as a reminder not only that "Haiti Matters," as President Barack Obama said in the January 25, 2010, edition of the U.S. magazine, *Newsweek*, but that Haitians matter, too.

Epilogue

Two Archives and the Idea of Haiti

ANTHONY BOGUES

> Through Haiti we take possession of the world.
> —*Revue des Colonies*

> The struggle of Toussaint Louverture was this struggle for the transformation of a juridic right into a real right, the struggle for the *recognition* of man, and that is why it both inscribes itself and inscribes the revolt of the black slaves of Saint Domingue in the history of world civilization.
> —Aimé Césaire, *Toussaint Louverture*

Introduction

Haiti is/was an idea. Before Haiti, there was *Ayti*, then *Hispaniola*, then *Saint Domingue*—the richest colony in the eighteenth-century global system of European colonial empires. St. Domingue, the "Pearl of the Antilles," was the exemplary plantation colony—a land of untold riches, racial slavery, and colonial fantasy. This fantasy was so powerful that it is said that some French metropolitan elites sent their clothes to Haiti to be washed in a special river every six months. With its theater life, St. Domingue was considered the "Paris" of the Atlantic world. It was a fantasy without specters since both the planters and French colonial power thought it impossible for the black slaves to revolt. Haiti, then, was always about an idea.

For the colonial empires of the time, that idea was about the possibility of a rich colony—a space where everything in Europe's colonial fantasy was both possible, and real. For the slaves in the Atlantic world, the transformation of St. Domingue into Haiti was another idea; in the words of an 1827 editorial in the *Freedom Journal*: "The Revolution in St. Domingo . . . taught the world that the African, though trodden down in the dust by the foot of the oppressor, yet had not entirely lost the finer sensibilities of his nature, and still possessed the proper spirit and feelings of man."[1] As an idea of freedom about the capacity of the black body for sovereignty and as a colonial fantasy, Haiti generated multiple archives that regularly collided. One archive was about the "horrors" of St. Domingue; the other archive concerned the Haitian Revolution and the regeneration of the African world and therefore was about possibility in the midst of a dominant system of colonial racial slavery. This second archive was, in the words of Aimé Césaire, about the recognition of the slave "as a man." Horrors and regeneration are not separate sides of the same coin. Certainly there is a dialectical relationship between them produced by the same source—the Haitian Revolution—but the archives of horrors and of possibilities mark two distinct spaces in the history of Haiti as an idea. And as the various essays in this volume illustrate, these archives did not yield a single story.

When Michel-Rolph Trouillot posited that the Haitian Revolution was "unthinkable" and had been silenced in Western historiography, he did so reflecting on the way in which, within mainstream historiography, the revolution was muted and the event itself was thought impossible by the planters of St. Domingue. But all major revolutions are unthinkable by elites. The seductions of power blind one to the possibilities of change. In this sense, the Haitian Revolution was not unique. However it was unique in another sense because for the elites of St. Domingue and French colonial power, the seductions of power were harnessed to an epistemology of racial knowledge and a human schema of classification in which the African was a being of lack. Thus, the figure of the revolutionary slave—not the rebellious slave, but the revolutionary slave—was not just unthinkable but impossible. The elements of this impossibility resided in two other places as well. The first had to do with conventional narratives about modernity and revolution: How could a narrative about modernity and revolution accommodate the revolutionary slave? And secondly, even within a radical historiography in which the French Revolution was exemplary, how could a slave revolution pose fundamental questions about politics and society?

Edmund Burke notes that prior to the French Revolution, revolutions were about the restoration of lost liberties. Likewise, the political theorist Hannah Arendt points out that the American Revolution was fought "to restore liberties" and that, furthermore, this was primarily a political question, one in which the core political objective was the "establishment of a new body politic."[2] The convulsions of the French Revolution placed on the table of Western political thought the question of the social. "Liberty, Equality, and Fraternity" required equality of a different kind together with the intervention of the people as sovereign and thereby concretely posing new questions. Certainly it was the Jacobin wing of the revolution that sharply posed these issues, but, although loudly proclaiming the "rights of man," they did not extend those rights to the colonial native nor to the black slave. This in spite of Jules Michlet's observation in the *History of the French Revolution* that "the Revolution especially, in her rapid apparition, wherein she realized so little, saw, by the flashes of lightning, unknown depths, abysses of the future."[3] It was the social question that forced the French Revolution into these flashes, making its historiography *the primary* one about eighteenth-century revolution and one that shapes different genres of radical political thought within the Western intellectual tradition.

The epistemology of racial classification meant that the French Revolution could not see its colonies and African slaves as subjected to unique forms of domination. And so when the revolutionary outbreak in the northern provinces of St. Domingue occurred and was eventually sustained by the revolutionary army of ex-slaves, forcing first the French colonial Civil Commissioner Léger-Félicité Sonthonax in 1793 and then the French National Assembly to proclaim the ending of slavery in 1794, it was a remarkable event. Thus it was not that the French Revolution had become universal, but rather that the revolutionary activities of the slaves had intervened. No wonder, then, that Danton could announce at the National Assembly meeting that proclaimed the abolition of slavery, "that until now our decrees of liberty have been selfish, and only for ourselves."[4] This now means we are forced to ask ourselves: In what ways can we understand the Haitian Revolution as distinct from the French and American Revolutions?

Colonial Modernity

It is conventionally argued that political modernity took shape in the late seventeenth and eighteenth centuries. The writings of John Locke, Jacques Rousseau, and Immanuel Kant, among others, laid foundations for modern

Western political thought. Additionally, the English Civil War and the emergence of the Levelers, the establishment of forms of representative democracy in the American Revolution, and the French Revolution were practices that opened up spaces for thinking about the citizen and the rights that constitute elements of liberal political modernity. All these ideas and practices drew their questions from various forms of despotism and were concerned with and circled around rule—political rule: What are its conditions? How can it be achieved and what are its best forms? In a profound sense, they were rehearsals of Aristotle's question about the best form of government emerging in the new context of the science of man and the "degodding" of thought. To put the question plainly: How was the human now to be governed? This was a legitimate question as the various newly formed European nation-states emerged. However it may be sanguine to recall Karl Marx's comment in 1842, that criticism looks at the questions not the answers. And so when we look at this matter of the foundations of modern political thought, we find the one question that is not posed in any fundamental way is about racial slavery and colonialism.

In this regard it should be noted that in all wings of the American abolitionist movement, collection boxes were used to collect funds at meetings. A caption on one such box reads: *"Free me from the Oppression of Man."* If the triggers for the French and American Revolutions were related to the despotism of monarchy, for the revolutionary slaves in St. Domingue, it was about a distinct form of oppression. The question the slaves posed therefore required a different set of logics. To put it another way, the revolutionary slave raised two of the most acute questions of the period: What was the status of the slave and the colonial native, and how would their political actions challenge dominant political notions of the period? St. Domingue as a colonial slave society was based upon a color hierarchy of 128 shades of distinctiveness. But whether the individual in the revolutionary army was a free black, a Creole, a Bossales, or a maroon, it was the revolutionary slave who posed the most fundamental social question of the time. Thus the Haitian Revolution becomes unthinkable not only for the elites but because it cleared new grounds for political thought was also not recognized in the history of political thought.

Archival Afterlife

In such a context, the revolution and its afterlife were not silenced but reformulated into a dominant archive in which the revolution became a disaster—the harbinger of chaos and an event that should never have occurred. If one reaction to the French Revolution was the lament of Edmund Burke in his *Reflections on the Revolution in France*, then for many the Haitian Revolution was unmitigated chaos with long-term global repercussions. One hundred and eighteen years after the 1804 Haitian Declaration of Independence, T. Lothrop Stoddard produced a book in the United States, *The French Revolution in San Domingo*, in which he argued that "the French Revolution in San Domingo—the first great shock between the ideals of white supremacy and race equality . . . erased the finest of European colonies from the map of the white world and initiated the most noted attempt at negro self-government, the black republic of Haiti."[5] Haiti as an idea was a shock to the social system of racial domination such that a hundred years after the revolution it still had to be framed by power as unsuccessful chaos.

Now, notice how the revolution was framed by Stoddard—as "The French Revolution." It was the "French Revolution in the tropics,"[6] and what can one expect when the heat of revolution meets the "unbearable" heat of the tropics? In the production of the archive of power about the revolution, other things of note occurred. First, the revolution was imagined as solely the consequence of the French Revolution, thereby making the revolutionary slave figure marginal: in the minds of colonial and planter power in the Atlantic world, this revolutionary slave figure did not have thought. Secondly, the "excesses" of the revolution were seen to reside not with the French nor with the planter class but with the revolutionary slave. In this frame, the revolution was archived to produce a specific historical knowledge about it—one that would be critical of black sovereignty. It is this haunting specter of black sovereignty and its possible meanings in all its various forms that continues to befuddle Western historiography and political thought.

To face this specter, it is proper again to turn to Aimé Césaire. In his essay on Toussaint Louverture, Césaire notes that "there is no French Revolution in the French colonies."[7] From the emergence of the revolution as a *full event* the following matter has been a conundrum. How to characterize the revolution? Fighting against the French and entering into negotiations with them at a moment when the military balance of forces was uneven, the leaders of the slave revolution attempted to make clear where they stood politically on questions of equality. The 1790s document drafted by Biassou, Jean-François, and Toussaint (who signs it in the name of his nephew, Belair) spoke to a common humanity, not to matters of citizenship. It proclaimed that they were free just like the French and that it is "only by avarice and our ignorance that anyone is still held in slavery." It further noted that all humans have the same father "created in the same image. We are your equals then by natural right."[8] Contrast this with Sonthonax's proclamation of the abolition of slavery in 1793: he invokes citizenship, stating that the blacks are now French citizens and additionally that they owe their freedom to the "free people of color." He continues: "Never forget, citizens, that you got from them the arms that have conquered your freedom; Never forget that it is for the French Republic you have fought for . . . that of all the whites in the universe, the ones who are your friends are the French."[9] We will leave Sonthonax's racial appeal alone, but one should note that, as in most of the emancipation processes from slavery in the Atlantic world, freedom is a gift bestowed from above upon the "suffering" slave.

It is fair to say that the radical republicanism of the French Revolution did have some sway amongst particular elements of leadership of the revolutionary slaves, specifically those who nurtured the fervent hope that the France they were dealing with was one that under their pressure had abolished slavery and would never revert to any attempt to reinstate it. It was a hope that was of course misplaced. So let us leave Sonthonax and turn to Toussaint. In a 1794 letter to Laveaux, Toussaint describes a moment when the ex-slaves go beyond the boundaries of order established by himself and others. Riding throughout the night to meet with dissident ex-slaves, he admonishes them for their behavior, reminds them that he is their metaphorical father, and as he relates, "I told them that if they wished to preserve their liberty, they would have to submit to the laws of the Republic, and be docile and work." The response of the ex-slaves was "Look how the whites and colored men who are with you are good and united with the blacks . . . that general is what we call equality. Here it is not the same."[10]

A profound political move is evident in this statement of ex-slaves. Freedom without equality is a chimera. This simple statement goes beyond the boundaries of citizenship and interprets natural right as universal without any qualifications. It is this twining of freedom with a radical form of equality that marks the distinctiveness of the first phase of the Long Haitian Revolution.[11] It notes the centrality of the social revolutionary changes that reorder social systems. The social that appears in the Haitian Revolution is not that of the poor as they seek to enter the political stage. It is a social of different character altogether. The slave was not the poor nor the voice not heard, but rather the slave was a "living corpse."[12] So how would this "living corpse" make revolution? To be a " living corpse" was to be paradoxically both socially dead and alive with voice and speech and therefore to have the capacity to intervene in a polity. Within this paradox resided practices of the political that would in the end confront some of the most central political ideas of the period.

The Political and the American Revolution

Following Hannah Arendt, we can safely say that the American Revolution as a political revolution raised acute questions about the best form of representative government. In 1774, Jefferson delivered his *Summary View of the Rights of British America*. The document works through the colonial position of America and argues with reference to Anglo-Saxon thought and history that Britain no longer had the right to legislate for the colonies. Jefferson reminded the British crown that "our ancestors before their emigration to America were the free inhabitants of the British Dominion and possessed a right which nature has given to all men."[13] Noting that the British Crown had no proprietary rights in the colonies, Jefferson demanded rights for the colonies to manage their own affairs and asserted that the "British parliament has no right to exercise authority over us."[14] The right that Jefferson addresses here is that of political equality, of representation; these are the "rights of Englishmen." George Mason puts the matter plainly when he states, "We claim nothing but the liberty and privileges of Englishmen in the same degree as if we had continued among our brethren in Great Britain."[15] This claim was the driving force of the initial stages of the American Revolution; thus when the thirteen states in 1776 agreed to the Declaration of Independence, the document would begin by acknowledging that "in the course of human events it becomes necessary for one people to dissolve the political bonds which have connected them to another, and to assume among the powers of the earth, the separate and equal station to which the Laws of nature and Nature's God entitle them."[16] The American Declaration of Independence does not make reference to any right other than political equality, and it was not until 1789 that a constitutional amendment promulgated a Bill of Rights setting out a series of articles about individual rights with reference to religion, speech, petition, and assembly along with others. These rights represent formal procedural equality and restraint on political power organized as representative power. This point is worthy of note because oftentimes we conflate the two processes rather than seeing that the Bill of Rights emerges as the newly independent U.S. state seeks to consolidate itself. If the initial arguments worked their way through an overarching frame of the "rights of Englishmen," then the logic of such a frame would shape the elision of racial slavery. I suggest therefore that two core social matters faced the white settlers: the conquest of the indigenous population and racial slavery. These were new issues posed by the inauguration of colonial modernity and were never fundamentally confronted in the American Revolution.

The French Revolution and the Social

For the French Revolution, the intervention of the social occurred with respect to the conditions of the ordinary French person. Arendt notes that once the revolution began to grapple with this question of the poor, "The men of the revolution were no longer concerned with the emancipation of citizens. . . . They believed that they had emancipated nature herself."[17] If, however, the American Revolution turned on the question of political equality based on a natural right, then in the French Revolution a new question emerged: Where did popular sovereignty reside? Or, to use Rousseau's language, where did the "general will" reside, and how could it be interpreted? It is this working through of notions of sovereignty that would propel French radical politics up until the Paris Commune. As the French Declaration of Rights notes, "The principle of sovereignty resides essentially in the nation. No body nor individual may exercise any authority which does not proceed from the nation." The revolution developed a standing army, abolished forced labor, and made attempts to tackle property ownership.

But the social, as we have noted before, did not take into account slavery or colonialism. Note that the 1798 law on the colonies, while making "Black or colored individuals" citizens, did so on the basis of turning them into *French* citizens. What operated here under the notion of universalism was a policy of assimilation. Such a universalism meant that it was not conceivable for the "other" to be a citizen and have rights on his or her own terms; rather citizenship became aligned with Frenchness. This conception of citizenship as Frenchness was emphasized as the law paid some attention to the notion of the "foreigner." And so if the American Revolution placed on the table in the eighteenth century questions about the politics of representation and what one may call representative democracy, the French Revolution posed the question of rights and how those rights are reposed in citizenship and popular sovereignty. The Haitian Revolution, however, posed the question of freedom writ large. It did so because for the slave colony of St. Domingue, the social question was rooted in two forms of attempts at total domination—racial slavery and colonialism. It is from these frames that we begin to think about the social in the Haitian Revolution and how it shaped the revolutionary process.

Slavery and the Social

Racial slavery was an attempt at an absolute form of human domination. W. E. B. Du Bois once remarked that slavery was about "the submergence below the arbitrary will of any sort of individual." Slavery was, he continued, "barter in human flesh. It was a sharp accentuation of control over men beyond the modern labor system."[18] It is this consistent arbitrariness and control, which could create horrors for human life, that was one hallmark of slavery. The slave as a figure was both normatively and judicially outside the bounds of humane societal norms. Slavery created a state of exceptionalism, but one in which the exception was the norm governed by law and custom. C. L. R. James, writing in *Black Jacobins*, tells the story of a barber "summoned to attend to a customer [who] appeared in silk attire hat under his arm, sword at his side . . . followed by four Negroes. . . . At the slightest slackness . . . he boxed the cheek of the slave so hard that he often knocked him over."[19] Slavery as a social system was one of social and civil death, a paradoxical system of both exclusion and inclusion: exclusion from the rights of society, inclusion in that the labor of the slave was central to the economic life of the colonial empires.[20] In such a system, power was exercised on the flesh. It was the black body that colonial and racial power had to harness, to tame, and to make work, in order to transform the self into what the Caribbean historian Elsa Goveia has called "property in the person."[21]

Thus we have in the system of slavery a form of domination in which the question is not about the political form of rule but rather about how the human is transformed into a thing, yet has to expend labor to work and create. Such a situation, contrary to Hegel's conception of slavery in the *Phenomenology of the Mind*, is not about a dance of recognition but rather is one of death or life. It is a situation in which, for the slave to have a human life, the slave master has to die not reformed into something else. The complexities of this form of human domination in the colonial world and the Americas were further compounded by race. The process of what Césaire has called "thingification" was a racialized one, and so to be black was to be a slave. Thus we are not talking about Aristotle's natural slave, but rather a slavery that was based upon a trade founded, in the words of the slave abolitionist Quobna Cugoano, on practices in which the slave traders were "robbers of men, kidnappers, and ensnarers."[22] Racial slavery as a social phenomenon was also political and economic. Therefore the neat distinctions made between the social and the political begin to collapse when one examines the full character of the system. St. Domingue as the "Pearl of the Antilles" was the epitome of this system in the eighteenth century. The Haitian Revolution was unique because the revolution successfully breached this system and placed on the table of political thought a new set of issues.

An overview of the Haitian Declaration of Independence and of the 1805 Constitution illustrates this. Jean-Jacques Dessalines's secretary, Louis Boisrond Tonnerre, wrote these documents in language that was a mix of radical republicanism, with the generals of the revolutionary army acting as the "interpreters of their will" (an obvious reference to the idea of the general will), while at the same time both drawing upon new political ideas of race not as biology but as a political concept (Article 14 of the constitution) and not taking into account any idea of popular sovereignty: this should make us aware that what was being enacted was a complex, many layered situation common to many profound revolutions that rest upon the social as their primary catalyst. In the case of Haiti, the situation was further compounded because the revolutionary instrument was a revolutionary army—one that accurately knew that the revolution faced external opposition in a world where colonialism and racial slavery were still the order of the day. In such political situations, revolutionary armies do not become instruments of popular sovereignty. Today this feature of the Haitian Revolution continues to haunt Haitian society and is of central importance as we assess the revolution. Yet thinking comparatively, we might want to see that racial slavery was only formally abolished in the United States in 1865, and that it took another one hundred years to abolish Jim Crow segregation. In other words, the American Revolution, in paying primary attention to the political, did not legally eradicate the last legal vestiges of racial slavery until 160 years after the Haitian Revolution. So we return to asking: What question did the Haitian Revolution place on the table, and why was it a specter that imperial and colonial power archived as an event of chaos?

I suggested earlier that perhaps this move was in part about the specter of black self-government, but I want to suggest that something else was at play, that black sovereignty was only one issue. The other I would suggest is this:

what the Haitian Revolution did was to create a new ground for thinking and practicing freedom. To put the matter in another way, in the seventeenth and eighteenth centuries, the notion of freedom was narrowly defined as political equality, and rights were distributed accordingly. What the Haitian Revolution did was to explode that limitation by generating change at the level of subaltern practices of freedom which conflicted with the plantation system in the Americas. In this regard we should pay attention where possible to the women Carolyn Fick identifies in the north who argued for equal pay for equal work along with the vigorous attempts to develop different forms of land practices and ownership—not simply, I would argue, as "peasant forms of agricultural egalitarianism," but as attempts to work thorough the matter of labor itself and its meaning in the modern world.

At these levels and perhaps in these practices, we may see questions about freedom and equality being posed. All revolutions, Arendt tells us, are about new beginnings. I would put this differently. All revolutions are about new questions or old ones reformulated. What the Haitian Revolution did was to place on the table of political thought and practice the question of what freedom might look like—not political liberty. If emancipation was about a process of abolition from above in which elements of the old found new ways of working themselves into the pores of the new formation, then freedom was about making a new ground for a different life and possibility.

Thus to think about the Haitian Revolution is to reframe our understanding of the so-called master/slave dialectic. Here what is significant is not Toussaint facing Hegel in some kind of thought experiment; rather it is the ordinary slave, now ex-slave, making an effort to practice freedom. In the end we do not really know, and perhaps never will, what Boukman Dutty said on that August night of 1791 when the insurrection began. What we do know is that what he is supposed to have said about liberty was the catalyst that created the logics of the Long Haitian Revolution.

If we return to Césaire and the epigraph at the start of this essay in which he ponders the "struggle for the recognition of man," may we not pose the possibility that the Haitian Revolution was a revolution about the human? And if it is so, what does the archive of such a revolution look like? The unprecedented, multilayered historical practices of the Haitian Revolution created a breach in colonial modernity. This makes it a world–historical event—one perhaps yet to be fully grasped, not in its narrative forms, but in its meanings. It is this archive that requires deep exploration. This exploration would foreground a dimension of political thought that needs to be placed alongside the conventional narratives of political ideas of the period—that is, of black abolitionism.

The Long Haitian Revolution was one instance of black abolitionism in the Americas. It was the most significant and was part of a current of thought and ideas about the abolition of slavery. The threads of radical thought in the early Americas are many, and we have often placed the struggles against slavery outside these boundaries. The Long Haitian Revolution opens once again our imagination to the possibility of what might seem impossible. This is what it means to probe the archive of this revolution and the actions of the revolutionary slave.

NOTES

INTRODUCTION

1. Martineau, "Other Occupation."
2. Trouillot, "The Odd and the Ordinary," 6.
3. For recent histories of the Haitian Revolution, see Dubois, *Avengers of the New World*, and Popkin, *You Are All Free*; for an excellent collection of primary source documents on the Haitian Revolution, see Dubois and Garrigus, eds., *Slave Revolution in the Caribbean*.
4. James, *Black Jacobins*, 60.
5. See Gilmore, *Black Patriots and Loyalists*, and Frey, *Water from the Rock*.
6. Edmund Morgan argues that "the most ardent American republicans were Virginians, and their ardor was not unrelated to their power over the men and women they held in bondage.... Racism thus absorbed in Virginia the fear and contempt that men in England... felt for the inarticulate lower classes. Racism made it possible for white Virginians to develop a devotion to the equality that English republicans had declared to be the soul of liberty" (*American Slavery, American Freedom*, 381, 386).
7. For further discussion of these events, see Popkin, *You Are All Free*, 189–216.
8. For further consideration of the Atlantic dimensions of the Haitian Revolution, see the essays collected in Geggus, ed., *Impact of the Haitian Revolution in the Atlantic World*.
9. For extended discussion of Toussaint's political and economic strategy vis-à-vis the United States (and vice versa) during this period, see Carolyn Fick's essay in this volume, "Revolutionary St. Domingue and the Emerging Atlantic: Paradigms of Sovereignty."
10. Johnson, "A Revolutionary Dinner," 126–127.
11. Donald R. Hickey reports that in 1797, more than six hundred U.S. vessels were engaged in trading with St. Domingue, carrying as much as $5 million of imported merchandise. See Hickey, "America's Response," 365.
12. Brown, *Toussaint's Clause*.
13. Napoleon reinstated slavery in Martinique in 1802 and in Guadeloupe in 1803. He did not ever overtly attempt to reinstate slavery in St. Domingue, but many speculated (at the time) that he intended to do so. For further discussion, see Dubois, "Haitian Revolution," 18–41.
14. Napoleon Bonaparte to Leclerc, July 1, 1802, *Lettres du Général Leclerc*, ed. Paul Roussier (Paris: Société de l'Histoire des Colonies Françaises, 1937), 305–306, as cited in Dubois, "Haitian Revolution." Dubois's article includes an extended discussion of the reestablishment of slavery in the French colonies.
15. Roederer, *Oeuvres du Comte P. L. Roederer*, 3:461.

16. Library of Congress, *Guide to the Louisiana Purchase*; Cayton, "'Relations of Blood and Affection,'" 151. Note that Cayton is here ventriloquizing popular understandings of the Louisiana Purchase rather than arguing for this view.

17. Adams, *History of the United States of America*, 1:378, 406.

18. For an extended discussion of the relation between the Haitian Revolution and the Louisiana Purchase, and historiographical debates related to this issue, see the essay by David Geggus in this volume, "The Louisiana Purchase and the Haitian Revolution."

19. For discussion of Jefferson's shifting position with respect to Toussaint, see Matthewson, "Jefferson and the Nonrecognition of Haiti," 22–48.

20. Speech of George Logan, December 20, 1805, *Annals of Congress*, 9th Cong., 1st sess., 26–29, as cited in Hickey, "America's Response," 375.

21. According to Matthewson:

> The value of American exports to the French islands stood at $6.7 million in 1806, but fell to $5.8 in 1807, to $1.5 in 1808. These were nothing more than official trade statistics, collected at a time when it was illegal to trade with the Haitians. Obviously, they do not consider the substantial illicit trade, which was pervasive in the West Indies, but they did reflect a trend, for they were echoed by observers on the ground. At the end of the decade, a British merchant, William Doran, noted that the combined impact of the embargoes and other restrictions "at length put us in possession of this branch of commerce." ("Jefferson and the Nonrecognition of Haiti," 35)

22. Gallatin cited in ibid., 34.

23. "The southern conservative reaction was embodied in legislation, which included laws passed by Virginia (1801, 1802, 1804, 1805, 1806), North Carolina (1802), South Carolina (1800, 1805), Georgia (1802, 1804), Maryland (1805), and the Mississippi Territory (1805). This new body of legislation was aimed at slaves and free coloreds, requiring, for example, recently manumitted slaves in Virginia to leave the state within one year. It also encouraged new systems of surveillance and control, especially for free blacks, whom southerners thought to be dangerous incendiaries, owing to their role in the Dominguan revolution" (Matthewson, "Jefferson and the Nonrecognition of Haiti," 25). Jed Handelsman Shugerman notes that South Carolina reopened the African slave trade immediately following the Louisiana Purchase in a move that, he argues, was calculated by southern slaveholding interests to facilitate the spread of slavery westward by supplying ample slave labor and simultaneously preempting any increase in the illicit smuggling of slaves (and revolutionary antislavery sentiment) from the Caribbean into the port of New Orleans. According to Shugerman, South Carolina slaveholders concluded that "Louisiana either would continue to smuggle slaves from the Caribbean (and thus increase the risk of revolt as South Carolinians had fears), or South Carolina could provide the legal alternative by opening the African slave trade" ("Reopening of the Slave Trade," 276).

24. For important histories of the cotton frontier and the second slavery in the United States see Baptist, *Half Has Never Been Told*; Beckert, *Empire of Cotton*; and Johnson, *River of Dark Dreams*.

25. Matthewson, "Jefferson and the Nonrecognition of Haiti," 26. For more extensive treatment of this point, see Rugemer, *Problem of Emancipation*, as well as David Brion Davis's statement that "the myth that abolitionists were directly responsible for the bloodbath of Santo

Domingo became an entrenched part of master class ideology, in Latin America as well as the United States" (*Slave Power Conspiracy*, 35).

26. The term "second slavery" was coined by Dale Tomich; see Tomich, *Through the Prism of Slavery*. Anthony Kaye describes the second slavery as follows:

> After 1790, slavery expanded onto new ground, slaves tended new crops and new machinery, and the planter classes gained dominance in rising world markets and acquired new powers from reconstituted states in Cuba, Brazil, and the South. Profits reaped from sugar, coffee, and cotton derived, in part, from burgeoning industrial production in two ways. First, upturns in output met increased demand from the growing populations of industrial workers. The transition of tropical commodities from elite luxuries to common necessities reached midcourse around 1800 and was completed during the nineteenth century. Second, planters integrated industrial machines with slave labor. In the new techniques and increased scale of production and the sheer mobility and adaptability of slave labor, the second slavery was, in a word, modern. ("Second Slavery," 627)

27. Beckert, "Emancipation and Empire," 1408.
28. Baptist, "Second Slavery," 6.
29. Berlin, *Generations of Captivity*, 166–169.
30. Baptist, *Half Has Never Been Told*, 142.
31. Baptist, "Second Slavery," 19.
32. Baptist writes:

> From 1804, cotton climbed rapidly in importance until it became in most years 50% or higher of all U.S. exports by value. It would remain that way all the way until the Civil War. It was the main source of the foreign exchange needed to repay the imported manufactured goods brought in each year from British factories. The patterns and cycles of cotton, credit and other commodities would suffer astonishing crises, and would be rebuilt repeatedly. But in each version, the cycle of overseas goods and credit exchanged for cotton made on slavery's frontier, was still the driving piston that pushed the U.S. economy forward each year. For cotton brought not only income, activity, and the ability to repay short-term commercial debts. The world market for cotton was so large, and growing so quickly—and U.S. enslavers were demonstrating the ability to extract from the enslaved not only more cotton but higher-quality cotton than could be bought from free-labor peasants in other parts of the world—that the southwestern frontier began to look like an ideal place to invest money. Outsiders wanted to invest money in generating additional cotton-making capacity. ("Second Slavery," 19)

See also Beckert, *Empire of Cotton*.

33. Schoelcher, *Colonies étrangères et Haïti*, 279–280, as cited by Dubois, *Haiti*, 103.
34. Robinson, *Unbroken Agony*, 22. Robinson writes, "After extended negotiations, in 1838, under the Traité d'Amitié the original obligation of 150 million francs was reduced to 90 million francs, with the government of Haiti required to make thirty annual payments of 2 million francs in order to pay off the 60 million franc balance. Haiti had to make these payments in addition to the payments it had been making to a succession of private banks

from which it had to borrow at onerous interest rates in order to meet the terms of its original unjust obligation to France.... The Haitian economy has never recovered from the financial havoc France (and America) wreaked upon it, during and after slavery" (21–22).

35. Dubois, *Haiti*, 103.

36. Beauvois, "L'Indemnité de Saint-Domingue," 109–124. Beauvois's conclusions are drawn on the basis of analyzing the extent (or lack thereof) of French governmental repayments to former land-owners in St. Domingue; the insignificant nature of these payments leads him to conclude that the French government was pursuing political ends rather than seeking repayment for individuals who lost property during the Haitian Revolution.

37. Dubois, *Haiti*, 102.

38. On the use of racism for the workings of capitalism, see Wallerstein, "Ideological Tensions of Capitalism," 29–36.

39. In 2003, Haitian President Jean-Bertrand Aristide demanded that France repay the indemnity to Haiti (close to $22 billion in current value), given that the indemnity was initially exacted for the cost of slaves lost by French colonists, and that slavery is now recognized as a crime against humanity. The French were dismissive of Aristide's demand. See Charles, "Aristide Pushes for Restitution from France," *Miami Herald*, December 18, 2003.

40. Trouillot, "The Odd and the Ordinary," 6 (emphasis added).

41. See Rugemer, "Slave Rebels and Abolitionists," 179–202.

42. Jackson and Bacon, *African Americans and the Haitian Revolution*. Essays by Ivy Wilson and Marlene Daut included in this collection also describe the substantive connections between the United States and Haiti (despite the U.S. official non-recognition of Haiti) in the period following 1806.

43. Fischer, *Modernity Disavowed*; Dayan, *Haiti, History, and the Gods*; Buck-Morss, *Hegel, Haiti, and Universal History*; Nesbitt, *Universal Emancipation*; and Scott, *Conscripts of Modernity*.

44. Trouillot, *Silencing the Past*.

45. Massey, *For Space*, 89.

CHAPTER I. REVOLUTIONARY ST. DOMINGUE AND THE EMERGING ATLANTIC

1. Fick, "Haitian Revolution," 407–408.

2. Ibid., 402–403.

3. Ibid., 409–411.

4. Ardouin, *Études sur l'histoire d'Haïti*, 4:11–12. For a comprehensive treatment of the structural complexities that characterized and handicapped Haiti's colonial economy in its relations to international commerce, see Saint-Louis, *Aux origines du drame d'Haïti*.

5. De Conde, *Quasi-War*, 130–136; Logan, *Diplomatic Relations*, 64–67; Brown, *Toussaint's Clause*, 130–132; Saint-Louis, *Aux origines du drame d'Haïti*, 115–121; James, *Black Jacobins*, 207–212.

6. James, *Black Jacobins*, 214–223.

7. Toussaint Louverture, Général en chef de l'Armée de Saint Domingue à Monsieur Adams, Président du Congrès des États-Unis d'Amérique, le Cap, 16 brumaire An 7, in Jameson, ed., "Letters of Toussaint Louverture and Edward Stevens, 1798–1800," 66.

8. Brown, *Toussaint's Clause*, 18–22, 27–30. For the extent of commercial relations between Philadelphia merchants, in particular, and Saint Domingue during the 1790s, see Dun, "'What avenues of commerce,'" 357–364.

9. Brown, *Toussaint's Clause*, 73–75; Logan, *Diplomatic Relations*, 32–44.

10. Quoted in Logan, *Diplomatic Relations*, 44.

11. The "XYZ Affair" refers to the scandal that erupted when it became known in the United States that the three commissioners President Adams had sent to Paris in an effort to ease tensions between the two countries during the Quasi-War were rebuffed, insulted, and expected to pay a bribe if they wished to begin negotiations with Minister of Foreign Affairs Charles Talleyrand. See Brown, *Toussaint's Clause*, 124–127.

12. Cabon, *Histoire d'Haïti*, 4:88–89; Saint-Louis, *Aux origines du drame d'Haïti*, 131.

13. For a fuller discussion of militarized agriculture under the regime of Toussaint Louverture, see Moïse, *Le projet national de Toussaint Louverture et la Constitution de 1801*, 62–65; James, *Black Jacobins*, 242; Saint-Louis, *Aux origines du drame d'Haïti*, 150–155; and Fick, "Emancipation in Haiti," 26–27.

14. Bibliothèque Nationale [BN] (France), MSS 12102, Correspondance de Toussaint Louverture, v. 2, no. 415; *Ordonnance du Citoyen Toussaint Louverture, Général en chef de l'Armée de Saint-Domingue*, le Cap, 27 brumaire An 7 (November 17, 1798).

15. Ibid. On Toussaint's administrative initiatives, also see Ardouin, *Histoire d'Haïti*, 4:11–12; Moïse, *Le projet national de Toussaint Louverture*, 56–57; and Saint-Louis, *Aux origines du drame d'Haïti*, 133–134.

16. Logan, *Diplomatic Relations*, 95; De Conde, *Quasi-War*, 138–140; Brown, *Toussaint's Clause*, 144–161.

17. Saint-Louis, *Aux origines du drame d'Haïti*, 139.

18. Edward Stevens to Timothy Pickering, le Cap, September 30, 1799, in Jameson, ed., "Letters of Toussaint Louverture and Edward Stevens," 82–85.

19. Ibid., 84.

20. Edward Stevens to Brigadier-General Maitland, Gonaïves, May 23, 1799, in Jameson, ed., "Letters of Toussaint Louverture and Edward Stevens," 73.

21. For a fuller discussion of the complex underlying and immediate causes of the civil war between the two rivals, see James, *Black Jacobins*, 224–231; Sannon, *Histoire de Toussaint Louverture*, 2:191–205, 219–223; Ardouin, *Études*, 4:3–11, 19–26; and Saint-Louis, *Aux origines du drame d'Haïti*, 122–131.

22. Edward Stevens to Timothy Pickering, Arcahaye, June 24, 1799, in Jameson, ed., "Letters of Toussaint Louverture and Edward Stevens," 79, 80.

23. Ibid., 80.

24. Ibid., 77.

25. Edward Stevens to Timothy Pickering, le Cap, February 13, 1800, in Jameson, ed., "Letters of Toussaint Louverture and Edward Stevens," 93.

26. Logan, *Diplomatic Relations*, 82.

27. Quoted ibid., 83. Additional quotations in this paragraph are also quoted in Logan, *Diplomatic Relations*, 83, 84.

28. Logan, *Diplomatic Relations*, 85–88; Brown, *Toussaint's Clause*, 145–154.

29. Thomas Jefferson to James Monroe, January 23, 1799, in Oberg, ed., *Papers of Thomas Jefferson*, 30:633–637.

30. Thomas Jefferson to John Page, Philadelphia, January 24, 1799, in Oberg, ed., *Papers of Thomas Jefferson*, 30:640. See also Thomas Jefferson to Nicholas Lewis, Philadelphia, January 30, 1799, in Oberg, ed., *Papers of Thomas Jefferson*, 30:663–664.

31. Thomas Jefferson to Aaron Burr, Philadelphia, February 11, 1799, in Oberg, ed., *Papers of Thomas Jefferson*, 31:22–23.

32. Thomas Jefferson to James Madison, February 12, 1799, in Oberg, ed. *Papers of Thomas Jefferson*, 31:30.

33. Toussaint Louverture, Général en chef de l'Armée de Saint-Domingue à Monsieur John Adams, Président des États-Unis de l'Amérique, Port-de-Paix, 27 thermidor An 7 (August 14, 1799), in Jameson, ed., "Letters of Toussaint Louverture and Edward Stevens," 82.

34. Edward Stevens to Timothy Pickering, Léogane, January 16, 1800, in Jameson, ed., "Letters of Toussaint Louverture and Edward Stevens," 91.

35. De Conde, *Quasi-War*, 209.

36. Quoted in Logan, *Diplomatic Relations*, 104. Additional quotations in this paragraph are also quoted in Logan.

37. Quoted ibid., 105.

38. Ibid.

39. De Conde, *Quasi-War*, 209; Logan, *Diplomatic Relations*, 106–110.

40. Quoted in Brown, *Toussaint's Clause*, 65; and in Logan, *Diplomatic Relations*, 100.

41. Adams, *History of the United States*, 2:14.

42. Quoted in Logan, *Diplomatic Relations*, 143.

43. Adams, *History of the United States*, 2:21.

44. Trouillot, *Haiti, Nation Against State*, 44–45.

CHAPTER 2. (MIS)READING THE REVOLUTION

1. *General Advertiser*, July 20, 1791 (Philadelphia); *Federal Gazette*, July 20, 1791 (Philadelphia); reprinted in *Gazette of the United States*, July 23, 1791. All newspapers cited here were published in Philadelphia unless otherwise noted. The *Hetty* arrived on July 19. See Records of Arrivals and Clearances (entry 1057), vol. 1, Records of the U.S. Customs Service, Philadelphia, 1789–1791, Record Group 36, National Archives and Records Administration (NARA), Mid-Atlantic Regional Branch, Philadelphia, PA. For the *Hetty*'s cargo, see Inward Foreign Manifests (entry 1059b), box 8, Record Group 36, NARA. For Davis's logbook of this and other voyages to and from St. Domingue, see Dutilh and Wachsmuth Papers, IV Dut 2, 69.120.5, Independence Seaport Museum, Philadelphia, PA.

2. *Federal Gazette*, July 21, 1791. This captain was John Davidson, of the schooner *Charming Sally*. See Records of Arrivals and Clearances (entry 1057), vol. 1, Record Group 26, NARA.

3. In addition to those accounts quoted elsewhere, notices of the decree in this period include *Federal Gazette*, July 22, 1791 ("FOR THE FEDERAL GAZETTE"), reprinted in *General Advertiser*, July 23, 1791; *General Advertiser*, July 26, 1791 ("France. NATIONAL ASSEMBLY May 14"); *General Advertiser*, July 28, 1791 ("France. NATIONAL ASSEMBLY May 16"); *Federal Gazette*, July 30, 1791 (Philadelphia and Montego Bay, June 25 headings). Between August and December 1791 the decree was discussed in at least twenty-five writings in Philadelphia newspapers.

4. I use this phrase, rather than "free colored," "mulatto," or *affranchi*, to refer to people of mixed parentage in St. Domingue. After a certain point the categories of "free" and "freed" are no longer sufficiently specific when various groups were actively fighting on their own behalf. "Mulatto," though the term usually used by contemporary white Americans, was considered derogatory in St. Domingue.

5. For the question of the number enfranchised, see James, *Black Jacobins*, 77, who suggests four hundred; see also Blackburn, *Overthrow of Colonial Slavery*. Fick, *Making of Haiti*,

85, suggests a "few hundred." Geggus, "Racial Equality," 1303 n. 83, however, finds that number "scarcely credible." Dubois, *Avengers*, 89, finds the question irrelevant, except as an index of the various agendas at work in Paris. For the plight of the *gens de couleur* more generally, see Garrigus, *Before Haiti*.

6. Geggus, "Racial Equality"; Blackburn, *Overthrow of Colonial Slavery*, 185–190; and Dubois, *Avengers*, 89–90. See also Garrigus, *Before Haiti*, 352–359.

7. See *Federal Gazette*, April 2, 1791 (New York, March 31), and *General Advertiser*, April 2, 1791 (New York, March 31), in which the colonel killed is not named. See also *Federal Gazette*, April 4, 1791 (Baltimore), reprinted in *General Advertiser*, April 5, 1791, and *Pennsylvania Gazette*, April 6, 01791. For further details, see *General Advertiser*, April 11, 1791 (New London, April 1), *Federal Gazette*, May 7, 1791 (Boston, May 2, "*From the Moniteur Colonial, a paper printed at Cape Francois, of the 10th March, a gentleman of this town has been pleased to favor us with the following translation.*"). These sources were presumably the basis of contemporary accounts of this episode, most notably that provided in Edwards, *Historical Survey*, ch. 5, Rainsford, *Historical Account*, ch. 3. See also James, *Black Jacobins*, 82–84.

8. See *Gazette of the United States*, March 16, 1791, *General Advertiser*, March 19, 1791, reprinted in *Federal Gazette*, March 21, 1791, and *Pennsylvania Gazette*, March 23, 1791. See also Edwards, *Historical Survey*, ch. 4.

9. For cockades, see, for example, *Gazette of the United States*, November 11, 1789 ("*Extract of a letter from a gentleman in Martinique, to his correspondent in this town*"), *Pennsylvania Gazette*, November 18, 1789 ("BY order of the Excellencies the Governor and Intendent . . ."), and *Pennsylvania Gazette* December 16, 1789 (Kingston, October 10). For "the People," see *Federal Gazette*, May 4, 1790 ("American Intelligence"). For the National Assembly, see *Gazette of the United States*, September 8, 1790. See also *Pennsylvania Gazette*, September 15, 1790, in which a commentator noted that "one party are for declaring themselves independent from France altogether, the other are for the National Assembly, which has altered this place amazingly." For an example of notice of tyranny, see *Pennsylvania Gazette*, December 16, 1789 (Montego Bay, October 17). For "the cause of liberty," see *Federal Gazette*, October 14, 1790 ("FRENCH WEST INDIES"). For a parallel drawn between the *blanc* Intendent and the "governor" of the Bastille, see *Federal Gazette*, November 25, 1789 (Boston, November 13).

10. *Pennsylvania Gazette*, December 16, 1789 (Montego Bay, October 17).

11. *Federal Gazette*, October 14, 1790 ("FRENCH WEST INDIES").

12. Readers learned of this development in the text of the National Assembly's decree of October 12, which castigated the St. Marc Assembly and praised Mauduit. See Philadelphia *Gazette of the United States*, December 29, 1790 (Paris, October 12). The General Assembly at St. Marc was reacting to the National Assembly's decree of March 8, 1790, which gave legislative power to local entities for local issues. See *Federal Gazette*, June 1, 1790 ("By This Day's Mail. Foreign Intelligence. Paris"), reprinted in *Gazette of the United States*, June 2, 1790. For the National Assembly's subsequent instructions, issued on March 28, warning against pushing towards independence, see *Gazette of the United States*, July 28, 1790 ("Paris: Instructions for the Colonies"). Dubois, *Avengers*, 85–87; Fick, *Making of Haiti*, 81.

13. For their reception in Paris, see *Gazette of the United States*, December 4, 1790 (Paris, September 18). For their defense, see *Federal Gazette*, December 8, 1790 (Paris, October 2, "Colonial Committee"). For their castigation, see *General Advertiser*, January 4, 1791 (National Assembly, October 15, "FRENCH WEST INDIES").

14. *General Advertiser*, December 24, 1790 ("*Extract of a letter from Cape Francois, dated November 1, 1790*"), reprinted in *Pennsylvania Gazette*, December 29, 1790.

15. Blackburn, *Overthrow of Colonial Slavery*, 182–183; Dubois, *Avengers*, 87–88; Fick, *Making of Haiti*, 80–84.

16. *General Advertiser*, December 2, 1790 (Philadelphia, "Extract from Cape Francois"). See also *General Advertiser*, December 13, 1790 ("*Extract of a letter from a gentleman in Cape Francois, to the Printer of the Independent Gazetteer, &c. dated November 3*"), in which "Ojay" was maligned as an "ambitious villain" whose efforts were based on the decrees for freedom and equality given by the National Assembly—a "dangerous step" that would give the *gens de couleur* "the balance of power on the island."

17. *General Advertiser*, March 3, 1791 (Charleston, February 15, Savannah, February 3).

18. *General Advertiser*, March 3, 1791 (Savannah, February 3).

19. *General Advertiser*, April 29, 1791 ("Concise Sketch of the POLITICS of St. Domingo"). Bache was fluent in French, having lived in France from 1776 to 1785 while traveling with Benjamin Franklin, his grandfather. He had to relearn English after returning to the United States. Few, if any, of Philadelphia's other newspaper editors could claim fluency in French. On Bache, and on French language competency in general during this period, see Spurlin, *French Enlightenment in America*, 29–48 and Daniel, *Scandal and Civility*, 109–147.

20. *Federal Gazette*, December 8, 1790 (Boston, November 26). This was the opinion of officials on Martinique.

21. See, with different emphases, Newman, *Parades and Politics*; Waldstreicher, *Perpetual Fetes*; and Cleves, *Reign of Terror*. See also Ziesche, *Cosmopolitan Patriots*.

22. For newspapers, reading, and ideas about national identity, see Hale, "On Their Tiptoes," and Cotlar, *Tom Paine's America*. On Philadelphia's importance as a source of information, see Mott, *American Journalism*, 116–131; and Pasley, "*Tyranny of Printers*," passim and especially 74–95, 109–118, and 438 n. 49. For Philadelphia as a cultural center, see, for example, Branson, *These Fiery Frenchified Dames*.

23. This is noted in Nash, *Forging Freedom*, 7.

24. See, for example, Richard How to John Pemberton, August 8, 1789, Pemberton Papers, vol. 52, p. 167, Historical Society of Pennsylvania (HSP), Philadelphia, PA, in which the British correspondent hoped that "the most commendable Example of ye Pennsylvanians will at length be as universally imitated as it is extolled, till not a single negro remain in Bondage." See also de Warville, *New Travels*, passim.

25. *Federal Gazette*, June 2, 1791. *Federal Gazette*, April 4, 1791 (Baltimore), reprinted in *General Advertiser*, April 5, 1791, and *Pennsylvania Gazette*, April 6, 1791.

26. *Federal Gazette*, June 2, 1791 (Philadelphia).

27. *General Advertiser*, August 2, 1791 ("Address of the Municipality of Port-au-Prince, to the National Assembly").

28. *General Advertiser*, November 9, 1792 ("St. Domingo"); *Federal Gazette*, November 9, 1792 ("ST. DOMINGO"). Similar accounts are continued in *General Advertiser*, November 14, 1792 ("St. Domingo") and *Federal Gazette*, November 14 and 15, 1791 ("ST. DOMINGO").

29. This charge was made by the *blanc* governor Blanchelande. *General Advertiser*, May 12, 1791.

30. Blackburn, *Overthrow of Colonial Slavery*, 186–187; Davis, *Problem of Slavery*, 142–144; Fick, *Making of Haiti*, 84–85; Geggus, "Racial Equality," 1302–1303.

31. *General Advertiser*, June 17, 1791 (Baltimore, June 10).

32. *General Advertiser*, July 16, 1791 (London, May 6). That Burke's speech was given during debate over Parliament's right to create a constitution for Canada indicates the extent to

which the issues raised in St. Domingue penetrated into other discussions around colonial issues. Though this speech was given before the decree was passed, it was read in Philadelphia contemporaneously with its reception.

33. Bache's chief competitor was John Fenno's *Gazette of the United States*. The space devoted to St. Domingue and French debates over the colonial question in the *General Advertiser* far outpaces that in other papers in this period.

34. *General Advertiser*, July 30, 1791 ("Abstract of a letter from a gentleman in Cape Francois to his friend in this city, dated July 9th, 1791"), reprinted in *Federal Gazette*, August 1, 1791, and *Pennsylvania Gazette*, August 3, 1791. The scraps of debate in the National Assembly that Bache printed were suggestive. The July 26, 1791 issue ("France. *NATIONAL ASSEMBLY*") reported a debate on May 14 in which a letter from the *gens de couleur* delegates was read, but not discussed. Two days later, under the same heading, the debate of May 16 was recorded, in which the Assembly received notice from Parisian Jews "who, encouraged by the decree which raised a number of mulattoes to the rank of active citizens, begged that a similar favour might be conferred on them."

35. *General Advertiser*, August 8, 1791 ("Translated for the Independent Gazetteer," Cape Francois, July 10). This issue also supplied a translation of the text of the May 15 decree. The *Gazette of the United States* reprinted some of this material in its August 10, 1791 issue, but did not include the Bordeaux merchants' address.

36. These phrases were from a French merchant group. See *National Gazette*, December 5, 1791 (Paris, September 6), reprinted in *General Advertiser*, December 7, 1791. See also *Gazette of the United States*, August 24, 1791 ("*A Letter from the Provincial Assembly of the North of St. Domingo, to the King of the French*"); *Gazette of the United States*, September 10, 1791; and *General Advertiser*, September 13, 1791. For accounts placing *gens de couleur* at the head of the insurgent slaves, see, for example, *Gazette of the United States*, September 24, 1791 in which Cap-Français is described in the Pennsylvania Legislature as "closely besieged by an enraged and brutal multitude of Negroes and Mulattoes."

37. This agreement came about when Western *gens de couleur* organized a confederation with local free blacks (including a maroon band) to confront the *rouge* leadership of the city. Local *blanc* factions, sensing an opportunity, offered to ally with this confederation and to support the Decree of May 15. In response, the *rouge* in Port-au-Prince signed a concordat in September 1791 with the confederates that went well beyond the decree in its recognition of *gens de couleur* citizenship. Violence began when jealous nonslaveholding whites in the city (*petits blancs*) refused to honor the agreement. Faced with alarming signs of slave unrest, however, *rouge* leaders regained control and offered additional promises of recognition to the *gens de couleur* in October. Shortly afterwards, when news that the National Assembly had repealed the May 15 Decree, the whites of Port-au-Prince reneged again. In the ensuing riot the city burned. Dubois, *Avengers of the New World*, 119–122; Fick, *Making of Haiti*, 118–134; James, *Black Jacobins*, 96–103; Stein, *Sonthonax*, 64–65. For the quotation, see *Gazette of the United States*, October 19, 1791. For news of the concordats in Philadelphia, see *Federal Gazette*, October 18, 1791 ("Agreement between the White Citizens of Port-au-Prince and the Citizens of Color, September the 11th, 1791"), and *Pennsylvania Gazette*, October 19, 1791. Readers would have noticed that, in addition to mandating a broad acceptance of the Decree of May 15, they included provisions that explicitly adopted the *gens de couleur* interpretation of the March 8 and March 28, 1790, decrees of the National Assembly, as well as measures designed to rehabilitate Ogé's reputation.

38. *General Advertiser*, January 4, 1791.

39. For the debates in the Legislative Assembly, see *General Advertiser*, November 18, 1791 ("Affairs of the Colonies"), reprinted in *National Gazette*, November 24, 1791, and *Gazette of the United States*, December 10, 1791. Robespierre, by this account, "giving a loose to his violent temper," charged that Barnave and Lameth were "*traitors to their country*" because they had actively prevented the Decree of May 15 from being enforced. For threats of secession, see *Federal Gazette*, February 13, 1792 ("*INSURRECTIONS in ST. DOMINGO*"). See also *General Advertiser*, December 2, 1791 ("*Extract of a letter from London, Sept. 16*"). For the Decree of September 24 as a measure against the "counter-revolution," see *National Gazette*, December 22, 1791 (Paris, September 24), reprinted in *General Advertiser*, December 23, 26, 1791. See also *General Advertiser*, December 19, 1791 (Paris, September 8), in which sources suggest the British navy, in league with reactionaries in St. Domingue, would open the island's ports simultaneously with attacks by the counter-revolutionary forces massed along France's borders.

40. See, for example, *Federal Gazette*, December 19, 1791 ("*Extract of a letter from Cape-Francois, of the 16th of November, 1791, received by the brig Keziah, Capt. Robert Brown*"), reprinted in *General Advertiser*, December 20, 1791, *Gazette of the United States*, December 21, 1791, and *Pennsylvania Gazette*, December 21, 1791. See also *General Advertiser*, January 18, 1792 (Boston, January 4).

41. For the news of the Decree of April 4, see *National Gazette*, June 4, 1792 (Paris, March 24). For the wave of optimism, see, for example, *General Advertiser* and *Federal Gazette*, August 8, 1792, *Federal Gazette*, August 11, 1792 (Providence, August 4), reprinted in *Gazette of the United States* and *Pennsylvania Gazette*, August 15, 1792; summarized in *National Gazette*, August 15, 1792.

42. For the "newspaper war" in Philadelphia in 1792, see Pasley, "*Tyranny of Printers*," 48–78; and Daniel, *Scandal and Civility*, 116–128. For Jefferson's and Madison's roles, see Boyd, "Jefferson, Freneau, and the Founding of the National Gazette." For an overview, see Elkins and McKitrick, *Age of Federalism*, 82–92, 239–240.

43. *National Gazette*, August 11, 1792, reprinted in *Federal Gazette*, August 21, 1792.

44. *General Advertiser*, August 14, 1792. It is tempting to correlate Bache's shift in opinion on "levelling principles" and "pretentions" between this writing and his depictions, using the same phrases, of Ogé in late 1790. I find the general shift more convincing than this suggestive, but singular, moment when his rhetoric flip-flopped.

45. Popkin, *You Are All Free*; Stein, *Sonthonax*, 41–62.

46. *General Advertiser*, November 17, 1792 ("ST. DOMINGO").

47. *National Gazette*, November 17, 1792.

48. *General Advertiser*, December 17, 1792.

49. *General Advertiser*, December 5, 1792 ("ST. DOMINGO"). The specific reference here was the creation of the Intermediate Commission, a body that would replace the provincial assembly in the north. All accounts stressed the break this body represented with the past because of its make up "without distinction of colour." See *General Advertiser*, November 9, 1792 ("ST. DOMINGO"), November 12, 1792 ("ST. DOMINGO"), November 12, 1792 ("PROCLAMATION,—In the name of the NATION").

50. For material maligning both governor Blanchelande and Mauduit, see *General Advertiser*, November 9, 1792 ("ST. DOMINGO, Succint ACCOUNT of the MISFORTUNES of the COLONY in a letter from the Colonial Assembly to the French National Assembly, agreed to on the 4th"); *General Advertiser*, November 10, 1792 ("St. Domingo"); *National Gazette*, November 17, 1792; and *General Advertiser*, November 23, 1792 ("ST. DOMINGO").

These accounts intimate connections between the counter-revolution in France, to include Louis XVI's actions, and in St. Domingue.

51. *General Advertiser*, November 9, 1792 ("ST. DOMINGO").

52. Bache printed a call to Americans for contributions by a society on the island, but interrupted the plea by widening the call. "American Reader, go and do thou likewise!" he wrote. France had served "the cause of American freedom"; now its citizens should not "call in vain for our aid against a merciless foe.—Forbid it honor, forbid it justice, humanity forbid it!" *General Advertiser*, November 23, 1792 ("ST. DOMINGO").

53. *National Gazette*, July 6, 1793.

54. This alien sensibility was embodied in Bache's report of his apparent meeting in mid-1791 with a *gens de couleur* delegate from Martinique. The man was visiting the city in order to speak with George Washington, having what appeared to be an invitation, "distributed throughout the French colonies" via a printed leaflet, to "such oppressed people of colour, as chose to remove, and form a colony in Virginia." Bache explained to his readers that this plan was obviously "nothing less than a gross imposition" and that it appeared that "the Mulattoe" had been tricked. *General Advertiser*, June 4, 1791. See Cox, "British Caribbean," 282–283.

55. On white antislavery in the United States in this period, see, for example, Melish, *Disowning Slavery*, 50–118; Nash and Soderlund, *Freedom by Degrees*; Newman, *Transformation of American Abolitionism*, 1–59. More generally, see Davis, *Problem of Slavery*. For African American freedom efforts, see Egerton, *Death or Liberty*, and Pybus, *Epic Journeys of Freedom*.

56. *National Gazette*, March 12, 1792, reprinted in *General Advertiser*, March 14, 1792, and *American Museum*, July 1792.

57. See, for example, *General Advertiser*, August 8, 1791 ("Translated for the Independent Gazetteer," Cape Francois, July 10.).

58. *National Gazette*, March 12, 1792, reprinted in *General Advertiser*, March 14, 1792, and *American Museum*, July 1792.

59. *General Advertiser*, March 14, 1792 ("*Translation of an address [from* M. Gregory, *Deputy to the National Assembly of France &c.] to the* Colored Citizens *and* Free Negroes *of the* French Islands *in* America, *upon the subject of the* Rights *of* Man, *confirmed to them by the* National Assembly *of France*."). For Grégoire, see Sepinwall, *Abbé Grégoire*.

60. See Trouillot, *Silencing the Past*, esp. 70–107.

CHAPTER 3. "THE MISCHIEF THAT AWAITS US"

1. *Washington Federalist* (Georgetown, District of Columbia), October 20, 1802.

2. For a detailed survey of the U.S. concerns about the impact of the Haitian Revolution on the domestic order, see Elizabeth Maddock Dillon and Michael J. Drexler's introductory essay in this volume.

3. *New-York Evening Post*, August 10, 1802.

4. For more information on how the XZY Affair and the Quasi-War impacted Franco-American relations, see Hale, "'Many Who Wandered in Darkness'"; Ray, "'Not One Cent for Tribute'"; and DeConde, *Quasi-War*.

5. The Convention of 1800 or the Treaty of Mortefontaine, Article I, *The Avalon Project: Documents in Law, History, and Diplomacy*, http://avalon.law.yale.edu/19th_century/fr1800.asp.

6. Ray, "'Not One Cent for Tribute,'" 412.

7. See *New-York Evening Post*, August 10, 1802.

8. For more information on the relationship between the Haitian Revolution and domestic slave uprising see Hunt, *Haiti's Influence on Antebellum America*.

9. *Daily Advertiser* (New York), August 11, 1802; *Commercial Advertiser* (New York), August 11, 1802; *New-York Gazette and General Advertiser*, August 11, 1802; *New-York Evening Post*, August 11, 1802; and *Philadelphia Gazette & Daily Advertiser*, August 12, 1802.

10. *New-York Gazette and General Advertiser*, August 14, 1802.

11. *Mercantile Advertiser* (New York), August 16, 1802; and *Commercial Advertiser* (New York), August 16, 1802.

12. *New-York Gazette and General Advertiser*, August 16, 1802 (emphasis in the original).

13. *New-York Gazette and General Advertiser*, August 16, 1802. See *Philadelphia Gazette and Daily Advertiser*, August 17, 1802; *Alexandria Advertiser and Commercial Intelligencer* (Alexandria, VA), August 19, 1802; *Connecticut Journal* (New Haven), August 19, 1802; *Albany Centinel*, August 20, 1802; *Republican or, Anti-Democrat* (Baltimore), August 20, 1802; *Columbian Advertiser; and Commercial, Mechanic, and Agricultural Gazette* (Alexandria, VA), August 16, 1802; *Independent Chronicle* (Boston), August 16, 1802; *The Commercial Register* (Norfolk, VA), August 23, 1802; *Salem Register* (Massachusetts), August 16, 1802; *Connecticut Courant* (Hartford), August 16, 1802; *Providence Gazette* (Rhode Island), August 21, 1802; *Eastern Herald & Maine Gazette* (Portland), August 23, 1802; *Middlebury Mercury* (Vermont), August 25, 1802; *New-Hampshire Sentinel* (Keen), August 21, 1802; *Balance, and Columbian Repository* (Hudson, NY), August 17, 1802; *Courier* (Norwich, CT), August 18, 1802; *New-Jersey-Journal* (Elizabethtown), August 17, 1802; *United States Oracle, and Portsmouth Advertiser* (New Hampshire), August 21, 1802; *Greenfield Gazette* (Massachusetts), August 23, 1802; *True American* (Trenton, NJ), August 23, 1802; *OLIO* (Georgetown, DC), August 19, 1802; *Columbian Courier* (New Bedford, MA), August 20, 1802; *Farmers' Museum, or Literary Gazette* (Walpole, NH), August 24, 1802; and *Kentucky Gazette* (Lexington), September 10, 1802 (the late August and early September editions of the *Kentucky Gazette* are not accessible through Readex's on-line Early American Newspapers Series 1–7, 1690–1922, but it seems likely from the presentation of the September 10 narrative that the paper had carried notice of the event at some earlier date).

14. It may have been a fear of these deportation schemes that fueled the desire to proceed with the Louisiana Purchase, with acquisition of the territory being imagined as a preemptive means of foreclosing Louisiana as a dumping ground for forcibly deported French slaves from the West Indies. See Dubois, *A Colony of Citizens*, 404.

15. For information about the reported murder see, for example, *New-York Gazette*, September 10, 1802, and *Virginia Argus*, September 22, 1802. For the story about the escapees spotted near Hoboken, see *New-York Evening Post*, September 13, 1802. The story was shortly thereafter reprinted in Philadelphia (two papers), Boston (two papers), Connecticut, New Jersey, Newport, RI, Salem, MA, Concord, NH, Kennebunk, ME, Washington, Norfolk, VA, Augusta, ME, Keene, NH, and Burlington, VT.

16. *New-York Evening Post*, September 13, 1802.

17. *United States Chronicle* (Providence, RI), September 23, 1802. The story carried by the *Chronicle* reprints an article that first appeared in the *New-York Evening Post* two weeks prior (September 6, 1802).

18. *New-York Evening Post*, September 10, 1802 (emphasis in the original).

19. As I will discuss in more detail below, Fontaine Maury and Wade Hampton jointly authored a letter to Secretary of State James Madison about the situation in New York on

August 21, 1802. Madison forwarded the letter to Jefferson less than a week later, and references to the Hampton-Maury letter (and the situation in New York more broadly) appear intermittently in Madison's correspondence for the next several weeks. In his exchange with Jefferson, Madison underscores that both Secretary of War Henry Dearborn and Secretary of the Treasury Albert Gallatin were quickly apprised of the situation. Jefferson's initial reply to Madison on August 27, 1802 openly references both the Hampton-Maury letter and the correspondence between Mayor Edward Livingston and French officials in New York. In his letter to James Monroe (the governor of Virginia), Maury suggests that he and Hampton had sent either individual or jointly authored letters to the governors of Maryland, Virginia, the Carolinas, and Georgia. See Wade Hampton and Fontaine Maury to James Madison, August 21, 1802, and Thomas Jefferson to James Madison, August 27, 1802, in *The Papers of James Madison* 3:503 and 3:522. See also Fontaine Maury to James Monroe, August 21, 1802, *The Papers of James Monroe* 4:609–10.

20. *New-York Evening Post*, August 16, 1802.

21. The press loudly decried any attempts to discharge the prisoners. While a few New Yorkers reportedly tried to acquire some of the prisoners (presumably taking advantage of the flotilla's dire need for supplies to purchase slaves cheaply), no one agitated for their conditions to be improved.

22. *New-York Evening Post*, August 16, 1802.

23. The exchange of letters was reprinted in virtually every paper published in New York City. In addition, the exchange appeared in *Gazette of the United States* (Philadelphia), August 18, 1802; *Federal Gazette* (Maryland), August 19, 1802; *Poulson's American Daily Advertiser* (Philadelphia), August 19, 1802; *Columbian Advertiser; and Commercial, Mechanic, and Agricultural Gazette* (Alexandria, VA), August 20, 1802; *New-Jersey-Journal* (Elizabethtown), August 24, 1802; *Connecticut Journal* (New Haven), August 26, 1802; *South-Carolina State Gazette and Timothy's Daily Adviser* (Charleston), August 31, 1802. On August 20, the *Albany Centinel* carried the news of the accident, and on the following day Boston's *Columbia Centinel* ran its story about the collision in New York harbor.

24. A copy of Livingston's letter to Dearborn (dated September 1, 1802) was forwarded to James Madison on September 7, 1802. See Mayor Edward Livingston to Secretary of War Henry Dearborn, September 1, 1802 (copied by Daniel Brent and forwarded to James Madison), in *The Papers of James Madison*, 3:556.

25. Fontaine Maury was living in Fredericksburg when Gabriel's Rebellion shook nearby Richmond—and quickly unnerved the entire southern region. Fredericksburg's local paper, the *Virginia Herald*, in which Fontaine Maury's name frequently appeared in advertisements, notices, and letters to the editor, openly speculated that the French Revolutionary mantras of "Liberty and Equality" had "been infused into the minds of the negroes," and spurred Gabriel's uprising in 1800. Many southerners equated these French revolutionary slogans with contagions, which if not successfully quarantined could potentially ravage the United States, and it is likely that Maury's panic about the influx of revolutionary prisoners into New York harbor was inflected by his experiences in Virginia during Gabriel's Rebellion. See Wade Hampton & Fontaine Maury to James Madison, August 21, 1802, in *The Papers of James Madison*, 3:503. For more detailed information about the devastating effects of the Haitian Revolution on the French economy, see Trouillot *Silencing the Past* and Dubois *Colony of Citizens*.

26. Maury's letter to Monroe is perhaps the most charged of his extant letters about the situation in New York harbor, although it closely resembles the others (as well as those he

coauthored with Wade Hampton) in shape and detail. The difference in tone is likely attributable to Maury's personal relationship with Monroe. Fontaine Maury to James Monroe, August 21, 1802, *The Papers of James Monroe* 4:609–10. Drayton sent a letter to Thomas Jefferson on September 12, 1802, which begins by saying he has just received a letter from Colonel Wade Hampton about the situation in New York; see John Drayton to Thomas Jefferson, September 12, 1802, *Thomas Jefferson Papers* 38:385.

27. Fontaine Maury was just three years younger than Monroe, and they would surely have known one another when Monroe was a resident at his father's school. Maury's father officiated at the wedding of Jefferson's daughter, and his brother James Maury was the first U.S. consul to England—all of which suggests the level of familiarity between the Maury family and members of both Jefferson's administration and the planter elite of Virginia. See James Monroe to Fontaine Maury, September 6, 1802, James Monroe to William Davies, September 6, 1802 and James Monroe to Thomas Newton, September 6 1802, *James Monroe: Papers in Virginia Repositories*, microfilm reel no. 9.

28. Brown, *Toussaint's Clause*, 195.

29. Egerton, *Gabriel's Rebellion: The Virginia Slave Conspiracies of 1800 and 1802*, 48. Winthrop Jordan argues that "while" the Gabriel plot "confirmed [Virginians'] fears about the Negro, it jarred their picture of slavery and themselves," because it shattered the illusion that they lived in an "enlightened day when slaves were better treated and there were relatively fewer of them" (*White over Black*, 394).

30. Virginia had been a popular haven for refugee Creole planters since the initial outbreaks of violence in Haiti, largely because it lacked the prohibitions against both West Indian slaves and free "French Negroes" that other southern states, notably Georgia in 1793, South Carolina in 1794, and Maryland in 1797, had enacted as precautionary restraints. Despite the wariness of Virginia's slaveholders about the infection of revolutionary contagions—especially in the aftermath of Gabriel's Rebellion—they, inexplicably, remained "the only southern state not to adopt preventive measures" prohibiting the importation of West Indian slaves (Egerton, *Gabriel's Rebellion*, 169).

31. James Monroe to William Vaughan, March 17, 1802, *James Monroe: Papers in Virginia Repositories microfilm*, reel no. 8

32. *Daily Advertiser* (New York), October 26, 1802.

33. Ibid.

34. Ibid.

35. For more detailed information on the population history of Georgetown County, see George C. Rogers, *The History of Georgetown County*.

36. Ohline, "Georgetown, South Carolina," 131.

37. John Drayton to Thomas Jefferson, September 12, 1802, *Thomas Jefferson Papers* 38:385.

38. *Edes' Kennebec Gazette* (Augusta, ME), November 4, 1802. For more information on how information was suppressed in order to keep it from the domestic slave population see Aptheker, *American Negro Slave Revolts*, 155–158; and Jordan, *White over Black*, 391–399.

39. Shugerman, "The Louisiana Purchase," 263. See also Ohline, "Georgetown, South Carolina," 130–131.

40. *Courier* (Norwich, CT), November 10, 1802.

41. Loughran, *Republic in Print*, 9, 14, and 9.

42. See Girard, *Slaves Who Defeated Napoleon*, 190. Girard has done extensive work in French naval archives in Brest and Paris, but does not list any information about particular ships in his volume.

43. See Girard, "Ugly Ducklings."

CHAPTER 4. "ENTIRELY DIFFERENT FROM ANY LIKENESS I EVER SAW"

This essay has benefitted from generous conversations with a number of colleagues. I am grateful for audiences at Cornell University (especially Cheryl Finley and Hortense Spillers) and Yale University (espcially Jill Campbell, Wai Chee Dimock, Jackie Goldsby, and Caleb Smith) as well as the keen insights of the volume's editors, Elizabeth Maddock Dillon and Michael J. Drexler.

1. "An Authentic Portrait of Toussaint," *New Orleans Tribune*, November 10, 1864, 1.
2. Clavin, *Toussaint Louverture and the American Civil War*, 117.
3. "An Authentic Portrait of Toussaint," 1.
4. Davis and Starn, Introduction, 2.
5. Foucault defines "subjugated knowledges" as having two primary characteristics: "When I say 'subjugated knowledges' I mean two things. On the one hand, I am referring to historical contents that have been buried or masked in functional coherences or formal systemizations. . . . Second, when I say 'subjugated knowledges' I am also referring to a whole series of knowledges that have been disqualified as . . . insufficiently elaborated knowledges: naïve knowledges, hierarchically inferior knowledges, knowledges that are below the required level of erudition or scientificity" (*Society Must Be Defended*, 7).
6. Foucault, "About the Beginnings," 202; Foucault, *Language, Counter-Memory, Practice*, 139.
7. As Foucault writes, "Genealogies are, quite specifically, antisciences. . . . They are the insurrection of knowledges. Not so much against the contents, methods, or concepts of a science; this is above all, primarily, an insurrection against the centralizing power-effects that are bound up with the institutionalization and workings of any scientific discourse organized in a society such as ours" (*Society Must Be Defended*, 9).
8. In this sense, this essay approaches "literary portraiture" in ways that are indebted to W. J. T. Mitchell's notion of "iconology," especially where he outlines a methodological approach to iconology as the "ways that images in the strict or literal sense (pictures, statues, works of art) are related to notions such as mental imagery, verbal or literary imagery, and the concept of man as an image and maker of images," Mitchell, *Iconology*, 2.
9. The essays that comprise Jackson and Bacon's recent volume *African Americans and the Haitian Revolution* are the best single source glossing the wide range of African American responses to Haiti from the revolution to the early twenty-first century.
10. Nash, "Reverberations of Haiti," 65.
11. The first article in the series on Haiti was published on April 20, 1827, and seems to have run for the next six weeks. The first piece in the three-part installment of the Louverture biographical sketch was published on May 4, 1827. And installments of the short story "Theresa—A Haytien Tale" were published on January 18, January 25, February 8, and February 15, 1828. See Bacon, "'Revolution Unexampled,'" 81–92.
12. Walker, *Walker's Appeal*, 63.

13. For further discussion in broader context, see Wilson, "On Native Ground," 454.
14. "Toussaint L'Ouverture," *North Star*, February 18, 1848, 4.
15. See Trouillot, *Silencing the Past*.
16. Matthiessen, *American Renaissance*, ix. On the transnational dimensions of the American Renaissance, see Brickhouse, *Transamerican Literary Relations*, 25.
17. For more on African Americans and the Civil War, see Clavin, *Toussaint Louverture and the American Civil War*.
18. Stowe, *Uncle Tom's Cabin*, 300 (emphasis in the original). The effect of George's words on Eliza is reminiscent of an earlier scene with Mr. Wilson, his former boss at the bagging factory, inasmuch as they (Wilson and George) are both impassioned but the content of their words are markedly different. In the earlier episode with Mr. Wilson, George's tenor is purposely meant to sonically echo Patrick Henry and, as such, authorize George's actions through the sanctioned discourse of the Founding Fathers. The chapter, then, in which George "gets into an improper [revolutionary] state of mind" is not underwritten by his having been influenced by the Haitian Revolution or modeling himself after Louverture—which is to say that Stowe prefigures George's understanding of the right of revolution on a version based more on a circumscribed national model rather than other instances of black insurrection by the likes of figures such as Denmark Vesey, Joseph Cinque, and others.
19. Stowe, *Uncle Tom's Cabin*, 75–76.
20. Foucault, *Society Must Be Defended*, 9.
21. "Toussaint L'Ouverture," *Freedom's Journal*, May 4, 1827, 1.
22. As Srinivas Aravamudan argues, Wordsworth's sonnet, which finds Louverture imprisoned in Joux, "attempts to 'turn' Toussaint into Nature but apotropaically acknowledges the realities of a 'tropical' oppression both poetic and historical" (*Tropicopolitans*, 312).
23. "Toussaint L'Ouverture," *North Star*, February 18, 1848, 4.
24. "Tousaint [sic] L'Ouverture," *North Star*, June 13, 1850, 4.
25. Stepto, *From Behind the Veil*, xv.
26. "Toussaint L'Ouverture," *North Star*, February 18, 1848, 4.
27. Brown, *St. Domingo*, 12.
28. Phillips, "Toussaint l'Ouverture" (1861), 468.
29. Stowe, *Uncle Tom's Cabin*, 76.
30. Webb, *The Garies and Their Friends*, 122–123.
31. "An Authentic Portrait of Toussaint," 1.
32. Wallace, *Constructing the Black Masculine*, 72.
33. Phillips, "Toussaint l'Ouverture," 483.
34. Otter, *Philadelphia Stories*, 262.
35. Mitchell, *Iconology*, 2.
36. "The history of Toussaint, placed by the side of that of Napoleon, presents many striking parallels," Brown noted. "The parallels, however, have their contrast" too (*St. Domingo*, 36).
37. "Toussaint L'Ouverture," *North Star*, February 18, 1848, 4.
38. "And, lastly," offered Brown,

> Toussaint's career as a Christian, a statesman, and a general, will lose nothing by comparison with that of Washington. Each was the leader of an oppressed and outraged people, each had a powerful enemy to contend with, and each succeeded in founding a government in the New World. Toussaint's government made liberty its watchword, incorporated it in its constitution, abolished the slave-trade, and made

freedom universal amongst the people. Washington's government incorporated slavery and the slave-trade, and enacted laws by which chains were fastened upon the limbs of millions of people. Toussaint liberated his countrymen; Washington enslaved a portion of his, and aided in giving strength and vitality to an institution that will one day rend asunder the UNION that he helped to form. (*St. Domingo*, 37)

39. Smith, *A Lecture on the Haytien Revolutions*, 44, 46 (emphasis added).
40. Phillips, "Toussaint l'Ouverture," 468, 493–494.
41. Brown, *St. Domingo*, 28–29.

CHAPTER 5. FREDERICK DOUGLASS, ANTÉNOR FIRMIN, AND THE MAKING OF U.S.-HAITIAN RELATIONS

1. Baur, "Geffrard," 438–439.
2. Clavin, *Toussaint Louverture*, 51–53, 201 n.85.
3. Ibid., 121; Polyné, *From Douglass to Duvalier*, 5–7 (emphasis in the original).
4. Baur, "Geffrard," 445.
5. I draw here and in the following paragraphs on my overview of Haitian history in *Haiti: The Aftershocks of History*.
6. Nicholls, *Dessalines to Duvalier*, 102–107.
7. Firmin, *Lettres de Saint-Thomas*, 111–115; Firmin, *Equality*; Janvier, *La République d'Haïti*.
8. Firmin, *Equality*, 325–328.
9. Ibid., 198.
10. Polyné, *Douglass to Duvalier*, 25–26, 38; May, *Southern Dream of a Caribbean Empire*.
11. Denis, "100 Ans," 22–24. "Vous autres, vous créez facilement des machines, mais difficilement des idées."
12. Manigat, "La Substitution de la prépondérance américaine," 323.
13. Montague, *Haiti*, 147; Logan, *Diplomatic Relations*, 426.
14. On the role of descendants of migrants from Saint-Domingue in politics in Louisiana, see Scott, *Degrees of Freedom*.
15. Logan, *Diplomatic Relations*, 429–430.
16. Ibid., 432–433; Montague, *Haiti*, 147.
17. Logan, *Diplomatic Relations*, 438.
18. Douglass, "Haïti and the United States," 456; Logan, *Diplomatic Relations*, 406–407, 433–434.
19. Douglass, "Haïti and the United States," 339–340; Logan, *Diplomatic Relations*, 447–448.
20. Montague, *Haiti*, 148–149; Logan, *Diplomatic Relations*, 436, 442, 447–448; Douglass, "Haïti and the United States," 343–344.
21. Logan, *Diplomatic Relations*, 442.
22. The full correspondence is published in Firmin, *Roosevelt*, 497 and 501. See also Logan, *Diplomatic Relations*, 448–450. Benjamin, *Diplomatie*, 91–96: "Le Gouvernement d'Haïti n'afferme aucun port ou autre portion de son territoire, ni n'en dispose autrement, n'y accordant aucun privilège spécial ou droit d'usage à aucun pouvoir, état ou gouvernement." "L'acceptation de votre demande avec une telle clause serait, aux yeux du Gouvernement d'Haïti, un outrage à la souveraineté de la République d'Haïti et une violation flagrante de l'article 1er de notre

Constitution, car en renonçant au droit de disposer de son territoire, il en aurait consenti l'aliénation tacite"; "sans paraître céder à une pression étrangère et compromettre ipso facto notre existence de peuple indépendant, d'autant plus que plusieurs journaux américains, dans un but indevinable, font une propagande mensongère tendant à faire croire qu'il y a eu des engagements signés"; "de mauvaise volonté "; "à la plus glorieuse et la plus généreuse république du Nouveau Monde et peut-être du Monde Moderne."

23. Denis, "100 Ans," 14; Péan, *L'Echec du Firminisme*, 52–53.

24. Firmin, *Roosevelt*, 497–501; Logan, *Diplomatic Relations*, 437–438, 451.

25. The original passage is as follows:

Toutefois l'Haïtien intelligent, au lieu de s'emballer dans une méfiance irraisonnée des Etats-Unis, à cause de leur 'impérialisme' et de leur 'préjugé de couleur,' doit-il étudier la question, l'histoire en mains, avant de prendre une posture qui, pour digne qu'elle puisse paraître, ne prêterait pas moins à l'ironie, si ceux dont il se plaint avec le plus d'humeur, étaient encore les plus respectueux de son droit de peuple indépendant, en supposent même que cette attitude correcte ne fût que de pures formes. C'est, en effet, for significatif que les Américains gardent les formes là où les Européens s'en passent avant tant de cavalière aisance. . . . L'Amérique n'en a pas besoin. (Firmin, *Roosevelt*, 468–469)

26. The original passages are as follows:

Haïti, la République noire, libre et indépendante, peut vivre et elle vivra, à côté de l'Union américaine, sans que l'ombre colossale de sa grande voisine la fasse disparaître dans la lumière resplendissante de l'Archipel des Antilles. Au contraire, à cette ombre elle doit grandir, elle doit se développer, sans s'y laisser jamais absorber. Et, pour cela, que faut-il ? Du bon sens, de la sagesse et de l'intelligence. Les États-Unis, par force des choses, ont un intérêt actuel et capital à voir notre nation s'affermir et se civiliser, afin d'enlever tous les prétextes que les autres grandes puissances mettent ordinairement en avant, pour nous molester et surtout menacer notre autonomie nationale. (Firmin, *Roosevelt*, 478)

Les États-Unis ont tout ce dont nous avons besoins pour nous lancer dans le sillon d'une civilisation active et laborieuse. Ils ont les capitaux de toute sorte: argent, machines, expérience du travail hardi et énergie morale à résister contre les difficultés. Pourquoi, s'ils désirent notre amitié,—notre conservation étant devenue solidaire à leurs plus puissants intérêts,—ne nous offriraient-ils pas cette main secourable que nous cherchons depuis un siècle, sans trop le crier, il est vrai, mais en dépensant en pure perte nos amabilités et nos concessions souriantes envers les nations riches et civilisées, qui n'auraient qu'à laisser descendre jusqu'à nous leur bienveillance philanthropique, pour assurer notre ascension au milieu des peuples christianisés? (Ibid., 480)

27. Ibid., 131; Denis, "Les 100 Ans," 17–18.

28. "Ce n'est que dans le cas où notre indépendance nationale menacerait de s'anéantir par une impéritie, une infirmité interne aussi avilissante qu'irrémédiable, que l'Oncle Sam tendrait ses longs bras, pour ne point nous laisser choisir d'autre mains. Mais est-ce là une fatalité historique?" (Firmin, *Roosevelt*, 477). See also:

On ne peut résister contre l'évidence. Cette évidence actuelle, pour nous, c'est que les Etats-Unis ont acquis une prépondérance presque indiscutée dans les affaires internationales des deux Amériques. Qu'on s'en réjouisse ou qu'on s'en attriste— et nous n'avons aucune raison de nous en réjouir ni de nous attrister—il faut en prendre son parti et agir en conséquence. Au lieu donc de nous mettre en posture de barrer la voie à un torrent impétueux et irrésistible, c'est notre intérêt de le laisser suivre son cours, en nous tenant de façon à en être fructueusement arrosés; sans nous exposer à être emportés, en essayant d'y faire obstacle, dans un geste où notre impuissance n'égalerait que notre inconscience. (Ibid., 480)

29. "Homme je puis disparaitre sans voir poindre à l'horizon national l'aurore d'un jour meilleur. Cependant même après ma mort, il faudra de deux choses l'une : ou Haïti passe sous une domination étrangère, ou elle adopte résolument les principes au nom desquels j'ai toujours lutté et combattu. Car, au vingtième siècle et dans l'hémisphère occidental aucun peuple ne peut vivre indéfiniment sous la tyrannie, dans l'injustice, l'ignorance et la misère" (Moïse, *Constitutions*, 2:12).

CHAPTER 6. THE LOUISIANA PURCHASE AND THE HAITIAN REVOLUTION

1. Benot, *Révolution française*; Blackburn, *Overthrow of Colonial Slavery*; Trouillot, *Silencing the Past*.
2. Compare Palmer, *Age of the Democratic Revolution*; Godechot, *France and the Atlantic Revolution*; and Liss, *Atlantic Empires*, with Langley, *Americas in the Age of Revolution*; Calderón and Thibaud, *Revoluciones en el mundo atlántico*; Benjamin, *Atlantic World*; and Klooster, *Revolutions in the Atlantic World*.
3. Dubois, *Colony of Citizens*; Nesbitt, *Universal Emancipation*; Fischer, *Modernity Disavowed*; and Buck-Morss, *Hegel, Haiti, and Universal History*.
4. McLynn, *Napoleon: A Biography*; Blaufarb, *Napoleon: Symbol for an Age*; and Belaubre, Dym, and Savage, *Napoleon's Atlantic*.
5. Quinn, *French Overseas Empire*, 77; Lachance, "Repercussions of the Haitian Revolution," 210–211; Hernández Guerrero, "La Révolution haïtienne," 453–467; Brown, *Toussaint's Clause*, 224–228; Dubois, "Haitian Revolution and the Sale of Louisiana," 18; and Belaubre, Dym, Savage, *Napoleon's Atlantic*, 5, 9. See also below, n.68.
6. Adams, *History of the United States*, 1:378, 2:23.
7. Hosmer, *History of the Louisiana Purchase*, 45, 58, 71; Bruce, *Romance of American Expansion*, 46; Lyon, *Louisiana in French Diplomacy*, 194–195; Priestley, *France Overseas*, 353; Logan, *Diplomatic Relations*, 142–146; Handlin, *Chance or Destiny*, 27–48; Pratt, *History of United States Foreign Policy*, 96; Graebner, *Ideas and Diplomacy*, 82; Peterson, *Thomas Jefferson*, 759–761; LaFeber, "Foreign Policies of a New Nation," 34–35; Sprague, *So Vast, So Beautiful*, 299–300; Morison, Commager, and Leuchtenburg, *Growth of the American Republic*, 340; Burns, *Vineyard of Liberty*, 176; Liss, *Atlantic Empires*, 280 n.17; Kennedy, *Orders From France*, 126; Thernstrom, *History of the American People*, 1:225; Tucker and Hendrickson, *Empire of Liberty*, 92, 120, 281; Hoffman, *Luisiana*, 295, 306; Zuckerman, *Almost Chosen People*, 218; and Richard, *Louisiana Purchase*, 28–30.
8. Geggus, "French Imperialism," 31, 272 n.32. Logan, *Diplomatic Relations*, 143, 146, notes some exceptions but see, most recently, Garnier, *Bonaparte et la Louisiane*.

9. Lyon, *Louisiana*, 147.

10. Paquette, "Revolutionary Saint Domingue," 210, 221 n.3; Dubois, "Haitian Revolution," 18. Paquette cites only one case of such "Eurocentric interpretation," and Dubois cites only Paquette.

11. Even general U.S. history textbooks of half a century ago relate it to France's loss of troops in St. Domingue. See, e.g., Canfield, *Making of Modern America*, 166; Morris, *Encyclopedia of American History*, 132; Graff and Krout, *Adventure of the American People*, 171–172 (which completely ignores the "European" factor); Current et al., *American History*, 197–199; Carman et al., *History of the American People*, 322; and Kraus, *United States to 1865*, 304–306. Tucker and Hendrickson, *Empire of Liberty*, 92, exaggerate only slightly in affirming that St. Domingue "has of course always been acknowledged" as a contributory factor.

12. Dubois, "Haitian Revolution," 18.

13. Barbé-Marbois, *Histoire de la Louisiane*, 287–289, 299.

14. Geggus, "French Imperialism," 26–27.

15. Ibid., 27–28.

16. Benot, *Démence coloniale*, 9, 100; Benot, "Bonaparte et la démence coloniale," 13–35.

17. Barbé-Marbois, *Histoire de la Louisiane*, 290.

18. This view is expressed in Gaffarel, *Politique coloniale*, 133–138, 154; Hanotaux and Martineau, *Histoire des colonies françaises*, 1:535; Adams, *History of the United States*, 1:390; Benot, *Démence coloniale*, 21–31; and by most historians of the Haitian Revolution.

19. Deschamps, *Histoire de la question coloniale*, 70–71; Roloff, *Kolonialpolitik Napoleons*, 69–74, 249–252; Saintoyant, *Colonisation française*, 70–76; Leclerc, *Lettres du général Leclerc*, 33; Pluchon, *Toussaint Louverture*, 446–453.

20. See the chapters by Bélénus, Benot, and Elisabeth in *1802 en Guadeloupe*.

21. Girard, *Slaves Who Defeated Napoléon*, 46–47, 186–191; quotations from 187, 188.

22. See Leclerc, *Lettres du général Leclerc*, 287. This partly encoded dispatch was disguised as an "agricultural plan" but obviously referred to slavery. What remains unclear is the degree to which the hapless and disapproving Leclerc had been forewarned before leaving France.

23. Pluchon, *Toussaint Louverture*, 447. Other historians who have expressed similar views include Maurice Besson, Robert Paquette, and Dolores Hernández Guerrero.

24. Emmanuel de Las Cases, *Mémorial de Sainte-Hélène*, 1:687–688, 2:685–686. The idea is hinted at in official correspondence drafted in March 1801 but never sent. Other evidence suggests Bonaparte's attitude toward Toussaint radically changed during this month.

25. Dubois, "Haitian Revolution and the Sale of Louisiana," 18–41. Moreover, historians who emphasize that Toussaint presided over an economic revival usually forget that the colony's export figures for 1801–1802 benefited from the recent incorporation of regions where British occupiers had maintained slavery down to 1798.

26. Roloff, *Kolonialpolitik Napoleons*, 254.

27. DeConde, *This Affair of Louisiana*, 108–109; Smith, "Napoleon and Louisiana," 61.

28. The official instructions for the intended Captain-General of Louisiana, written in November 1802, recommend merely the defense of Louisiana and maintaining the colony's existing trade links with Spanish possessions. See Robertson, *Louisiana Under the Rule of Spain*, 359–376.

29. Talleyrand appears to have played along with Dupont so as to defuse American hostility. Inconclusive evidence, suggestive of an early willingness to sell, is summarized in Lyon, *Louisiana*, 141 n.52; DeConde, *This Affair of Louisiana*, 96, 119, 130.

30. The argument was made in Lyon, *Louisiana*, 191–192, and given primacy in Stenberg, "Napoleon's Cession of Louisiana: A Suggestion," 354–361.

31. See Benot, *Démence*, 331 n.2; Bruce, *Romance of American Expansion*, 46; Hernández Guerrero, *Revolución haitiana*, 115, which relied on the lightweight and unreliable Chidsey, *Louisiana Purchase*, 133–134, which presents St. Domingue as just a "pause" en route to Louisiana.

32. Montague, *Haiti and the United States*, 43; Barbé-Marbois, *Histoire de la Louisiane*, 184.

33. Roloff, *Kolonialpolitik Napoleons*, 244–254 (instructions); Leclerc, *Lettres du général Leclerc*; Napoléon Ier, *Correspondance de Napoléon*, vols. 7 and 8.

34. Leclerc, *Lettres du général Leclerc*, 143.

35. Lyon, *Louisiana*, 120–125; DeConde, *This Affair of Louisiana*, 103–105.

36. Napoléon Ier, *Correspondance de Napoléon*, 7:210, 226, 293, 345–346, 442, 532.

37. Lyon, *Louisiana*, 132–134, argues he took the need for paperwork seriously.

38. Tucker and Hendrickson, *Empire of Liberty*, 92; see also above, n.6.

39. Ibid., 120.

40. Girard, *Slaves Who Defeated Napoléon*, 277.

41. Napoléon Ier,, *Correspondance de Napoléon*, 8:5, 145–147, 199.

42. Smith, "Napoleon and Louisiana," 57–59; Lyon, *Louisiana*, 134–140.

43. Roederer, *Journal du Comte P.-L. Roederer*, 165; Lyon, *Louisiana*, 193–194; DeConde, *This Affair of Louisiana*, 151.

44. Benot, "Bonaparte et la démence coloniale," 19 n.11; Lyon, *Louisiana*, 194; Hoffman, *Luisiana*, 295, 306. Sprague, *So Vast, So Beautiful*, 300, wrongly claims that the French were driven out of St. Domingue at this time. This did not happen until November 1803.

45. Roloff, *Kolonialpolitik Napoleons*, 142–144; Thomas Ott, *Haitian Revolution*, 179–180, 186; Fleming, *Louisiana Purchase*, 56; Lyon, *Louisiana*, 137.

46. Paquette, "Revolutionary Saint Domingue," 205–206, 209; Barbé-Marbois, *Histoire de la Louisiane*, 271.

47. Napoléon Ier, *Correspondance de Napoléon*, 8:200–202. He proposed to take a levy from the 276 infantry battalions in Europe that had not yet sent troops to the colonies.

48. Lyon, *Louisiana*, 141–142. This activity is claimed to have been a smokescreen in Adams, *History of the United States*, 2:16–17.

49. One on-the-spot assessment reckoned that the army and navy had lost 30,000 of 43,000 men by May 1803. See Arango y Parreño, *Obras*, 1:354–355.

50. See ibid., 1:369–370; Barbé-Marbois, *Histoire de la Louisiane*, 293–297.

51. Marbois does not identify the minister in question. Almost all writers have assumed he was Denis Decrès, the minister of the navy and colonies, or Charles-Maurice Talleyrand, the foreign minister, but mention of his military service in North America leaves little doubt it was Berthier.

52. Lyon, *Louisiana*, 202–204, 214; DeConde, *This Affair of Louisiana*, 110–145, 155. See also Matthewson, *Proslavery Foreign Policy*, 113–115. DeConde stresses Jefferson's bellicosity and provides the best detail on French knowledge of U.S. opinion, but also observes that the American and European factors were interdependent.

53. Pichon's role is emphasized in Lyon, *Louisiana*, and in Bowman, "Pichon, the United States, and Louisiana," 257–270, which nonetheless corrects Lyon in showing that Pichon's most important dispatches arrived too late to affect the decision to sell.

54. Lyon, *Louisiana*, 203, 214; DeConde, *This Affair of Louisiana*, 157; David A. Carson, "The Role of Congress," 369–383; Bowman, "Pichon," 267; Paquette, "Revolutionary Saint Domingue," 221 n.4.

55. Williams, *Shaping of American Diplomacy*, 77–79; Lewis, *Louisiana Purchase*, 49–52; and Lyon, *Louisiana*, 152–157. The supposed weakness of Jefferson's diplomacy is the focus of Tucker and Hendrickson, *Empire of Liberty*.

56. Benot, *La Démence coloniale*, 102; Barbé-Marbois, *Histoire de la Louisiane*, 285–287, 335.

57. Roloff, *Kolonialpolitik Napoleons*, 149; Renaut, *Question de la Louisiane*, 117. Jefferson himself later mentioned he had not expected the French to sell until after war broke out with Britain. See Peterson, *Thomas Jefferson*, 761.

58. Lyon, *Louisiana*, 196, 199–201; Bowman, "Pichon," 269; Smith, "Napoleon and Louisiana," 59–62. The documents Lyon cites (202–207) to show Bonaparte's "prime motive was to placate the United States" suggest just as much the centrality of the British threat.

59. Barbé-Marbois, *Histoire de la Louisiane*, 2, 269–287, 298, 307.

60. Roloff, *Kolonialpolitik Napoleons*, 141–142.

61. Lyon, *Louisiana*, 141–142; Smith, "Napoleon and Louisiana," 59.

62. Barbé-Marbois, *Histoire de la Louisiane*, 2, 269–287, 298, 307.

63. DeConde, *This Affair of Louisiana*, 156–157 (on Monroe); Barbé-Marbois, *Histoire de la Louisiane*, 275, 282, 284–287, 299.

64. Adams, *History of the United States*, 2:13–17; Lyon, *Louisiana*, 195–196, 199–200; Paquette, "Revolutionary Saint Domingue," 205–211. The fact that the maintenance of French troops on Dutch soil was the main casus belli, and that Napoleon justified their presence by stating they were awaiting departure for Louisiana, suggests another link. However, for financial reasons, Napoleon stationed many troops abroad, and the Louisiana expeditionary force constituted less than a third of those in the Netherlands. Cf. Deutsch, *Genesis of Napoleonic Imperialism*, 87–88. Paquette makes a causal link by arguing the cost of the Saint Domingue expedition was a major factor in the regime's financial problems but he provides no figures.

65. Signaling renewed plans of conquest in the Middle East, the report increased British reluctance to withdraw from Malta, which was a major cause for the resumption of hostilities. Deutsch, *Genesis of Napoleonic Imperialism*, 116–120, tentatively suggests that the report should not be seen as a turning point but a petulant outburst that the French rapidly sought to excuse. A similar media-related puzzle was created the previous spring, when, although the retrocession of Louisiana was officially denied, the government-controlled *Gazette de France* argued that France should curb U.S. westward expansion by occupying Louisiana and detaching Kentucky and Tennessee. Bowman, "Pichon," 266; Lyon, *Louisiana*, 151.

66. Quotes from Bruce, *Romance of American Expansion*, 46; Bemis, *Diplomatic History*, 134–137.

67. The phrase comes from a 1799 letter to Aaron Burr and was an ironic reference to the French. See Scherr, "Jefferson's 'Cannibals' Revisited," 251–282.

68. See Hochschild, *Bury the Chains*, 294; Davis, *Inhuman Bondage*, 270; and Palmié and Scarano, eds., *Caribbean*, 310, 417.

CHAPTER 7. REPUBLIC OF MEDICINE

1. For a discussion about the influence of smallpox on the outcome of the American Revolution, see Fenn, *Pox Americana*. For a history of the relation of yellow fever, malaria, and the growth of empire in the Caribbean, see McNeill, *Mosquito Empires*.

2. The precise length of the pandemic is difficult to pinpoint, but lasts from 1793 to about 1820. I focus on the decade of the Haitian Revolution because the movement of soldiers and refugees across the Atlantic world during that decade was central to the outbreak, and helped make it visible in the imaginations of people on both sides of the ocean. For more on the yellow fever in particular, see McNeill, *Mosquito Empires*, and Arner, "Making Yellow Fever American," 447–471.

3. It has by now become a cliché that yellow fever determined the ultimate success of the revolution. While the impact of yellow fever on European troops was unquestionably a major factor in their failure to take and hold the colony, such claims ultimately oversimplify the tactical and strategic strength of St. Domingue's black fighters. For a further discussion of this issue—which verges on immunological determinism—see McNeill, *Mosquito Empires*, 236, 260–261.

4. Arner argues that transatlantic debates about the contagiousness of yellow fever were central to emergent strains of U.S. nationalism, but that these strains can only be properly understood by positioning "American medicine in a more 'multi-centered' Atlantic world" ("Making Yellow Fever American," 448).

5. See Rush, *Account of the Bilious Remitting Yellow Fever*, 323.

6. Geggus, "Yellow Fever in the 1790s," 38–58, 38. See also McNeill, *Mosquito Empires*, 32, and Carter, *Yellow Fever*.

7. See, for example, McNeill, *Mosquito Empires*, 64–65.

8. Geggus, "Yellow Fever in the 1790s," 41.

9. See Geggus, "Yellow Fever in the 1790s," Howard, *Haitian Journal of Lieutenant Howard*, 137.

10. McLean, *Enquiry into the Nature*, 79–80.

11. Ibid., 80.

12. Geggus, "Yellow Fever in the 1790s," 48, 50. McNeill cites the following statistics in his study: "in the course of the occupation, 1793–1798, the British multinational army committed a total of about 23,000 to 25,000 troops to St. Domingue. Roughly 15,000 or 60 to 65 percent, died there" (*Mosquito Empires*, 247). For an eyewitness account of this mortality, see Howard.

13. Carter, *Yellow Fever*, 6–7.

14. Geggus, "Yellow Fever in the 1790s," 39, 44; and Carter, *Yellow Fever*, 10.

15. For more on herd immunity, see Timmreck, *Introduction to Epidemiology*, 49–51, and Lilienfeld and Lilienfeld, *Foundations of Epidemiology*, 61. See also Wald, *Contagious*, 48–49, and Silva, *Miraculous Plagues*, 111–116. McNeill also writes of herd immunity, but describes its effects in terms of the useful phrase "differential immunity" (*Mosquito Empires*, 4).

16. Monnier, *Observations sur quelques epidémies*, 6: "Très-rarement un seul échappe au tribut qu'elle exige pour se *créoliser*, suivant l'expression du pays." Unless otherwise noted, all translations are my own. On the "seasoning fever," see, for example, Pinckard, *Notes on the West Indies . . . with Remarks upon the Seasoning or Yellow Fever of Hot Climates*; William Pym, *Observations upon the Bulam Fever*, 3; and Williamson, *Medical and Miscellaneous Observations*, 1:291.

17. Geggus, "Yellow Fever in the 1790s," 43.

18. Gilbert, *Histoire Médicale de l'armée française*, 81: "On évitera avec le plus grand soin la promenade du bord de mer le soir, temps où la fraîcheur précipite les émanations marécageuses que le soleil a tenues en évaporation dans la journée. Les militaires se souviendront toujours que rien n'est plus dangereux que de se coucher et s'endormir sur la terre humide."

19. For an extended discussion of the Philadelphia outbreak, see Otter, *Philadelphia Stories*; Estes and Smith, *Melancholy Scene of Devastation*; and Powell, *Bring Out Your Dead*.

20. Pernick, "Politics, Parties, and Pestilence," 559–586, 562. As Arner argues in "Making Yellow Fever American," this was an important debate that played out beyond the borders of Philadelphia and the United States to the greater Atlantic world.

21. Pernick, "Politics, Parties, and Pestilence," 568.

22. Ibid., 570.

23. Rush, *An Enquiry into the Origin of the Late Epidemic Fever*, 14.

24. Rush, *Observations upon the Origin of the Malignant Billious*, 19.

25. Devèze, *An Enquiry into, and Observations upon the Causes and Effects of the Epidemic Disease*, 36.

26. Rush, *Account*, 20, 94.

27. François, *Dissertation sur la fièvre jaune*, 6: "Aux Antilles, à la Terre-Ferme, elle épargne les habitants du pays, tandis qu'elle tue avec fureur les étrangers, quelquefois très-peu de jours après leur arrivée. Aux Etats-Unis d'Amérique, c'est tout le contraire: l'indigène seul paraît susceptible de contracter la fièvre jaune, tandis que l'étranger en est exempt."

28. Nassy, *Observations sur la cause*, 39. This text was published in French with English translations on facing pages.

29. Ibid., 41.

30. Wald, "Imagined Immunities," 189–208, 190. See also Wald, *Contagious*.

31. Wald, "Imagined Immunities," 208.

32. Jackson, *A Treatise on the Fevers of Jamaica*, 162–163.

33. Rush, *Account*, 96.

34. Carey, *A Short Account of the Malignant Fever*, 62–63. For a further discussion of the debates among Carey, Absalom Jones, and Richard Allen, see Otter, *Philadelphia Stories*.

35. See Jones and Allen, *A Narrative of the Proceeding of the Black People*.

36. For more on the formation of black community during the outbreak, see Gould, "Race, Commerce, and Literature," 157–186.

37. Rush, *Account*, 97.

38. Pym, *Observations upon the Bulam Fever*, 154.

39. Mézière, *Le Général Leclerc*, 230.

40. Ibid., 275 n.72.

41. Ibid., 205.

42. Quoted in James, *Black Jacobins*, 314–315.

43. McLean, *An Enquiry into the Nature*, 1.

CHAPTER 8. THE OCCULT ATLANTIC

1. Fargeaud, *Balzac*, 194–196.

2. McClellan, *Colonialism and Science*, 4–5. Traces of mesmerism in St. Domingue date back to at least 1782; see Regourd, "Mesmerism in Saint-Domingue," 326.

3. Moreau de Saint-Méry, *Description topographique*, 45–52. Page numbers are from the French edition and modified translations are from Moreau de Saint-Méry, *A Civilization that Perished*.

4. She is "possessed [*pénétrée*] by God. She shakes, her whole body is convulsed, and the oracle speaks through her mouth." A convulsive dancer later experiences what Saint-Méry refers to as "mount Vaudoux" (*monter Vaudoux*), 48–49.

5. Moreau de Saint-Méry, *Description topographique*, 50 (emphasis added).

6. Mesmer, *Mémoire*.

7. Méheust calls "l'évènement Puységur" the emergence of the unconscious as an object of study which would eventually revolutionize the notion of the self during the nineteenth century. See his preamble in *Somnambulisme et médiumnité*. See also Chertok and de Saussure, *The Therapeutic Revolution*.

8. For a complete history of magnetic somnambulism see Edelman, *Voyantes*.

9. Later, the famous Puységur will actually attribute to his seafaring brother the honor of having penetrated Mesmer's "secret" first and discovering the crucial and surreptitious influence of the magnetizer's "will" on the patient and in provoking a state of artificial or magnetic somnambulism (Puységur, *Du Magnétisme animal*, 134–135).

10. McClellan, *Colonialism and Science*, 177–178.

11. Moreau de Saint-Méry, *Description topographique*, 274.

12. Weaver, *Medical Revolutionaries*, 112.

13. Darnton, *Mesmerism and the End of the Enlightenment*, 83–85.

14. Touchard, *L'Hermès*, vols. 3–4 (emphasis in the original).

15. Touchard, *L'Hermès*, 3–4:367–370. I would like to thank Garret T. Murphy for the help with this translation.

16. Franklin et al., "Rapport des commissaires chargés par le Roi de l'examen du magnétisme animal."

17. See Azouvi, "La Polémique du magnétisme animal."

18. Mesmer's "baquet" was a large container or "bucket" that was filled with water and contained iron filings, ground glass, and other materials that were supposed to channel the "magnetic fluid" between patients who were holding cables attached to the apparatus. With such sensational tools, Mesmer achieved great placebo effects. Anne Chastenet also brought the "baquet" to Saint Domingue.

19. Crabtree, *From Mesmer to Freud*, 213–214.

20. Gottschalk, *Lafayette*; Helmut Hirsch, "Mesmerism and Revolutionary America"; Darnton, *Mesmerism*, 65–66, 88–89.

21. Zwarg notes that we still do not know much about the early influence of mesmerism in North America. She suggests that another early surge of mesmerism probably arrived in North America along with white and black refugees who were fleeing the slave insurrection in St. Domingue. The knowledge they brought with them about magnetic somnambulism may have been a key factor in the mesmeric context informing Charles Brocken Brown's *Edgar Huntly; or, Memoirs of a Sleep-Walker* (1799); see Zwarg, "Vigorous Currents," 32 n.57.

22. McClellan, *Colonialism and Science*, 179–197, 226.

23. Moreau de Saint-Méry, *Description topographique*, 347–348.

24. Ex-Haitian president François Dénis Légitime is an early commentator who brings support to this claim:

> Even more miserable than the inhabitants of ancient Délos, they [Haitians] are continually tormented, no longer by that same python, but by reptiles which though smaller are no less dangerous, and we would like to speak about those

demented writers who march in the footsteps of Moreau de St-Méry, those who have taken malicious pleasure in broadening the scope, then falsifying or amplifying his texts so as to render their virulent effects even more noxious, without even trying to understand whether, at the time when the master was composing those works, Mesmer's 'baquet', transported to Santo Domingo by a French naval officer, was not, without the participation of all those snakes, performing as many magnetically induced wonders as the so-called box of *couleuvres*. (Légitime, *Vérité sur le vaudoux*, 34)

Couleuvre is a small snake, the name of which has come into the vernacular to mean humbug and trumpery.

25. Regourd, "Mesmerism in Saint-Domingue," 324.
26. Cited in Hirsch, "Mesmerism and Revolutionary America," 5.
27. "Haiti indeed stands at the vanguard of the history of modernity. The Haitian experience was not a modern phenomenon *too*, but *first*" (Susan Buck-Morss, *Hegel*, 137–138).
28. Dayan, *Haiti*, 242.
29. Ibid., xix, 54, 9–10, 267.
30. Ibid., 51, 54, 56, 72. Dayan writes: "A vodou history might be composed from materials such as oral accounts of the possession of Dessalines and his emergence as lwa, god, or spirit, and equally ambivalent accounts of figures like Ezili, Jean Zombi, or Défilée. Sinkholes of excess, these crystallizations of unwritten history force us to acknowledge inventions of mind and memory that destroy the illusions of mastery, that circumvent and confound *any* master narrative" (ibid., 54).
31. Ibid., 37, 72 (emphasis in the original).
32. Citing works by Karen McCarthy Brown and Kesner Castor, Benedicty-Kokken nuances Dayan's account of Vodou possession as "reciprocity" when she writes "Vodou is as much about power relations as it is about equality. To be ready to accept the spirits into one's body . . . is nonetheless uncomfortable and even physically dangerous" (*Spirit Possession*, 320).
33. Dayan, *Haiti*, 67–68.
34. *Le Vaudou haïtien*, 108–113.
35. Bourguignon, "Spirit Possession" 384–385. See also Hurston, *Tell My Horse*, 221.
36. Ramsey, *The Spirits and the Law*, 17.
37. Bourguignon, "Spirit Possession," 378.
38. "To be mounted by the *lwa*—that is, to be temporarily released from of one's earthly soul, of one's worldly knowledge of one's day-to-day burden, oppressions, and subjugations—is the ultimate release from the chains of servitude to an oppressive system" (Benedicty-Kokken, *Spirit Possession*, 317).
39. Franketienne, *Les Affres d'un défi*; Depestre, *Le Mât de cocagne*.
40. Since the Haitian Revolution "Vodou practice was pushed to the margins, an embarrassment for 'modern' Haitian elites, yet it has remained a way of manipulating the poor peasantry, hence a source of power for political oppositions of every persuasion. To narrate Haiti's history as good versus evil stunts our capacity for moral judgment. Past suffering does not guarantee future virtue. Only a distorted history is morally pure" (Buck-Morss, *Hegel*, 138).
41. Ibid., 70–71.
42. "None of Vodou's precedents in Africa ever conceived of eliminating the institutional arrangement of master and slave altogether. No European did either. The radical anti-slavery articulated in Saint-Domingue was politically unprecedented" (ibid., 132–133).

43. Ibid., 126, 123–133.

44. Ibid., 150, 144.

45. Ibid., 150 (emphasis in the original).

46. Rickels, *I Think I Am*, 34.

47. The master's skin fetish and arbitrary naming process resurface in the malevolent side of Haitian lore: "The gods, monsters, and ghosts spawned by racial terminology redefined the supernatural. What colonists called sorcery was, rather, an alternative philosophy. The most horrific spirits of the Americas came out of the perverse logic of the master, reinterpreted by slaves who had been mediated to their bones by the colonial myths" (Dayan, *Haiti*, 237). Through Haitian esoteric beliefs, the paranoid fantasies of the agents of colonial power transpire, as do, in turn, the arbitrary and domineering components that made up white enlightenment.

48. Rickels, *I Think I Am*, 21.

49. Kerner, *The Seeress of Prevors*. Edgar Allan Poe's *The Facts in the Case of M. Valdemar*, where Valdemar appears to survive his own death due to his magnetic connection to the narrator, would probably not have worked as a hoax if not for the international success of Kerner's book on the extraordinary magnetic gifts of the clairvoyant from Prevorst: "As early as 1855 the anonymous author of *Rambles and Reveries of an Art Student in Europe* pointed to the last page of Justinus Kerner, *The Seeress of Prevorst* . . . as the source for Poe's gruesome finale [in *The Facts in the Case of M. Valdemar*]" (Beaver, *The Science Fiction of Edgar Allan Poe*, 394).

50. Rickels, *I Think I Am*, 34–37.

CHAPTER 9. IN THE SHADOW OF HAITI

My thanks to Peter Reed, Hsuan Hsu, and Chris Iannini for their helpful insights on earlier drafts and to Phil Lapsansky of the Library Company of Philadelphia for his invaluable research assistance.

1. Kazanjian, *Colonizing Trick*, 27–28.

2. Fischer, *Modernity Disavowed*, 12.

3. Untitled, *Daily National Journal*, December 25, 1824, 3.

4. Douglass, "Lecture on Haiti," 206. Further references will be cited parenthetically in text as "*LH*."

5. Lesser-known slave rebellions and plots periodically erupted in the slaveholding south. Charles Deslonde, a slave from St. Domingue, led the largest of these recorded slave uprisings, which occurred in 1811 outside of New Orleans (Dixon, *African America*, 28).

6. Brown, *Black Man*, 142.

7. Egerton, *Gabriel's Rebellion*, 169.

8. For a critical overview of the historiographical debates over the Vesey archive, see Hyde, "Novelistic Evidence," 32–36.

9. The *Official Report* was not a verbatim transcript of the June, July, and September trials. It introduced information not found in the surviving manuscripts of the Vesey Court (Johnson, "Denmark Vesey and His Co-Conspiration," 925).

10. Schoeppner, "Legitimating Quarantine," 81.

11. Sinha, *Counterrevolution of Slavery*, 15.

12. "Legislature of South Carolina," *Niles' Weekly Register*, December 25, 1824, 261.

13. "Hayti—And the Emancipation of the Blacks," *New-York Literary Journal, and Belles-Lettres Repository*, December 1820, 93.

14. Bolster, *Black Jacks*, 4–6.

15. "Free People of Color," *Niles' Weekly Register*, August 23, 1823, 392 (emphasis in the original).

16. Hamer, "Great Britain," 6.

17. "Art. VII.—Mr. Hoar's Mission," *Southern Quarterly Review*, April 1845, 455 (emphasis in the original).

18. "Debate in the Senate on the Admission of Florida and Iowa," *Cincinnati Weekly Herald and Philanthropist*, April 2, 1845, 1.

19. Kennedy and Parker, *An Official Report of the Trials of Sundry Negroes*, viii. Further references will be cited parenthetically in text as *"OR."* Over the June sessions, the Court of Freeholders and Magistrates ordered six executions, including Vesey's; the July sessions convicted an additional twenty-six men to the gallows and the August sessions another man—William Garner—to hang (Johnson, "Denmark Vesey" 939, 940–941).

20. Johnson, "Denmark Vesey," 952.

21. According to David Robertson, the alleged presence of "French Negroes" brought by masters fleeing St. Domingue may have provided another source for the rumored connections between the Vesey conspiracy and Haiti (Robertson, "Inconsistent Contextualism," 155).

22. Sidbury, "Plausible Stories and Varnished Truths," 183.

23. Clavin, "Race, Rebellion, and the Gothic," 14.

24. Johnson, "Denmark Vesey," 916.

25. Corporation of Charleston, *An Account of the Late Intended Insurrection*, 17.

26. Sidbury, "Plausible Stories," 182.

27. "An Account," *Republican Star and General Advertiser* (September 10, 1822), 2.

28. It is likely that such reports came from local newspapers. The April 11, 1822, *Charleston Courier*, for example, carried just such a report "relative to the occupation of the Spanish port of the island of St. Domingo, by the troops of President Boyer" (Johnson, "Denmark Vesey," 964).

29. Corporation of Charleston, *An Account*, 37.

30. Holland, *A Refutation of the Calumnies Circulated Against the Southern Western States*, 62.

31. Ibid., 83.

32. Ibid., 61 (emphasis in the original).

33. The British Consul brought charges against the Charleston Sheriff Francis Deliesseline and petitioned Johnson for a writ of habeas corpus to release Elkison after authorities, at the urging of the South Carolina Association—an extralegal organization of private citizens (many of whom were Charleston public officials)—arrested him off the Liverpool merchant vessel *Homer*.

34. Paquette, "Jacobins of the Lowcountry," 186.

35. Untitled, *Charleston Mercury*, August 11, 1852, 2.

36. "Massachusetts and South Carolina," *Liberator*, December 12, 1845, 197.

37. Ibid.

38. Fears over the influx of "people of colour" from St. Domingue who were "dangerous to welfare and peace of the state" had even prompted the governor to issue a 1793 proclamation ordering all free blacks who had arrived in South Carolina less than a year to leave (Alderson, "Charleston's Rumored Slave Revolt of 1793," 98–99). For an account of one refugee household from St. Domingue, see Jones, "Time, Space, and Jurisdiction," 1031–1060.

39. Nash, "Reverberations of Haiti," 46.

40. Trouillot, *Silencing the Past*, 83, 91.
41. Ibid., 73.
42. "Massachusetts and South Carolina," *New Englander*, April 1846, 203.
43. Ibid., 204 (emphasis in the original).
44. Gaffield, "Haiti and Jamaica," 584–585.
45. Baur, "Mulatto Machiavelli," 324.
46. Dayan, "Few Stories about Haiti," 160.
47. Baur, "Mulatto Machiavelli," 325.
48. Alexander, "'The Black Republic,'" 67.
49. "President of Hayti," *National Advocate, for the Country*, August 13, 1822, 2.
50. "Hayti," *Village Register and Norfolk Country Advertiser*, July 19, 1822, 22.
51. Alexander, "'Black Republic,'" 66.
52. Baur, "Mulatto Machiavelli," 321, 324.
53. "Hayti," *Portsmouth Journal of Literature & Politics*, November 18, 1826, 2.
54. Trouillot, *Silencing the Past*, 95.
55. "President Boyer, of Hayti," *Connecticut Courant*, August 27, 1822, 2.
56. Ibid.
57. "Republic of Hayti. Proclamation," *Independent Chronicle & Boston Patriot*, April 12, 1823, 2.
58. Lacerte, "Xenophobia and Economic Decline," 504; and "From Hayti," *Aurora and Franklin Gazette*, April 26, 1826, 2.
59. "From Hayti," *Aurora and Franklin Gazette*, 2.
60. "Hayti," *Aurora General Advertiser*, February 16, 1824, 2.
61. Ibid.
62. Fischer, *Modernity Disavowed*, 237.
63. Geggus, preface, xiii.
64. "Of Hayti," *Boston Commercial Gazette*, May 7, 1821, 2.
65. Untitled, *Freedom's Journal*, March 16, 1827, 3.
66. Ibid.
67. Dixon, *African American*, 37, 39.
68. "From the Baltimore Federal Gazette," *Daily National Journal*, September 6, 1824, 2.
69. Dewey, *Correspondence Relative to the Emigration to Hayti*, 7–8. Further references will be cited parenthetically in text as "CR."
70. Walker, *Walker's Appeal*, 24.
71. Ibid., 76, 62–63.
72. Dayan, "'A Receptacle,'" 805.
73. Untitled, *New-Bedford Mercury*, June 30, 1824, 1.
74. Stowe, *Uncle Tom's Cabin*, 300.
75. "Colonization of the Blacks," *Portsmouth Journal of Literature & Politics*, July 3, 1824, 2.
76. "Agent from Hayti," *Essex Register*, June 24, 1824, 2.
77. Dewey, "Notice," in *Correspondence*, n.p.
78. Baur, "Mulatto Machiavelli," 318.
79. Paul founded Boston's African Baptist Church. Prince Saunders used the first floor of the church for his African school. In 1823, Paul traveled with Saunders to Haiti on a mission for the Baptist Missionary Society (White, "Prince Saunders," 527, 534).
80. "Hayti," *Gazette & Patriot*, July 10, 1824, 2.

81. Dixon, *African America*, 37.
82. Dayan, "Few Stories," 162. The Code Rural declared rural inhabitants not under contract to a proprietor or renter to be vagabonds and subject to imprisonment until they were bound to a contractor, presumably of their own choice. Those vagabonds who refused to be bound were to be put on public works construction until they agreed to contract (Baur, "Mulatto Machiavelli," 333).
83. Hunt, *Remarks on Hayti as a Place of Settlement*, 11–12; and Baur, "Mulatto Machiavelli," 326–327.
84. "For the Freedom's Journal. Hayti.—No. VI. From the Scrap Book of Africanus," *Freedom's Journal*, October 12, 1827, 122–123.
85. Cole, "Theresa and Blake," 160.
86. "From the Christian Watchman. Hayti, No. I. From the Scrap Book of Africanus," *Freedom's Journal*, April 20, 1827, 22.
87. "Hayti," *Freedom's Journal*, 291.
88. Foster, "How Do You," 635.
89. Kachun, "Antebellum African Americans," 256–9.
90. Gilroy, *Black Atlantic*, 55.
91. Cole, "Theresa and Blake" 160; and McHenry, *Forgotten Readers*, 101.
92. Foster, "How Do You," 636.
93. White, "Prince Saunders," 527. In the 1850s, Holly emerged as one of the most vocal proponents of emigration to Haiti. He spearheaded the emigration movement of the 1850s, which led to the establishment in 1860 of the U.S. Haitian Bureau of Emigration overseen by Scottish-American abolitionist James Redpath (Dixon, *African America and Haiti*, 3, 8–9). Unlike the 1820s movement, Christian evangelism played a significant role in the 1850s emigration movement, which figured black American emigrants as a source of spiritual salvation for benighted Haitians (Dixon, *African America*, 9, 36).
94. White, "Prince Saunders," 528–529.
95. Saunders, *Haytien Papers*, vii, ix.
96. Saunders, *Memoir*, 8.
97. Ibid., 12–13.
98. Ibid.
99. Dixon, *African America*, 46.
100. Foster, ed., "Theresa—A Haytien Tale," 639. Further references will be cited parenthetically in text as "*THT*."
101. Douglass's "Lecture on Haiti" reads: "The Mole St. Nicolas [sic] of which we have heard so much and may hear much more, is a splendid harbor. It is properly styled the Gibraltar of that country. It commands the Windward Passage, the natural gateway of the commerce both of the new and old world. Important now, our statesmanship sees that it will be still important when the Nicaragua Canal shall be completed. Hence we want this harbor for a naval station" (204). Henceforth, Douglass's work will be cited in the text as "*LH*."
102. Marlene Daut argues that the "miscegenated 'oedipal drama' of slavery described in Sejour's story was distinctly . . . associated with the Haitian Revolution" (Daut, "'Sons of White Fathers,'" 5). See also Castronovo, *Fathering the Nation*.
103. Like "Theresa—a Haytien Tale," Delany's militant novel was also serially published in the New York–based African American periodicals the *Anglo-African Magazine* (1859) and the *Weekly Anglo-African* (1861–1862) (Cole, "Theresa and Blake," 158, 163–164).
104. Ibid., 161.

105. Saunders, *Memoir*, 14.
106. Foster, "How Do You," 632.
107. McHenry, *Forgotten Readers*, 102.
108. Trouillot, *Silencing the Past*, 88.
109. Brown, "St. Domingo," 33. Further references will be cited parenthetically in text as "*SD*."
110. In 1854, British abolitionist Ellen Richard raised funds to purchase Brown's manumission from his master, Enoch Price, so that Brown might return to the United States without fear of recapture and reenslavement. Richard was a member of the same British family who secured Frederick Douglass's manumission (Jefferson, "Introduction," 18).
111. "A Fugitive Slave Turned Author," *Liberator*, January 12, 1855, 11.
112. Brown, *Three Years in Europe*, xxi.
113. "William Wells Brown at Philadelphia," *Liberator*, January 26, 1855, 14.
114. Cohen, "Notes," 164, 168.
115. Ibid., 69; Wisecup, "Progress of the Heat," 10–11.
116. Ibid., 10.
117. Nabers, "Problem of Revolution," 86.
118. Webb, *Garies and Their Friends*, 123.
119. Ibid., 122.
120. Wisecup, "Progress of the Heat," 2.
121. Cohen, "Notes," 170. In *Clotel*, Brown draws upon Beard's description of the black Haitian revolutionary Lamour de Rance to craft the fictional runaway slave Picquilo, a participant in Turner's Revolt, who takes refuge in the Great Dismal Swamp. Brown's fictionalization also signified upon the Haitian dimensions of Turner's revolt. After the violent suppression of the revolt, Virginia Governor James Floyd received a letter signed by "Nero," which predicted additional slave revolts under a leader who was once a slave in Virginia and "escaped to St. Domingo, where his noble soul became warmed by the spirit of freedom, and where he imbibed a righteous indignation, and an unqualified hatred for the oppressors of his race" (Jackson and "Fever and Fret," 14).
122. Fischer, *Modernity Disavowed*, 35.
123. Brown, "St. Domingo," 25.
124. Fischer, *Modernity Disavowed*, 236.
125. Brown returned to this material during the Civil War. In the first of two biographical race histories, *The Black Man: His Antecedents, His Genius, and His Achievements* (1863) and *The Rising Son; or, The Antecedents and Advancements of the Colored Race* (1874), the entry on Nat Turner reenergizes the specter of slave uprising through the present threat of arming black soldiers in the Union war effort (Cohen, "Notes," 172).
126. Trouillot, *Silencing the Past*, 89.
127. Brickhouse, "Writing of Haiti," 411.
128. Meelish, "Frederick Douglass and the Consequences of Rhetoric," 38, 39–40.

CHAPTER 10. *THE HAYTIAN PAPERS* AND BLACK LABOR IDEOLOGY IN THE ANTEBELLUM UNITED STATES

1. Prince Saunders, *Haytian Papers*, iii. Henceforth cited in the text as "*HP*."
2. Saunders, born in Vermont in the late eighteenth century, studied in England and became acquainted with prominent abolitionists Thomas Clarkson and William Wilberforce,

among others, then traveled to Haiti to help Henri Christophe create a system of public schools. In 1816, he returned to England. The epigraph is from a letter he received from an English abolitionist; Saunders cites this passage in his *Memoir Presented to the American Convention for Promoting the Abolition of Slavery*, an address presented in the United States in 1818. This information comes from Maxwell Whiteman's biographical note in the facsimile of Saunders's United States writings, republished in one volume in 1969. There is some speculation that Saunders was a contributor to *Freedom's Journal*, which featured numerous articles about Haiti and Africa. Saunders's invocation of Divine Providence to assert an African American destiny of freedom and peace in Haiti certainly resembles the argument of those articles. As Jacqueline Bacon explains, citing Craig Wilder, "Haiti represented 'the culmination of God's plan for African freedom'" for many of the readers and writers of *Freedom's Journal*. Bacon, *Freedom's Journal*, 148.

3. Ramsey, *Spirits and the Law*, 67.

4. Ibid, 67.

5. For further discussion of agricultural labor policies and peasant resistance, see Ramsey and Dupuy, *Haiti in the World Economy*, 86–91.

6. As Laurent Dubois points out, Thomas Clarkson, who had recommended Saunders to Christophe as an agent to bring African American settlers, expressed some reservations about how they might adjust. Specifically, "Clarkson admitted that some American emigrants might have some trouble adjusting to Haiti. For one thing, being 'free men' in the United States, they were 'accustomed to go where they pleased in search of their livelihood without any questions being asked them or without any hindrance by the Government. No passports are even necessary there.' That was not the case under Christophe's regime, which policed movement assiduously: plantation laborers were, after all, required to stay on their plantations and could not move about freely looking for work" (*Haiti*, 75).

7. I have discussed the problem of the idea of "paternal solicitude" previously. Certainly, Christophe or Boyer did not solicit the opinion of Haitian peasants when they invited African American settlers to their county. My point in this case, however, is to understand Saunders's appeal to a free black audience and the ways in which his portrayal of Haiti plays on desires for autonomous land ownership and freedom from masters. See O'Brien, "Paternal Solicitude," 32–54.

8. Smith, *African American Environmental Thought*, 19.

9. Bogues, "Haitian Revolution," 28.

10. Bogues has also pointed out the differences in the articulation of natural rights philosophy by Black Atlantic writer Quobna Cugoano. Well aware that natural rights philosophy was distorted by Atlantic slavery, Cugoano asserted that progress and civilization would enhance, rather than diminish, natural rights because he did not differentiate them from civil rights. Bogues states, "For Cugoano, the fundamental natural right was the right of the individual to be free and equal, not in relationship to government, but in relationship to other human beings" (*Black Heretics*, 45).

11. As Jonathan Glickstein points out, antebellum labor ideology in the United States was hemmed in by "the centuries-old division between mental and manual labor" and a belief that "differential rewards and esteem attended this division," While the Jacksonian assumption that "an individual" would use his "education to leave his laboring status behind him" as well as to gain property reconfirmed the ideology of social mobility in the United States, "the sanctity of private property and the rights of capitalists and other mental laborers to their

superior rewards" were intrinsic to free labor ideology. See Glickstein, *Concepts of Free Labor*, 8.

12. Ruffin, *Black on Earth*, 29. Kimberly K. Smith makes similar claims about black agrarianism in *African American Environmental Thought*.

13. James McCune Smith's alternative view of civilization emerges as a collaborative project carried out by manual and intellectual laborers.

14. Bethel, "Images of Hayti," 827–841.

15. Ibid, 832.

16. Bacon, *Freedom's Journal*, 168.

17. See Girard, "Black Talleyrand," 87–124; and "Jean-Jacques Dessalines and the Atlantic System," 549–582.

18. Dubois, *Avengers*, 250.

19. Roediger, *Wages of Whiteness*, 45, 48.

20. Dubois, *Haiti*, 107.

21. Fick, *Making of Haiti*, 180.

22. Nesbitt, *Universal Emancipation*, 162.

23. As Daniel Schafer explains, "The government encouraged immigration of free persons of color from the United States and permitted them to lease land upon arrival. After a one-year residence, leaseholders would become eligible for Haitian citizenship and for legal purchase of Haiti's abandoned lands" (*Anna Madgigine Jai Kingsley*, 67).

24. Beard, *Toussaint L'Ouverture*, 308.

25. Vincent, *Transatlantic Republican*, 129 (emphasis in the original).

26. Ibid., 154 (emphasis in the original). Moses defines Ethiopianism (a sense of black racial pride founded in biblical accounts of African greatness) as a literary-religious tradition common to English speaking Africans, regardless of nationality (see *Golden Age*, 156). Moses explains elsewhere that "The Ethiopian' tradition sprang organically out of certain shared political and religious experiences of English-speaking Africans during the late eighteenth and early nineteenth centuries, finding expression in slave narratives and folk culture. As prophecy, it was supposedly common knowledge among free blacks before the Civil War" ("Poetics of Ethiopianism," 411–426).

27. Moses, *Golden Age*, 48.

28. According to Leslie Harris, Smith's success as a doctor and pharmacist "did not remove him from the problems of the black working class in New York; rather, he went out of his way to address their needs in his medical practice and in his writings in newspapers, most notably in Frederick Douglass's papers, and as physician for the Colored Orphan Asylum from 1842. Perhaps his experiences with self-directed working-class parents and children of the asylum caused him to become an imaginative and outspoken supporter of all types of black labor, as well as a proponent of ways for black workers to improve themselves" (*In the Shadow of Slavery*, 231).

29. Smith, *A Lecture on the Haytien Revolutions*, 9. M'Cune is an alternate spelling of his name. Henceforth, references to this work will be made in the text as "*LHR*."

30. This example of the black freedmen of Haiti organizing and establishing a productive community in the absence of white oversight or influence reflects Smith's own belief in black self-reliance and political autonomy. As C. Peter Ripley and the editors of *The Black Abolitionist Papers: Volume 3* note, "Smith defended the autonomous black press and directed efforts to establish the National Council of the Colored People in the early 1850s. He promoted black

education and self-help principles through his writings and his work" with various community organizations, including the Colored Orphan Asylum (350).

31. The rhetorical situation is also significant; he is addressing supporters of a "Colored Orphan Asylum" who need to educate their charges. Similarly, Saunders addressed societies formed for the express purpose of creating free schools. The economic and educational connection is significant.

32. In a 1930 article entitled "Education in Haiti," Rayford Logan refutes the ongoing charge that "the Negro's inherent incapacity for self-government" is best evidenced by conditions in Haiti" (401). To the contrary, he draws from Saunders's *Haytian Papers* to illustrate that Haiti has struggled to succeed since the early nineteenth century, as evidenced by "Christophe's sincere desire and intelligent determination to provide an adequate system of schools" (416).

33. *Anglo-African Magazine*, 1.1 (January 1859), 5–17.

34. Ibid.

35. Ibid., 25.

36. Ibid., 142.

37. The spectacle of Haiti in the white American political imaginary, what Smith refers to as the "Horrors of St. Domingo," emanates in part from the anxiety about whether the romanticized notion of what Joseph Schumpeter calls "that semi-mystic entity endowed with a will of its own-the 'soul of the people'" could manifest among black Haitians as it had, ostensibly, among white Americans (*Capitalism, Socialism, and Democracy*, 252).

38. The hemispheric labor ideology that emanates from this comparison between Haiti and the United States took a more concrete shape when, in 1846, McCune Smith joined fellow New Yorker and future cofounder of the Radical Abolition Party, Gerrit Smith, as well as black newspaper editor Charles Ray and Theodore Wright, to allot 120,000 acres of Gerrit Smith's land to free blacks in New York State. Gerrit Smith's philanthropy was also influenced by stories of West Indian emancipation. Endowing 250 free black New Yorkers with land reaffirmed their potential as self-sufficient, productive laborers (if not yeoman farmers) and secured their status as eligible voters. Gerrit Smith's choice to announce his land reform plan on the anniversary of West Indian emancipation, combined with a perfectionist religious worldview that included the global manifestation of what Saunders understood as "God's plan" for Haiti, connects his and McCune's vision for New York State to the agrarian demands of Haitian freedom fighters. Gerrit Smith's and James McCune Smith's vision coincides with the West Indian work ethic. According to John Stauffer, they and West Indians defined freedom as the right "to work on small plots of land on which they could earn their subsistence and resist the authority of former masters" (*Black Hearts of Men*, 140).

39. Foner, *Free Soil*, xxviii.

40. See also Roediger, *The Wages of Whiteness*, 57.

41. Sundquist, *To Wake the Nations*, 32.

42. Whittier, *Anti-Slavery Poems*, 12–13, 15.

43. Alfred Hunt, for example, notes the abstract concept of enlightenment, saying "Saunders chose to publish laws and proclamations, hoping that readers would see how enlightened was the constitutional monarchy of Henri Christophe." He attends, briefly, to the issue of Toussaint's "forced-labor policy under martial law," but he does not consider the implications of Saunders's extended attention to issues of labor and freedom and subtle criticism of Christophe. See Hunt, *Haiti's Influence*, 89, 160.

44. A notable exception to this rule might be Leonora Sansay's 1808 novel, *Secret History: or, The Horrors of St. Domingo*, which takes place during Dessalines's reign. Elizabeth Maddock Dillon argues that the most pressing form of violence in the novel is a patriarchal/colonial one connected to "the dynastic model of marriage associated with the European aristocracy and the sterile colonial model of extractive production" that suppresses the development of a creolized social reproduction in which women can be active agents ("Secret History," 94).

45. Bogues, "Haitian Revolution," 7. As Bogues also points out, Cugoano's anticolonial insistence that conquest and domination are forms of evil—little more than robbery and plunder—contrasts with his plan to replace the slave trade with agricultural trade (*Black Heretics*, 41–42, 44). If Haitian revolutionaries were to avenge the island's original inhabitants, they would be entitled to fruits of their agricultural labor.

46. Trouillot, *Silencing the Past*, 73.

47. On the one hand, proslavery authors invoked a gothic tradition to recount the violence of the Haitian Revolution as a cautionary tale about the dangers of freedom; on the other hand, abolitionists "finding slave owners and white soldiers culpable for the 'horrors of St. Domingo'" argued "that whites who brutally enslaved Africans sowed the seeds of their own destruction" (Clavin, "Race, Rebellion, and the Gothic," 2).

48. Clavin also notes that abolitionists "marginaliz[ed] the role of Dessalines and other rebel leaders, as well as the nameless and faceless black masses" in favor of creating an image of Toussaint as a "Great Man, a slave who compared favorably to other Great Men of the Age of Revolution" (Clavin, "Race, Rebellion, and the Gothic," 2; and "Second Haitian Revolution," 118).

49. Bethel, "Images of Hayti," 830.

50. Ibid.

CHAPTER II. THE CONSTITUTION OF TOUSSAINT

1. The first American edition of Olaudah Equiano's *Interesting Narrative* (1791) had subscription orders numbering only 336 copies. There were two later reprints that precede Douglass's *Autobiography*, the first in 1829 and another in 1837.

2. The 1786 edition was an unchanged reissue of the first edition of 1773. It was sold out of the shop of Benjamin Crukshank in Philadelphia.

3. Carretta, "Early African-American Literature?," 99.

4. We pass over here another, but perhaps the weakest, possible objection to consideration of Toussaint's Constitution: that it was written in French. At a moment that sees a collection like Sollors and Shell's *Multilingual Anthology of American*, not to mention common inclusion of French and Spanish texts in U.S. literature anthologies, this criticism does not seem to warrant much attention.

5. Toussaint's name appears in Title 6 §16, Title 8 §§ 28, 30 (twice), and 31, and Title 13 § 77. His signature concludes the text.

6. Almost certainly apocryphal.

7. Our numbers are based on searches of the Readex Newspaper Database, and of several papers not included in that database, like Philadelphia's *Aurora*; we assume that the text appeared in more papers than we have listed.

8. We note, too, the publication of Mason Locke Weems' *The Life of Washington* in 1800, which continued through nine editions in the first decade of the nineteenth century.

9. Paine's critical letter to Washington, written in 1796, was widely reprinted following the announcement of Paine's return.

10. Reprinted from the *Gazette of the United States*, May 7, 1801. Here, the piece gets reactivated by the appearance of Toussaint's Constitution.

11. The original is slightly edited, and the passage about the shoe-blacks appears much earlier in the original text.

12. Tise, *American Counterrevolution*.

13. *Aurora General Advertiser*, August 17, 1801.

14. Emphasis in the original.

CHAPTER 12. HAITI AND THE NEW-WORLD NOVEL

1. Quoted in Geggus, "The Naming of Haiti," 207. Geggus cites the Archives de la Guerre, Vincennes, MS 597, ANOM, CC9B/23, proclamation of April 28, 1804. He explains, "Exceptions were made for certain whites who had allied themselves with the blacks. In the constitutions of 1805, 1806, and 1816, the ban on Europeans was rephrased to exclude 'whites of whatever nation,' but it was omitted in the 1807 and 1811 constitutions of Henry Christophe, ruler of northern Haiti between 1807 and 1820" (295).

2. Gulick's essay "We Are Not the People" reads the 1805 Constitution formally and rhetorically, as an "emerging legal and political genre," which places the newly independent nation at the center of revolutionary studies.

3. Thomas Newton to Governor Henry Lee, May 10, 1792, Executive Papers, Box 74, 1–10 May Folder, quoted in Sidbury's *Ploughshares into Swords*, 14–49.

4. Edwards, *Historical Survey*, 63.

5. Ibid., 91; Jefferson, *Notes on the State of Virginia*. Jefferson writes, "Deep rooted prejudices entertained by the whites; ten thousand recollections, by the blacks, of the injuries they have sustained; new provocations; the real distinctions which nature has made; and many other circumstances, will divide us into parties, and produce convulsions which will probably never end but in the extermination of the one or the other race" (264).

6. "The Vision," *New York Magazine, or Literary Repository*, April 2, 4, 1791, 198.

7. Charles Brockden Brown's "On the Consequences of Abolishing the Slave Trade to the West Indian Colonies," cites the Haitian Revolution as evidence for why slavery should be abolished in the states. In his edition of Leonora Sansay's *The Secret History; or, The Horrors of St. Domingo* (1808), Michael Drexler highlights Sansay's use of slave revolution as a way of allowing for Clara to "speak for herself" rather than through her husband or lover, Aaron Burr.

8. See Haywood's *Bloody Romanticism*. He argues that out of two primary strains of British Romanticism—sensibility and the sublime—comes the "bloody vignette," which uses "hyperbolic realism" to negotiate the spectacular violence of the revolutionary period.

9. See Cotlar's "Reading the Foreign News," 307–338.

10. Haywood, *Bloody Romanticism*, 8.

11. See Gibbons, "Ireland, America, and Gothic Memory," 25–47. Gibbons locates the source of the American gothic in Irish underground groups, such as the United Irishmen, which I discuss in my analysis of William Cobbett's pamphlets. See also Leask, "Irish Republicans and Gothic Eleutherarchs," 347–367.

12. Quoted in List, "Role of William Cobbett," 4. List argues in her dissertation that we misread Cobbett as a conservative Federalist in America when we should understand his

changed political proclivity as a Tory, the result of his sense of Britishness in the face of what he felt was an "immoral and empty" American culture. See also Swanwick, *A Rub from Snub* and *A Roaster*; Bradford, *Imposter Detected*, xii, xiii; and Carey, *Pill for Porcupine*.

13. Madison quoted in Gaines, *William Cobbett and the United States*, xiv; Coleridge quoted in Hughes, ed., *Cobbett*, 15.

14. Gaines, "William Cobbett's Account Book," 299–312.

15. All quotations from Cobbett come from Wilson, ed., *Peter Porcupine in America*, 145.

16. Ibid., 144.

17. Emphasis in the original.

18. Ibid., 146.

19. See Backus, *Gothic Family Romance*, 1–21.

20. "Letter to William Stephens Smith, November 13, 1787." Here, Jefferson refers both to Shays's Rebellion in Western Massachusetts and the subsequent fear of insurrection generally.

21. As in Edmond Burke's *Reflections* on the French Revolution, Jefferson understands revolution as posing a choice between two poles: accepting the status quo or jeopardizing civil liberties, civilization, and white culture. His statements here reflect his acceptance of inevitable change to the status quo while attempting to manage and delimit the scope and quality of these changes brought on by slave violence and ultimate emancipation.

22. "Letter to St. George Tucker, August 28, 1797." He begins the letter by situating his warning in inevitable revolution: "the first chapter of this history, which has begun in St. Domingo."

23. Wilson, *Peter Porcupine*, 241–257. The full title is *Detection of a Conspiracy, Formed by the United Irishmen, with the Evident Intention of Aiding the Tyrants of France in Subverting the Government of the United States of America. By Peter Porcupine*.

24. In an answer to why the role of "system" comes to be so important to narrative, Clifford Siskin suggests that "in the late eighteenth and early nineteenth centuries, two genres mixed. As novels took on the constitutive force of systems—making [Anna] Barbauld's nation—systems assumed causal roles in novels. Embedded within Romantic-era fictional narratives, system was rewritten into something that could be blamed—even something that could kill" ("Novels and Systems," 203). The intermixing of form (for Siskin, system and novel) is a central premise of my thesis on the transformation of the American gothic novel, as something which uses different forms of print, especially those which attempt to narrate collective violence. As I suggest, however, for Burke and Cobbett system is coterminous with revolutionary violence.

25. Burke, "Speech on the Occasion of the recommitment of the Quebec Bill, 6 May 1791," *Speeches of the Right Honourable Edmund Burke, in the House of Commons, and in Westminster-Hall* (London: Longman, Hurst, Rees, Orme, and Brown, 1816): 4:8.

26. Cobbett, *Peter Porcupine's Gazette*, 244.

27. Ibid., 254.

28. Stern's *Plight of Feeling* identifies the source of American romance as the French Revolution but, as I am arguing, this ignores the impact of the Haitian Revolution on early American literature.

29. Miles, "The 1790s: The Effulgence of Gothic," 44.

30. Godwin, *Caleb Williams*, 3.

31. Godwin's invocation of "terror" was also a clear reference to the Jacobin "terror," which was still in full force during at the time of the novel's publication. Ibid., 4.

32. Marquis de Sade wrote in his notes that the Gothic seemed to be "the necessary fruit of the Revolutionary terrors felt by the whole of Europe." Extracts from "Idée sur les romans" in *Les Crimes de l'amour*, quoted in Sage, *Gothic Novel*, 48–49; Mathias, *Pursuits of Literature*, 194. For a discussion of the rise of the gothic in 1790s British culture, see Miles and Clery's *Rise of Supernatural Fiction*, 124.

33. Ian Duncan's *Modern Romance and the Transformation of the Novel* presents two theories of gothic origins: "more than anything else, this romance revival involved the confrontation with cultural origins that were at once native and alien" (21).

34. Ibid., 2.

35. Ibid.

36. Following Duncan's argument, I am making a distinction between premodern Romance as archetypal and mythological, and post-novel, modern romance, which renders these archetypes tropes, one of many features of its rhetorical structure.

37. Duncan, *Modern Romance*, 7.

38. My argument builds upon Teresa Goddu's incisive study *Gothic America*, in which she changes the critical register from the psychoanalytic to the historical, arguing that "the site of slavery" is a crucial locus for the genre's horror. I am less convinced by Edwards, *Gothic Passages*, in which he considers the gothic a "mode" rather than a genre, a move that diminishes many of its contours and much of its potency. See also Davidson's seminal *Revolution and the Word*, which argues for the specifically national character of the gothic novel, one in which the critique of "individualism" is fairly limited. Elizabeth Maddock Dillon offers a significant challenge to this enduring nationalist frame suggesting that the "correspondence between nation and novel in early America should be reconsidered" in order to account for the persistence of "colonial and creole social reproduction" in early American novels ("Secret History," 78–79).

39. See Dimock, *Through Other Continents*, 3–4.

40. Fiedler, *Love and Death in the American Novel*, 144 (emphasis in the original).

41. Ibid., 137.

42. I borrow these terms from Richard Slotkin's influential *Regeneration through Violence*. But as more an "archetype" than a fully-fleshed character, "neither demonic nor a disturbing figure by the time he has been naturalized in popular literature," the "noble savage," gets replaced by the terrifying specter of blackness in the earliest articulations of the novel (Fiedler, *Love and Death*, 159).

43. Brown, *Rhapsodist*.

44. Ibid., 7.

45. Ibid., 7.

46. Brown, *Edgar Huntly*, 3–4.

47. Brown, *Rhapsodist*, 7.

48. Hawthorne, *House of the Seven Gables*, 2.

49. See Goudie, "On the Origin of American Specie(s)," 60–87. He argues that "no development is more disturbing to the reader . . . than his subsequent awakening to a racially supremacist consciousness" (60).

50. See Kenny's *American Irish*. The chapter on the eighteenth century details the different waves of immigration and their numbers, argues for an increased critical focus on the Scotch-Irish and their Presbyterianism as something apart from the Catholic, South Carolinian settlers, and suggests that over one quarter of the Irish immigrants settled in Philadelphia by 1790. Kenny briefly discusses the role of the United Irishmen and their contribution to radicalism in Philadelphia, as "an important catalyst for the radicalism of the contemporary At-

lantic world" (41). See also Bric, "Irish and the Evolution of the 'New Politics,'" 147. To be sure, two waves of immigration threatened to contaminate American slaves: the Irish (250,000 came from Ireland, 1717–1775) and thousands of Creole refugees and black slaves after the onset of revolution in St. Domingue in August 1791. Arriving in port towns such as Charleston and New Orleans, St. Dominguan refugees very quickly migrated to larger cities such as Boston, New York, and Philadelphia.

51. Samuels, *Romances of the Republic*, 29.
52. See Powell, *Bring Out Your Dead*, 30–46.
53. Brown, *Arthur Mervyn*, 147.
54. Ibid., 148.
55. Ibid. The immediacy of the violence collapsed into a brief moment echoes both Jefferson's and Cobbett's warnings of the mere "single spark" required to obliterate the nation in the "twinkling of an eye."
56. Ibid.
57. Ibid.
58. Goudie, "On the Origin of American Specie(s)," 60–87.
59. Brown, *Arthur Mervyn*, 370.
60. Ibid.
61. Ibid., 350.
62. Brown's novel anticipates the terror of slave conspiracies, like Gabriel's Rebellion (1800), Denmark Vesey's Conspiracy (1822), and Nat Turner's Revolt (1831), which influence much antebellum print. After such events, the concealed agency of murderous black slaves haunt more and more literature perhaps none more seamlessly than Herman Melville's gothic novella, *Benito Cereno* (1855).
63. See Levine, "Race and Nation," 332–353.
64. Brown, *An Address to the Government of the United States*, 5.
65. Ibid., 6.
66. Ibid.
67. Ibid., 31–32.
68. Ibid., 32.
69. See Tragle, *Southampton Slave Revolt*. Tragle devotes almost 150 pages to newspaper articles and notices published in the days and months following Nat Turner's insurrection (27–170). For example, in the aftermath of Turner's insurrection, a Baltimore paper, *Niles' Register*, published this notice: "Incendiary Publications—The 'Vigilance Association of Columbia,' (South Carolina), composed of gentlemen of the first respectability, have offered a reward of fifteen hundred dollars for the apprehension and prosecution to conviction, of any white person who may be detected in distributing or circulating within the state the newspaper called, 'The Liberator,' printed in Boston, or the pamphlet called 'Walker's Pamphlet' or any other publications of a seditious tendency" (quoted in Tragle, *Southampton Slave Revolt*, 131).
70. See Chakrabarty's *Provincializing Europe*, where he argues that historicism is a process that translates modernity (or capitalism) as something that has developed over time, a temporal plane constructed as "first in Europe, then elsewhere." He writes, "Historicism thus posited historical time as a measure of the cultural distance (at least in institutional development) that was assumed to exist between the West and the non-West" (7). Drawing on John Stuart Mill's "On Liberty," which argues that the pinnacle of civilization is self-rule, a position not quite suitable—"not yet"—for African or Asian colonial subjects, Chakrabarty

explains: "Some historical time of development and civilization (colonial rule and education, to be precise) had to elapse before they could be considered prepared for such a task. Mill's historicist argument thus consigned Indians, Africans, and other 'rude' nations to an imaginary waiting room of history. In doing so, it converted history itself into a version of this waiting room. . . . That was what historicist consciousness was: a recommendation to the colonized to wait" (8).

CHAPTER 13. DISPOSSESSION AND COSMOPOLITAN COMMUNITY IN LEONORA SANSAY'S *SECRET HISTORY*

1. In a recent overview of the critical trends organizing the field of early American literature, Stephen Shapiro summarizes the cultural work of sentimental fiction in these terms: "The problematic enshrined at the heart of eighteenth century sentimental tales involves the nexus of new associative relations made possible by the bourgeois subject freed from aristocratic lineage and status hierarchies" (Shapiro, *Culture and Commerce*, 21).

2. As Elizabeth Barnes puts it, "For American authors, a democratic state is a sympathetic state, and a sympathetic state is one that resembles a family" (Barnes, *States of Sympathy*, 2).

3. Beginning with Terence Martin's *The Instructed Vision*, which draws together Scottish Common Sense philosophy and American fiction, the presence of Enlightenment language and ideas in American letters has been given its most extensive consideration in Brown's *Consent of the Governed*; Weinstein's *Family, Kinship, and Sympathy in Early American Culture*; Tennenhouse's *The Importance of Feeling English*, and Boudreau's *Sympathy in American Literature*.

4. Tennenhouse has argued that broken and makeshift families are an indelible fact of the late eighteenth-century American experience, causally connected to the kind of international migration we see in *Secret History*: "the British diaspora in America was made up of a large number of partial families, transplanted second sons, as well as a disproportionately large ratio of single men to unmarried women who emigrated to America under a variety of contracts and conditions. As a result, during and immediately following the very substantial emigrations from Britain from the 1750s to the 1770s, and again after 1781, there was a sizeable population of fractured and makeshift families" (*Importance*, 44).

5. Gilroy, *Black Atlantic*, 4. In her article on *Secret History* and the form of the early American novel, Elizabeth Maddock Dillon construes the novel's "fractured domestic scenes" ("Secret History," 79) and the mobility of its women in terms of "the difficulties and the possibilities of creole social reproduction in the colonial Atlantic world" ("Secret History," 96). This paradigm invites us to rethink, in particularly generative ways, the politics of domestic relations in the early American novel: "Any consideration of domestic reproduction in the colonial New World would entail an effort to think against, through, or around the presumed sterility of the creole and the racialized and gendered ideologies that comprised the substance of [the] colonial doxa" ("Secret History," 99). Like Dillon, I am invested in integrating Sansay into a continuous literary tradition in the colonial Atlantic world in such a way that revises the nationalist coordinates that have persisted in early American criticism and challenges the more canonical readings of domestic literature as the narrative expression of a new American democracy. To my mind, Sansay is part of a literary tradition that reaches back to the captivity narrative and received ideas about Enlightenment sociability that exposes the model of the

self-enclosed individual as a measure of life particularly ill-suited to the exchanges and displacements characteristic of the Atlantic colonial world.

6. Cheah and Robbins's collection *Cosmopolitics* offers a thorough overview of the problems and possibilities at stake in cosmopolitanism. Goodlad's "Trollopian 'Foreign Policy'" contains a concise account of the current critical views shaping the discussion.

7. Drexler, "Brigands and Nuns," 184–185. In *Haiti, History, and the Gods*, Joan Dayan similarly credits Sansay's "insights into the relations between castes and colors during the last days of Saint-Domingue" as revealing "more about the kinds of mixtures and erosions of boundaries that prevailed there more than any other document about this period" (172). To this point, conventional historiographies of the Haitian revolution have largely centered on its ideological relation to the French Revolution and contemporary debates over the hypocrisy of Enlightenment principles of equality and liberty, or the potentially disastrous repercussions to the slave trade anticipated by Southern slaveholders. Dayan's book and James's *Black Jacobins* remain two of the most influential historical accounts of the revolution, while Popkin's "Facing Racial Revolution" offers a helpful overview of the white colonists' and black revolutionaries' engagement with French popular radicalism. Woertendyke, "Romance to Novel," and Dillon, "Secret History," offer particularly helpful readings of *Secret History*'s synchronic political dimensions—the novel, in other words, "both activates and depends upon two geopolitical spaces at once, Early America and Early Haiti" (Woertendyke, "Romance to Novel," 258). See also Matthewson, "Jefferson and Haiti."

8. As Woertendyke has artfully demonstrated, *Secret History* is a generically composite text whose temporal, spatial, and formal scope "obsessively resists both the consolidating impulses of the novel and the attendant compulsion toward a totalizing progressive historicism" (Woertendyke, "Romance to Novel," 263). For Woertendyke, the text's chief generic coordinates can be found in the British tradition of the secret history.

9. For this line of thought, I am particularly indebted to Nancy Armstrong and Leonard Tennenhouse, whose article "The Problem of Population and the Form of the American Novel" offers a compelling theoretical paradigm for reading the early American novel as a cosmopolitan form that draws on captivity narrative traditions to articulate the growing tensions between competing social bodies that included "the population." It is my aim to broaden this paradigm in such a way as to recuperate the hitherto neglected cultural and political history of Caribbean revolution and its impact on North American literary production. To this end, I am less concerned with the more overt objects of Sansay's critique—namely, the humanitarian abuses and social excesses of a postrevolutionary French colonial elite. To be sure, that critique places *Secret History* in a much larger context of transatlantic revolutionary history, slave insurrection, and early republican political paranoia, but we should resist succumbing to the mimetic fallacy that the novel reflects deeply encoded political and social anxieties that precede their articulation in writing. Rather, I want to consider how the text's formal qualities perform specific ideological functions. On the recent Americanist turn to historical formalism, see especially Weinstein and Looby, *American Literature's Aesthetic Dimensions*, and Cahill, *Liberty of the Imagination*.

10. Locke, "Second Treatise of Government," 111–112.

11. When he proclaims that "in the beginning all the world was America" (ibid., 117), Locke tacitly acknowledges that nothing less than a new act of creation is necessary to create a fiction of origins for the modern individual.

12. This is how Locke describes the paternal household: "Let us therefore consider the master of a family with all these subordinate relations of wife, children, servants, and slaves,

united under the domestic rule of a family; which [resembles] a little common-wealth" (ibid., 126). In a statement that neatly reproduces the operations of the contract, *The Coquette*'s Mrs. Richman makes a case for just such a formation: "It is the glory of the marriage state . . . to refine, by circumscribing our enjoyments. Here we can repose in safety. . . . True, we cannot always pay that attention to former associates, which we may wish, but the little community which we superintend is quite as important an object; and certainly renders us more beneficial to the public" (Foster, *Coquette*, 123). In exchange for relinquishing certain freedoms of association, a woman is compensated with protection and authority over a "little community" that mirrors society at large and perfects the citizenship of its constituents under the governance of a paternal head. As the sum of its rational individuals assembled at the level of the household, this is civil society in Lockean terms.

13. The works I have in mind, such as Stern's *The Plight of Feeling* or Barnes's *States of Sympathy*, successfully challenged the peripheral place of sentimental writing in an almost exclusively masculinized canon by assigning a progressive social agenda that was anchored to and predicated on sentiment's essentially "feminine" qualities. Critics continue to revise this enormously influential work from the early 1990s by challenging its gendered ideal of a democratic nation built on a horizontal model of shared human feeling.

14. Foster, *The Coquette*, 123.

15. Wood, *Julia*, 225.

16. Sansay, *Secret History*, 73–74. Hereafter this work will be referred to in the text as *SH*.

17. It seems plausible that Clara's description of the "countless multitudes" (*SH*, 145) of land crabs that swarm over the mountains of Cuba is an allegorical allusion to the slave revolutionaries that likewise draws on the language of undifferentiated masses. Clara relates the tale of a Spaniard whose local knowledge of the crabs' migratory patterns helps him successfully dupe credulous English soldiers into believing that the sound of the crustaceans' scuttling is, in fact, an opposing military "army." Much like the black revolutionary army that expels the invading French colonial powers, this "brown stream," Clara observes, cannot be deflected or redirected. In this sense, the revolutionaries, much like the crabs, offer a collective force that observes many of the principles of Deleuze and Guattari's rhizome, a multidirectional network, or "weave," that changes in nature according to the circuits it incorporates and abandons.

18. As Michael Drexler notes, Clara "is surprised to find a wholly different system of land ownership and property management [in central Cuba] than that present before the revolution on Saint-Domingue," offering her new insights into how different "collectives get started, gain strength, and move into action" ("Brigands and Nuns," 190).

19. The revolution in France turned all questions of citizenship in St. Domingue, for free *gens de coleur*, Creoles, and colonial whites alike, into a highly vexed subject. The white inhabitants had long resented the trade restrictions placed upon them by royal administrators in the metropole, yet they just as readily recognized the dangers inherent in the popular rhetoric of liberty and equality. Popkin explains that "the violent disagreements among the whites themselves" ("Facing Racial Revolution," 514) over the colony's relationship to France and the future of slavery in the Caribbean precluded any meaningful public debate over granting the rights of citizenship to the island's free mixed-race population. Indeed, the island was institutionally organized in such a manner as to make such issues prohibitively complicated: as Drexler tells us, "Saint Dominguan society recognized a staggering 128 racial categories to discriminate all conceivable gradations from white to black" as part of "an elaborate system of regulations severely restrict[ing] anything resembling civic equality" ("Introduction," 17).

20. Sansay's comment about such rapacious greed is an accurate reflection of French colonial practices in St. Domingue both before and during the slave revolt. The island's chief commodities, coffee and sugar, made easy fortunes for whites whose disdain for Creole culture—a phrase considered something of an oxymoron—sent them back with haste to the Parisian metropole, where fortunes could be spent on luxurious aristocratic lifestyles. Perversely, this fueled the demand for increased slave labor, until enslaved blacks outnumbered whites and free *gens de coleur* ten to one by 1790. The voracious exploitation of St. Domingue's commodities and slave labor force by the French in the revolutionary years is discussed in Drexler, "Brigands and Nuns," Dillon, "Secret History," and Blackburn, *Overthrow of Colonial Slavery*.

21. It is striking that Sansay's character shares her name with Samuel Richardson's famous protagonist, another dead sentimental heroine whose death arguably results from a deficiency of male figures capable of recognizing her unique brand of interiority.

22. As several historians have documented, the kind of domestic violence we encounter in Clara's marriage has a social history outside the gothic. Such hidden forms of cruelty became more visible during the nineteenth century through court cases and publicized first-hand accounts. Those cases offer insight into the nature of gendered domestic relations, property rights, legal procedure, and the changing nature of paternal authority in the eighteenth and nineteenth centuries. See Foyster, *Marital Violence*, and Daniels and Kennedy, *Over the Threshold*.

23. Foucault, *Society Must be Defended*, 242–243.

24. Ibid.

25. Ibid., 245. Giorgio Agamben builds on Foucault's discussion of the population by first challenging Foucault's insistence that the eighteenth century marked a epistemic shift toward biopolitics. In *Homo Sacer*, Agamben traces an idea of biopolitics back to classical political theory, making the notion of sovereignty over "bare life" a long-held political assumption.

26. Foucault, *Society Must Be Defended*, 246.

27. In *Fictions of Mass Democracy*, Stacey Margolis makes the case that there is a constitutive relationship between "diffuse, informal, and largely disorganized" (2) social networks of modern democratic power and the formal structures of nineteenth-century U.S. fiction. The early American novel, she argues, returns time and again to the political potential of decentered networks of exchange, in such a way that "transform[s] the very notion of political agency, making it possible to rethink what counts as a political action and who counts as a political actor" (30). The question of who counts as a political actor, I would argue, lies at the heart of the figure of the "population," which *Secret History* construes as its own decentered form of political agency.

28. Historian Jeremy Popkin has documented several important, albeit rare, contemporary eyewitness accounts of the uprising, which he classifies as captivity narratives insofar as they are told from the perspective of white colonists imprisoned by the former slaves. I find it wholly plausible that Sansay was familiar with this form of writing given its general popularity at the time, the existence of these contemporary local versions, and the language of *Secret History* itself.

29. Tyler, *Algerine Captive*, 124.

30. Since first appearing in 1684, Mary Rowlandson's narrative was republished fifteen times before 1811. Twelve of those were in the last thirty years of the eighteenth century. John Williams' narrative, first published in 1707, reappears eleven times before 1811. Nine of these editions appeared after 1770. See Evans' *American Bibliography* and Armstrong and Tennenhouse, "Problem of Population," 668–669.

31. I am indebted here to Ezra Tawil's compelling reading of racial and cultural identity in Jemison's captivity narrative. See Tawil, *Making of Racial Sentiment*, 100–108.

32. Seaver, "Narrative of the Life of Mrs. Mary Jemison," 209.

33. *Secret History* therefore shares conceptual ground with a form of cosmopolitanism resembling Immanuel Kant's laws of universal hospitality. In 1795, Kant claimed in *Perpetual Peace* that "the right to visit, to associate, belongs to all men by virtue of their common ownership of the earth's surface; for since the earth is a globe, they cannot scatter themselves infinitely, but must, finally, tolerate living in close proximity, because originally no one had a greater right to any region of the earth as anyone else" ("Perpetual Peace," 118). As refugees, the sisters' survival comes to depend on such principles of universal tolerance: in every "strange country" to which they retreat, Mary and Clara find "asylum" with "strangers" (*SH*, 105, 106). Thus the novel evokes a late eighteenth-century notion of cosmopolitan sociability to suggest that all humans are fundamentally the same by nature but potentially different by culture and will encounter one another in a transnational system of international communication.

34. Agamben, *Homo Sacer*, 4.

CHAPTER 14. THEATRICAL REBELS AND REFUGEES

1. *Philadelphia Gazette and Universal Daily Advertiser*, May 22, 1795. Murdock's script was printed with the support of "a number of gentlemen," and advertised for sale beginning September 25, 1795. The introduction to another play by Murdock, *The Beau Metamorphized*, gives the author's perspective on the reception of *Triumphs of Love*.

2. See Nathans, "Trampling Native Genius," 29–43. Murdock's script circulated in print the year before its stage production, supported by subscribers including Charles Wilson Peale, Benjamin Rush, Benjamin West, and even Pennsylvania governor Thomas Mifflin. For more on the early American stage and its social contexts, see Nathans, *Early American Theatre* and Johnson, *Absence and Memory*.

3. Nathans, *Early American Theatre*, 93. As Nathans has elsewhere argued, American theater's customary anglophile repertoire, class biases, and limited desire for local authorship limited the play's popularity ("Trampling Native Genius," 29–43).

4. *Gazette of the United States*, September 25, 1795.

5. See White, *Encountering Revolution*. The figures appear in White, "'A Flood of Impure Lava,'" 37. By that same count, a third of them were people of color.

6. Nash, "Reverberations of Haiti," 67 n.14. As Nash and others observe, St. Domingue's refugees joined preexisting French expatriate communities in Philadelphia. The ambiguities involved in identifying the different Franco-Atlantic populations should remind us that contemporary Anglo-American discourse used "French" loosely to designate a diverse assortment of francophone or Franco-Atlantic people. As an identity category, "French" could modify or overwrite other political, geographical, cultural, and racial labels. Such relaxed usage habits accommodated a reality in which many of the revolutionary era's people, characters, and identities were mobile, rapidly changing, or never firmly anchored in fixed geopolitical categories in the first place.

7. Philadelphia's passenger lists, a partial enumeration at best, identify 3,084 refugees between 1791 and 1794, of whom 848 were slaves or free blacks. Ibid., 50.

8. On the influence of these refugees, see Childs, *French Refugee Life*; Dessens, *From Saint-Domingue to New Orleans*; Branson and Patrick, "Étrangers dans Un Pays Étrange," 193–208. The differences seem to have been particularly noticeable in terms of racial practices. French Caribbean immigrants, for example, brought different social categories and understandings of race, and the considerable numbers of slaves and servants of color they brought to Philadelphia augmented the city's black population by about 25 percent (Nash, "Reverberations of Haiti," 47).

9. A character in *André: a Tragedy, in Five Acts* by William Dunlap, for example, refers obliquely to revolutions in other "climes" (73). At the end of the decade, a number of Anglo-Atlantic plays addressed slave unrest, but they staged individual banditry rather than organized revolution. Such plays typically imagine slave revolt as local, isolated, and dispersed forms of marronage or banditry. Francophone theater appears also reticent on the topic, although one notable exception is Charles de Rémusat's published but never-performed 1825 play, *The Saint-Domingue Plantation, or, The Insurrection: a Drama in Five Acts*.

10. Murdock, *Triumphs of Love*, 37–38. Henceforth all page references to this work will be made directly in the text.

11. Nathans, *Early American Theatre*, 95.

12. See Hunt, *Haiti's Influence*. More recently, see Clavin, *Toussaint Louverture*; Garraway, *Tree of Liberty*; Gaspar and Geggus, *Turbulent Time*; Geggus and Fiering, *World of the Haitian Revolution*; Jackson and Bacon, *African Americans and the Haitian Revolution*; Kachun, "Antebellum African Americans," 249–273.

13. Fischer, *Modernity Disavowed*, 2.

14. Trouillot, *Silencing the Past*, 27.

15. My sense of how theater works in this context is informed by theoretical discussions about the relationships among sites of performance—between on- and offstage performances that we might characterize as more or less "theatrical" or "performative"—conducted by interdisciplinary thinkers in the arts and social sciences such as Erving Goffman, Victor Turner, Richard Schechner, and Judith Butler. More recently, performance studies scholars such as Tracy Davis, Marvin Carlson, Janelle Reinelt, and Thomas Postlewait have questioned the definitions of and boundaries between formal theater and unconscious social acts (to pose one sort of performance continuum), discussing issues such as political meaning, authenticity, artificiality, and imitation.

16. Freeman, *Character's Theater*, 196–197.

17. The mask's nose is "as big as the man of Strasburgh," an allusion to book 4 of Sterne's *Tristam Shandy*, in which an enormous, phallic nose inspires comical curiosity and desire.

18. The patriotic turn also helps Murdock's play deploy St. Domingue refugees in a for-profit display that supports his claim to "native genius" as an American playwright. That American exceptionalism is also the subject of White, "Saint-Domingue Refugees," 248–260.

19. See Matthewson, "Abraham Bishop," 148–154; Waldstreicher and Grossbart, "Abraham Bishop's Vocation," 617–657.

20. White, "Saint-Domingue Refugees," 249; see also Newman, "American Political Culture," 72–89. For a fuller picture of St. Domingue's French Creole culture, see Garraway, *Libertine Colony*.

21. On black responses to the Haitian Revolution, see Scott, "Common Wind"; and White, "'It Was a Proud Day," 13–50.

22. *Philadelphia General Advertiser*, August 9, 1793, boasts of donations collected from theaters, circuses, and the "French patriotic Society" in excess of $10,000.

23. Philadelphia, for example, saw more than 110 francophone publications during the 1790s (Hébert, "French Publications in Philadelphia," 38). Anglo-American newspapers made figures such as Genêt, Talleyrand, La Rouchefoucauld-Liancourt, and M. L. E. Moreau de St. Méry household names during the 1790s. In *French Refugee Life* Childs amply describes the celebrity French refugee social scene of diplomats, intellectuals, aristocrats, religious figures, and merchants of both Creole and European origins.

24. *Philadelphia General Advertiser*, April 18, 1794.

25. Sansay, *Secret History*, 118.

26. *New-York Journal, & Patriotic Register*, January 25, 1792. Brockett, "European Career of Alexandre Placide," 306–313, surveys Placide's two decades of English and French success before his arrival in America. Sodders, "Theatre Management of Alexandre Placide," 10–11, gives a brief overview of Placide's Caribbean career. See also Hoole, *Ante-Bellum Charleston Theatre*; Curtis, "John Joseph Stephen Leger Sollee," 285–298; Willis, *Charleston Stage*.

27. *Charleston City Gazette and General Advertiser*, February 8, 1794.

28. The advertisement for Gardie's "first appearance on this stage" does not elaborate upon her Caribbean routing to American theaters, promoting her origins in "the Theatre at Paris" (*Gazette of the United States*, April 28, 1794). Scholars have not fully explored the implications of Gardie's story; she has received brief mentions in Brooks, "Decade of Brilliance," 333–365; Winter, "American Theatrical Dancing," 58–73; Shapiro, "Action Music in American Pantomime," 49–72.

29. Dunlap, *History of the American Theatre*, 1:402–404. Gardie pursued an acting career in France, St. Domingue, New York City, Philadelphia, and Boston until her sensational murder by her second husband in 1798.

30. Benefit performance for Gardie and Willems advertised in the *Philadelphia Gazette*, June 26, 1794. Dunlap identifies Willems as coming from England (ibid., 1:234).

31. Sonneck examines the French influences on American opera in *Early Opera in America*, 197–219.

32. Foster, *Choreography and Narrative*, 128–130, and Meglin, "'Sauvages, Sex Roles, and Semiotics,'" 87–132, describe the European versions of *Mirza*, the first two choreographed by Maximilien Gardel in 1779, and a shortened 1781 *Fête de Mirza*. The earlier versions staged lurking black "assassins," although American performances do not specifically indicate their presence.

33. Sodders, 68.

34. When the play appeared first in the Boston, it was simply billed a "military pantomime" and apparently revolved around a demonstration of swordsmanship (*Boston Argus* April 16, 1793). Beginning in June 1794, a more elaborate version appears in Charleston; theatergoers could read elaborate descriptions beginning with the Charleston *City Gazette* of June 6, 1794.

35. Lailson's production appears in the *Philadelphia Gazette*, July 18, 1797.

36. *New York Daily Advertiser*, June 13, 1796.

37. Newman, "American Political Culture," 78.

38. Lewis Hallam Jr., acted Mungo to great acclaim, reportedly after making a study of African American character. See Richards, *Drama, Theatre, and Identity*, 217.

39. For a detailed discussion of racialized performances in various London settings, see Worrall, *Politics of Romantic Theatricality*, 68–106. See also Carlson, "New Lows," 139–147.

40. Prologue preceding *Triumphs of Love* in theatrical performance; the text (included in some, but not all, printed versions of the play) does not indicate who spoke the prologue.

41. Review printed in *Gazette of the United States*, May 25, 1795.

42. Paul Gilmore describes the "type of imitation and repetition staged by the minstrel show" that rendered race "simultaneously a mask and an essential identity" (*Genuine Article*, 50).

43. Ibid., 69.

44. In what might be a sign of Murdock's regard for his patron's views, the list of subscribers displays Rush's name prominently, out of strict alphabetical order at the top of the names beginning with "R."

45. Rush, letter to Nathanael Greene, September 16, 1782, quoted in Nash, *Forging Freedom*, 3.

46. For more on the pleasures and perils of nineteenth-century minstrelsy, see Lott, *Love and Theft*; Lhamon, *Raising Cain*; Lhamon, *Jump Jim Crow*.

47. Marx, *Eighteenth Brumaire*, 15.

48. James, *Black Jacobins*. On the ways in which both French and American historiography have reconceived the Haitian Revolution, see Sepinwall, "Specter of Saint-Domingue," 317–338.

49. Sonneck, *Early Opera in America*, 145; Richards, *Drama, Theatre, and Identity*, 70–71. Ads for performances of the *Poor Soldier* featuring Domingo appear in the *Polar Star and Boston Daily Advertiser*, January 2, 1797, and the *Boston Columbian Centinel*, April 12, 1797, "for the last time this season." The next year saw a return to Bagatelle, the original white character, "as originally written" (*Boston Gazette, and Weekly Republican Journal*, June 4, 1798).

50. Murdock recycled this satire in his 1798 play *The Politicians*. Caesar, Pompey, and Sambo reappear, this time debating the relative merits of French and English allegiances (19–20). There is no evidence that the play ever appeared on stage.

51. Newman, *Parades and the Politics of the Street*, 157–160 describes white support and celebration of the French Revolution alongside the increasingly diminishing possibilities of black political expression during the 1790s. In response to such shifts in political culture, black Americans performed their own celebrations of Haitian independence and the end of the slave trade.

52. See Alderson, "Charleston's Rumored Slave Revolt," 93–111; Sidbury, *Ploughshares into Swords*; Genovese, *From Rebellion to Revolution*; Linebaugh and Rediker, *Many-Headed Hydra*.

53. Nash, "Reverberations of Haiti," 47.

54. Ashli White examines the implications of "French Negroes" in North American discourse. Reports of black St. Dominguans frequently used the label to signal vaguely threatening, exotic or foreign (often, though not exclusively, francophone) characters. The xenophobic designation broadly associates threatening outsiders with radical revolution and slave revolt (*Encountering Revolution*, 138–154).

55. Nash, "Reverberations of Haiti," 57.

56. White, *Encountering Revolution*, 39–40.

57. *Baltimore Evening Post*, September 18, 1793.

58. *New York Spectator*, July 14, 1804. There has been significant debate over the nature and the extent of African American awareness of Haiti. As a reprinted anecdote, this account

indicates more reliably the ways that white onlookers imagined and narrated reenactments of Haitian-style insurrection in their midst.

59. Freeman, *Character's Theater*, 194–195.

CHAPTER 15. THE "ALPHA AND OMEGA" OF HAITIAN LITERATURE

1. Trouillot, "Odd and the Ordinary," 7.
2. A transcript of this broadcast can be found at: The Haiti Democracy Project, http://haitipolicy.org/printversions/1637.htm?PHPSESSID=837d5f2252549fa2f1549d8cd3699494.
3. Jenson, "From the Kidnapping," 165.
4. See the transcript at Haiti Democracy Project.
5. Dow, "Occupying and Obscuring Haiti," 5–22.
6. Bellegarde-Smith, "Overview of Haitian Foreign Policy," 265–281.
7. Anna Brickhouse has recently written about the connection between the discourse of blame and disgust surrounding Haitian refugees in the U.S. and Hurricane Katrina victims. See, "L'Ouragan de Flammes (The Hurricane of Flames)," 1121.
8. Jenson, "From the Kidnapping," 169.
9. Lawless, *Haiti's Bad Press*, 51.
10. For apparent states, see Glick-Schiller and Fouron, *Georges Woke Up Laughing*, 27; and Braziel, "Haiti, Guantánomo,'" 12.
11. In an article entitled "Mulatto Literature," which appeared in *The Albion* on July 9, 1853, the Haitian writer Ignace Nau was referred to as "one of the cleverest of the negro novelists" and Dupré was called the "Haytian Molière." When the playwright Pierre Faubert's son won the French prize of honor at the Sorbonne in 1858—"the highest prize ... at the concourse of all the colleges"—it was widely reported in the U.S. press. The northern kingdom of Haiti's *Gazette Royale d'Hayti* was referred to repeatedly in the U.S. press as well. There are also numerous mentions of J. S. Milscent's *L'Abeille Haytienne*, the first Haitian review, in the U.S. press, particularly around the time of Pétion's death. For Faubert's son in the U.S. press see, *Littell's Living Age*, May 7, 1859; *Liberator*, December 24, 1858; *Friends' Review*, December 11, 1858; *Liberator*, October 8, 1858; *African Repository*, December 1858; *Independent*, September 30, 1858; *Farmer's Cabinet*, October 28, 1858. For *L'Abeille Haytienne* see, *Newbury Port Herald*, August 16, 1816; *Baltimore Patriot*, August 17, 1816; *Rhode Island American*, August 16, 1816; *City Gazette*, August 16, 1816; *New England Palladium*, August 13, 1816; *Nantucket Gazette*, August 17, 1816; *Boston Gazette*, August 19, 1816; *Carlisle Gazette*, August 21, 1816; *Hallowel Gazette*, August 21, 1816; *Plattsburgh Republican*, August 24, 1816; *Union*, September 6, 1816; *Vermont Gazette*, September 10, 1816; *Baltimore Patriot*, November 5, 1816; *National Advocate*, November 5, 1816. For mentions of the *Gazette Royale*, see *Nantucket Gazette*, July 8, 1816; *Sun*, July 6, 1816; *Franklin Herald*, July 9, 1816; *Delaware Gazette and Peninsula Advertiser*, July 11, 1816; *Independent American*, July 17, 1816; *Otsego Herald*, July 18, 1816; *Commercial Advertiser*, September 11, 1816.
12. *Le Système colonial dévoilé* (1814); *Notes à M. le Baron V.P. de Malouet* (1814); *Le Cri de la conscience* (1815); *Le Cri de la patrie* (1815); *A Mes Concitoyens!* (1815); *Réflexions adressées aux Haytiens de partie de l'ouest et du sud, sur l'horrible assassinat du Général Delvare, commis au Port- au-Prince, dans la nuit du 25 décembre, 1815, par les ordres de Pétion* (1816); *Communication officielle de trois lettres de Catineau Laroche, ex-colon, agent de Pétion* (1816); *Relation de la fête de la Reine S.M. d'Hayti* (1816); *Réflexions sur une lettre de Mazères, ex-colon français, ... sur les*

noirs et les blancs, la civilization de l'Afrique, le Royaume d'Hayti, etc. (1816); *Réflexions politiques sur quelques ouvrages et journaux français concernant Hayti* (1817); and *Essai sur les causes de la Révolution et des guerres civile d'Hayti* (1819).

13. "Review of New Books," *Literary Gazette; or Journal of Criticism, Science, and the Arts*, February 17, 1821. "Review of New Books." *The Literary Gazette; or Journal of Criticism, Science, and the Arts*, February 17, 1821.

14. "The Namesakes," *Baltimore Patriot*, May 19, 1815.

15. "Boston: Friday Morning, Sept. 15," *Boston Daily Advertiser*, September 15, 1815, 2; repr. *Alexandria Gazette*, September 26, 1815.

16. For the *North American Review*, see Brickhouse, *Transamerican Literary Relations*, 3–4.

17. Cushing, "Article VI—*Refléxions politiques*," 112. Cushing's article on Vastey was very influential and was either referenced or quoted several times in the northern United States. See, for example, "Review of New Books," *Literary Gazette; or Journal of Criticism, Science, and the Arts*, February 17, 1821; "From the Catskill Recorder: Revolutionary Incidents. St. Domingo," *Rhode Island American*, February 13, 1821; "From the Catskill Recorder: Revolutionary Incidents. St. Domingo," *Essex Patriot*, August 18, 1821.

18. "Article V—*Reflexions sur une Lettre de Mezeres* [sic], *Ex-Colon français, addressee à* M. J. C. L. Sismonde de *Sismondi*, etc.," *Analectic Magazine*, May 1817, 403.

19. "Mulatto Literature," *Albion: A Journal of News, Politics, and Literature*, July 9, 1853, 326.

20. Many newspaper articles like the one printed in the *Weekly Visiter* [sic] also referred to "numerous publications" that they had "received from Cape François" (see the issue dated February 1, 1817). Most articles that criticized Vastey or other Haitian writings from the north did so because of what they perceived as the northern kingdom's "false defamation of Pétion." This is particularly the case with those who referred to Vastey's *Le Cri de la Patrie*. See also *Weekly Recorder*, July 10, 1816.

21. McGill, *American Literature*, 1.

22. See Bacon, *Freedom's Journal*, 151, and Fanning, "Roots of Early Black Nationalism," 70.

23. Pasley, *Tyranny of the Printers*, 2.

24. The northern kingdom of Haiti had a very distinct relationship to the northern United States, which differed considerably from its relationship to the southern states. The southern United States maintained a hostile, fear-driven attitude toward Haiti. Evidence of this exists in a report in *L'Abeille Haytienne*, which stated, "Captain Mackenzie reports also that the appearance of the Haitian pavilion in New Orleans had the effect of water on a hydrophobe. The view of our emblematic colors caused them to have violent convulsions" (see the issue dated September 1, 1817). The historian Logan tells us that in fact "most of the trade was between the Northern ports of the United States and Haiti since the attitude of the Southern states was not conducive to the coming of ships and sailors from the free Negro republic" (see Logan, *Diplomatic Relations*, 195). In addition, an article entitled "Look Sharp!" (published in the *Federal Republican & Commercial Gazette*, March 28, 1810) reported that "the mulatto general Rigaud arrived at Philadelphia from France on the 7th" and that "attention is anxiously drawn towards him, by a report that he was lately in this state. . . . It is not for the sake of persecuting an individual that we introduce this article, but the safety of this and the southern states imperiously requires that he should be expelled, if he has really entered them, and that at any rate his motions should be closely watched." This last article was

reprinted in the *Repertory* on April 3, 1810; the *Connecticut Mirror* on April 9, 1810; the *Berkshire reporter* on April 11, 1810; and in the *Sun* on April 21, 1810.

25. For Dessalines in the U.S. press, see Jenson, "Before Malcom X," 331. In 1809 King Henry Christophe sought to counteract his negative image abroad by issuing a heart-felt plea to U.S. merchants. The article stated that its purpose was "to make known the truth, and to bring to light the falsity of the infamous impostures my enemies have spread with so much profusion against me." Christophe's letter was reprinted in the *Observer*, July 30, 1809, and the *American*, August 4, 1809. An additional article in the *New-England Palladium* on August 4, 1809, which made reference to this letter, stated that Christophe's address to the merchants was brought to the United States by a "gentleman from the *West-Indies*." This last article was also reprinted several times. See *Boston Patriot*, August 5, 1809; *Providence Gazette*, August 5, 1809; *Massachusetts Spy; or Worcester Gazette*, August 9, 1809; and *Rutland Herald*, August 19, 1809.

26. Jenson, "Before Malcom X," 33; Desormeaux, "First of the (Black) Memorialists," 135.

27. See Paryz, "Beyond the Traveler's Testimony."

28. Bakhtin, *Dialogic Imagination*, 262–263.

29. For "collective bovarysme," see Price-Mars, *So Spoke the Uncle*, 8. The Haitian literary historians Pradel Pompilus and Dieudonné Fardin have each written that Haitian literature, like all literature, owes something to the literatures that have come before it. J. Michael Dash, who makes one of the principal arguments against using negritude as the dominant mode of understanding nineteenth-century Caribbean literature, has explained that the dismissal of early Haitian literature is largely because "revolutionary ideologies in the francophone Caribbean in the 1930s were constructed around myths of rupture and innovation" leading to a condemnation of nineteenth-century texts that outwardly resembled European literature as "a time blind imitation" (Dash, "Marvelous realism," 70; Dash, "Nineteenth-Century Haiti," 46). See Pompilus, *Manuel Illustré de la littérature haïtienne*, 1; Fardin, *Histoire de la littérature haïtienne*, 8.

30. For the absence of audience, see Bernabé et al. *Eloge de la créolité / In Praise of Creoleness*, 76; and Laroche, *L'Avènement de la littérature haïtienne*, 162–174. For literacy in the nineteenth century, see Egerton, "Politics and Autobiography," 229.

31. Clinton, *Logic and Historic Significance*, 52–53.

32. For Hegel, see Buck-Morss, *Hegel, Haiti, and Universal History*, 60. For Spinoza, see Nesbitt, *Universal Emancipation*, 22–23; and Hutton for Louverture quotation, 54.

33. Jenson, "Before Malcom X," 331.

34. Dash, *Literature and Ideology*, 5.

35. "Annual Report of the Library Company," 52.

36. Boyce-Davies, "Beyond Uni-Centricity," 99.

37. Sheller, "'The Haytian Fear,'" 286.

38. Much of the scholarship on U.S.-Haiti relations is concerned with the reactions of scared southerners, northern abolitionists, or African American activists, but rarely do early Haitian authors significantly figure. For southerners, see Sidbury, "Saint Domingue in Virginia," 539–541; Hunt, *Haiti's Influence on Antebellum America*, 101; Sheller, "'The Haytian Fear,'" 287; and White, "Limits of Fear," 363. For northern abolitionists, see Sheller, "'The Haytian Fear,'" 286; and Clavin, *Toussaint Louverture*, 118. For African Americans, see Fanning, "Roots of Early Black Nationalism," 63; and Dixon, *African America and Haiti*, 8.

39. Drexler, "Haiti, Modernity, and U.S. Identities," 453.

40. Boyce-Davies, "Beyond Uni-Centricity," 96 (emphasis added).

41. Brickhouse, *TransAmerican Literary Relations*, 2.
42. Buell, "American Literary Emergence," 429.
43. Nau, "Littérature," 152–156.
44. Buell, "American Literary Emergence," 424.
45. Brickhouse, *TransAmerican Literary Relations*, 6–7 (emphasis in the original).
46. Glissant, *Caribbean Discourse*, 98.
47. Goudie, *Creole America*, 11.
48. Anderson, *Imagined Communities*, 25 (emphasis in the original).
49. Bellegarde, as quoted in Bellegarde-Smith, "Overview of Haitian Foreign Policy," 58.
50. Brickhouse, *TransAmerican Literary History*, 6.
51. Nau, "Littérature," 155–156.
52. Vastey, *Réflexions politiques*, 32. Henceforth cited in the text as "*RP*."
53. For the authors who do this, see Trouillot, "Odd and the Ordinary," 3.
54. Gillman, "Otra vez Caliban/Encore Caliban: Adaptation/Translation/Americas Studies," 205, 193.
55. Vastey, *Système coloniale*, 95.
56. It was not only Vastey who recognized the difficult subject position of Haitian authors. The following review of *Colonial System*, published in the *Antijacobin Review* in 1818, acknowledges the complicated relationship of the Haitian Revolution to vengeance:

> Of the cruelties practised [*sic*] by the French in St. Domingo, Europe had, in a great measure, till now, been totally ignorant. The mask has, however, been withdrawn, by the liberty which the Haytians have given themselves, and perhaps the most signal vengeance they can now take of their ancient oppressors, is to give an impartial history. In reading over the tract before us we have doubted whether we were in the society of men or of wild beasts; but a little reflection easily convinced us that the brutes of the field could not act as the monsters we have been placed in company with. (315; repr. *Port-Folio*, April 1819).

57. Vastey, *Réflexions sur une lettre de Mazères*, 90. Henceforth cited as "*RM*" in the text.
58. Patterson, *Slavery and Social Death*, 38.
59. *Republican Farmer*, November 26, 1816.
60. *Evening Post*, May 25, 1810.
61. "Royalty," *Niles Weekly Register*, November 9, 1816, 168 (emphasis in the original).
62. Hofmman, *Le Nègre romantique*, 32.
63. Ibid. The article from *Niles Weekly* was published in response to the *Boston Palladium*'s report of a birthday party given for Henry Christophe's wife, Queen Marie-Louise, in 1816. Vastey had published a pamphlet detailing the event, and parts of it appeared in translation in the Boston paper; the article was reprinted in the *Daily National Intelligencer*, October 16, 1816.
64. According to Alyssa Goldstein Sepinwall, the Abbé Grégoire was "disgusted with the return of monarchy" in northern Haiti, and for this reason he was an ardent supporter of Pétion. Sepinwall writes that Grégoire was "appalled that as much of the world was slowly adopting republican principles, the North of Haiti was abandoning them. He was especially incensed at the irony of blacks' creating a system based on arbitrary titles" ("Exporting the Revolution," 48). Grégoire's disdain and unwillingness to correspond with the northern kingdom derived from the fact that he viewed Haiti as a "laboratory for republicanism" (ibid.) and saw Christophe's

kingdom as an obstacle to spreading a republican message throughout the Atlantic World, just as he saw the United States's continued slavery as a similar obstacle. See Grégoire (abbé de), *De la noblesse de la peau*, 86. See also Vastey's letter to Thomas Clarkson, in which he complained that the French priest ignored his letters in Griggs and Prator, *Henri Christophe and Thomas Clarkson*, 180.

65. Vastey, *Essai*, 147–148. Henceforth, cited as *"Essai"* in the text.
66. Vastey, *Réflexions politiques*, 32–33.
67. Pease, "Exceptionalism,"108.
68. Cushing, "Article VI," 124.
69. Ibid., 116. Cushing was not the only U.S. newspaper editor to print positive reviews of Christophe after 1817, as evidenced by the following extract from a letter written by a U.S. person from Virginia who lamented the glowing reports of the Haitian monarch in the northern press: "It astonishes me a great deal to see that the editors of our newspapers treat the name of that monster, Christophe, the soi-disant king of Hayti, with the shadow of respect" (*Boston Daily Advertiser*, June 26, 1816; repr. *Enquirer*, July 6, 1816).
70. Cushing, "Article VI," 119.
71. Rufus as quoted in Zuckerman, "Power of Blackness," 194. Thomas Jefferson, once a proponent of "Toussaint's Clause," which allowed the United States to continue to trade in arms and other goods with Toussaint Louverture during the Haitian Revolution, changed his tune remarkably after Haitian independence, when he began attempting to have a bill imposing a trade embargo on Haiti passed in Congress. The Logan Bill was passed in February of 1806, and it forbade U.S. merchants from trading with any portions of the colony not in possession of France. See Matthewson, "Jefferson and the Nonrecognition of Haiti," 32. Official trade statistics (which do not take into account the illegal trade, of course) show that U.S. exports to the French islands stood at $6.7 million in 1806 but fell to $5.8 million in 1807 and to $1.5 million in 1808 (ibid., 35). When the trade embargo expired in 1810 and was not renewed, trade resumed between the two countries. For a table indicating the trade statistics after 1810, see Logan, *Diplomatic Relations*, 194–195.
72. "Miscellaneous and Literary Intelligence," *North American Review* 1.1 (May 1815): 134.
73. See, "Article V," *Analectic Magazine*, 406.
74. Adams, "Defence of the Constitutions of the Governments of the United States."
75. Cushing, "Article VI," 125.
76. For "century of isolation," see Leyburn, *Haitian People*, 11; and Mintz, Foreword to Leyburn, *Haitian People*, vi.
77. For hostilities, see Logan, *Diplomatic Relations*, 195; Sidbury, "Saint Domingue in Virginia," 551; Farmer, *Uses of Haiti*, 69; Matthewson, *Pro-Slavery Foreign Policy*, 129–140; and Fanning, "Roots of Early Black Nationalism," 73.
78. Farmer, *Uses of Haiti*, 68.
79. McGill, "Market," 150.
80. According to Logan, by 1821, "American interests in the northern part of Haiti were sufficiently important to make it a topic of national interest." Logan tells us that "Haitian trade [with the U.S.] generally ranked above that of Norway and Denmark, Sweden and the Swedish West Indies; South America, Austria, Turkey and the Levant; Egypt, Mocha and Aden; Morocco and the Barbary States; Africa, generally; the South Seas; and the northwest coast of America" (*Diplomatic Relations*, 194). Farmer adds to this that "with brief exception . . . the United States and Haiti have been trading partners from the first decade of the nineteenth century, when they were the only independent republics in the hemisphere. That the United

States did not officially recognize Haiti did little to alter the fact that, by 1851, the United States sold more goods to Haiti than it did to any other Latin American country, including Mexico" (*Uses of Haiti*, 51).

81. Hickey, "America's Response," 373.

82. Fanning, "Roots," 78. For more information about this, see also Logan, *Diplomatic Relations*, 198; and Hickey, "America's Response," 373, where he argues that this campaign actually began much earlier than the 1820s. Hickey writes that as early as 1804 the Philadelphia newspaper the *United States Gazette* led the way with support among the Federalists of the north for opposing limited trade with Haiti.

83. Milscent, "Suite des Considérations sur l'île d'Haiti," 3.

84. See Limonade's letter as translated in Griggs and Prator, *Henri Christophe*, 174.

85. Clay as quoted in Matthewson, "Jefferson and the Nonrecognition of Haiti," 234.

86. This tacit recognition was politically important precisely because it was understood among the three governments that to treat with Christophe as a king or Pétion as a president was to recognize the independence of the country. This much was evident by the conflict between the U.S.-appointed agent Septimus Tyler's refusal to address Christophe as the king after the latter seized the property of some U.S. merchants in 1810 (for more historical details, see n.88 below). This situation led to an eventual showdown between John Quincy Adams and Christophe in 1817 (see Logan, *Diplomatic Relations*, 189–190), ending with the former boldly refusing to address Christophe as the king of Haiti, ever. The same problem of discursive, "tacit" recognition was an issue for France when Thomas Clarkson agreed to act as an emissary between Christophe's kingdom and the French monarch. First, the French government refused to treat with Clarkson formally as long as he presented himself as a government agent of Haiti. Christophe wanted Clarkson to transmit his proposal for the conditions of opening negotiations with respect to French recognition (written by the Duke of Limonade) to Louis XVIII and the French cabinet. Clarkson's response was this: "With respect to the Diplomatic Paper by which your Majesty authorized me to act as your Envoy at Paris . . . we were unanimously of the opinion that the French Cabinet would not receive it. By receiving it the . . . Cabinet would be acknowledging the independence of Hayti at the very outset" (translated in Griggs and Prator, *Henri Christophe*, 97–98). It goes without saying that Clarkson, a frequent correspondent of Christophe, recognized the independence of Haiti, but he also recognized that he was acting as an "individual" rather than a government agent (translated in Griggs and Prator, *Henri Christophe*, 161). Vastey, Limonade, and Christophe, too, understood the implications of treating with France under these circumstances—that is to say, without an emissary. Both Vastey (as a private citizen) and Limonade (in an official capacity) wrote that it was impossible for the Haitians to treat with France without the country first recognizing Haiti's independence because to do so would have been to have "tacitly recognized their rights of sovereignty and have renounced independence" (Vastey, *RM*, 134). To enter into negotiations with France upon a point that Haitians wanted a priori recognized would have been to legitimate France's position in the first place. In this way, Haiti and France were engaged in bold stand-off since neither side felt it could even communicate directly with the other side without losing some of its justification.

87. Berlant, "Citizenship," 40.

88. Quotation from Pasley, *Tyranny of the Printers*, 317. As far as the U.S. government was concerned, U.S. merchants were free to recognize the independence of Haiti only when acting as commercial or private individuals. The minute they stepped into the role of government agent, as in the case of Septimus Tyler, Christophe, Pétion, and Haiti ceased to exist as separate

and sovereign. Beginning in 1812, Henry Christophe was engaged in a dispute with the U.S. government over $125,000 dollars that he claimed he had sent there for the purchase of supplies in 1810. In "retaliation" Christophe seized U.S. cargoes valued at $132,000. When the U.S. government attempted to intervene on behalf of the merchants, Christophe refused to respond to the claim. Christophe charged that Tyler, the agent who had been appointed to oversee the matter in 1817, had addressed his letter to Christophe rather than to King Henry I. Subsequent attempts to collect the claim failed because John Quincy Adams refused to give Tyler the authority to address Christophe as the king. The dispute was never resolved because Adams determined that the two rulers were at an impasse, finding that "no further measures" would be "practicable on the part of the Executive in th[at] case" (quoted in Logan, *Diplomatic Relations*, 184–190). This conflict was widely reported in U.S. newspapers when it first occurred. Each of these newspapers published one of three versions of the story in which Christophe wanted to start a "predatory war" of commerce with the United States. See *New York Commercial Advertiser, Mercantile Advertiser, New York Herald*, April 28, 1810; *Connecticut Mirror*, April 30, 1810; *Fredonian, New England Palladium, Repertory*, May 1, 1810; *New York Spectator*, May 2, 1810; *Newburyport Herald, Northern Whig, Virginia Patriot*, May 4, 1810; *Essex Register, Freedman's Friend, Merrimack Intelligencer, Weekly Visiter* [sic], May 5, 1810; *Eagle, Herald of Liberty, Independent American*, May 8, 1810; *Berkshire Reporter, Political Barometer*, May 9, 1810; *Connecticut Journal*, May 10, 1810; *Cooperstown Federalist, Portsmouth Oracle, True American*, May 12, 1810; *Supporter*, May 19, 1810; *Reporter*, May 21, 1810; *New-Hampshire Gazette*, May 22, 1810; *Evening Post*, May 25, 1810; *Alexandria Daily Gazette*, May 29, 1810; *Courier*, May 30, 1810.

89. "Article V—*Reflexions sur une Lettre de Mezeres* [sic], *Ex-Colon français, addressee à M. J. C. L. Sismonde de Sismondi*, etc.," *Analectic Magazine*, May 1817, 410.

90. "History of Hayti," *Boston Commercial Gazette* 62.43 (October 31, 1822): 1; hereafter referred to as "*BCG* et al." in the notes. This article was reprinted several times. See *Times and Weekly Advertiser*, November 11, 1822; *Nantucket Inquiror* [sic], January 7, 1823; *Hampshire Gazette*, November 13, 1822; *New Hampshire Observatory*, February 3, 1823.

91. According to Matthewson, Timothy Pickering of Massachusetts, who had helped to broker Toussaint's Clause, disagreed with the trade embargo of 1805 and 1806, noting that it would harm the trade for which he had arduously labored during the Adams administration; he claimed that the Haitians' only fault was "having black skin" (as quoted in Matthewson, "Jefferson and the Non-Recognition of Haiti," 235–236.

92. For a newspaper article that made precisely this argument, see the *Northern Whig*, December 2, 1817. In 1817, when the United States began to support and recognize the former Spanish colonies of South America, a couple of U.S. newspapers drew explicit connections to the situation in St. Domingue/Haiti, noting that the difference was that Haitians were black. Others, like the *Dedham Gazette* on November 21, 1817, for example, wrote that the United States should not recognize "St. Domingo" or the Spanish colonies either.

93. "From a Late English Paper," *City of Washington Gazette*, May 21, 1818, 2; repr. in the *Philanthropist*, March 20, 1819, 228.

94. "'State of Hayti,'" Review of "La [sic] Système colonial dévoilé"—Par le Baron de Vastey," *Port-Folio* 7.4 (April 1819): 315.

95. *BCG* et al. Reprinted in *Times and Weekly Adviser*, November 12, 1822; *Nantucket Inquiror* [sic], January 7, 1823; *Hampshire Gazette*, November 13, 1822; *New Hampshire Repository*, February 3, 1823.

96. See the *Analectic Magazine*, May 1817.

97. "St. Domingo," *New York Herald*, April 7, 1804, 2. For additional examples of the many articles in which this was done, see *Green Mountain Patriot*, March 28, 1804; *Oracle Post*, April 10, 1804; *Bee*, April 10, 1804.

98. Milscent, "Considérations sur l'île d'Haiti, par J.S. Milscent, Haitien," *L'Abeille Haytienne*, August 1, 1817, 7.

99. The most telling conflation of the government with the people occurs when Vastey uses an article that was written in the *Gazette Royale d'Hayti*, the official publication of Henry Christophe's kingdom, to express his disdain over the actions of a U.S. merchant ship from New York named the *Sidney Crispin*, which was under the captainship of Elesha Kenn. Reprinted in his *Essai*, Vastey's article stated that on October 17, 1816, Crispin along with his crew brought a letter from two French warships hovering off the coast of Cap-Henry to the Count of Marmelade seeking to open negotiations with Christophe. Because the letter did not recognize the sovereignty of Christophe, addressing him as General Christophe rather than King Christophe, the count naturally refused to transmit the letter. In the article Vastey conflated the "dishonorable" actions of these merchants with their government when he stated that Christophe "was astonished that Americans who had been trading with Haiti for so many years, and who enjoy the protection of the government, and who, like us, had been brought to liberty and independence, could have burdened themselves with a commission that was as dishonorable as it was disturbing for men who belong to a nation that is friends with Haiti" (Vastey, *Essai*, 351–356). This event was widely reported in the U.S. press. See *New-England Palladium & Commercial Advertiser*, December 3, 1816; *Albany Advertiser*, December 4, 1816; *Boston Patriot and Morning Advertiser*, December 4, 1816; *Essex Register*, December 4, 1816; *American Advocate and Kennebec Advertiser*, December 7, 1816; *People's Advocate*, December 7, 1816; *Weekly Visiter* [sic], December 7, 1816; *Recorder*, December 10, 1816; *Newburyport Herald*, December 10, 1816; *American*, December 11, 1816; *Burlington Gazette*, December 12, 1816; *Merrimack Intelligencer*, December 14, 1816; *Columbian Register*, December 21, 1816; *American Beacon and Commercial Diary*, December 23, 1816; *People's Advocate*, March 22, 1817. See also the captain's defense of his actions, which was printed in several U.S. newspapers: *Commercial Advertiser*, December 3, 1816; *Baltimore Patriot*, December 5, 1816; *Boston Daily Advertiser*, December 6, 1816; *New-England Palladium*, December 6, 1816; *Alexandria Gazette*, December 9, 1816; *Lancaster Journal*, December 9, 1816; *American Beacon and Commercial Diary*, December 10, 1816.

100. See Vastey, *Notes*, 10.

101. See Vastey, *Essai*, 265.

102. Ardouin, *Études sur l'histoire d'Haiti*, 25.

103. Even though both Vastey and Christophe publicly maintained that non-recognition from both the United States and England was merely a fable, they still actively sought formal recognition. See, for example, Vastey's letter to Clarkson, November 29, 1819, translated in Griggs and Prator, *Henri Christophe and Thomas Clarkson*, 180–181, and Christophe to Clarkson, November 20, 1819, translated in ibid., 169.

104. For abolitionist publications, see, *Christian Observer*, December 1817; *Anti-Slavery Record*, November 1835; *Freedom's Journal*, February 7, 1829, and February 14, 1829).

105. *City of Washington Gazette*, May 21, 1818; repr. in the *Philanthropist*, March 20, 1819. These words, however, were reprinted from the 1818 English translation of Vastey's *Reflexions politiques* published in London. See *Political Remarks*, 10.

106. See Hunt, *Haiti's Influence*, 91.

107. Nesbitt, "Idea of 1804," 38.

108. Cushing, "Article VI," 114. British reviews of Vastey's works often used a similar language. The *British Review* (1820) equally applauded Vastey's writing by saying that "a black" who had once been "deplorably illiterate" stood as a "specimen of the native black genius," while the *Monthly Repository of Theology and General Literature* (1819) wrote of Vastey's *Reflexions*, "We have here a great curiosity, a vindication of the Negroes by a Negroe." See "History, Literature, and Present State of Hayti," *British Review and London Critical Journal* 15 (1820): 74; and "Article VI," *Monthly Repository of Theology and General Literature* 14 (1819): 329.

109. Cushing, "Article VI," 120.

110. Sepinwall, "Exporting the Revolution," 45.

111. Buffon's naturalist writings were premised on the assumption that the "Negro" represented a "degenerate" form of the white race. The French author even proposed racial mixing to speed up the process of regeneration, writing that if miscegenation were promoted, "the Mulatto would have only a light trace of brown that would disappear altogether within the next generations; it would only take therefore 150 or 200 years to clean the skin of a Negro by this method of mixing with white blood" (*Histoire naturelle générale et particuliére*, 14:313–314). It was not long before racial mixing was proffered as a possible solution to help end slavery and to hasten the "regeneration" of the black race. In his *Études des races humaines*, Michel-Hyacinthe Deschamps wrote, for example:

> The *regeneration* of the *human species*, or the return of all the colored races to the white type, is possible, suppressing the odious prejudice, by means of perpetual crossing of the métis with the primordial white, now European, race. We would whiten the natives of an island, of a country, of a vast colony. The Negroes would not have to be born slaves, our *inferior brothers*; they are our equals in the order of creation; they have the right—as do we—to the sun, to liberty, and to the banquet of life. . . . Glory to the promoters of the emancipation of the slaves! (135, emphasis in the original)

A reviewer of John R. Beard's biography of Toussaint Louverture also encouraged miscegenation as a way to help end slavery in the United States, writing that "many sensible men who have lived in Hayti are of opinion that an increase of the mulatto stock, by legitimate and permanent sanctions would vastly improve it, in as much as the public interests fare well at the heads of these men of mixed blood who are not, as we commonly supposed, faded copies of both black and white, but specimens of an original ability as yet but imperfectly displayed" ("Toussaint L'Ouverture," *North American Review*, 1864, 596).

112. Fanuzzi, "Taste, Manners, and Miscegenation," 580.

113. See, Grégoire, *De la noblesse*, 52, 82.

114. Vastey, *Système*, vi.

115. See Vastey, *RP*, 1.

116. See Goudie, *Creole America*, 77–78; and Slotkin, *Regeneration Through Violence*, 5.

117. Ames, *Works*, 458.

118. Ibid., 460.

119. Emerson, "The American Scholar," 51 and 70–71.

120. Whitman, "Democratic Vistas."

121. For literacy as humanity, see Chukwudi, Introduction, 5; and Aravamudan, *Tropicopolitans*, 270.

122. *City of Washington Gazette*, May 21, 1818; repr. in the *Philanthropist*, March 20, 1819.
123. Emerson, "Nature," 7 (emphasis in the original).
124. Brickhouse, *Transamerican Literary Relations*, 7.
125. *BCG* et al.
126. Farmer, *Uses of Haiti*, 72.
127. *BCG* et al.
128. Grégoire, *De la noblesse*, 86.
129. Brissot de Warville, as quoted in Fanuzzi, "Taste," 582.
130. Nesbitt, "Idea of 1804," 8, 17.
131. For revolution as incomplete, see Fanuzzi, "Taste," 582. For virtues of the revolution, see Fischer, *Modernity Disavowed*, 9.
132. Vastey, *Système*, vi.
133. Bauer, "Hemispheric Studies," 236.
134. During, "Literature—Nationalism's Other?" 139 (emphasis in the original).
135. See Vastey's letter as translated in Griggs and Prator, *Henri Christophe*, 180–181. See also, Farmer, *Uses of Haiti*, 69.
136. Moten, "Democracy," 77.
137. Vastey, *Réflexions sur une lettre de Mazères*, 36. For an intriguing argument about Dessalines's desire to export the revolution in Haiti elsewhere in the Americas, see Jenson, "Before Malcom X," 340.
138. Vastey, *Notes*, 7. Here, Vastey specifically refutes the writing of the former French colonist Pierre Victor Malouet, who had written that "the [Haitian] revolution has transferred from the whites to the blacks the question of control over the Caribbean, and our unfortunate rivalries [*nos misérables rivalités*] must give way in the face of the great interest in the region that is obviously developing" (*Collection de mémoires*, 4:2).
139. Hobsbawm, *Nations and Nationalism*, 31.
140. Glissant, *Introduction à une poétique du divers*, 17.
141. Césaire, *Discourse on Colonialism*, 56.
142. Saint-Rémy, Foreword, xxi.

EPILOGUE

1. Cited in Jackson and Bacon, *African Americans and the Haitian Revolution*, 170.
2. Arendt, *On Revolution*, 24.
3. Michelet, *History of the French Revolution*, 17.
4. Dubois and Garrigus, *Slave Revolution*, 131.
5. Stoddard, *French Revolution in San Domingo*, preface.
6. This phrase is taken from the title of a 1989 exhibition in Paris done by the Haitian artist Edouard Duvall Carrié.
7. Césaire, *Toussaint Louverture*.
8. Cited in Nesbitt, *Caribbean Critique*, 3.
9. Cited in Garraway, *Tree of Liberty*, 70.
10. See L'Ouverture, *Haitian Revolution*, 23.
11. For a discussion of the idea of the Long Revolution of Haiti, see Bogues, "And What About the Human?," 29–47.

12. I develop the idea of the slave as a "living corpse" drawing from the poetry of Nicolas Guillen particularly his poem, "I Came on a Slave Ship." For a further discussion of this, see Bogues, "And What About the Human?"

13. Teaching American History, www.archives.govt/exhibits/charters.

14. Ibid.

15. Letter to London Merchants (1766), http://www.gunstonhall.org/library/archives/manuscripts/letter_London_Public_Ledger.html.

16. Declaration of Independence, www.archives.govt/exhibits /charter/declaration.

17. Arendt, *On Revolution*, 109.

18. Du Bois, *Black Reconstruction*, 11.

19. James, *Black Jacobins*, 33.

20. As Elizabeth Maddock Dillon writes, slaves might be considered "bare labor" because, although treated inhumanly, they had economic and juridical value. See Dillon, *New World Drama*, 26–27.

21. For a further discussion of this see Bogues, "And What About the Human?"

22. Cugoano, *Thoughts and Sentiments*, 17.

WORKS CITED

1802 en Guadeloupe et à Saint-Domingue: Réalités et mémoire. Gourbeyre: Archives Départementales, 2003.
Adams, Henry. *History of the United States of America*. Vol. 1. New York: Charles Scribner's Sons, 1889–1891.
———. *History of the United States of American during the First Administration of Thomas Jefferson* [1891–1896]. 2 vols., reprint ed. New York: Antiquarian Press, 1962.
Adams, John. "Defence of the Constitutions of the Governments of the United States." 1787. http://press-pubs.uchicago.edu/founders/documents/v1ch11s10.html.
Agamben, Giorgio. *Homo Sacer: Sovereign Power and Bare Life*. Translated by Daniel Heller-Roazen. Stanford, CA: Stanford University Press, 1995.
Alderson, Robert. "Charleston's Rumored Slave Revolt of 1793." In *The Impact of the Haitian Revolution in the Atlantic World*, edited by David Patrick Geggus, 93–111. Columbia: University of South Carolina Press, 2001.
Alexander, Leslie M. "'The Black Republic': The Influence of the Haitian Revolution on Northern Black Political Consciousness, 1816–1862." In *African Americans and the Haitian Revolution: Selected Essays and Historical Documents*, edited by Maurice Jackson and Jacqueline Bacon, 57–79. New York: Routledge, 2010.
Ames, Fischer. *The Works of Fisher Ames, Compiled by a Number of His Friends*. Oxford: Oxford University Press, 1809.
Anderson, Benedict. *Imagined Communities: Reflections on the Origin and Spread of Nationalism*. London: Verso, 1999.
Anderson, Fred. *The Crucible of War: The Seven Years' War and the Fate of Empire in British North America, 1754–1766*. New York: Knopf, 2000.
"The Annual Report of the Library Company of Philadelphia for the Year 1971." Philadelphia: Library Company of Philadelphia, 1972.
Aptheker, Herbert. *American Negro Slave Revolts*. New York: Columbia University Press, 1943.
Arango y Parreño, Francisco de. *Obras*. 2 vols. Havana: Ministerio de Educación, 1952.
Aravamudan, Srinivas. *Tropicopolitans: Colonialism and Agency, 1688–1804*. Durham, NC: Duke University Press, 1999.
Ardouin, Beaubrun. *Études sur l'histoire d'Haïti* [1853–1860]. Vol. 4. Port-au-Prince: François Dalencourt, 1958.
Arendt, Hannah. *On Revolution*. London: Penguin Books, 1965.
Armstrong, Nancy, and Leonard Tennenhouse. "The Problem of Population and the Form of the American Novel." *American Literary History* 20 (2008): 667–685.

Arner, Katherine. "Making Yellow Fever American: The Early American Republic, the British Empire and the Geopolitics of Disease in the Atlantic World." *Atlantic Studies* 7.4 (December 2010): 447–471.
Azouvi, François. "La Polémique du magnétisme animal." Foreword to *Le Magnétiseur amoureux*. Paris: J. Vrin, 2006.
Backus, Margot Gayle. *The Gothic Family Romance: Heterosexuality, Child Sacrifice, and the Anglo-Irish Colonial Order*. Durham, NC: Duke University Press, 1999.
Bacon, Jacqueline. "'A Revolution Unexampled in the History of Man': The Haitian Revolution in *Freedom's Journal*, 1827–1829." In *African Americans and the Haitian Revolution: Selected Essays and Historical Documents*, edited by Maurice Jackson and Jacqueline Bacon, 81–92. New York: Routledge, 2010.
———. *Freedom's Journal: The First African American Newspaper*. New York: Lexington Books, 2007.
Bakhtin, M. M. *The Dialogic Imagination*. Edited by Michael Holquist. Translated by Caryl Emerson and Michael Holquist. Austin: University of Texas Press, 1981.
Baptist, Ed. *The Half Has Never Been Told: Slavery and the Making of American Capitalism*. New York: Basic Books, 2014.
———. "The Second Slavery and the First American Republic." *Almanack Braziliense*, North America, n. 5 (May 2013). http://www.almanack.unifesp.br/index.php/almanack/article/view/1001.
Barbé-Marbois, François. *Histoire de la Louisiane et de la cession de cette colonie par la France aux États-Unis de l'Amérique septentrionale*. Paris: Firmin Didot, 1829.
Barnes, Elizabeth. *States of Sympathy: Seduction and Democracy in the American Novel*. New York: Columbia University Press, 1997.
Bauer, Ralph. "Hemispheric Studies." *PMLA* 124 (January 2009): 234–250.
Baur, John Edward. "Mulatto Machiavelli, Jean Pierre Boyer, and the Haiti of His Day." *Journal of Negro History* 32.3 (July 1947): 307–353.
———. "The Presidency of Nicolas Geffrard of Haiti." *Americas* 10.4 (April 1954): 425–461.
Beard, J. R. *The Life of Toussaint L'Ouverture, the Negro Patriot of Hayti*. Westport, CT: Negro Universities Press, 1970.
———. *Toussaint L'Ouverture: A Biography and Autobiography*. Boston: J. Redpath, 1863.
Beauvois, Frédérique. "L'Indemnité de Saint-Domingue: 'Dette d'indépendance' ou 'rançon de l'esclavage'?" *French Colonial History* 10 (2009): 109–124.
Beckert, Sven. "Emancipation and Empire: Reconstructing the Worldwide Web of Cotton Production in the Age of the American Civil War." *American Historical Review*, 109.5 (December 2004): 1405–1438.
———. *Empire of Cotton: A Global History*. New York: Knopf, 2014.
Belaubre, Christophe, Jordana Dym, and John Savage, eds. *Napoleon's Atlantic: The Impact of Napoleonic Empire in the Atlantic World*. Leiden: Brill, 2010.
Bellegarde-Smith, Patrick. "Overview of Haitian Foreign Policy and Relations: A Schematic Analysis." In *Haiti: Today and Tomorrow: An Interdisciplinary Study*, edited by Charles Foster and Albert Valdman, 265–281. Lanham, MD: University Press of America, 1984.
Bemis, Samuel Flagg. *A Diplomatic History of the United States*. New York: Henry Holt, 1953.
Benedicty-Kokken, Alessandra. *Spirit Possession in French, Haitian, and Vodou Thought: An Intellectual History*. Lanham, MD: Lexington Books, 2015.

Benjamin, Georges J. *La Diplomatie d'Anténor Firmin: Ses péripeties, ses aspects.* Nancy, France: Imprimerie Grandville, 1957.
Benjamin, Thomas. *The Atlantic World: Europeans, Africans, Indians and Their Shared History.* Cambridge: Cambridge University Press, 2009.
Benot, Yves. "Bonaparte et la démence coloniale." In *Mourir pour les Antilles: Indépendance nègre ou esclavage, 1802–1804*, edited by Michel Martin and Alain Yacou. Paris: Éditions Caribéennes, 1991.
———. *La Démence coloniale sous Napoléon.* Paris: La Découverte, 1991.
———. *La Révolution française et la fin des colonies.* Paris: La Découverte, 1987.
Berlant, Lauren. "Citizenship." In *Keywords for American Cultural Studies*, edited by Glenn Hendler and Bruce Burgett, 37–42. New York: New York University Press, 2007.
Berlin, Ira. *Generations of Captivity: a History of African-American Slaves.* Cambridge, MA: Belknap Press of Harvard University Press, 2003.
Bernabé, Jean, et al. *Eloge de la créolité / In Praise of Creoleness.* Paris: Gallimard, 1993.
Bethel, Elizabeth Rauh. "Images of Hayti: The Construction of an Afro-American Lieu de Mémoire." *Callaloo* 15.3 (Summer 1992): 827–841.
Blackburn, Robin. *The Overthrow of Colonial Slavery, 1776–1848.* London: Verso, 1988.
Blaufarb, Rafe. *Napoleon: Symbol for an Age.* Boston: Bedford, 2008.
Bogues, Anthony. "And What About the Human?: Freedom, Human Emancipation, and the Radical Imagination." *Boundary 2* 39.3 (Fall 2012): 29–47.
———. *Black Heretics, Black Prophets: Radical Political Intellectuals.* New York: Routledge, 2003.
———. "The Haitian Revolution and the Making of Freedom in Modernity." Speech, presented at University of Pennsylvania, Philadelphia, March 25, 2005.
Bolster, W. Jeffrey. *Black Jacks: African American Seamen in the Age of Sail.* Cambridge, MA: Harvard University Press, 1997.
Boudreau, Kristin. *Sympathy in American Fiction: American Sentiments from Jefferson to the Jameses.* Gainesville: University of Florida Press, 2002.
Bourguignon, Erika. "Spirit Possession." In *A Companion to Psychological Anthropology: Modernity and Psychocultural Change*, edited by Conerly Carole Casey and Robert B. Edgerton. 374–388. Malden, MA: Blackwell Publishing, 2005.
Bowman, Albert H. "Pichon, the United States, and Louisiana." *Diplomatic History* 1 (1977): 257–270.
Boyce-Davies, Carol. "Beyond Uni-Centricity: Transcultural Black Presences." *Research in African Literatures* 30.2 (1999): 96–109.
Boyd, Julian. "Jefferson, Freneau, and the Founding of the *National Gazette*." In *The Papers of Thomas Jefferson*, edited by Julian Boyd, 20:718–753. Princeton, NJ: Princeton University Press, 1950–2013.
Bradford, Samuel. *The Imposter Detected, or, A Review of Some of the Writings of "Peter Porcupine," By Timothy Tickletoby.* Philadelphia: Free and Independent Political and Literary Press of Thomas Bradford, 1797.
Branson, Susan. *These Fiery Frenchified Dames: Women and Political Culture in Early National Philadelphia.* Philadelphia: University of Pennsylvania Press, 2001.
———, and Leslie Patrick. "Étrangers dans un Pays Étrange: Saint-Dominguan Refugees of Color in Philadelphia." In *The Impact of the Haitian Revolution in the Atlantic World*, edited by David Patrick Geggus, 193–208. Columbia: University of South Carolina, 2001.

Braziel, Jana Evans. "Haiti, Guantánomo, and the 'One Indispensable Nation': U.S. Imperialism, 'Apparent States,' and Post-Colonial Problematics of Sovereignty." *Cultural Critique* 64 (Fall 2006): 127–160.

Bric, Maurice J. "The Irish and the Evolution of the 'New Politics.'" In *The Irish in America: Immigration, Assimilation, Impact*, edited by P. J. Drudy, 143–168. Cambridge: Cambridge University Press, 1985.

Brickhouse, Anna. "L'Ouragan de Flammes (The Hurricane of Flames): New Orleans and Transamerican Catastrophe, 1866/2005." *American Quarterly Review* 59.4 (2007): 11–21.

———. *Transamerican Literary Relations and the Nineteenth-Century Public Sphere*. Cambridge: Cambridge University Press, 2004.

———. "The Writing of Haiti: Pierre Faubert, Harriet Beecher Stowe, and Beyond." *American Literary History* 13.3 (Fall 2001): 407–444.

Brockett, O. G. "The European Career of Alexandre Placide." *Southern Communication Journal* 27.4 (1962): 306–313.

Brooks, Lynn Matluck. "A Decade of Brilliance: Dance Theatre in Late-Eighteenth-Century Philadelphia." *Dance Chronicle* 12.3 (1989): 333–365.

Brown, Charles Brockden. *An Address to the Government of the United States on the Cessation of Louisiana to the French, and on the Late Breach of Treaty by the Spaniards, Including the Translation of a Memorial, on the War of St. Domingo, and the Cessation of Mississippi to France, Drawn up by a Counselor of State*. Philadelphia: John Conrad and Co., 1803.

———. *Arthur Mervyn, or, Memoirs of the Year 1793*. Edited by Sydney J. Krause and Norman S. Grabo. Kent, OH: Kent State University Press, 1977.

———. *Edgar Huntly; Or, Memoirs of a Sleep-Walker*. New York: Penguin Classics, 1988.

———. "On the Consequences of Abolishing the Slave Trade to the West Indian Colonies." *Literary Magazine, and American Register* 4.26 (November 1805): 375–381.

———. *The Rhapsodist and Other Uncollected Writings*. Edited by Harry R. Warfel. Delmar, NY: Scholars' Facsimiles & Reprints, 1977.

Brown, Gillian. *The Consent of the Governed: The Lockean Legacy in Early American Culture*. Cambridge, MA.: Harvard University Press, 2001.

Brown, Gordon S. *Toussaint's Clause: The Founding Fathers and the Haitian Revolution*. Jackson: University of Mississippi Press, 2005.

Brown, William Wells. *The Black Man, His Antecedents, His Genius, and His Achievements*. New York: Thomas Hamilton, 1863.

———. *St. Domingo: Its Revolutions and Its Patriots* [1855]. Philadelphia: Rhistoric Publications, 1969.

———. *Three Years in Europe; or, Places I Have Seen and People I Have Met*. London: Charles Gilpin, 1852.

Bruce, H. Addington. *The Romance of American Expansion*. New York: Moffat, 1909.

Buck-Morss, Susan. *Hegel, Haiti, and Universal History*. Pittsburgh, PA: University of Pittsburgh Press, 2009.

———, Sibylle Fischer, and David Scott. Book Discussion: "Susan Buck-Morss, *Hegel, Haiti, and Universal History*." *Small Axe* 14.3 (2010): 152–185.

Buell, Laurence. "American Literary Emergence as a Postcolonial Phenomenon." *American Literary History* 4.3 (1992): 411–442.

Buffon, Georges Louis Leclerc, Comte de. *Histoire naturelle générale et particuliére, avec la description du cabinet du roy*. [1766]. Vol. 14. http://www.buffon.cnrs.fr/?lang=.

Burke, Edmund. *The Speeches and Writings of Edmund Burke.* 9 vols. Oxford: Clarendon Press, 1991–1997.
Burns, James M. *The Vineyard of Liberty.* New York: Knopf, 1982.
Cabon, R. P. Adolphe. *Histoire d'Haïti* [1895–1919]. 4 vols. Port-au-Prince: Éditions de la Petite Revue, 1940.
Cahill, Edward. *Liberty of the Imagination: Aesthetic Theory, Literary Form, and Politics in the Early United States.* Philadelphia: University of Pennsylvania Press, 2012.
Calderón, María Teresa, and Clément Thibaud, eds. *Las Revoluciones en el mundo Atlántico.* Bogotá: Taurus, 2006.
Canfield, Leon H. *The Making of Modern America.* Boston: Houghton Mifflin, 1950.
Carey, Matthew. *A Short Account of the Malignant Fever, Lately Prevalent in Philadelphia*, 4th ed. Philadelphia, 1794.
Carlson, Julie A. "New Lows in Eighteenth-Century Theater: The Rise of Mungo." *European Romantic Review* 18.2 (2007): 139–147.
Carman, Harry J., et al. *A History of the American People*, 3rd ed. New York: Knopf, 1967.
Carretta, Vincent. "Early African-American Literature?" In *Beyond Douglass: New Perspectives on Early African-American Literature*, edited by Michael J. Drexler and Ed White, 91–106. Lewisburg, PA: Bucknell University Press, 2008.
Carson, David A. "The Role of Congress in the Acquisition of the Louisiana Territory." *Louisiana History* 26 (1985): 369–383.
Carter, Henry Rose. *Yellow Fever: An Epidemiological and Historical Study of Its Place of Origin.* Edited by Laura Armistead Carter and Wade Hampton Frost. Baltimore: Williams & Wilkins Co., 1931.
Castronovo, Russ. *Fathering the Nation: American Genealogies of Slavery and Freedom.* Berkeley: University of California Press, 1996.
Cayton, Andrew. "'Relations of Blood and Affection': The Origins of Patriotism in the Age of Jefferson." In *The Louisiana Purchase and Its Peoples: Perspectives from the New Orleans Conference*, edited by Paul E. Hoffman. Lafayette: Louisiana Historical Association, 2004.
Césaire, Aimé. *Discourse on Colonialism.* New York: Monthly Review Press, 2000.
———. *Toussaint Louverture: La Révolution Française et le Problème Colonial.* Paris: Presence Africaine, 1981.
Chakrabarty, Dipesh. *Provincializing Europe: Postcolonial Thought and Historical Difference.* Princeton, NJ: Princeton University Press, 2000.
Cheah, Pheng, and Bruce Robbins, eds. *Cosmopolitics: Thinking and Feeling Beyond the Nation-State.* Minneapolis: University of Minnesota Press, 1998.
Chertok, Léon, and Raymond de Saussure. *The Therapeutic Revolution, from Mesmer to Freud.* New York: Brunner/Mazel, 1979.
Chidsey, Donald B. *Louisiana Purchase.* New York: Crown, 1972.
Childs, Frances Sergeant. *French Refugee Life in the United States, 1790–1800.* Baltimore: Johns Hopkins University Press, 1940.
Clavin, Mattew J. "Race, Rebellion, and the Gothic: Inventing the Haitian Revolution." *Early American Studies* 5.1 (Spring 2007): 1–29.
———. "A Second Haitian Revolution: John Brown, Toussaint Louverture, and the Making of the American Civil War." *Civil War History* 54.2 (2008): 117–145.
———. *Toussaint Louverture and the American Civil War: The Promise and Peril of a Second Haitian Revolution.* Philadelphia: University of Pennsylvania Press, 2009.

Cleves, Rachel Hope. *The Reign of Terror in America: Visions of Violence from Anti-Jacobinism to Antislavery*. Cambridge: Cambridge University Press, 2009.

Clinton, A. *The Logic and Historic Significance of the Haitian Revolution and the Cosmological Roots of Haitian Freedom*. Kingston, Jamaica: Arawak Publications, 2005.

Cobbett, William. *Detection of a Conspiracy, Formed by the United Irishmen, with the Evident Intention of Aiding the Tyrants of France in Subverting the Government of the United States of America. By Peter Porcupine*. Philadelphia: Published by William Cobbett, 1798.

———. *Tit for Tat, or, A Purge for a Pill: being an answer to a scurrilous pamphlet, lately published, entitled "A Pill for Porcupine."* Philadelphia: Published by William Cobbett, 1796.

Cohen, Lara Langer. "Notes from the State of Saint Domingue: The Practice of Citation in *Clotel*." In *Early African American Print Culture*, edited by Lara Langer Cohen and Jordan Stein, 161–177. Philadelphia: University of Pennsylvania Press, 2012.

Cole, Jean Lee. "Theresa and Blake: Mobility and Resistance in Antebellum African American Serialized Fiction." *Callaloo* 34.1 (2011): 158–175.

Corporation of Charleston. *An Account of the Late Intended Insurrection Among a Portion of the Blacks of This City; Published by the Authority of the Corporation of Charleston*. Charleston, SC: A. E. Miller, 1822.

Cotlar, Seth. "Reading the Foreign News, Imagining an American Public Sphere: Radical and Conservative Visions of 'the Public' in Mid-1790s Newspapers." In *Periodical Literature in Eighteenth-Century America*, edited by Mark L. Kamrath and Sharon M. Harris, 307–338. Knoxville: University of Tennessee Press, 2005.

———. *Tom Paine's America: The Rise and Fall of Transatlantic Radicalism in the Early Republic*. Charlottesville: University of Virginia Press, 2011.

Cox, Edward L. "The British Caribbean in the Age of Revolution." In *Empire and Nation: The American Revolution in the Atlantic World*, edited by Eliga H. Gould and Peter S. Onuf, 275–294. Baltimore: Johns Hopkins University Press, 2005.

Crabtree, Adam. *From Mesmer to Freud: Magnetic Sleep and the Roots of Psychological Healing*. New Haven, CT: Yale University Press, 1993.

Cugoano, Quobna. *Thoughts and Sentiments on the Evil of Slavery*. London: Penguin, 1999.

Current, Thomas, et al. *American History: A Survey*, 2nd ed. New York: Knopf, 1967.

Cushing, Caleb. "Article VI—*Réflexions politiques sur quelques ouvrages et journaux français.*" *North American Review and Miscellaneous Journals* 3.1 (January 1821): 112–134.

Curtis, Julia. "John Joseph Stephen Leger Sollee and the Charleston Theatre." *Educational Theatre Journal* 21.3 (1969): 285–298.

Daniel, Marcus L. *Scandal and Civility: Journalism and the Birth of American Democracy*. New York: Oxford University Press, 2009.

Daniels, Christine, and Michael V. Kennedy. *Over the Threshold: Intimate Violence in Early America*. London: Routledge, 1999.

Darnton, Robert. *Mesmerism and the End of the Enlightenment in France*. Cambridge, MA.: Harvard University Press, 1968.

Dash, J. Michael. *Literature and Ideology in Haiti*. London: Macmillan, 1981.

———. "Marvelous Realism: The Way Out of Negritude." *Caribbean Studies* 13.4 (1973): 57–70.

———. "Nineteenth-Century Haiti and the Archipelago of the Americas: Antènor Firmin's Letters from St. Thomas." *Research in African Literatures* 35.2 (2004): 44–53.

Daut, Marlene L. "'Sons of White Fathers': Mulatto Vengeance and the Haitian Revolution in Victor Séjour's 'The Mulatto.'" *Nineteenth-Century Literature* 65.1 (June 2010): 1–37.

Davidson, Cathy. *Revolution and the Word: The Rise of the Novel in America*. New York: Oxford University Press, 1986.
Davis, David Brion. *Inhuman Bondage: The Rise and Fall of Slavery in the New World*. New York: Oxford University Press, 2006.
———. *The Problem of Slavery in the Age of Revolution, 1770–1823*. Ithaca, NY: Cornell University Press, 1975.
———. *The Slave Power Conspiracy and the Paranoid Style*. Baton Rouge: Louisiana State University Press, 1969.
Davis, Natalie Zemon, and Randolph Starn. Introduction. "Memory and Counter-Memory," special issue. *Representations* 26 (Spring 1989): 1–6.
Dayan, Joan. "Few Stories about Haiti, or, Stigma Revisited." *Research in African Literatures* 35.2 (Summer 2004): 157–172.
———. *Haiti, History, and the Gods*. Berkeley: University of California Press, 1995.
———. "Paul Gilroy's Slaves, Ships, and Routes: The Middle Passage as Metaphor." *Research in African Literatures* 27.4 (1996): 7–14.
———. " 'A Receptacle for that Race of Men': Blood, Boundaries, and Mutations of Theory." *American Literature* 67.4 (December 1995): 801–813.
Debien, Gabriel. "Assemblées nocturnes d'esclaves à Saint-Domingue." *Annales historiques de la Révolution* 44 (1972): 273–284.
DeConde, Alexander. *The Quasi-War: The Politics and Diplomacy of the Undeclared War with France, 1797–1801*. New York: Scribner's, 1966.
———. *This Affair of Louisiana*. New York: Charles Scribner's Sons, 1976.
Deleuze, Gilles, and Felix Guattari. *A Thousand Plateaus: Capitalism and Schizophrenia*. Translated by Brian Massumi. Minneapolis: University of Minnesota Press, 1987.
Denis, Watson. "Les 100 ans de Monsieur Roosevelt et Haïti." *Revue de la Société Haïtienne D'histoire et de Géographie*, 226 (September 2006): 1–41.
Depestre, René. *Le Mât de cocagne*. Paris: Gallimard, 2005.
Deschamps, Léon. *Histoire de la question coloniale en France*. Paris: E. Plon, Nourrit et Cie, 1891.
Deschamps, Michel-Hyacinthe. *Études des races humaine: Méthode naturelle d'ethnologie*. Paris: Leiber et Comelin, 1859.
Desormeaux, Daniel. "The First of the (Black) Memorialists: Toussaint L'Ouverture." *Yale Nineteenth-Century French Studies: The Haiti Issue*. 107 (Spring 2005): 131–145.
Dessens, Nathalie. *From Saint-Domingue to New Orleans: Migration and Influences*. Gainesville: University Press of Florida, 2007.
Deutsch, Harold C. *The Genesis of Napoleonic Imperialism*. Cambridge, MA: Harvard University Press, 1938.
Devèze, Jean. *An Enquiry into, and Observations upon the Causes and Effects of the Epidemic Disease, which Raged in Philadelphia from the Month of August till Towards the Middle of December, 1793*. Philadelphia, 1794.
De Warville, J. P. Brissot. *New Travels in the United States of America. Performed in 1788. Translated from the French*. Dublin: By W. Corbet, For P. Byren, A Grueber, W. McKenzie, J. Moore, W. Jones, R. McCallister, and J. Rice, 1792.
Dewey, Loring D. *Correspondence Relative to the Emigration to Hayti, of the Free People of Colour, in the United States. Together with the Instructions to the Agent Sent out by President Boyer*. New York: Mahlon Day, 1824.
Dillon, Elizabeth Maddock. *New World Drama: The Performative Commons in the Atlantic World, 1649–1849*. Durham, NC: Duke University Press, 2014.

———. "The Secret History of the Early American Novel: Leonora Sansay and Revolution in Saint Domingue." *Novel* 40 (Fall 2006/Spring 2007): 77–103.
Dimock, Wai-Chee. *Through Other Continents: American Literature Across Deep Time.* Princeton, NJ: Princeton University Press, 2006.
Dixon, Chris. *African America and Haiti: Emigration and Black Nationalism in the Nineteenth Century.* Westport, CT: Greenwood Press, 2000.
Douglass, Frederick. "Haïti and the United States. Inside History of the Negotiations for the Môle St. Nicolas. I." *North American Review* 153.418 (September 1891): 337–345.
———. "Haïti and the United States. Inside History of the Negotiations for the Môle St. Nicolas. II." *North American Review* 153.419 (October 1891): 450–459.
———. "Lecture on Haiti." In *African Americans and the Haitian Revolution: Selected Essays and Historical Documents*, edited by Maurice Jackson and Jacqueline Bacon, 202–211. New York: Routledge, 2010.
Dow, Mark. "Occupying and Obscuring Haiti." *New Politics* 5.2 (Winter 1995): 12–22.
Drexler, Michael J. "Brigands and Nuns: The Vernacular Sociology of Collectivity after the Haitian Revolution." In *Messy Beginnings: Postcoloniality and Early American Studies*, edited by Malini Johar Schueller and Edward Watts, 175–199. New Brunswick, NJ: Rutgers University Press, 2003.
———. "Haiti, Modernity, and U.S. Identities." *Early American Literature* 43.2 (2008): 453–465.
———. Introduction to *Secret History; or, The Horrors of St. Domingo*. Orchard Park, NY: Broadview, 2007.
———, and Ed White. *The Traumatic Colonel: The Founding Fathers, Slavery, and the Phantasmatic Aaron Burr.* New York: New York University Press, 2014.
Du Bois, W. E. B. *Black Reconstruction in America.* New York: Atheneum, 1962.
Dubois, Laurent. *Avengers of the New World: The Story of the Haitian Revolution.* Cambridge, MA: Harvard University Press, 2004.
———. *A Colony of Citizens: Revolution and Slave Emancipation in the French Caribbean, 1787–1804.* Chapel Hill: University of North Carolina Press, 2004.
———. *Haiti: The Aftershocks of History.* New York: Metropolitan Books/Henry Holt and Co., 2012.
———. "The Haitian Revolution and the Sale of Louisiana." *Southern Quarterly* 44.3 (2007): 18–41.
———, and John Garrigus, eds. *Slave Revolution in the Caribbean, 1789–1804: A Brief History with Documents.* New York: Palgrave Macmillan, 2006.
Dun, James Alexander. "'What Avenues of Commerce, Will You, Americans, Not Explore!': Commercial Philadephia's Vantage onto the Early Haitian Revolution." *William and Mary Quarterly* 62.3 (2005): 357–364.
Duncan, Ian. *Modern Romance and the Transformation of the Novel: The Gothic, Scott, Dickens.* Cambridge: Cambridge University Press, 1992.
Dunlap, William. *André: A Tragedy, in Five Acts.* New York, 1798.
———. *History of the American Theatre.* 2 vols. London: Richard Bentley, 1833.
During, Simon. "Literature—Nationalism's Other? The Case for Revision." In *Nation and Narration*, edited by Homi K. Bhabha, 138–153. New York: Routlege, 1990.
Edelman, Nicole. *Voyantes, guérisseuses et visionnaires en France: 1785–1914.* Paris: A. Michel, 1995.

Edwards, Bryan. *An Historical Survey of the French Colony in the Island of St. Domingo: Comprehending a Short Account of Its Ancient Government, Political State, Population, Productions, and Exports; a Narrative of the Calamities Which Have Desolated the Country Ever Since the Year 1789, with Some Reflections on Their Causes and Probable Consequences; and a Detail of the Military Transactions of the British Army in That Island to the End of 1794.* London: John Stockdale, Piccadilly, 1797.

Edwards, Justin. *Gothic Passages: Racial Ambiguity in the American Gothic.* Iowa City: University of Iowa Press, 2003.

Egerton, Douglas R. *Death or Liberty: African Americans and Revolutionary America.* New York: Oxford University Press, 2009.

———. *Gabriel's Rebellion: The Virginia Slave Conspiracies of 1800 & 1802.* Chapel Hill: University of North Carolina Press, 1993.

Egerton, George. "Politics and Autobiography: Political Memoir as Polygenre." *Biography: An Interdisciplinary Quarterly* 15.3 (1992): 221–242.

Elkins, Stanley, and Eric McKitrick. *The Age of Federalism: The Early American Republic, 1788–1800.* New York: Oxford University Press, 1993.

Emerson, Ralph Waldo. "The American Scholar." In *The Portable Emerson*, edited by Carl Bode and Malcolm Cowley, 51–71. New York: Penguin Books, 1981.

———. "Nature." In *The Portable Emerson*, edited by Carl Bode and Malcolm Cowley, 7–50. New York: Penguin Books, 1981.

Estes, J. Worth, and Billy G. Smith, eds. *A Melancholy Scene of Devastation: The Public Response to the 1793 Philadelphia Yellow Fever Epidemic.* Canton, MA: Science History Publications/USA, 1997.

Evans, Charles. *American Bibliography: Chronological dictionary of all books, pamphlets, and periodical publications printed in the United States of America from the genesis of printing in 1639 down to and including the year 1820.* Chicago: Blakely Press, 1903–1959.

Eze, Emmanuel C. Introduction to *Race and the Enlightenment: A Reader.* Edited by Emmanuel Chukwudi Eze. Malden, MA: Blackwell Publishing, 1997.

Fanning, Sara. "The Roots of Early Black Nationalism: Northern African Americans' Invocations of Haiti in the Early Nineteenth Century." *Slavery & Abolition* 28.1 (April 2007): 61–85.

Fanuzzi, Robert. "Taste, Manners, and Miscegenation: French Racial Politics in the U.S." *American Literary History* 19.3 (2007): 573–602.

Fardin, Dieudonné. *Histoire de la littérature haïtienne.* Port-au-Prince: Editions Fardin, 1967.

Fargeaud, Madeleine. *Balzac et "La Recherche de l'absolu."* Paris: Hachette, 1968.

Farmer, Paul. *The Uses of Haiti.* Monroe, ME: Common Courage Press, 1994.

Fenn, Elizabeth. *Pox Americana: The Great Smallpox Epidemic of 1775–82.* New York: Hill and Wang, 2001.

Fick, Carolyn. "Emancipation in Haiti: From Plantation Labour to Peasant Proprietorship." *Slavery & Abolition* 21.2 (2000): 11–40.

———. "The Haitian Revolution and the Limits of Freedom: Defining Citizenship in the Revolutionary Era." *Social History* [UK] 32.4 (2007): 394–414.

———. *The Making of Haiti: The Saint Domingue Revolution from Below.* Knoxville: University of Tennessee Press, 1990.

Fiedler, Leslie. *Love and Death in the American Novel.* New York: Stein and Day, 1966.

Firmin, Joseph-Anténor. *The Equality of the Human Races.* New York: Garland, 2000.

———. *Lettres de Saint-Thomas: Études sociologiques, historiques et littéraires*. Port-au-Prince: Imprimerie Centrale, 1976.

———. *M. Roosevelt, Président des États-Unis et la République d'Haïti*. Paris: F. Pichon et Durand-Auzias, 1905.

Fischer, Sibylle. *Modernity Disavowed: Haiti and the Cultures of Slavery in the Age of Revolution*. Durham, NC: Duke University Press, 2004.

Fleming, Thomas. *The Louisiana Purchase*. Hoboken, NJ: Wiley, 2003.

Foner, Eric. *Free Soil, Free Labor, Free Men*. New York: Oxford University Press, 1995.

Foster, Frances Smith. "How Do You Solve a Problem Like Theresa?" *African American Review* 40.4 (2006): 631–645.

———, ed. "Theresa—A Haytien Tale." *African American Review* 40.4 (2006): 639–645.

Foster, Hannah Webster. *The Coquette*. New York: Penguin, 1996.

Foster, Susan Leigh. *Choreography and Narrative: Ballet's Staging of Story and Desire*. Bloomington: Indiana University Press, 1996.

Foucault, Michel. "About the Beginnings of the Hermeneutics of the Self: Two Lectures at Dartmouth." *Political Theory* 21.2 (1993): 198–227.

———. *Language, Counter-Memory, Practice: Selected Essays and Interviews*. Translated by D. Bouchard and S. Simon. Ithaca, NY: Cornell University Press, 1977.

———. *Society Must Be Defended: Lectures at the Collège de France 1975–1976*. Edited by Mauro Bertani and Alessandro Fontana. Translated by David Macey. New York: Picador, 2003.

Foyster, Elizabeth. *Marital Violence: An English Family History, 1660–1857*. Cambridge: Cambridge University Press, 2005.

François, André. *Dissertation sur la fièvre jaune observée à Saint-Domingue pendant les années XI et XII*. Paris: De l'Imprimerie de Didot Jeune . . . , an XII, 1804.

Frankétienne. *Les Affres d'un défi*. Paris: J.-M. Place, 2000.

Franklin, Benjamin, Antoine Laurent Lavoisier, and Jean Sylvain Bailly. "Rapport des commissaires chargés par le Roi de l'examen du magnétisme animal." In *Histoire académique du magnétisme animal*, edited by Claude Burdin and Frédéric Dubois, 26–91. Paris: J.-B. Baillière, 1841.

Freeman, Lisa A. *Character's Theater: Genre and Identity on the Eighteenth-Century English Stage*. Philadelphia: University of Pennsylvania Press, 2002.

Freud, Sigmund, and Joseph Breuer. *Studies on Hysteria*. In *The Standard Edition of the Complete Psychological Works of Sigmund Freud*, vol. 2. Edited and translated by James Strachey. London: Hogarth Press, 1955.

Frey, Sylvia R. *Water from the Rock: Black Resistance in a Revolutionary Age*. Princeton, NJ: Princeton University Press, 1991.

Gaffarel, Paul. *La Politique coloniale en France de 1789 à 1830*. Paris: Félix Alcan, 1908.

Gaffield, Julia. "Haiti and Jamaica in the Remaking of the Early Nineteenth-Century Atlantic World." *William and Mary Quarterly* 69.3 (July 2012): 583–614.

Gaines, Pierce W. *William Cobbett and the United States*. Worcester, MA: American Antiquarian Society, 1970.

———. "William Cobbett's Account Book." *Proceedings of the American Antiquarian Society* 78 (1968): 299–312.

Garnier, Michaël. *Bonaparte et la Louisiane*. Paris: Kronos, 1992.

Garraway, Doris Lorraine. *The Libertine Colony: Creolization in the Early French Caribbean*. Durham, NC: Duke University Press, 2005.

———. *Tree of Liberty: Cultural Legacies of the Haitian Revolution in the Atlantic World*. Charlottesville: University of Virginia Press, 2008.
Garrigus, John D. *Before Haiti: Race and Citizenship in French Saint Domingue*. New York: Palgrave Macmillan, 2006.
Gaspar, David Barry, and David P. Geggus. *A Turbulent Time: The French Revolution and the Greater Caribbean*. Bloomington: Indiana University Press, 1997.
Geggus, David P. Preface to *The Impact of the Haitian Revolution in the Atlantic World*, edited by David P. Geggus, ix–xviii. Columbia: University of South Carolina Press, 2001.
———. "French Imperialism and the Louisiana Purchase." In *The Louisiana Purchase and Its Peoples: Perspectives from the New Orleans Conference*, edited by Paul E. Hoffman, 25–34. Lafayette: Louisiana Historical Association, 2004.
———. *Haitian Revolutionary Studies*. Bloomington: Indiana University Press, 2002.
———. "The Naming of Haiti." *New West Indian Guide* 71.1/2 (1997): 43–68.
———. "Racial Equality, Slavery, and Colonial Secession during the Constituent Assembly." *American Historical Review* 94 (1989): 1290–1308.
———. "Yellow Fever in the 1790s: The British Army in Occupied Saint Domingue." *Medical History* 23 (1979): 38–58.
———, and Norman Fiering, eds. *The World of the Haitian Revolution*. Bloomington: Indiana University Press, 2009.
Genovese, Eugene D. *From Rebellion to Revolution: Afro-American Slave Revolts in the Making of the Modern World*. Baton Rouge: Louisiana State University Press, 1979.
Gibbons, Luke. "Ireland, America, and Gothic Memory: Transatlantic Terror in the Early Republic." *Boundary 2* 31.1 (Spring 2004): 25–47.
Gilbert, [Nicolas Pierre]. *Histoire médicale de l'armée française, a Saint-Domingue, en l'an dix; ou mémoire sur la fièvre jaune, avec un apperçu de la topographie médicale de cette colonie*. Paris, 1803.
Gillman, Susan. "Otra vez Caliban/Encore Caliban: Adaptation/Translation/Americas Studies." *American Literary History* 20.1–2 (2008): 187–209.
Gilmore, Alan. *Black Patriots and Loyalists: Fighting for Emancipation in the War for Independence*. Chicago: University of Chicago Press: 2012.
Gilmore, Paul. *The Genuine Article: Race, Mass Culture, and American Literary Manhood*. Durham, NC: Duke University Press, 2001.
Gilroy, Paul. *The Black Atlantic: Modernity and Double Consciousness*. Cambridge, MA: Harvard University Press, 1993.
Girard, Philippe R. "Black Talleyrand: Toussaint Louverture's Diplomacy, 1798–1802." *William and Mary Quarterly* 66.1 (2009): 87–124.
———. "Jean-Jacques Dessalines and the Atlantic System: A Reappraisal." *William and Mary Quarterly* 69.3 (2012): 549–582.
———. *The Slaves Who Defeated Napoleon: Toussaint Louverture and the Haitian War of Independence, 1801–1804*. Tuscaloosa: University of Alabama Press, 2011.
———. "Ugly Ducklings: The French Navy and the Saint-Domingue Expedition, 1801–1803." *International Journal of Naval History* 9.3 (2010). http://www.ijnhonline.org/2010/12/01/the-ugly-duckling-the-french-navy-and-the-saint-domingue-expedition1801-1803/.
Glick-Schiller, Nina, and Georges Fouron. *Georges Woke Up Laughing: Long Distance Nationalism and the Apparent State*. Durham, NC: Duke University Press, 2001.
Glickstein, Jonathan. *Concepts of Free Labor in Antebellum America*. New Haven, CT: Yale University Press, 1991.

Glissant, Édouard. *Caribbean Discourse: Selected Essays.* Translated by J. Michael Dash. Charlottesville: University Press of Virginia, 1989.

———. *Introduction à une poétique du divers.* Paris: Gallimard, 1996.

Goddu, Teresa. *Gothic America: Narrative, History, and Nation.* New York: Columbia University Press, 1997.

Godechot, Jacques. *France and the Atlantic Revolution of the Eighteenth Century, 1770–1799.* New York: Free Press, 1965.

Godwin, William. *Caleb Williams; or Things As They Are.* Edited, with an Introduction by Maurice Hindle. London: Penguin Books, 1988.

Goodlad, Lauren M. E. "Trollopian 'Foreign Policy': Rootedness and Cosmopolitanism in the Mid-Victorian Global Imaginary." *PMLA* 124 (2009): 437–454.

Gottschalk, Louis Reichenthal. *Lafayette between the American and the French Revolution (1783–1789).* Chicago: University of Chicago Press, 1950.

Goudie, Sean X. *Creole America: The West Indies and the Formation of Literature and Culture in the New Republic.* Philadelphia: University of Pennsylvania Press, 2006.

———. "On the Origin of American Specie(s): The West Indies, Classification, and the Emergence of Supremacist Consciousness in Arthur Mervyn." In *Revising Charles Brockden Brown: Culture, Politics, and Sexuality in the Early Republic,* edited by Philip Barnard, Mark L. Kamrath, and Stephen Shapiro, 60–87. Knoxville: University of Tennessee Press, 2004.

Gould, Philip. "Race, Commerce, and the Literature of Yellow Fever in Early National Philadelphia." *Early American Literature* 35.2 (2000): 157–186.

Graebner, Norman A. *Ideas and Diplomacy.* New York: Oxford University Press, 1964.

Graff, Henry, and John Krout. *The Adventure of the American People.* New York: Rand McNally, 1959.

Grégoire, Henri (abbé de). *De la noblesse de la peau.* [1820]. Paris: J. Millon, 1996.

Griggs, Earl Leslie, and Earl Clifford H. Prator. *Henri Christophe and Thomas Clarkson: A Correspondence.* New York: Greenwood Press, 1968.

Gulick, Anne. "We Are Not the People: The 1805 Haitian Constitution's Challenge to Political Legibility in the Age of Revolution." *American Literature* 78.4 (December 2006): 799–820.

Hale, Matthew Rainbow. "'Many Who Wandered in Darkness': The Contest over American National Identity, 1795–1798." *Early American Studies* 1.1 (2003): 127–175.

———. "On Their Tiptoes: Political Time and Newspapers During the Advent of the Radicalized French Revolution, circa 1792–1793." *Journal of the Early Republic* 29.2 (2009): 191–218.

Hamer, Philip M. "Great Britain, the United States, and the Negro Seamen Acts, 1822–1848." *Journal of Southern History* 1.1 (February 1935): 3–28.

Handlin, Oscar. *Chance or Destiny: Turning Points in American History.* Boston: Little, Brown & Co., 1955.

Hanotaux, Gabriel, and Alfred Martineau, eds. *Histoire des colonies françaises et de l'expansion de la France dans le monde.* Vol. 1. Edited by Joannès Tramond. Paris: Plon, 1929.

Harris, Leslie. *In the Shadow of Slavery.* Chicago: University of Chicago Press, 2003.

Hawthorne, Nathaniel. *The House of the Seven Gables.* New York: Penguin Classics, 1981.

Haywood, Ian. *Bloody Romanticism: Spectacular Violence and the Politics of Representation, 1776–1832.* New York: Palgrave Macmillan, 2006.

Hébert, Catherine. "French Publications in Philadelphia in the Age of the French Revolution: A Bibliographical Essay." *Pennsylvania History* 58.1 (January 1991): 37–61.

Hernández Guerrero, Dolores. *La Revolución haitiana y el fin de un sueño colonial.* Mexico: UNAM, 1991.

———. "La Révolution haïtienne et l'expansion territoriale des Etats-Unis." In *Rétablissement de l'esclavage dans les colonies françaises, 1802,* edited by Marcel Dorigny, 387–402. Paris: Maisonneuve & Larose, 2003.

Hickey, Donald R. "America's Response to Slave Revolts in Haiti." *Journal of the Early Republic* 2.4 (Winter 1982): 361–379.

Hirsch, Helmut. "Mesmerism and Revolutionary America." *American-German Review* 10 (1943): 11–14.

Hobsbawm, Eric. *Nations and Nationalism since 1780: Programme, Myth, Reality.* Cambridge: Cambridge University Press, 1992.

Hochschild, Adam. *Bury the Chains: Prophets and Rebels in the Fight to Free an Empire's Slaves.* Boston: Houghton Mifflin, 2005.

Hoffman, Paul E. *Luisiana.* Madrid: Editorial MAPFRE, 1992.

Hofmman, Léon-François. *Le Nègre romantique.* Paris: Payot, 1973.

Holland, Edwin C. *A Refutation of the Calumnies Circulated Against the Southern Western States, Respecting the Institution and Existence of Slavery Among Them to Which Is Added, a Minute and Particular Account of the Actual State and Condition of Their Negro Population.* Charleston, SC: A. E. Miller, 1822.

Hoole, William Stanley. *The Ante-Bellum Charleston Theatre.* Tuscaloosa: University of Alabama Press, 1946.

Hosmer, James K. *The History of the Louisiana Purchase.* New York: Appleton, 1904.

Howard, Thomas Phipps. *The Haitian Journal of Lieutenant Howard, York Hussars, 1796–1798.* Edited by Roger Norman Buckley. Knoxville: University of Tennessee Press, 1985.

Hughes, A. M. D., ed. *Cobbett.* Oxford: Clarendon Press, 1923.

Hunt, Alfred N. *Haiti's Influence on Antebellum America: Slumbering Volcano in the Caribbean.* Baton Rouge: Louisiana State University Press, 1988.

Hunt, Benjamin S. *Remarks on Hayti as a Place of Settlement for Afric-Americans; and on the Mulatto.* Philadelphia: T. B. Pugh, 1860.

Hurston, Zora Neale. *Tell My Horse: Voodoo and Life in Haiti and Jamaica.* New York: Perennial Library, 1990.

Hyde, Carrie. "Novelistic Evidence: The Denmark Vesey Conspiracy and Possibilistic History." *American Literary History* 27.1 (2014): 26–55.

Jackson, Maurice, and Jacqueline Bacon, eds. *African Americans and the Haitian Revolution: Selected Essays and Historical Documents.* New York: Routledge, 2010.

———. "Fever and Fret: The Haitian Revolution and African American Responses." In *African Americans and the Haitian Revolution: Selected Essays and Historical Documents,* edited by Maurice Jackson and Jacqueline Bacon, 9–23. New York: Routledge, 2010.

Jackson, Robert. *A Treatise on the Fevers of Jamaica, with some Observations on the Intermitting Fever of America, and an Appendix, Containing Some Hints on the Means of Preserving the Health of Soldiers in Hot Climates.* Philadelphia, 1795.

James, C. L. R. *The Black Jacobins: Toussaint Louverture and the San Domingo Revolution,* 2nd rev. ed. New York: Vintage Books, 1963.

Jameson, J. Franklin, ed. "Letters of Toussaint Louverture and Edward Stevens, 1798–1800." *American Historical Review* 16.1 (1910): 64–101.

Janvier, L.-J. *Les Constitutions d'Haiti.* Paris: C. Marpon et Flammarion, 1886.

———. *La République d'Haïti et ses visiteurs (1840–1882).* Paris: Marpon et Flammarion, 1883.

Jefferson, Thomas. *Notes on the State of Virginia*. Edited by Merrill D. Peterson. New York: Library of America, 1984.

———. *Thomas Jefferson Papers, 1606–1827*. Microfilm. Washington, DC: Library of Congress.

———.*Jefferson: Political Writings*. Joyce Appleby and Terence Ball, Eds. Cambridge: Cambridge University Press, 1999.

Jenson, Deborah. "Before Malcolm X, Dessalines: A 'French' Tradition of Black Atlantic Radicalism." *International Journal of Francophone Studies* 10.3 (2007): 329–344.

———. "From the Kidnappings of the Louvertures to the Alleged Kidnapping of Aristide: Legacies of Slavery in the Post/Colonial World." *Yale French Studies* 107 (2005): 162–186.

———. "Placing Haiti in the Geopsychoanalytic Space." In *Unconscious Dominions: Psychoanalysis, Colonial Trauma, and Global Sovereignties*, edited by Warwick Anderson, Deborah Jenson, and Richard C. Keller, 167–198. Durham, NC: Duke University Press, 2011.

Johnson, Michael P. "Denmark Vesey and His Co-Conspirators." *William and Mary Quarterly* 58.4 (October 2001): 915–976.

Johnson, Odai. *Absence and Memory in Colonial American Theatre: Fiorelli's Plaster*. New York: Palgrave Macmillan, 2006.

Johnson, Ronald Angelo. "A Revolutionary Dinner: U.S. Diplomacy Toward Saint Domingue, 1798–1801." *Early American Studies* 9.1 (Winter 2011): 114–141.

Johnson, Walter. *River of Dark Dreams: Slavery and Empire in The Cotton Kingdom*. Cambridge, MA: Harvard University Press, 2013.

Jones, Absalom, and Richard Allen. *A Narrative of the Proceeding of the Black People, During the Late Awful Calamity in Philadelphia, in the Year 1793: And a Refutation of some Censures, Thrown upon Them in Some Late Publications*. Philadelphia, 1794.

Jones, Martha S. "Time, Space, and Jurisdiction in Atlantic World Slavery: The Volunbrun Household in Gradual Emancipation New York." *Law & History Review* 29.4 (2011): 1031–1060.

Jordan, Winthrop. *White over Black: American Attitudes Toward the Negro, 1550–1812*. Chapel Hill: University of North Carolina Press, 1968.

Kachun, Mitchell A. "Antebellum African Americans, Public Commemoration, and the Haitian Revolution: A Problem of Historical Mythmaking." *Journal of the Early Republic* 26.2 (2006): 249–273.

Kant, Immanuel. "To Perpetual Peace." In *Perpetual Peace, and Other Essays on Politics, History, and Morals*. Translated by Ted Humphrey, 107–144. Indianapolis. IN: Hackett Publishing Co., 1983.

Kaye, Anthony. "The Second Slavery: Modernity in the Nineteenth-Century South and the Atlantic World." *Journal of Southern History* 75.3 (August 2009): 627–650.

Kazanjian, David. *The Colonizing Trick: National Culture and Imperial Citizenship in Early America*. Minneapolis: University of Minnesota Press, 2003.

Kennedy, Lionel H., and Thomas Parker. *An Official Report of the Trials of Sundry Negroes Charged with an Attempt to Raise an Insurrection in the State of South-Carolina: Preceded by an Introduction and Narrative*. Charleston, SC: James R. Schenck, 1822.

Kennedy, Roger G. *Orders from France: The Americans and the French in a Revolutionary World, 1780–1820*. New York: Knopf, 1989.

Kenny, Kevin. *The American Irish: A History*. Harlow, Essex, UK: Longman, 2000.

Kerner, Justinus. *The Seeress of Prevorst: Being Revelations Concerning the Inner-Life of Man, and the Inter-Diffusion of a World of Spirits in the One We Inhabit*. Translated by Catherine Crowe. London: J. C. Moore, 1845.

Klooster, Wim. *Revolutions in the Atlantic World: A Comparative History*. New York: New York University Press, 2009.

Kraus, Michael. *The United States to 1865*. Ann Arbor: University of Michigan Press, 1969.

Lacerte, Robert K. "Xenophobia and Economic Decline: The Haitian Case, 1820–1843." *Americas* 37.4 (April 1981): 499–515.

Lachance, Paul. "Repercussions of the Haitian Revolution in Louisiana." In *The Impact of the Haitian Revolution in the Atlantic World*, edited by D. P. Geggus, 209–230. Columbia: University of South Carolina Press, 2001.

LaFeber, Walter. "Foreign Policies of a New Nation." In *From Colony to Empire: Essays in the History of American Foreign Relations*, edited by William Appleman Williams, 9–37. Chicago: Rand McNally, 1956.

Langley, Lester D. *The Americas in the Age of Revolution, 1750–1850*. New Haven, CT: Yale University Press, 1996.

Laroche, Maximilien. *L'Avènement de la littérature haïtienne*. Port-Au-Prince: Editions Mémoire, 2001.

Las Cases, Emmanuel de. *Mémorial de Sainte-Hélène*. 2 vols. Paris: Bourdin, 1842.

Lawless, Robert. *Haiti's Bad Press*. Rochester, VT: Schenkman Books, 1992.

Leask, Nigel. "Irish Republicans and Gothic Eleutherarchs: Pacific Utopias in the Writings of Theobald Wolfe Tone and Charles Brockden Brown." *Huntington Library Quarterly* 63.3 (2000): 347–367.

Leclerc, Charles Victor Emmanuel. *Les Lettres du général Leclerc, commandant en chef de l'armée de Saint-Domingue*. Edited by Paul Roussier. Paris: Leroux, 1937.

Légitime, François Dénis. *La Vérité sur le vaudoux*. Port-au-Prince, 1892(?).

Levine, Robert S. "Race and Nation in Brown's Louisiana Writings of 1803." In *Revising Charles Brockden Brown*, edited by Philip Barnard, Mark L. Kamrath, and Stephen Shapiro, 332–353. Knoxville: University of Tennessee Press, 2004.

Lewis, James E. *The Louisiana Purchase: Jefferson's Noble Bargain?* Charlottesville, VA: Thomas Jefferson Foundation, 2003.

Leyburn, James. *The Haitian People*. New Haven, CT: Yale University Press, 1966.

Lhamon, W. T. *Jump Jim Crow: Lost Plays, Lyrics, and Street Prose of the First Atlantic Popular Culture*. Cambridge, MA: Harvard University Press, 2003.

———. *Raising Cain: Blackface Performance from Jim Crow to Hip Hop*. Cambridge, MA: Harvard University Press, 1998.

Library of Congress. *Guide to the Louisiana Purchase*. Web Guide to Primary Documents in American History. http://www.loc.gov/rr/program/bib/ourdocs/Louisiana.html.

Lilienfeld, Abraham M., and David E. Lilienfeld. *Foundations of Epidemiology*. New York: Oxford University Press, 1980.

Linebaugh, Peter, and Marcus Rediker. *The Many-Headed Hydra: Sailors, Slaves, Commoners, and the Hidden History of the Revolutionary Atlantic*. Boston: Beacon Press, 2000.

Liss, Peggy K. *Atlantic Empires: The Network of Trade and Revolution, 1713–1826*. Baltimore: Johns Hopkins University Press, 1983.

List, Karen K. "The Role of William Cobbett in Philadelphia's Party Press, 1794–1799." Ph.D. diss., University of Wisconsin–Madison, 1980.

Locke, John. "The Second Treatise: An Essay Concerning the True Original, Extent, and End of Civil Government." In *Two Treatises of Government and A Letter Concerning Toleration*, edited by Ian Shapiro, 100–210. New Haven, CT: Yale University Press, 2003.
Logan, Rayford W. *The Diplomatic Relations of the United States with Haiti, 1776–1891*. [1941], reprint ed. New York: Kraus Reprint Co., 1969.
———. "Education in Haiti." *Journal of Negro History* 15.4 (October 1930): 401–460.
Lott, Eric. *Love and Theft: Blackface Minstrelsy and the American Working Class*. New York: Oxford University Press, 1993.
Loughran, Trish. *The Republic in Print: Print Culture in the Age of U.S. Nation Building, 1170–1870*. New York: Columbia University Press, 2007.
L'Ouverture, Toussaint. *The Haitian Revolution/Toussaint L'Ouverture*. Introduction by Jean-Bertrand Aristide. Edited by Nick Nesbitt. New York: Verso, 2008.
Lyon, E. Wilson. *Louisiana in French Diplomacy, 1759–1804*. Norman: University of Oklahoma Press, 1934.
Madison, James. *The Papers of James Madison*. Edited by David B. Mattern, J. C. A. Stagg, Jeanne Kerr Cross, and Susan Holbrook Perdue. Charlottesville: University of Virginia Press, 1995.
Malouet, Pierre Victor. *Collection de mémoires et correspondences officielles sur l'administration des colonies et notamment sur la guerre française et hollandaise*. Paris: Baudouin, 1802.
Manigat, Leslie F. "La Substitution de la prépondérance américaine a la prépondérance française en Haïti au début du XXe siècle: La Conjoncture de 1910–1911." *Revue d'histoire moderne et contemporaine* 14.4 (December 1967): 321–355.
Margolis, Stacey. *Fictions of Mass Democracy in Nineteenth-Century America*. Cambridge: Cambridge University Press, 2015.
Martin, Terrence. *The Instructed Vision: Scottish Common Sense Philosophy and the Origins of American Fiction*. Bloomington: Indiana University Press, 1961.
Martineau, Jean-Claude. "The Other Occupation: The Haitian Version of Apartheid." Third World Traveler. 2005. http://www.thirdworldtraveler.com/Haiti/Special_Apartheid.html.
Marx, Karl. *The Eighteenth Brumaire of Louis Bonaparte: With Explanatory Notes*. New York: International Publishers, 1963.
Massey, Doreen B. *For Space*. London: SAGE, 2005.
Mathias, T. J. *The Pursuits of Literature*, 5th ed. London: T. Becket, 1798.
Matthiessen, F. O. *The American Renaissance: Art and Expression in the Age of Emerson and Whitman*. New York: Oxford University Press, 1941.
Matthewson, Tim. "Abraham Bishop, 'The Rights of Black Men,' and the American Reaction to the Haitian Revolution." *Journal of Negro History* 67.2 (1982): 148–154.
———. "Jefferson and Haiti." *Journal of Southern History* 61 (1995): 209–248.
———. "Jefferson and the Nonrecognition of Haiti." *Proceedings of American Philosophical Society* 140.1 (March 1996): 22–48.
———. *A Proslavery Foreign Policy: Haitian-American Relations During the Early Republic*. Westport, CT: Praeger, 2003.
May, Robert E. *The Southern Dream of a Caribbean Empire, 1854–1861*, 2nd ed. Gainesville: University Press of Florida, 2002.
McClellan, James E. *Colonialism and Science: Saint Domingue in the Old Regime*. Baltimore: Johns Hopkins University Press, 1992.

McGill, Meredith. *American Literature and the Culture of Reprinting, 1834–1853*. Philadelphia: University of Pennsylvania Press, 2003.

———. "Market." In *Keywords for American Cultural Studies*, edited by Glenn Hendler and Bruce Burgett, 149–152. New York: New York University Press, 2007.

McHenry, Elizabeth. *Forgotten Readers: Recovering the Lost History of African American Literary Socie*ties. Durham, NC: Duke University Press, 2002.

McLean, Hector. *An Enquiry into the Nature, and Causes of the Great Mortality Among the Troops at St. Domingo: with Practical Remarks on the Fever of that Island; and Directions of the Conduct of Europeans on Their First Arrival in Warm Climates.* London, 1797.

McLynn, Frank. *Napoleon: A Biography*. New York: Arcade, 2002.

McNeill, J.R. *Mosquito Empires: Ecology and War in the Greater Caribbean, 1620–1914*. New York: Cambridge University Press, 2010.

Meelish, Glen. "Frederick Douglass and the Consequences of Rhetoric: The Interpretive Framing and Publication History of the 2 January 1893 Haiti Speeches." *Rhetorica: A Journal of the History of Rhetoric* 30.1 (Winter 2012): 37–73.

Meglin, Joellen A. "'Sauvages, Sex Roles, and Semiotics': Representations of Native Americans in the French Ballet, 1736–1837; Part One: The Eighteenth Century." *Dance Chronicle* 23.2 (2000): 87–132.

Méheust, Bertrand. *Somnambulisme et médiumnité, 1784–1930*. In *Collection les empêcheurs de penser en rond*. 2 vols. Le Plessis-Robinson: Institut Synthélabo pour le Progrès de la Connaissance, 1999.

Melish, Joanne Pope. *Disowning Slavery: Gradual Emancipation and "Race" in New England, 1780–1860*. Ithaca, NY: Cornell University Press, 1998.

Mesmer, Franz Anton. *Mémoire de F. A. Mesmer, Docteur En Médecine Sur Ses Découvertes*. Paris: Fuchs, 1799.

Métraux, Alfred. *Le Vaudou haïtien* [1958]. Paris: Gallimard, 2003.

Mézière, Henri. *Le Général Leclerc (1772–1802) et l'expédition de Saint-Domingue*. Paris: Tallandier, 1990.

Michelet, Jules. *History of the French Revolution*. Charleston, SC: BiblioBazaar, 2008.

Miles, Robert. "The 1790s: The Effulgence of Gothic." In *The Cambridge Companion to Gothic Fiction*, edited by Jerold Hogle, 41–62. Cambridge: Cambridge University Press, 2002.

———, and E. J. Clery. *The Rise of Supernatural Fiction, 1762–1800*. Cambridge: Cambridge University Press, 1995.

Milscent, Jules Solime. "Suite des Considérations sur l'île d'Haiti." *L'Abeille Haytienne* 16 (August 1817): 3–7.

Mintz, Sidney. Foreword to *The Haitian People*, by James Leyburn, rev. ed. New Haven, CT: Yale University Press, 1966.

Mitchell, W. J. T. *Iconology: Image, Text, Ideology*. Chicago: University of Chicago Press, 1986.

Moïse, Claude. *Constitutions et luttes de pouvoir en Haïti, 1804–1987: La Faillite des classes dirigeantes (1804–1915)*. 2 vols. Montreal: Éditions du CIDIHCA, 1988.

———. *Le projet national de Toussaint Louverture et la Constitution de 1801*. Montreal: Les Éditions du CIDIHCA, 2001.

Monnier, René le. *Observations sur quelques epidémies de Saint-Domingue, compliquées de symptômes de la fièvre dite jaune*. Paris, 1810.

Monroe, James. *The Papers of James Monroe, 1776–1831*. Microfilm. Washington, DC: Library of Congress, 1963.

Montague, Ludwell Lee. *Haiti and the United States, 1714–1938*. Durham, NC: Duke University Press, 1940.
Moreau de Saint-Méry, M. L. E. *A Civilization that Perished: The Last Years of White Colonial Rule in Haiti*. Translated by Ivor D. Spencer. Lanham, MD: University Press of America, 1985.
———. *Description topographique, physique, civile, politique et historique de la partie Française de l'isle Saint-Domingue: Avec des observations générales sur sa population, sur le caractère & les mœurs de ses divers habitans ; sur son climat, sa culture, ses productions, son administration, &c. &c. Accompagnées des détails les plus propres à faire connaître l'état de cette colonie à l'époque du 18 octobre 1789 ; et d'une nouvelle carte de la totalité de l'isle*. 2 vols. Edited by I. Sonis and J. Vallance. Philadelphia, 1797.
Morgan, Edmund. *American Slavery, American Freedom: The Ordeal of Colonial Virginia*. New York: Norton, 1975.
Morison, Samuel E., Henry S. Commager, and William Leuchtenburg. *The Growth of the American Republic*, 7th ed. New York: Oxford University Press, 1980.
Morris, Richard B. *Encyclopedia of American History*. New York: Harper, 1953.
Moses, Wilson Jeremiah. *The Golden Age of Black Nationalism, 1850–1925*. Hamden, CT: Archon Books, 1988.
———. "The Poetics of Ethiopianism: W. E. B. DuBois and Literary Black Nationalism." *American Literature* 47.3 (November 1975): 411–426.
Moten, Fred. "Democracy." In *Keywords for American Cultural Studies*, edited by Glenn Hendler and Bruce Burgett, 76–79. New York: New York University Press, 2007.
Mott, Frank Luther. *American Journalism: A History of Newspapers in the United States through 250 Years, 1690–1940*. New York: Macmillan Company, 1941.
Murdock, John. *The Beau Metamorphized, or, The Generous Maid: An After-Piece in Two Acts*. Philadelphia: Printed by Joseph C. Charless for the author, 1800.
———. *The Politicians; or, A State of Things. A Dramatic Piece*. Philadelphia: Printed for the author, 1798.
———. *The Triumphs of Love; or, Happy Reconciliation. A Comedy in Four Acts*. Philadelphia: R. Folwell, 1795.
Murphy, Kieran. "Magic and Mesmerism in Saint Domingue." *Paroles Gelées: UCLA French Studies* 24 (2008): 31–48.
Nabers, Deak. "The Problem of Revolution in the Age of Slavery: *Clotel*, Fiction, and the Government of Man." *Representations* 91 (Summer 2005): 84–108.
Napoléon Ier. *Correspondance de Napoléon Ier*. 32 vols. Paris: Plon, 1856–1869.
Nash, Gary B. *Forging Freedom: The Formation of Philadelphia's Black Community, 1720–1840*. Cambridge, MA: Harvard University Press, 1988.
———. "Reverberations of Haiti in the American North: Black Saint Dominguans in Philadelphia." *Pennsylvania History* 65.5 (1998): 44–73.
———, and Jeanne R. Soderlund. *Freedom by Degrees: Emancipation in Pennsylvania and Its Aftermath*. New York: Oxford University Press, 1992.
Nassy, David de Isaac Cohen. *Observations sur la cause, la nature, et le traitement de la maladie epidemique qui regne a Philadelphie*. Philadelphia, 1793.
Nathans, Heather S. *Early American Theatre from the Revolution to Thomas Jefferson: Into the Hands of the People*. Cambridge: Cambridge University Press, 2003.
———. "Trampling Native Genius: John Murdock Versus the Chestnut Street Theatre." *Journal of American Drama and Theatre* 14.1 (2002): 29–43.

Nau, Emile. "Littérature." In *Panorama de la littérature haïtienne de 1804 à nos jours*, edited by Christophe Charles, 152–156. Port-au-Prince: Editions Choucounes, 2003.

Nesbitt, Nick. *Caribbean Critique*. Liverpool: Liverpool University Press, 2013.

———."The Idea of 1804." In *Haiti Issue: 1804 and Nineteenth-Century French Studies*, edited by Deborah Jenson. Special issue of *Yale French Studies* 107 (2005): 6–38.

———. *Universal Emancipation: The Haitian Revolution and the Radical Enlightenment*. Charlottesville: University of Virginia Press, 2008.

Newman, Richard S. *The Transformation of American Abolitionism: Fighting Slavery in the Early Republic*. Chapel Hill: University of North Carolina Press, 2002.

Newman, Simon P. "American Political Culture and the French and Haitian Revolutions: Nathaniel Cutting and the Jeffersonian Republicans." In *The Impact of the Haitian Revolution in the Atlantic World*, edited by David Patrick Geggus, 72–89. Columbia: University of South Carolina, 2001.

———. *Parades and Politics of the Street: Festive Culture in the Early Republic*. Philadelphia: University of Pennsylvania Press, 1997.

Nicholls, David. *From Dessalines to Duvalier: Race, Colour, and National Independence in Haiti*, rev. ed. New Brunswick, NJ: Rutgers University Press, 1996.

Oberg, Barbara, ed. *The Papers of Thomas Jefferson*. 40 vols (to date). Princeton, NJ: Princeton University Press, 2003–2004. Vols. 30–31.

O'Brien, Colleen C. "Paternal Solicitude and Haitian Emigration: The First American Occupation?" *South Central Review* 30.1 (2013): 32–54.

Ohline, Howard A. "Georgetown, South Carolina: Racial Anxieties and Militant Behavior, 1802." *South Carolina Historical Magazine* 73.3 (July 1972): 130–140.

Ott, Thomas. *The Haitian Revolution, 1789–1804*. Knoxville: University of Tennessee Press, 1972.

Otter, Samuel. *Philadelphia Stories: America's Literature of Race and Freedom*. New York: Oxford University Press, 2010.

Palmer, Robert R. *The Age of the Democratic Revolution*, 2 vols. Princeton, NJ: Princeton University Press, 1959, 1964.

Palmié, Stephan, and Francisco A. Scarano, eds. *The Caribbean: A History of the Region and Its Peoples*. Chicago: University of Chicago Press, 2011.

Paquette, Robert L. "Jacobins of the Lowcountry: The Vesey Plot on Trial." *William and Mary Quarterly* 59 (January 2002): 185–192.

———. "Revolutionary Saint Domingue in the Making of Territorial Louisiana." In *A Turbulent Time: The French Revolution and the Greater Caribbean*, edited by D. B. Gaspar and D. P. Geggus, 204–225. Bloomington: Indiana University Press, 1997.

Paryz, Marek. "Beyond the Traveler's Testimony: Emerson's English Traits and the Construction of Postcolonial Counter-Discourse." *The American Transcendental Quarterly* (September 2006). http://www.accessmylibrary.com/coms2/summary_0286-26681429_ITM.

Pasley, Jeffrey L. *"The Tyranny of Printers": Newspaper Politics in the Early American Republic*. Charlottesville: University of Virginia Press, 2001.

Patterson, Orlando. *Slavery and Social Death: A Comparative Study*. Cambridge, MA: Harvard University Press, 1982.

Péan, Marc. *L'échec du Firminisme*. Port-au-Prince, Haïti: H. Deschamps, 1987.

Pease, Donald. "Exceptionalism." In *Keywords for American Cultural Studies*, edited by Glenn Hendler and Bruce Burgett, 108–112. New York: New York University Press, 2007.

Pernick, Martin S. "Politics, Parties, and Pestilence: Epidemic Yellow Fever in Philadelphia and the Rise of the First Party System." *William and Mary Quarterly* 29.4 (October 1972): 559–586.

Peterson, Merrill D. *Thomas Jefferson and the New Nation: A Biography*. New York: Oxford University Press, 1970.

Phillips, Wendell. "Toussaint l'Ouverture." In *Speeches, Lectures, and Letters*, edited by Wendell Phillips. Boston: James Redpath, 1863.

Pinckard, George. *Notes on the West Indies, Including Observations Relative to the Creoles and Slaves of the Western Colonies, and the Indians of South America; Interspersed with Remarks upon the Seasoning or Yellow Fever of Hot Climates*, 2nd edition with additional Letters from Martinique, Jamaica, and St. Domingo, 2 vols. London: Baldwin, Cradock, and Joy, 1816.

Pluchon, Pierre. *Toussaint Louverture: Un révolutionnaire noir d'Ancien Régime*. Paris: Éditions Fayard, 1989.

Poe, Edgar Allan. *The Science Fiction of Edgar Allan Poe*. Edited by Harold Lowther Beaver. Harmondsworth: Penguin, 1976.

Polyné, Millery. *From Douglass to Duvalier: U.S. African Americans, Haiti and Pan Americanism, 1870–1964*. Gainesville: University Press of Florida, 2010.

Pompilus, Pradel. *Manuel illustré de la littérature haïtienne*. Port-au-Prince: Editions Henri Deschamps, 1961.

Popkin, Jeremy D. "Facing Racial Revolution: Captivity Narratives and Identity in the Saint-Domingue Insurrection." *Eighteenth-Century Studies* 36 (2003): 511–533.

———. *You Are All Free: The Haitian Revolution and the Abolition of Slavery*. Cambridge: Cambridge University Press, 2010.

Powell, J. H. *Bring Out Your Dead: The Great Plague of Yellow Fever in Philadelphia in 1793*. Philadelphia: University of Pennsylvania Press, 1949.

Pratt, Julius. *A History of United States Foreign Policy*. New York: Prentice-Hall, 1955.

Price-Mars, Jean. *So Spoke the Uncle*. Translated by Magadaline W. Shannon. Washington, DC: Three Continents Press, 1983.

Priestley, Herbert I. *France Overseas Through the Old Regime*. New York: Appleton-Century, 1939.

Puységur, Armand-Marie-Jacques de Chastenet de. *Du Magnétisme animal: Considéré dans ses rapports avec diverses branches de la physique générale*, 2nd ed. Paris: J. G. Dentu, 1820.

Pybus, Cassandra, *Epic Journeys of Freedom: Runaway Slaves of the American Revolution and Their Global Quest for Liberty*. Boston: Beacon Press, 2006.

Pym, William. *Observations upon the Bulam Fever, which Has of Late Years Prevailed in the West Indies, on the Coast of America, at Gibraltar, Cadiz, and Other Parts of Spain: with a Collection of Facts Proving It to Be a Highly Contagious Disease*. London, 1815.

Quinn, Frederick. *The French Overseas Empire*. Westport, CT: Praeger, 2000.

Rainsford, Marcus. *An Historical Account of the Black Empire of Hayti Comprehending a View of the Principle Transactions in the Revolution of Saint Domingo; with Its Antient and Modern State*. London: Albion Press for James Cundee, 1805.

Ramsey, Kate. *The Spirits and the Law: Vodou and Power in Haiti*. Chicago: University of Chicago Press, 2011.

———, and Alex Dupuy. *Haiti in the World Economy: Class, Race, and Underdevelopment since 1700*. Boulder, CO: Westview Press, 1989.

Ray, Thomas M. "'Not One Cent for Tribute': The Public Addresses and American Popular Reaction to the XYZ Affair, 1798–1799." *Journal of the Early Republic* 3.3 (1983): 389–412.

Regourd, François. "Mesmerism in Saint-Domingue: Occult Knowledge and Vodou on the Eve of the Haitian Revolution." In *Science and Empire in the Atlantic World*, edited by James Delbourgo and Nicholas Dew, 311–332. New York: Routledge, 2008.

Rémusat, Charles de. *The Saint-Domingue Plantation, or, The Insurrection: A Drama in Five Acts*. Edited by Doris Y. Kadish. Translated by Norman R. Shapiro. Baton Rouge: Louisiana State University Press, 1828.

Renaut, Francis P. *La Question de la Louisiane, 1796–1806*. Paris: E. Champion, 1918.

Richard, Carl J. *The Louisiana Purchase*. Lafayette: Center for Louisiana Studies, 1995.

Richards, Jeffrey H. *Drama, Theatre, and Identity in the American New Republic*. Cambridge: Cambridge University Press, 2005.

Rickels, Laurence A. *I Think I Am: Philip K. Dick*. Minneapolis: University of Minnesota Press, 2010.

Robinson, Randall. *An Unbroken Agony: Haiti, from Revolution to the Kidnapping of a President*. New York: Basic Books, 2007.

Robertson, David. "Inconsistent Contextualism: The Hermeneutics of Michael Johnson." *William and Mary Quarterly* 59.1 (January 2002): 153–158.

Robertson, James A. *Louisiana Under the Rule of Spain, France, and the United States, 1785–1807*. Cleveland: Arthur Clark, 1911.

Roederer, A. M., ed. *Oeuvres du Comte P. L. Roederer*. Vol. 3. Paris: Firmin, 1854.

Roederer, Pierre-Louis, *Journal du Comte P.-L. Roederer, Ministre et Conseiller d'Etat*. Paris: Daragon, 1909.

Roediger, David R. *The Wages of Whiteness: Race and the Making of the American Working Class*. London: Verso, 1991.

Rogers, George C. *The History of Georgetown County, South Carolina*. Columbia: University of South Carolina Press, 1970.

Roloff, Gustav. *Die Kolonialpolitik Napoleons I*. Munich: Oldenbourg, 1899.

Ruffin, Kimberly. *Black on Earth: African American Ecoliterary Traditions*. Athens: University of Georgia Press, 2010.

Rugemer, Edward Bartlett. *The Problem of Emancipation: The Caribbean Roots of the American Civil War*. Baton Rouge: Louisiana State University Press, 2008.

———. "Slave Rebels and Abolitionists: The Black Atlantic and the Coming of the Civil War." *Journal of the Civil War Era* 2.2 (June 2012): 179–202.

Rush, Benjamin. *An Account of the Bilious Remitting Yellow Fever, as It Appeared in the City of Philadelphia in the Year 1793*, 2nd ed. Philadelphia, 1794.

———. *An Enquiry into the Origin of the Late Epidemic Fever in Philadelphia*. Philadelphia, 1793.

———. *Observations upon the Origin of the Malignant Billious, or Yellow Fever in Philadelphia*. Philadelphia, 1799.

Sage, Victor, ed. *The Gothic Novel: A Casebook*. Basingstoke: Macmillan, 1990.

Saint-Louis, Vertus. *Aux origines du drame d'Haïti: droit et commerce maritime (1794–1806)*. Port-au-Prince: L'Imprimeur II, 2006.

Saintoyant, Jules-François. *La Colonisation française pendant la période napoléonienne, (1799–1815)*. Paris: La Renaissance du Livre, 1931.

Saint-Rémy, Joseph. Foreword to *Mémoire pour servir à l'histoire d'Haïti*, by Louis-Félix Boisrond-Tonnèrre. Port-au-Prince, 1804.

Samuels, Shirley. *Romances of the Republic: Women, the Family, and Violence in the Literature of the Early American Nation.* New York: Oxford University Press, 1996.
Sannon, H. Pauléus. *Histoire de Toussaint Louverture* [1920]. Vol. 2, 2nd ed. Port-au-Prince: Collection Patrimoine, 2003.
Sansay, Leonora. *Secret History, or, The Horrors of St. Domingo.* Edited by Michael J. Drexler. Orchard Park, NY: Broadview, 2007.
Saunders, Prince. *Haytian Papers: A Collection of the Very Interesting Proclamations and Other Official Documents, Together with Some Account of the Rise, Progress, and Present State of the Kingdom of Haiti* [1818]. Philadelphia: Rhistoric, 1969.
———. *A Memoir Presented to the American Convention for Promoting the Abolition of Slavery, and Improving the Condition of the African Race, December 11th, 1818.* Philadelphia: Dennis Heartt, 1818.
Schafer, Daniel. *Anna Madgigine Jai Kingsley: African Princess, Florida Slave, Plantation Owner.* Gainesville: University Press of Florida, 2003.
Scherr, Arthur. "Jefferson's 'Cannibals' Revisited: A Closer Look at His Notorious Phrase." *Journal of Southern History* 77.2 (2011): 251–282.
Schoelcher, Victor. *Colonies étrangères et Haïti: Résultats de l'émancipation Anglaise,* Vol. 2. Paris: Pagnerre, 1843.
Schoeppner, Michael. "Legitimating Quarantine: Moral Contagions, the Commerce Clause, and the Limits of *Gibbons v. Ogden.*" *Journal of Southern Legal History* 17 (2009): 81–120.
Schumpeter, Joseph A. *Capitalism, Socialism, and Democracy.* New York: Harper & Row, 1942.
Scott, David. *Conscripts of Modernity: The Tragedy of Colonial Enlightenment.* Durham, NC: Duke University Press, 2004.
Scott, Julius Sherrard. "The Common Wind: Currents of Afro-American Communication in the Era of the Haitian Revolution." Ph.D. diss., Duke University, 1986.
Scott, Rebecca J. *Degrees of Freedom: Louisiana and Cuba After Slavery.* Cambridge, MA: Belknap Press of Harvard University Press, 2005.
Seaver, James Everett. "A Narrative of the Life of Mrs. Mary Jemison." In *Women's Indian Captivity Narratives,* edited by Kathryn Zabelle Derounian-Stodola, 117–210. New York: Penguin Books, 1998.
Sepinwall, Alyssa Goldstein. *The Abbé Grégoire and the French Revolution: The Making of Modern Universalism.* Berkeley: University of California Press, 2005.
———. "Exporting the Revolution: Grégoire, Haiti, and the Colonial Laboratory, 1815–1827." In *The Abbé Grégoire and His World,* edited by Richard Popkin and Jeremy H. Popkin, 41–69. Boston: Kluwer Academic Publishers, 2000.
———. "The Specter of Saint-Domingue: The Impact of the Haitian Revolution in the United States and France." In *The World of the Haitian Revolution,* edited by David Patrick Geggus and Norman Fiering, 317–338. Bloomington: Indiana University Press, 2009.
Shapiro, Anne Dhu. "Action Music in American Pantomime and Melodrama, 1730–1913." *American Music* 2.4 (Winter 1984): 49–72.
Shapiro, Stephen. *Culture and Commerce in the Early American Novel: Reading the Atlantic World-System.* University Park: Penn State University Press, 2008.
Shell, Marc, and Werner Sollors. *The Multilingual Anthology of American Literature: A Reader of Original Texts with English Translations.* New York: New York University Press, 2000.

Sheller, Mimi. "'The Haytian Fear': Racial Projects and Competing Reactions to the First Black Republic." *Politics and Society* 6 (1999): 283–301.
Shugerman, Jed Handelsman. "The Louisiana Purchase and South Carolina's Reopening of the Slave Trade in 1803." *Journal of the Early Republic* 22.2 (2002): 263–290.
Sidbury, James. "Plausible Stories and Varnished Truths." *William and Mary Quarterly* 59.1 (January 2002): 179–184.
———. *Ploughshares into Swords: Race, Rebellion, and Identity in Gabriel's Virginia, 1730–1810*. New York: Cambridge University Press, 1997.
———. "Saint Domingue in Virginia: Ideology, Local Meanings, and Resistance to Slavery, 1790–1800." *Journal of Southern History* 63.3 (1997): 539–541.
Silva, Cristobal. *Miraculous Plagues: An Epidemiology of Early New England Narrative*. New York: Oxford University Press, 2011.
Sinha, Manisha. *The Counterrevolution of Slavery: Politics and Ideology in Antebellum South Carolina*. Chapel Hill: University of North Carolina Press, 2000.
Siskin, Clifford. "Novels and Systems." *Novel: A Forum on Fiction* 34.2 (Spring 2001): 202–215.
Slotkin, Richard. *Regeneration Through Violence: The Mythology of the American Frontier, 1600–1860*, rev. ed. Norman: University of Oklahoma Press, 2000.
Smith, James McCune. *A Lecture on the Haytien Revolutions; with a Sketch of the Character of Toussaint L'Ouverture*. New York: Daniel Fanshaw, 1841.
Smith, Kimberly K. *African American Environmental Thought*. Lawrence: University of Kansas Press, 2007.
Smith, Ronald D. "Napoleon and Louisiana: Failure of the Proposed Expedition to Occupy and Defend Louisiana, 1801–1803." In *The Louisiana Purchase and its Aftermath, 1800–1830*, edited by Dolores Labbé. Lafayette: University of Southwestern Louisiana, 1998.
Sodders, Richard Phillip. "The Theatre Management of Alexandre Placide in Charleston, 1794–1812." Ph.D. diss., Louisiana State University, 1983.
Sonneck, Oscar. *Early Opera in America*. Boston: G. Schirmer, 1915.
Sprague, Marshall. *So Vast, So Beautiful a Land: Louisiana and the Purchase*. Boston: Little, Brown, 1974.
Spurlin, Paul Merrill. *The French Enlightenment in America: Essays on the Times of the Founding Fathers*. Athens: University of Georgia Press, 1984.
Stauffer, John. *The Black Hearts of Men*. Cambridge, MA: Harvard University Press, 2002.
Stein, Robert L. *Léger Félicité Sonthonax: The Lost Sentinel of the Republic*. Rutherford, NJ: Fairleigh Dickinson University Press, 1985.
Stenberg, Richard. "Napoleon's Cession of Louisiana: A Suggestion." *Louisiana Historical Quarterly* 21 (1938): 354–361.
Stepto, Robert B. *From Behind the Veil: A Study of Afro-American Narrative*, rev. ed. Urbana: University of Illinois Press, 1991.
Stern, Julia. *The Plight of Feeling: Sympathy and Dissent in the Early American Novel*. Chicago: University of Chicago Press, 1997.
Stoddard, T. Lothrop. *The French Revolution in San Domingo*. Boston: Houghton Mifflin, 1914.
Stowe, Harriet Beecher. *Uncle Tom's Cabin; or, Life Among the Lowly*. Boston: John P. Jewett, 1852.
Sundquist, Eric. *To Wake the Nations: Race in the Making of American Literature*. Cambridge, MA: Harvard University Press, 1993.
Swanwick, John. *A Rub from Snub, or, A Cursory Analytical Epistle: Addressed to Peter Porcupine*. Philadelphia, 1795.

Tawil, Ezra. *The Making of Racial Sentiment: Slavery and the Birth of the Frontier Romance.* Cambridge: Cambridge University Press, 2006.
Tennenhouse, Leonard. *The Importance of Feeling English: American Literature and the British Diaspora, 1750–1850.* Princeton, NJ: Princeton University Press, 2007.
The Black Abolitionist Papers. Vol. 3. Edited by Peter C. Ripley. Chapel Hill: University of North Carolina Press, 1991.
Thernstrom, Stephan. *A History of the American People.* San Diego: Harcourt Brace, 1989.
Timmreck, Thomas C. *An Introduction to Epidemiology,* 3rd ed. Boston: Jones, 2002.
Tise, Larry E. *The American Counterrevolution: A Retreat from Liberty, 1783–1800.* Mechanicsburg, PA: Stackpole Books, 1998.
Tomich, Dale. *Through the Prism of Slavery: Labor, Capital, and World Economy.* Lanham, MD: Rowman & Littlefield, 2004.
Touchard, H., ed. *L'Hermès: Journal du magnétisme animale.* Paris: Levi, 1828.
Tragle, Henry Irving. *The Southampton Slave Revolt of 1831: A Compilation of Source Material.* Amherst: University of Massachusetts Press, 1971.
Trouillot, Michel-Rolph. *Haiti, State Against Nation: The Origins and Legacy of Duvalierism.* New York: Monthly Review Press, 1990.
———. *Silencing the Past: Power and the Production of History.* Boston: Beacon Press, 1995.
———. "The Odd and the Ordinary." *Cimarrón* 2.3 (1990): 3–12.
Tucker, Robert W., and David C. Hendrickson. *Empire of Liberty: The Statecraft of Thomas Jefferson.* New York: Oxford University Press, 1990.
Tyler, Royall. *The Algerine Captive; Or, The Life and Adventures of Doctor Updike Underhill: Six Years a Prisoner Among the Algerines.* Edited by Caleb Crain. New York: Modern Library, 2002.
Vastey, Baron Pompée Valentin de. Appendix. *Essai sur les causes de la revolution et des guerres civiles d'Hayti, faisant suite au Réflexions politiques sur quelques ouvrages et journaux français concernant Hayti.* Sans-Souci, Haïti: L'Imprimerie royale, 1817.
———. *Le Cri de la conscience.* Cap-Henry: Chez P. Roux, 1815.
———. *Le Cri de la patrie.* Cap-Henry: Chez P. Roux, 1807.
———. *Essai sur les causes de la revolution et des guerres civiles d'Hayti, faisant suite au Réflexions politiques sur quelques ouvrages et journaux français concernant Hayti.* Sans-Souci, Haïti: L'Imprimerie royale, 1817.
———. *Notes à M. le Baron V. P. de Malouet.* Cap-Henry: Chez P. Roux, 1814.
———. *Political Remarks on Some French Works and Newspapers, Concerning Hayti.* London, 1818.
———. *Réflexions politiques sur quelques ouvrages et journaux français concernant Hayti.* Cap-Henry: Chez P. Roux, 1816.
———. *Réflexions sur une lettre de Mazères, ex-colon français Adressée à M. J.c.l. Sismonde De Sismondi. sur les noirs et les blancs, la civilization de l'Afrique, le Royaume d'Hayti, etc.* Sans Souci: L'Imprimérie Royale, 1817.
———. *Relation de la fête de la Reine S. M.dD'Hayti.* Cap-Henry: Chez P. Roux, 1816.
———. *Le Système coloniale dévoilé.* Cap-Henry: P. Roux Imprimerie du Roi, 1814.
Vincent, Bernard. *The Transatlantic Republican: Thomas Paine in the Age of Revolutions.* Amsterdam: Rodopi, 2004.
Wald, Priscilla. *Contagious: Cultures, Carriers, and the Outbreak Narrative.* Durham, NC: Duke University Press, 2008.
———. "Imagined Immunities." In *Cultural Studies and Political Theory,* edited by Jodi Dean, 189–208. Ithaca, NY: Cornell University Press, 2000.

Waldstreicher, David. *In the Midst of Perpetual Fetes: The Making of American Nationalism, 1776–1820*. Chapel Hill: University of North Carolina Press, 1997.

———, and Stephen R. Grossbart. "Abraham Bishop's Vocation; or, the Mediation of Jeffersonian Politics." *Journal of the Early Republic* 18.4 (1998): 617–657.

Walker, David. *Walker's Appeal, in Four Articles; Together with a Preamble, to the Coloured Citizens of the Worlds, But in Particular, and Very Expressly, to Those of the United States of America*. Boston: Printed for the Author, 1830.

Wallace, Maurice. *Constructing the Black Masculine: Identity and Ideality in African American Men's Literature and Culture, 1775–1995*. Durham, NC: Duke University Press, 2002.

Wallerstein, Immanuel Maurice. "The Ideological Tensions of Capitalism: Universalism Versus Racism and Sexism." In *Race, Nation, Class: Ambiguous Identities*, edited by Étienne Balibar and Immanuel Maurice Wallerstein. 29–36. New York: Verso, 1991.

Weaver, Karol K. *Medical Revolutionaries: The Enslaved Healers of Eighteenth-Century Saint Domingue*. Urbana: University of Illinois Press, 2006.

Webb, Frank J. *The Garies and Their Friends* [1857]. Edited and introduced by Robert Reid-Pharr. Baltimore: Johns Hopkins University Press, 1997.

Weinstein, Cindy. *Family, Kinship, and Sympathy in Nineteenth-Century American Literature*. New York: Cambridge University Press, 2004.

———, and Christopher Looby. *American Literature's Aesthetic Dimensions*. New York: Columbia University Press, 2012.

White, Arthur O. "Prince Saunders: An Instance of Social Mobility Among Antebellum New England Blacks." *Journal of Negro History* 60.4 (1975): 526–535.

White, Ashli. *Encountering Revolution: Haiti and the Making of the Early Republic*. Baltimore: Johns Hopkins University Press, 2010.

———. "'A Flood of Impure Lava': Saint Dominguan Refugees in the United States, 1791–1820." Ph.D. diss., Columbia University, 2003.

———. "The Limits of Fear: The Saint Dominguan Challenge to Slave Trade Abolition in the United States." *Early American Studies: An Interdisciplinary Journal* 2.2 (2004): 362–397.

———. "The Saint-Domingue Refugees and American Distinctiveness in the Early Years of the Haitian Revolution." In *The World of the Haitian Revolution*, edited by David Patrick Geggus and Norman Fiering, 248–260. Bloomington: Indiana University Press, 2009.

White, Shane. "'It Was a Proud Day': African Americans, Festivals, and Parades in the North, 1741–1834." *The Journal of American History* 81.1 (June 1994): 13–50.

Whitman, Walt. "Democratic Vistas." 1871. http://xroads.virginia.edu/-hyper/whitman/vistas/vistas.html.

Whittier, John Greenleaf. *Anti-Slavery Poems: Songs of Labor and Reform*. Boston: Houghton Mifflin, 1848.

Williams, William Appleman. *The Shaping of American Diplomacy*. Chicago: Rand McNally, 1956.

Williamson, John. *Medical and Miscellaneous Observations Relative to the West India Islands*, 2 vols. Edinburgh, 1817.

Willis, Eola. *The Charleston Stage in the XVIII Century*. Columbia, SC: State Company, 1924.

Wills, Gary. *Negro President: Jefferson and the Slave Power*. Waterville, ME: Thorndike Press, 2004.

Wilson, David, ed. *Peter Porcupine in America: Pamphlets on Republicanism and Revolution*. Introduction by David Wilson. Ithaca, NY: Cornell University Press, 1994.

Wilson, Ivy G. "On Native Ground: Transnationalism, Frederick Douglass, and 'The Heroic Slave.'" *PMLA* 121.2 (2006): 453–468.
Winter, Marian Hannah. "American Theatrical Dancing from 1750 to 1800." *Musical Quarterly* 24.1 (January 1938): 58–73.
Wisecup, Kelly. "'The Progress of the Heat Within': The West Indies, Yellow Fever, and Citizenship in William Wells Brown's *Clotel*." *Southern Literary Journal* 41.1 (Fall 2008): 1–19.
Woertendyke, Gretchen. "Romance to Novel: A Secret History." *Narrative* 17.3 (2009): 255–273.
Wood, Sally Sayward Barrell Keating. *Julia and the Illuminated Baron. A Novel: Founded on Recent Facts, Which Have Transpired in the Course of the Late Revolution of Moral Principles in France, by a Lady of Massachusetts*. Portsmouth, NH: Oracle Press, 1800.
Worrall, David. *The Politics of Romantic Theatricality, 1787–1832: The Road to the Stage*. New York: Palgrave Macmillan, 2007.
Ziesche, Philipp. *Cosmopolitan Patriots: Americans in Paris in the Age of Revolution*. Charlottesville: University of Virginia Press, 2010.
Zuckerman, Michael. *Almost Chosen People: Oblique Biographies in the American Grain*. Berkeley: University of California Press, 1993.
Zwarg, Christina. "Vigorous Currents, Painful Archives: The Production of Affect and History in Poe's 'Tale of the Ragged Mountains.'" *Poe Studies* 43.1 (2010): 7–33.

CONTRIBUTORS

Anthony Bogues is Asa Messer Professor of Humanities and Critical Theory and director of the Center for the Study of Slavery and Justice at Brown University. He is the author of *Empire of Liberty: Power, Freedom and Desire* (2010) and editor of *From Revolution in the Tropics to Imagined Landscape: The Art of Edouard Duval-Carrié* (2014).

Marlene L. Daut is associate professor of English and Cultural Studies at Claremont Graduate University, where she also directs the Graduate Certificate Program in Africana Studies. She is the author of *Tropics of Haiti: Race and the Literary History of the Haitian Revolution in the Atlantic World, 1789–1865* (2015).

Elizabeth Maddock Dillon is professor of English at Northeastern University. She is the author of *New World Drama: The Performative Commons in the Atlantic World, 1649–1849* (2014) and *The Gender of Freedom: Fictions of Liberalism and the Literary Public Sphere* (2004).

Michael J. Drexler is professor of English at Bucknell University. He is the author (with Ed White) of *The Traumatic Colonel: The Founding Fathers, Slavery, and the Phantasmatic Aaron Burr* (2014) and editor of Leonora Sansay's *Secret History; or, The Horrors of St. Domingo and Laura* (2007).

Laurent Dubois is Marcello Lotti Professor of Romance Studies and History. He is the author of *Haiti: The Aftershocks of History* (2012) and *Avengers of the New World: The Story of the Haitian Revolution* (2004).

James Alexander Dun is assistant professor of history at Princeton University. He is the author of *Dangerous Neighbors: Making the Haitian Revolution in Early America* (2016) and "Atlantic Antislavery, American Abolition," in Andrew Shankman, ed., *The World of the Revolutionary Republic* (2014).

Duncan Faherty is associate professor of English and American studies at Queens College and the City University of New York Graduate Center. He is the author of *Remodeling The Nation: The Architecture of American Identity, 1776–1858* and the co-curator of the *Just Teach One* textual recovery project housed at the American Antiquarian Society.

Carolyn Fick is associate professor of history at Concordia University in Montreal. She is the author of *The Making of Haiti: The Saint Domingue Revolution from Below* (1990), recently translated and published in French, titled: *Haïti: Naissance d'une Nation. La Révolution de Saint-Domingue vue d'en bas* (2013/2014).

David Geggus is professor of history at the University of Florida, Gainesville. Among his most recent publications are *Haitian Revolutionary Studies* (2002) and *The Haitian Revolution: A Documentary History* (2014).

Kieran M. Murphy is assistant professor of French and comparative literature at the University of Colorado–Boulder. He is the author of "Electromagnetic Thought in Balzac, Villiers de l'Isle-Adam and Joseph Breuer" (2011) and "White Zombie" (2011).

Colleen C. O'Brien is associate professor of American literature at the University of South Carolina–Upstate. She is the author of *Race, Romance, and Rebellion: Literatures of the Americas in the Nineteenth Century* (2013).

Peter P. Reed is associate professor of English at the University of Mississippi. He is the author of *Rogue Performances: Staging the Underclasses in Early American Theatre Culture* (2009) and essays on Atlantic theatre, racial performance, and Haiti's influence on nineteenth-century American culture.

Siân Silyn Roberts is associate professor of English at Queens College, City University New York. She is the author of *Gothic Subjects: The Transformation of Individualism in American Fiction, 1790–1861* (2014), and has contributed to the edited volume *The Transatlantic Turn of the Gothic* (2013).

Cristobal Silva is assistant professor of English and comparative literature at Columbia University. He is the author of *Miraculous Plagues: An Epidemiology of Early New England Narrative* (2011).

Ed White is Pierce Butler Professor of English at Tulane University. He is the author of *The Backcountry and the City* (2005) and (with Michael J. Drexler) *The Traumatic Colonel: The Founding Fathers, Slavery, and the Phantasmatic Aaron Burr* (2014).

Ivy G. Wilson is associate professor of English and director of the program in American studies at Northwestern University. He is author of *Specters of Democracy: Blackness and the Aesthetics of Politics in the Antebellum U.S.* (2011) and editor (with Dana Luciano) of *Unsettled States: Nineteenth-Century American Literary Studies* (2014).

Gretchen J. Woertendyke is associate professor of English at the University of South Carolina. She is the author of *Hemispheric Regionalism: Romance and the Geography of Genre* (2016).

Edlie Wong is associate professor of English at the University of Maryland–College Park. She is the author of *Racial Reconstruction: Black Inclusion, Chinese Exclusion, and the Fictions of Citizenship* (2015) and *Neither Fugitive nor Free: Atlantic Slavery, Freedom Suits, and the Legal Culture of Travel* (2009).

INDEX

ACS (American Colonization Society), 163, 175–77, 207
Adams, Henry, 8, 117, 123
Adams, John, 24, 28, 31, 35, 39, 117–18, 125, 223, 226; "Defence of the Constitution of the Government of the United States," 301
Adams, John, Quincy, 380n88
Adams administration, 5, 8, 28, 223, 380n91
Africa, 175, 177–80, 184, 194, 196–97, 199, 201, 206, 229, 233, 352n42; emigration to, 186–87
African-American intellectuals, 81, 83–84, 94
African-American labor discourse, 190–99
African-American literature, 213–15
African Americans, 96, 176–77, 179–80, 206–7, 282, 358n2
African-American writers, 115
African colonization, 163, 177, 180–81, 284
African nationality, 85, 88, 93
Africans, 87, 131, 139–42, 155, 177, 198, 203–4, 235, 294, 297, 307–8, 310, 315, 365–66n70
African slaves, 62, 71, 74, 113, 144, 316, 361n47
agrarian, 192, 195–96
Aiken, William, 172
Allen, Richard, 141, 178, 208
American Civil War, 11–12, 84–85, 92–93, 96, 103, 185, 289–90, 329n32
American emigrants, black, 163, 182–83
American identity, 10, 260–61, 310–11
American independence, 113, 168, 170
American literature, 232, 241, 291, 308, 366n1
American merchants, 29, 291
American novel, 265; early, 211, 264–65, 364, 366–67n5, 367n9, 369n27
American Renaissance, 84, 293
American Revolution, 11, 48, 92, 229, 310–11, 316–17; politics of, 320–21, 323; relationship to Haitian independence, 2–3, 14, 168–69, 176, 232, 308
American vessels, 29, 31–32, 166
Anderson, Benedict, 76–77
animal magnetism, 145–50, 152–53
Arendt, Hannah, 320–21, 324
Arthur Mervyn, 244, 246–47, 265
assassination, 183, 195, 217
asylum, 178–79, 273–74, 370n33
Atlantic world, 3, 5, 130–33, 140, 263–65, 314–15, 318–19, 349nn2, 4, 350n20, 366n5

Bache, Benjamin Franklin, 47, 49, 51–53, 55–56, 334n19, 335n34, 337n52
Bacon, Jacqueline, 14, 193, 358–59n2
Baltimore, 66, 70, 172, 246, 282, 365n69
Baptist, Edward, 11–12
Barnave, Antoine, 43
Barnes, Elizabeth, 366n2
Bauer, Ralph, 311
Beard, John R., 185, 382n111
Benito Cereno, 85, 365n62
Benot, Yves, 117, 119, 124
Berlant, Lauren, 303, 305
Bickerstaff, Isaac, 278
Bigelow, John, 80–81
Black Jacobins, 86, 145, 281, 322
black militancy, 163, 184–86
blackness, 56, 192, 202–3, 228, 232, 234, 237, 249, 278, 281, 285, 297, 364n42
black revolutionaries, 59, 66, 71, 76, 200, 367n7
black sailors, 115, 165–66, 169
Bonaparte, Napoleon, 6–7, 142, 225, 247–48, 297–98, 327nn13, 14, 342n36, 348n24; French empire, 6–7, 39–40; comparison with Toussaint Louverture, 90, 221; role in Louisiana purchase, 114, 118–28

Borgella, Bernard, 216, 219–20
Bossales, 194
Boyer, Jean-Pierre, 12, 163, 169–70, 173–79, 182–83, 186, 196–97, 358n7
Breuer, Joseph, 152
Brickhouse, Anna, 293, 374n7
Britain, 31, 46, 53, 114, 119, 121, 123, 126–30, 166, 222, 234–35, 239, 320, 348n57, 366n4
Brown, Charles Brockden, 242–49, 265, 362n7
Brown, John, 92, 95, 186
Brown, William Wells, 83–84, 88, 115, 163–64, 215
Buck-Morss, Susan, 14, 146, 154, 158–59
Bunel, Joseph, 28, 36
Burke, Edmund, 50, 238, 316, 318, 363n21
Burr, Aaron, 223, 261, 264, 275, 348n67, 362n7

Cap-Français, 43, 45–46, 53
Carey, Matthew, 141
Césaire, Aimé, 312, 314–15, 318, 322, 324
Charleston, SC, 61–62, 163–64, 166–72, 175, 177, 179, 275, 277; Corporation of, 168, 170
Chastenet, Armand-Marie-Jacques de, 148–50, 152, 351n18
Christophe, Henry, 206–7, 297–98, 301, 303–4, 357–58n2, 358nn6, 7, 360nn32, 43, 362n1, 376n25, 377n63, 378n69, 379n86, 379–80n88, 381n99; *Haytian Papers*, 195–97, 202; re-institution of plantation economy, 98, 189–91, 193
Cinque, Joseph, 93
citizenship, 40, 60, 84, 130–31, 139–41, 252–53, 255, 318–19, 321, 368n12; rights of, 40–41, 368n19
civic equality, 20, 44, 46, 50–54, 56, 368n19
Clarkson, Thomas, 303, 312, 358n6, 379n86
Clavin, Matthew, 95, 207, 361n48
Clay, Joseph, 303
Clotel, 184–85, 251, 357n121
Clyde, William, 104, 106
Cobbett, William, 234–39, 244, 249, 362–63n12
Code Henri, 181, 189–91, 195
coffee, 7, 33, 42, 61, 99, 329, 369n20
colonialism, 6, 20, 146, 155, 188; and slavery, 29, 39, 102, 312, 317, 321–23
colonial power, 146–47, 151, 153–54, 247, 323, 353n47

colonists, 2–3, 42, 45, 295, 300, 353; white, 46, 50–52, 55, 186, 367n7, 369n28
Colored Orphan Asylum, 91, 359n28, 359–60n30
Congress, U.S., 6, 29, 31, 34, 96, 166, 170, 174, 225, 234, 302–3, 328
Consolante, 61–66, 69–71, 75, 78
conspiracy, 65, 145, 167–69, 172–73, 217, 234, 238
constitution, 45, 299, 323, 342n38, 344–45n22, 362n1. *See also* Toussaint's Constitution
contract, 180, 253, 256–57, 259, 356n82, 366n4, 368n12
Coquette, The, 250, 253, 368n12
Cornish, Samuel, 163, 176, 208
cotton, 11–13, 61, 119, 196, 328–29
counter-memories, 20, 81–82, 86, 93
counter-revolution, 51–52, 336n39, 336–37n50
counter-revolutionary St. Domingue, 162–65, 167–68, 170, 173–74, 188
Crummell, Alexander, 186
Cuffee, Paul, 181, 198
Cushing, Caleb, 299–301, 307, 375n17

dance, 146–47, 269, 277, 280, 322; vaudoux dance, 146–49, 153, 159
Darnton, Robert, 149–50
Davis, William, 42–44, 334, 337, 341, 348, 391
Dayan, Colin (Joan), 14, 146, 154–56, 158–60, 367n7
DeConde, Alexander, 125
Decrès, Denis, 125, 347n51
Delany, Martin R., 182, 186, 215
Deliesseline, Francis G., 171
Devèze, Jean, 138, 350n25
Dewey, Loring D., 176–77, 179
disease, 14, 114, 130–40, 142, 144, 244, 246
Douglass, Frederick, 97, 99, 101, 103, 105–9, 188, 215, 356n101
drama, 284
Drayton, John, 75–76, 340n26
Duncan, Ian, 240–41, 364nn33, 36
Dunlap, William, 371n9, 372n29

Early American Republic, 40–41, 77–78, 236, 246, 249; academic history of, 1, 132, 243; black revolution in, 232–34, 239
Edgar Huntly, 235, 246, 265
Edwards, Bryan, 164, 233–34, 364n38

emigration, 85, 175–77, 181, 203, 320, 356n93, 366n4
England, 85, 92, 100, 183–84, 186, 296, 300–301, 357–58n2; and Napoleon, 6, 114, 118–19; and United States, 12, 126–29, 294, 306
epidemic, 130, 132–33, 135–40, 142
Equiano, Olaudah, 214, 216, 230
Europe, 7, 124–25, 127–28, 132–33, 184, 187, 206–7, 294–95; migration, 99, 136; slavery in, 54–55, 102; war in, 23–24, 27, 29
exiles, 38, 108, 146, 167, 179, 273–78, 287

Faubert, Pierre, 203, 312
Federalists, 215, 222–23, 226, 228, 234, 247, 300, 379n82; anxiety about Haiti, 60, 137, 230; trade with Haiti, 8–9, 36
Firmin, Anténor, 97, 99, 101–5, 107–10
Forten, James, 198, 207, 215
Foucault, Michel, 81–82, 257–58, 341n7, 369n25
France, 5–7, 103–4, 118–19, 125–27, 129–30, 329–35, 378n71, 379n86; National Assembly of, 42, 45–46, 49–52, 333n12, 334nn16, 27, 335n37, 337n59; response to Haitian Revolution, 12–13, 23–29, 34–41, 44–47, 49–50, 52–56
Franco-American relations, 61, 121
Franklin, Benjamin, 223–24, 295, 299, 334n19; relationship to the occult, 114, 145–46, 149, 152–54, 159, 161
Franklin Commission, 146, 149, 151–53
freedom, 55–56, 168–69, 186–88, 191–201, 203–4, 206–7, 258–59, 278–81, 319, 324, 357n121, 358n7, 360n43, 361n47
Freedom's Journal, 83, 86, 163, 176, 180, 183, 193, 207, 358n2
French Directory, 25, 32–35, 120
French frigates, 58–61, 64, 66–68, 70, 75–78
French General Assembly's Decree of May 15th, 43–44, 49–50, 52, 55–57, 336n39
French Negroes, 58, 62, 67, 69, 73–74, 77–78, 282–84, 340n30, 354n21, 373n54
French refugees, 274, 277–78, 372n23
French Revolution, 20, 43–50, 56–57, 119, 199–200, 220–22, 236, 239–40, 281, 311, 315–19, 321, 363n21, 367n7
Freneau, Philip, 52–53, 55, 336n42
Freud, Sigmund, 160

Gabriel's Rebellion, 73, 339n25, 365n62
Garies and Their Friends, 88–89, 181, 185

Geffrard, Fabre, 97
Genêt, Edmond, 29, 372n23
genre, 15, 211, 234, 241, 249, 316, 363n24, 364n38
gens de coleur, 4, 20, 43–44, 46–57, 162, 204, 273, 332–33n5, 334n16, 335n37, 337n54, 368n19, 369n20
Georgia, 19, 165, 214, 338–39n19, 340n30
Gilroy, Paul, 180, 211
Girard, Philippe, 120, 123, 193, 341n42
Godwin, William, 240, 363n31
gothic, 67, 232, 234–35, 239, 241–43, 249, 363n24, 364nn32, 38, 369n22
Grant, Ulysses S., 103
Great Britain, 31–34, 36, 38–40, 133–34, 166, 320; relationship with Haiti, 19, 23, 27–29; role in Louisiana Purchase, 113, 118, 122
Grégoire, Henri, 55–56, 377–78n64

Haitian Declaration of Independence, 318, 323
Haitian emigration, 176–78, 181, 195, 197
Haitian exceptionalism, 1–2, 14, 287, 295–96
Haitian independence, 97–98, 159, 162, 172, 212, 282, 288, 290, 295–96, 299, 302–4, 308, 310, 373n51, 378n71
Haitian literature, 287, 289, 291, 293, 295, 297, 299, 301, 303, 305, 307, 309, 311, 313, 376n29
Haitian modernity, 163, 179–81
Haitian sovereignty, 109, 174, 294, 305–6
Hall, Prince, 202
Hamilton, Alexander, 34, 122–23, 137, 222–24
Hampton, Wade, 72, 338–39n19, 339–40n26
Hawthorne, Nathaniel, 211, 243, 265
Haytian Papers, 181, 189, 192, 195–97, 206–7, 357n1
Hegel, Georg Wilhelm Friedrich, 158, 291, 324
Hemings, Sally, 224
herd immunity, 114, 135–36, 138–40, 142, 144, 349n15
history, universal, 82, 90, 158–59

immigration, 99, 177, 244, 364–65n50
immunity, 114, 132, 135, 137, 139–42, 144, 179

Jacmel, 36–38
Jefferson, Thomas, 6–8, 39–40, 121, 123, 226, 228, 237–38, 320, 338–39n19, 339–40n26, 348n55, 362n5, 363nn20, 21, 378n71

Jemison, Mary, 261
Jenson, Deborah, 291
Jim Crow, 188
Johnson, Michael P., 164, 167, 171
Jones, Absalom, 141, 214, 230, 350n34

King, Rufus, 34, 300

labor ideology, free, 192–93, 203–5, 359n11
land ownership, 115, 192, 196–97, 199, 206, 368n18
Leclerc, Charles, 7–8, 122–23, 142
Liberia, 85, 163, 176–77, 208
Livingston, Edward, 68–71, 75, 339n24
Locke, John, 251–52, 254, 316, 367n11, 367–68n12
Logan, George, 9
Louisiana Purchase, 8–10, 114, 117–19, 121–23, 125, 127–29, 346n25

Madison, James, 72, 223, 236, 338–39n19, 339nn24, 25
magnetism, 147, 149, 154
Maitland, Peregrine, 27, 31–32, 35
manumission, 184, 280–81
maroons, 93, 201–2, 317
Martineau, Harriet, 206
Mauduit du Plessis, Antoine de, 44, 46, 49, 53, 333n12
Maury, Fontaine, 68, 71–72, 75, 338–39n19, 339n25, 339–40n26, 340n27
McCune Smith, James, 83, 87, 192–93, 199, 202–4, 207–8, 359n13, 29, 360n38
McLean, Hector, 134, 143
Melville, Herman, 211, 265, 365n62
merchants, 36, 43, 51; U.S. merchants, 104, 302–3, 305–6, 372n23, 376n25, 378n71, 379–80n88, 381n99; U.S. merchants trade with Haiti, 6, 8, 19, 28–29, 71, 96
Mesmer, Franz, 145–46, 148–50, 152, 154, 159, 161, 351n18
mesmerism, 114, 145–46, 148–49, 151–55, 158, 160–61
Milscent, Jules Solime, 294, 303, 305–6
mimicry, 278–79, 281, 298
miscegenation, 285, 382n111
modernity, history of, 3, 14–15, 41, 117, 145–46, 154–56, 158–60, 315, 352n27
monarchy, 24, 297–301, 317, 377n64
Monroe, James, 72, 75, 127, 331, 338–39n19, 339–40n26, 340n27

Moses, Wilson, 198
mulattoes, 42, 52, 54–56, 109, 335n34
Murdock, John, 212, 266–73, 276, 278–80, 282, 284–86, 370nn1, 2, 373nn44, 50

National Assembly of France. *See* France
national identity, 77, 114, 130–32, 139–40, 144, 214, 270, 290, 307
nationalism, 198
Native Americans, 154, 156, 242, 249
natural rights, 55, 192, 198–200, 204, 291, 297, 358n10
Nau, Ignace, 374n11
Negro Seamen Acts, 162, 165–66, 171–73, 175, 185, 188
New England, 113, 180, 223–24
New Orleans, 121–24, 126–27, 129, 185, 328n23, 353n5, 365n50, 371n1, 375n24
newspapers, 19, 50, 234, 274, 288–90, 297–98, 379–80n88, 381n99; coverage of Haitian revolution, 174–76, 215, 221–22; coverage of French frigates, 59, 62–64, 66–67; of Philadelphia, 44–45, 48
New York, 61, 63–64, 68–72, 74–75, 78, 172, 177, 183, 199, 203–5, 275–76
Norfolk, VA, 66, 73, 172, 244, 338nn13, 15
North Star, 84, 87

Ogé, Vincent, 45–47, 50, 57, 336n44

pandemic, 131–35, 140–41, 144, 349n2
Paquette, Robert, 118, 124, 126
Paul, Thomas, 178, 355n79
Pétion, Alexandre, 190, 215, 288, 292, 299, 303, 374–75n12, 375n20, 377n64, 379n86, 379–80n88
petit blancs, 4, 199, 204–5
Philadelphia, 42–44, 47–50, 131–32, 137–39, 141–42, 244–46, 267–69, 271–75, 334n19, 370nn6, 7, 371n8, 372n23
Philadelphia's American Philosophical Society, 152–53
Phillips, Wendell, 83, 88–93
Pichon, Stephen-Jean-Marie, 126
Pickering, Timothy, 380n91
Placide, Alexandre, 275–77
Port-au-Prince, 31, 49, 51, 95, 100, 104, 107–8, 169, 175, 335n37
portraits, 43, 49, 80–81, 86–88, 192, 197, 219

Prosser, Gabriel, 164, 215
Puységur, Marquis de, 148–49, 351nn7, 9
Pym, William, 142

Quasi-War, 5, 23, 28, 35, 39, 61, 331n11, 337n4

race, 20–21, 86, 229–30, 234, 239, 241, 249, 308–9, 322–23, 361–62, 371
racial slavery, 162–63, 170, 187, 314–15, 317, 321–23
racism, 9, 13, 199, 204, 254, 327n6
recognition of Haiti, 34–35, 40–41, 97, 174, 291–92, 301–6, 310, 379n86, 381n103
refugees, 14, 19, 130, 132–33, 137–38, 262, 266–69, 271, 273–77, 279, 281, 283–86, 349n2, 370–71n33
retrocession, 123, 125–26, 348n65
revolutionary antislavery, 166, 186–87
Revolutionary St. Domingue, 23, 25, 27, 29, 31, 33, 35, 37, 39, 41, 187, 238; counter-revolutionary St. Domingue, 170
Rigaud, André, 32, 36–37, 39, 215, 375n24
romance, 226, 234–35, 239–44
Rowlandson, Mary, 260–62, 369n30
runaways, 282–84
Rush, Benjamin, 132, 137–38, 140–41, 280, 370n2, 373n44

Saint-Méry, Moreau de, 146–48, 153–54, 350n4, 372n23
San Ildefonso, Treaty of, 121
Sansay, Leonora, 164, 250–51, 253, 255–62, 265, 275; *Secret History; or The Horrors of St. Domingo*, 182, 211, 361nn44, 45, 367nn7, 9, 368nn17, 18, 369nn20, 21, 22
Saunders, Prince, 115, 163, 181–83, 189–99, 202–3, 206–7, 360n31
second slavery, 9, 11, 329n26, 332
self-ownership, 250, 252–53, 265
slave code, 218
slave cultures, 146–47, 153
slave emancipation, 26, 28, 31–32, 35, 39, 41, 162, 167, 174
slaveholding, 4, 35, 41, 164, 193
slave insurrection, 43, 49, 56–57, 114, 151, 161, 244, 251, 253, 286, 351n21, 367n9
slave labor, 5, 11, 13, 195, 328n23
slave population, 60, 73–75, 145–46, 158, 165, 246

slave revolts, 19, 24, 29, 120, 163–64, 172–73, 212–13, 232–33, 237–38, 254, 266–68, 270–73, 275–76, 278, 284–86, 369n20, 371n9
slave rituals, 146–47, 153, 158
slavery, abolition of, 25, 175, 178, 181, 197, 308, 316, 319, 325, 358n2
slaves, 3–5, 9–13, 95–98, 149, 155–56, 167–70, 172–73, 199–202, 247–48, 252–54, 278–80, 282–83, 315–17, 322, 328n23, 328–29n25; freed, 5, 267, 279, 284; rebellious, 271–72, 274, 286, 315; revolutionary, 315, 317–19, 325
slave states, 166, 171, 175, 188
slave-trade, 9, 11, 25, 114, 187, 196, 224, 312, 328nn21, 23, 342–43n38, 361n45, 367n7, 373n51
slave trade, internal, 11
slave traders, 233, 323
slave violence, 247, 363n21
Smith, Gerrit, 206, 360n38
social relations, contractual, 252, 255, 258, 260, 263
Sonthonax, Léger-Félicité, 4–5, 319
Southampton Slave Revolt, 365n69
sovereignty, 20, 23, 40, 82, 84, 154, 250, 254–55, 303, 305, 312, 315, 321, 379n86, 381n99; national, 19, 23, 107; popular, 4, 20, 24, 40, 321, 323
Spain, 24, 39, 118–21, 124–26, 130, 173, 186, 296, 346n28
spirit possession, 155, 157
Staten Island, 64, 66–67, 70–71
Stevens, Edward, 31–35, 37, 330–32, 397
Stowe, Harriet Beecher, 85–86, 90, 265; *Uncle Tom's Cabin*, 85, 88, 90, 342n18

terror, 86, 147, 156, 162, 176, 236–37, 239–40, 244, 246–47, 363n31, 365n62
theaters, 108, 268–71, 274, 371n15
Theresa, 83, 182–83
Toussaint Louverture, 5–8, 23–40, 80–84, 86–93, 185–86, 205–7, 213–21, 223–25, 227–31, 318–19, 330n7, 331n15, 343n38
Toussaint's Clause, 6, 225, 228, 378n71, 380n91
Toussaint's Constitution, 211, 213–15, 217–19, 222–25, 228–31, 361n4, 362n10
Triumphs of Love, 212, 266–67, 269–71, 274–76, 278, 281, 285–86, 370–71n1
Trouillot, Michel-Rolph, 15, 84, 118, 188

United Irishmen, 238–39, 362n11

Vastey, Pompée Valentin, 212, 287–301, 303–4, 306–9, 311–13, 375n20, 377nn56, 63, 377–78n64, 379n86, 381n99, 382n108, 383nn132, 138
Vaudoux. *See* Vodou
Vesey, Denmark, 93, 163–64, 168, 187, 342n18, 354n19; Vesey conspiracy, 164, 167, 172–73, 175, 179
Virginia, 62, 66, 68, 70–73, 215, 244, 249, 327n6, 328n23, 337n54, 338–39n19, 339n25, 357n121, 378n69
Vodou, 114, 146–47, 153–61, 352n42

wage labor, 190–92
Walker, David, 83, 176, 215, 249
warships, 36, 61, 107–8
Washington, D.C., 66, 70, 91–92, 105, 108, 223–24, 226, 229–30, 294–95, 299
Washington, George, 80, 90–91, 137, 152, 186, 224, 226, 337n54, 342–43n38
Webb, Frank J., 84, 88–90, 181, 185
West Indian emancipation, 166, 172, 360n38
Wordsworth, William, 86, 90

yellow fever, 7, 114, 130–44, 244–45, 248

zombie, 156, 158–59

ACKNOWLEDGMENTS

We are delighted to acknowledge the many people who have helped this volume on its path to appearing in print. We offer our thanks, first and foremost, to the contributors to the volume, who have been patient during the long gestation of this work and whose essays have made the wait worthwhile. We are grateful to Robert Lockhart at the University of Pennsylvania Press for shepherding the collection to publication. Our thanks, as well, to Max Cavitch and two anonymous reviewers for their clarifying comments on the collection. We are also grateful for the assistance of Amanda Ruffner, Tracy Kellmer, and Erica Ginsburg at the University of Pennsylvania Press and Brian Ostrander at Westchester Publishing Services. We are pleased to acknowledge the support received from the Office of the Dean and the Office of the Provost at Bucknell University and from the Office of the Dean of the College of Social Sciences and Humanities at Northeastern University. Our thanks to Nick Salvo, who assisted with compiling the index.

A number of the essays (or portions thereof) included in the volume have appeared elsewhere in previous versions including Marlene Daut, "'The Alpha and Omega of Haitian Literature': Baron de Vastey and the U.S. Audience of Haitian Political Writing," in *Comparative Literature* 64.1 (2012); Michael J. Drexler and Ed White, "The Constitution of Toussaint," in *A Companion to African American Literature*, ed. Gene Jarrett (New York: Wiley-Blackwell, 2010); Carolyn Fick, "Revolutionary Saint Domingue and the Emerging Atlantic: Paradigms of Sovereignty," in *Review: A Journal of the Fernand Braudel Center* 31.2 (2008); and David Geggus, "French Imperialism and the Louisiana Purchase," in *The Louisiana Purchase and Its Peoples: Perspectives from the New Orleans Conference*, ed. Paul E. Hoffman (Lafayette: Louisiana Historical Association, 2004). We thank the publishers for permission to reprint these materials.

Finally, it is our great good fortune that the brilliant Haitian artist, Edouard Duval-Carrié, created an original image for the cover of the book—one that invokes and refracts the complex history of relations between Haiti and the United States that is the subject of this volume. We are deeply grateful to Edouard for this creation, and to the vivid embodiment it gives to the long and entwined relation of the United States and Haiti, across laboring bodies, land- and seascapes, commodity regimes, revolutions, aesthetics, and, most important, imaginaries.